Thinking Sex
with the Early Moderns

Thinking Sex

with the

Early Moderns

———— ❧ ————

Valerie Traub

PENN

UNIVERSITY OF PENNSYLVANIA PRESS

PHILADELPHIA

A volume in the Haney Foundation Series, established in
1961 with the generous support of Dr. John Louis Haney.

Copyright © 2016 University of Pennsylvania Press

Published by
University of Pennsylvania Press
Philadelphia, Pennsylvania 19104-4112
www.upenn.edu/pennpress

Printed in the United States of America on acid-free paper
1 3 5 7 9 10 8 6 4 2

Library of Congress Cataloging-in-Publication Data

Traub, Valerie, author.
   Thinking sex with the early moderns / Valerie Traub.
      pages cm.— (Haney Foundation series)
   Includes bibliographical references and index.
   ISBN 978-0-8122-4729-9
   1. Sex in literature. 2. English literature—Early modern,
1500–1700—History and criticism. 3. Sex
(Psychology)—History—16th century. 4. Sex
(Psychology)—History—17th century. 5. Gender
identity—England—History—16th century. 6. Gender
identity—England—History—17th century. 7. Language and
sex—History. 8. Renaissance—England. I. Title. II. Series:
Haney Foundation series.
   PR428.S48T73   2016
   820.9'353809031—dc23
                                                      2015017216

To

Gina
Theresa
Maureen
Jennie
Holly
Sabiha
Marjorie
Laura
Gavin
Amy
Chad
Ari
Stephen
Sarah
Tiffany
Emily
Charisse
Lauren
Amanda W
Amanda O
Leah
Jennifer
Jonathan
Andrew
Katie
Angela
Kate
Amrita
Hamit
Eliza

CONTENTS

This book was written during a particular moment in U.S. cultural and political history—after the initial efflorescence of academic gay/lesbian/queer studies and during a socially conservative and sex-negative political backlash that extended from the media and medicine to schools and the arts. This was a time of severe social and discursive contradiction around sex, with sex phobia contending in equal measure with the sex saturation of a celebrity-obsessed culture. It began—although I did not know it at the time—in conversations with Mark Schoenfield at Vanderbilt University, who gamely agreed to read all of Shakespeare's sonnets with me. A turning point came when Julie Crawford suggested that an early version of "The Joys of Martha Joyless" allegorized my own scholarly and pedagogical career. Its overall design began to coalesce during the Bush II era (2001–2009), a period characterized by governmental disavowals of the existence of anything other than reproductive marital sexuality, contributing to persistent underfunding of research into and prevention programs for HIV/AIDS and to abstinence-only policies of so-called sex education. Over the first decade of the new millennium, politicians in the United States were relieved of office for seeking out sex workers, panics about pedophilia moved from the schools into the Catholic Church to the football locker room,[1] the feminist critique of sexual harassment was co-opted to prohibit most consensual sexual conduct within the workplace and schools, and teenagers increasingly were incarcerated for engaging in consensual erotic acts that their parents' generation performed with impunity. Across the globe political conflicts intensified over homosexual civil rights, the treatment of sex workers, HIV transmission, and women's and girls' access to sexual information and health care. Women were stoned to death for adultery and men executed for sodomy. The right to sexual and other forms of education was exploited by the U.S. government to justify the geopolitical incursions of the post-9/11 security state. The book was finished as President Obama struggled to address the crises that arose out of Bush neglect—of infrastructure, of ethical and financial oversight, of education—in ways that could only disappoint a feminist and queer Left, even as the more mainstream demands of gay organizing began to bear fruit in local, state, and national policies on gays and lesbians in the military, civil unions, and marriage equality. Contradictions were everywhere: the same year that the governor in the state in which I live signed legislation barring health-care benefits to domestic partners of public employees, National Public Radio declared it a "good year to be gay." I finished revising the manuscript while we await the Supreme Court decision on marriage rights; having first married my partner in 1986 and made it legal in my natal state of California in 2014, I am cautiously hopeful that she and I will gain access to each other's Social Security benefits before I retire. But who knows?

Sex, needless to say, has been much on my mind.

My ideas began to cohere into something like an "argument" during the six years I chaired the Women's Studies Department at the University of Michigan. One of the oldest and best resourced of such departments in the United States, composed in equal parts of humanists and social scientists in addition to several medical practitioners, this vibrant, collegial, and contentious community honed my understanding of interdisciplinarity—what it is, what makes it possible, what its limits are. Whereas I had long considered myself to be an interdisciplinary scholar, I quickly found that providing leadership to a group composed of scholars with such different perspectives and expertise required not only attentive listening but risky acts of mediation. Much of what I discovered about my colleagues in the social science and medical fields countered humanists' stereotypes of them. For one thing, they were more adept at integrating feminist and queer theory (as developed in the humanities) into their research and teaching than humanists are at integrating social science research, and their training in different methodologies made them routinely self-reflexive about the stakes of their research design. I was especially intrigued to find that they, too, are pursuing sexuality as a form of difficult knowledge. (Not that I was entirely won over; they remain tireless in lampooning the limitations of humanists, most especially our obscurantist "jargon" and our demonstrated inability to intuit the meaning of information presented on x/y axes.)

During this time, and with the help of some amazing faculty and office staff, I strove to institutionalize LGBTQ/Sexuality Studies through a variety of programmatic means, including developing a stable of undergraduate courses, devising an LGBTQ/Sexuality Studies graduate certificate, and harnessing the energies of queer faculty across campus to teach sexuality courses under the institutional umbrella of Women's Studies. My experience of the possibilities for and pitfalls of institutional change comprises a biographical substrate of the pages that follow. Another exhilarating and ambivalent effort involved collaborating with colleagues in Women's Studies and History to develop and co-teach a large undergraduate lecture course on the history of sexuality. That we attempted to forgo chronology and sexual identity as organizing rubrics was as utopian as our "global" spatial-temporal design, which mandated that we "cover" much of the world through most of recorded time. My own pedagogical failures in that endeavor were as serendipitous to my thinking as were invitations to organize a conference on the topic of "gay shame" and respond in print to queer scholarship situated in the fields of comparative literature and Islamic studies. Each of these collaborations, for different reasons, pushed my thinking beyond the bounds of my expertise and comfort zone.

Indeed, a variety of affective investments have punctuated this undertaking, including alienation and anger. But these negative affects have been leavened by the intense joy sometimes experienced in my teaching, in conversations with colleagues, and in the course of engaging with a host of talented graduate students. My debts to specific colleagues and friends are noted in my Acknowledgments. Here I want to flag for special thanks those students involved in a Women's Studies graduate course on making sexual knowledge. Through discussions about contemporary sex surveys, DSM (Diagnostic and Statistical Manual) controversies about diagnosing sexual pathologies, and SIECUS (Sexuality Information and Education Council of the United States) position statements, my awareness that the frameworks through which we construct our research objects direct the questions that we ask was transformed into an organizing principle of my scholarship and teaching. Thinking in that course about the contemporary meanings of age of sexual consent laws, contemporary pornography, sex education, and discourses of sexual health deepened my appreciation of both the perennial quality of the symbolic functions of sex, as well as the import of its historical specificity. Our conversations clarified my understanding of the productive as well as constraining effects of academic disciplines while increasing my appreciation for both the pleasures and tripwires of interdisciplinary dialogue—including our different understandings of and investments in theory, history, methods, experience, and activism. At the same time, teaching students who are unaccustomed to thinking historically—or whose sense of the past is radically attenuated—reaffirmed my belief that a historical approach to sexual knowledge relations can usefully inform, nuance, and texture our approach to contemporary problems. The hope that understanding such processes of knowledge production in other times and other places might provide a conceptual framework for intervening in contemporary discourses of sex and sexuality underlies the pedagogical intent of what follows.

Post-Stonewall queer pedagogy typically has focused on whether or how to come out in the classroom. As someone who was, early in my career, forbidden by my (closeted gay male) department chair to come out to my students, I acknowledge the political import and personal significance of negotiating such everyday, banal acts of self-disclosure, which, as others have remarked, take the form of performative speech acts that require continual reiteration. Even within the supposedly queer-friendly academy today, coming out through word, implication, personal style, bodily acts, or reading assignments involves a delicate and sometimes stressful choreography of revelation and concealment, exposure and withholding, of strategizing across the boundaries of private and public for both students and teachers. Those teachers and students whose gender presentation, style, or comportment depart most radically from dominant norms no doubt dance to a somewhat different tune than those of us who could, if we so choose, pass as straight.

In its pedagogical investments, however, this book is interested less in the performance of sexual (or gender) identity than in the performance of sexual speech. Whether we come out in the classroom or pass, are straight or would like not to be, central to our pedagogical strategies is our felt experience when speaking sex. Like the performative act of coming out, candor in such speech involves a complex choreography of personal revelation and concealment of erotic interests and affiliations.[2] Teaching sexually explicit materials involves not only deep contextualization, but forthrightness. Fellatio, cunnilingus, blow jobs, finger or fist fucking: whether couched in a high or low idiom, these words, or others like them, voiced in an academic setting (no matter whether during an undergraduate lecture, graduate seminar, conference panel, or keynote address), violate tacit assumptions about academic protocol and decorum. However progressive, feminist, or queer their views, many auditors and interlocutors react to what they perceive as a breach of etiquette, or to an imagined assault, or to the contagious quality of sexual shame. I have encountered widened eyes, downcast glances, deafening silence, and nervous as well as appreciative laughter.

It is within such contradictory contexts that my engagements with peda-gogy, history, knowledge practices, and the relationship between feminist and queer modes of thinking, acting, and being have evolved. In gratitude for the opportunity to speak sex, to think sex, and to make sexual knowledge, I dedicate this book to my Michigan graduate students who, more than anyone else, have taught me what it means to teach.

Note on Spelling

I have mainly retained original spellings and punctuation in quotations from early modern texts except when quoting from modern editions. Given my hope that readers less familiar with early modern English will read this book, I have expanded contractions, distinguished *i/j*, *u/v*, and *vv/w*, and replaced long *s* for *f*. I also have translated typeface into modern roman type. All citations of the *Oxford English Dictionary* refer to the *OED Online*.

CHAPTER I

Thinking Sex

Knowledge, Opacity, History

> If you tasted it, it would first taste bitter,
> then briny, then surely burn your tongue.
> It is like what we imagine knowledge to be:
> dark, salt, clear, moving, utterly free,
> drawn from the cold hard mouth
> of the world, derived from the rocky breasts
> forever, flowing and drawn, and since
> our knowledge is historical, flowing, and flown.
> —Elizabeth Bishop, "At the Fishhouses"

Is sex good to think with? Over the past thirty years, historians, literary critics, and scholars of gay, lesbian, queer, and sexuality studies have demonstrated that there is much to be gained, conceptually and politically, in thinking *about* sex. They have shown the extent to which sexual attitudes, concepts, and practices have been influenced by and are indices of societal concerns specific to time, place, and discursive context. Whether investigating historical lives or imaginative fictions, medicine or pornography, visual or textual representations, they have provided ample demonstration of the diversity of sexuality and the complex ways in which that diversity has been and continues to be represented, claimed, contested, and refused.

But what about *thinking sex*? That is, using sex as *a way to think* and, further, as a means by which to analyze what such thinking entails? Is it possible or desirable to use sex itself as an analytical guide for thinking about bodies, histories, representations, and signification? Can "sex" as a conceptual category help us apply pressure to the question of how we make sex *into knowledge*? To these questions, *Thinking Sex with the Early Moderns* answers in the affirmative. Playing on the double meaning of thinking and knowing about sex and mobilizing sexuality as a form of knowledge and thought, this book explores how thinking *about* sex is related to thinking *with* sex, and how both activities affect a range of knowledge relations—especially the affective, embodied, cognitive, and political interactions among those who supposedly know and those who decidedly don't.

Given the capaciousness of the concepts of "sex" and "knowledge," inquiry into how sex is made into knowledge potentially could comprise a vast and unwieldy project, traversing several fields of endeavor. Indeed, the inquiry pursued in this book is one without a stable or coherent referent. In what ways are sexual knowledge and knowledge practices about sex "research objects"? Given sexuality's relationship to the body and the psyche, nature and culture, what are its borders and boundaries? In order to narrow the field of inquiry, I have focused my study of sexual knowledge on three questions: What do we know about early modern sex? How do we know it? And what does such knowledge mean? As forthright as each of these questions appears, each extends outward into separate, yet overlapping, intellectual domains. To ask what we *know* about early modern sex is to ask a question that is simultaneously epistemological (having to do with the contents, conditions, and practices of knowledge) and historical (having to do with a precise time and space, including the here and now as well as the then and there). To ask *how* we know what we think we know is to venture into the domains of methodology (the analytical procedures we employ) and theory (the conceptual frameworks that inform our methods). It is to ask not only what sexual knowledge we make but how we might make history through the analytic provided by sexuality. And to ask what such knowledge *means* is to query what we do with it, how we make it both signify and significant, in individual, interpersonal, and social contexts. It is to query *why* we want to know what we hope to know, as well as to query what we do with that knowledge. The processes of meaning and doing thus raise questions about the effects of knowing and of the transmission of knowledge—questions infused not only with political but, as I will show, ethical and pedagogical dimensions. In thus reframing the history of sexuality as an epistemological problem, this book aims to reorient the ways by which historians and literary critics, feminists and queer studies scholars, approach the historicity of sex.

When considered epistemologically, sexual knowledge becomes a conceptual problematic, one that I will refer to as "sex-as-knowledge-relation." I approach this problematic by means of some related premises: that *how* we access and produce the history of sexuality is as important as *what* we discover about prior organizations of erotic desire; that sex, like gender, is best approached as a flexible and capacious category of analysis (rather than a delimited or fixed object of study);[1] and that methods used to write the history of sexuality—that is, historiography as practiced by both historians and literary critics—will benefit from sustained consideration of what it means to "know" sex in the first place. Because my conception of history includes our own historical moment, I approach the relations between thinking sex and making sexual knowledge as both sequential (thinking comes first, making knowledge out of thought comes second) and recursive (how we make knowledge affects how we think, including what questions we can imagine).

Such are my central questions and premises—and if they appear, in their initial formulation, unduly abstract, I strive in this study to provide compelling demonstrations of how and why thinking sex-as-knowledge-relation might speak to a range of interests and projects. Over the course of the next nine chapters, my answers to these questions resolve into several arguments about the analytical challenges and stakes involved in making sexual knowledge out of the material traces of the past. My argument begins with the observation that many of us engaged in the effort to make sexual knowledge regularly hit up against conceptual difficulties: opacity, absence, gaps, blockages, and resistances. Whether we seek to acquire knowledge of sex in the past or to understand the past through the analytic of sexuality, such moments of impasse are often experienced as our own private research problem—albeit a problem we might acknowledge over e-mail or dinner with friends. *Thinking Sex with the Early Moderns* argues that sexual knowledge is difficult because sex, as a category of human thought, volition, behavior, and representation, is, for a variety of reasons, opaque, often inscrutable, and resistant to understanding. Rather than attempt to surmount or conceal such obstacles, or grant them only minimal due as a matter of what is missing (whether in the archives or in our understanding), this book leverages the notions of opacity, obscurity, obstruction, and impasse in order to explore what such barriers to vision, access, and understanding might entail for the production and dissemination of knowledge about sex. It seeks in such obstacles what social scientists call "methodological release points,"[2] using them as an analytical wedge with which to open new questions about sex-as-knowledge-relation and devise new strategies to confront some of the ways it is possible *not to know*. The principle I seek to mobilize throughout the book is this: *sex may be good to think with, not because it permits us access, but because it doesn't.*

Opaque Knowledge

Why might sex be hard to know? Why is sex opaque—and, as I shall argue, obstinate and implacable in its opacity? While this book will provide some detailed answers to these questions, I begin by noting that obstacles regarding sexual knowledge do not all derive from the same place, nor are they all of the same conceptual order.[3] *Thinking Sex with the Early Moderns* takes its bearings from the fact that sex is an experience of the body (and hence fleeting) and that individual sexual acts are likewise local and ephemeral. Furthermore, there is the basic fact of psychic variation: to put it simply, what turns one person on may turn another one off. The extent of erotic diversity necessarily renders any instance of sexual experience or representation a highly contingent matter of interpretation. These two realities subtend the analyses that follow. Nonetheless, this is not a book about subjectivity, and thus not a book about desire. Nor is it about the emotional needs of the desiring subject except insofar as certain affects—particularly frustration and disappointment—can prompt inquiry into structural conditions of knowledge production. When attending to the past, this shift in focus away from "the subject" shifts attention from the question of what people (or literary characters) want to the knowledge relations they inhabit and perform. When attending to the present, this shift broadens the optic to include the disciplinary structures we inhabit and the questions we ask of past lives and texts.

The chapters that follow demonstrate that the opacities of eroticism—not just those aspects of sex that exceed our grasp, but those that manifest themselves as the *unthought*—can serve as a productive analytical resource. The epistemological orientation enacted here derives not only from hitting up against such impasses, but from intuiting that these structures of occultation and unintelligibility *are also the source of our ability to apprehend and analyze them*. In short, the obstacles we face in *making* sexual history can illuminate the difficulty of *knowing* sexuality, and both impediments can be productively adopted as a guiding principle of historiography, pedagogy, and ethics.

Given that sex may be good to think with precisely because of its recalcitrant relation to knowledge, the sense of "making" heralded in the book's first part is slightly ironic: any knowledge *made* necessarily carries within it, as a hard, inviolate kernel, those impediments by which it is also constituted. Such constitutive impediments explain why I evoke Elizabeth Bishop's description of the "taste" of knowledge as "bitter" and "briny," able to burn one's tongue. At the same time, my conception of the difficulty involved is guided by the apprehension that, as Bishop writes, "our knowledge is historical, flowing, and flown." It might seem that Bishop idealizes knowledge as ultimately "clear" and "utterly free." Yet, in pausing with her over the verb that qualifies her invocation of knowledge—that is, to "imagine"—we might find reason to pause as well over the task of drawing knowledge from "the cold hard mouth" and "rocky breasts" of the world. What is at stake, in her poem and my project, is precisely what "we *imagine* knowledge to be." At stake as well is what stymies us and what it means to go on "tasting" knowledge, despite its salt-soaked bitterness.

By moving through an instructive range of difficulties (including the archival, the historiographic, and the hermeneutic) and by subordinating the question of the desiring subject, *Thinking Sex with the Early Moderns* engages in an extended thought experiment. It proposes, first, that we approach the conceptual status of sex (its meaning, its ontology, its significance) not only as a problem of representation (of what can be expressed or textualized or *not* expressed or textualized)[4] or as a problem of signification (as something made intelligible or unintelligible by means of particular conceptual categories) but as an epistemological problem. An epistemological approach—asking *what* can be known as well as *how* it is known—recasts the dynamics among sex, representation, signification, and historiography as a problem of knowledge relations: constituted not only by social interchange but by implicit understandings of what counts as knowledge and what eludes or baffles as ignorance. Tracing the contours of a structural dynamic between knowledge and ignorance back in time before the "epistemology of the closet," I advocate that we confront what we *don't* know as well as what we *can't* know about sex in the past.[5] This confrontation with the variety of ways that it is possible not to know implicates the investigator, if willing, in various considerations of pedagogy and ethics.

These epistemological, pedagogical, and ethical propositions come into especially sharp focus when we attempt to think sex, as my title designates, with the early moderns. My title pays homage to Gayle Rubin's "Thinking

Sex: Notes for a Radical Theory of the Politics of Sexuality,"[6] which proposed "elements of a descriptive and conceptual framework for thinking about sex and its politics."[7] "Thinking Sex" is often credited as one of the founding documents of queer theory, in no small measure because it provides a general blueprint for investigating sex through the conceptual categories by which it is thought.[8] In attempting to "build rich descriptions of sexuality as it exists in society and history" and "to locate particular varieties of sexual persecution within a more general system of sexual stratification," Rubin anatomizes six conventional ways of thinking sex: sexual essentialism (belief in its biologically mandated and universal status); sex negativity (fear of the dangerous effects of sex on peoples and cultures); the fallacy of misplaced scale (which mandates disproportionate punishment for sexual crimes); the hierarchical valuation of sex acts (whereby monogamous heterosexuality is elevated over "promiscuity" or "perversions"); the domino theory of sexual peril (whereby sexual contagion is thought to spread restlessly through the body politic); and the lack of a concept of benign sexual variation (whereby people mistake their own sexual preference for a universal system). Sex for Rubin is simultaneously a matter of representation and reality, discourse and embodiment, metaphor and phenomenological acts. If what results from Rubin's capacious focus seems particularly portable—applicable to cultures and times far removed from the twentieth-century United States—and thus becomes recognizable as "theory," this theory is derived and abstracted from the lived situation of bodies and the acts in which they engage.[9]

Rubin's concepts have motivated an enormous body of work on sexuality, particularly within queer studies. Beyond their utility for contesting sexual normativity, the method that activates them provides a model for scrutinizing the conceptual categories whereby we can think sex. My analytical mode, accordingly, is not primarily narrative or hermeneutic, but anatomizing, as I attempt to parse the ways in which certain concepts enable or disable our methods and understandings. Like Rubin, I have located my analysis within the frameworks provided by very specific modes of embodiment, believing that theories and methods—however brilliantly conceived and argued—are best tested and tempered within the forge of temporal and spatial particularity.

Even as I develop theoretical and methodological principles that I hope will prove useful to scholars' investigation of other times and cultures,[10] my archive is composed of texts and discourses produced in England from the late sixteenth to the later part of the seventeenth century. The configuration of "the early modern" situates the scholar of sex in a particular relationship not only to other scholars but to literary culture and to history, with the iconic figures of "Shakespeare" and "the Renaissance" looming large. No doubt the view looks different from other times and places, where questions of sexual definition, historical alterity, sexual modernity, new media and genres,[11] and the availability of archival materials contour the terrain along distinctive tracks.[12] I maintain, however, that the particular synergy of, on the one hand, *differences* between early modernity and our own time (e.g., the lack of widely legible sexual identities in the early modern period) and, on the other hand, *similarities* between then and now (e.g., the existence of a diverse erotic repertoire) offers an advantageous prospect from which to scrutinize fissures in and obstructions to our knowledge.[13]

The chapters that follow hone in on two questions: What are the contours of sexual knowledge—its contents, syntaxes, and specificities—for the early moderns? And which social, intellectual, and institutional processes are involved in creating and exchanging it—for them and for us? Attention to the second question, in particular, entails focusing on the overlaps and contradictory injunctions that divide and conjoin literary and historical study.[14] What processes constitute "the history of sexuality" as a research object? Is it a field of inquiry with agreed-upon methods? How does it function as a point of contention within and between disciplines? And which objects of inquiry within the history of sexuality particularly stymie our efforts to know them? By means of three rubrics, I have organized my exploration of these questions along related conceptual axes. In Part I, "Making the History of Sexuality," the accent falls primarily on historiographic issues—that is, the methods and protocols by which historians and literary critics investigate and pursue knowledge about sex in the past. Given the interdisciplinary nature of lesbian/gay/queer studies, it is peculiar that reflections on historiographic method often seem silently embedded in scholarship, present implicitly in the mode of argumentation and the means of marshaling evidence, rather than being fully aired. In this section, I bring method to the forefront by articulating my own preferences and choices, which arise from within the interdisciplinary dialogues among the protocols of close reading, the investments of queer and feminist theories, and the proffering of historical claims. Part II, "Scenes of Instruction; or, Early Modern Sex Acts," sustains this interest in historiography but layers on to it questions about what it means to "know" sexuality, both in the early modern period and today.[15] Grounded in a concept of erotic tutelage and linked by the effort to examine various forms of presumptive knowledge about sex as well as an interest in the material acts that comprise "sex," these chapters treat both analytical presumptions and sex acts themselves as scenes of instruction. The pedagogical relations with which I am concerned toggle between those represented within early modern texts, between texts and their original readers or audiences, and between scholars who study such texts and our students and readers. Part III, "The Stakes of Gender," shifts into a more explicitly theoretical mode in order to focus on the difference that gender specificity makes to the now twenty-year-old project of "queering the Renaissance." Engaging in close readings of lyric poetry and a range of other scholars' work, this section demonstrates the stakes of a literary and historical practice that is simultaneously feminist and queer.

Signifying Sex

Once one considers the possibility that there is something to be gained from highlighting and mobilizing methodological opacities rather than attempting to surmount or ignore them, one cannot help but notice that they have something significant in common with the incoherence, intransigence, and unintelligibility of eroticism itself—whether conceived as libido, eros, a fantasy structure, or sexual act. Indeed, the concept of "sex" is founded on numerous, sometimes incongruent, ideas. We regularly speak of sex as: anatomy, gender, desire, fantasy, making love, reproduction, violence, and individual erotic acts.[16] Although feminist and queer studies scholars have become adept at separating and flagging these meanings, this doesn't bring confusion to a halt, because "sexuality" in academic discourse often implies an additional set of concepts: affect, kinship,[17] or a particular "regime" of modernity.[18] I use "sexuality" interchangeably with "sex" and "eroticism" throughout this book for I intend these terms to cover a range of erotic feelings and corporeal practices; indeed, part of the task of this book is to think by means of their overlaps and ambiguities. For this reason, whereas I use "sexual" and "erotic" as predicates that are sufficiently stable in the relations they signify to hold up across time, my emphasis will be on their historically varying contents and rhetorics, as well as the fact that the actions they name are not necessarily "the same" or known in advance.

"Knowledge," too, can signify in various ways. In the early modern period, the word could convey acknowledgment, recognition, and awareness, as well as friendship and intimacy; not incidentally, it also referred to what Genesis 4 calls "carnal knowledge." Repeatedly in the period sex is likened to a form of knowledge, as in the 1540 act of Parliament that refers to "such mariages beyng . . . consummate with bodily knowledge" (Act 32 Hen. 8, c. 38) or rape victims' testimonies that "he had knowledge of my body." In our own time, as Ludmilla Jordanova notes, knowledge refers to "awareness, information, understanding, insight, explanation, wisdom," each of which involves "distinct relationships between knowers and known."[19] Central to the conceptions guiding this book is the multiplicity of "knowledge," "knowing," and "knowers," as well as the dynamic historical relations among knowledge and sex. In this regard, *Thinking Sex with the Early Moderns* shares with feminist philosophers of epistemology a concern with what is known, how it is known, differential access to knowledge, and the terms by which knowledge is expressed. It departs from their collective project by concerning itself less with the establishment of truth claims (or their contestation) than in exploring the techniques of knowledge production educed by sex.[20] Furthermore, the concept of knowledge motivating this book includes not only official discourses but knowing that is "made by trial and error, drift, unforeseen by-products, crazy inventions, play, and frivolous speculation."[21] Most especially, epistemology as I conceive it is concerned with the *categories* and *concepts* by which early moderns, and scholars of early modernity, think sex.[22]

Framing the question as how sexuality sets up obstacles to knowledge involves revisiting how queer studies has approached the concept of epistemology. In *Feeling Backward: Loss and the Politics of Queer History*, Heather Love maintains that queer historiography has moved away from an epistemological focus, which she defines as the quest to find identities, toward a focus on affect and identification.[23] Love's definition of identity knowledge as an epistemologically based method makes a certain kind of sense, but it also risks confusion. I would suggest that earlier LGBT scholarship was driven less by a concern with knowledge relations than with sexual *ontology*, insofar as it tended to treat sexual identity as a form of being, whether in the form of social identity or individual subjectivity. Lesbian studies, to be sure, did tend to focus on acts of knowing, but its central historical question, "Was she a lesbian?" was less an opening onto knowledge relations in the past, or between the past and the present, than a question of wanting to know whether the identity category fit, as Martha Vicinus memorably put it, "for sure."[24] My return to epistemology brackets precisely the concept of identity that Love used to define epistemology's salience in order to zero in on the conceptual categories and maneuvers that are implicated in knowledge's production.

The conceptual terms available to signify sexual knowledge, and thus the terms available to signify what sex *is* or might *mean* both in the early modern period and today, are thus crucial to what follows. Beyond the hard-to-pin-down definitional nature of sex and knowledge, I seek to leverage the idea that sex itself poses an interrelated problem of signification and knowability. Indeed, the epistemology of sex is intensely bound to the issues of sexual representation and signification—by which I mean the capacity of language to denote and connote meanings about erotic affect, embodiment, desires, and practices, through practices of articulation as well as silence, and by means of conceptual categories that implicitly organize what can be known and circulated. Recognition of the various discursive means by which sex is (un)intelligible has been central to theorizing the cultural symbolics and ideological work of sexuality.[25] Homosexuality especially has been viewed as "occasioning a crisis in and for the logic of representation itself."[26] Lesbianism has been seen as constituted by dynamics of insignificance, unaccountability, invisibility, and inconsequence.[27] Historically distinct forms of unintelligibility have been important to queer theorists reading "the tropologies of sexuality that are put into play once the field of sexuality becomes charged by the widespread availability of a 'homosexual' identity."[28]

This book, however, investigates a discursive system in which the "widespread availability" of *any* sexual identity had yet to come to the fore. For this reason, early modernists confront what might be called distinctly *presuppositional* discursive contexts—by which I mean how the past is both like and unlike, "not yet like" and "not ever like," the present.[29] It is perhaps especially the case that, within the bounds of early modern English, one cannot safely assume that a given word, phrase, speech, or bodily act is erotic—or, for that matter, not erotic. "Sodomy" might or might not mean sodomy; "lesbian" might or might not mean lesbian; "whore" might or might not mean whore.[30] For, as literary critic Laurie Shannon, following the historian Alan Bray, has noted, there is nothing actually "dispositive" about the capacity of sex in the early modern period to signify particular meanings.[31] Or, as I rephrased this insight in earlier work through the concept of (in)significance: "Erotic acts *come* to signify . . . through a complex and continual social process."[32] What is true at the level of signifying systems is true as well for individual subjects and the specific conditions of communication in which they participate.[33]

Because erotic desires and acts are unreliable as modes or catalysts of signification, they have seemed to require supplemental discursive framing in
order to reveal the meanings and values they may, or may not, convey. Historicist scholars have tended to negotiate the uncertainty of sexual signification by describing erotic concepts through a period's own languages and
idioms, as well as by locating sexuality within densely contextualized
domains—in essence, momentarily stabilizing the meanings of sex through
other discourses: legal statutes and trials of sodomites and tribades, medical
descriptions of the use and "abuse" of genitalia, and prescriptive literature
that articulates dominant sexual mores. They have expended critical energy
attempting to decode period-specific lexicons, hoping to pierce through
cryptic allusions, linguistic codes, and playful innuendo to recover sexual
subjectivities and evidence of erotic acts. This focus on signification and context—that is, on the *way* things mean—has now settled into what one critic
calls "the routines of discursive contextualization,"[34] a habitual strategy with
both gains and losses.[35]

Over the past decade or so, a number of historicist scholars have moved
beyond identity as the governing question of the history of sexuality, shifting
the analytical imperative away from inclusion, for instance, of lesbians in
history or dating the "birth of the homosexual," and toward how sex signifies
in ways eccentric to modern identity logics.[36] In my previous book *The
Renaissance of Lesbianism in Early Modern England*, I analyzed the instability
of sexual signification by exposing the dynamics that, I argued, governed
representations of female same-sex desire in early modern England. Intent on
resisting the way that narrow definitions of evidence preclude an understanding of female sexuality prior to the development of identity regimes, I traced
the fates of figures of same-sex eroticism by composing a cultural history,
arguing for a capacious designation of what "counts" as erotic for women.

As was true of that book, *Thinking Sex with the Early Moderns* elaborates
questions of sexual signification as a way to explore something other than
identity history—not only because identity is haphazardly relevant to the
early modern period but because it can constrain the questions that we ask
of sexuality.[37] To be initially schematic about it (in terms that subsequent
chapters will complicate): one strand of scholarship on sex—call it the
historical/historicist/genealogical strand—focuses on what we can know
about sexuality in the past, often in terms of its difference from the present.
Another strand—call it the psychoanalytic and/or queer one—is concerned
with how sexuality messes with signification, particularly in terms of the

stability of identity categories. This latter emphasis is evident not only in queer theory focused on modernity but in historical studies of more distant periods. (Many studies, of course, enact both impulses.) Despite these differences, however, both strands have viewed the primary question about *the past* to be the appropriateness of adducing the force of sexual identity categories for earlier time periods.[38] In part, this is because influential genealogists have maintained that it is the aim of sexual genealogies to explore *"the multiplicity of possible historical connections between sex and identity*, a multiplicity whose existence has been obscured by the necessary but narrowly focused, totalizing critique of sexual identity as a unitary concept."[39] The possible connections between sex and identity—related to but not put to rest by the anti-identitarian claims of queer theory—have thus served as the governing question of the history of sex, even when the motive is to show that such identities are unstable or contingent.

This book travels a different path to demonstrate that historical, even genealogical, projects need not concern themselves exclusively (or even at all) with connections between sex and identity, sex and subjectivity, or the truth relations they instantiate. Rather than adducing how early modern sexuality defies modern categories or is anti-identitarian, I untether sex from identity as the main historical question. Setting aside the issue of identity has also enabled me to set aside the issue of sexual nomenclatures. This does not mean the book is uninterested in language, much less in concepts: one chapter explores early modern lexicons for their representational dynamics, scrutinizing the ways by which sex is represented through language, while another takes up the term "lesbian" as a critical sign. But this book approaches signification mainly as a way to move closer to the shadowy borders and uneven edges where words-as-concepts rub up against bodies and the erotic acts they perform.

Many of the questions animating *Thinking Sex with the Early Moderns* arose out of my previous immersion in and confusion about early modern signifying practices. Because discourses about female-female desire were structured through rhetorics of absence, invisibility, and insignificance, I developed an almost allergic sensitivity to the potentials and pitfalls of the methods by which we research the sexual past. My nascent awareness of the importance of opacity in knowledge began when I had occasion to ask: How are we to locate the lines between passionate friendship and eroticism, especially insofar as women were generally disenfranchised from the classical ideology of friendship (*amicitia*) and often vilified for expressing self-motivated

desire? Or, to move from the register of prevailing social discourses to that of
the desiring individual: How, as the historian Anna Clark has asked, are we
to positively identify the look, the caress, the sigh?[40] What is the basis for
interpreting kissing, touching, embracing, or sharing a bed (all common practices in the early modern era) as erotic—or not?[41] What, if any, is the erotic
valence of flogging, in a period when theological, medical, pedagogical, and
legal discourses approach the use of the whip and the rod through their own
quite varied understandings?[42] And whatever happened to chin chucking, a
pervasive ancient and early modern practice that no longer seems to even
signify in the modern world?[43] Or, to move to the realm of critical practice:
On what basis can we differentiate between libertine sexism and libertine
sexiness, particularly if we recognize that power differentials can have, and
certainly have had, a constitutive role in sexuality? Does the widespread use
of the term "homoerotic" for periods prior to modernity—a critical practice
in which I participate—function, at least in part, as a cover for our confusion
about the meanings of erotic desire? These questions—which are obviously
hermeneutic, historical, and historiographic—are also, I have come to
believe, epistemological.

   Thinking Sex with the Early Moderns is concerned less with subjects' desires
for other subjects or the contexts within which those desires are granted
meaning than with the articulation of desires for sexual *knowledge* and the
various ways those desires are affirmed, ignored, or repelled. It retains my
prior interest in the oscillating dynamics of significance and insignificance,
intelligibility and unintelligibility, but here I approach the historicity of these
dynamics along a parallel route located on a "meta" conceptual register.
Rather than devise a chronological cultural history of sexuality or of the
pursuit of sexual knowledge, I tarry with the synchronic contradictions of
early modern knowledge relations, believing that it is by so doing that a
diachronic history of thinking sex might become possible.

Historicizing Sex

Historians and literary critics understandably tend to avoid acknowledging
in print how the conceptual, methodological, and archival impasses they
encounter affect their interpretations and narratives.[44] In part this is because
our scholarly instinct is to work toward revelation, to fill in gaps and make
lacunae speak. Those of us working outside of a strictly philosophical register

(and philosophy's subfield of epistemology) don't really have a vocabulary for talking about *not* knowing—except, that is, by means of psychoanalysis, which, at least within early modern studies, continues to struggle against perceptions of a disqualifying ahistoricism. But our reticence is also a result of the dominant preoccupation of most historical scholars (literary critics as well as historians), which has been to explore erotic *attitudes, affects, identities,* and *ideologies*—rather than confront what happens to interpretative practice when we look for the details of actual sexual practices. There are good reasons for this tendency: when we look for evidence of attitudes, we actually find it! Yet, when we start to scrutinize the details of such attitudes—or their concretization into dominant ideologies—they don't necessarily tell us what people *did* with one another or what specific bodily acts *meant to them.* Despite this obvious obstacle, for literary critics and historians alike, the *content* of sex in the early modern era has been all too presumable, supposedly interpretable through such ready-to-hand, transhistorical rubrics as "homo-eroticism," "heterosexuality," "sodomy," "masochism," "sadism," "re-production," "heteronormativity," and "cruising." Such vague referents function as placeholders for a sexual activity and set of relational practices everywhere assumed, but rarely actually described. The material, corporeal aspects of sexual activity—not merely the ecstasy, pain, or ennui it occasions, but the nitty-gritty bodily acts of which it consists—remain surprisingly underarticulated and often subject to a presumptive, tacit form of knowing.[45]

Although I believe that the more historical evidence we accrue of specific erotic acts the better, I do not think that a diligent compilation of sexual practices will resolve this issue. For the opacity of sex, while it certainly has an archival dimension, is not merely a matter of evidentiary lack. When it comes to sex, even I don't know what I've done, much less what my friends or neighbors do. And despite sociological surveys that purport to present an accurate snapshot of sexual behaviors, what the larger population does is also a mystery. This is less because people lie (although of course they do) than because we don't have much of a language, even now, to narrate our experiences in anything but the baldest possible terms—which is one reason why historical scholars resort to handy transhistorical placeholders in the first place.[46]

The use of such concepts has fostered important analytical work. But the time has come to demand more congruence between our theoretical concepts and the historical practices they are employed to name, and not just in pursuit of greater linguistic accuracy. Given the pervasive critical recourse to "heteronormativity," for instance, we might well ask: what was normative about early modern cross-gender sex? Whatever it was, it was not belief in the self-evident naturalness of desire across the gendered categories of male and female. As literary critic Ben Saunders notes: "in the Renaissance, the love that dare not speak its name is not homosexuality but rather any love that dares to posit a woman as worthy of a man's complete devotion."[47] A number of pre- and early modernists have shown the extent to which the concept of "heterosexuality" fundamentally misidentifies the way in which sexual relations were understood, and thus leads scholars to misconstrue the societal norms aimed at regulating sexual behavior.[48] Similar pressure could be put on the concept of the "homoerotic," which, as a critical term, serves to designate *some*thing, but in point of fact *not too precisely*. It thus simultaneously registers and deflects our confusion over the thorny problem of identifying what may look like homosexuality to us, but in certain respects isn't. The resort to "queerness," opportune as it has been, does not resolve this issue. A related problem is raised by invocations of terms derived from the discourse of sexology. To what does "masochism" refer? An interiorized desire for suffering? A form of bodily pleasure? An explicit erotic act, such as bondage? A sexual orientation and, by extension, a community of like-minded individuals? One impetus of this book is to suggest the payoff in coming clean about the extent to which these concepts are *our* categories, based on our projections of what the past was like. But no less a crucial impetus is to challenge the presumptive knowledge that these categories each, in their own way, sustain.

This book's commitment to history and historiography thus runs deeper than the dominant historicist mandate to infuse literary scholarship with cultural and temporal specificity. While not neglecting that mandate, I believe that a literary critic's commitment to history can also involve matters of method central to and challenging of the discipline of history itself. Beginning with my second chapter on Alan Bray's histories of male homosexuality and friendship, my engagement with modes of historical understanding as well as techniques of historical analysis provides a baseline for the anatomizing analyses of the ensuing chapters.[49] Indeed, the rest of this book attempts to make good on the invitation issuing from Bray's historiographic legacy. By taking up several different historiographic problems, I aim to historicize sexuality, engage with historically contingent questions about sexuality, analyze and critique the methods used to historicize sexuality, and ask what it means to historicize sexuality. The precise opacities that appear by means of these questions may be distinctive to the early modern period, but figuring out how to leverage them is a task relevant to every historical scholar concerned with erotic desires and practices or gendered embodiment.

It is no accident that questions about historiographic method have been central to the field of sexuality studies since its beginnings, with history, historicism, and historiography situated in complex tension with the hermeneutic priorities of literary studies. Debates about the relations between representation and "real life," metaphors and materiality, texts and their mediation, signification and social practice have been central to how these disciplines and fields intersect, interpret, and misinterpret each other. One of the objectives of *Thinking Sex with the Early Moderns* is to affiliate the approach toward sex as a complex issue of representation and a remarkably malleable social metaphor (as typically practiced in literary studies and some versions of anthropology and history) with the view of sex as an empirically verifiable, material and social practice (as emphasized in sociology and psychology, as well as in history and anthropology). The ensuing pas de deux is simultaneously conceptual, historical, and interdisciplinary.

In the face of an institutional climate of intense (and at times mindless) championing of interdisciplinarity,[50] it is perhaps unsurprising that influential literary critics have championed the separation of literary from historical study in the name of a "queerer" historicism. Parts I and II proffer ways of thinking sex that direct attention to the points of contact and divergence between these two disciplines. Cross-disciplinary affiliation as I practice it here does not presuppose harmony or paper over differences; indeed, I often dwell on differences, precisely to explore the unique affordances offered by each method. The historical questions addressed in these sections include the relation between eroticism and friendship; the relative salience of acts versus identities; the decision to privilege historical alterity or continuity; the assumption of a correlation between periodization and subjectivity; the varied meanings and functions of temporality; ambivalence about comprehensive period chronologies; the problem of historical teleology; the methodological resources provided by language; and the politically fraught relation between pastness, particularly the premodern, and sexualized formations of racial, ethnic, religious, and national otherness. Among the historiographic arguments developed in these pages is the idea that to do the history of sexuality is not to turn a blind eye to perennial features of the erotic system; but neither is it too quickly to assume similarity or homology in such a way that historical distance and difference are rendered inconsequential. Relations between similarity and difference in historiography might be construed less as an imperative choice than as shimmering tension. To think about resemblance can open an inquiry up to alterity—especially to how something differs from itself. To think about alterity can lead one back to similarity—to ghostly echoes and uncanny resemblances. Similarity and difference, so construed, are metabolic and metamorphic; they are not "up against" each other in the sense of opposition, but "up against" each other in the sense of up close and personal—with all the fraught tensions that this can entail.[51]

My effort to think sex beyond the protocols of identity history and social contextualization has involved unsettling the boundaries between hetero and homoeroticism, as well as licit and illicit, transgressive and orthodox, sexualities. Abandoning strict division between such notions, as well as between men and women, same-sex bonds and heterosexual marriage, enables different configurations of relationship to come to the fore. Emphasizing the erratic and wayward transitivity of erotic desires and acts, and questioning the categories by which "the sexual" is defined, I enact a version of "queering" now common among early modernists and queer studies scholars, advancing the idea that *queer* is that which most "confounds the notion of being as being at one with oneself."[52] Nonetheless, there are crucial differences in my approach that trouble a presumed consensus about what it means, methodologically and theoretically, to queer. As I have already begun to suggest, rather than focusing on how early modern sexuality defies modern categories or is itself anti-identitarian, I focus on how sexuality sets up obstacles to knowledge, not in terms of *identity* but in terms of *sex*. Second, in my effort to deploy "queer"—as a verb, a method, and a category—with analytical rigor and precision, I explore, rather than assume, its oppositional stance toward normativity. Given the principled undefinability of "queer," its infinite mobility and mutability, one notion has provided ballast for its centrifugal expansion: the idea that it is always posed against the "normal." Other queer studies scholars have begun to explore how "queer mobility and indefinition function within queer studies as both *a disciplinary norm* and *a front*," and that rather than being "endlessly open-ended, polyvalent, and reattachable," it is "sticky . . . with history."[53] Aligned with their efforts to explore the field habitus of queer studies but with more distant historical periods in mind, I explore what is normal for the early modern period. Third, because I attend "to sexuality's governance across multiple and contradictory regulatory norms,"[54] I also retain gender as a crucial modifier of sexuality and the meanings of queer.

Knowing Women's Bodies

It is a central premise of what follows that our conceptual resources are impoverished when it is maintained that *any* attempt to account for sexuality in precisely gendered or corporeal terms results in an unwelcome policing of desire, an epistemological violence against the libido, or an exasperating confinement of bodies. My resistance to the trend to ignore, despecify, or dispatch gender in the name of queer is theoretically grounded in an appreciation of the multiple vectors (gender, sexuality, race, class) that historically have underpinned and crosshatched embodiment in sometimes congruent, sometimes incongruent ways. It also stems from a historical sense that queer studies misrecognizes its own conditions of emergence when it categorically rejects affiliation with feminism in the name of analytically separating sexuality from gender. Yes, gender and sexuality are not the same,[55] and there are good reasons for initiating their tactical divergence for certain questions and certain projects.[56] Nonetheless, to "distinguish sexuality from gender analytically is not [necessarily] to deny their relationship but is in fact the precondition for undertaking the study of that relationship."[57] The question of how gender and sexuality do and do not interanimate at any particular time and place remains a live question.[58] This is in part because gender is continuously materialized through social and psychic practices and will operate contingently for different communities and individuals. Indeed, the intransigence of gender, as both embodied materiality and as analytic tool, is one of the opacities with which this book is most concerned. For all of these reasons, the feminism animating these pages is fueled not only by theoretical investments but by a historicist interest in the ongoing *work* of gender.[59]

One of the main arguments of this book is that the gendered specificity of female embodiment offers an especially valuable resource for thinking sex. We can approach this resource in historicist terms, noting how often early modern discourses constitute the female body as a knowledge problem. Consider the early modern medical and theological controversies about the existence of the hymen, as well as the hymen's controversial status in the effort to "prove" virginity.[60] As Margaret Ferguson argues, "for centuries, the hymen has been alleged to give 'proof' of a virgin's existence; from the early modern period to the present, however, the proof is riddled by doubt. The hymen may have been destroyed by the digital searches of those charged with finding it; or it may have been lost 'innocently,' and in a way the female subject has forgotten; and/or it may never have existed (as an object available to 'ocular proof') at all."[61] Early modern medical texts also attribute the breaking of the hymen to the use of illicit "instruments" such as dildos, to overly vigorous masturbation, to the "defluxion of sharp humors,"[62] and to the illicit penetration of the vagina by sexual partners, male and female.[63] But such acts are not, in the end, conclusive of the presence or absence of the hymen. Who knows how a woman has lost her hymen? Who knows if it even exists? Regularly presented in medical texts as a matter of "controversy," the existence of the hymen stymied physicians' most dedicated efforts to secure medical "fact."[64]

Representing a basic threshold of human knowledge, the enigma of the hymen is only one of a number of commonly noted "female mysteries." Foremost among them is the truism that only women can definitely know the paternity of their children: while the reproductive effects of certain sex acts might seem obvious, the ascription of paternity onto a single man depends, absent the physical resemblance of child to father, on the performance of a woman's word.[65] Likewise dependent upon women's performative acts is the enduring question of women's orgasm. Because it was commonly believed that women emitted seed during orgasm, this inquiry took the form of medical debates about the physical nature of female seed (including its confusion with vaginal lubrication, secretions, menses, and leukorrhea), its comparative quality (generally thought to be thinner and weaker than men's), the extent to which emission of seed was the source of female erotic pleasure, and the age-old question of whether women's pleasure in sex was greater than man's. Add to this the ability of women to fake it and the ways in which anxiety about that ability bleeds into Renaissance concerns about women's insincerity and capacity to deceive,[66] and women's orgasm becomes another early modern sexual-knowledge problem. Such queries, controversies, and thematizations of the mystery of female bodies register the impossibility of knowing sex through them.[67]

The photograph included here encapsulates some of what is at stake in using women's embodiment to think more broadly about the historical conjunctions of sex and knowledge. It depicts a statue on a column outside the Paris cathedral of Notre Dame in which a gorgeous, female-headed, amply breasted snake is in the process of enticing Eve.[68] The seduction of Eve by the snake in the Garden of Eden stands in Western Christian traditions as an Ur-story not only of humankind's fall from divine grace through knowledge of good and evil but also a fall into the knowledge of sex. Medieval commentators regularly interpreted the knowledge to which Eve and Adam became

FIGURE 1. The seduction of Eve, Notre Dame de Paris. Photograph by Pascal Lemaître.

privy as understanding not only mortality and sin, but sexual desire, arousal, frustration, and pleasure. Augustine, for instance, materialized the origins and transmission of sin in the semen from which humans are propagated, arguing that "the sexual desire (*libido*) of our disobedient members arose in those first human beings as a result of the sin of disobedience."[69] Indeed, for Augustine, spontaneous sexual arousal was clear evidence of the effect of original sin, both its proof and its penalty, for it materially evinced the triumph of the passions.[70]

This interpretation of the Fall as not only introducing mortality but fallen flesh (signified by the naked genitals) was an important strain of Christian thought throughout the seventeenth century.[71] The conceptual marriage of mortal with carnal knowledge helps to explain why the postlapsarian modesty topos—whereupon knowing themselves to be naked, Eve and Adam cover their genitals in shame—becomes so conventional in textual and visual representations across a wide swath of genres. It also provided convenient theological support for the common belief in women's sexual insatiability, thought to result from deficient powers of reason. Insofar as lust was a mark of weakness and inconstancy, it not only was projected onto women, but was gendered feminine in ways that also redounded on men: excessive desire became a correlate of effeminacy.[72] Fears of female insatiability, however, were not merely the result of misogynous fears of women's erotic power over men. They are part of a larger epistemological configuration in which sex not only is the means of possessing knowledge but is its own form of knowledge. This knowledge is of a very particular kind: of and through the body and thus, according to church fathers, devoid of the reason that distinguishes humans from the rest of the animal world. Concerns about maintaining the distinction between humans and animals informed controversies, including commentaries by Clement of Alexandria, Augustine, and Thomas Aquinas, over how to maintain the rational will while in the throes of passion and the degree to which sex does or does not momentarily turn humans into beasts. Given the associations among women, lust, and animality, the theological debate about the "beastliness" of sex is replete with gendered distinctions and implications.

It is in this context that the depiction of the snake as female-headed and female-breasted becomes particularly arresting, for the colloquy between female serpent and Eve positions women in a special relationship to sexual knowledge.[73] It transforms the seduction of Eve into a gendered double whammy: on the one hand, the first woman is responsible for the Fall through her weakness, inconstancy, ambition, and the feminine wiles by which she tempts Adam to succumb; on the other hand, the snake as Eve's seductress mirrors the temptress image while doubling down on the associations of female embodiment with duplicity, inconstancy, and rebelliousness. Authorized by the belief that "like" is most persuasive and effective with "like," the image of the Eve-serpent interaction is also eroticized. According to the Jewish Midrash, the serpent was one of the two species of animals to have sex, as humans are conventionally thought to do, face-to-face.[74] The representation of two females engaged in such intimacy comes close to implying that Eve engaged in bestiality, a category of sexual sin that since Aquinas in the thirteenth century has been considered by many as the most grievous.[75] The unnatural human-animal conjunction implied in the snake's homoerotic appeal thus spirals morally ever downward, turning sexual knowledge into something that is not only embodied but caused by the conjunction of two errant female wills.[76] And because the Fall is also a fall into human history, into temporality itself, the seduction of Eve registers women's erotic embodiment and sexual knowledge as ambivalent agents of historical time. It is because of women, in this cultural narrative, that sex becomes intertwined with embodiment, sin, femininity, knowledge, and history.

This nexus of associations is a far cry from the modern dispensation in which sex is the privileged site of truth—the truth of the subject, the repository of the secrets of the individual self. In contrast, the knowledge of sex associated with early modern women was a *fallen* truth, one that moved the desiring subject away from God, the progenitor of all meaning. In this context, sexual knowledge could only be fraught for early modern women—an ensnaring catch-22. In intellectual and theological terms, female bodies represented something that could not and should not be known (except by a privileged few), as well as something that should not be talked about (except by a growing community of male "experts"). Women not only inhabited this position of nonknowledge; they were thought to personify it. In the medieval period, women's bodies were considered to be repositories of secrets: the secrets of nature, the secrets of knowledge, the secrets of sex.[77] As the quest for greater and more sufficient explanatory knowledge began to be pursued outside of the monastery through medical practice, the theme of secrets lodged within the female body became an authorizing topos for science itself.[78]

This official discourse, whereby sexual knowledge was assumed to be both lodged within the female body yet was supposedly known and articulated only by male elites, was contravened in practice. In domestic life, expert knowledge of the body and of sex was in fact the province of "ordinary women," who, "through their practice of midwifery and of kitchen physic or medical care in the household" gained, practiced, and disseminated sexual knowledge.[79] Yet, the body that they supervised was simultaneously a source of knowledge shared with other women and a troubling source of vexed intimacy among them. It was also a frequent source of friction in their dealings with men. For women to express sexual knowledge in most public arenas, in particular, was self-incriminating, for it was virtually impossible to reveal such knowledge, particularly during legal processes, without seeming to confirm one's own lack of chastity. "This was a culture," in the words of Laura Gowing, "in which it was positively virtuous not to be able to describe sex."[80]

Awareness of such gendered paradoxes and epistemological double binds inform the affective, analytical, and political substrate that has generated much of this book. Early modern women are descendants of the seduced, seducing Eve *and* simultaneously that of her mirror image, the female-headed snake. Such figures are desirous of knowledge and either lack the wisdom and restraint that would tell them what they don't (need to) know or resist the presumption of such limits. At the same time, in Eve's listening to the seductions of the serpent, in her grasping for that apple, we can see her foredoomed effort to push beyond the constraints on permitted knowledge, on the terms of her embodiment and sexuality. Precisely because Eve and her progeny are damned for it, *Thinking Sex with the Early Moderns* reclaims the legacy of these figures, figured intimately in colloquy, on behalf of sexual knowledge itself.

These knowledge relations take the feminist concerns of this book beyond a focus on positive and negative representations of women (and men) to ask about the structural, epistemological dynamics that constitute the possibility of representation of sex in the first place. These dynamics are mobile, unstable, and thus subject to the deconstructive work that often is allied with that of "queering." Thus, one important strand of the analytical work of this book is to pause at the moments when the practice of queering meets up with the entailments of gender, where the fact of gendered embodiment and its relationship to ignorance and knowledge, power and authority, are both destabilized and materialized. Such a pause doesn't merely challenge the universalizing pretensions of queer theory, which has based much of its intervention on distancing queerness from the minoritizing claims of identity.[81] It encourages us to scrutinize the diacritical relations of gender to sexuality, while recognizing that gender itself is diacritical insofar as masculinity and femininity are knowable only through their difference and interaction.[82]

Identification Histories

One way I have pursued a diacritical approach to gender and sexuality is by mobilizing a concept of cross-gender identification. Hazily defined in queer and gender studies, cross-gender identification involves a process—psychic, affective, analytical, and political—of transiting across gender boundaries. An important feature of early modern performances of gender,[83] cross-gender identification—when repurposed as a method—directs attention to several investments. Thinking in terms of cross-gender identification, first, assembles useful perspectives generated out of one gender on behalf of another. In practice, this means that one might recognize in the specificity of male embodiment some dispositions toward knowledge and sex that can benefit women, or that one might deploy pressure on a universal, nongendered category such as queer by considering women's relation to it.

Second, cross-gender identification trains our eye on the fact that desires are not endlessly fluid and free-floating, but mobile across and through specific sites of embodiment and enunciation.[84] Indeed, given that my interest in cross-gender identification is less in the deconstruction of the male/female binary than in the transit across sites whose specificity is precisely what is at issue, this concept may help us refine the work that we want the concept of queer to do.[85]

While these investments derive from thinking of cross-gender identification in terms of identities, cross-gender identification also facilitates the critical move beyond that terrain by shifting the focus to dynamic social and psychic processes.[86] Understood as the "play of difference and similitude in self-other relations," identification both produces resemblance and self-recognition and disrupts them.[87] As Marjorie Rubright describes the critical turn this involves in relation to ethnicity, "attending to the process of identification . . . reframes our object of analysis by shifting analytic pressure from the 'what' (groups, identities, ethnic distinctiveness) to the 'how' (the dynamic processes wherein questions of identity and ethnicity emerge)."[88] For my purposes, identification (and disidentification) are particularly useful insofar as they call attention to the *work* involved in any relationship as it seeks to negotiate difference and achieve momentary stasis, balance, or coherence.[89]

This dynamic notion of psychic process inflects the scholarship of historians and historicist literary critics when they construe "history" as something imaginatively knit together through active engagement with material fragments and traces. Whether they stress the alterity of the past or its connection to us, such scholars reasonably aver that the selection, organization, and interpretation of archival remains are subject to our identifications and desires.[90] The following chapters build on this insight but morph it for additional purposes. First, I am intent on showing that identification and disidentification enable us to hone in on the kinds of psychic, cultural, and historiographic labor of making sexual history. Second, I assume that disidentification and disavowal are as crucial as affirmative desire and recognition in that process of making. Third, I show that the play of similarity and difference within dynamics of psychic (dis)identification provides analytical purchase on the unpredictable oscillation of similarity and difference within historiographic practice.

Proceeding from the conviction that the future of feminist, queer sexuality studies lies in an enhanced ability to identify across rather than solely along the vectors of gender and sexuality, the historiography I've practiced here is both retrospective and prospective; it recognizes, on the one hand, that "the past exists in a state of infinite regress" and, on the other hand, that "the past is always coming at us."[91] We are the pivot between past and future, their point of vital and vitalizing connection. What is at stake in this perception is a certain way of critically inhabiting a relation to a distant "other" (who can in various ways seem a lot like the self). Most especially, this practice includes not only recognition of the "blind spots in our current understanding,"[92] as is often suggested, but an injunction to explore how blind spots condition the very possibility of thought. For this reason, for all my interest in defamiliarizing the present, the historiography I advocate doesn't so much put all its "faith in exposure"[93] as presume that deconstructive disclosure must be accompanied by recognition of those impasses that resist being thought.

The Questions of Psychoanalysis

So conceived, historiography, like sex, names a knowledge relation. It also bears a certain relationship to psychoanalytic thought. To approach identification and disidentification as psychic fuel in the project of making sexual

knowledge suggests the utility of psychoanalysis for historiography. Psychoanalysis takes many forms and has a century-long, multifarious, and contentious history of its own. It names, simultaneously, a theory of how things
work (e.g., the drives and its affects), a set of analytic concepts (e.g., the
unconscious, repression, displacement), and a program of action (e.g., therapy, hermeneutics). It is the second of these—psychoanalysis as a set of
concepts—that is most relevant to my project, as I occasionally take recourse
in the analytical resources offered by specific concepts regarding the mechanisms of psychic process (particularly identification, transference, and displacement). I approach psychoanalytic concepts and techniques as themselves
historical phenomena and thus part of an evolving and internally self-critical
method.[94] Far from being the explicit framework of the analysis contained
herein (or assuming a total congruence between psychoanalytic methods and
the history of sexuality),[95] psychoanalysis provides this book with a certain
disposition toward knowledge.[96]

The largest departure of this book from most psychoanalytic work is that
its focus is not the desiring subject; its greatest debt is to the idea that knowledge is opaque and recalcitrant.[97] Knowledge, in psychoanalysis, is believed
to develop through anxiety, resistance, refusal, dependence, disavowal, hate,
frustration, and abjection, as well as through identification, desire, attachment, gratitude, fantasy, pleasure, and love. One might opine that the idea
of sex as inscrutable and resistant to understanding is merely the mythology
of psychoanalysis itself: sex resists understanding so that we can mobilize
more techniques to know it. Shifting from the attempt to discover the truth
of the subject to exploring how we practice sex-as-knowledge-relation, however, enables us to scrutinize and to think more carefully about the specific
forms that resistance and attachment take.

When approached as a mode of knowledge relation, psychoanalysis can be
employed not for its prepositional contents (the Oedipal complex, the mirror
stage), but for its *propositional syntax*. This syntax is valuable to the extent
that it elicits a questioning attitude not only toward the "incognito of the
unconscious"[98] but toward processes of knowing and making knowledge.
Indeed, a propositional syntax directs attention to the kinds of psychic and
social *work* involved in *making sex mean*, whether in the past or in the present.
If there is one thing this emphasis on labor entails, it is recognition that
sexual knowledge is elusive, that it requires us to slow down to catch its
peculiar tempo, and that, far from functioning as "the sinecure of self presence,"[99] sex is just as likely to disrupt such certitude.

One premise of this book is that the psychoanalytic concept of transference—that dynamic exchange of energies (affective, erotic, and cognitive) between any two interlocutors—as well as the related concept of "working through" can be leveraged for the purposes of historiographic practice. The concepts of transference and countertransference offer a structural understanding of some of the strategies and stakes of one's engagement with the past. Whether transferential energies exist between analyst and analysand, reader and text, or historian and event, whether they are construed as erotically charged or not, they compose a dynamic and tensile knowledge relation.[100] Reversing classic psychoanalytic treatments of "history," it is helpful to think of the past in the position of the analyst, the historian/critic in that of the analysand. The analysand's desires, identifications, and unconscious wishes may be foregrounded in the analytic encounter, as the analysand may "identify with, repeat, or performatively reenact forces active in it,"[101] but they are understood to be only one aspect of the complex negotiation between "pastness" and the scholar. And yet, certain aspects of the traditional position of analyst to history-as-analysand remain relevant to this encounter. To the extent that the historiographic impulse is an orientation toward a distant and inscrutable "other" (whether construed as similar to or different from oneself), it can adopt an attitude akin to that of psychoanalysis in its listening mode: actively attending to what is and is not spoken, by whom, and in what context. A psychoanalytic orientation to the past, then, entails scholars taking up the position of both the analyst (who listens, who inquires, who is conscious of countertransference) and the analysand (who desires, who identifies with, who engages in transference).

If, as psychoanalytic thinkers are apt to aver, the process of analysis involves closeness and distance, "extreme intimacy and extreme impersonality,"[102] this spatialized tension nicely captures the posture toward the past that the following chapters attempt to enact: attentive to the "working through" of issues within early modern texts alongside the "working through" of problems extant between those texts and the present moment. Such a working through does not lead to closure, but to the examination of ongoing forms of relationality and perceptual, psychic, and political processes. Within this intimate yet not-personal encounter, it is not just that the unconscious desire of the observer changes the object of study but that analysis of such desire can produce knowledge about both the observer and the past as an object—including what it is impossible to know.[103] This feedback loop, in short, involves and depends upon the transferential historicity of knowledge relations.[104]

Faithful attention to the past, one might counter, is the aim of all rigorous historical and historicist scholarship. So much is true. But there is one important distinction that underlies my yoking of historiography with a psychoanalytic disposition: when pursued as a method of open-ended interpretation rather than of pinning down meaning; when pausing over the tensions between knowing and not knowing; when lingering with the implications of the limits of knowledge—history making can be seen to perform psychoanalysis in a different key. What draws these strategies into paratactic relation is a process of thinking *with*. Strolling alongside and pausing along the way, this stance encourages a critical aptitude attentive to the caesuras, the gaps and false starts, the moments of inarticulacy, that structure and punctuate narratives, methods, and analyses of sex.[105]

Psychoanalysis, Early Modernity, Queer Studies

My emphasis on psychic work and on thinking sex transferentially aligns *Thinking Sex with the Early Moderns* with certain tendencies within both early modern studies and queer studies. Early modern critics whose interests in desire and its vicissitudes are frankly epistemological provide the closest cognate to my own.[106] For instance, I share with Ben Saunders a wish to understand "the relation of desire to understanding"[107] and recognize with him that this relation is caught up in the unknowable "wild card" of our own desires.[108] The subject's failure to know likewise motivates Graham Hammill's observation that "while Freud and Lacan are both very sure of what sexuality is not, neither is very sure at all of what it is. What makes psychoanalysis of great interest to the study of sexuality is this uncertainty."[109] Furthermore, "the difficulty that psychoanalytic thought has with sexuality is symptomatic of sexuality itself as an object of critical knowledge and historical analysis."[110] But having torqued the framework away from desire-as-subjectivity to sex-as-knowledge-relation, my synthesis of psychoanalysis with historiography attempts a balancing act unconsidered by these critics. If psychoanalysis urges us to stay with contradictions and to mind the epistemological gap, not by stepping over it but by stepping *into* it,[111] an appreciation of historical contingency reminds us that there might be some good reasons on occasion to climb out in order to reach firmer ground. The method I strive to enact greets the charisma of answers with charitable interest but also generous skepticism; it greets naïveté with patience and warm regard; and by taking time to dwell in *im*possibility, it tries as long as possible to keep multiple options available—while also recognizing when it is necessary to take a stand.

Such stands feel especially urgent in queer studies right now. In my effort to explore the psychic work entailed by thinking sex in and as history, this book pushes against a governing, if underarticulated, assumption in queer studies: that erotic desires and practices are best characterized as *pleasure*. And here, both Foucault's separation of pleasure from desire,[112] and psychoanalysis, whose concept of *jouissance* often serves as a touchstone, have a lot to answer for. I have two objections to the queer uptake of *jouissance*. First, in psychoanalytic thought, *jouissance* is a far more complex, self-contradictory concept than its anodyne translation as "enjoyment," "pleasure," or even "orgasm" (*jouir* is the French term for orgasm) would suggest. As L. O. Aranye Fradenburg writes: "The concept of *jouissance* has little in common with the notion of satisfaction. It is libidinal rapture at or beyond the limit of our endurance—most obviously orgasm, but by extension, any ecstasy that depends in some way on the exacerbation of sensuous experience. *Jouissance* is not pleasure, because it involves unpleasurable excesses of sensation. . . . Nor does it satisfy 'me': 'I' lose 'myself' in it. 'I' am even, all too often, averse to it, because 'I' do not *want* to lose myself in it."[113] As a radical divestiture of the self, *jouissance* is opposed to the kinds of ego- and identity-affirming gestures that, despite its anti-identitarian polemics, underwrite much queer scholarship.

More important, the queer celebration of *jouissance* often seems intent on promoting the counterfactual notions that erotic desire inevitably will be experienced in ways that stimulate ascending excitation (either as a continuous arc, movement from plateau to plateau, or through ebbs and flows) and lead, indispensably and inexorably, to a climax of bodily and mental arousal and satisfaction.[114] Even Leo Bersani—whose influential analysis of erotic self-shattering "which disrupts the ego's coherence and dissolves its boundaries"[115] is framed by the crucial insight that "there is a big secret about sex: most people don't like it"[116]—implies that sex is fundamentally, essentially, about pleasure.[117] When presuming enjoyment and gratification as the sine qua non of sex, queer studies might be said to enforce its own it-goes-without-saying: after all, if it weren't for pleasure, why would we be queer?[118] Needless to say, this presumption is based on a convenient forgetting of another psychoanalytic premise upon which much queer theory was founded:

that desire, psychically emerging out of the experience and management of loss, as well as negotiations of the boundaries between self and other, repeatedly entails significant evasions of satisfaction. (Queer studies scholars tend to accept this as a tenet of the formation of subjectivity but forget its implications for bodily experience.) Yet, rather than ontologize the notion that desire is always in excess of the capacity to satisfy it, as queer Lacanians are apt to do, I translate this insight into a methodological compass, one that directs our orientation toward obstacles and limits.

To be prosaic about it, the taking for granted of orgasmic "achievement" and sexual "satisfaction" fails to confront the force of compulsions and aversions that animate, direct, and constrain people's erotic lives—whether these constraints are felt in terms of object choice (including unconscious predilections for certain gendered, raced, and classed bodies), particular body parts or prosthetics (dildos, nipple or cock rings), explicit corporeal activities (looking, sucking, rubbing, penetration), or sites and social contexts (bedroom, bathhouse, hotel, public toilet, park). For every affirmative experience of desire ("I want that"), there implicitly are posed other desires ("I *don't* want *that*), which may be more or less inflexible or aversive ("I might like that with this person or that object, but not here, not now"). For all the thought that has been expended on the cultural penchant for classifying people according to the gender of their erotic partners (and these preferences are now, for good reasons, generally understood to be *not* born of antipathy), with the exception of psychological and therapeutic discourses, relatively little serious attention has gone into understanding the function of *dis*pleasure— not to mention dissatisfaction, disappointment, making do, boredom, and privation—that exist as an undercurrent of many people's erotic lives.[119] Sex for many is a matter of perennial trial and considerable error, not only in respect to attaining "good enough" sex with particular partners, but in terms of preferred bodily acts. Indeed, as Sedgwick noted on behalf of erotic difference, "Many people have their richest mental/emotional involvement with sexual acts that they don't do, or even don't *want* to do."[120] If the thriving market for self-help books, magazine stories, and online advice columns indicates anything, it is that sex remains for many a mysterious domain—even a *problem*—with basic understandings of anatomy, physiology, affective and sexual response in question throughout the life span.

To the extent that queer studies assumes rather than analyzes the pleasures of sex and implicitly relegates sexual frustration, sexual unhappiness, and *bad sex* to the domain of therapeutic intervention,[121] it not only leaves something important out of its domain of inquiry, implying that the question of sexual ineptitude and dissatisfaction aren't worth theorizing,[122] but fails to benefit from the ways that trial and error provide a means for theorizing sex itself.[123] This book proposes that it is by attending to various obstacles to sexual satisfaction, very broadly construed, that we might devise new questions and alternative ways of thinking sex. In short, it hopes to persuade that queer theory could exploit the conceptual payoff of bad sex by including within its sphere of attention sex that is frustrating, dissatisfying, even aversive—for it is out of these affective states, and the quotidian adjustments they require, that queer worlds also emerge.[124]

Thinking Sex with the Early Moderns

Thinking Sex with the Early Moderns has been impelled by my political commitments as a feminist, my previous research on the cultural history of lesbianism, my training as an early modern literary critic, and my cross-disciplinary institutional location. Posing these commitments in various relations to one another, it enacts an interdisciplinary vision of critical and historical practice: one that is simultaneously feminist and queer, that mines the analytical value of cross-gender identification, and is as respectful of the protocols of archival research as of psychic indeterminacy and close reading. Its meta-level register, however, is perhaps more akin to that of "theory" than is usually the case in literary criticism or historical scholarship. Indeed, because it is hard to outline the contours of an opacity—it refers, after all, to a shadowy presence, with murky edges subject to fluctuating degrees of illumination—I approach sexual knowledge obliquely, through the varying interpretative practices it occasions. Because the latter chapters assume familiarity with terminology, historiographic issues, and critical debates introduced earlier, they are best read in the order they appear. Although certain concerns of the sections overlap, their arguments do not so much repeat as become refracted through the prism of various angles of vision and interpretation; certain issues telescope in and out, as I use literary readings to theorize and historicize, and use history and literature to test the limits of theory.

The book's first part, "Making the History of Sexuality," takes up problems of historiographic method as pursued by historians and literary scholars. It does so first from the standpoint of the history of male homosexuality, then by investigating the effort to queer temporality, and third from the perspective of lesbian historiography. These approaches, though distinct, are interrelated, and by the end of Part I they accrue into something close to a methodological desideratum. That desideratum is itself interdisciplinary: if Chapter 2 engages with historiography as practiced by a historian, and Chapter 3 engages with literary critics who position their projects against disciplinary history, Chapter 4 offers my own proposal for "how to do" the history of sexuality at the intersection of these disciplines by focusing on the particular problems of lesbian history. Together these chapters suggest ways to balance historical sameness and difference, continuism and alterity, queer theory and the history of sexuality, and they bring clarity to the principles of selection by which one idea, figure, or trope is made to correspond to another.

Part II, "Scenes of Instruction; or, Early Modern Sex Acts," builds on Part I's historiographic inquiries, while also querying what it means to assert historical knowledge. Postulating that the scrutiny of sex acts enables special access to the obscured substrate of sexual historiography, I comprehensively survey the state of our knowledge about early modern sexual practices and offer a framework for how to productively work the constitutive contradictions first adduced in the scholarship of Bray. If Part I focuses on sex as represented *in* history, Part II begins to make a case for construing sex not only as the effect of historical processes or as a precise set of practices, but as an agent *of* history—that is, an agent in historical processes of knowledge production. But in order to apprehend this agency, we need to consider whether what "presents" as a historiographic problem is in fact an epistemological one. To consider this issue by means of specific examples, Part II focuses on what we still do not know about early modern sex, asking what this "lack" might tell us. It closely reads early modern language and texts and scrutinizes literary and historical scholarship, attending in particular to the role of presumptive knowledge in the making of sexual knowledge. Advocating the import of what we don't know as well as what we *can't* know, Part II explores the meanings of sexual acts, sexual language, sexual publics, and sex education both in the early modern period and today. In addition, by modeling cross-gender identification as a critical practice on behalf of women, and by managing the gap between treatments of sex as representation and sex as material practice, Part II puts into critical practice some of the methods introduced in Part I.

Part III, "The Stakes of Gender," pairs two chapters that might seem to have nothing to do with one another, insofar as one is about the relationship between male homoerotic and heteroerotic desire in an early modern sonnet sequence and the other is about lesbianism in contemporary critical discourse. This counterintuitive pairing, however, allows me to capitalize on the methodological payoff of the previous sections, bringing into explicit theorization the diacritical relationships between gender and sexuality, and both to history. These chapters build methodologically on Annamarie Jagose's proposition in *Inconsequence: Lesbian Representation and the Logic of Sexual Sequence* that sexuality "is culturally produced as a sequential fiction."[125] Viewed from the perspective of sequence, all sexual identifications are "always secondary, always back formations, always belated."[126] This belatedness is projected specifically onto the representation of lesbianism, which typically is viewed as inconsequential and imitative, thereby masking a "disavowal of precisely that derivativeness which . . . is the heart of sexuality itself."[127] Whereas Jagose's consideration of sequence hinges its critique of the terms of lesbian visibility on the precedential ordering of first and second, origin and derivation, I have repurposed her deconstructive analytic. Splitting the terms of her analysis apart, Chapter 8 focuses on the import of sequence in Shakespeare's sonnets, while Chapter 9 focuses on the secondariness of lesbianism in current critical dispensations. My reading of the difficulties involved in diacritically reading Shakespeare's sonnets no less than "the sign of the lesbian" demonstrates that both, in fact, function as exquisite metonymies of the problem of sexual opacity to which this book is dedicated.

"Sex Ed; or, Teach Me Tonight" concludes the book by meditating on the opacity of sexual knowledge in the current moment. An extempore rejoinder at a sexuality studies conference provides an occasion to consider the impossible pedagogical imperatives involved in queer studies as well as in a more capaciously conceived "sex education." While collating and distilling the argumentative energies of the preceding chapters, this chapter ties the analysis of history to the larger stakes—of pedagogy, ethics, and futurity—that motivate the book as a whole. It returns us to the intellectual, historiographic, and pedagogical disposition that would recognize in what we don't know, as well as what we can't know, not only the partiality of our methods and a spur to future inquiry but an intractability that has been constitutive of the history of sex and that continues to inform our relations to that history and to each other.

By attempting to think sex with the early moderns, this book aims to show that the obstacles we face in making sexual history can illuminate the difficulty of knowing sexuality and that both impediments can be adopted as a guiding principle of historiography, pedagogy, and ethics. It is not just that the truth of sex is not fully attainable or representable in words or images, as the contingencies of sexual signification manifest. Nor is it just that sexuality is socially constructed or a product of manifold historical processes. From the second chapter dedicated to the scholarship of Alan Bray to the tenth chapter dedicated to sexual pedogogy, I hope to persuade that the projects of knowing sex, thinking sex, and making sexual knowledge are situated within the space of an irresolvable contradiction. Other queer studies scholars have asserted and analyzed the "the unknowability of the sexual,"[128] sexuality's "epistemic uncertainty,"[129] and the "unfathomable nature of the erotic."[130] They have provocatively raised "the question of sexuality *as a question*,"[131] noting the radical incommensurability between self-knowledge, erotic desire, and the social shapes desire assumes.[132] It is one task of those of us in historical sexuality and queer studies to work this contradiction, to render its constitutive irony resonant and productive. Rather than deploy the apprehension of uncertainty and inscrutability to defend psychoanalysis as a method, to situate theory and literature against history, to extract an archival ethics of eroticism out of Foucault, or to separate feminism from queer studies, I use the opacity of sex to draw queer and psychoanalytic theory, history and literature, feminist and queer interests, closer together.

This book represents my effort to think my way not out but by means of a series of epistemological dead ends. As critics, many of us are a lot better at critique than in collaboratively envisioning, much less creating, structures that would stimulate analysis of the recalcitrant knowledge relations considered in these pages.[133] To the extent that this book engages in critique,[134] I have been motivated by the belief that energy is gained not only when scholars enthusiastically agree about the animating force of a new concept or a renewed method, but when we disagree, when we are not all intent on the same general project, and when pressure is put on existing as well as emerging concepts and methods. If some of this book takes the form of critique, however, most of it gambles on envisioning a different scholarly horizon, where ignorance is productive, inarticulacy is treasured, and bewilderment beckons us toward different questions to ask of the relationship between sex and bodies in time. In recasting the issues as ones of epistemology and pedagogy rather than subjectivity and identity, of knowledge and ignorance rather than norms and their transgression, of erotic dissatisfaction as much as erotic pleasure, of sequence and syntax alongside semiotic content, and of *how* we know as much as *what* we know, *Thinking Sex with the Early Moderns* strives to enact an ethical relation, finally, to *sex*, that is worthy of and accountable to its ongoing history.

PART I

Making the History
of Sexuality

CHAPTER 2

Friendship's Loss

Alan Bray's Making of History

Explaining the motives and procedures of an "intellectual history that is correlated with critical theory," Dominick LaCapra emphasizes that such a project focuses "on modes of conceptualization and argument—the way material is or is not thought out, 'emplotted,' worked over, and set forth."[1] Furthermore, it "often moves on the 'meta' level by inquiring into its objects of study, along with the ways they have been studied, through interrogating and at times contesting their assumptions or sense of what is or is not worthwhile and valid. Thought here takes an insistently dialogic form in interrogating the work of others and in opening itself to interrogating in the interest of both disclosing questionable assumptions or arguments and enabling intellectual movement toward more desirable alternatives."[2]

I am not an intellectual historian. And my poles of orientation are less post-structuralism and disciplinary history than queer theory and feminism. However, the impetus for the chapters that follow share with LaCapra an interest in "modes of conceptualization and argument," and they enact my response to "the very way problems are articulated."[3] This motive necessitates returning to constitutive formulations of a field, as well as raising basic questions about its genesis in order to examine the "prereflective disciplinary habitus" within which practitioners engage.[4] I thus begin with some of the concepts devised by one of the originators of the history of early modern sexuality in an effort both to honor his intellectual legacy and to ask how scholars might work with and through the questions that this legacy raises.

❧   ❧   ❧

In the headnote that precedes his essay "The Body of the Friend," Alan Bray describes the painful occasion that gave impetus to his work:

> In 1987 I heard Michel Rey, a student of J.-L. Flandrin in the University of Paris, give a lecture entitled "The Body of My Friend." The lecture was only an outline, and his early death left his doctoral thesis uncompleted and his loss keenly felt by many. But in the years that followed that lecture Michel and I often discussed the history of friendship, and I have sought in this paper to complete that paper as he might have done had he lived, as a tribute to his memory. It is a paper about the body of the friend at the onset of the modern world and its loss.[5]

In a position not unlike that of Bray, I—along with you—confront the loss of a scholar who has done more, perhaps, than any other to return the body of the friend, and with it the complex meanings of intimacy, to historical consciousness. Although it did not fall to me to complete the monumental piece of scholarship that is *The Friend*, the manuscript Alan Bray was finishing at the time of his death, it does fall to me to try to do justice to a scholarly legacy that has had a singular, indispensable, and galvanizing effect on the history of sexuality, and that has, in its complete form, transformed the histories of friendship and the family.[6]

Bray's first book, *Homosexuality in Renaissance England*, forcefully exposed a cultural contradiction: whereas sodomy was associated apocalyptically with debauchery, heresy, foreignness, and sedition, and thus the dissolution of the social order, intimate male friendship enabled all manner of legitimate social ties and mutually beneficial obligations, advancing homosocial relations within the patriarchal social order.[7] There was nonetheless an affinity and a symmetry between representations of universally admired masculine friendship and officially condemned sodomy—as Bray later put it, "they occupied a similar terrain."[8] The result of this "unacknowledged connection between the unmentionable vice of Sodom and the friendship which all accounted commendable" was widespread cognitive dissonance, a reluctance to recognize in idealized friendship the dreaded signs of sodomy.[9] The disparity between the rhetoric of unspeakability that governed public discourses and those social and erotic practices in which many men engaged indicated to Bray a "quiet, nominal adjustment," perhaps unique to Renaissance England.[10] This accommodation began to show signs of strain by the end of the sixteenth century, when changes in social relations and modes of symbolizing them caused the overlap in legitimate and illegitimate forms of male intimacy to become an identifiable social problem. With the rise of economic individualism and social pluralism—represented most visibly in the advent of London molly houses—male homoeroticism was dissociated from the broad nexus of homosociality. Newly legible as a secular social ill, it increasingly was prosecuted, as raids on molly houses arranged by the Society for the Reformation of Manners from 1699 to 1738 attest.

In advancing this thesis, Bray's book demonstrated that homosexuality is not a stable, unchanging fact of sexual life, but a dynamic field of signification that possesses a history of its own, a history closely tied to other social phenomena: the structure of the household, the growth of cities, the emergence of individualism. To make these connections was to extricate the historiography of homosexuality from its preoccupation with the identification of gay individuals and to refocus it on the analysis of social structures and processes that regulate the intelligibility of same-gender attachments. Thus, despite the proliferation of scholarship on male homoeroticism and queer readings since the publication of Bray's book in 1982, what Jonathan Goldberg said in his 1994 introduction to *Queering the Renaissance* is still true today: "*Homosexuality in Renaissance England* remains the groundbreaking and unsurpassed historical investigation for the period."[11]

As if to make explicit the larger historical narrative of which *Homosexuality in Renaissance England* is a part, *The Friend*, offered as volume 2 to Bray's history of male bonds, broadens out temporally in both directions. Tracing protocols of masculine friendship from the eleventh to the nineteenth century, Bray constructs an immensely learned archaeology of the "formal and objective" expressions of intimacy and obligation that are part of a forgotten history of the family, religion, and what he calls traditional society.[12] Rather than function as the only basis of social cohesion, the early modern family subsisted within larger structures of relation, including those of Christian ritual, service, and "voluntary kinship"—the kinship created by ritual or promise, as in the bonds forged by adoption or sworn brotherhood.[13] Insofar as the role of Christianity in traditional society was, according to Bray, to help members of the community to live in peace, its rites recognized several forms of binding commitment, including marriage, kinship, and friendship.[14] Focused on the public witnessing of such unions in baptism, the Eucharist, the kiss of peace, and burial, as well as the sharing of beds and familiar correspondence, *The Friend* demonstrates friendship's equivocal role not only in giving a social shape to masculine bonds but in threatening them. Friendship, Bray insists, was not an unreserved good; it could be compromised by expectations of material interest, influence, and advancement. Given the precariousness of relations in the public sphere, he argues, even the best of friendships could be shadowed by suspicions of collusion, misuse, and enmity, imparting an ethical uncertainty to friendship even when it was most clearly a matter of love. In a characteristic hermeneutic move, Bray discovers traces of the equivocal nature of friendship not only in the rites of traditional Christianity but in the idealized rhetoric of love and fidelity through which friendship was inscribed in letters, poetry, and burial monuments. Such idealized constructions, which we might assume to be empty conventions, were, in part because of their conventionality, replete with affect; in particular, they negotiated the fear that one's friend might prove to be one's enemy. By excavating the remains of friendship in public sites and rituals heretofore obscured by a historical enterprise intent on recognizing only the kinship created by marriage, by locating the family within an encompassing network of friendship that kinship also created, and by interpreting friendship from the standpoint of the Christian ethics it embodies, Bray's compelling narrative returns to the praxis of friendship a social and historical efficacy that, until his work, had largely been forgotten. *Why* it was forgotten as the Enlightenment ushered in civil society will be of considerable interest to those who seek to understand how the past paved the way for our present.

The influence of Bray's first book and published essays can be seen in all subsequent treatments of male homoeroticism from 1550 to 1800 in England, in no small part because of his activist commitment to "play[ing] a part in changing" "the world around us as history has given us it."[15] Yet it implies a serious underestimate of the value of *Homosexuality in Renaissance England* that the book most often is cited only for its exposure of cognitive dissonance and its narrative regarding the emergence of a homosexual identity. Because of the stranglehold that questions of identity and the dating of its consolidation have had on the history of homosexuality, and because the critical accent has been on the content of Bray's historical scheme rather than the method by which he composed it, the considerable conceptual advances he made in charting an epistemic shift in the intelligibility of male bonds have not been fully assessed.[16] By highlighting some of his additional contributions to historiographic method, I hope to draw attention to the opportunities and challenges they offer for future engagement and critical dialogue, including the extent to which his work intersects with yet also challenges certain dispositions within queer studies.

It is one of the paradoxes of Bray's scholarly career that the history of sexuality is not the discipline in which he would have located his work. Repeatedly he insists that to begin with the question of sexuality is to miscon-strue the issue.[17] The point, articulated throughout his corpus, is to view sexuality in a wider social and interpretive frame, whereas "the effect of a shaping concern with sexuality is precisely to obscure that wider frame."[18] This is true because "what is missing [in Renaissance discourses] is any social expression of homosexuality based on the fact of homosexuality itself. . . . What we look for in vain are any features peculiar to it alone."[19] Bray's determined ambivalence regarding the disciplinary field of sexuality studies is, I suggest, simultaneously a product of his historical inquiry and the ground out of which his historiography emerged. His insistence that sexuality—by which I mean not only the identity categories of homo and hetero, but the very idea of an autonomous field of erotic relations—was a post-seventeenth-century phenomenon motivates what I believe is his most decisive contribu-tion: the location of male intimacy in a range of early modern social systems. Having described in his first book the forms of social life in which homosexu-ality was embedded—the village, the household, the educational system, apprenticeship, prostitution, the theater—in subsequent work he situates male bonds within the symbolic gift systems of patronage, preferment, and service associated with the medieval great house. What he calls "the gift of the friend's body"—signified by public kisses and embraces, eating at the common table, the sharing of beds, the familiar letter—functioned up through the sixteenth century as a crucial form of "countenance."[20] Such public signs of favor and intimacy, Bray argues, were not only normative but instrumentally oiled the wheels of social relations. With the demise of the openhanded household—a change both architectural and social—the public conveyance of countenance through the friend's body ceased to be advanta-geous; lacking its prior symbolic capital, it became unintelligible. As England was transformed into a modern, civil society, friendship was recast as a nonin-strumental affinity: "rational, objective, universal," and for the most part irrelevant to Christian ethics and public affairs.[21] Situating this change within a new regime of visibility—the disappearance of lower servants from view, of gentlemen from service, of crowds drinking in the great hall—Bray offers a causal explanation for the growth of suspicion regarding behaviors previously deemed unexceptional, as well as for the persecution of mollies. Just as the "sodomite" took on a "new actuality," so too a "radically new meaning to the desire for the body of the friend" took shape.[22] As Bray memorably describes this shift, the public kiss and embrace were replaced by the handshake.[23]

Michel Foucault's corpus is often credited, rightly, with articulating the theoretical import of reading for silences, absences, and exclusions. Alan Bray's corpus, it seems to me, demonstrates the payoff of this approach. Characteristic of Bray's rhetorical stance is the adoption of the persona of the sleuth, embarked on a slow process of detection: painstakingly following a "forensic trail" of clues, sharing his mind as it works through assumptions and doubts, examining evidence from multiple angles, entertaining objections, and devising alternative methods in light of them.[24] The discovery of clues, of course, often is an effect of what is not said, and Bray's favored trope for this function in his own work—as well as that of others—was "the detective story where the clue was that the dog did *not* bark."[25] With steady tough-mindedness, he draws significance out of what is, and what is not, available in the archive. In so doing, the archive is reconfigured: it is not a storehouse or treasure chest waiting to be opened but a palimpsest of fragments, on the ragged edges of which hang unexpected meanings. Bray's articulation of the difference between Elizabethan and later discourses of male intimacy, for instance, hinges on "what is left out" in idealized expressions of friendship: the "tactful omission of those bonds of mutual interest of which the everyday signs were such conventions."[26] When suspicion *is* generated by accounts of friendship, as it increasingly was, it is because "some of the conventions of friendship are missing . . . and the missing ones are precisely those that ensured that the intimacy of these conventions was read in an acceptable frame of reference."[27] What could convert signs of male friendship into signs of sodomy, it turns out, was partly the mixing of status or degree—and it was only by looking for "the silence between the lines" that Bray hit upon the significance of social inequality to the sodomy-friendship interrelation.[28] For a social historian generally committed to traditional protocols of evidence, this emphasis on silence and insignificance, on traces and fragments and the difficulties of intelligibility they pose, was, especially at the time, a strikingly unconventional move.[29]

That erotic behavior might not signify in or by itself implicitly links the problem of representation to the issue of social embeddedness. The combined effect of this connection is to emphasize the uncertainty of sexuality's power of signification. As I noted in Chapter 1, Laurie Shannon has cogently rearticulated and extended Bray's argument, maintaining that there is nothing fully dispositive about eroticism to convey particular meanings; erotic acts operate only unreliably as a trigger for articulation.[30] Correlating the gift of the friend's body to the changing fate of homosexuality, for instance, Bray argues that the proximity of exalted and excoriated male bonds means that erotic affects and acts *could* be an element of both—it depends on how you look at it. How you look at it is itself influenced by historical factors, including what counts as sex in a given culture. What counts, of course, can be highly contingent, variable, and incoherent, even within a single culture and historical moment—as was brought home to everyone in the United States when President Bill Clinton avowed that whatever he did with Monica Lewinsky, it was not sex.[31]

One effect of showing that sodomy and friendship could be recognized at one moment as utterly distinct and at another moment as close to the same thing was to deconstruct, from a historically specific angle, the boundary between them. The complex elaboration of male intimacy throughout early modern society, coupled with the potential for erotic acts *not* to signify, creates the interpretative field into which *all* erotic behaviors fall: "Mediated as homosexuality then was by social relationships that did not take their form from homosexuality and were not exclusive to it, the barrier between heterosexual and homosexual behaviour . . . was in practice vague and imprecise."[32] One might expect, then, that changes in the social articulation of male bonds might affect the meanings of male intimacy with women—and indeed they did. Just as the sodomite became identifiable as a perversion of normative cross-sex alliance, so these alliances increasingly relied on the sodomite to secure their own status as natural and inevitable. Arguing that the transformation in male intimacy "placed a burden of social meaning on the heterosexual bond between husband and wife that before it had not been required to carry alone," and that, with the ascendance of civil society, the gift of the body came to be acknowledged "only as a sexual gift between men and women,"[33] Bray brings to the theoretical dictum of the dependence of the hetero on the homo a historical specificity it otherwise often lacks.[34]

Yet, it is important to acknowledge that, despite this deconstructive impulse, Bray never adopted the inversive desideratum of queer theory: that the burden of proof belongs to those who assume the presence of *hetero*sexuality. Committed as he was to the historian's protocols of evidence, and taking seriously sexuality's lack of dispositive power, he was cautious about assigning erotic signification to particular gestures, behaviors, texts, people. He especially discounted the truth value of Renaissance accusations of sodomy, whose evidentiary basis he rightly judged to be unreliable:

We will misunderstand these accusations if, beguiled by them, we uncriti-
cally assume the existence of the sexual relationship which they appear to point
to, for the material from which they could be constructed was rather open and
public to all. . . . Homosexual relationships did indeed occur within social
contexts which an Elizabethan would have called friendship. . . . But accusations [of sodomy] are not evidence of it.[35]

It is here, perhaps, that we can catch a glimpse of an unacknowledged
tension in Bray's corpus: on the one hand, the open and public nature of
friendship protected early modern men from suspicion of sodomy; on the
other, it somehow provides an indication in the present that they were not
involved in a "sexual relationship." In his first book, after noting the difficulties involved in using modern conceptual categories, Bray adopted the solution of using "the term homosexuality but in as directly physical—and hence
culturally neutral—a sense as possible."[36] How "culturally neutral" derives
from "directly physical" has long puzzled me, especially since the meaning
of "physical" seems here, by default, to imply anal intercourse—perhaps the
least culturally neutral, most overdetermined erotic activity during the early
modern period and today. Throughout the first book, then, homosexuality,
implicitly conflated with a single erotic practice, is also functionally equated
with sodomy. One result of this series of conflations is that the baseline
meaning of homosexuality, its status as an analytical object, is foreknown and
foreclosed—even as the locations in which it is expressed and the significations it accrues change over time.[37] Another result is that friendship—for all
its structural affinity with and proximity to homosexuality—is definitionally
posited as something *other* than homosexuality: not, as it were, "directly
physical."[38]

This is in fact Mario DiGangi's critique of the way that Bray manages the
tension between sodomy, homosexuality, and friendship: "Bray effectively
conflates 'homosexuality' with 'sodomy,' implicitly reduces both to the com-
mission of sexual acts, and then cordons off these proscribed sexual acts from
the nonsexual intimacy appropriate for 'friends.' "[39] In contrast, Jonathan
Goldberg confidently affirms that the combined theses of *Homosexuality in
Renaissance England* and the influential essay "Homosexuality and the Signs
of Male Friendship in Elizabethan England" imply that "much in the ordinary transactions between men in the period . . . took place sexually."[40] The
possibility of two such opposed interpretations of Bray's core argument is

symptomatic not of misreading or misappropriation but of a pervasive ambiguity animating his work. The analytic tension between eroticism and friendship became clearer to me while reading the manuscript of *The Friend*, where the embedding of intimacy in a vast range of social relations and the foregrounding of ethical considerations had the subtle but persistent effect of minimizing the possibility that the bonds being described were at all sexual. Throughout Bray's work, there is a recurring expression of concern that the reader might be "misled" by the appearance of erotic meanings, leading him or her to "misconstrue" the forces at work in the construction of male intimacy.[41] *The Friend's* brief for the ethical import of friendship is particularly punctuated by such cautions against misconstruction. Indeed, the ambiguities and tensions present in Bray's earlier work are heightened in his final book.

On the one hand, the intense emotional affects Bray excavates in *The Friend*—affects that give rituals and conventions their experiential salience and contribute to their social efficacy—would seem to belie any strict dichotomy between friendship and eroticism.[42] Early on Bray notes that the ethical praxis he aims to uncover need not have excluded the erotic: "The ethics of friendship in the world I describe began with the concrete and the actual, and the only way to exclude anything would be by abandoning that starting point. That hard-edged world included the potential for the erotic, as it included much else."[43] And, throughout the book he acknowledges the erotic *potential* of the physical closeness that, at any given moment, might signify one way or the other: bonds that, because of their association with social excess and disorder, signified sodomy; bonds that, due to their coherence with legitimate forms of social organization, signified friendship, kinship, obligation, love. On the other hand, sometimes Bray dismisses the historian's access to "the possible motives and nature of [a] physical relationship" by reducing such interpretation to "no more than speculations"—as in his discussion of Amy Poulter's marriage to Arabella Hunt.[44] Sometimes the potential eroticism of friends is specifically, even categorically, denied—most emphatically, perhaps, in the exposition of John Henry Cardinal Newman's shared grave with Ambrose St. John, which forms the coda of Bray's book: "Their bond was spiritual. . . . Their love was not the less intense for being spiritual. Perhaps, it was more so."[45] Whereas Bray in his final chapter pointedly asks (in response to the sexual escapades recorded in the diary of Anne Lister), "Would a sexual *potential* have stood in the way of the confirmation of a sworn friendship in the Eucharist? The answer must be that it would not, in that it evidently did not do so here,"[46] at the telos of his argument he resurrects, seemingly without hesitation, a stark division between spiritual and carnal love.[47] This division is apparent as well in Bray's objections to John Boswell's scholarship on same-sex unions; one of Boswell's mistakes was his inability to grasp "that the expected ideals of the rite would not have comprehended sexual intercourse."[48] Here, however, the circumspection of the qualifier "expected" perhaps carries Bray's central point: that is, the ease with which a distinction between love and sodomy was maintained in the official discourse of traditional society, whatever the actual nature of the relation.[49] The analytic ambiguity at the heart of *The Friend*'s emphasis on erotic *potential* thus pulls in two contradictory directions. At times this ambiguity expands the meaning of homoerotic affect, rendering it as something more than "just sex," a point about which Bray was explicit: "The inability to conceive of relationships in other than sexual terms says something of contemporary poverty."[50] But when this ambiguity slides into a categorical denial of eroticism, it risks conceding the defining terms of the argument to those who would protect the study of intimacy from eroticism's embodied materiality.

The risk of dematerializing eroticism was articulated two decades ago when Goldberg warned that sexuality "can always be explained in other terms, and in ways in which anything like sex disappears."[51] This caution will be examined in Chapter 6. It is worth noting that, despite the symbolic centrality of the gift of the friend's body in Bray's book, bodies themselves play a very small part in his discussion. One is tempted to say that the materiality of the body is displaced onto the memorials—the gravestones and churches—that populate his account.[52] Nonetheless, I wonder what Bray would have made of the triumphant proclamation on the inside dust jacket cover of *The Friend*: "He debunks the now-familiar readings of friendship by historians of sexuality who project homoerotic desires onto their subjects when there were none."[53] Certainly, Bray warned repeatedly against anachronism and misconstrual: he considered them bad history. But his own negotiation of this problem was considerably more nuanced than an effort to "debunk" the assertions of others; nor does the preemptive rejection of the mutual engagement between past and present implied in the term "projection" accurately convey his own historical method.[54] "Readers of this book can and will appropriate the past for themselves, if I stick to my job of presenting the past first in its own terms," he declares in the introduction to *The Friend*, and he follows up that remark with a pointed reference to the politics of the present: "Could it be that that very appropriation might prelude a resolution of the conflict between homosexual people and the Christian church today?"[55] Insofar as Bray stressed repeatedly that his scholarship grew out of an activist engagement with contemporary gay life, I suspect that any denigration of contemporary identification with a homoerotic past may have given him pause.[56]

It is not just that leveling a charge of projection in this way is inaccurate and offensive; more important, it circumvents, and thereby obscures, questions tacitly raised by Bray's scholarship but not resolved in it: namely, the relations between emotional and bodily intimacy, and what we make of them. Indeed, it is one of the legacies of his work that, although the tension between friendship and eroticism informs it at almost every turn, nowhere is the unstable line separating these forms of intimacy brought into direct focus and treated as an object of analysis. Bray casts his eye first on the conventions of friendship and then on those of sodomy, but in analyzing their connection, he seems to take his cue from early moderns themselves, who were unwilling "to take seriously the ambiguous borderland between the 'sodomite' and the shared beds and bonding of its male companionship."[57] For a historian to "take seriously" this "ambiguous borderland" would mean to submit to analytic scrutiny the movement across borders, the places where and the moments when (and not simply the processes by which) one thing becomes another. Bray's apparent preference was much like that of the early modern society he describes, which "knew that the gaps—and the overlaps—between one thing and its other had their utility."[58] Rather in the manner of the "accommodating ambiguity" he identifies elsewhere,[59] Bray does not parse his terms too precisely, as evinced by the sleight of hand in his remark that "the word 'love' in this society could comprehend as easily the public relation of friends as the more private meaning we give the word today, but wherever on that wide spectrum the gift of a friend's body might lie, it gestured toward a place of comforting safety in an insecure world."[60] Indeed, if one substitutes the term "eroticism" for "friendship" in Bray's statement that "the indirection of the language of friendship provided a circumspect path around it,"[61] one comes close to describing the rhetorical strategy he deployed in regard to the confused relations among the sexual, the physical, the subjective, and the affective.

Examining the ambiguous borderland, the overlap, between one thing and another might particularly have paid off in relation to one of Bray's key terms: voluntary kinship. It is striking that Bray ignores the applicability of voluntary kinship to the social structure of the molly house. Because of the tight link between sodomy and social disorder—a link that for Bray goes to the heart of what sodomy is—he fails to consider whether the vows of mollies, some of which follow the traditional script of marriage, might not also operate as an alternative form of kinship. The analytic division between friendship and sodomy, social disorder and social cohesion, enables him to recognize bonds of kinship only within the received structure of traditional society: in the form of male couples whose formal vows are backed by Christian ritual.

It may well be wrong to characterize Bray's circumspection in this regard as reticence or reluctance to confront the radical implications of his own work. As a historian, he appears to have approached the relation between friendship and eroticism primarily from the standpoint of evidence. In his final chapter, for instance, he asks of the body of the friend:

> But did it not also have the body's genitals? Did its symbolic significance stop short there? The laughter that closed an earlier chapter suggested that it did not. Yet the sexual potential in these gestures has repeatedly come into view only to slip away again. . . . This is not, of course, to say that the erotic has not been part of this history. But sexuality in a more narrow sense has eluded it whenever it has come into view. With the diary of Anne Lister that problem falls away.[62]

Yet even as the evaluation of evidence must persist as a preoccupation of historians, important questions of method and theory remain untouched by it. Whether Bray's disinclination to probe, rather than work adroitly around, the precise means of the overlap of friendship and eroticism *as a theoretical problem* indicates the historian's discomfort with the deconstructive ramifications of his own radical history or whether, conversely and paradoxically, it is a further measure of his own deconstructive commitments is a question about which I remain unsure. Bray delights, for instance, in the enigma of Shakespeare's Sonnet 20, which he calls a "dazzling tour de force" that "can be read *both* as asserting the chastity of friendship in the most transcendent of terms *and* as rejecting it in the most bawdy and explicit of terms."[63] In puzzling through this problem, I am reminded that Goldberg recognized that Bray's early work raised "formidable questions" of "ontology and epistemology": "what sodomy is and how it may be recognized."[64] In its performance of what appears to be a strategic ambiguity carried out in the name of ethics,

Bray's final book invites, if only to defer, questions just as formidable about the ontology and epistemology of friendship, eroticism, and sexuality.

In this regard, it is useful to unpack Bray's concluding comments in a review of books on homosexuality in which he notes, with what appears to be mixed appreciation and apprehension, that the books "have succeeded in undermining their very starting point in the questions they have steadily been drawn into asking. What then is the nature of sexual identity, or of any personal identity? What is the difference between the sexual and the nonsexual? . . . The history of sexuality will not provide answers to these questions, if indeed there are any, but it has disturbingly raised them; and it is there that its importance lies."[65] It is telling that Bray's skepticism regarding the history of sexuality as a field of knowledge production is articulated in the same breath as his apparent doubt regarding the field's ability to resolve ontological questions about the identity of and relations between sexuality and friendship. Both, I believe, are worthy cautions, and both insights inform the chapters that follow. Nonetheless, as the charge of "projection" of homoerotic desires that has been leveled in Bray's name vividly suggests, a countervailing epistemological and political danger is that *not* to pursue such ontological questions—what is sexuality? what is friendship? what is the nature of the difference between them?—risks ceding authority for answering them to those who would assert their own tendentious criteria for how sexuality is to be known. Rather than "[debunk] the now-familiar readings of friendship by historians of sexuality," Bray's historical scholarship intersects with the theoretical work of Eve Kosofsky Sedgwick in inviting several queries that are simultaneously epistemological and methodological: How do we *know* when there were no homoerotic desires between historical figures? What is the basis of our knowledge of the eroticism of the past? How *do* we know what (we think) we know?

Thinking Sex with the Early Moderns represents my own response to these questions, but the impetus for working them out was anticipated and inspired by Alan Bray. For the logic of Bray's corpus (if not the deliberate proffering of methodological dicta) implies certain propositions. First, if eroticism is always embedded in other forms of social relation, if acts of bodily intimacy are rendered intelligible only from within a precise social location, if the power of eroticism to signify is variable and uncertain, if we cannot always be confident that we have interpreted its presence or absence correctly, then eroticism, like sodomy and friendship, is apprehensible as a knowledge relation—one existing not only between people but between people and history. Not only will our desires for a usable past necessarily inform the history of sexuality we create, but the epistemological opacity of sexuality will be constitutive of the methods by which we investigate it. This recognition leads me, as it did not, apparently, lead Bray, to a second proposition. If we do not know the extent to which relations may have been erotic, it is as mistaken to assume that they were not as it is to assume that they were. In her afterword to *Queering the Renaissance*, Margaret Hunt urged scholars to "scramble the definitions and blur the boundaries of the erotic, both so as to forestall the repressive uses to which rigid understandings of it almost inevitably lend themselves, and to gain access to a much larger analytical arena."[66] In *The Renaissance of Lesbianism in Early Modern England*, I took that invitation as far as seemed historically responsible by adopting, as a heuristic axiom, a studied skepticism about any a priori dividing line between female friendship and female homoeroticism. It may be that the difference gender makes in this regard is particularly salient: not only did cultural images of tribades have little of the apocalyptic force conveyed by images of sodomites, but the practices of female friendship may have been more congruent with the expression of female eroticism than masculine friendship was with sodomy.[67] What counts as erotic, in other words, may involve gender differentials of which we are only now becoming sufficiently aware.

Insofar as the precise criteria one might use to sequester friendship from sexuality are nowhere theorized in Bray's work, we might approach the question of their relation as a productive fault line upon which his corpus is built—the "blindness" that enabled his considerable insight. If, as I have argued, Bray negotiated this fault line by deploying a strategic ambiguity—by seeming at one point to concede or advance an erotic interpretation while at other points explicitly denying that possibility—it may be because of some criteria of evidence known only to him. The fact remains that nowhere does he submit to *systematic* comparison any evidence of erotic affect in order to better delineate the homosocial from the homoerotic. Rather than preclude further investigation, the identification of this problem—and the hijacking of Bray's work to privilege asexual friendship over sexuality—should spur us on. Indeed, just how far the rhetoric and practice of masculine friendship comprehended the expression of erotic desire and the performance of erotic acts and whether it is possible to construct a legitimate definition of such criteria remain two questions unanswered by Bray's corpus—questions, in other words, for the rest of us.[68]

Additional questions embedded in Bray's work likewise deserve consideration. In the afterword to the 1995 edition of *Homosexuality in Renaissance England*, for instance, Bray boldly asserts that "attitudes to homosexuality unquestionably have been symptomatic of fundamental changes in European society and in substantial part *constitutive* of them."[69] Sexual representation is not merely mimetic; it has an efficacy, an agency, of its own. Such an assertion urges a greater appreciation of sexuality's ideological utility—not only its pliability and susceptibility to pressure but its ability to exert pressure on practices, discourses, and institutions external to it. But from where, one might ask, does this agency derive? Of one thing we can be sure: it is not a function of desire. Strikingly absent from Bray's work is any concept of desire as an internal, generative mechanism or drive. Such a concept is, to his mind, alien to the psychic, emotional, and ideological landscape of early modern culture. In his discussion of the sexual dreams and fantasies expressed in the diary of Michael Wigglesworth, for instance, Bray argues that the sexual impulses over which Wigglesworth agonized (the "filthy lust . . . flowing from my fond affection to my pupils") were experienced by this colonial subject as unbidden, separate from his will, not a matter of his own *desire* at all.[70] As Bray notes in *The Friend*, the "desire for the gift of the friend's body . . . does not correspond easily to anything in our culture several centuries on."[71] Even as Bray may contribute to what David Halperin has called "the possibility of a new queer history of affect,"[72] his contribution is not to explain what intimacy tells us about the desires of an individual subject (or, for that matter, to historicize emotion), but to describe the instrumentality of intimacy in creating (or threatening) social cohesion. Sworn brotherhood, for example, is a response to the ethical uncertainty of friendship, and its meaning exists primarily in the wider social responsibility assumed by friends when they formalize their vows. So too, the "desire for the gift of the friend's body" functions, much like the homosocial desire anatomized by Sedgwick, as the glue that holds early modern society together.

Yet, the question remains: What does it mean to assert for representations of sexuality an agency that does not depend on a subject of desire? The answer to this question is everywhere implied by the dense historical interconnections Bray excavates among religion, ethics, the family, and friendship, but the most trenchant indication of it is recorded in a memorial headnote to an essay he published in an anthology that appeared after his death. According to Katherine O'Donnell and Michael O'Rourke, when Bray asked himself, "*How would [his current work] change the exploratory maps constructed twenty years ago?* he said this: it would be a shift from studies of sexuality into ethics and from the politics of identity into the politics of friendship."[73] There is much for historians of sexuality to ponder in that proposed shift, including the presence or absence of the body and erotic desire in ethics and friendship and the risks involved in leaving their material histories behind. Addressing that risk is a motivating force behind Chapter 6, which, in an explicit departure from Bray's own strategy, contemplates early modern sex *acts* in order to advance the epistemological direction inaugurated by his historical work.

A further consideration is the relation of Bray's work to the category of gender. On the face of it, Bray's corpus seems to offer little to the history of female friendship or female sexuality. Although I tend to think otherwise, certain problems with his approach to gender deserve acknowledgment. Bray duly noted the restricted scope of *Homosexuality in Renaissance England*: "Female homosexuality was rarely linked in popular thought with male homosexuality, if indeed it was recognized at all. Its history is, I believe, best to be understood as part of the developing recognition of a specifically female sexuality."[74] This may have been true when this book was written; whether it remains true is a question to which I will return. To his credit, Bray recognized then that the dissonance between friendship and sodomy was in part a function of gender: "So long as homosexual activity did not disturb the peace or the social order, and in particular so long as it was *consistent with patriarchal mores*, it was largely in practice ignored."[75] Yet, because of the asymmetrical application of the legal and theological category of sodomy to early modern English men and women, Bray's first book does not provide ready analytical purchase to scholars working on women. Perhaps predictably, major studies of female homoeroticism have limited their engagement with his thesis primarily to the perception of parallels between a growing stigma regarding female intimacies and the increasing legibility of sodomy.[76]

Bray's published essays on friendship likewise retain a focus on men, in part because the formal displays of intimacy that characterized male patronage in the sixteenth and seventeenth centuries were, he argues, less relevant to women, who on the whole were denied access to the public sphere. As Bray remarks in "The Body of the Friend," it was precisely because of the male body's privileged ability to confer cultural capital that the gift of the friend's body was definitively male. In addition, much of Bray's analysis of the symbolic gift exchanges among men hinges on the fact that "the daily cycle of working, eating and drinking, the bodily functions, and sleeping was carried on outside the marital home." "Service in the great houses was men's work," Bray contends, and although women served as washerwomen, herds-women, and traders, they did so from outside the great house walls.[77] Where, one might ask, did these women live? Given the importance of the patriarchal household, it seems unlikely that they resided in all-female collectives. Does the mere fact that they were not mentioned in household records provide sufficient support for Bray's claim?[78]

A portion of *The Friend*'s long final chapter concerns female relations, mainly by means of the figure of Anne Lister. Prior to this chapter the book treats female friendship as "the silence between the lines" of male friendship, referring briefly and sporadically to a few female burial monuments.[79] Lister's voluble diary breaks this silence, both because of its erotic explicitness and because Lister was intent on enacting with two of her lovers the kind of formal, public, and binding union that sworn brothers had vowed for centuries. She thus provides Bray with a "vantage point" for reconsidering the congruity between a relationship that was "unquestionably sexual" and "the confirmation of a sworn friendship in the Eucharist," as well as a frame for thinking about the extent to which "that traditional world of kinship and friendship at the heart of religion's role" survived in the byways of the nineteenth century.[80] Nonetheless, the criteria Bray uses to admit women's entrance into the historical picture imply that there is little evidence with which to track the path of female friendship prior to Lister's relatively late incarnation. Bray admits that the friendship between Ann Chitting and Mary Barber "had a sufficiently formal and objective character for them to be buried together" in the early seventeenth century, but this does not impact his general view that women's role in the history of friendship is the "silence between the lines."[81] One is left to wonder whether Lady Anne Clifford's apology, in a letter to her mother, for her inability to travel "to Oxford, according to your Ladyship's desire with my Lady Arbella [Stuart], and to have slept in her chamber, which she much desired, for I am the more bound to her than can be," demonstrates something of the public conveyance of countenance that Bray charts in familiar letters between men.[82] In other words, there is the question of how Bray actually reads the lives of the women whom he includes, and what these readings do to broaden the terms of feminist and lesbian histories. Finally, one is left to wonder about the historiographic irony that a woman should have been the means to reinsert sex back into the historical narrative. Early in the historiography of homosexuality, the boys had sodomy and the girls had romantic friendship; in *The Friend*, as in other recent work, the history of male homosexuality is all about love.

If we shift our focus from what Bray *says* about women to what his work *makes available* to those of us working on women, however, a more enabling set of procedures emerges. As Chapter 5 will demonstrate, methods of analysis and interpretation derived from scholarship on men can be usefully applied on behalf of women; such methodological cross-gender identification, I argue, may even have some advantages over the supposedly gender-neutral rubric of "queer." Adoption of Bray's insights about the unstable nature of erotic signification and consideration of the ontological and epistemological issues raised by his work would greatly nuance scholarship on women's sexuality, which has tended to presuppose a certain knowingness about it. Indeed, insofar as a central question in the history of female homoeroticism has been how to talk about "lesbianism" before the advent of modern identity categories, we would do well to consider how this question of anachronistic terminology can morph into an ontological question—what *is* lesbianism in any given era?—as well as how these queries might be supplemented with the epistemological question: how do we know it?

Although nothing in Bray's corpus provides clear answers to these questions, in its performance of ambiguity, tension, and irresolution his work urges us to ask them. In the expanse of its historical sweep, *The Friend*, in particular, gestures in a direction that might draw us closer to some answers. Perhaps not since Lillian Faderman's *Surpassing the Love of Men: Romantic Friendship and Love Between Women from the Renaissance to the Present* has a responsible scholar of gay/lesbian/queer history approached large-scale historical change and continuity with such confidence and ambition. In part because the postmodern suspicion toward the explanatory power of metanarratives has taken firm hold in those subfields where the history of homosexuality is most often written (social and cultural history, gender and women's history, cultural studies, literary studies),[83] the creation of densely local and socially contextualized knowledges has been constitutive of the field.

Bray's widening of the temporal lens in *The Friend* allows us to consider anew how the retrospective fiction of periodization has functioned as an epistemic force field, permitting certain questions to advance while occluding others. To the extent that the suitability of assuming a longer vantage has been raised within the history of homosexuality, it has been approached primarily via the debate between acts and identities or, in its more historiographical formulation, between the assertion of alterity or continuism. In the context of this debate, responsible reconsideration of taking the long view has gone precisely nowhere. Yet, as archival materials come to light that support more nuanced conceptions of identity, orientation, and predisposition than early social constructivist accounts would have allowed, these debates have begun to diminish in importance.[84] Recent attempts to move beyond the impasse produced by these debates have demonstrated that it is the precise nature and interrelations of continuities and discontinuities that are of interest, not the analytical predominance of one over the other.[85]

Bray's final book is perhaps the most subtle mediation between the claims of historical continuity and historical difference in this field to date. It thus provides the springboard for the consideration of historiography, including issues of alterity, continuism, and periodization, pursued in the next two chapters. In addition, by insisting that friendship can be understood only in terms of the wider context that gives it meaning, *The Friend* confutes a basic, if undertheorized, premise of the historiography of homosexuality: that we must conceptualize our object of analysis by provisionally isolating its parameters and claiming for it, however tacitly, a relatively independent social status. That is, whether one historicizes the sodomite or the molly, tribadism, sapphism, or queer virginity, in order to gain a foothold for these phenomena in a landscape unmarked by modern identity categories, scholars have tended to approach the phenomena as discrete, internally unified, and relatively bounded. Despite our adoption of Bray's argument that homoeroticism is part of a networked system of social relations, we have failed to recognize the full ramifications of that insight and so have treated homoeroticism much like the historical periods in which we locate it.

Could it be that this bounded conceptualization of our analytical object is related to the problem of period boundaries? I am not sure, but it seems no accident that Bray's final book flouts both at once. There is no question that many of the issues prominent in the history of homosexuality traverse historical domains. Chapter 4 will enumerate these issues with a particular focus on lesbianism, identifying them as "perennial axes of social definition" that crop up as "cycles of salience," while also arguing against a view of seamless continuity by which the past is directly laminated onto later social formations. While the mandate of that chapter is to advance analytically the history of women's sexuality, the more general point is to foster the creation of a temporally capacious, conceptually organized, gender-comparative history of sexuality. Fitted together in a dialogic rather than a teleological mold, this history might not only find a form that is conceptually coherent yet rife with tensions; through its parataxis and juxtapositions, it might also energize new areas of inquiry, ones that beckon beyond the protocols that have organized research for the past two decades. The conversation I want to enable is not principally one between the past and the present—queer theory, influenced by Foucaultian genealogy, has provided an ample set of procedures for that, usable even by as devout a social historian as Bray. What requires new theorizing, I suggest, is how to stage a dialogue between one past and another. It is to this problem that the next two chapters turn.

It may seem that I have strayed far from the terrain mapped out by Alan Bray. These were not his questions, to be sure. Nonetheless, they are the questions that arise out of the exploratory maps that he so diligently and generously offered. Following the signposts in his work, much of what follows attempts to chart more precisely the overlapping coordinates of love, friendship, eroticism, and sexuality present in his historiographic vista, while also placing these coordinates in more compelling relation to gender, as well as in relation to issues that have emerged since his death. Perhaps the most humbling legacy of the friend whom we have lost—and of friendship's loss—is this: just as Alan Bray's first book provided guidance for much of the historical work that followed, his final gift of friendship beckons us to a new landscape, which is also, as he eloquently testifies, quite old yet, because of his work, quite near.

CHAPTER 3

The New Unhistoricism in Queer Studies

FOR DAVID HALPERIN

Since around 2005, a specter has haunted the field in which I work: the specter of teleology. On behalf of a *queerer* historiography, some scholars of French and English early modern literature have charged other queer studies scholars with promoting a normalizing view of sexuality, history, and time. This normalization allegedly is caused by unwitting imprisonment within a framework of teleology. A teleological perspective views the present as a necessary outcome of the past—the point toward which all prior events were trending.[1] The antiteleologists challenge any such proleptic sequel as a straitjacketing of sex, time, and history, and they announce their critique as a decisive rupture from previous theories and methods of queer history (especially Foucault-inspired genealogy). Given the high profile of the scholars involved, as well as the high octane of their polemics, it is not surprising that their assessment has been embraced enthusiastically by many other scholars, inside and outside of early modern literary studies, who aim "to free queer scholarship from the tyranny of historicism."[2] Whereas there are other hot topics within queer studies right now—including whether queer theory should "take a break" from feminism, whether it should "just say no" to futurity, whether it is irremediably impervious to racial and class diversity, and whether the moment of queer theory is over—these issues are all subject to explicit debate in various forums, from conferences and blogs to books and journals. What is curious about this queer teleoskepticism is that, to date, no one has actually responded to the charge—and thus there has been a notable absence of debate.[3]

It thus seems important to ask: Of what does this queer critique of teleology consist? How did it evolve? What strategies and solutions are being proposed, and what is their analytic and political purchase on the relations of sex, time, and history? Using the accusation of teleology as an analytical fulcrum, I parse in what follows some of the assumptions regarding temporality, representation, periodization, empiricism, and historical change implicit in the alleged relationship of teleological thinking to what has been called "straight temporality." Ascertaining the conceptual work that the allegation of teleology performs, I reconsider the meanings and uses of the concept "queer," as well as "homo" and "hetero," in the context of historical inquiry. I also assess some of the unique affordances of psychoanalysis and deconstruction for the history of sexuality. At stake, I hope to show, are not only emerging understandings of the relations among chronology and teleology, sequence and consequence, but some of the fundamental purposes and destinations of queering.

To queer history within the terms of this body of scholarship is no longer simply to identify subjects in the past who do not comport with normative expectations of gender or heterosexuality; or to identify past actors whose desires and behaviors may or may not conform to modern categories of sexual identity; or to demonstrate the range of erotic practices—sodomy, tribadism, flagellation, mystical ecstasy—in which past historical actors might have engaged. To queer history rather has come to be seen as coterminous with and expressive of the need to queer temporality itself. As such, the scholarship I review here is part of a broader trend within queer studies. Variously called the "turn toward temporality" or the elucidation of "queer time," a diverse range of work across disciplines and periods has focused on "time's sexual politics." Shifting away from the spatial modes underwriting much previous scholarship (theories of intersectionality and social geography, for instance), important books have explored backward emotional affects, lateral queer childhoods, and reproductive futurism.[4] Although diverse in topic and method, this scholarship argues that temporal and sexual normativities, as well as temporal and sexual dissonance, are significantly, even constitutively, intertwined. Queer temporality, in the words of Annamarie Jagose, is "a mode of inhabiting time that is attentive to the recursive eddies and back-to-the-future loops that often pass undetected or uncherished beneath the official narrations of the linear sequence that is taken to structure normative life."[5] Collectively, this curvature of time has fueled significant epistemological as well as methodological innovations, productively disturbing developmental and progressive schemas, whether conceived in psychological, narratological, social, or historical terms.

Nonetheless, the theoretical rationales, specific methodologies, and political payoff of this bending of time are far from clear. Indeed, even to speak of it as a "turn" may unduly homogenize scholarly projects that are keyed to different disciplinary registers and that display varying investments in the history of sexuality, literary criticism, and cultural studies. Some scholars working on queer temporality seem motivated primarily by resistance to narratives of the history of sexuality, while others are primarily interested in time, but not especially concerned with history. Some are speaking to debates about historical method within the historical periods in which they work, while others are speaking primarily to other queer studies scholars. The relationship to "the literary"—as a source for accessing both history and temporality—varies as well. Despite this heterogeneity, teleoskepticism is positioned in much of this work as a potent challenge to heteronormativity and "straight time."

To my mind, the broad claims of theory, however intrinsically interesting or valuable, are best assessed in their applicability to specific historical contexts and fields of inquiry. For this reason, I scrutinize in what follows the arguments of three early modernists who maintain that teleological thinking present in queer historicism undergirds a stable edifice of temporal normativity. That a particularly intense critique of teleology has arisen within the context of early modern studies is partly due to scholars' efforts to contend with the force of historicism, which has been the field's dominant (but by no means exclusive) method since the 1980s. Furthermore, pre- and early modern studies have been the site of vigorous debate about historiographic method since volume 1 of Michel Foucault's *The History of Sexuality* upped the critical ante on understandings of sexual modernity. The arguments described in these pages thus arise from within a distinct temporal and professional frame, and I leave to others the task of assessing whether my perspective generates questions pertinent to the explanatory potential of queer temporality more generally.[6]

Because the rest of this chapter focuses on the writings of Carla Freccero (who works mainly in French literature and culture) and Jonathan Goldberg and Madhavi Menon (whose expertise is in English), I state from the outset that I find much of their work, including some of their assertions regarding temporality, trenchant and thought provoking. In this I am far from alone: the quick uptake of their interventions bespeaks enormous enthusiasm among a diverse range of scholars. What follows unavoidably involves a certain amount of generalization that elides differences among them (especially regarding the role of gender and psychoanalysis) and fails to convey the insight and verve with which they read particular texts and cultural phenomena. My impetus for treating them as a collective stems from the fact that they have vigorously published on this theme and, despite their differences, share a common line of argumentation regarding teleology, regularly and approvingly cite one another regarding it, and are treated by other scholars as providing a unified perspective on it. The point is not to attack individual scholars, delineate strict methodological camps, or propose a single way of doing the history of sexuality. Indeed, part of what is confusing is that some of these scholars' recent pronouncements run against the grain of their previous work.[7] My aim, then, is to advance a more precise collective dialogue on the unique affordances of different methods for negotiating the complex links among sexuality, temporality, and history making. What are the possible different ways of queering history and temporality? What, if any, are the specific procedures that eventuate out of these different paths? And what are the stakes of those differences? If I answer critique with critique and, in the end, defend genealogical approaches to the history of sexuality—arguing in particular that we can read chronologically without straitjacketing ourselves or the past—I hope to do justice to these scholars' innovations by engaging seriously with their polemics and acknowledging the value of certain hermeneutic strategies for which they are eloquent advocates.

In many respects, the projects of these early modernists reiterate familiar queer theoretical investments. They share with countless others a desire to promote the capacious analytical capacity of *queer* to deconstruct sexual identity, to illuminate the lack of coherence or fixity in erotic relations, and to highlight the radical indeterminacy and transitivity of both erotic desire and gender. Like many others, they find their warrant in Eve Kosofsky Sedgwick's assertion that "one of the things that 'queer' can refer to" is "the open mesh of possibilities, gaps, overlaps, dissonances and resonances, lapses and excesses of meaning when the constituent elements of anyone's gender, of anyone's sexuality aren't made (or *can't be* made) to signify monolithically."[8] Drawing on Sedgwick as well to privilege the universalizing over the minoritizing aspect of sexualities, these critics maintain that we should not "take the object of queering for granted."[9] In Freccero's words, her "work has been mostly about advocating for queer's verbally and adjectivally unsettling force against claims for its definitional stability, so theoretically anything can queer something, and anything, given a certain odd twist, can become queer."[10] Similarly, Menon maintains that "if queerness can be defined, then it is no longer queer."[11] In historiographic terms, these critics refuse to countenance the emphasis on historical difference often attributed to historicist scholars. Collaborating on an article published in *PMLA*, for instance, Goldberg and Menon call for "acts of queering that would suspend the assurance that the only modes of knowing the past are either those that regard the past as wholly other or those that can assimilate it to a present assumed identical to itself." They also share a resistance to the conventional historical periodizations that typically organize the disciplines of history and literature: "We urge," Goldberg and Menon say, "a reconsideration of relations between past and present that would trace differential boundaries instead of being bound by and to any one age."[12]

Although similar statements appear in the historical work of other scholars, including some they critique, Freccero, Goldberg, and Menon charge these scholars with a failure to deliver. According to Menon, "the ideal of telos continues to shape even the least homonormative studies of Renaissance sexuality."[13] According to Freccero, "what [has] most resisted queering in my field . . . was a version of historicism and one of its corollaries, periodization."[14] And, according to Goldberg, other queer historicist scholars "remain devoted to a historical positivity that seems anything but the model offered by queer theory."[15] In these scholars' view, this alleged "ideal of telos"—and its reputed corollaries, periodization and positivism—underwrites work governed by a genealogical intent that treats any earlier figures (for example, the sodomite, the tribade, the sapphist) as precursors of, in the words of Freccero, a "preemptively defined category of the present ('modern homosexuality')."[16] Stating that they find a lingering attachment to identity that unduly stabilizes sexuality and recruits earlier sexual regimes into a lockstep march toward the present, they adduce in others' work a homogeneous fiction of "modern homosexuality" that inadvertently, and through a kind of reverse contamination, conscripts past sexual arrangements to modern categories. And although certain deconstructive tendencies motivate much queer historical scholarship, these critics are further distinguished by the manner in which they champion the specific capacities of formal textual interpretation—especially the techniques of deconstruction and psychoanalysis—to provide a less teleological, less identitarian, and in their view, less normalizing historiographic practice. The alluring name that Goldberg and Menon give to their counterstrategy is "homohistory," defined as a history that "would be invested in suspending determinate sexual and chronological differences while expanding the possibilities of the nonhetero, with all its connotations of sameness, similarity, proximity, and anachronism."[17] In sum, they call for a queering of history that would be, in Goldberg and Menon's words, an "unhistoricism"—or, to use Freccero's term, an "undoing" of the history of homosexuality (in ironic homage to David Halperin's *How to Do the History of Homosexuality*, a main target of her critique).

ᘐᘐ ᘐᘐ ᘐᘐ

Before I explore these arguments, I note that this critique has a history of its own. Although the question of teleology in organizing historical understanding has long vexed historians,[18] this question gained momentum in queer studies by means of Sedgwick who, in *Epistemology of the Closet*, proposed as her axiom 5 that "the historical search for a Great Paradigm Shift may obscure the present conditions of sexual identity."[19] Directed at the work of several gay male historians, Sedgwick's critique focused not only on the work of Michel Foucault, but also Halperin's *One Hundred Years of Homosexuality*, with its social constructionist effort to differentiate premodern forms of sexual desire and behavior from a distinctively modern homosexual identity. Comparing Halperin's work to Foucault's, she observed that "in each history one model of same-sex relations is superseded by another, which may again be superseded by another. In each case the superseded model then drops out of the frame of analysis." Sedgwick's critique of the "birth of the homosexual" and the model of supersession to which it was joined had as its ultimate goal the recognition of the "unrationalized coexistence" of incommensurate models of sexuality: "the most potent effects of modern homo/heterosexual definition tend to spring precisely from the inexplicitness or denial of the gaps *between* long-coexisting minoritizing and universalizing, or gender-transitive and gender-intransitive, understandings of same-sex relations."[20] Concerned with what she termed the "unfortunate side effect" of historical studies (despite their "immense care, value, and potential"), she noted that whereas "'homosexuality as we *conceive of it* today,' has provided a rhetorically necessary fulcrum point for the denaturalizing work on the past done by many historians," such formulations risked "reinforcing a dangerous consensus of knowingness about the genuinely *un*known" in modern discourses of sexuality.[21]

Sedgwick's critique had two conceptual targets: narratives of supersession, in which each prior term drops out, and the conceptual consolidation of the present (or the modern). A third target—the perceived emergence of the homosexual locatable in a specific moment in time—can be inferred from the irony that limns her descriptive lexicon of "birth" and "Great Paradigm Shift." Compelling as her critique was, however, Sedgwick did not endorse a particular form of historiography. She neither asserted the likelihood of transhistorical meanings, made arguments about historical continuity and change, or advocated on behalf of synchronic over diachronic methods. Despite other scholars' characterization of her critique as a "refusal of the model of linearity and supersession,"[22] she did not address temporal linearity or chronology per se, much less advance a standard of total chronological suspension. By attending to "the performative space of contradiction," Sedgwick deployed deconstructive strategies in her encounter with the past not as a way of doing history but rather "to denaturalize the present."[23]

Sedgwick's discussion of the Great Paradigm Shift received a direct response from Halperin in *How to Do the History of Homosexuality*, where he offered a pluralist model of four distinct paradigms of male gender and eroticism, all of which, he argued, are in various ways subsumed by or conflated with the modern category of homosexuality. Answering Sedgwick's objection regarding supersession while also integrating her primary insight regarding synchronic incoherence, Halperin writes:

A genealogical analysis of homosexuality begins with our contemporary notion of homosexuality, incoherent though it may be, not only because such a notion inevitably frames all inquiry into same-sex sexual expression in the past but also because its very incoherence registers the genetic traces of its own historical evolution. In fact, it is this incoherence at the core of the modern notion of homosexuality that furnishes the most eloquent indication of the historical accumulation of discontinuous notions that shelter within its specious unity. The genealogist attempts to disaggregate those notions by tracing their separate histories as well as the process of their interrelations, their crossings, and, eventually, their unstable convergence in the present day.[24]

In other words, Halperin's genealogy is committed to the view that modern sexual categories provide not just an obstacle to the past but also a window on to it. In positioning the present in the relation to the past, a queer genealogist might adduce similarities or differences, continuities or discontinuities, all in pursuit of the contingency of history.

In the decade between Sedgwick's critique and Halperin's response, skepticism about the functions of historical alterity and periodization grew among pre- and early modernists. In 1996, Freccero and Louise Fradenburg challenged queer historicists to "confront the pleasure we take in renouncing pleasure for the stern alterities of history."[25] Rejecting as essentialist the insistence on the radical incommensurability of past and present sexualities, they proposed a historiographic practice conscious of the role of desires and identifications across time. Echoing Sedgwick in asking "Is it not indeed possible that alteritism at times functions precisely to stabilize the identity of 'the modern'?" they argued that "it might, precisely, be more pleasurable *and* ethically resonant with our experience of the instabilities of identity-formation to figure a particular historical 'moment' as itself fractured, layered, indeed, historical."[26] Related motives animated the work of Carolyn Dinshaw, who sought to "show that queers can make new relations, new identifications, new communities with past figures who elude resemblance to us but with whom we can be connected partially by virtue of shared marginality, queer positionality."[27] Dinshaw's "sensible" historiography, which depended on a "process of touching, of making partial connections between incommensurate entities" across the medieval and postmodern, also privileged a view of sexuality as indeterminate, constituted as much by disidentification and misrecognition as by identification and mimesis.[28]

Such work forged an implicit alliance among two forms of queerness: one directed at subjectivity—affirmatively courting the contingency of desire and rejecting identity's stabilizations—and one directed at historiography, with the aim of resisting alterity and periodization in favor of similitude, resemblance, and identification. Yet, none of these scholars set themselves the task of writing a historical account that traversed large expanses of time. Even as they challenged periodization, their own analyses remained bounded, whether within one or, in the case of Dinshaw, two temporally distinct time frames. By offering either a synchronic analysis or one that paratactically juxtaposed and connected modernity with premodernity, they could bracket the question of any intervening time span—indeed, the *point* was to bracket it. The brilliance of this move was that it enabled affective relations with the past to come to the fore—a move the consequences of which I will explore in Chapter 6. But this innovation also allowed these and subsequent scholars to avoid all matters associated with chronology, including how to explain the endurance or recurrence of some of the very similarities that interested them. Propelled by the desire to defamiliarize modern identity categories while finding new affiliations between the past and the present, the emerging field of queer historiography did not, at this point, directly engage with but rather sidestepped this central issue. This is a problem to which Chapter 4 turns, where I offer a positive model for negotiating the play of difference and similarity over the long temporal term.

Only after queer historiography adopted the postcolonial critique of an imperialist Western history did teleology per se gravitate to the center of discussion. In addition to confronting Eurocentrism and its geopolitical exclusions, postcolonial historians and historians of non-Western cultures followed Johannes Fabian in querying the ideological fit between spatial and temporal alterity, whereby spatially "othered" cultures are judged as inhabiting a time "before" Western modernity. Metanarratives emanating from the metropole have, indeed, inscribed a version of history as developmental telos, whereby a tight conceptual link exists between modernity, progress, and enlightenment, or inversely, between premodernity and what Anjali Arondekar terms "the time(s) of the primitive in a post-colonial world."[29] Among those working on sexuality, the critique of Western timelines focused initially on debating the applicability of Western models of sexual identity to non-Western contexts. Troubling the Foucaultian division between a supposedly Eastern *ars erotica* and a Western, Christian *scientia sexualis*, historians of India, China, and the Middle East have refuted the discursive construction of non-Western sexualities as anterior, traditional, primitive, and inevitably developing toward Western models.[30] Resisting the "sedimented politics of time" that "often reproduces subjects, critical genealogies and methodological habits that duplicate the very historiographies we seek to exceed,"[31] these scholars are striving toward a decolonization that is simultaneously archival, methodological, and temporal.

In part because the "Middle Ages" has been treated as the abject other of modernity, medievalists were quick to adopt the postcolonial critique of historical timelines for queer studies. In 2001, Glenn Burger and Steven F. Kruger emphasized the politically fraught relationships among the premodern, primitivity, and sexual positioning, calling into question "straight (teleological) narration, causal explanations, and schemes of periodization."[32] Since then, more scholars working on Western cultures have begun to look beyond sexual identity to ask questions about concepts in the history of sexuality that do and do not transit across cultural as well as historical borders. Querying what such differential presences and absences tell us about culturally distinct modes of comprehending and organizing sexuality, they are exploring how our recognition of them might promote alternative genealogies of sexual modernity.

By the middle of the last decade, then, the various strands emerging out of queer theory, pre- and early modern literary studies, and postcolonial history had converged in a critically conscious queer historicism that not only brought the past into provocative relations with the present but provided powerful incentive for scholars' recognition of the role of similarity and identification in the act of historicizing. The notion that time might have, in its asynchronicities, warpings, and loops, something akin to queer dimensions, or be susceptible to queering through the productive juxtaposition of distant times and places, or in its linear flow be intriguingly coincident with other phenomena such as reproductive futurity and modernist progress, or may help us think about the uneven temporalities of sexual geographies and their tendentious transnational periodizations are ideas that have initiated a range of provocative meditations on the forces of historical alterity and similitude, identification and disidentification, affect and analysis, in the making of history. Indeed, my elucidation of "cycles of salience" in Chapter 4 responds appreciatively to this body of work, even as I aim to supplement the forms of eroticism considered to include female-female desire.

⁊꤮   ⁊꤮   ⁊꤮

So why do I part company with the new "unhistoricism"? The unhistoricists' implicit query of genealogy—what might be occluded by it?—is a vital one,[33] and no doubt speaks to a more general fatigue regarding the injunction "always historicize!" Furthermore, I have considerable sympathy with the critical methods, psychoanalysis and deconstruction, that the unhistoricists employ to oppose that hegemony.[34] I agree that "psychoanalysis, as an analytic, is also a historical method,"[35] and would point to increased appreciation for its utility as one of the more appealing trends in early modern queer criticism.[36] I share, as well, their interest in the capacity of *queer* to denaturalize sexual logics and expand the object of study through untoward combinations and juxtapositions; recognition of the role that affect and desire, particularly identification, play in the work of historical reconstruction; confidence in the specific capacities of literary language and literary form to contribute to historical understanding; and belief that the past can speak meaningfully to the present.

Despite these areas of agreement, I remain unconvinced that a teleological imperative is what impedes our understanding of past sexualities. In part, my skepticism stems from my understanding of genealogy as it was theorized and put into practice by Foucault. Since the publication of his initial description (articulated through a reading of Nietzsche), genealogy has come to mean a lot of different things to different people—some of it identifiable as Foucaultian, some of it not. Linguistically connoting "descent," genealogy for Foucault "postulates conditions of possibility in the past for some synchronic feature of the present."[37] More particularly, it concerns how the identity of something is dispersed over time through mixing, repurposing, and contingency. Drawing a distinction between the organic development traceable back to an origin (*Ursprung*), descent (*Herkunft*), and emergence (*Entstehung*), he argued that the genealogist should seek to "dispel the chimeras of the origin" by "cultivat[ing] the details and accidents that accompany every beginning."[38] Due to his emphasis on power, "details and accidents" tend in Foucault's corpus to be produced by violence, pettiness, meanness, and quarrels, but to my mind they stand more generally for the principle of contingency and the way history proceeds by fits and starts. "Beginnings" refers to those moments when one thing is repurposed into another through practices of power-knowledge. Pressing for recognition of historical rupture and discontinuity, especially in terms of events and episodes "situated within the articulation of the body and history,"[39] Foucault traced epistemic breaks of intelligibility that fundamentally altered what could be thought.[40] Practices of repurposing necessarily involve dispersion, and the point of genealogy is "to maintain passing events in their proper dispersion," while also recognizing in those passing events that which "gave birth to those things that continue to exist."[41] With the inevitability of the present disrupted, so too is the idea that the past actively inheres in or secretly animates the present.[42] What is at stake in these productive contradictions is precisely the distinction Foucault drew between writing a history of the past *in terms of* the present (that is, conventional history) and writing a history *of* the present (genealogy).[43] The latter recognizes that there is no firm ontological or epistemological ground for our identifications with the past—they, too, are historically contingent. The accusation, then, that genealogy, in the form that Foucault wrote it, is teleological runs against the grain of Foucault's own project. Indeed, nothing could be further from teleology than Foucault's own genealogies, which understand historical processes in full light of their conditionality.

With Foucault's own genealogical project in mind,[44] I now want to scrutinize how the unhistoricists build their indictment of teleological misprision,

first by presenting their projects through their own words. Recognizing that
an "altericist reaction" among pre- and early modernists "was undoubtedly
necessary insofar as it sought to enable analyses of gender and sexuality rather
than foreclose them through a presumption that 'we know whereof we
speak,'" Freccero nonetheless worries "that altericism is sometimes accompanied by an older, more familiar claim that periods—those confections of
nineteenth-century disciplinarization in the West—are to be respected in
their time- and context-bound specificity. This is the historicism I speak of,
the one that, in the name of difference smuggles in historical periodization
in the spirit of making 'empirical' claims about gender and sexuality in the
European past."[45]

Here Freccero forges a close correlation between a prior, apparently principled, commitment to alterity (thus, "altericism") and periods (those time- and
context-bound Western confections), while also suggesting that periodicity
becomes the vehicle by which scholars make "empirical" claims. Freccero's
formulation "in the spirit of" leaves ambiguous whether periodization necessitates empiricism or empiricism necessitates periodization, but her point seems
to be that altericists pass off periodization as something empirical, whereas it
actually is something conceptual and metaphysical. Whichever way it works,
empiricism and periodization are judged to be inimical to queer. I will return
to the status of periods and empiricism later, but for now simply offer Freccero's own description of her project in *Queer/Early/Modern*, which "set itself
the task of critiquing historicisms and troubling periodization by rejecting a
notion of empirical history and allowing fantasy and ideology an acknowledged place in the production of 'fantasmatic' historiography."[46] Approaching
historical affects as persistence and repetition, and situating subjects in a more
"promiscuous" and asynchronic relationship to temporality, she fashions a
historiographic method she calls "queer spectrality—ghostly returns suffused
with affective materiality that work through the ways trauma, mourning, and
event are registered on the level of subjectivity and history."[47] As a historiographic method, queer spectrality is a flexible, alluring, and often moving
hermeneutic. For instance, Freccero's application of spectral (or as she also
calls it, figural) historiography charts the "transspecies habitus" of dogs and
humans through their manifestations of violence in colonialism and the contemporary prison-industrial complex; this reading implicates racism, transnational capital, virile masculinity, queer heterosexuality, and lesbian domestic
relations in a complex affective network that is "comparatively queer relative
to any progressive, ameliorative rational accounts of historical process."[48]

Rejecting progressive narratives as well as remedy and rationality, Freccero maintains that she is motivated by an ethical impulse to produce "queer time"[49] by means of "a suspension, a waiting, an attending to the world's arrivals (through, in part, its returns), not as a guarantee or security for action in the present, but as the very force from the past that moves us into the future."[50]

Less devoted to a psychoanalytic concept of fantasy but equally invested in nonidentitarian modes of thought, Goldberg, like Freccero, construes temporality as asynchronic, noncontinuous, and nonidentical. At least since his 1995 essay "The History That Will Be," he has attempted to think beyond periodization, arguing that "historic possibilities must depend upon mobilizations that would be unthinkable if history were segmented across uncrossable divides."[51] Striving to keep "temporal multiplicity in play," he objects that recent projects in the history of sexuality may "have shown that the present draws upon various incommensurate strands, [but] have tended nonetheless to divide these strands among previous discrete moments and to draw them in relationship to a consolidated present."[52] "Discrete moments"—that is, periods—are defined by Goldberg not only by their boundedness but by their relationship to a "consolidated present." Periodization thereby is identified with "teleological similarity," which "can imagine the past under the sign of difference, but not the present." Extending "Sedgwick's insistence that any time period is characterized by the 'unrationalized coexistence of different models'" to the unrationalized coexistence of "different temporalities," he maintains that "the relationship between queer theory and the history of sexuality still remains unresolved terrain. Or, rather, the resolutions, fastening either on the model of absolute alterity or on the model of ultimate identity, have yet to imagine the possibility of writing a history that attends to the possibility of the non-self-identity of any historical moment."[53] Rather than a spectral haunting that seeks a reciprocal relation with the past, Goldberg explores the multitemporality, nonidentity, and noncorrespondence of the early modern, the recognition of which can expose the "imbrication of alternative possibilities within normative sexualities."[54] In his 2009 book *The Seeds of Things*, Goldberg seeks the queer within the hetero by exploring, as he puts it in a related essay, the "multiple materialisms to be found in early modernity," extending the meaning of "queer" to a consideration of physics because "queer theory is not and never was just about sex in itself."[55]

Menon makes many of the same theoretical and rhetorical moves as Freccero and Goldberg, but her special interest is in pressing against all forms of desire's confinement, whether that of sexual identity, terminology, literary form, chronological boundaries, or historical method. Because desire, in her view, always exceeds identity and is "synonymous . . . with queerness," she "insists that we refrain from identifying sexuality, and revel in pursuing the coils of a desire that cannot be contained in a binary temporal code."[56] *Unhistorical Shakespeare: Queer Theory in Shakespearean Literature and Film* begins by arguing that "our embrace of difference as the template for relating past and present produces a compulsory heterotemporality in which chronology determines identity."[57] In other words, scholarly attention to historical difference produces a relationship to time in which sexual identity is causally related to chronological explanations; correlatively, queer studies scholars who do not suspend all chronology are not only normativizing but, in her words, "governed by dates."[58] Subjection to the datelines of chronological time is then translated into teleology: "Defined as the doctrine of ends or final causes, teleology depends on a sequence leading to an end that can retrospectively be seen as having had a beginning."[59] Disrupting this purported causal chain via "homohistory, in which desires always exceed identitarian categories and resist being corralled into hetero-temporal camps,"[60] Menon exploits what she sees as the tight congruence of literary form with historical and political structures, in order to access what she calls, in her book's final sentence, "the homo in us all."[61] Her term "compulsory heterotemporality," echoing Adrienne Rich's "compulsory heterosexuality," reactivates sexual normativity as the cause and effect of "straight" temporality and historiography. Adopting the rhetoric of postcolonial studies,[62] Menon writes that "the temporal version of decolonization—what may be termed dechronolization—would involve taking anachronism seriously and defying difference as the underwriter of history."[63] Under the banners of homohistory and unhistoricism, Menon rejects not only historical difference but what she sees as its theoretically suspect corollaries—facts, origins, authenticity, and citation or naming—to which she believes historicists naively adhere.

Composing what increasingly seems a united front, these scholars resist historicism on the grounds that it exaggerates the self-identity of any given moment and therefore exaggerates the differences between any two moments. Against what they view as a compulsory regime of historical alterity, they elevate anachronism and similitude as the expression of queer insurgency. Their readings offer persuasive examples of how queerness animates and troubles ostensibly heterosexual literary texts and cultural discourses. Their strengths as critics reside in the ability to see beyond heterosexuality's inscription on textual form as well as their attentiveness to the vicissitudes of desire and the failures of sexuality. Their contributions as theorists include their fashioning of a queer analytic that encompasses a range of relations that do not conspire to *any* intelligible identity. Furthermore, a deep ethical commitment to deconstructive exposure—as a mode of reading, as politics, as theory—informs their provocations. Whether one applauds, as I do, or abhors, as others might, the political implications of continually exposing identity's contradictions and indeterminacy (a debate now three decades old), their readings amply demonstrate the stresses and fractures within the normative, as well as the distinctive capacity of literary texts to solicit our awareness of such productive contradictions.

Readings, however, are not the same thing as history; more precisely, deconstructive and psychoanalytic interpretations of literary texts, while they contribute much to historical understanding, do not necessarily conduce to a historical explanation. For all the undeniable utility of deconstruction, in particular, as an interpretative protocol, these critics, I submit, overestimate its analytical capacity and explanatory power. Although deconstruction exposes the contingency of—and thus implicitly historicizes—truth claims, the extent to which its largely synchronic hermeneutic can succeed as a full-scale historiographic method remains unresolved. Whereas deconstruction may be an extraordinary technique for elucidating queerness *in* time, it has not, at least not yet, demonstrated a satisfying capacity for analyzing temporality in *all* of its dimensions, including elucidating forms of queerness *across* time.[64]

So how is it that these scholars make their argument with such persuasive force? To understand this, we need to attend to the rhetorical maneuvers and conceptual conflations that underlie their indictments of difference, chronology, and periodization. First, an associational logic pervades their work, wherein historical difference, chronology, periodization, and empirical facts are positioned in an endlessly self-incriminating and disqualifying feedback loop. These conflations reflect a general tendency toward analogical argumentation. As should be clear from their own words, Goldberg, Menon, and Freccero's rejection of "straight temporality" forges a tight metonymic chain among the alleged operations of sex, time, and history. They accomplish these linkages via rhetorical maneuvers whereby difference and sameness are constellated with concepts that stand in as near cognates: not only hetero and homo, but distance and proximity, multiplicity and self-identity, change and stasis, disidentification and mimesis. These close cognates allude to both abstract theoretical principles and specific material realities. Yet, drawn as they are from different epistemological registers—psychic, social, temporal, formal, historiographic—and abstracted from contexts of space or time, they are rhetorically deployed so as to cross seamlessly from one conceptual domain to another. This unmarked analogic process forges a metonymic chain, whereby a tug on one link causes movement in another. However, because these analogies are asserted presumptively rather than argued, and sustained by the play of metaphors rather than by discursive or material connections, when the conceptual space or difference between these concepts becomes inconvenient, they are silently sundered—allowing great latitude for equivocation.

It remains unclear why analogical argumentation—familiar to readers of medieval and Renaissance texts as a dominant style of reasoning[65]—might be especially suited for queer analysis. Nor is it clear why a particular mode of analogical thinking, that signified by the rhetorical trope *metalepsis*, is heralded by Freccero and Menon as an exemplary queer analytical tool. Metalepsis occurs when a present effect is attributed to a remote cause; it links A to D but only by eliding B and C. Since several steps intervene between the cause and effect, metalepsis comprises a "compressed chain of metaphorical reasoning."[66] Metalepsis can be rhetorically powerful (as has been shown to be the case in Shakespearean drama),[67] but nonetheless is vulnerable to critique as fuzzy logic. Freccero, for instance, suggests that metalepsis is particularly queer and theoretical: "the reversal signified by the rhetorical term *metalepsis* could be seen to embody the spirit of queer analysis in its willful perversion of notions of temporal propriety and the reproductive order of things. To read metaleptically, then, would be to engage in queer theorizing."[68] More interested in its status as a repressed or failed rhetorical device, Menon uses metalepsis as an interpretive crux for reading absent sex scenes in Shakespearean drama, scenes of implied consummation, which, despite their failure to be staged, nonetheless link social cause to tragic effect. While there is much to admire in the way these critics demonstrate that "the 'far-fetched' nature of metalepsis telescopes time so that the far appears near, and vice versa,"[69] their willingness to "embrace the accusation of metalepsis"[70] fails to translate into a cogent defense of metalepsis as a mode of queer argument.

To the contrary: a metaleptic sleight of hand enables the ground of critique to keep shifting.[71] At times, it seems that the allegation of teleology is directed against scholars who invoke *any* form of sexual identity, even one located in the present, and even if construed as indeterminate and internally riven. At other times, the accusation appears aimed at scholars' attempts to track terms, concepts, and forms of intelligibility by means of the temporal frame of chronology or diachrony. At times, it appears that the complaint is scholars' failure to treat sex solely as representation, an interpretative choice that renders them immediately vulnerable to charges of empiricism and positivism. At other times, the indictment widens to encompass the entire discipline of history and the concerns and methods of historians. Through an on-again, off-again associational reasoning dedicated to the wholesale rejection of alterity-cum-heterotemporality, these investments mingle, come together, merge, and sometimes fall apart.

Recognizing that such rhetorical maneuvers underpin the charge of teleology,[72] we might be justified in asking just what forms of similarity are being celebrated and what kinds of difference are discarded. A case in point is the talismanic invocation of "the homo." Despite the catchy phrase "homohistory," it remains unclear how expanding the possibilities of "the homo," "with all its connotations of sameness, similarity, proximity, and anachronism," automatically enacts resistance to "a present assumed identical to itself." Nor is it clear why "the homo" necessarily would be queerer than alterity, unless the corresponding shorthand of "hetero" is so essentialized as to be always already normativizing. Might historical alterity not sometimes offer its own pleasures (as well as accurately describe certain pre- and early modern modes of intelligibility)? How is it that "the homo" signifies similarity and identification across time while simultaneously signifying resistance to any such identification with sexual categories in the present? Just what *is* conveyed, in psychic, social, temporal, formal, and historical terms, by the über-concepts "homo" and "hetero"? How much analytical weight and presumed congruence can these master terms and their pseudocognates bear? To what extent are they in sync, when, and why? In these scholars' hands, "homo" and "hetero" serve as mobile conceptual lynchpins, used theoretically to suture together diverse phenomena; but they fail to attach to, much less elucidate, specific social conditions or material embodiments.

Sexuality, the diverse enactments of erotic desire and physical embodiment; temporality, the various manifestations of time; and history, historicism and historiography, the aggregate repertoire of cognitive and affective approaches to the past, are not intrinsically connected. Neither straight identity nor heterosexual desire is the same as linear time. Not every diachronic or chronological treatment of temporality need be normativizing, nor is every linear arc sexually "straight." A scholar's adherence to chronological time does not, in and of itself, have any necessary relationship to sexuality, much less to sexual normativity. Neither does a scholar's segmentation of time into periods. The act of periodizing is of routinized professional significance, functioning for many historians and literary critics as rote convenience, not to mention a structure underlying the academic job market. It is worthwhile to question the value of any conceptualization that has been reified in this way, as well as to insist that scholars recognize their complacency and complicity with its arbitrary application. Periodization produces some unfortunate effects, including misrecognitions of the exemplarity and/or novelty of one's chosen purview, as well as falsely universalizing claims based on ignorance of what scholars concerned with other times actually do. But conventional periods are only one way to slice and dice the past; time, conceived as "the phenomenal ordering of events,"[73] is both ontological and epistemological; as such, it can be segmented in multiple ways, with the concept of "the period" changing according to the question and time frame considered.[74] To periodize is not, in and of itself, a brief on behalf of a particular method. Although it has become common to refer to the act of periodization as "not simply the drawing of an arbitrary line through time, but a complex practice of conceptualizing categories, which are posited as homogeneous and retroactively validated by the designation of a period divide,"[75] the identity that periodicity imposes need not be inevitably problematic—as long as it is understood to be contingent, manufactured, invested, and not produced by othering what came before. The wholesale characterization of periodization as a straightening of the past races over such issues while making light of historical contingency—that is, the ways in which practices, representations, and discourses happen to gather in particular places and times.

Although certain problematic allegiances among sexuality, temporality, and historiography *do* exist—as when invocations of the future are enrolled in the service of reproductive generation[76]—these links, far from being immanent in either sex or time, are historically and discursively produced. If temporality has been harnessed to reproductive futurity, this is due to an operation of ideology, not to the formal procedures of diachronic method (which, while not exempt from ideology, is not the same thing as ideology). However coimplicated, mutually reinforcing, and potentially recursive, the relations of sex to time are the effects of a historical process, not the preconditions to history. We thus need to ask: by which analytical and material *processes* do history and historiography become teleological, heterotemporal, or straight?

History is polytemporal not only because each synchronic moment is riddled with multiple, and sometimes contradictory, *a*synchronicities, but because time, like language, operates simultaneously on synchronic and dia-chronic axes. Although it is true, as Menon argues, that "time does not neces-sarily move from past to future, backward to forward,"[77] it also is true that time moves *on*. Any ethics we might wish to derive from a consideration of temporality must contend with the irreducible force of time's movement on our bodies, our species, and the planet.[78] Queer or not, we remain in many respects *in* time. Analytics dedicated to charting time's cultural logics can be organized via lines, curves, mash-ups, juxtapositions. Nonetheless, writing the history of sexuality by means of asynchronicities located within a syn-chronic frame or by vaulting over huge expanses of time may bypass chronol-ogy, but it generally fails to break out of the binary of "then" and "now" that thus far has constituted queer studies' engagement with the past.[79]

The sequential process that constitutes diachrony is, I would argue, a cru-cial and often tendentious element of sex, texts, and history. Sequence is a formal elaboration, made possible by a syntactical arrangement, the purpose of which is to imply connections, highlight or manage disconnections, and drive a temporal movement along. But sequence in one domain—for instance, narrative or poetic form—may or may not equate to, or even imply, sequence in another—such as that which structures erotic concepts like "fore-play" and "consummation." What is the relationship between unconven-tional literary or cinematic form and queer eroticism? *How* and *why* might the operations of sexuality and form be coincident, and what is at stake in apprehending them as *identical*?[80] What mechanism or process—aesthetic, erotic, political, historical—enables their equation? Are all "points," consum-mations, and closures (textual, erotic, political, historical) necessarily co-implicated, and do they all possess the same degree of inevitability?

Absent investigation of these questions, the presumptive metonymies of sexuality, temporality, and historiography confuse chronology and conse-quence with teleological progress. In constructing this specter, the advocates of homohistory assert, ironically, a new essentialism. Chapter 8 of this book will address the relationships between sexuality and textuality by means of an alternative analytic of sequence. For now, suffice it to say that it may not be so very queer to bind such disparate phenomena into a single unitary ontol-ogy. To invoke Sedgwick once more: "What if the richest junctures weren't the ones where *everything means the same thing*?"[81] That these conflations occur under the banner of queer should not go unnoticed. Queer's free-floating, endlessly mobile, and infinitely subversive capacities may be one of its strengths—accomplishing strategic maneuvers that no other concept does—but its principled imprecision poses considerable analytic limitations. Simply at the level of politics, for instance, queer's congeniality with neoliberalism has been well documented.[82] However mutable as a horizon of possibility, queer is a position taken up in resistance to specific configurations of gender and sexuality. If queer, as is often said, is intelligible only in relation to social norms,[83] and if the concept of normality itself is of relatively recent vintage,[84] then queer needs to be defined and redefined in relation to those changing configurations.[85] To fail to specify these relations is to ignore desire's emergence out of distinct cultural and material configurations of space and time, as well as what psychoanalysis calls libidinal predicates. It is to celebrate the instability of queer by means of a false universalization of the normal.

The analytic capacity of queer can only be elevated to ontology if it is abstracted and dehistoricized.[86] One of the more dubious forms this abstraction takes is to insist that sexual identity is completely irrelevant to contemporary queer life. Opines Menon: "a homosexuality that is posited as chronologically and sexually identifiable adheres to the strictures of heterohistoricism and is therefore not, according to the logic of my argument, queer at all."[87] Although Goldberg and Freccero have no doubt that sexual identities generate real effects, they tend to interpret them as exclusively pernicious. If, as Lee Edelman maintains, "queerness can never define an identity; it can only ever disturb one,"[88] it remains the case that queerness today is imbricated with and tethered to a range of identities, in complex relations of support, tension, and contest.[89] However problematic, regulatory, and incoherent modern identity categories may be, this does not obviate their cogency as palpable discursive and social constructions. That we remain under modernity's sway is clear from contemporary debates about the globalization of gay identity,[90] as well as by the pervasive institutionalization of sexual identities in laws, social policies, and clinical therapies. For this reason, a queer historicism that refuses, on principle, to countenance the existence of the category "modern homosexuality" invests too much descriptive accuracy in the transhistorical truth value of queer theory.[91]

Rather than continue a zero-sum game of identity versus nonidentity, queer scholars might gain some analytical purchase by recognizing that the material, social, and psychic conditions of queer life might not always be served by the presumption of an *exclusive* queerness: perhaps at least some of us, and the worlds within which we live, are queer and gay, queer and bi, queer and trans, queer and lesbian, queer and heterosexual. This is not only a matter of recognizing the import of social emplacements and embodied desires—or even the contingency of queer theory itself—but the give-and-take of psychic processes. Identities may be fictions—or in Freccero's term, phantasms—but they are weighty ones, and they still do important work. That they also break down, become unhinged, is understood in psychoanalysis as part of a lifelong process of formation and deformation, not an either-or proposition.

To clarify this tension in less psychoanalytic terms, it may be useful to return to the theorist who has done more than anyone to render explicit the stakes of a queer hermeneutic. Following her description of the "open mesh of possibilities" with a long list of possible self-identifications that "queer" might compass, Sedgwick noted that "given the historical and contemporary force of the prohibitions against *every* same-sex sexual expression, for anyone to disavow those meanings, or to displace them from the term's definitional center, would be to dematerialize any possibility of queerness itself."[92] Sedgwick's queer is positioned in relation to both universalizing and minoritizing axes; its radical potential is relative to the political work of identity, which is seen as simultaneously enabling and disabling, self-empowering and disciplinary. As is usual with her caveats, there is something important at stake here, and it has to do with politics and ethics. Intent on promoting the universalizing over the minoritizing aspects of eroticism, those who would celebrate "the homo in us all" seem unaware of, or perhaps untroubled by, the asymmetrical disposition of privileges and rights attached to sexual minority status. Furthermore, to argue, as Menon does, that sexual identity categories are themselves an effect of a misguided queer historicism[93] is to misrecognize the processes by which identities are produced, as well as the political force of their application and dissemination.[94]

Only by failing to attend to historicism as it is actually practiced can such an accusation stand.[95] But rather than engage *with* history or historiography, unhistoricists seem more interested in refiguring abstract temporality. This would be entirely appropriate, were it not the case that they pursue queer temporality as a wholesale substitute for history and historiography. Posing unhistoricism against what they call "hegemonic history," Goldberg and Menon take as "axiomatic"[96] the critique of the traditional historical enterprise proffered by Hayden White's *Metahistory* from 1973, whose work functions as the primary touchstone for Freccero as well.[97] Their reiteration of this reference against "History" writ large implies that historians have ignored White's critique, when in fact it has been widely discussed and to some degree integrated into cultural history, intellectual history, gender history, the history of sexuality, and queer historiography—as practiced by historians. Disciplinary history has witnessed as well a sustained engagement with time and temporality in recent years.

The "un" of unhistoricism disregards these engagements in order to produce a binary for the sake of deconstructing it. Moreover, this project bespeaks an antipathy to empirical inquiry, which, viewed as the primary tool of the historian, is posed as antithetical to acts of queering—as if queerness could not live in the details of empirical history. Needless to say, plenty of scholars in queer studies do practice various forms of empirical inquiry—not only historians, but anthropologists, sociologists, psychologists, legal theorists, critical race theorists, and, yes, literary critics—and some of them have offered astute analyses of the relationship between their methods and those of queer theory. Without delving into *that* bibliography, one can simply ask: Where would queer theory be without the anthropology of Esther Newton, the history of George Chauncey, the sociology of Steven Epstein, the legal writings of Janet Halley? Where would queer theory be without Gayle Rubin's "Thinking Sex"?[98]

Rejecting out of hand the methods used by most social scientists, unhistoricism's hostility to empiricism adorns itself in the resurgent prestige of "theory." Freccero proposes to not "take seriously the pieties of the discipline that would require the solemn, even dour, marshalling of empirical evidence,"[99] while Menon laments that "by grafting chronological history onto theory, Renaissance queer theorists *confine* themselves to being historians of sexuality."[100] Rendering explicit the hierarchical division of labor informing their critique, this conceptual and affective elevation of (sexy) theory over (dour) history is never fully explained, nor are the key practitioners of the history of sexuality—those trained as historians, those who identify as historians, or those working in history departments—cited and directly engaged. Indeed, one might probe what history stands for in this body of work. For many scholars, history is, on the one hand, an academic discipline, a knowledge community, a professional locus from which to investigate the past; on the other hand, it refers to the collective, highly mediated understandings of material, ideational, and discursive "events" of past cultures, achieved through various methods.[101] But for the unhistoricists, history stands in for a very specific, self-delimiting, and ultimately caricatured set of methods, becoming an abject emblem crowned with a capital letter—in other words, a cliché.

It is not my purpose here to mount a defense of the work of historians, although Chapter 6 will engage directly with their work as it overlaps with and diverges from that of literary critics. For now, suffice it to say that the discipline of history is as varied and contentious as any literature department, and its internal debates regarding the "cultural turn," "narrative," "teleology," "evidence," "objectivity," and "theory" are complex, nuanced, and ongoing. Others are doing a better job thinking through the particular affordances of disciplinary history, including its methods and protocols, for queer endeavors than I ever could.[102] And historians of sexuality are more than capable of explaining their own investments and methods.[103] I doubt, however, that historians will direct those explanations to the unhistoricists, for the latters' lack of genuine interest in the discipline of history assures that most historians will feel free to ignore them.[104] Their mischaracterization of the historian's enterprise threatens not only to stall productive exchange between literary and historical studies (thereby contributing to the mutual disciplinary estrangement that in the past produced some of the problems of historical practice so abhorred by them), but to deflect attention away from the substantive methodological challenges still faced by those intent on crafting a queer historicism.[105]

Demeaning the disciplinary methods employed to investigate historical continuity and change does not advance the cause of queerness. Moreover, it has led to unnecessary confusion by implying that to queer *temporality* is necessarily to queer *history* and *historiography*. Historiography, of course, refers to the methods we use to adduce, narrate, and reactivate the past. But the past, history, and temporality—despite their obvious interrelations—are not the same. The past is whatever actually happened, to which we have only mediated access in the form of texts, artifacts, memories (a problem that will be addressed in Chapter 6). Time is the phenomenological dimension in which the ever-receding present becomes the past, even as the present tends toward the future. As simultaneously ontological and epistemological, it is an abstraction, yet also something we know feelingly through our own aging, mortality, future-leaning aspirations, and retrospective memories. And history denotes the narratives that we construct about the past and past times, narratives that take shape according to the precepts of a variety of historiographic methods, from archival sleuthing and textual analysis to interviews and demographics.

To insist on the need to distinguish between pastness, time, history, and historiography is to suggest that the effort to queer temporality may not be

about queering history at all. The structure and movement of time is not the
only means of access to the past nor the only way to negotiate our mediated
relationship to it. Nor does a concern with temporality sum up the kinds of
queer-friendly transactions that can be forged between past and present by
historians and literary critics. Indeed, the effort to queer temporality charts a
very particular itinerary, motivated by distinctive aims—disrupting developmental continuity and teleology prime among them—with only the most
oblique relationship to other historical questions such as temporal contingency and change over the long term. Given these distinctions, the question
might be how to negotiate the conceptual and methodological tensions
between the projects of queering time and writing history. Any such negotiation would involve some difficult methodological decisions: whether and how
to balance the claims of historical similitude and alterity when engaging with
the past, whether and how to use psychoanalysis and deconstruction to enable
not only synchronic but diachronic understandings across time, and whether
and how sequence, chronology, and periodization might have utility for
queer studies. Beyond these specifically historiographic issues, at stake more
broadly are the role of empirical inquiry in queer studies, the adequacy of
"homo" and "hetero" as descriptors of incommensurate phenomena, and the
tension between identity and nonidentity in contemporary understandings
of queerness.

However these issues are addressed, for both those invested in the project
of queering temporality and those who remain skeptical about it, it might be
the better part of valor to desist from couching the issues in terms of a
rhetoric of "normalization." For those committed to fostering a range of
nonnormative modes of being and thought, the derision implicit in this accusation can only be construed as an attempt to foreclose the very possibility of
resistance.[106] While proclaiming a uniquely queer openness to experimentation and indeterminacy, this rhetoric disqualifies others' ways of engaging
with the past, suggesting that the effort to account for similarities and change
over time can only be motivated by a hegemonic, if defunct, disciplinarity.
Indicted by association as inimical to the agenda of queering are a wide
range of methodological practices and tools: empiricism, periodization and
chronology, large-scale historical narration, disciplinary-specific competencies, and attachment to logic itself. Paradoxically, unhistoricism arrogates to
itself the only appropriate model of queer history even as its practitioners
imply that history is not something they are interested in making. The categorical quality of their polemic, which implicitly installs queer as a doctrinal

foundation and ideological litmus test, goes to the heart of historiographic and queer ethics. It goes to the heart of academic and queer politics. It goes to the heart of interdisciplinarity and its future.

⁓ ⁓ ⁓

Rather than practice "queer theory as that which challenges all categorization,"[107] I believe there remain ample reasons to practice a queer historicism dedicated to showing *how* categories, however mythic, phantasmic, and incoherent, *came to be*. To understand the chance nature of coincidence and convergence, of sequence and consequence, and to follow them through to the entirely contingent outcomes to which they gave rise: this is not a historicism that creates categories of identity or presumes their inevitability; it is one that seeks to explain such categories' constitutive, pervasive, and persistent force. Resisting unwarranted teleologies while accounting for resonances and change will bring us closer to achieving the difficult and delicate balance of apprehending historical sameness and difference,[108] continuism and alterity, that the past, as past, presents to us. The more we honor this balance, the more complex and circumspect will be our comprehension of the relative incoherence *and relative power* of past and present conceptual categories, as well as of the dynamic relations among subjectivity, sexuality, and historiography.

Such a queer historicism need not segregate itself from other methods, such as psychoanalysis, with its crucial recognition of the role of the unconscious in historical life, and its aim may well be the further deconstruction of identity categories. But any such rapprochement would require enhanced discernment regarding the ways our bodies remain in time, as well as regarding the use to which different theorists of sex, time, and history are put. In this regard, the exchange I have attempted to advance in these pages cannot help but touch upon the generative legacy of Eve Sedgwick. In its citational circulations, that legacy has become ever more diffuse—and at times attenuated or diluted. The question of how we utilize the multiple "Sedgwicks" we have known is thus one issue at stake. That this is so might give sufficient reason to pause over the prospect of yoking the future of queerness so tightly to *un*historicism. What we create out of the *copia* bequeathed by Sedgwick—as well as by those with whom she was in dialogue—merits something more scrupulous. After all: what we remember, what we forget, what we retain, what we omit, and what we finally acknowledge as our debts—this is no less than history in the making.

CHAPTER 4

The Present Future
of Lesbian Historiography

This chapter builds on the critique offered in the previous chapter by offering some new strategies for negotiating the apprehension of similarity and difference in the history of sexuality. It does so by means of the particular case of lesbian historiography. The genesis for this chapter, as for the book as a whole, lies in my sense that the future of studies of sexuality demands more deliberate reflection about how we go about constructing historical narratives. To the extent that historiographic method has been a topic of debate, for a long time it took the form of the by now notorious distinction between acts versus identity, and its corollary, alterity versus continuism. Scholars whose historical accounts take a continuist form tended to emphasize a similarity between past and present concepts of sexual understanding; those who instead highlight historical difference or alterity (as it is termed by literary scholars) tended to emphasize problems of anachronism, changing terminologies and typologies, and resistance to teleology.[1] In my estimation, the relative weight accorded to alterity or continuism has had a more pronounced impact on the practice of lesbian history than any other issue (including debates about what counts as evidence of same-gender desire).

The premise of the present chapter is that the methodological assumption of a sameness/difference polarity has outlived its utility. Indeed, as the previous chapter's critique of unhistoricism suggested, what now requires methodological scrutiny is how queer historicism, and the history of sexuality more generally, can pursue both synchronic and diachronic explanations by using a range of different methods. The historiographic choice is no longer between a supersessionist continuous history and an examination of synchronic complexities and contradictions, for few scholars of sexuality are indifferent to the simultaneous existence of incoherent discourses of sexuality, whether in the past or in the present. Nor would many commit to writing a teleological history, in which one model of identity seamlessly supersedes the next. I have begun to intimate that attention should focus on how to think about multiple similarities and differences, whether conceived as continuous or discontinuous, not by juxtaposing periods but by constructing an analytic focused on the "across" of time.

But first, let us recall how the opposition between alterity and continuism evolved within lesbian history, for it took a very decided form that has influenced, under cover, as it were, the terms of subsequent debate. As was true in the previous chapter, the point of this historical exercise is not to reenact old debates, but to take stock of where they have led us and where we might go. The first implicitly continuist approach was Lillian Faderman's groundbreaking 1981 *Surpassing the Love of Men,* which, as its subtitle announced, traced romantic friendship and love between women from the Renaissance to the present. Terry Castle's 1993 *The Apparitional Lesbian,* although it opposed Faderman's desexualized paradigm of romantic friends, nonetheless reiterated her continuist premises by provocatively collapsing eighteenth-century representations with twentieth-century cultural formations.[2] The continuist approach was extended backward in time through Bernadette Brooten's magisterial *Love Between Women,* which, even as it treads cautiously through the historical specificities of ancient Rome, in its effort to demonstrate a lesbian identity in antiquity nonetheless implicitly employs concepts of 1970s lesbianism to read the early Christian West.[3]

Castle and Brooten, in particular, were critical of the influence of Michel Foucault on the periodization of homosexual identity, including his notorious pronouncement in *The History of Sexuality,* volume 1, that "the sodomite was a temporary aberration; the homosexual is now a species,"[4] which has served as a banner cry for the alterist position. The critique of methodologies that stress historical difference, however, has also taken a form less dismissive of Foucault and the historical methods he inspired. In a thoughtful challenge to the practices of women's history, Judith Bennett has argued that a "patriarchal equilibrium" has "worked to maintain the status of European women in times of political, social, and economic change."[5] Writing as a social historian who views history as necessarily a story of both continuity and change, Bennett proposes a distinction between changes in women's experiences and structural transformations of women's social status, while also proposing the term "lesbian-like" to resolve the issues of alterity posed by the distant past.[6] Diagnosing various reasons for gender historians' penchant for focusing on change, Bennett suggests that European women's history may be profitably viewed as "a history of change without transformation."[7] From a rather different angle, Louise Fradenburg and Carla Freccero, editors of the collection *Premodern Sexualities*, critique the fascination with alterity that, they argue, had taken hold of queer historical studies. Suggesting that identification with the past is an important motivation for historicist work, they advocate a practice that observes "similarities or even continuities" while eschewing "an ahistoricist or universalizing effect."[8] Carolyn Dinshaw's *Getting Medieval* similarly advocates the affective need for apprehending similarities, this time through the metaphor of "touches across time."[9] And Martha Vicinus echoes these sentiments in *Intimate Friends*, maintaining that "attitudes toward and behaviors by lesbians show a rich combination of change and continuity."[10] Arguing that "we gain a better sense of intimate friendship by tracing repetitive patterns," she notes that "even though the *structures* of intimacy remained in place, their *meanings* changed over time."[11]

I rehearse these forays into lesbian, women's, and queer history because I believe they indicate that, methodologically speaking, we are poised to enter a new stage, wherein some of the theoretically motivated and archivally supported claims that have absorbed the attention of scholars over the past twenty-five years can be reassessed. As more archival materials support more subtly calibrated concepts of identity and orientation, debates about acts versus identities, alterity versus continuism, have—at least for some scholars—begun to recede in importance, while other scholars, as the previous chapter makes clear, have given these debates new life in reconfigured forms.[12] I want to suggest that what I call the present future of lesbian historiography—by which I mean those methods that might enable us to imagine a future historicist practice—necessitates analyzing recurring patterns across large spans of time in the identification, social statuses, behaviors, and meanings of women who erotically desired other women. Doing so, I believe, could result in a new paradigm for lesbian history.[13]

I thus want to register a shift in my own thinking (which in *The Renaissance of Lesbianism* had fallen more on the side of emphasizing alterity) toward an engagement with the following tripartite hypothesis:

- There exist certain recurrent explanatory metalogics that accord to the history of lesbianism over a vast temporal expanse a sense of consistency and, at times, uncanny familiarity.

- These explanatory metalogics draw their specific content from perennial axes of social definition, which become particularly resonant or acute at different historical moments.
- The recurring moments in which these metalogics are manifested might profitably be understood as *cycles of salience*—that is, as forms of intelligibility whose meanings recur, intermittently and with a difference, across time.

This chapter will attempt to fill in the contours of these hypotheses by drawing on the work of a number of scholars. Before doing so, however, I want to suggest what is at stake in such patterns of discourse for current historiographic practices. Such cycles of salience are what lead us to encounter what can look a lot like "lesbianism" in the distant historical periods in which we work. They indicate, I propose, not lesbianism per se—by which I mean the canonical form that now circulates globally as a modern identity category[14]—but the presence of symptomatic preoccupations about the meanings of women's bodies and behaviors. The appearance of consistency and familiarity produced by these metalogics, the axes of social definition from which they draw their energy, and the cycles of salience during which they reappear are not, therefore, simple or self-evident. Nor are these cycles, precisely, continuity—if by that we mean an unbroken line connecting the past to the present.[15] I am not, in other words, forgoing an alterist conception for a continuous or transhistorical one. It is less that there exist transhistorical categories that comprise and subsume historical variation than that certain perennial logics and definitions have remained useful, across time, for conceptualizing the meaning of female bodies and bonds.[16] Emerging at certain moments, silently disappearing from view, and then reemerging as particularly relevant (or explosively volatile), these recurrent explanatory logics seem to underlie the organization, and reorganization, of women's erotic lives. Sometimes these preoccupations arise as repeated expressions of identical concerns; sometimes they emerge differently or under an altered guise. Recurrence, in other words, does not imply transhistoricity, and cycles can be nonidentical to themselves. As endemic features of erotic discourse and experience, these logics and definitions, as well as the ideological fault lines they subtend, not only contribute to the existence of historically specific types and figures but also enable correspondences across time. At the same time, the forms these metalogics take, their specific content, the discourses in which they are embedded, and the angle of relations among them all are subject to change. Social preoccupations come in and out of focus, new political exigencies emerge, discourses converge and the points of contact between them shift—and in the process, the meanings of female-female desire are reconfigured.

The methodological reassessment I am offering is made possible by a wealth of published studies. Thanks to social and cultural history, as well as to an even larger body of work by literary critics analyzing cultural representations, we now possess a densely textured picture of what it might have meant for women to love, desire, and have sex with each other at various times in specific communities.[17] The research that has taken place in almost every historical period, particularly for England, France, and North America, offers a heretofore unimagined opportunity to confront the conceptual challenges of change and continuity on a larger, more capacious scale than typically has been tried—including pushing against the analytical paradigms and geographic boundaries of the Anglo-European West. Lesbian history will continue to locate its subjects in specific temporal and spatial contexts, while also addressing how their histories intersect and diverge across national, ethnic, racial, and geographical borders. However, by identifying certain axes of definition that have been developed largely out of the histories of white women in western Europe and the United States, analyzing the reasons for their recurrence, and then submitting these narratives to comparative analysis across the boundaries of race, religion, and geography, it may, over time, be possible to fashion a broadly synoptic account of historical regimes of eroticism—without losing sight of each regime's specificity, complexity, relative coherence, and instability. In short, recognition of these periodic cycles of salience—flaring up and abating—could provide us with a means to collectively write that which, for good reason, has not been attempted since Faderman's inaugural study: a transnational, culturally specific, and comparative history of lesbianism over the *longue durée*.

ʕ੮   ʕ੮   ʕ੮

A search for "types" has framed much of the scholarship on lesbian history of England and the United States. From my own book on the relations between representations of the "masculine tribade" and the "chaste feminine friend" in the sixteenth and seventeenth centuries,[18] to Susan Lanser's work on the "sapphist" as a flashpoint for modernity in the eighteenth century,[19] to Martha Vicinus's early delineation of four antecedents to modern lesbianism and, more recently, her exploration of nineteenth-century familial models for female intimacy such as mother/daughter and husband/wife,[20] to Judith Halberstam's exploration of twentieth-century forms of female masculinity,[21] an implicit typological impulse has framed efforts to render female-female desires intelligible—both in their own historical terms, and in ours.

In part this typological inclination results from the medical taxonomies from which the modern category of homosexuality was derived.[22] Thus, a reliance on systems of classification similarly has dominated studies of male homosexuality, both within the West and cross-culturally.[23] David M. Halperin has provided the most explicit description and theorization of typologies of male homosexuality across a broad temporal expanse. Halperin—previously one of the most influential advocates of historical *dis*continuity—attempts in *How to Do the History of Homosexuality* "to rehabilitate a modified constructionist approach to the history of sexuality by readily acknowledging the existence of transhistorical continuities, reintegrating them into the frame of the analysis, and reinterpreting their significance within a genealogical understanding of the emergence of (homo)sexuality itself."[24]

Revisiting his own historicist practice in order to balance the conceptual appeals of historical continuity and change, Halperin offers a sophisticated analytical paradigm based on four "transhistorical" "pre-homosexual categories of male sex and gender deviance": effeminacy; pederasty or active sodomy; friendship or male love; and passivity or inversion.[25] This rehabilitation implicitly relies on classical models of male-male relations, which are viewed as variously applicable at different times and places. Halperin proposes, however, a transhistorical model only up to the emergence of modern homosexuality—when, owing to a "long historical process of accumulation, accretion, and overlay," the relations among these categories definitively changed.[26]

Although I have been inspired by Halperin's engagement with continuist arguments, my current interest lies not in creating a transhistorical taxonomy of categories or figures—or, at least, this would only be one task in a larger project I envision. I am less interested in describing the *contents* of typologies and exposing the conceptual strands that contribute to them than in investigating the cultural conditions that render such types culturally salient at particular moments.[27] This reflects my desire to build methodologically on the project pursued in *The Renaissance of Lesbianism in Early Modern England* while also moving beyond it. There I argued that, under the auspices of divergent discourses circulating in England, a symptomatic break in the representation of female homoeroticism occurred over the course of the seventeenth century, a shift in the terms of female embodiment, which led to a "cultural perversion" of female-female desire. This process of perversion, which involved particular negotiations of significance and insignificance, articulation and negation, intelligibility and unintelligibility, provided some of the primary materials out of which modern identity categories were fashioned. I also argued, however, that early modern representations are definitively estranged from modern conceptual categories. Rather than attempt to forge links between the tribade, the tommy, the invert, and the butch, for instance, I focused on certain conceptual axes that, within the temporal parameters of two centuries, organized the meanings of tribadism and female friendship. Building on the work of Annamarie Jagose on the terms of "lesbian inconsequence,"[28] the book attempts to expose the fragile nature of a governing regime of visibility (and its corollary, invisibility) by focusing on the specific incoherences that have governed the intelligibility—and lack of intelligibility—of female-female desire.

The two figures whose genealogies I traced nonetheless appear strangely similar to subsequent emanations of female homoerotic desire. Figures that, since the foundational work in lesbian history, have been treated as prototypical for the nineteenth century (the passing woman and the romantic friend), as fundamental to the pathologizing discourses of sexology and early psychoanalysis (the invert and the pervert), and as vital to twentieth-century self-definitions (butch and femme) seem to have been cut from much of the same cloth as the early modern tribade and friend. Noting such resemblances linking various manifestations across time, I asked in closing: why do such apparent resonances assert themselves?

It would seem that certain representational features of female bodies and bonds slip into and out of historical view; some acquire more importance and visibility as others decline and fade, only to reappear in a different guise under changed social conditions. The discourses in which they are articulated shift and mutate as well. By the late eighteenth century, for instance, the sexually deviant figure that arguably had the most potential to signify transgressively—the tribade who supposedly used her enlarged clitoris to "imitate" the sex acts of men—had almost disappeared from the medical discourse that first gave her cultural intelligibility. Given the changes during this period to the practice of anatomy and physiology, it makes sense that she waned as an object of medical curiosity; but why did she linger in other genres, such as literature, and then later reappear in medicine (albeit in much different form) as the invert of sexology and psychoanalysis? The differences between the tribade and the invert, of course, are as considerable as those between Galen and Freud, but the metalogic of a figure composed by a masculinized style of desire persists. No longer diagnosed routinely, as she was in the early modern period, through the presence of an oversized clitoris, the tribade's "monstrous" abuse of her body and other women was refigured by sexology as the mannish invert's hypervirility, her masculine characteristics imbuing not only her physical nature, but her very soul.[29] Nonetheless, the common recourse to a physiological explanation for a masculinized desire, as well as the projection of such desire onto women of Africa and the Middle East in both the seventeenth and nineteenth centuries, has been striking enough to invite continuist narratives.

In order to defend the hypothesis of continuity, however, one would need to analyze the intervening period and the discursive regimes at work within it. What happened to the terms of cultural representation between the production of the masculine tribade and the masculine invert? For one thing, the emergence of a new type: the sapphist. Susan Lanser has located the cultural production of the sapphist in a historical moment when "private intimacies between women became public relations."[30] Rather than residing in the pages of medical textbooks, the sapphist's "publicity" was largely a construction of a variety of fictional forms, from picaresque novels to satiric pornography, which alternately celebrated and condemned her.[31] By the latter part of the eighteenth century, so notorious was the figure of the sapphist that, as Martha Vicinus maintains, "women's intimate friendships were divided into two types, sensual romantic friendship and sexual Sapphism."[32] Nonetheless, as Lisa Moore argues, sapphism and romantic friendship "continued to exhibit a dangerous intimacy."[33] What separated romantic friendship from suspect sapphism, contends Lanser, was less the masculinized gender performance of the sapphist than her deviation from class propriety. Indeed, Lanser argues that it is only through a kind of back-formation that figures suspected of sapphism—because of their violations of genteel respectability—were later deemed "masculine."[34]

Over this same period, the intimate female friend was reconstituted as something both akin and alien to the innocent, chaste, yet desiring adolescent who is represented widely in sixteenth- and seventeenth-century literature. By the late eighteenth century, under the auspices of a culture of manners, sensibility, and taste, the idioms of chastity and innocence that figured early modern friendship seem to have been channeled into the twin virtues of propriety and sentiment. Fictionally immortalized by that hypervirtuous exemplar of moral womanhood, Samuel Richardson's Clarissa, the "particular friend" of the Enlightenment appears to be both libidinally attached to and tragically barred from those female intimacies that might protect her from the worst abuses of patriarchal masculinity.[35] A real-life Clarissa may have had access to "sensual romantic friendship" with such a friend as Anna, but it is the project of Richardson's text—as it was of many eighteenth-century novels—to explicitly frustrate such desire.[36]

Yet, in their attempts to contain and stave off intimate female friendships, such texts had more in common with early modern literature than with later configurations of desire. For, by the next century, sensual romantic friendship—or, to invoke its function as an effect of domestic ideology, the "female world of love and ritual"—subsisted hand in glove with the Victorian bourgeois ideal of female passionlessness. Bolstered by a socioeconomic investment in women's domesticity and the separation of spheres, the expectation of women's lack of interest in sex with men paradoxically fostered the fervid expressions of love and desire among girls and women characterized by Carroll Smith-Rosenberg as "socially acceptable and fully compatible with heterosexual marriage."[37] Indeed, the nineteenth century, in Vicinus's terms, "saw a concerted effort to spiritualize all love."[38] Out of the contradictory idioms of romantic friendship and sapphic sexuality, women in the nineteenth century were, as Vicinus asserts, able "to fashion something new—a personal identity based upon a sexualized, or at least recognizably eroticized, relationship with another woman."[39]

This eroticized personal identity and public persona often depended on a form of gender inversion signified through sartorial and behavioral style. As both objects of and agents in the formation of modern identity categories, sapphists and inverts sought to make themselves legible (to themselves and to others) through the adoption of masculine dress. Yet, at the beginning of the modern era, as Vicinus argues, "gender inversion was the most important signifier of same-sex desire, but interpretations of the so-called mannish woman varied considerably."[40] As Laura Doan has shown, especially during the relaxation of gender conventions during World War I, certain British women who adopted masculine fashion neither perceived themselves nor were perceived by others as sapphists.[41] Following the postwar tightening of gender ideology, and especially after the notorious 1928 obscenity trial of Radclyffe Hall, many sapphists proclaimed their erotic independence by means of closely cropped hair, starched shirts, jackets, ties, cigarette lighters, and monocles.[42] Their manipulation of the tropes of masculine dress drew upon prior preoccupations with the cultural signification of gendered clothes, yet did so within the context of a different gender regime and by means of vastly different material technologies. Tribades, one might say, did not smoke.

Why do certain figures and tropes of eroticism (and gender) become culturally salient at certain moments, becoming saturated with meaning, and then fade from view? Why do suspicions of deviant behavior sometimes seep into the most innocuous-seeming of friendships, and why are such friendships at other times immune from suspicion? Why do certain figures, separated by vast temporal expanses, appear to adumbrate, echo, or reference one another? To adequately address these questions, we need to sharpen our analytical focus. Which characteristics of their social formation actually recur? Which social forces foster an interest in bodily or expressive acts among women, and through which discursive domains and by means of which material technologies are such intelligibilities circulated?

A focus on lesbian typologies, I have come to feel, enables only partial answers to these questions.[43] For instance, from one set of concerns, the female-oriented (although mixed-sex) "Society of Friendship" formed by seventeenth-century poet Katherine Philips looks a lot like an avatar of late nineteenth-century Boston marriage; both social forms spiritualize female emotional bonds; both derive sustenance from women's intellectual capacities; both arise from within the confines of feminine domesticity; both defer to class decorum in matters of the desiring body. But from another angle— say, the freedom to advocate for female intimacy as a political alternative to patriarchal marriage—the gulf between them is profound.

Or consider the ways that the same-sex intimacies that occurred among certain women living in medieval and early modern convents appear to provide a prototype for the fervid romantic friendships of nineteenth-century women. In both cases, intimacies were authorized by a tight relation between spirituality and eroticism, and both were materially supported by gender segregation. Yet the erotic spirituality of the nun is very different from that professed by romantic friends, and the domesticity enforced on bourgeois women as they were shunted out of the public sphere was a wholly different matter from the (largely) voluntary rigors of monastic life. Whereas the "particular friend" of the medieval monastery was debarred by the rules of her religious order from embracing or even holding hands, her nineteenth-century counterpart was likely to be encouraged by family and kin to kiss and caress her "particular friend."

So too, the gender-bending common to the medieval virago, the early modern tribade, the female husband or the passing woman of the eighteenth and nineteenth centuries, the mannish invert of sexology, the 1950s bar dyke, the stone butch, and the transgender subject of today suggests one powerful line of historical and affective connection. Yet, several other lines—including concepts of bodily morphology, extent or desirability of gender passing, relations between secrecy and disclosure, economic imperatives, and claims to an erotic subjectivity—crosscut them in such a way as to disrupt the appearance of similitude.[44] In this respect, rhetorics, vocabularies, and conventions matter as much as do wide-scale changes in material conditions. Within the frame of a particular set of identifications, for instance, a lesbian drag king might claim as historical precursor the gender-bending passing woman of eighteenth-century narrative; but if she were to submit herself to the narrative conventions structuring earlier discourses of gender passing, she quickly would find that the gulf of history is wide.[45] For one thing, as Sally O'Driscoll has argued, the passing woman depicted in eighteenth-century ballads is associated almost exclusively with *hetero*sexuality.[46]

The ideological utility of body parts to social discipline is another case in point. The metonymic logic that governed the representation of the early modern tribade's enlarged clitoris can be seen in the determination of nineteenth- and twentieth-century sexologists to discover the reasons of behavioral aberrations in a particular bodily source. Like the tribade's clitoris, the essentialized characteristics attributed to the invert attest to a will to discover in the body an explanatory mechanism for its own deviations. From this perspective, the quest, during our contemporary age of biogenetics and psychobiology, for a "gay gene" (supposedly manifest in a specific gene on the X chromosome or in the hypothalamus) and for hormonal sources of sexual orientation reiterates a desire to pin the mystery of sexuality onto a discrete physical essence. This twenty-first-century means of understanding the relation between desire and biology, psychology and the body echoes earlier cultural formations, as Siobhan Somerville has argued: "the current effort to re-biologize sexual orientation and to invoke the vocabulary of immutable difference" has its origins in the "historically coincident" yet "structurally interdependent" discourses of nineteenth-century sexology, comparative anatomy, and scientific racism.[47] Those nineteenth-century discourses, I would add, trace some of their structural components—for instance, their anatomical essentialism—back to early modern attempts to diagnose the tribade's transgression as a function of bodily morphology and, at times, racial difference.[48]

At the same time, the material technologies by which gay genes can even be thought *as such*—much less investigated—are profoundly modern in orientation. Yet material technologies need not be particularly sophisticated or "scientific" to affect the range of available discourses. During the sixteenth and early seventeenth centuries, for example, tales of tribades would have remained a fairly elite knowledge had they not made their way through the new genre of travel literature and into vernacular medical advice books. So too, an even wider array of print media—newspapers, scandal sheets, published trial records, novels, and pornography—disseminated an epistemology of suspicion about alleged sapphists in the eighteenth century.[49]

Resemblances, then, shimmer unsteadily and unevenly, moving closer or receding, depending on the axes of definition that inform one's perspective or capture one's attention. Such attention may be the result of forces extrinsic to sexuality itself. Certain axes of social definition may become more pronounced during eras when social discourse about sexuality draws into its orbit concerns and signifiers external to it. Like the periodic moral panics first adduced by Gayle Rubin and Jeffrey Weeks,[50] cycles of salience may be linked temporally and conceptually to moments of social crisis which have their source in anxieties peripheral to eroticism, such as reactions to feminism and changing gender roles, reservations about redefinitions of the family, nationalist or racist fears of contamination, concerns about morality and social discipline, and violent upheavals in the political order.[51] Conversely, a resurgence of salience for other axes of social definition may be more likely to occur precisely when such anxieties are absent.

I do not propose that we create rubrics (e.g., a paradigm of bodily morphology or gender inversion or intimate friendship) under which all historical variants would be gathered, organized, and codified. To offer the tribade, the invert, and the romantic friend, for instance, as transhistorical figures of lesbian history would move us only a small step beyond models of a single, unified lesbianism. To do the history of sexuality is not to turn a blind eye to perennial features of the erotic system in the name of historical alterity. But neither is it to too quickly assume homology when not every facet repeats.

❧   ❧   ❧

As noted in Chapter 2, with the exception of Alan Bray's *The Friend*, a history of homosexuality over the *longue durée* largely has been avoided since

Faderman's foundational survey. Such avoidance stems from the association
of overarching historical narratives with the "gay ancestors" approach to history, as well as from a postmodern suspicion toward the explanatory power
of metanarratives. There have, to be sure, been histories of sexuality more
generally that traverse several centuries (such as John D'Emilio and Estelle
Freedman's *Intimate Matters* and Richard Godbeer's *Sexual Revolution in
Early America*; Anna Clark's *Desire: A History of European Sexuality*; Leila
Rupp's introductory overviews, *A Desired Past: A Short History of Same-Sex
Love in America* and *Sapphistries: A Global History of Love Between Women*;[52]
Joseph Boone's *The Homoerotics of Orientalism*; as well as sourcebooks such
as Alison Oram and Annmarie Turnbull's *The Lesbian History Sourcebook:
Love and Sex Between Women in Britain from 1780 to 1970*). There also have
been temporally broad, theoretically inflected studies, such as Jonathan Dollimore's *Sexual Dissidence*, Lee Edelman's *Homographesis*, and Annamarie
Jagose's *Inconsequence*. With the exception of Boone, however, none of these
has explicitly theorized the implications of connecting the strands of gay,
lesbian, or queer history across multiple historical periods. To the extent that
a longer vantage has been raised as a methodological or theoretical question,
it largely has been framed within the context of the acts-versus-identity
debate. Dominated by the impulse to create densely local and socially contextualized interpretations, the field's center of gravity has resulted in some
remarkable period-based studies that will inform our understanding for a
great while.[53]

But note the phrase "period-based studies." Since the move away from the
famous-gay-people-in-history approach, the history of homosexuality—both
male and female—mainly has been written by means of research segmented
along traditional period lines. Even as queer theory, post-structuralism, and
the "linguistic turn" have pressured many of the methodological premises of
literary critics and traditional historians, the power of periodization has not
been shaken—as titles such as *Queering the Renaissance, Queering the Middle
Ages*, and *Queering the Moderns* attest.[54] Although it has become a tenet of
historicist queer studies to disrupt the "straight," reproductive logic of
sequential temporality, to expose periodization as a fetish, and to keep one
eye on our contemporary situation, the ensuing conversation between past
and present generally has been accomplished by relying on a period-bound
concept of the past: one historical moment, situated in proximity to modernity (or postmodernity).[55] To queer the Middle Ages, for instance, is also to
historicize the modern—with the injunction to "get medieval" pursued by

considering how medieval concepts inhabit, resonate, or are at odds with contemporary categories and crises: the U.S. military policy of don't ask, don't tell; the sexual politics of the Clinton impeachment; the discourse of HIV/AIDS; the love lyrics of rock star Melissa Etheridge.[56]

Queer historiography, in other words, has enabled a provocative conversation between the past and the present, history and (post)modernity. Notwithstanding this provocation, the retrospective fiction of periodization has functioned epistemologically as a force field, encouraging certain questions while obstructing others.[57] In particular, the common sense of periodization has kept our analytical attention off those problematic areas where historical boundaries meet: the ragged edges, margins, and interstices of periodization that frame our narratives.[58] It is here that historical claims, especially about the advent of change or novelty, can rub uncomfortably against one another—sometimes calling into question the basic premises and arguments of temporally discrete historical studies and sometimes leading to charges of scholarly ignorance or special pleading. Yet, as understandable as is the desire to expose other scholars' epistemic privileging of their own turf, a strategy of border surveillance does not help us learn to speak across period divides.[59]

I want to suggest a different strategy—one based on acknowledgment of perennial axes of social definition and their temporal appearance as cycles of salience, and which is in pursuit of the explanatory metalogics that such definitions manifest. Many of the issues in gay/lesbian/queer history that have structured the asking of questions and the seeking of answers traverse historical domains. Whereas these issues may not all function as axes of social definition, they provide one means of access to them as well as to a better understanding of the moments when they accrue social significance. Presented as a large set of substantive themes, they include:

- the relationship between erotic acts and erotic identities;
- the quest for the etiology of erotic desire in the physical body, including the role of anatomy;
- the status accorded to the genitals in defining sexual acts;
- the relations of love, intimacy, and friendship to eroticism, including the defensive separation of sex from friendship;
- the fine line between virtue and transgression, orderly and disorderly homoeroticism;
- the relationship of eroticism to gender deviance and conformity;
- the symbolic and social functions of gendered clothing;

- the relevance of age, class/status, and ethnic/racial hierarchies to erotic relations;
- the composition and effects of familial, marital, and household arrangements;
- the role of voluntary kinship and familial nomenclatures in mediating and expressing erotic bonds;
- the relationship of homoeroticism to homosociality;
- the role of gender-segregated spaces, including religious, educational, criminal, and medical institutions;
- the existence of communities and subcultures, including public sexual cultures and spaces;
- the division between public and private sexualities;
- the effects of racial, geographical, religious, and national othering;
- the effects of social and geographical mobility;
- assessments of appropriate erotic knowledge, including the ambiguous line separating medicine from obscenity;
- the credibility of religious, medical, scientific, and legal discourses in the production of sexual categories, including definitions of nature, the unnatural, normality, and the abnormal;
- the differences between concepts of erotic identity, predisposition, and habitual behaviors;
- the dynamic of secrecy and disclosure, including covert signs, coding, and open secrets;
- the efficacy of representations of (homo)sexual contamination and/or predation to the body politic;
- the impact of sexually transmitted diseases on fears of mortality and social catastrophe;
- the interdiction against and circulation of sexual prostheses and supplemental technologies of sex;
- the relationship of hermaphrodites and the intersexed to same-sex desires and practices;
- the attractions of aesthetic conventions of erotic similitude versus erotic difference and/or hierarchy;
- the effects of narrative, poetic, and visual form on representations of homoeroticism.

Because of pervasive gender asymmetries, additional themes have had more consequence for the history of female bodies, experiences, and representations:

- the misogynist logic of female imperfection, excessive appetite, susceptibility to seduction, and inconstancy;
- the role of female anatomy, especially the clitoris, in cultural representations;
- the import of chastity, reproductive marriage, and the sexual double standard on women's erotic options;
- women's unequal access to sex education and sexual knowledge, including sexual language, anatomical definitions, and medical taxonomies;
- the effects of reproductive choice and constraint on women's erotic welfare;
- the gendering of propriety, emotion, and sensibility;
- the derivative, secondary order of lesbian visibility, which underpins conceptual misrecognitions such as lesbian "impossibility" and "imitation";
- the social power of lesbians (and representations of female homoeroticism) relative to that of men;
- the relation of women's erotic ties to their political subjectivity—that is, to feminism;
- the potential threat that female-female eroticism poses to patriarchal relations and male dominance.

This list is unwieldy, but even so, it is not comprehensive. Each of these themes assumes different contours, contents, and emphases when examined from historically specific locations.[60] Some of them have been discussed at length in queer scholarship; others hardly have been raised. Some have settled in one or another historical location; others have been assumed to possess no past. Not only does each one provide a specific angle for investigating how subjects might have understood—or not understood—themselves, but in the aggregate they allow us to appreciate the extent to which their powers of definition extend across discrete historical moments and, thus, beyond the subjects so defined by them. They are substantive and constitutive: organizing the self-perceptions and contributing to the intelligibility of same-sex desire (as both representation and lived experience) for people in the past, while also providing the terms by which we have identified those subjects and made the past intelligible to ourselves. To the extent that they precipitate the establishment of temporal patterns of meaning making, they have been complicit in framing queer historical investigation as an inquiry into an already constituted object: as Laura Doan has put it, "identity history" as "a hunt for x."[61]

At the same time, the range and diversity of these themes enable us to see that social constructivist claims regarding the emergence of modern homosexuality—whatever the date proposed—have been founded on the basis of a relatively limited set of preoccupations (e.g., identity, subcultures, medical concepts, and legal codes), which have been used to stand in, metonymically, as evidence of homosexuality *tout court*. In the aggregate, these themes prod us to query whether the different dates that have been proposed for the "birth" of the modern homosexual may not result from their separate temporal arcs. Upsetting the premises of identity history by proliferating the range of relevant issues, they urge us to ask whether what is sometimes presented as whole-scale diachronic change (before and after sexuality, before and after identity, before and after modernity) might rather be a manifestation of ongoing synchronic tensions in conceptualizations about bodies and desires (and their relations to the gender system). As these tensions are confronted with the material realities of new social formations—attacks on monastic culture, the rise of empirical science, the emergence of print and media technologies, the public sphere, political satire and pornography, secularism, mandatory schooling, scientific racism, transnational gay and lesbian movements, the resurgence of religious fundamentalisms—they are played out, differently, yet again.

※ ※ ※

This list of substantive themes is intended to bring more clarity to the principles of selection by which one figure might be made to correspond to another across time. It aims to bring more exactitude to the practice of genealogy within queer historicism by encouraging more precise definition of terms and setting of conceptual parameters. As should be clear to readers of Chapter 3, the proposal I am advocating runs counter to others' efforts to confront the challenges posed by teleology, chronology, and periodization. Rather than "dispense with periodization" as Carolyn Dinshaw and Karma Lochrie suggest,[62] I suggest we instead use the significant period-based studies published over the past twenty years in order to piece together the questions, concepts, and propositions that have emerged from them into a multilayered genealogy of sexuality. This involves a perspective that is simultaneously synchronic and diachronic: perennial axes of social definition are the synchronic materials out of which diachronic cycles of salience emerge. Poised between the no-win options of attempting to manufacture a coherent, seamless, successionist metanarrative or of eschewing chronological temporality altogether, the genealogy I envision would derive out of and retain the questions, issues, arguments, and contradictions of our fragmented, periodized, discontinuous research. This process of piecing together would encourage us to scrutinize multiple points of intersection, both temporal and spatial, forged from a variety of angles, among different erotic regimes, while also requiring analysis of the ways these linkages are disrupted or crosscut by other angles of vision. Viewed from a wide angle but with all the rough edges showing, this genealogy would necessitate a method of historiography that is literally dialogical; it would be motivated, in both form and content, by the question: how might we stage a dialogue between one queer past and another?[63]

It is, admittedly, difficult to imagine how such a multifaceted dialogue might happen or take place. Given the highly periodized institutional conditions within which we pursue our scholarly work, and given, as well, the mandate to examine such an enormous temporal and spatial expanse, its creation clearly is not the task of any one scholar. Such a complex act of creation would require a collective conversation, or, rather, many conversations imbued with multiple voices, each of them engaged in a proliferating and contestatory syntax of "and, but, and, but." This collaboration, born of a common purpose, would not erase friction but embrace it. I imagine such voices and the histories they articulate coming together and falling apart, like the fractured and vacillating images of a rotating kaleidoscope: mimetic, repetitive, but changing, with each of its aspects reverberating off others, but nonetheless possessed of their own autonomy. Such a kaleidoscopic vision of historiography is, no doubt, a utopian dream. But like all dreams, it gestures toward a horizon of possibility, provocatively tilting our angle of vision and providing us with new questions and, perhaps, new ways of answering them.

Moving toward this horizon is not the sole direction for lesbian historiography; our approaches need not, indeed should not, be mutually exclusive. Not all questions related to the writing of queer history would be resolved by joining in this effort. Gaps in our knowledge remain and may never be filled; archives remain to be investigated in even greater abundance than we were aware prior to digitization; different racial, national, geographic, and linguistic traditions call out for specification and comparison (including comparisons made available by historicism).[64] Significant methodological problems require more analysis, including the complex role of emotional affect in our construction of the past.[65] Perhaps the largest questions of the moment concern how to continue to hone methods appropriate to investigating homoerotic desires and experiences specific to various ethnic and racial groups in the past[66] (especially the construction of female-female desire in non-Western cultures),[67] as well as how to best situate the history of sexuality in a transnational and comparative frame.[68] Just as the historical object of study is implicated in the temporal issues addressed above, so too it is framed by spatial configurations. To the extent that teleological history has positioned non-Western sexualities as anterior, primitive, and inevitably progressing toward Western models, resistance to that paradigm must involve a decolonization that is not only archival but methodological.[69]

It is my hope that the identification of perennial axes of social definition and the metalogics they reflect will help scholars investigating different racial, ethnic, national, linguistic, and religious traditions to further develop methodological tools appropriate to their own questions and contexts. Which of these axes of definition function across cultural as well as historical boundaries? Which are culturally specific to Europe and North America? What do such differential presences and absences tell us about indigenous modes of comprehending and organizing sexuality, and how does recognition of them promote alternative genealogies of sexual modernity?

The implication of lesbian historiography in both space and time thus raises additional questions regarding its present future. Most pertinent to the dialogue I have advocated: Would its aim be to create a single lesbian historiography which produces multiple histories that intersect at different points? Or would its goal be to create multiple lesbian historiographies which refract and bounce off of one another in continual oscillation? Finally, how might a reconceived lesbian historiography pressure the development of a global history of sexuality? Whatever our answers to these questions, the future of lesbian historiography will require a more ambitious and capacious response to our growing historical knowledge. The past deserves no less than this; the future demands this and more.

PART II

———— ❧ ————

Scenes of Instruction;
or, Early Modern Sex Acts

CHAPTER 5

The Joys of Martha Joyless

Queer Pedagogy and the (Early Modern) Production of Sexual Knowledge

I want to inspire queers to be more articulate about the world they
have already made, with all its variations from the norm, with its
ethical understanding of the importance of those variations, with its
ethical refusal of shame or implicitly shaming standards of dignity,
with its refusal of the tactful silences that preserve hetero privilege,
and with the full range of play and waste and public activity that
goes into making a world.

—Michael Warner, *The Trouble with Normal*

Teachers and writers might better serve the claims of knowledge if
we were to resist not sex but the impulse to split off sex from
knowledge.

—Jane Gallop, *Feminist Accused of Sexual Harassment*

"A Wanton Mayd Once Lay with Me"

In Richard Brome's stage play *The Antipodes*, a comedy first performed in
1638, a theme of sexual distress is introduced by a reference to two women
lying in bed together. Martha Joyless, a countrywoman suffering from a virgin's melancholy straight out of Robert Burton,[1] is dismayed that her marriage of three years has never been consummated; she reports to her new

London acquaintance, Barbara, of her equally melancholic husband, Peregrine: "He nere put child, nor any thing towards it yet / To me to making."[2]
At the same time, she expresses ignorance about the actual means of conceiving children: "For were I now to dye, I cannot guesse / What a man do's in
child-getting" (1.3.319–20). Joyless and clueless as she is, however, she is not
altogether without sexual experiences, as becomes clear when she relates to
Barbara this memory:

> I remember
> A wanton mayd once lay with me, and kiss'd
> And clip't, and clapt me strangely, and then wish'd
> That I had beene a man to have got her with childe.
> What must I then ha' done, or (good now tell me)
> What has your husband done to you?
>
> (1.3.320–25)

In an aside, Barbara directs the audience's perceptions: "Was ever / Such a
poore peece of innocence, three yeeres married?" (1.3.326–27). She then asks
Martha directly: "Does not your husband use to lye with you?" Martha's
earnest answer further displays her ignorance:

> Yes, he do's use to lye with me, but he do's not
> Lye with me to use me as he should, I feare;
> Nor doe I know to teach him, will you tell me,
> Ile lye with you and practise, if you please.
> Pray take me for a night or two, or take
> My husband and instruct him, But one night.
> Our countrey folkes will say, you London wives
> Doe not lye every night with your owne husbands.[3]
>
> (1.3.328–36)

Despite Martha's unwitting, if nonetheless thoroughly conventional, jab at
the promiscuity of city wives, the dramatic focus throughout her request for
erotic instruction is her astonishing "innocence." So eager for knowledge that
she would place both herself and her husband in Barbara's bed, Martha's
rural simplicity is posed against Barbara's urban sophistication. Clearly, Martha is the butt of this sexual joke.[4] Yet, her lack of understanding of the

mechanics of procreation is nonetheless accommodating of her fond recollection of a "wanton mayd" who kissed, clipped, and clapped her. Modern
editors gloss "clip't and clapt" as "embraced and fondled passionately," as
well as "embraced and patted"—with the added suggestion that "clapt"
"may imply something more firmly administered"; and one editor suggests
that "'slap' is a recent equivalent"—still so used, I am told, in contemporary
Ireland.[5] Apparently, this unnamed maid's behavior took the form of passionate, even forceful caresses that were not incompatible with her own desire to
be penetrated and impregnated. Like Barbara's urbane sophistication, this
maid's erotic desires and actions contrast comically to Martha's erotic ignorance and dependence on the knowledge of others.

The play's thematization of Martha Joyless's sexual dilemma invites us to
consider anew the historical production of sexual knowledge: the conditions
of collecting, creating, and disseminating information about sexuality, in the
past as well as in the present. Although the intent of Brome's play is to satirize
Martha's "innocence" and to pity her marital lot,[6] I want to resist its satiric
pull long enough to consider the implications of the fact that she does articulate knowledge about sex, although not the kind her culture readily acknowledges. Of what does Martha's knowledge and ignorance consist?[7] On the one
hand, she is inexperienced in the mechanics of sex with men—so much so
that although she is, by her own admission,

> past a child
> My selfe to thinke [children] are found in parsley beds,
> Strawberry banks or Rosemary bushes,

she nonetheless confesses to "have sought and search'd such places / Because
I would faine have had one" (1.3.306–8). On the other hand, she *is* experienced, however briefly, in the erotic caresses of a woman; but other than
realizing that this is *not* the way to procreate, she possesses little understanding of what such contact signifies. Indeed, given her incomprehension, one
hesitates to call it knowledge at all.

Martha's asymmetrical position of knowing and not knowing (or more
precisely, of having experienced a form of "sex" eccentric to the dominant
discourse that is then overwritten as simplicity) introduces sexual knowledge
as a problem of pedagogy: Martha seeks tutelage from Barbara because she
has not been properly taught by her husband. At the same time, in its lack
of accommodation to both dominant discourses of reproductive sexuality and

to the counterdiscourses generated by queer scholarship, Martha's situation forces us to confront, as an epistemological problem, the function of sexual knowledge as an analytical category within historiography. One only has to inquire whether the conceptual categories thus far made available by the history of sexuality help to elucidate Martha's erotic situation to see the difficulty, given the present state of our knowledge, of doing her analytical justice. As prior chapters have detailed, within the history of sexuality, debate has focused largely on whether same-sex sexualities in eras prior to the nineteenth century are best understood as connoting sexual identities or sexual acts. Yet, neither the logic of sexual identities (that is, the self-perception or social ascription of being a "lesbian," "heterosexual," or even a "sapphist") nor the idiom of sexual acts (in which all nonreproductive contact is simply a form of carnal sin) adequately comprehends or describes the complex meanings of Martha's experience.

Nor are the analytical categories that have illuminated the relationship of modern homosexuality to knowledge of particular help here: this is not the "open secret" analyzed by D. A. Miller, nor is it precisely the "privilege of unknowing" anatomized by Eve Kosofsky Sedgwick—not only because the epistemology of the closet requires homosexuals, that is, sexual identities, in order to enact its discipline, but because Martha is so very open about what is not a secret.[8] Nor is it sufficient to fall back on the tired trope of inconceivability that has dominated understanding of lesbianism in the past; erotic acts between women are part of what is at stake, albeit comically, in Martha and Barbara's exchange, or the joke would lose its effectiveness. We are in undefined territory here, where the relations of knowledge to subjects, and both to eroticism, have yet to be charted.[9]

Indeed, to what extent is it possible to apprehend Martha's subjective *desire* at all? The passage from *The Antipodes* inscribes nothing of her possible pleasure and is equally silent about her possible *dis*pleasure. Only Martha's ambiguous descriptors of the "wanton" maid and her "strange" behavior offer any clue—and both of these could signify approval, disapproval, or neither.[10] Other than her wish to learn what her husband must do to conceive a child, Martha gives us little access to her desire or interiority. Indeed, her indifference as to whether Barbara bed down with her or her husband underscores that nothing essential about the state of Martha's erotic subjectivity is revealed in her remembrance.[11]

Even when we broaden the analytical optic beyond the question of Martha's subjectivity to survey the wider implications of her recollection, its significance remains obscure. Indeed, the status of her erotic remembrance is a prime example of the principle that eroticism need not signify or convey particular meanings. Is Martha's experience with her unnamed bedmate a transgressive act? Is her narrative a tale of misconduct? To the contrary: no repugnance on the part of other characters is generated by her story of clipping and clapping, nor is any stigma attached to it. Barbara's pity is explicitly directed toward the sorry state of Martha's marriage:

Poore heart, I gesse her griefe, and pitty her.
To keepe a Maiden-head three yeares after Marriage,
Under wed-locke and key, insufferable! monstrous,
It turnes into a wolfe within the flesh.

(1.3.261–64)

Contrary to modern expectations, the homoerotic experience recalled by Martha is neither cause nor symptom of her illness; rather, it is the protracted keeping of her "Maiden-head" that has given rise to her virgin's melancholy and obsession with "child-getting." It is not just that Martha's ignorance is its own form of knowledge or that her knowledge is overwritten as a form of ignorance, but that her ill health is a result of her ignorance. It is from this position that her "virgin's melancholy" authorizes her quest for carnal knowledge.[12]

The play is quite clear about the need for Martha's marriage to be consummated, and it pursues this end via a medical discourse and therapeutic intervention that diagnoses Martha as "full of passion," "distracted," "mad for a child," and, my personal favorite, *"sicke* of her virginity" (1.2.211; 2.1.769; 2.1.770, 2.1.770, emphasis mine). Under the dominant Galenic medical dispensation, the conventional treatment for virgin's melancholy was a wedding, the presumption being that legitimate sexual congress would bring about the orgasm that purges the sexually congested body of its built-up humors.[13] Absent regular vaginal intercourse, an alternative treatment prescribed in several medical textbooks was the manual manipulation of the genitals by a female midwife;[14] given that Martha's sexless marriage is diagnosed as the cause of her melancholy, it is significant that *The Antipodes* does not allude to this method of cure. To do so, of course, would be to call further attention to the same-sex contact that the play introduces only in order to forget. Instead, Martha's narration calls little attention to itself and is quickly passed over as the text focuses on the means of bringing Peregrine back to a state of mental health capable of the penetrative sexual performance demanded by the tight early modern linkage of marriage to reproduction.[15]

Despite the fact that Martha "presents" as both a melancholic and hysteric, and, in seeking Barbara's help, positions herself as a patient, it is Peregrine who is judged to be sicker than his wife, and it is he who holds the promise of the couple's return to sexual health. Peregrine's melancholy, initially caused by an overindulgence in reading travel literature, was exacerbated by his parents' refusal to allow him to travel the world; instead, seeking to bind him close to home—and in spite of his overdetermined name—they married him off to Martha. Forbidden to travel, he is now "in travaile" (1.3.230), his mind fully taken up in wandering "beyond himselfe" (1.2.198). His refusal to consummate his marriage apparently derives from an overly credulous reading of Mandeville's *Travels*, which includes a description of the "Gadlibriens" who employ other men to deflower their wives because of the risk of being stung by a serpent lodged within the female body.[16] There is much that could be said about Peregrine's resistance to marital sexuality and the specific form that his resistance takes. Motivated in part by the desire for travel,[17] his "*Mandevile* madnesse" (4.10.2400) could also be motivated by other desires—homoerotic ones, perhaps—that would render this unhappy family multiply queer. Given that travel in this period offered Englishmen opportunities for a variety of sexual encounters—travel narratives are full of descriptions of both cross-sex and same-sex liaisons, whether fantasized or real, consensual or coercive—it would be a mistake to view Peregrine's resistance to marital sexuality as a rejection of sex altogether.

Nonetheless, the play enacts Brome's customary belief that the best way to remedy madness is by humoring delusions through metatheatrical fantasy. Under the direction of a doctor and a rather eccentric lord, Peregrine's family and a troupe of actors collude in convincing the patient that he has journeyed to the Antipodes (when he actually has been under the influence of a sleeping potion). Not surprisingly, the Antipodes, also called anti-London in the play, provides Brome with the opportunity for an extended dramatization of the world turned upside down, where lawyers are honest, servants govern their masters, and men are ducked as scolds.[18] The climax of this theatrical inversion therapy occurs when Peregrine, who, in good colonialist fashion, proclaims himself king of the realm, marries and takes to bed the Antipodean queen: Martha, thinly disguised.[19] Thus tricked into consummating his marriage by committing mock adultery, Peregrine is cured of his melancholy. As the lord Letoy surmises, Peregrine's

much troubled and confused braine
Will by the reall knowledge of a woman
        . . . be by degrees
Setled and rectified.

(4.12.2444–47)

In fulfillment of the expectations of Galenic psychophysiology, coitus proves to be a potent restorative. The newly unified spouses emerge from their bedroom kissing, caressing, and cooing, to the obvious delight of the other characters, who, throughout much of the stage action, have functioned as onstage voyeurs. Peregrine confirms his cure: "Indeed I finde me well." While Martha responds: "And so shall I, / After a few such nights more" (5.2.3016–18).

The Antipodes is extremely canny about staging its interest in sex through metatheatrical means. Although the consummation of the Joyless marriage takes place offstage, this does little to minimize its erotic interest;[20] indeed, the play's dramatization of onstage voyeurs who are deeply invested in the success of the coital cure saturates the performance space with eroticism.[21] A subplot dramatizing the attempted seduction of another woman, Diana, by the fantastic lord Letoy (who turns out to be her long-lost father) adds to the erotic effect.[22] In addition, roughly half of the vignettes staged to convince the delusional Peregrine that he has voyaged to the end of the earth concern sexual matters: courtiers who complain of being "jested" sodomically from behind (4.6.2105–11); old women who "allow their youthfull husbands other women. . . . And old men [who] give their young wives like license" (2.7.1085–86); a maid who attempts to sexually assault a gentleman (4.2.1934–72); and a tradesman who procures a gentleman to sexually pleasure his wife, to the acclaim of the gentleman's lady (2.7, 2.8, 3.8). With its sexual thematic and innuendos, with its treatment of voyeurism as entertainment and entertainment as cure, *The Antipodes* publicizes sex in such a way as to come very close to making sex public.

At issue, of course, is not only what Martha or Peregrine knows, but, given that this play was written for the stage, what the performers and audience know. What kind of sexual knowledge is being produced and exchanged, not only among the characters involved in this metatheatrical sex play, but also among the performers, and between them and the audience? Given the cultural context of the original production—wherein cross-dressed boy actors played the female parts—some audience members may have experienced an additional homoerotic frisson. Yet, while transvestite boy actors may ironize Martha's assertion of erotic ignorance, their performance of femininity does not resolve the issues raised by it. Evidently, *The Antipodes* was designed to meet the needs of Christopher Beeston's company with its large numbers of children.[23] One might well ask, how did this play function pedagogically for these young players? Just what *was* it that they were learning? No less salient is the pervasive interpretation of Brome's drama, which, based on the play's Jonsonian commitment to theater as comic therapy, submits that the "real patients" are those who are watching the play.[24] To what kind of "therapy" is the audience being subjected through *The Antipodes'* public discourse about sex?

To speak of public sexual discourse in the early modern era may seem odd, especially insofar as modern relations between public and private were only beginning to emerge.[25] Yet certain aspects of sexual life that we now tend to consider private were performed "publicly" in a variety of ways, including the sexual contact that arose, either consensually or through acts of violence, out of the practice of sharing beds (especially common among servants and between servants and masters); the sex unwittingly witnessed by travelers, both male and female, sleeping in communal inn rooms; and deliberate acts of group sex and voyeurism in taverns, fairs, and, later in the century, molly houses.[26] More conventionally, the early modern community was unabashedly concerned with the status of marital consummation. Until the urban elite started to separate themselves off from communal celebrations after the Restoration, wedding festivities across all status groups were accompanied by a good deal of sexual innuendo and erotic play, not least of which was the customary ritual of wedding guests escorting the bridal couple to bed, relieving them of the ribbons and laces that served as clothing fasteners, and "throwing the stocking," or relieving them of their hose.[27] As David Cressy notes, these actions were meant both "to help them to their happiness, and to help establish plausible evidence of their consummation."[28] The public theater likewise promoted its own discourse of sex, in no small part through stage comedy's focus on physicality, bodily senses, domestic scenarios, and, more often than not, erotic desire. A traditional comedic plot device, the bed-trick, makes comic hay out of sexual knowledge relations. Temporarily inverting the usual patriarchal hierarchy in order to reintegrate the recalcitrant man into the reproductive community, the conventional Renaissance bed-trick dramatizes male ignorance about particular female bodies while asserting female knowingness over the duped male. *The Antipodes* trumps this convention by exploiting Peregrine's delusion and making Martha pose as his sexual fantasy, the Antipodean queen. Depending less on male ignorance and female duplicity than the collusion of an entire community, the bed-trick in Brome's play functions like the ritual festivities of the wedding night, forging ties of communal sexual knowledge through the approbation of marital consummation.

Within the play's context of marital dis-ease, theatrical sex therapy, publicity about sex, and communal investment in it, it is striking that Martha's narration of her prior homoerotic encounter with the "wanton mayd" elicits no overt condemnation—indeed, it seems to exist in some field of discretion untouched by moral, medical, religious, or legal judgment. We would err in judging the application of this discretion to be a form of tolerance, for tolerance assumes recognition of the object of forbearance—precisely what is lacking here. Nor is such discretion explained by other conceptual safety nets that might seem to minimize the threat of female-female sex: that Martha's sexual experience is presented in the past tense; that she now is safely married. After all, she has just asked Barbara to repeat, if in a more pedagogical guise, the bedroom performance of the "wanton mayd," and it is the miserable state of her marriage that has led her to look outside it for erotic instruction. We need only imagine the direction the plot might have taken if, in the adulterous mode of Restoration comedy, Barbara had capitalized on maximizing her own erotic pleasure and, in response to Martha's plea, bedded down with Peregrine, or Martha, or with both of them; the fact that the play entertains no such possibility for comic entanglement confronts us with the particular indifference with which Martha's reminiscence is met.

I am not suggesting that a patriarchal teleology or heterosexual privilege fail to organize the logic of Martha's situation: Martha's naïveté expresses an altogether conventional form of early modern femininity; her friend's embraces are positioned narratively as a precursor to marital intercourse; and her request for Barbara's tutelage likewise has the restoration of procreative sexuality as its end. Nonetheless, Martha's predicament forces us to acknowledge a decided disjunct between marriage and sex. Of what does Martha's marriage of three years consist? Whatever it is, it is not sex: and this absence of joy, of *jouissance*, is quite literally driving her mad. Even though Brome's play craftily brings about a three-years-delayed consummation to great communal fanfare and tendentiously maps erotic *jouissance* onto a reproductive imperative, the fact remains that Martha's journey to erotic satisfaction can hardly be called straight. And having turned to her friend Barbara for erotic instruction once, it is certainly conceivable, if we permit ourselves the intellectual indulgence of thinking outside the plot, that she might do so again.

That, at least, is a conceit made possible by Martha's erotic remembrance, embedded as it is in a scene of erotic yearning—a yearning simultaneously for knowledge and sex—that the play both gestures toward and disavows.

"What Must I Then Ha' Done, or . . . What Has Your Husband Done to You?"

By raising marital sexuality to the status of a question and by posing that question by means of female-female eroticism, Brome's representation of the state of Martha's knowledge urges us to reconsider the state of *our* knowledge about early modern sex: not only what we know, but also how we know it. I thus turn away from the possible pleasures we might infer from Martha's fictional biography to pursue instead the knowledge relations that the representation of her ignorance performs. Within this inquiry, Martha functions less as a character or a subject—indeed, her flat characterization all but precludes that—than as a heuristic for accessing strategies of knowledge production. To treat her in this way no doubt accords to Brome's play more intellectual heft than it deserves. Nonetheless, this strategy propels analysis further than does simply rehearsing the terms of early modern patriarchy or, alternatively, fantasizing a queer erotic elsewhere for women beyond patriarchy's frame.

To begin, then, with the current state of historical knowledge. If, as I've begun to intimate, the historiography of sexuality fails to do justice to Martha's situation, so too does the work of most feminist and social historians. Taking gender as its primary term of analysis, for instance, feminist scholars have tended to focus on sexuality as it pertains to women's so-called "life cycle" as maid, wife, mother, or widow.[29] The patriarchal "life cycle" likewise informs the work of most social historians, whose studies of marriage, gender identity, and social transitions generally are organized along the lines of wooing, wedding, birth, and maternity.[30] Were they to read *The Antipodes*, such scholars would likely emphasize Martha's obsession with child-getting, thereby implicitly privileging a reproductive imperative over sexual pleasure. Those scholars of sexuality who attempt to work outside the logic of the female reproductive life cycle tend to do so by deploying categories of deviance or transgression: premarital sex, bastardy, adultery, prostitution.[31] Whether the critical accent is on the disciplining of women's bodies or opportunities for female agency, transgression has functioned heretofore as the primary analytical means for conceptualizing erotic conduct that fails to conform to patriarchal mandates. Yet, because notions of norms and their transgression are structured by a binary of the licit and the illicit, they necessarily are indexed to the dominant social orthodoxy—even when the intention is to uncover the existence of those who would defy it.

But what of Martha's memory of kissing and clipping? Some forms of female eroticism are neither subsumed under marital exigencies nor performed in defiance of them; not primarily organized by the neat logic of a life cycle lived in compliance with patriarchal ideology *or* its transgression, they cannot adequately be comprehended within the licit/illicit divide.[32] Thus, simply adding female homoeroticism to a list of deviant acts or identities would fail to account for Martha's desire for marital sexuality and procreation *alongside* her experience of sex with a woman. Nor does this divide help us to map the complex relations inscribed in Martha's sexual history: casual sex with an unnamed woman; marriage utterly devoid of sex; request to a female acquaintance for erotic instruction; marital consummation with an unfaithful husband. Much less does it account for the erotic improvisation of Martha's anonymous bedmate, who passionately embraced and slapped her companion while expressing her own desire to conceive a child. Was she as ignorant about the means of procreation as Martha? How are we to understand the maid's desire to be impregnated by Martha and Martha's desire to learn how to conceive by having sex with Barbara? How do we account for the queer circuit whereby these characters' desires, frustrations, and hopes are represented?

The representation of Martha's sexual history urges a recognition that none of the bicameral rubrics through which we routinely process early modern sex—the licit and the illicit, the homo and the hetero, the queer and the normative, erotic acts and erotic identities—provide us with much analytical purchase on the sexual and knowledge relations enacted in this play. Let us ask, then: What *are* the historical conditions of the production of erotic knowledge in the early modern period? To date, the most analytically generative method for approaching this question has been Michel Foucault's distinction between "two great procedures for producing the truth of sex": an *ars erotica*, supposedly pursued by premodern and non-Western cultures through practices of initiation, secrecy, and mastery; and a *scientia sexualis*, the distinctively modern, Western disciplinary apparatus, based on confession, which elicits and produces knowledge of sexuality in order to administrate it.[33] Yet, despite the therapeutic intent of Brome's play, Martha's homoerotic experience is not subject to any particular procedure for producing truth. Her request for erotic initiation, after all, is denied; and if the *ars erotica* proves unavailable to her, also unavailable is the disciplinary effect of confession. It is striking that Martha's confession is one that *no one wants to hear*—not Barbara, not the Doctor, perhaps not even Brome, so quickly does he pass over it. It would appear that Martha's problems, experiences, and queries exist outside of the nexus of knowledge, truth, and power that both the *ars erotica* and the *scientia sexualis*, however distinct their methods, tend to produce. Martha's tenuous and ambiguous relation to erotic knowledge thus calls for a mode of analysis eccentric to Foucault's opposition of initiation to discipline.

Although Brome denies Martha access to an *ars erotica*, some knowledge of continental Renaissance pornography seems to inform his approach to the relation between sexual knowledge and sexual pedagogy. As pornography has developed in the West, it has seemed to possess an overdetermined relationship to pedagogy; not only, as Sarah Toulalan remarks, is "one person's pornography . . . another person's sex education,"[34] but one of the defining features of "modern" Western pornography from its inception in the sixteenth century is the extent to which it thematizes and dramatizes sex as tutelage. The enduring tropes of early modern literary obscenity were created by Italians such as Pietro Aretino, whose *Ragionamenti* (1534) depicts an older, experienced woman initiating a young, "innocent" girl into the arts of love—first by talking, then by doing.[35] Her own desire for pleasure drawn forth from a homoerotic scene of instruction, the girl then is emboldened to seek out more "mature" pleasures with men. While female naïveté is a compelling trope that invites instruction, mature women are also imagined as telling men how best "to do it" in Aretino's *Sonnetti lussuriosi* and Thomas Nashe's narrative poem "The Choise of Valentines."[36] If, in Aretino's sonnets, the women are simply egging their male partners on to try greater variety, in Nashe's poem, the hapless male lover, Tomalin, is clueless about the mechanics of sex, specifically about how to pleasure a woman. Francis helpfully instructs him in what is needed, crying out "Oh not so fast" (line 179), and then directing: "Togeather lett our equall motions stirr / Togeather let us live and dye, my deere" (lines 183–84).[37] Considerably elaborated by the French later in the seventeenth century,[38] the pedagogical conventions of pornography pursue their purpose by means of a variety of narrative strategies: loquacious female speech; graphic nomination of body parts; sequential movement from sex talk to sex acts; a metaphoric inventiveness that mirrors the inventiveness of bodily postures and activities; and the eroticization of narrative itself.[39] And women, for whatever reason, often play the role of instructor.[40]

All of this inventiveness and loquaciousness is denied to Martha. On the one hand, as Laura Gowing remarks, "this was a culture in which it was positively virtuous not to be able to describe sex"—particularly, one might note, for women.[41] Even within women's unofficial oral culture, marital status tended to regulate the circulation of knowledge about sexual matters: "The key rituals of the female body, those where knowledge was shared and experiences were public, were organized by and for married women. Being single meant exclusion from the exchanges of reproductive knowledge."[42] Although alternative ways to gain entrance to such knowledge existed, especially among communities unconcerned with social legitimation (such as bands of rogues or prostitutes), Martha remains outside of such circuits of verbal instruction. And her plea to another wife for information results not in the sharing of women's secrets but the communal orchestration of her husband's sexual performance.

On the other hand, like so much else during the period prior to the civil wars, the representation of Martha's predicament sits on the cusp of two different public cultures. In the first four decades of the seventeenth century, sexual knowledge circulated primarily by means of gossip, ballads, chapbooks, jestbooks, and vernacular medical texts. Bawdy verse was sung, recopied, and recorded in commonplace books; sexually suggestive libels and insults were pinned on posts and church doors, read or sung aloud to crowds. But "the widespread use of allusion and metaphor" in such materials, as Gowing notes, "served as a partial barrier to the participation of the young and the single."[43] Thus, to my earlier description of the public culture of sex, we need to factor in the ways that sexual knowledge and its expression were regulated according to gender, age, and status. Young women, in particular, might witness sexual acts but not have the language to describe what they saw; they might hear allusions to sexual conduct but not know precisely what was implied.

These barriers to knowledge and expression began to break down in the 1640s and 1650s, when a scurrilous political satire, arising out of social unrest and temporarily free from censorship, mined the sensational possibilities of conflating political with sexual slander, giving rise to far more explicit representations. So, too, vernacular medical texts, including ones directed toward women, became increasingly available and sexually explicit, read as much for their sexual advice as for their medical information.[44] Together, the languages of satire, medicine, and sexual advice reconfigured the terms of what could be said and written about sex in public. After the Restoration, the rise of a courtly libertine culture, the increased availability of vernacular pornography, and the growth of molly houses all gave birth to what we might call a nascent sexual public.

The extent of Brome's investment in dramatizing Martha's ignorance is such that she enjoys no access to sexual discourse. Recognition of this prohibition gains critical traction beyond the obvious feminist one once we note that Martha's articulation of her sexual past and her request for tutelage generate the operations of a tacit knowledge (the implied, supposedly self-evident, dominant discourse that "goes without saying"). As a result of these operations, her effort to satisfy her desire is ignored, deflected, passed over. This "nonresponse" in the face of her attempt at sexual agency enacts a process of disqualification all too familiar to contemporary queers. So let us pause at the moment of deflection and disqualification to ask: What goes (sexually) without saying? What are the tacit processes by which certain sexual knowledges are rendered intelligible, legitimate, and enabling, while other knowledges are rendered unintelligible, illegitimate, and disqualifying? How do the relations between sexual knowledge and ignorance produce unpredicted knowledge like Martha's—consigned, on the one hand, to irrelevance or insignificance, but which, on the other hand, might hold within itself a future possibility of articulation and power? How do irrelevant or insignificant knowledges become counterhegemonic and agential? And how does that possibility, then and now, relate to publicity about sex, to public sexual cultures, indeed, to public sex?

By raising such questions, I am suggesting that our epistemology of early modern sex is not nearly as supple, nuanced, or complex as its representations warrant. Eroticism in this period was more "wanton" in its forms and more "strange" in its effects than we tend to recognize. Our reluctance to credit early modern sex with sufficient diversity persists despite the explosion of interest among literary critics in queering early modern texts—especially purportedly heterosexual ones—and despite the most important advance in queer historiography: namely, the effort to articulate the extent to which homoeroticism was embedded in a variety of early modern social systems, such as domesticity, apprenticeship, authorship, patronage, and politics.[45]

The recognition that homoeroticism was one point in a networked system of social relations, as powerfully formulated by Alan Bray, has enhanced our understanding of the meanings of sexuality to individuals and to social polities, as well as our appreciation of sexuality's ideological utility, pliability, and susceptibility to pressure. Yet, despite the invocation of networked relations, scholarship generally does not make good on its promise of detailing processes of mutual constitutiveness; we tend to analyze the relation of "sex" to "society" only from the angle of the social formation with which sexuality is imbricated. Conceived as a discrete, unified, bounded, and essentially passive object of inquiry, sexuality is *embedded in, deployed, made use of* by other discourses and systems. Thus positioned, sexuality becomes an epiphenomenon of gender, rank, family, patronage, politics; it is to these domains, not eroticism, that social agency accrues.[46]

The Antipodes' enactment of a belabored, inefficient, *sick* marital sexuality invites us to consider whether eroticism is not only *embedded* in systems of knowledge (in this case, medical, domestic, theatrical), but itself is an *agent* of knowledge production. Rather than embodying an innate desire whose meaning is self-evident—something we all already know—sexuality in Brome's play is a question to be asked, an answer to be given, as well as a task to be learned and performed. "What must I then ha' done, or . . . What has your husband done to you?" queries Martha; and, with a cluelessness that is as provocative as it is disarming, she attempts to direct her own training: "Ile lye with you and practise, if you please." Insisting that sex is a matter of *doing something*, Martha introduces the practical approach toward sexual pedagogy enacted by others throughout the play. The fact that Martha's request for hands-on instruction is silently denied and then deflected onto the therapeutic elicitation of Peregrine's desire—a desire that he quickly learns how to direct—renders no less significant the play's overall interest in what might be called "sex education." (This displacement merely reminds us that sex education tends to render intelligible and popularize only particular forms of sex.)[47] Indeed, the successful performance of sex in *The Antipodes* is, as I have noted, a communal effort: it requires the combined resources and diligent attention of family and neighbors, as well as the intervention of the medical and theatrical communities. If marital sexuality is figured by the end as a remedy for all that ails Martha and Peregrine, if procreative intercourse is therapeutically reinstalled as the only legitimate sexual practice, these nonetheless are revealed to be the result of a particular social production, a process of knowledge construction—one that draws its energy from seeking a friend's advice and, when that fails, submitting to the professional expertise of an early modern psychotherapist.

The play's intervention proceeds by a route more circuitous and more self-consciously metatheatrical than the shaming rituals that generally enforce early modern sexual and household discipline—the stocks, the cucking stool, the charivari. However, it is not as though the politics of shame are absent from the reception of Martha's reminiscence—either by the other characters or by literary critics. On the contrary. But rather than shame being directed primarily toward Martha's subjectivity, it is directed toward her inadequate grasp of tacit knowledge.[48] Having confounded, in the words of Mary Poovey, "what counts as acceptable knowledge about sex,"[49] Martha breaks, in the words of Michael Warner, her culture's "tacit rules about what can be acknowledged or said in public."[50] Those rules are not exactly ours, but they nonetheless work, as they do in the present, to privilege certain knowledges and to discredit, by means of condescension, pity, or shame, unofficial or dissident knowledges. As Warner remarks, "isolation and silence are among the most common conditions for the politics of sexual shame." Combating these conditions requires "the circulation and accessibility of sexual knowledge, along with the public elaboration of a social world."[51] Absent such circulation and such worlds, it is all too possible for the dominant culture to enforce a collective amnesia about the pervasiveness of erotic variation, routinely asking us, as Warner puts it, to "forget everything [we] know about sex."[52]

The belief that sexual pleasure is a source of knowledge motivates Warner's and others' exposé of the "geography of shame" and sexual paranoia that, through zoning laws and real-estate transactions, has remapped the sexuality of New York City.[53] Their defenses of gay male cruising, of the importance and creativity of public spaces of and for sex, are part of a defense of the unpredictable exchanges that can take place—simultaneously public and intimate—in what Warner calls the "world-making project of queer life."[54] I want to draw out of Warner's defense of a queer ethos of public sex the importance of sexual pedagogy to such world-making projects:

> The naive belief that sex is simply an inborn instinct still exerts its power, but most gay men and lesbians know that the sex they have was not innate nor entirely of their own making, but *learned*—learned by participating, in scenes of talk as well as of fucking. One learns both the elaborated codes of a

subculture, with its rituals and typologies . . . but also simply the improvisational nature of unpredicated situations. As queers we do not always share the same tastes or practices, though often enough we learn new pleasures from others. What we do share is an ability to swap stories and learn from them, to enter new scenes not entirely of our own making, to know that in these contexts it is taken for granted that people are different, that one can surprise oneself, that one's task in the face of unpredicted variations is to recognize the dignity in each person's way of surviving and playing and creating.[55]

Although there is a tendency here to idealize the nurturing aspects of queer culture, I agree that, because we bring to sexual activity a shared disqualification from the norm, a broadly empathic ethos of generosity tends to inform queer sex. Whatever ideological divisions and tensions around race, class, and gender fracture political alliances and propel us to blame and shame one another, sexual variation tends to enjoy a policy of nonpolicing. In the erotic realm, at least, queers are apt to recognize as an axiom (and not merely a theoretical one) that, as Eve Kosofsky Sedgwick memorably put it, "people are different from each other."[56]

The ethics of queer sexual culture are derived in part from the ways that knowledge and disclosure are used by and against queers. What Martha Joyless's position vis-à-vis erotic knowledge shares with the epistemology of the closet is the extent to which that intersubjective space is constructed "by dominant assumptions about what goes without saying, what can be said without a breach of decorum, who shares the onus of disclosure, and who will bear the consequences of speech and silence."[57] Making sex public, insisting on the publicity of sex through a reasoned defense of the right to a public sexual culture, moves the consideration of sex beyond a matter of private appeals (for instance, Martha's request of Barbara) or sexual therapy (such as that deceptively enforced upon Peregrine). This movement beyond the private and the therapeutic challenges the presumptive onus of disclosure and refigures public discourses of sex—both doing it and talking about it—as a question of sexual pedagogy.[58]

Eroticism isn't just something that people do (or, in the case of Peregrine, refuse to do); it is something that people learn; it requires initiation, experimentation, education—in Martha's words, practice. Erotic encounters, including discursive encounters about sex, teach particular skills, some of which have cultural capital (the simultaneous orgasm recommended in early modern prescriptive literature, for example); others of which do not (the clipping and kissing of women). Yet, the history of sexuality over the *longue duree* suggests that under certain conditions the information made available by doing, making, and talking about sex can translate into nascent forms of counterknowledge, capable of dissident effects and future, and as yet unknown, possibilities.

How knowledge of and about sex becomes sexual dissidence,[59] how one might identify the precise mechanisms by which this occurs, are questions to which I don't have an answer—although I believe any such answer will derive from the practices and insights of specific collectivities. What I do know is that we need to conceptualize erotic pedagogy more expansively and flexibly, and, even in the face of recurring sex panics, with less paranoia about the potential overlap of sex and words. Such self-protection is an understandable reaction to the cultural situation within the United States: resurgent homophobia; moralistic redeployments of feminist critiques of sexual harassment, incest, and child molestation; and the sacrifice of sexual justice for political self-interest. Yet, we concede the terms of public discourse about sex at our peril. The contemporary United States remains a sex-obsessed yet sex-negative culture, one that is simultaneously seduced by sexual scandal and enamored of punitive measures that make people pay, sometimes tragically, for their sexual desires. It is a culture in which adolescents enjoy unprecedented access to sexual imagery, both hetero and homosexual, in the media, yet they are often denied basic information about sex itself. It remains a culture in which the surgeon general can be fired for suggesting that discussion of masturbation might be included in publicly funded sex education. It is a culture in which sexual responsibility has become defined as sexual abstinence before marriage and where abstinence is the primary public health strategy for combating sexually transmitted diseases and unwanted pregnancy. Not surprisingly, it is a culture in which the transmission of HIV continues unabated and the correlation between teen pregnancy and poverty high. Conservatives have been extraordinarily effective in using sex education as a forum in which to push their social agenda; they have succeeded in part by deploying a rhetoric that renders talk about sex, especially sexual speech, as sexual abuse.[60]

As the right-wing equation of sexual language with sexual immorality makes clear, there are dangers to forging an intimate analytic connection between sex acts and sex talk.[61] While language and acts obviously are related, collapsing sexual speech with sexual behavior is, I believe, a category error, one that elides important differences between the incitement to discourse and the incitement of bodies.[62] Chapter 7 will consider the relations among sexual acts and the language used to describe them within the purview of early modernity. From this end of the historical spectrum, we can note the difficulties that can arise when talk about sex is interpreted as sexual behavior. These problems were vividly put in relief, for example, when Jane Gallop was accused of sexually harassing a female graduate student. Gallop's defense against the charge of sexual harassment hinged, first, on a denial of having committed unwanted sexual acts; second, on a critique of sexual harassment policies that conflate sex ("harassment on the basis of sex") with sex ("sexual advances"), thereby confusing sexism with sexuality;[63] and third, on her contention that the "unprofessional, personal behavior that ran afoul of sexual harassment policy was in fact my application of feminist pedagogical methods."[64] Arguing that "breaking down the barrier between the professional and the personal has been central in the feminist effort to expand the institution of knowledge to include what and how women know,"[65] Gallop maintains that it is in the overlapping zone of talk and sex, pedagogy and eroticism, that knowledge production is, for her, most "productive."[66] Whatever our own preferred bodily boundaries as learners and teachers, as well as our collective interest in preventing those abuses of power that can occur by means of sex, it is crucial to acknowledge how wide and hazy the overlap of sex and talk can be, and how much disservice we do to both eroticism and knowledge when we too quickly collude with the institutional policing of their categorical separation.[67] In the present social milieu, such policing not only provides an easy vehicle for political gain but also is often motivated more by fear of litigation than concerns about the abuse of power.[68] Rather than capitulate to these forces, then, we need to respond by refining our understandings of the relations between sexual speech and sexual pedagogy; analyze the different forums in which viewing sex and reading and talking about it might operate ethically; and publicly affirm our pedagogy, especially insofar as it depends upon sex talk, as ethically motivated social action.

Several commitments impel my advocacy of a capaciously conceived sex education as a rich epistemological resource in the present and on behalf of the past. One aim of *Thinking Sex with the Early Moderns* is to supplement the usual understanding of sex as power with an understanding of sex as a knowledge relation. This does not involve advocating a classroom pedagogy of personal confession or the development of a queer *ars erotica*. Nor am I attempting to add yet another chapter to the *scientia sexualis* through the further proliferation and visibility of modern erotic taxonomies.[69] Rather than use sex to produce the truth of the subject, this and subsequent chapters detail the processes by which sex and sex talk function as forms of knowledge relations—by which I mean not only knowledge of or about sex but also knowledge through and by means of sex. Knowledge so conceived is not only a set of sexual *contents*—for instance, historical knowledge about erotic acts, identities and non-identities, bodily positions and hierarchies, erotic rituals and their forms of circulation—but, perhaps more important, an intellectual disposition and mode of comportment toward sexual variation that is accessed through the complex mediations of history.[70]

For instance, in posing the question of marital sexuality in the terms provided by Martha's seduction at the hands of a woman, *The Antipodes* confronts us with the inadequacy of one strand in the history of sexuality that would position homoeroticism in opposition to histories of the family and reproduction. I hope to have shown that this analytic is out of touch with the situation depicted in Brome's play and with many aspects of early modern culture. Without subsuming the homo under the hetero or so extending the boundaries of the queer that it is emptied of all specificity, we need to ask more of queer studies than that it provide access to homoerotic subjects or enable the queering of heterosexuality. As queer theory has long maintained, the capacious and flexible analytic of queer provides modes of understanding that exceed contemporary discourses of erotic identity, pushing beyond the concerns of any identity-based constituency (L, G, B, or T). At the same time, as I argued in Chapter 3, in the current academic drive to queer *everything*, and to do so in such a way that the entailments of identity are denied, queer studies risks forgetting its history and its accountability. One way to circumvent this either-or dilemma is to apprehend sexuality as a form of knowledge production, as an agent in the construction of knowledge. Homoeroticism and heterosexuality are not just theoretically imbricated and historically constitutive of one another,[71] not just contingent and unstable and, in their differing ways, queer; they also pose similar and interrelated epistemological and pedagogical problems that require the development of more nuanced analytical strategies.

In transiting from a feminist reading of Martha Joyless to contemporary discourses of public sex, I have implied, however obliquely, that a cultural phenomenon indicatively, if not exclusively, inflected as male might be useful for articulating the possibilities and stakes of female sexual knowledge and agency. Building on Sedgwick's axiom 7—"The paths of allo-identification are likely to be strange and recalcitrant"[72]—I have followed the contours of one such wayward path.[73] The conjunction of public sexual knowledge—that which women, historically, have been denied—and the culture of public sex—which gay men, in particular, seek to defend—may seem perverse. To read both of these through a feminist resistance to the misuse of sexual harassment discourses as they police sexual pedagogy may seem even more so. But it is only through such perverse affiliations across sex, gender, sexuality, and history that I have been able to explore how the production of sexual knowledge relies so heavily on an undertheorized process of making sex public—on a publicity, in other words, that is also a pedagogy.

What draws me on in forging these conjunctions is the historical elusiveness and epistemological opacity of sex. Despite the common assumption that we all know what sex is, I conclude this chapter by insisting that there is much about sex that we *don't know*: of what acts sex consists, what pleasures it affords, what difficulties it encounters, and what inventiveness it engenders.[74] As Peter Coviello has argued:

> From the determination to approach sex as something not known in
> advance—not circumscribed in an already-given set of acts or affects, or for
> that matter an already-given set of disruptions, displacements, and
> inarticulabilities—there follows . . . a series of potentially revelatory shifts in
> critical perspective. One comes into a sense of sex as, for instance, an unfin-
> ished project, a set of possibilities constrained but unpredetermined by locally
> available terms and modes of expression; or as comprised of dispositions and
> affects that might not know themselves *as* sex in any but retrospective
> appraisals; or as the point of entry for a host of constraints and subjections but
> also for varieties of *surprise*, of uncertainty, of intensities that are forever
> unwriting the codes by which we become legible to ourselves, our present
> tense, and our imagined future.[75]

It is with acceptance of such surprise, as one of the most significant affects honored by a queer analytic, that I offer Martha's cluelessness—reconceptualized as a precocious if unwitting ordinariness, an undertheorized resistance to tacit knowledge, a persistent curiosity about the yet-to-be-known—as a figure for the disposition we might adopt in order to more attentively interpret earlier—and current—sexual regimes.

In appropriating Martha Joyless to raise questions about the conditions of knowledge production, in bringing the homo and the hetero, the cruising gay man and the unhappily married woman, into closer analytical contact, I have traversed diverse sites of sexual pedagogy: the early modern stage, the public spaces of gay intimacy, and the contemporary classroom. I will return to the classroom in Chapter 10. Suffice it for now to say that I have traced these paths in order to offer an alternate route for bridging the historical divide separating the queer past from the queer present. In framing the historiographic issues as ones of epistemology and pedagogy rather than subjectivity and identity, of knowledge and ignorance rather than norms and their transgression, of erotic dissatisfaction as much as erotic pleasure, of how we know as much as what we know, the situation of Martha Joyless gestures toward a pedagogy and ethics, as well as a history, of sexuality. Martha's dogged attempt to transform her joyless state has had an effect on me that can only be called pedagogical. As such, it calls out for a pedagogically attuned response that is also an ethically motivated one. Her naive quest for knowledge—enacted through the exposure of ignorance, pursued in the name of joy, and revealing a life crosscut by strange circuits of desire—performs its own scene of instruction, inviting us to consider what it might mean to develop an ethics, a pedagogy, adequate to the complexity of sex in history, as well as in contemporary culture.

CHAPTER 6

Sex in the Interdisciplines

You must go on, I can't go on, I'll go on.
— Samuel Beckett, *The Unnamable*

When I was in my second year of an English literature doctoral program, a young, personable, fast-talking assistant professor offered the department's first "theory" course. As a postcolonial, deconstructive, neo-Marxist critic, R. Radhakrishnan performed a pedagogy that vacillated between discussions of passages of Foucault, de Man, Derrida, and Said, and recitations of quotations drawn from his encyclopedic familiarity with global literary traditions. The final phrasing of Samuel Beckett's *The Unnamable*, "You must go on, I can't go on, I'll go on,"[1] was among his favorites: to him its sequence of externally imposed imperative, adamant refusal, and determined if resigned acceptance offered a concise synopsis of the post-structuralist ironies of language, signification, and the pursuit of meaning. For me, struggling to create logical arguments out of the unfamiliar morass of my coursework, the aphorism expressed something closer to the bone; it quickly became my mantra for my failure to understand the central insights, much less the literary and philosophical traditions, of contemporary theory.

"You must go on, I can't go on, I'll go on" has reappeared, unbidden, at subsequent moments of personal and intellectual crisis. I offer its resonant paradox of (im)possibility, as well as the irony that suffuses it, as an epigraph for this chapter, which intensifies this book's effort to think *in terms of*, rather than around or even through, an impasse. In France, streets that have no outlet—in English, "dead ends"—are called impasses. Having ventured down such a street, the only way out is to go back, to retrace one's steps, in order to continue on one's way. This book has already headed down a number of such paths. My aim has not been to break down the barriers or scale the walls, but to pause at the moments of blockage, to note the signs of others' journeys, and to retrace my steps—back and forth and back again. The impasse itself, I've tried to show, can productively function as a site of investigation for understanding the circumstances that have led us to it.

Taking up the pedagogical disposition introduced in the previous chapter, I now reframe the impasse of sex as a potential scene of instruction. What happens when we linger with an unanswerable question about sex, and not attempt to answer it? What does it mean to *not* pursue sex in terms of hermeneutic or historical interpretation but rather in terms of epistemology? Just as the "making" of this book's first section "Making the History of Sexuality" is slightly ironic in view of its unfulfilled and unfulfillable promise, the chapters that compose Part II, "Scenes of Instruction; or, Early Modern Sex Acts," are a bit of a tease. I am not going to make good on the promise ostensibly implied by this reference to "sex acts." I will not provide a detailed or comprehensive view of past sexual practices, prove what really happened in early modern beds, or demonstrate, yet again, the historical contingency of forms of desire. Nor will I present any original archival research to supplement what other scholars have said about this topic. Rather, my aim is to outline a strategy for working with the interlinked problems of method and knowledge posed by the historicity of sex (as something that both happened and was represented as happening) by honing in on a set of discursive conditions that currently stymie the production of our knowledge.

As readers of Chapter 3 will recognize, the scholarly atmosphere of historical sexuality studies is pervaded with suspicion. Within this loosely defined, interdisciplinary endeavor, certain positions have become relatively fixed. Many queer theorists, generally trained as literary critics, increasingly ignore, dismiss, or disparage literary historicism and history. Some queer literary critics who work on the distant past have posed history as inimical to theory. And many historians tend to ignore or find fantastical the interpretative flights of literary critics, while maintaining ambivalence toward queer theory.

For heuristic purposes, we might describe both the congruence and antagonisms of these positions through a classic Venn diagram of what I am calling, following Robyn Wiegman, "academic field formations" (Figure 2).[2] While this image elides questions of relative weight and scale, unduly homogenizes each area, and ignores the fact that certain scholars cleave more closely to an area's borders than to its center, it conveys, first, that these fields do

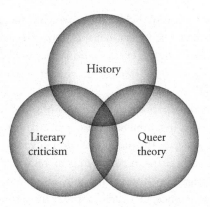

FIGURE 2. Academic field formations.

overlap, and second, that the area representing the overlap of all three is extremely small.

One way to characterize the work of this chapter is that it represents the efforts of one scholar, located at the center of that tiny overlap, trying to make sense of what is going on around her.[3] Aiming to articulate what the view looks like from the vantage of someone as much engaged with the work of historians as with the work of literary critics and queer theorists, I follow up on the proposal of historian Sarah Maza that "instead of repeating unexamined bromides about the benefits of cross-disciplinary work, we need to approach other disciplines with an educated and open-minded appreciation of differences. Navigating between disciplines demands a deep immersion in the practices of another field, and a clear understanding of the points at which 'translation' between disciplines is most difficult."[4] In an effort to generate some methodological wherewithal out of others' intellectual and archival labor, I remain mindful of, as Laura Doan puts it, "the vital operations of disciplinarity in producing historical knowledge in relation to sex."[5] And yet, I also insist that, at the present moment, it is neither accurate nor adequate to explain what stymies us in terms of disciplinary differences. Indeed, I want to shift the critical conversation from disciplinary boundaries to the less reified notion of academic field formations. Queer theory, after all, is not a discipline—indeed, it has a strong antidisciplinary bias. Literary studies is a discipline whose centrifugal capaciousness has led to the implosion of a common core. And history, which alone among the three continues to hold a strong disciplinary identity, is nonetheless fragmented into various methodological and topical subfields, one of which is the history of sexuality. Nonetheless, these field formations depend upon, generate, and reproduce not only particular methods but critical rationalities, styles of reasoning, ways of thinking—indeed, *identifications*—with which the scholar of past sexualities needs to contend.

In zeroing in on these rationalities and identifications, my aim is not to reconcile or synthesize incommensurate perspectives; nor, as has become common in dialogues across the disciplines, do I advocate in a partisan manner for one over another. Instead of trying to resolve the dilemma posed by incompatible designs on history, my aim is to stay with their jostling and unsettling incoherence in order to prod the problem toward fuller disclosure—not to surmount the impasse, but to explore and rearticulate it. If the impasse impedes our understanding, it is not because the thing we seek to understand lies on the other side and we simply need to break down the barrier or vault ourselves over it to resolve all difficulties. Rather, the impasse itself—its nature, its history, and its impact—is what requires analysis.

Acting on Sex

Like the preceding chapters, this one offers some pointed questions and historiographic principles that might guide future work; but it and Chapter 7 pursue this aim by reorienting certain threads of argument around the question of *sex acts*—the most stubbornly material aspect of the composite phenomenon we call sex. It is a curious fact that sex acts—what people actually do with one another's bodies, or with their own, at particular moments in time—seem to have been particularly vulnerable to the forces of presumptive knowledge. Like Chapter 5's scrutiny of the predicament of the clueless, my inquiry here focuses both on the fact of presumptive knowledge—exploring further what such knowledge assumes and entails—and what its presence can tell us about the problem of knowing sex historically. The previous chapter explored the costs exacted by habits of foreknowledge regarding women's sexuality, arguing that the opposition between heterosexuality and homosexuality, as well as the Foucaultian framework of the *ars erotica* and the *scientia sexualis*, have overdetermined our categories of analysis, leading to a failure to attend to the details of sexual knowledge relations. The present chapter broadens the optic to consider the effects of presumptive knowing about sex in general, both in the early modern period and today. Postulating that the scrutiny of sex acts enables special access to the obscured substrate of sexual historiography, I ask, in a deliberately metacritical way, *what constitutes the history of sexuality as an object?* What critical aptitudes have shaped the horizon of scholarly expectation and the field of knowability about early modern sex? What historiographic procedures have accrued and sedimented into the *not said?*

To retrace our steps thus far: "Friendship's Loss" (Chapter 2) assessed the virtues of a long diachronic perspective on friendship, while identifying the line dividing friendship from eroticism as a hermeneutic crux in the history of sexuality. "The New Unhistoricism in Queer Studies" (Chapter 3) advocated a method capable of negotiating the relations among sexual sameness and difference in historical inquiry. "The Present Future of Lesbian Historiography" (Chapter 4) put this method into practice, linking disparate forms of embodiment and social practice to explore how and why certain forms of same-sex desire become socially salient at certain moments. The present chapter demonstrates the continuing relevance of a historical approach to early modern sex; but rather than explore problems that arise when adducing eroticism across incongruent or discordant time frames or when negotiating the tension between alterist and continuist methods, I integrate the epistemological challenges that were broached in Chapter 5. Layering epistemology onto historiography, I show that historical specificity pushes us to reconsider the limits of the knowable, while attention to the conditions of knowledge pushes us to reconsider the limits and promise of historical inquiry. I thereby return to the broad questions posed in my first chapter: What *is* sex? Through which conceptual categories is it known? How do those categories and concepts organize what it means *to know?* How should we approach the silences and resistances of the archive, as well as the temporal distance between the back then and the here and now?[6] In short, how, when, and why does sex *become* history?

This chapter's consideration of the relations between method and epistemology was sparked by the vertigo induced by two divergent propositions for engaging with past sexualities: a historian's injunction to "find the bodies"[7] and several literary critics' proposals for what one of them calls an "archival *ars erotica.*"[8] These two mandates represent sophisticated, complex, yet entirely different critical dispositions with which to confront sex as a matter of referential facticity and sex as a historical experience that is ultimately inaccessible. On the one hand: if one could only ever "find the bodies," one might be able to answer the questions we have of past sexualities through rigorous documentation, comprehensive archival sleuthing, and analytical expertise. Disciplinary differences notwithstanding, this desire to locate bodies is not solely the wish of historians; it informs the approach of literary critics who engage in ingenious readings of metaphor to prove that sex occurred between the speaker and beloved of Shakespeare's sonnets, as well as those who hinge their interpretations of *Othello* on whether Othello and Desdemona "consummated" their marriage.[9]

On the contrasting other hand, proponents of a queer archival *ars erotica* imply that if we could affectively immerse ourselves in a thoroughly eroticized relationship to history, we need not be concerned with our failure to find evidentiary proof at all. Rather, we can discover both intellectual and affective pleasures in the connections we forge with past writers and texts. This provocative proposal issues from the domain of queer literary and cultural studies by scholars focused on a range of writers and texts, from medieval mystics to Mary Shelley's *Frankenstein*.

The vertigo induced in me by these divergent proposals—a vertigo caused not by recoil or disbelief, but by the apparent fact of their irreconcilability—only increased the more I considered them in light of conversations between historians and literary critics about how best to handle evidentiary protocols given the transdisciplinary consensus that the past is unrecoverable in its totality and is accessible to us only through textual mediation. Coming from very different angles, such propositions seem to speak past one another as they speed along in parallel universes.

The next section of this chapter queries the epistemological and methodological stakes of imagining acts of retrieval and interpretation as an archival *ars erotica*. I next take a "time-out" from methodological differences in order to survey the state of knowledge about early modern sex, as aggregated equally by literary critics and historians. I then turn to methodological issues evinced in the work of those scholars, often but not exclusively historians, who hope to locate and recover the sexual meanings of bodies in the past. My aim is to suggest that these divergent responses can be usefully approached as reactions to the same intractable epistemological problem: the temporally simultaneous, logically contradictory, and irreducibly dual status of sex as *material embodiment* (a matter of corporeal behaviors) and sex as *representation* (whether construed as text, language, discourse, narrative, image, or trope). This problem poses not only an obstacle but an opportunity—one that can be exploited if we focus on sex acts themselves as an analytically productive resource. For sex acts, I argue, carry within their stubborn materiality a means to access sex-as-knowledge-relation, as well as a means to throw off kilter certain habits and effects of presumptive knowing about sex—including, as the final pages of this chapter will argue, what counts as queer.

For, when it comes to making sexual knowledge historically, we *all* encounter the subtle but abiding differences between "real life" and "representation," whether under the guise of "fact" and "fiction," "materiality" and "metaphor," or "literality" and "figuration"—even if we dismiss the relevance of these distinctions, pay them no mind, or follow well-worn paths for circumventing the problems they pose. I have come to feel, however, that rather than actually confront what stymies us, we collectively make an end run around it. One particularly well-worn path is our common recourse to analytically hazy concepts such as *the body, desire,* and cultural or textual *mediation*—about which more in a moment. Another common path is resorting to the procedures of social *contextualization,* generally upheld as the sine qua non of historical research on sex. By questioning the routinized application of these terms and methods, I do not mean to impugn any scholar with inattentiveness or bad faith: these have been the best conceptual tools at hand and they have enabled significant work.[10] I am not even suggesting that, despite their predictability, we jettison them. Nonetheless, their recurrent, calcified use has permitted us to bypass certain issues. Rather than evade or smooth the friction between sex as materiality and sex as representation, I propose to translate it into an occasion for thinking sex in the interdisciplines. Our disparate investments and methodologies, I submit, at times seem irreconcilable not only because of the gulf of intelligibility that often separates history from literary studies from queer theory, but because the methods we have devised are symptomatic of a dissonance within sexuality itself. The impasse with which I am concerned, in other words, is not only that of historiographic method but of sex. Working with and by means of this impasse, the rest of this chapter delves into that gap, as I strive to think my way into the logics and illogics it imposes.[11] In pursuit of what we cannot know, alongside what we can, I approach sex acts as an especially charged site of investigation of how obstacles to knowing have been, are, and will continue to be constitutive of our knowledge, thereby recasting tensions between literary, historical, and queer modes of knowing as a manifestation of the more general sexual opacity with which *Thinking Sex with the Early Moderns* is concerned.

Archival *Ars Erotica*

In the final pages of *The Renaissance of Lesbianism*, I had occasion to ask (hypothetically, as I made no effort to answer it): "What if we approached the works of Katherine Philips (and other early modern women whose traces are waiting for us in the archive) not as subject *to* our identifications, but as objects *of* our desire?"[12] In retrospect, that "what if?" seems to have been part of a queer zeitgeist because answers had already begun to appear from queer literary critics intent on capitalizing on the force of both identification *and* desire in history making. Now seen as part of a larger trajectory of affect studies, the beginnings of this method as a matter of historiography were heralded by Carolyn Dinshaw's influential analysis of a "queer touch" arcing discontinuously from the medieval period to the postmodern.[13] Since then, a growing group of critics have proposed a number of related strategies for bridging the distance between past and present that exploit historiography as affect: Carla Freccero's practice of a "spectral historiography," which is particularly attentive to the impact of uncanny persistence and haunting repetitions;[14] Elizabeth Freeman's proposal for an "erotohistoriography," which privileges the body as a means to engage with and apprehend the past;[15] and Dinshaw's recent rearticulation of history-as-affect in terms of queer temporality.[16] Lynne Huffer likewise extols an erotic encounter with the past, finding her warrant for an "archival *ars erotica*" in Foucault's description of his emotional responses to the traces of lives he discovered in dusty records.[17] And Lara Farina proposes "erotic reading" as a way for scholars of premodern lesbianism to move beyond the constraint of "conventional recognition of what is 'in' given medieval texts."[18]

These scholars are less intent on how it was possible to "know" sexuality in the past than in how it might be possible to forge affectively replete and analytically productive links between then and now. Dinshaw's *How Soon Is Now?*, for instance, focuses on the asynchrony of "amateur medievalists" in order to demonstrate that not only does queerness have "a temporal dimension" but that "temporal experiences can render you queer."[19] Throughout this collective corpus, animating energies, seductive sympathies, and haunting hallucinations attest to the complex "structures of feeling" involved in queer historicist work.[20] While not all literary historicists have taken up this "affective turn," and some queer scholars of affect focus less on connection and attachment than on *dis*connection and antipathy, the provocation to read texts and history through the critic's embodied and, in particular, erotic responses has quickly become a popular strategy of queer literary historicism.[21]

The problems confronted by this body of work are real, and its practitioners have applied considerable ingenuity in negotiating them. As Peter Coviello remarks, their willingness to suspend foreknowing about sex has "helped to dislodge the inclination to read moments of the past, and particularly the sexual past, in lockstep coordination with their contextual determinations, and has sponsored in turn a desire to explore some counter-moves: to *touch* the past, for example, in identification and desire, or . . . in anguish and shame; or to grant something of the past's alterity to the present tense, but to approach that alterity as itself something unstable and incomplete, fissured by points of connection and continuity."[22] They have taken up fundamental tensions between difference and sameness, distance and intimacy, alienation and attachment, identification and disidentification, and devised novel means to address them—creating, in essence, a proposal for a new historiographic method. By foregrounding the affects informing the tensions at the basis of most historiographic inquiry, they productively elaborate the extent to which their impact on historiographic practice is always with us—which is why there is little point in trying to maintain an austere detachment from the past. Indeed, their focus on affect implicitly answers the question posed by historian Joan Scott when she asks how we can "account for our attraction to (or repulsion from) specific events, philosophies, figures, or, for that matter, figures of speech" in historical research.[23] Helping to explain why we pursue some questions and not others, affect might be said to be the unstated premise upon which all historicizing projects build. That the histories with which these critics are concerned—generally queer and lesbian ones—can be apprehended only from a present vantage that for a long time was, and still in many respects is, hostile to it gives their work an added urgency. Many who encounter their readings might concur with Robyn Wiegman, who confesses that she is "enthralled anytime the sensorious can overtake the epistemological."[24] Furthermore, this scholarship, composed against the grand, progressive projects of modernity, grants the abstract concept of temporality greater texture, heft, and weight, suffused as it is with emotions, desires, subjects, and objects. And not least, this collective project, in the words of Dinshaw, "values various ways of knowing that are derived . . . from desires to build another kind of world."[25]

By alluding to the archival *ars erotica* as a collective project, I do not mean to conflate these scholars' different strategies and purposes or imply a more homogeneous "movement" than is the case. Indeed, I would except from some of what follows Heather Love's *Feeling Backward: Loss and the Politics of Queer History* for, while it "take[s] impossible love as a model for queer historiography,"[26] its focus is on negative affects, disaffection, and disconnection as historiographic procedures. So, too, Carla Freccero's notion of queer spectrality emphasizes mourning and is keen to confer on history's ghosts their own subjectivity and alterity.[27] Nor by raising some concerns about aspects of this work do I mean to criticize any particular study. Unlike Chapter 3, where I scrutinized individual arguments proffered against teleological thinking, here I want to raise some general questions from within the ambit of a shared set of concerns for which history-as-affect has become the term of art. As detailed in Chapter 1, I have my own investments in thinking about identification and disidentification as modes of historiography, particularly in terms of what I called the transferential historicity of knowledge relations; indeed, other scholars have alluded to my work as part of the trend of historical affect studies.[28] It is in this spirit of a collective project in which I include my own work that I ask: How do the proposed analogies between sex, affect, and knowledge production negotiate the various methodological impasses that confront us? What knowledge relations ensue from privileging our own desires for and identifications with a past? How do erotic transactions between past and present, as experienced by the contemporary scholar, translate into practical procedures? And what might be the epistemological and methodological stakes of imagining historical inquiry as partaking in an erotic "archive fever"?[29]

These questions direct attention to the possibility that, rather than the "sensorious" overtaking the "epistemological," when it comes to history, the sensorium itself may be laden with unacknowledged epistemological freight. What, then, might be some of the risks of equating historical research with an erotic encounter? First, the construction of research as a phenomenological experience of desire often (although not inevitably) equates desire with pleasure; it thus participates in the more general privileging of pleasure that, as I noted in Chapter 1, problematically underwrites much queer theory itself. To be somewhat prosaic about it, I do not encounter the archive as an especially aphrodisiac site.[30] Furthermore, the supposition of an affective response during the labor of research strikes me as too quick to presume on the affects of others and too prone to translate into an implicit injunction that scholars *feel something*. It seems an unwarranted leap to assume we know in advance what affects historical texts open onto. Furthermore, however passionate one's attachment to ideas, to specific texts, and to history, the acts of researching and writing are hard work, full of tedium and self-denial—in my experience most often registered in concrete bodily sensations of a tight neck, aching back, tingling wrists, and blurry eyes. I fear that we mystify the conditions of our labor when, in pursuit of connection, we wax too ecstatic about it. Indeed, Dinshaw's repetition in *How Soon Is Now?* of the resonant phrase "I want more life" explicitly acknowledges the tedious labors of historical research (archival, textual, hermeneutic);[31] her moving articulation of her felt "kinship" with amateur medievalists,[32] her appreciation of the more leisured pace of their inquiries and the absorption, attachments, and passions that motivate their labors, accurately diagnoses the conditions of, while proffering its own remedy against, professional business as usual.[33] Nonetheless, some of us may *never* experience the pleasures Dinshaw celebrates, and for a variety of reasons—some institutional, some cognitive, some affective, some idiosyncratic. And some of us may never want to.

Beyond the particular experiential affects assumed, projected, and promoted in this scholarship, the relative weight accorded to the scholar's own affects can be equally problematic when considered in terms of the past. Although, as I've suggested, I am interested in what happens when we approach earlier texts as objects of our desire, I wonder what happens to the lives of past historical agents under the influence of its gravitational pull. Especially when such affects become the orbit around which a research project revolves, might it be that the perception of the past as something we think primarily *in relation to ourselves* risks subordinating it under the planetary influence of our own identifications and desires?[34] Might it be that, in an effort to actualize one's own desire, one ends up producing a fantasy of the past that annuls the past, and that, more specifically, dematerializes the corporeality of those distant others' sexual experiences? Might it be that the lateral energies and democratic openings heralded in such scholarship obscure the vertical hierarchies that continue to obtain between now and then? We, after all, are living; they, after all, are dead. In short, what happens to the past, *as past*, when scholars are interested mainly in producing a map of their own affective relation to it? Self-reflexivity about one's critical desire, of course, can take different forms. My point is not that these mappings necessarily are projections, for, as my discussion of transference as a dynamic mode applicable to historiography suggests, that much is inevitable: the past is often inscrutable and in its finitude ultimately irrecoverable. My point is that we do not overcome this difficulty by ignoring or dismissing the past's relative autonomy.

By "relative autonomy," I refer to whatever happened in the past irrespective of our encounter with it. As Fredric Jameson famously cautioned during early debates about the textuality of history: "One does not have to argue the reality of history: necessity, like Dr. Johnson's stone, does that for us. That history—Althusser's 'absent cause,' Lacan's 'Real'—is *not* a text, for it is fundamentally non-narrative and nonrepresentational; what can be added, however, is the proviso that history is inaccessible to us except in textual form, or in other words, that it can be approached only by way of prior (re)textualization."[35] If, in the present context, it seems important to return to the initial part of Jameson's statement in order "to argue," precisely, for "the reality of history," it is to indicate my demurral from those who seem willing to dismiss that autonomy.[36] Although I continue to believe, as I wrote in *The Renaissance of Lesbianism*, that there is an "*extent* to which our desire for these [past] representations constitute[s] them as objects,"[37] I would emphasize that to recognize such an "extent" is to affirm that the past is not cut whole cloth from our desires. However much we construe the past through our desires, those desires remain *ours*, not those of historical subjects.[38]

To insist on the relative autonomy of the past while admitting the necessity of making rather than revealing history is not necessarily a brief on behalf of historical alterity, in the sense that the past is only interesting or worth pursuing when it is different from the present.[39] It *is* an argument on behalf of the element of surprise and, more particularly, of *impasse*: of the irreducible, intransigent quality of any given other's experience, including experiences lodged in the past. This impasse, as I've suggested throughout this book, is as much epistemological as historical and hermeneutic. Moreover, the really interesting thing about engaging with the past is when our projections encounter something that cannot be accounted for—that is, when they come up short, hit a block, an obstacle, a wall.[40] Indeed, I suspect that it is in reaction to such historical, hermeneutic, and epistemological impasses that scholars first began to feel the need to practice and theorize an archival *ars erotica*. But rather than sit with that obstacle and scrutinize its contours and cracks, they have attempted to use their desire and their reparative readings as a vehicle by which to transcend temporal distance.

This fantasy resolution, I submit, is incongruent in ways that could be methodologically productive. For what is most useful about proposals for an archival *ars erotica* is not the erotic transactions they celebrate but the light they collectively shed on the historiographic mandate to privilege either the alterity of the past or its resemblance to us. Taken as a group, practitioners of history-as-affect clearly hold opposed attitudes toward the concepts of historical difference and similitude: some, like Huffer, make claims on behalf of the strangeness of the past or, like Love, of its resistance to our desires; some, like Dinshaw and Freccero, are intent on the past's asynchronic presentism. Readers of Chapters 3 and 4 will recall my claim that alterity and similitude have come to function in queer studies as corollaries to other critical claims and investments, carrying with them considerable conceptual baggage, with arguments demonstrating one or the other assumed to be produced by means of a set of a priori suppositions.[41] That is, certain affects tend to be described as *necessarily consequent* to seeking the past's alterity or, conversely, to seeking the past's resemblance to ourselves. Yet, as evinced by the divergence among these scholars, such affective consequence seems less a logical necessity than an indication of the work of critical desire. This observation, far from a critique, offers up a methodological release point. For, precisely because the play between similarity and difference is the element out of which desires and identifications are generated, we might want to resist translating either into a historiographic mandate.

The questions I have raised about an archival *ars erotica* as an emergent field habitus are intended to provoke some calculation of and a greater appreciation for its specific analytical capacities and payoff. For some projects—those focused, for instance, less on history than on the phenomenology of reading—the benefits of an archival *ars erotica* might be well worth the risks. Moreover, work that posits historiographic relations in terms of *negative* affects (such as disidentification, feeling haunted or refused) not only resists an overestimation of pleasure,[42] but provides a salutary reminder of the resistances from which all work on history-as-affect proceeds. My point is that this resistance of the past to our efforts to know it seems both to motivate the archival *ars erotica* and to defy its modes of redress. As a fantasy structure, it illuminates less the past than the epistemological constraints and contradictions in which our scholarship is caught.

Knowing Early Modern Sex

To better apprehend the conceptual problems that an archival *ars erotica* can and cannot address, I now turn from historiography as affect/desire and the erotic phenomenology of the researcher to historiography as the elucidation of sex *acts* locatable in the past. To raise the issue of acts is to confront one of the reasons that, as I noted in Chapter 1, sex remains obscure: namely, that sex acts are of the body, and hence mortal, ephemeral, highly individualized, and local; and that within this already individualized phenomenon, psychic variation plays an unusually powerful and provocative role. We know, of course, that what turns any particular person on may turn another one off, but our methods have not yet come to terms with the fact that the transient materiality of sex and the extent of erotic diversity necessarily render any manifestation of sexual experience or representation less a "thing" of which we can catch hold than a matter of hermeneutics—that is, of interpretative aptitudes and contingent choices.

When early modern literary critics and historians have paused to consider the difficulties involved in ascertaining knowledge of past sexual practices, they have tended to route the question of sex acts through the question of evidence. To adopt the words of literary critic Margaret Ferguson, any historicist or historian of sexuality faces "subtle but significant problems in constituting and navigating our evidentiary field."[43] Critics and historians alike have felt compelled to devise ways to circumvent the archival scarcity that is one of the constitutive conditions of producing knowledge about early modern sex. When hived off from the articulation of erotic desire—about which we have ample literary evidence—sex acts leave few sources or traces, except in registers of births, accusations of assault or breach of promise, and prosecutions for crime. Compared to the relative volubility about sex in the eighteenth century, as well as the protocols of politeness that organized the discursive proliferation of the Victorian period, records of sexual experience in the sixteenth and seventeenth centuries are both limited in quantity and unpretentious in tone. I will address the down-to-earth tenor of early modern "sex talk" in Chapter 7. For now, I note that the apparent restraint of the archive stems from various issues: a paucity of nonelite and female-authored writing, the scarcity of first-person sources such as letters and diaries, the brevity with which most sources describe sexual activities, and the use of formulaic stock phrases, particularly in official documents. The appreciation voiced by Graham Hammill regarding scholars of early modern same-sex desire thus should be extended to those early modernists composing the history of sexuality more generally: they have had to develop "sharper analytic tools and techniques for contextualizing and interpreting sexual desires and practices which are notoriously difficult to pin down in their particularities."[44] These techniques have been devised to address a number of different questions: How do the quotidian practices of daily life get recorded into and become represented in texts? Through what kinds of discourses (law, literature, medicine, visual culture) and genres (pornography, poetry, stage play, satire, romance, letter, diary, memoir, popular pamphlet and broadside) does sex become textualized? How does one discriminate—need one discriminate?—between the official and the popular, the literary and the judicial? In what ways do different discursive domains impose interpretative limits? What role should demographic data (rates of bridal pregnancy, bastardy, incarceration, population growth and decline) play in interpretation? How do the specifics of textual form and authorial intention, as well as the processes of circulation and consumption, affect our understanding? How does the language of sex—explicit, inexplicit, metaphoric, or punning—affect what sex means? Routed through such questions and retrieved in terms of them, textual and material traces of the past have been mined not only for official doctrine and imaginative flair, but for what they reveal about attitudes, beliefs, and changing social mores.[45]

The resulting picture, when collated across multiple discrete studies, is surprisingly comprehensive. In diachronic terms, the Protestant Reformation, steady migration to the capital, the burgeoning of print culture, loosening control of the church on sexual immorality, the upheavals of the civil wars and interregnum, and shifting medical conceptions of the body all contributed to changes in the social profile of sex. For England during the period of 1550 to 1680, scholars have demonstrated:

- the general desirability of sexual contact for adult men and women;[46]
- the importance of sexual control to household order, including the patriarch's self-control and governance of women and subordinates.[47]
- a general sense that sexual matters, especially those involved in courtship or impinging on household discipline, were community matters;[48]
- despite official proscriptions, general tolerance of premarital cross-gender sex, especially if the couple intended marriage and sex did not result in illegitimate births;[49]
- relatively late average ages of marriage (twenty-six years for women, twenty-eight for men);[50]
- relatively high rates of bridal pregnancy, bastardy, adultery, and marital dissolution;[51]
- medical and popular acceptance of the role of erotic pleasure for both men and women in maintaining good health and conceiving children;[52]

- the importance of understandings of heat, friction, and fluids to the psychophysiology of sex for men and women, from the mechanics of arousal to the spilling and reception of seed;[53]
- the Reformation's impact on promoting discourses of romantic love, companionate marriage, and domestic heterosexuality;[54]
- a tension between reproductive (testicular) and performative (penile) sexuality related to changing ideas of masculinity;[55]
- a range of factors impinging on children's choice of a spouse, including parental approval, financial considerations, and community values;[56]
- despite the importance of marital status to social status, high numbers of unmarried adults, at least one-fifth of whom never married, particularly in urban locales;[57]
- the importance of discourses of intimate friendship and kinship (both voluntary and through bloodlines) to the forging of erotic bonds;[58]
- complex shifts in public regulation of sexual conduct, including intensification in some areas (policing) and weakening in others (religion), especially in London, over the course of the seventeenth century;[59]
- the endurance of a sexual double standard regarding male honor and female reputation, enforced by women as well as men;[60]
- an official horror of sodomy, set against the widespread valorization of intimate male friendship;[61]
- the limited sexual options available to women, who nonetheless fashioned idioms to articulate their desires for men and for one another;[62]
- an eruption of interest, across discursive domains, in female-female desire around 1600;[63]
- the unspoken congruence of homoerotic desires with the domestic relations of the early modern household;[64]
- the eroticization of urban space,[65] including the pervasive presence of female and male prostitution, despite repeated crackdowns, in London;[66]
- the rise of an indigenous erotica and pornography to supplement materials circulated from the continent;[67]
- a medical culture eager to treat a range of sexual ailments, including genital infections, erectile dysfunction, amenorrhea, chlorosis, sterility, and syphilis;[68]

- intense anatomical interest in the sexed body, and a corresponding medical interest in causes of sex transformation, hermaphroditism, and "unnatural" sexual behaviors, with texts increasingly circulating in the vernacular;[69]
- relatively few prosecutions for male-male sodomy and none for female-female sex until the late seventeenth century;[70]
- an official horror of bestiality, with occasional prosecutions directed primarily at young men;[71]
- the omnipresent threat of rape and sexual coercion experienced by all females and by male youth;[72]
- all-too-quotidian acts of violence among domestic intimates, not least because "reasonable correction" was a prerogative of parents, husbands, masters, and mistresses against their subordinates;[73]
- the susceptibility of "sex" to religious and racialized rhetorics and the susceptibility of religion and "race" to sexualized ones.[74]

I present these conclusions as both a summary consensus and in the form of bullet points to underscore that much painstaking labor and methodological creativity—both individual and collective, and often across disciplinary divides—has been required to create this picture. In contrast to the profusion of themes pertinent to the history of lesbianism described in Chapter 4 —where my goal was to tease apart concepts that had been associatively conflated—each of these topics has tended to be approached as a question in its own right, and often pursued through different methodological means (deriving from literary, cultural, social, intellectual, and demographic history) that make it difficult to correlate any one set of conclusions with conclusions drawn from other perspectives.[75] Indeed, the details of any one of these themes have been a matter of considerable debate, even if what I suggest here is the emergence of a broad consensus. While further refining individual details is one worthy goal and will certainly continue apace, I suggest that another goal might be to correlate these themes with one another—not to create a synthetic history, but to apprehend which of these elements do and do not fit together, and where they rub each other the wrong way. With the exception of "textbook" surveys whose summary purpose is necessarily superficial, rarely are these various issues treated as interrelated or contradictory, much less as parts of a larger sexual landscape. Treatments of adultery, for instance, rarely consider sodomy; questions about the rise of molly houses at the end of this period are indifferent to female sexuality; scholars of legal discourse tend to disregard pornography. The tendency, rather, has been to give each of these topics its due, first by collecting and aggregating scattered references, and then by paying particular attention to the cause of attitudinal or social change. Regardless, in methodological terms, what was true for the list of themes in Chapter 4 is equally true here: scholars hoping to advance the history of sexuality might begin by setting their sights on the underresearched relations and conflicts among any two or three of these items.

My purpose, however, is less to nudge along such comparative research than to note that this body of work depends upon a default method of social "contextualizing." It has been nearly axiomatic for early modern scholarship across disciplines to define its goal as describing the ideological and material *contexts* within which sex occurs. Beyond its usual prestige in historical scholarship generally,[76] contextualization represents one strategy to deal with what Katherine Binhammer describes as "the difficulties of historical interpretation when the object of study is constituted by taboos, silences, and prohibitions."[77] It is not just the paucity of discourse about sex that generates these difficulties, however. For one of the peculiarities of knowledge about early modern sex is that it depends so heavily upon the ways knowledge was organized at the time. As Julia Garrett notes, such knowledge was "generally mediated and ancillary. Sexual behaviors, sensations, and phenomena [did] not constitute an autonomous category of knowledge that . . . might be investigated in their own terms. . . . Scholars who investigate early modern sexuality have thus found that in order to access such information, they must work through an enveloping discourse, one that may serve as a vehicle for sexual discourse but also subordinates such knowledge to its own priorities."[78]

Scholars thus have argued (and with increasing frequency have simply presumed) that to understand the meanings and functions of sex, they must identify the discourses in which it appears and range of relations in which it is embedded and to which it contributes. As noted in previous chapters, they accordingly have demonstrated that sexual activity in this period was tethered to, correlated with, and expressed a wide range of emotional affects and relations: love, coercion, masochism, violence, patriarchy, reproduction, apprenticeship, pedagogy, service, commerce, racialization, religion, monstrosity, witchcraft, theatricalization, language use, and court and national politics.[79] The center of gravity thus has been less on *sex* than on what early modern society can tell us about sexual *attitudes* or on what sex can tell us about the social formations to which it is tethered.[80] So axiomatic is this impulse that it serves at times as the only point of agreement between radically different scholarly projects—as can be seen when comparing queer literary historicist Mario DiGangi's complexly intersectional assertion that "although same-sex practices are the sine qua non of the sodomite and the tribade, both types are composed of discursive strands that engage categories of nationality, religion, status, and economics, as well as sexuality,"[81] to historian Faramerz Dabhoiwala's announcement that his concern "is not primarily to enter into the bedrooms and between the sheets of the past. It is to recover the history of sex as a central public preoccupation, and to demonstrate that how people in the past thought about and dealt with it was shaped by the most profound intellectual and social currents of their time."[82] Despite their differences, both scholars suggest that one of the most important things about sex is that it is not *just* about sex: rather, sex draws from and is embedded in larger social relations.[83] Obviously, the pervasive impulse to texture and nuance the social and psychic meanings of sex stems from a wish to do justice to its complexity as a social and collective, and not merely physical or individual, phenomenon. It derives in some cases from an understandable desire to do historical justice to the overlapping idioms (such as those signaled by *love, friend, kiss, embrace*) that refer to both sexual and nonsexual intimacies. But insofar as the appeal to context has operated as a methodological force field for the consideration of early modern sex, it has had some unintended, unfortunate consequences. Preeminent among them is that sex has been irradiated into its relations; it thus is construed and represented as *epiphenomenal*, as an *effect* of other historical processes—not as a historical agent in its own right.[84] And in the process, sex itself has become disembodied—or rather, embodied in only very particular ways.

Presumptive Knowledge

The historiographic imperative to contextualize sex is intensified by the fragmented nature of sexual utterance in the period and its dispersion across discursive domains. But it also is a response to the larger historiographic problem of textual mediation. Before I justify that causal statement, it is useful to link the method of contextualization to the epistemological problem of knowing what sex is. A tacit assumption across disciplines is that to speak of "the body" is necessarily to speak of sex, and to speak of sex is to speak of sexual practices. Yet, despite the number of books with beguiling titles like

Illicit Sex: Identity Politics in Early Modern Culture; Figuring Sex Between Men from Shakespeare to Rochester; Love, Lust, and License in Early Modern England; Imagining Sex: Pornography and Bodies in Seventeenth-Century England; and, crossing the channel, *The Sexual Culture of the French Renaissance* and *Sex Acts in Early Modern Italy,*[85] sex acts are not robustly represented in this scholarship. Each of these books offers considerable insight into any number of features of sexuality as a social, cultural, and/or literary phenomenon, but none of them actually elucidates sexual acts per se. Rather than identify, describe, and analyze sex acts, they identify, describe, and analyze the cultural meanings and contexts of the sex acts that they tend to presume.

The emphasis on context and interpretation, in other words, has contributed to scholarly circumspection regarding what early modern people actually did. Given the nature of the archive, this caution is understandable; nonetheless, it calls out for scrutiny. After all, specific bodily behaviors are what bring "sex" into being; without them, there would be only erotic desire and fantasy. So why do most scholars of early modern sexuality seem to avoid this fact? Why are the body's pleasures and displeasures a major lacuna in the history of sexuality? Why, in short, do scholars resort to presumptive knowledge about acts rather than investigate what such acts are?

The identification or accusation of presumptive knowledge generally is meant to discredit scholars for their failure to see, to recognize, to apprehend. But given this book's premise that failures may present opportunities and represent real achievement, I want to elucidate the spoken and unspoken categories—the structures of discourse—that impact the ways early modern sex is cognitively processed and presumptive knowledge encouraged. I concede that it is impossible to transcend all presumptions; in order to think at all, we need to presume some things and ignore others—all we can do is foreground and analyze the specific configurations of knowledge that such presumptions support or exclude. I offer just one example, selected out of scores of others, precisely because, *in its own terms,* it is a major contribution to early modern studies and, *in my terms,* it is sufficiently close to my own focus on epistemology to offer a subtle variation on it.

In the course of an argument regarding the construction of subjective inwardness through theatrical means, Katharine Eisaman Maus astutely notes that "in both Jonson and Shakespeare sexual experience becomes a *topos* of unknowable inwardness."[86] Analyzing the "bed-trick" in Shakespeare's *Measure for Measure,* upon which the plot's resolution turns (in which one woman, unbeknownst to the man, takes the place of another woman with whom he thinks he is having sex), she argues:

> This trick merely poses in a dramatically acute form a more general difficulty that plagues attempts at sexual policing throughout the play: the problem that bodily acts fail to have meaning in themselves, but acquire the significance participants and witnesses attach to them. Angelo compares Claudio's [sexual] offense to murder and counterfeiting; Lucio thinks it "a game of tick-tack." The sex act does not mean the same thing to Isabella and to Mistress Overdone, or even to Isabella and Mariana. The loving union of Juliet and Claudio seems importantly different from the commercial relationship of Lucio to his whore, and likewise from the vexed, covertly legitimate connection between Angelo and Mariana. Motives, outcomes, class position, religious conviction, temperamental imperatives, all complicate what Lucio calls "this downright way of creation." The problem is not merely how strictly the authorities ought to regulate particular sexual behaviors, but how that behavior is to be defined and interpreted.[87]

Maus's perspicacity regarding the interpretive and epistemological problems posed by the meanings of sex is rare in Shakespeare criticism. Nonetheless, intent on subjectivity, she does not pause to consider that the contents of "the sex act" to which both she and the play refer are similarly obscure and potentially just as multiple as the characters' moral perspectives on sex. Do all of these characters perform the same acts? Do they enjoy them in the same way? Subjective inwardness, she argues, is unknowable; but sex, it appears, functions as always already known.

Sexuality is not Maus's main focus in this essay, and she is not a scholar primarily of sexuality. But the implication that *we all know what sex is* is representative of countless other studies, including recent ones by scholars who take sex as their focus. As an antidote to this problem, Christine Varnado has asked us to reconsider the contents we supply to "the almost universally agreed on 'straight' invisible sex" in *Romeo and Juliet,* the offstage sex to which critics have access only through the morning-after bedroom scene (3.5).[88] Varnado argues that "*nothing* would have to be different in the text of the play to imagine the invisible sex act before this dialogue as something else: some nonpenetrative erotic act of a more diffuse and mutual *jouissance* or some suspended dilation of pleasure that gets cruelly interrupted by the lark. Nor would anything have to be different, for that matter, if the unseen act were an unclimactic fumble, a premature climax, an impossible penetration, or a dysfunctional episode. Nor would anything have to change if Romeo did the same thing (any of the things) with Juliet that he would do with a boy."[89] Furthermore, although Juliet seems happy about whatever transpired, a whole corpus of early modern texts do not share her glossy view of the "rites" of the wedding night. Examining what she calls a "discourse of 'hymeneal instruction,'" Margaret Ferguson notes that "it is easy for readers today to make unwarranted assumptions about what the wedding night meant in a past culture," and proposes, instead, that such nights were figured in a variety of texts as imbued with desire, dread, and anxieties about masculine self-control.[90] As Ferguson (and others) have pointed out, it is a staple of early modern comedy that it defers "consummation"; while she emphasizes that this deferral enables plays to use that "space/time to explore issues of sexual and gender politics,"[91] I would highlight the extent to which scholars have tended to impose their own erotic narrative of domestic and sexual harmony onto the "afterward" of plots.

One could, of course, chalk such presumptive knowledge up to the silences of the text, or the archive, or prevailing norms of speech within the academy. Varnado and Ferguson point instead to the presumptive heterosexuality—and its attendant idealization—that continues to govern critical discourse. But I think that something else is also going on. In addition to the heteronormativity of collective critical rationalities, presumptive knowledge about sex symptomatizes the limits to our knowledge: that is, sex tends to invite presumption, functioning as already known, *because it is unknowable*. It thus calls for an epistemological response, one that involves examining the implications of the power of discursive conditions to shape not only sex but our production of knowledge about it. Once considered epistemologically, plenty of good reasons for presumptive knowledge abound.

One such reason can be found in the language of sex. Here are some lists, none of them comprehensive, of popular terms alluding to sex. Terms in circulation prior to 1650 include "lust," "lewdness," "licentiousness," "lasciviousness," "lechery"; "incontinence," "concupiscence," "wantonness," "bawdry," "venery"; "coition," "fornication," "copulation," consummation"; "deflower," "devirginate," "lie with," "swive," "fuck"; "sodomy," "buggery," "bestiality," "pederasty," "tribadry," "masturbation"; "adultery," incest," "bigamy"; "whore," "cuckold," "cuckquean," "wittol," "libertine"; "unnatural villainy," "carnal knowledge," "carnal congression," and "rite of love." In specific contexts, words with broader meanings, including "abomination," "conversation," "occupy," "enjoy," "dalliance," "debauchery," "infidelity," "vice," "uncleanness," "use," and "abuse," also could be used to refer to sexual activity.

Many of the terms that we now regularly use to describe sex assumed their sexual connotations or were coined, according to the *Oxford English Dictionary*, much later. They include "coitus" (1713), "sexual intercourse" (1753), "sexual liaison" (1816), "fellatio" (1887), "cunnilingus" (1897), "sexual relations" (1897), "premarital sex" (1878), "extramarital sex" (1929), and "foreplay" (1929). Our common phrase "to make love" was used as early as 1567 to mean "to pay amorous attention; to court, woo," but apparently did not allude to engaging in sexual *acts* until 1929. "Sex" referred to the genitals as early as 1664, but did not refer to sexual *activity* until 1900. To all of these we might add compound terms that the *OED* does not include: "romantic tryst," "licit and illicit sex," "reputable and disreputable sex," "normal and deviant sex," "sexual contact," "sexual intimacy," "sexual transgression," "sexual immorality," and "sexual impropriety."

My point in offering these lists is not to emphasize the historicity of any individual term, or to restrict our usage to period-specific terms—although there is much to be learned from a consideration of any particular word's temporal contingency, longevity, and reversals of meaning.[92] My point, rather, is that most of these terms indicate less a specific *sexual activity* than the social lens of assessment through which conduct is cognitively and morally processed. Early modern "sex words" are largely devoid of specific corporeal information; instead, they gesture vaguely toward implied behaviors. "Fornication," "adultery," and "bigamy" refer not so much to sex as to its relation to marriage. "Relations" and "liaison" are more neutral than "impropriety" or "bawdry," and these are less judgmental than "promiscuity" or "debauchery." Viewed as conceptual categories, these terms refer our understandings back to attitudes and ideologies, not to acts. Covering over the hermeneutic activity by which sexual behavior is cognitively processed, they function, without anyone intending them to, as artful dodges that secure presumptive knowledge about what sex is and what it means. Through the force of implication, presumptive knowledge is aided and abetted by language itself.

A second reason for presumptive knowing is that sex, as Chapter 5 argues, continues to be overwritten either as a concept of sexual identity or as a more flexible erotic position nonetheless still specified by virtue of its object (homo,

hetero, bi, poly). Even as early modernists debated the relevance of identity
categories to eras "before homosexuality," and even though one might
assume the conceptual priority of acts to which one side of the "acts versus
identities" debate was supposedly dedicated, the consideration of sex acts was
circumscribed by the question of whether genital contact among members of
the same sex was adequate to impart a sense of sexual identity.

Third, lodged deep within both literary sensibilities and the project of queering is the fear that inquiry into what actually happens between bodies might
be misconstrued as a form of naive empiricism. The derision explicit in Mary
Poovey's critique of a "sociological" survey methodology that sees sex as "a
compound made up of separate but repeatable kinds of acts (kissing and touching, vaginal intercourse, masturbation, anal intercourse, and so on)"—in other
words, as independent variables—voices a broader humanist unease not just
about quantification, but about how the segmenting of sex acts might sunder
them from social and affective meanings.[93] To be sure, any experience of sex is
more complex and multidimensional than a single "act" can connote, and few
variables are actually isolatable.[94] Sexual contact can involve hands and mouths
as well as genitals, speech as well as sight, and sometimes, then as now, entail
the use of inducements, prosthetics, lubricants, and equipment. The use of
body parts other than the genitals can occur whether the sex is solitary, happening between two people, or in a larger group; it obtains whether sex is a matter
of commercial exchange or romantic love. Each embodied act comprises,
involves, and melds into other acts.[95] But, to extend Michael Warner's observation, quoted in Chapter 5, regarding the disjunction between what we know
firsthand and what we theorize: it seems that that which is obvious in our own
erotic lives—that we both engage in specific acts and that they overlap with
other acts—has not had much impact on scholars' treatments of early modern
sex. The unfortunate consequence of this is the tacit assumption that we know,
in each individual instance, how early moderns "did it."[96]

Finding the Bodies

In recognition of this tacit assumption's stranglehold on research, James
Bromley has noted: "Despite the proliferation of histories of identity, our
'backward gazes' at pre- and early modernity have not scrutinized sexual acts
themselves. . . . We continue to read Renaissance texts as though the field
of available sexual practices in Renaissance culture was already organized

according to modern Western culture's dominant narrative of sexual activity, which itself does not entirely account for the available forms of pleasure or attitudes toward those forms that currently circulate."[97] Bromley's assessment of critics' collective inattention was anticipated by the historian Cynthia Herrup, whose 1999 essay "Finding the Bodies" diagnosed a constitutive embarrassment among her colleagues about the physicality of sex. Chastising them for seeing something *other* than sex when they analyze early modern discourses, she critiqued the tendency to read the sexual body as a metaphor for concerns that extend beyond the body—a tendency that she attributed to self-consciousness about the object of study. "To date," she wrote, "the most successful (least threatening) way to make sex matter has been to disembody it. So we point out echoes of sex where it physically is not and claim to find something more than sex where it physically is."[98] Having discovered a rich documentary archive associated with the mid-seventeenth-century trial of the Earl of Castlehaven—including descriptions of anal sodomy, cross-gender rape, masturbation, voyeurism, and intercrural intercourse—Herrup urged her fellow historians to resist this hermeneutic error, to stop reiterating the reticence of the archive, and instead help it to speak. In her patient excavation of what early moderns are reported to have said about sex and her thoughtful analysis of how to read those utterances in light of one another and in light of the law, Herrup's book-length analysis of the Castlehaven trial provides a model of how to read sex in the archive. Although her main aim in *A House in Gross Disorder* is to resituate the case as less about sodomy than about violations of household order,[99] and although her main methodological intervention is to read trial records as stories, advise "agnosticism on the verdict," and shift the focus to which version of events "was persuasive to whom, when, and why,"[100] her book offers a telling example of what research into the seventeenth-century archive can yield in the matter of sex acts.

Herrup's injunction to "find the bodies" continues to stand as a salutary reminder to historians of what they supposedly value—that is, elucidating lived experience—but what the category of "sex" strangely has permitted them to elide. Taking Herrup's injunction to heart, I began assiduously collecting the references to sex acts that compose the archive from which this and Chapter 7 evolved. Most early modern historians of sexuality, however, have continued to produce research indifferent to Herrup's more wholesale prescription, composing histories based on context rather than acts, while also ignoring the methodological innovation of the archival *ars erotica* that was having such a pronounced effect in queer studies.

Nonetheless, there has emerged across literary and historical scholarship a range of representations of sex acts that defy any presupposition of early modern "heteronormativity." Although references to sex acts crop up as isolated instances and are dispersed across a wide range of texts (both early modern and scholarly), the collation of this research enables the following composite portrait. At least some of the early modern populace engaged in and/or fantasized about looking, rubbing, touching, kissing, penetrating, and being penetrated in various positions and via various orifices, alone, in couples, in groups, in private, and in public. In increasing numbers after 1660 but also present before, legal, medical, and literary texts, material objects, manuscripts, and "cheap print" refer to or depict solo and mutual masturbation,[101] tongue kissing,[102] tribadism, or "the game of flats,"[103] anal buggery of men and women,[104] cunnilingus and fellatio,[105] digital penetration,[106] vaginal penetration from behind,[107] intercrural sex,[108] chin chucking,[109] flagellation,[110] use of dildos,[111] rimming,[112] eroticized purging,[113] private and public voyeurism,[114] the reading of dirty manuscripts, books, pamphlets, and pictures in homes and brothels,[115] and the singing of bawdy songs in alehouses, taverns, and inns.[116] The "public cultures of sex" were alive and well and gaining steam; they included incidents of sexual display and group sex in rural and urban institutions.[117] Indeed, about the spatial geography of sex we have a fair amount of evidence: people had sex in their studies, in front of the fire, in beds and closets; in gardens, stables, fields and forests, behind hedgerows, in ditches, and in wood yards; in alehouses, taverns, and inns; in coaches and onboard ship; in brothels and, by the end of the century, in molly houses. Places of assignation included the streets and alleys of major cities, and, in London, barbershops,[118] public and private theaters,[119] the Royal Exchange,[120] and the aisles of Saint Paul's Cathedral.[121]

This brisk summary obviously fudges any firm distinction between the acts of engaging in such behaviors, fantasizing about them, and writing about them, as well as whether the tone used to describe these acts is celebratory or condemnatory. It fudges as well the numbers of people participating in any particular activity, and hence the question of its typicality. And it does not address the knotty issue of whether we are finding more diverse sex in the past now because it is something that we value or because we better know how to look for it.[122] But, for those who are concerned that critical desire, particularly on the part of literary critics, unduly inflates the available evidence, let us turn to the work of historians, and not cultural historians but those most interested in documenting "experience." A number of years ago,

Henry Abelove argued, mainly on the basis of demographic evidence, that the late eighteenth century saw a marked increase in the popularity of cross-sex vaginal intercourse, inside and outside of marriage, and a corresponding reconceptualization of nonpenetrative behaviors as "preliminary" to vaginal intercourse—a shift that, he maintains, gave rise to the notion of "foreplay."[123] Abelove's hypothesis forms one basis of Tim Hitchcock's argument that there was a "sexual revolution" in the eighteenth century, in which people equated sex "more firmly with activities that could lead to pregnancy," a revolution that began first in London and thereafter in the rest of the country.[124] Whether the popularity of vagina-penis intercourse in fact increased and whether this can be correlated to capitalist production, as Abelove surmises, concern me less than these historians' attempt to historicize sex acts themselves. We might well wish to query the hyperbolic rhetoric of "invention" that Abelove ascribes to the concept of foreplay,[125] the hyperbolic rhetoric of "revolution" promoted by Hitchcock, and a framework that seeks to correlate radical changes in sexual practices with definitive temporal boundaries—the dangers of which have been evident since Sedgwick's *Epistemology of the Closet*. Nonetheless, it does seem that people's sex lives in the sixteenth and seventeenth centuries were, for a host of reasons, not mainly or necessarily oriented around the penetration of vagina by penis.

As early as 1979, G. R. Quaife argued, based on court records and low birth rates in Somerset, that "heavy petting," which he defined as "mutual masturbation" and "the manipulation of the female genitals," while sometimes "a prelude, or hoped-for prelude, to sexual intercourse," became "an end in itself" for the "largely illiterate lower orders."[126] Based on church court depositions dealing with a wider social spectrum, Laura Gowing argues that "the persuasions and practices that witnesses talked about" suggest "a wide repertoire of behavior that avoided pregnancy and alleviated sin."[127] Surveying a large swath of visual and medical materials across western Europe, art historian Patricia Simons notes that "the visual display and manual manipulation of genitals occupied a great deal of libidinal energy in a pre-penetrative regime of contraceptive denial or interruption."[128] The first-person accounts of Samuel Pepys in the late seventeenth century and John Cannon in the early eighteenth both record a number of nonpenetrative sexual encounters with several female partners, domestic servants, and mistresses, willing and unwilling.[129] In the aggregate, this scholarship confirms Abelove's view that penis-vagina intercourse may have been less the telos of early modern sexual encounters, the end point of a presumed erotic sequence, than one act among a variegated repertoire. In fact, going further, we might speculate that nonprocreative, nonmissionary, and even nonprivate sex in the early modern period seems to have been *what most people actually did*.[130]

I have three motives for giving this composite portrait of sexual activity its due. First is to insist that the diversity it describes be taken more seriously, not only in terms of the picture it portrays but in terms of its methodological implications. It is time for scholars to begin to use this aggregate research to recalibrate the kinds of questions they ask of their subjects and texts.[131] I do not think it is overstating the case to say that the implications are every bit as far-reaching for a historical understanding of *sex* as Thomas Laqueur's *Making Sex* was for gender,[132] for it would radically refigure what sex *means* for those studying the early modern period. Research dedicated to detailing the diversity of sexual activity provides a foundation upon which scholars might construct a *historicized theory of sexual variation* capable of analyzing not only *what* early moderns did, but the reasons *why* they did what they did. The goal of such a theory would be to convey a detailed exposition of the multiple and conflicting factors that might have influenced any "decision" regarding sex: concepts and experiences of affective and power relations; knowledge and fears about bodily health; modes of scrutiny and surveillance by kin and neighbors; understandings of the law, prosecution, and redress; concepts of sin and salvation. Onto these qualitative indices could be layered statistical measures of health, illness, and disability, and the material stresses on householding, reproduction, and population. This project would need to be cognizant of the impact of the communication and dissemination of sexual knowledge, including its transmission orally and through various media. The aim would not be to approach these factors as "contexts" for a sex already assumed; nor would it necessarily be to trace generalizable patterns, achieve a holistic synthesis, or identify minoritized practices. Rather, by elaborating the multiple and contradictory factors potentially involved in any individual's pursuit of any given sexual taste, we would be closer to understanding not just the what and the how but the *why* of early modern sex.

My second motive, conversely, is to suggest that scholars not shy away from the methodological problems inherent within this evolving narrative that will impact any theory we might devise. For instance, we might decide to hold in abeyance the increasingly prevalent tendency to nominate such diversity as "queer." Resisting this ascription may enable appreciation of the fact that, far from spelling defiance of a secure hegemony, multifarious sex acts may have comprised the typical, the usual, the commonplace of early modernity. Indeed, their mundane, quotidian presence does not simply confirm our sense, articulated in scholarship since Bray's first book on sodomy, of the disjunction between precept and practice. It begins to unravel the very notions of norms and normativity for the early modern period. And with that unraveling, the definitional, canonical core of queer inquiry, as that which is always posed against the normative, begins to show its cracks. What new theories, we might ask, might be needed to respond to the fissures thus exposed by the pressures exerted by history?

Third, as my admission of "fudging" the distinction between experience and representation registers, our approach to the materiality of sex still remains an unresolved issue. I agree with Herrup that scholars' reiteration of archival difficulty may portend a larger problem, but I am not convinced that the problem was or is scholarly anxiety, or that diagnosing it as a problem of affect gets us very far. It is certainly true that some of the historical work on sex published in the 1970s can seem prurient,[133] and some historians may well have felt the need to distance themselves from it. But even if embarrassment *were* the primary obstacle to analyzing early modern sex acts, redressing it through more candid, open, liberal speech would not resolve the dilemma of what to do with the intractability of sex as a material phenomenon.

In order to dig deeper into that dilemma, we might turn back to literary-critical terrain, where critics aver that, as Bromley puts it, "an adequately historicized understanding of what 'counts' as sex in Renaissance texts can reveal the extent to which this division between 'sexual activity' and 'everything else' governs and is governed by representational logic itself."[134] It should be clear by now that *Thinking Sex with the Early Moderns* shares the view that "representational logic" can tell us a lot about what sex means and what it means to know it. But representational logics are only the starting place for an epistemological inquiry into "what 'counts' as sex." The next step is to take up, not only as a theoretical but a practical matter, the corollary proposition that we do not, indeed, cannot, know all of what sex means—and not just because its meaning, being past, is irrecoverable. And so, while I happily align my work with those scholars intent on "finding the bodies" in the early modern period, I aim to complicate that endeavor by shifting this discussion of critical rationalities from matters of the archive and representation to matters of epistemology—which in this case involves attending to the strategies of those who are concerned less with the production of history than with the historical production of knowledge.[135] But before we head there, we must tarry a bit longer with questions of method circulating among historians and literary critics, as well as in the legacy of Alan Bray.

Acts and Epistemologies

As I noted in Chapter 2, Bray came to believe that a focus *on* sexuality is not the right starting place for historians *of* sexuality. In response to his sense that questions of sexual identity were unduly circumscribing the field, Bray made a strategic turn away from his earlier focus on specifically sexual identities, ideologies, and practices to an orientation toward affect. Bray's shift anticipated similar moves by other scholars who, reacting to an early preoccupation with sodomy and gender transgression, began to emphasize homoerotic friendship and love.[136] Yet, the embedding of intimacy in a range of social relations also, as I have noted, had the effect of minimizing the possibility that the bonds Bray was describing were sexual. Affects—preeminent among them, love—analytically overtook whatever bodily acts might have been involved. As Helmut Puff describes it, Bray "dethrone[d] sex as an organizing principle for the history of same-sex relations, offering affective intimacy as its centerpiece instead."[137] In a sense, Bray made his own tactical end run around the roadblock of acts versus identity, for he not only veered away from sexual *identity* but also from sexual *acts*.

To reconsider Bray's end run is not to maintain that all same-sex friendship is necessarily erotic. As Sharon Marcus has shown in reference to Victorian women, differentiating between the experience of erotic desire and the experience of being "just friends" can bring welcome precision to our understanding of the historical relations among homosocial, homoerotic, and homosexual bonds.[138] But Bray's is not, like Marcus's, an insistence on clear-eyed distinctions; his is a refusal to scrutinize the gap separating erotic from non-erotic intimacies. This bypassing of sex acts has had the effect of stalling precisely the project toward which Bray's own work gestured: inquiry into the epistemology of sex.[139]

I now want to step into the hole he sidestepped. Part of what impels me is the sense that this historian's privileging of affect over sex as a historical question bears some similarities to queer literary critics' privileging of affect-as-sex as a historical method. Clearly, these two moves are tilted in different directions: Bray is interested primarily in affects in the past, while the critics promoting an archival *ars erotica* are interested primarily in affects in the here and now. But might both of these strategies be a response to the same historiographic problem?

One way to get at this question is by scrutinizing further the (generally unstated) conceptual categories that organize historiographic practices, for these represent one indication of what scholars collectively think it means to know early modern sexuality. Rather than canvass the conclusions of their research as previous sections have done, here I describe the conceptual paradigms that have organized its production. Historical research on early modern sex has been generated, with a few exceptions, under the aegis of five organizing rubrics:

- Sexual or social identity: here the focus has most often been sodomy and homoerotic desire (male or female) or, conversely, a presumptive heterosexuality with the occasional inclusion of a token reference to sodomy. Included as well is work on erotic friendship, which, while often posing itself as anti-identitarian regarding modern sexual identities, reiterates the conceptual logic of social identity via its recourse to "the friend."
- Gender identity: in work focused on "women" or "men," "femininity" or "masculinity," references to sexuality tend to appear as anecdotes or examples of the construction of masculine/feminine virtue or vice; of virginity, chastity, honor, and sexual reputation; of wooing, wedding, fertility, and reproduction; of singleness, marriage, and widowhood; of sexuality as a metonym of domestic or social order and disorder.
- "Class" identity: here scholars focus on the sexual attitudes and/or sexual experiences of the poor, the lower, middle, or upper ranks of society, with scholarly production weighted toward the experience of elites; generally sexuality is subordinated to problems of social discipline, economic viability, or familial dynasty.
- The social: here sexuality is illustrative of attitudes toward or practices of adultery, divorce, the family, the household, domestic service, religious belief, witchcraft, alcohol use, violence, or crime.
- Discursive domain or genre: these studies treat sex in the context of different types of texts: pornography, drama, love lyrics, popular pamphlets, legal depositions, medicine, witchcraft treatises, theology, and visual art.

These rubrics sometimes overlap, and my aim is not to distinguish them so as to create a rigid taxonomy, but instead to emphasize how much they govern scholarship. In particular, they allow us to see that (with the exception of the first rubric) "sex" tends to crop up, catch-as-catch-can, as a by-product of research on other topics. Furthermore, it is hardly adventitious that within these five rubrics, two forms of sex act rule the conversation: penis-vagina intercourse and male-male anal sodomy. Penis-vagina intercourse is, obviously, the handy historical default. That which is normative does not require explicit articulation—or so the thinking goes. When actual penises and vaginas, tongues and hands, do appear in scholarship (which is to say, rarely), most scholars tend to assume they know how they were employed, and in what order: in striking contrast to the portrait of early modern sex I just described, scholars assume that embracing, kissing, and caressing are teleological preludes to vaginal intercourse.[140] The upshot is not just more instances of presumptive knowledge. Through this sequential rendering, vaginal penetration comes to serve as a powerful metonymy for "heterosexuality" as a social institution.[141] That is, "intercourse" is taken to materially figure not merely the dominant mode whereby male and female bodies are sexualized but the hegemony of "heterosexuality" itself. Thus organized metonymically, "heterosexuality" (variously qualified by scholars as patriarchal, reproductive, or heteronormative) is thus reduced to a single sexual act. Moreover, its hegemony can be echoed and countered, but not undermined, by its illicit mirror images: premarital pregnancy, adultery, bastardy. In the logic of this representational system, pregnancy, adultery, and bastardy also function as metonymic assurances—evidence, yet again and in circular fashion, of a nearly universal "heterosexuality."

So, too, sodomy among men, generally equated with anal intercourse (in yet another act of metonymy), has operated as its own kind of scholarly default, largely because, of all early modern erotic behaviors, it is the most obviously aligned with oppositional notions of deviance and transgression. Furthermore, its apocalyptic signification, especially as represented in theology and the law, rendered its representation public and verbose enough that it has been relatively easy to document. For scholars first schooled in the seductions of "subversion and transgression" and more recently subject to the solicitations of the "queer," the scholarly appeal of sodomy is that it would seem to most obviously challenge normative heterosexuality.[142]

Two other forms of erotic activity, female homoeroticism and bestiality, have also been objects of inquiry, but from a much smaller cohort of scholars and with less obvious impact on the field. In previous work, I argued that representations of female-female erotic desire revolved around relations of social significance and insignificance. Within that signifying nexus, women's erotic contact in the period tended to take one of two forms: reciprocal erotic friendship or tribadism.[143] This is not to say that no other forms of "lesbianism" existed.[144] Nonetheless, what I have called "chaste femme love" typically was extolled for its chastity and innocence, whereas the tribade was almost universally condemned as monstrous: not only was this figure deemed a usurper of male prerogatives, but her body generally was imagined to be prosthetically "supplemented" either by her hypertrophic clitoris or the use of a dildo. Considered as a form of sodomy, tribadism was rarely publicly ascribed to Englishwomen prior to the late seventeenth century; rather, it was generally projected "elsewhere" in discourses of implicit racialization. As a research object, female homoeroticism is perhaps the most muted of sexual categories in early modern studies.

Bestiality, or, in the period's own idiom, "buggery with beasts," also was considered a subset of sodomy—an act of penetration (whether of the animal by the human or of the human by the animal) that supposedly contravened nature. Although the preeminent legal jurist of the time, Sir Edward Coke, included women in his buggery statute if they committed the act "with bruite beast,"[145] only two cases of female "bestial buggery" have been recorded, and scholarship has tended to interpret bestiality as involving a male agent and passive animal.[146] Bestiality captures scholarly attention in part because of the practice's purported alterity to modern sexual systems. With the growth of animal studies, bestiality and the associated rhetoric of "bestial sexuality" have been explored in light of a (provocative or abjected) transit across species boundaries, early modern beliefs in cross-species reproduction, and the deployment of rhetorics of animalistic desire to dehumanize racial and religious "others."[147]

Each of these forms of sex has exerted a particular hold on scholars' imaginations, and inquiry into each has yielded its own configurations of knowledge and intense scholarly debates. But what are the consequences of the hold they have had? First, although sex acts are often analyzed in this scholarship, they remain implicitly tethered to forms of identity (the sodomite, the tribade, the bestial bugger)—even if this identity does not take the form of a modern subjectivity. One result of this identitarian focus is the elision or illegibility of the erotics that Bromley cannily refers to as "everything else." Second, those acts that have garnered most scholarly attention generally are conceptualized by means of bodily penetration and a related binary of activity and passivity. In this, scholars echo early modern legal doctrine. Coke defined both cross-sex intercourse (crucial to legal annulments of marriage and to accusations of rape) and same-sex or cross-species buggery (capital crimes against the monarch) as legally punishable only if penetration had occurred. Ejaculation on its own was not sufficient to secure an indictment, "but the least penetration maketh it carnall knowledge."[148] Such definitional exactitude derives from the legal requirements for evidence and the ramifications for the parties involved, including the dissolving of the sacrament of marriage and the forfeiting of human or animal life. But just because the law cognitively processed sex through the implicitly gendered (and age) rubrics of activity and passivity,[149] it is not clear that this was the final or even the most prevalent word on what "sex" meant to early moderns. And, as the next chapter will suggest, it may not be the best rubric for us to process early modern sex.

The overarching rubrics that have defined and circumscribed how we think of early moderns thinking sex stand as testaments to the import of the concepts and categories by which *we make sex mean*. In an attempt to edge closer to the opacity of sexual knowledge, I now turn, with this desideratum in mind, to the work of certain scholars whose projects have led them to confront, in various ways, the difficulties of historical signification.

The Impasse of Textual Mediation

From early days in the history of sexuality, historians as well as literary critics have attempted to give credit to and negotiate the conceptual distance between subjects' lived experience and their signifying practices.[150] Many of them have followed their colleagues in anthropology and literary studies in disputing the rigidity of that binary, arguing, in the words of David Halperin, that "material conditions give rise to ideological formations," while, conversely and interrelatedly, "symbolic systems construct material reality."[151] Most scholars working in the history of sexuality would furthermore agree with queer theorist Lee Edelman that "interpretations of sexuality are necessarily determined by the rhetorical structures and the figural logics through which 'sexuality' and the discourse around it are culturally produced."[152] Indeed, Dagmar Herzog, a historian of modern German sexuality, credits historians of sexuality with advancing this awareness into disciplinary history:

because sexuality—whatever "it" was at various times and in various places thought to be—turned out to be one of those realms where interpretations and experiences, discourses and feelings, fantasies and sensations became inextricable . . . it was frequently historians of sexuality who refused to accept a dichotomy between representation and reality. Instead, they pioneered new ways of applying intellectual historical and literary critical methods to what had traditionally been social historical sources, and they analyzed legal frameworks and socioeconomic conditions in tandem with meaning-making processes.[153]

It thus has become common for historians to acknowledge that any semblance of "lived experience" is made accessible only through mediated representations and processes of source selection. An introduction to the disciplinary techniques of historians, for instance, announces its purpose as attempting "to unseat easy assumptions about the certainty of our knowledge about the past, and to make clear that the uncertainty lies not just in the stubborn opacity of sources but in our inherent inability to get beyond sources themselves."[154] Or, as Frances Dolan observes of other early modernists: "The mediated and textual nature of our access to historical knowledge has been much noted in recent decades and can now stand as a kind of given, as likely to be rehearsed by historians as by literary critics."[155] Noting some residual resistance to this idea, Dolan nonetheless points to many others who assume "'the textuality of history' in all its complexity" and thus indicating "some shared terrain."[156]

In Chapter 3 I argue that characterizations proffered in debates about queer temporality have obscured the extent to which early modern historians of sexuality have considered the role of textual mediation as a defining force with which to contend in their work.[157] With recognition of some "shared terrain" stipulated as a baseline, we can explore some of the ways both literary critics and historians construe and negotiate this conceptual tension. As we will see, the alleged disciplinary dispositions that would seem to direct our projects may not be the most salient factor when locating where accounts of textual mediation hit up against their own limits.

It may be useful to preface this scrutiny of textual mediation with some definitional premises. For the purposes of this discussion, I assume widespread agreement with Jameson's "proviso" that the past "is inaccessible to us except in textual form" and that we cannot "discover" or "recover" its meanings without recourse to textual mediation. I assume, as well, consensus

on the need to differentiate between the past as everything that happened—
the vast totality of pastness—and the narratives we construct of it. It nonetheless seems crucial to distinguish between claims of "creating" or "inventing"
the past versus claims of "reconstituting" or "narrativizing" it. Embedded
within this continuum of practices are consequences, including the kind of
dialogue with the past that we consider possible or desirable. We might
accordingly attempt to achieve greater lexical precision in our use of the terms
"the past" and "history" by asking scholars to define their usage and the
impetus behind it. To my mind, we do not create the past, but we *do* create
"history"—if by history we mean the narratives, the frames of analysis, and
the selection of particular aspects of the past as analytic objects.

In the early efflorescence of the new historicism, Louis Montrose influen-
tially proposed a cogent encapsulation of the movement's investments in the
"historicity of texts" and the "textuality of history."[158] But Montrose's chiastic formulation, so enabling at the time, seems to not so much tackle the
problem of mediation as enable an elegant means of evading it. What, after
all, activates and actualizes these recursive explanatory formulations within
historiographic practice? How are links formalized across this chiasmus? My
suspicion that this rhetoric symptomatizes a methodological quandary is iter-
ated by Dolan, who, in the context of reading court depositions, points to
the interpretative maneuvers involved in the use of the verb "mediate,"
which, she maintains, signals the presence of a methodological challenge
"that most scholars acknowledge and then ignore."[159] The scholars Dolan
examines dutifully register the fact of textual mediation, and then, seduced
by the dream of a first-person speaking subject, conveniently forget in the
course of their interpretations the specific ways those subjects' words are
transmitted.

Attending, as Dolan does, to the clues embedded in our ready-to-hand
rhetoric, I want to approach this problem from an obverse angle. For it is
just as common for scholars to denounce the error in treating historical documents as a *transparent* window on reality or as *definitively* delineating specific
attitudes as it is for them to gesture toward, then forget, textual mediation.
Such modifiers have usefully marked the distance from an unreconstructed
historicism, but they have also allowed scholars to hedge their bets. I myself
have used such a qualifier when I proposed earlier that we cannot know *all*
of what sex means—leaving unspecified the extent and limits of what kind
of knowledge *is* possible. While acknowledging the necessity of mediation,
these rhetorics allow us to avoid articulating with any degree of exactitude

the extent to which we can and cannot access the past. Windows, after all, may be cloudy, delineation need not be definitive, knowledge may be partial and inexact, yet still provide a plausible semblance and credible account of something that actually happened. If we tarry with the conceptual dodge lodged within this rhetoric, the question morphs from whether the past is mediated to how much of the Real, how much referentiality, how much accuracy, we are willing to commit to in a historiography that is self-conscious about its own methodological limits.

Dolan and I obviously are not the first to consider this question. What is new, I submit, is our refusal to frame this problem in purely disciplinary terms. Such disciplinary framing is evident, for instance, in historian Gabrielle Spiegel's examination of the ontological status of "history as text." Arguing for more precision in cross-disciplinary discussions about the "hermeneutic circle," she hazarded the observation that "the task facing the [historian] is broadly constructive" whereas that facing the literary critic is "broadly deconstructive."[160] These alleged methodological differences are elaborated by Maza: "while nearly all historians believe in the ultimate reality of the past, they approach that reality much more gingerly than do their literary colleagues. Fully aware of the many choices and extensive labor that go into the task of historical reconstruction, they are both less likely to invoke that past's 'reality' but also wary of acknowledging double and triple meanings or the self-subversion of a source: a document can only mean one thing if it is to serve as one element of a large pattern."[161] Or, as she summarizes: "literary scholars set their texts a-wobbling while historians nail theirs to the ground."[162]

Aware of textual mediation and the impact of their own desires on source and document selection, historians thus have been confronting, albeit according to a different set of priorities, the same impediments, the same conundrums, as those that have impelled queer literary critics to develop the call for an archival *ars erotica*.[163] Their strategies, of course, differ from those of critics and queer theorists, as the metaphor of "nailing" texts to the ground makes clear. Nonetheless, awareness of the problem as one common to both disciplines may enable a more productive dialogue about the difficulties and strategies of sexual knowledge production than has been typical thus far.[164] In fact, recognition of this shared conundrum may serve as a methodological release point, freeing literary critics, historians, and queer theorists alike from taking recourse in mutual accusations. Particularly within the history of sexuality, which numbers among its personnel at least as many literary critics as trained historians, the stability of disciplinary difference has, over the past decade, itself been set a-wobbling.

We might note, for instance, that it is historian Mark Salber Phillips who argues that "every representation of history, whatever its genre, incorporates elements of *making, feeling, acting*, and *understanding.* . . . Consequently, a more ramified analysis of historical representation needs to consider the problem of mediation as it relates to four fundamental dimensions of distance that shape our experience of historical time": history's "formal structures of representation, including its aesthetic qualities and rhetorical address"; its "affective character" (e.g., "cool appraisal or lively emotions"); its "implications for action," whether "political, religious or ethical"; and its "assumptions regarding explanation and understanding."[165]

Historians' recognition of the constitutive force of rhetoric, affect, ideology, and action does not, however, imply that there is agreement across disciplines regarding "how to evaluate the textual form in which history is accessible to us and how to understand the meanings of texts as documents *and* as literature"—in other words, how to assess their status as different kinds of *evidence*. In this quest, Dolan observes, the two disciplines "have reached something of an impasse."[166] Even in "the wake of the consensus that the real is constructed," she observes, "there has been surprisingly little reflection on principles for selecting evidence and standards for privileging some forms of evidence over others or sorting evidence in terms of the kinds of claims one is trying to support."[167] To surmount this impasse, Dolan proffers specific strategies and principles, modeled in part on early modern readers' own practice of thinking "across evidentiary registers."[168] Drawing from her work on ballads, for instance, Dolan describes her evidence as "scattered, random, and mobile," arguing that

we need to abandon the notion of an evidentiary point of origin or substratum, thinking instead about charting ripple effects, splatters, aftershocks, feedback loops, and contact networks rather than tracing a line to the beginning or digging down to the bottom. Each fragment of evidence is valuable as a piece of a larger puzzle; but its value does not depend on its proximity to the event, the facts, or the truth of what it represents. Each fragment, whether it is a deposition, a diary entry, or a ballad, has invariably been shaped by the process of its own production, by generic conventions, and by an awareness of audience or market. Everything needs to be read warily; everything requires interpretation; each morsel makes most sense when it is read against others, but a different sense depending on what others.[169]

Dolan's strategies of assessment shift the methodological register away from abstract or dutiful acknowledgments of textual mediation and toward practical plans for dealing with it. In this emphasis on practice, she shares a fair amount with strategies devised by historians out of their own skepticism about the reality/representation dichotomy. Several gender historians, for instance, describe their task as one of comparing stories from different discursive registers against each other.[170] As David Turner, a historian of adultery, describes it: "Rather than viewing 'representation' and 'reality' in dichotomous terms, this approach argues that each source establishes a different 'point of contact' with the wider social world. This point of contact is established by various means: in subject matter, modes of expression and language, authorial intention and sense of audience, and established forms and textual conventions developed over time."[171] Dolan's and Turner's methods dovetail with that of art historian Patricia Simons, who engages "the ways in which verbal language, visual rhetoric, material culture and living bodies constructed each other in mutual feedback loops of interchange and cross-fertilization."[172] Radiating out from the intersection of different disciplines, these lateral paths of affiliation, comparison, and feedback loops lead us toward a perspective on sexual knowledge production that is not only self-consciously interdisciplinary,[173] but aims to capitalize on the difficulties that historical knowledge-making throws in our way.[174]

Minding the Gap

Such interdisciplinary convergences provide one strategy for contending with the fact of historiographic limits, and recognition of such limits and potential strategies for dealing with them may have the benefit of prodding scholars toward greater exactitude when making claims about what particular historical methods can and cannot deliver. But this recognition does not provide much analytic purchase on the *epistemological* problem with which this chapter has been concerned. For if historians of sexuality have, to reiterate Herzog, "refused to accept a dichotomy between representation and reality," their refusal does not insure the irrelevance of what, I have argued, remains a fundamental fact about sex: its irremediably dual status as materiality and metaphor. Refusal of the terms of binary opposition does not dispel the tension; rather, the act of refusal indicates one attempt to think one's way around it. Indeed, in the absence of more direct confrontations of this problem, the history of sexuality appears to be bifurcating into two methodological "schools": one engaged with concepts of discourse and various modes of theory, and one that presents itself as primarily empirical, descriptive, and narrative.[175]

The collective strategies of historians and literary historians, in other words, have taken us only so far in remediating this tension. But what is so special about sex in this regard? Is it, as I have implied throughout, a special case? Are not the tensions between reality and representation, metaphor and materiality, relevant to other domains of existence? Would not the category of "experience," for instance, encounter the same problems, while providing a more ample investigative field, one on which historians have already expended considerable theoretical energy?[176]

While I would not reject this possibility, I believe that sex is, in fact, a special case, one in which the status of the "sex act" is striated with tensions between materiality and metaphor, signification and unknowability. For evidence of this, I turn to one of the least theorized objects of knowledge within the domain of sex acts: orgasm. Annamarie Jagose has recently observed that "despite the increasing amount of humanities scholarship during the 1990s on sexuality . . . about sex itself, it seemed there was relatively little to say."[177] Linking this elision to the conceptual hostility toward orgasm present in Foucault and Deleuze, Jagose excepts within queer theory only Leo Bersani for his "studied effort to think about sex on its own terms, rather than as a cipher for other, more serious, matters."[178] In words that echo Herrup's chastisement of historians, Jagose argues that queer theory needs to resist "the transubstantiation of sex into matter deemed more immediately or more recognizably political."[179] But what might be involved in thinking about "sex on its own terms"?

Jagose's answer arrives couched in an argument about the value of twentieth-century orgasm as a research object. This value, she writes, inheres in "its availability for rethinking the relationship between *sex as a set of bodily practices or techniques* and *sexuality as a field, both psychic and regulatory*."[180] Orgasm, in other words, presents an analytical opportunity precisely to the extent that it is understood "as a complexly contradictory formation."[181] In regard to "sex as a set of bodily practices," she argues that "thinking the biological with, rather than against, the cultural acknowledges orgasm's complex discursive profile, the often contradictory ways it is both experienced and apprehended."[182] The epistemological payoff of this strategy of confronting rather than smoothing over contradiction is twofold. First, literary critics and queer theorists might gain some analytical leverage were we to desensitize our allergy to empiricism. The methods used to understand the world through empirical means benefit us in countless ways, from our use of media interfaces to our understanding of biodiversity to our reliance on medical technologies. If it was once crucial for post-structuralists to critique empiricism for its pretension toward truth with a capital T (and if this provided the opportunity for theory to stretch in the direction of the queer), it may now be time to recall that empiricism is a mode of investigation, a set of techniques, that can be pursued with a variety of aims in mind. As Jagose points out, "there is no reason to presume that the cultural and the biological must be at loggerheads, nor that an emphasis on the cultural will lend itself to the open-ended possibilities of transformation while an emphasis on the biological will as inevitably become bogged down in the inertia of the status quo."[183]

Second and more specifically—as I have shown throughout this chapter—it is only by risking empiricism, and the charges of naïveté that are often the knee-jerk reaction to it, that scholars can spotlight specific embodied acts as historically knowable. Moreover, it is knowledge of these acts—however partial, mediated, and internally contradictory—that provides the basis upon which we might construct something that has yet to be attempted: a historicized theory of sexual variation.

This injunction, however, carries with it an important qualifier. For it is only a *historicized* theory—with the emphasis on history—that will effectively confute presumptive knowledge about the meanings and material contents of sex. Prior to Herrup's book, for instance, historians thought they knew what the Castlehaven scandal was about: sodomy. When Herrup reopened the archive of this trial, its contents revealed a Pandora's box of other forms of sex, as well as sex's mutually constitutive relations to patriarchal householding, sexual violence, relations of service, and religious identity.[184]

These arguments conduce to a further contradiction, one to which much of this book is dedicated: to rethink the relation between "bodily practices" and "sexuality as a field, both psychic and regulatory" is to recognize that any empirical spotlight, however extensive or bright, will not resolve the meanings of sex or vanquish the shadows of the archive.[185] Sexuality as an epistemological field works *precisely by means of this impasse*. If the incoherence attending orgasm, for instance, draws its specific "charge from the historic processes whereby sexuality has come to constitute a framework of intelligibility of sex," it is also the case that early modern sex, while not captured within the modern regime of sexuality as the truth-of-the-subject, is structured across the same body-representation divide. If "orgasm's structuring contradictions . . . cannot be explained away or even decisively arbitrated,"[186] neither can those contradictions that preexisted the modern seizure of "sex" by the epistemological apparatus of "sexuality." Certain historical research objects, like the seventeenth-century Castlehaven trial or Pepys's diary, likewise evince contours drawn by means of "understandings" and "fleshly experiences" that are, in Jagose's words, "equally strung on the warp of figuration as the weft of literality."[187]

This, finally, is why the effort to "find the bodies" will not serve as an ultimate methodological desideratum for those interested in thinking sex in the interdisciplines. Such methodological insufficiency bears emphasizing because it contravenes current trends in the history of sexuality. Recently, for instance, Tim Hitchcock, long a staunch advocate of concentrating on the "physical cultures" of eighteenth-century sex, has argued that attending to sexual practices will provide "an answer to an essentially historiographical conundrum," resolving incompatibilities between the "text-based and essentially relativistic work of cultural studies and the purportedly empirical understandings wrought by demographers and their social-historical fellow travellers."[188] In his laudable effort to attend to the "ragged and uncertain boundary around what [early moderns] thought was sex,"[189] Hitchcock promotes physical sex acts as the *solution* to this historiographic catch-22, one that would enable historians to compose "a single," synthetic "narrative of historical change."[190]

Yet, any effort to bring to light the physical cultures of sex is circumscribed not only by the fact of textual mediation and scholars' choice of which bodies to find, but by the fact that sex acts simultaneously index the materiality of the body and the lack of adequation of our signifying systems and historiographic methods to represent or enliven them. Finding the bodies, giving them visibility and voice, will not surmount these difficulties. But neither can we mitigate these limits or indemnify our conclusions by simply owning up to our desires and rendering more explicit our erotic attachments to what we find in the archive in the mode of an *ars erotica*. Attending simultaneously

to the weft of materiality and the warp of metaphor instead demands attending to the *texture* of contradiction, *the lack of fit*, the rough edges that emerge
when the threads of materiality and metaphor chafe against one another, fray,
or tie themselves in knots.

The epistemological skein of sex will not unravel through our analytical
efforts into discrete strands of different color, ply, and heft, or allow more
than patchy patterns to emerge. The crux of sex, its incongruities and obliquities, will not disappear or give way to some truth hidden away—whether in
the archive, within the scholar's own embodied affect, in the construction of
a better research object or a more coherent methodological synthesis. This is
because *any* question about sex is not merely historical, arising from within
the conceptual parameters of specific times and places, and knowable only
through fragments. Nor is it merely hermeneutic, a matter of developing
more subtle interpretative techniques, more sensitive tools to address archival
scarcity and textual mediation, or more deft lateral, comparative strategies.
Nor is it finally to be redressed by developing new critical concepts and
categories to render them more sophisticated or less identitarian, or by adopting, in a more robust fashion, the tenets of queer theory. The question posed
by sex, finally, is of sex *as such*.

To refer to "sex as such" is to affirm that there *is* such a thing as *sex qua
sex*—by which I mean sex that isn't reducible to power or discourse or the
truth-of-the-subject—even as I simultaneously affirm that this "thing" is not
ultimately knowable, much less an ontological or transhistorical essence. To
say this is to displace the analytical priority accorded to desire and to discourse under the modern apparatus of sexuality, as well as the methods we
have devised to deal with that apparatus, and to reorient the epistemological
problem of sex away from power-knowledge and toward sex's mysterious
materiality—the essence of which is that, paradoxically, *it cannot be known*.

If what I have just argued seems directed toward historians, the rub, I
insist, goes both ways. If an epistemologically oriented history of sexuality
would require historians to do something other than produce historical *explanations*, it also would prod literary critics to do something other than produce
literary *readings*. Furthermore, literary critics and queer theorists might find
some common incentive to reconsider the transhistoricity of one of their
most cherished concepts. For if what modernity would come to ontologize
as perversion, creating ever more elaborate etiologies for it, was in fact the
most common way that early modern people had sex, then it is not just that

"the normal" is a historical back-formation, but that the purpose and object of queering is more historically delimited than those who apply queer to early modernity might wish. Queering the Renaissance, in other words, becomes a less obvious, less satisfying strategy than it has seemed ever since it burst on the scene with Jonathan Goldberg's groundbreaking collection of 1994.

The form of interdisciplinarity I have enacted here is clearly not a utopic coming together in such a way that contestation and disciplinary affiliations disappear. The shared strategies of critics and historians have shortened some of the distance between the disciplines, but they have not thereby abolished what is essentially an epistemological gap. Nor does my effort to think sex in the interdisciplines result in a gesture of compromise (although I do not consider compromise a bad thing). Indeed, if my excursion into academic field formations began heuristically with a Venn diagram, I would now complicate that descriptive model in several ways. First, the stasis of the diagram fails to do justice to the multiple forms of identification (whether with fields, methods, disciplines, or identities) that animate each set. Nor does it do justice to the varied positions, alignments, and identities into which these forms of identification provisionally cohere. Second, I am not suggesting that the optimal result would be a more capacious field formation, wherein history, literary criticism, and queer theory would all reside companionably within a larger, all encompassing circle. In fact, the relations I have described and the mode of inquiry that I am advocating are more akin to a freeway interchange in the middle of Los Angeles, with its multiple entrances and exits, overpasses and underpasses of different heights and widths and degrees of curve, and people traveling at different speeds, as they veer off in divergent directions and with varied purposes in mind. While there is always the possibility of a jam or a crash or the mundane frustration of missing the right turnoff, there is also the possibility that this tangled infrastructure will provide the routes whereby we find ourselves someplace other than where we thought we were headed.

In the midst of this snarled interchange of identifications, critical rationalities, scholarly desire, and disciplinary training, I have attempted to draw disparate things together over the fact of an impasse. But adopting an epistemological perspective is not the only way to move forward, and I do not propose it to diminish the importance of scholarship forged from within the terms of disciplinary or field formations. I *do* mean to disrupt the security of performances of rectitude. For recognition of our common plight provides a reminder that the deficiencies that each modus operandi finds in others' methods may be projections of a blind spot, behind which lurks the obdurate withholding of sex from knowledge. The wager I have made is that by stepping *into* the aporia of sex-as-knowledge-relation, we might develop additional strategies to work *within* the gap between materiality and metaphor, historical, literary, and queer methods, the past and its mediations. This work begins with the mundane effort of challenging presumptive knowledge about sex; it honors both discipline-specific and cross-disciplinary competencies; it risks empiricism in order to tender the murky contours of sex in the past more susceptible to theorization; and it casts a skeptical eye on the conceptual categories with which we approach the archive and forge our interpretations. Most especially, this work demands and benefits from a willingness to linger within a state of uncertainty regarding *meaning* and a state of contradiction regarding *method*.

Claiming this degree of ambivalence as both hermeneutically and historiographically sound will not adjudicate the dual status of sex, much less between preferred disciplinary protocols. Rather, foregrounding the epistemological conundrums posed by sex renders such adjudication less of an issue by changing the terms of our questions: away from the polarizations that create climates of mutual suspicion and toward the concepts, categories, and processes by which knowledge is created. Neither the teasing out of hermeneutic complexity nor a diligent combing of the archives, neither the universalizing claims of theory nor the specificities of a temporally located sexual utterance, can secure the meanings of sex in the past. I would go so far as to hypothesize that dismissals of other fields for their methodological failures serve less to illuminate any discipline's unique affordances than to rhetorically shore up notions of disciplinary privilege that have, over the past decade, actually become less relevant or tenable. Indeed, I have come to believe that recourse to the idea of disciplinary difference no longer serves much useful purpose in the project of thinking sex. The problem is not disciplinarity but the reluctance on all sides to recognize that the problem of sex as a research object is a problem of one's *own*.

In a fundamental way, the project of knowing sex, thinking sex, and making sexual knowledge is situated precisely within that tensile space where the embodied specificity of erotic desires and corporeal acts that actually happened rub up against the impossibility of our ever knowing exactly what such desires and acts were or might mean. Whether we see this conundrum as an effect of our left brain failing to communicate with our right brain or of being bodies in the world, it is one task of those of us in historical sexuality and queer studies to work this mind-fucking contradiction, to render its multiple ironies resonant and productive. Given its irresolvability, our preferences for our own strategies of knowledge production warrant a little humility, our treatments of others' methods a bit more forbearance. As areas of contention about the meanings and significance of sex, the closely aligned but mutually suspicious fields of the history of sexuality, queer literary historicism, and queer theory require not a disciplinary détente, a methodological compromise, or an agreement to disagree. They need, rather, to take each other seriously. For if nothing else, the conundrum of sex as metaphor and sex as materiality holds us all captive to its constitutive irony.

CHAPTER 7

Talking Sex

> Sweet Dol,
> You must go tune your virginal, no losing
> O' the least time. And, do you hear? Good action.
> Firk, like a flounder; kiss like a scallop, close;
> And tickle him with thy mother-tongue. His great
> Verdugoship has not a jot of language.
> —Ben Jonson, *The Alchemist*

So the inimitable housekeeper Face instructs Dol Common in the arts of seduction in Ben Jonson's *The Alchemist* (1610). To perform "good action" with "Don of Spain" (3.3.10), she is instructed to "tune" her bodily instrument, with the musical metaphor sustained through references to "time" and "action," the mechanisms of a keyboard instrument.[1] The tropes quickly shift: she is instructed to "firk, like a flounder; kiss like scallop," then, "tickle" her sex partner with her "mother-tongue." But what do these instructions mean? How *does* one firk like a flounder?[2] Among the eleven editions I consulted, those editors who do more than explain that a flounder is a small flat fish define "firk" as "arouse, stir up"[3] and "excite sexually,"[4] while "like a flounder" is glossed as "the undulating motion of a flatfish swimming, or its habit of lying flat and face-upward," and, conversely, "the arching contortions of a flat fish out of water."[5] Swimming or dying, undulating or arching, a firking flounder poses a conundrum. The extension of the marine metaphor into scallop sex does little to clarify: the image of lips "close" together (or perhaps closed) may provide a thematic link, but is not a particularly sexy image.[6] Coping with this line leads editors in various directions: to the reputed resemblance between shellfish and female genitals,[7] the early modern use of shellfish as an aphrodisiac,[8] and the explanation, "with her lips sealing his, using suction like a bivalve mollusc."[9] With both facial and labial lips potentially involved, the imagined sexual "action" bifurcates—or perhaps pleasurably extends—across body parts. Is this what it means to "tickle" with "thy mother-tongue"? The phrase "Good action" is even more up for grabs once one considers the meaning of Dol's "mother-tongue," the anatomical difficulties of which are regularly fudged by the explanation, "Face plays wittily on kissing and speaking."[10] If her lips are shut tight, or acting as a seal or suction cup, how is she to use her actual tongue, to talk, to whisper, or to kiss? Or are these actions possibly sequential, kissing, then sucking, then tickling? Is the tongue in question her organ of speech, her native language, or both (as suggested by the gloss, "arouse him with erotic language; penetrate his mouth with your tongue")?[11] Does its allusive meaning rely on the reputed vulgarity of the vernacular? Or is the mother-tongue, as one editor asserts, "what lies between the vaginal labia"?[12]

Face is projecting a certain sexual lingua franca onto Dol: he imagines that she possesses a language, and a knowledge, common to all but the Don.[13] This purported fluency, composed as it would be of words, bodies, practices, and pleasures, enhances the erotic possibilities of his speech and the audience's imagining of what might ensue. But thinking about this passage solely in terms of *dramatic* action is not the only way to approach the relations of knowledge here. As this scene of erotic instruction shifts tropologically from a standard pun on virgin/virginal, to physical yet baffling figurations of several sexual acts, to the lack of a shared language among sexual partners, questions about what constitutes "good action" only multiply. Indeed, for contemporary readers and audiences, the passage shifts briskly from the hackneyed to the confusing to the incomprehensible. In so doing, linguistic excess seems to slip into epistemological aporia. Does sex itself somehow compensate for this aporia? Or is the production of incomprehension and, more particularly, the humor that results from a sexual suggestiveness at odds with itself, the aim of Jonson's language of sexual "action"? Has Jonson failed or succeeded in "talking sex" in this passage? Does Face offer viable instruction for "good action," or does he—like the image he conveys—*flounder*? And is whatever incomprehensibility thus conveyed locatable in the text itself, in the early modern audience, or in the minds of contemporary readers and critics today?

To ask such questions is to focus, more acutely than this book has done thus far, on the actual language of sex. In this pursuit, I join a handful of

early modernists who are attempting to theorize, rather than simply identify or describe, the imbrications of sex with language *at the level of the
word*. Through diverse modes of historicizing, they have pursued this aim
by examining particular words, terms, rhetorics, and ellipses;[14] the specific
functions of erotic wordplay, especially puns;[15] the orthographic and typographic materialities that literally inscribe erotic meanings into texts;[16] and
the resources of philology for queering early modern words.[17] In *Queer
Philologies: Sex, Language, and Affect in Shakespeare's Time*, Jeffrey Masten
argues that "there can be no nuanced cultural history of early modern sex
and gender, without spelling out its terms—for what alternatives of historical access do we have?"[18] Accordingly, he argues, "the study of sex and
gender in historically distant cultures is necessarily a *philological* investigation."[19] Taking my cue from his meticulously rendered "queer philology,"[20]
I ask what might happen when terms refuse to be spelled out—and, in
particular, what this refusal or resistance might mean for a history of early
modern sex. I hope to show that certain practices of reading for sex—
including some of those performed by feminist and queer-friendly critics—
evade the epistemological problems that sexual language throws up in its
wake. Critics and historians interested in gender have tended to emphasize
the misogyny of early modern sexual language, whereas queer critics have
tended to emphasize the creative exuberance of its metaphorical expansion.
In what follows, I apply a queer and feminist perspective to how we read
for sex by metacritically foregrounding the concepts and methods by which
we do so. By scrutinizing the interpretive habits that underlie assumptions
about how early modern sex and words intersect—including their rendition
as euphemism, stock phrases, "bawdy language," and wordplay—I aim to
render explicit the hermeneutic processes, protocols, and procedures that
render language *as* sex, whether that sex is understood as "erotic,"
"bawdy," "queer," "misogynous," or "normative."

The previous chapters have explored some of the conceptual frameworks
that organize and roadblocks that impede what early modernists do when
they attempt to make sex into knowledge. These obstacles, I've argued, result
from a number of disparate factors: silences in the archive, the gendering of
cultural logics, the instability of sexual signification, the materiality of sex
acts, and the abiding tension between representation and/as reality. They,
and the conceptual categories scholars have developed to deal with them,
are constitutive of our knowledge—organizing it in sometimes tendentious,
sometimes unwitting, but nevertheless consequential ways. Chapter 6, in

particular, approaches what we cannot know about sex by means of the irreducible materiality of bodily acts.

The present chapter likewise focuses on what we do not know, but its center
of gravity is a phenomenon that might seem to be the obverse of corporeal
acts: the language by which sex is expressed, represented, substantialized, and
materialized. Whereas the concept of mediated textuality explored in Chapter
6 implies the use of language,[21] in this chapter I hone in on the actual words
used to describe sexual activities.[22] Giving equal time to what scholars say about
early modern sex and what early moderns themselves said about it, asking to
what extent incomprehensibility is a modern reader's problem or one of early
modern readers and audiences, I toggle back and forth between then and now,
paying particular attention to the signifying capacities of early modern language, the related representational strategies of early modern texts, and scholars'
varied efforts to understand what those words and strategies might mean. My
method is simultaneously historical and epistemological, as I continue to challenge presumptive knowledge by scrutinizing how we come to know sex by
means of the language that puts it in circulation.

To raise epistemological questions about sexual language is to apply pressure to our interpretive categories and to place them in relation to the various
methodologies through which we access sex in the early modern past. Scholarly approaches to the sex-language nexus generally track different disciplinary and methodological investments. Early modern historians tend to
approach the relation of language to sex as a mandate to represent the period
"in its own terms"—although since the linguistic turn they increasingly have
been attuned to the play of metaphor, narrative, and genre.[23] Conversely,
literary critics tend to approach the centrality of language as a warrant to
interpret erotic tropes and metaphors, to unpack puns and innuendo,
although their procedures vary depending on critical modalities. In queer
and/or historicist work, the reading of tropes often takes the form of historicizing the alterity of early modern language. In psychoanalytic work, the
historicity of language often is subsumed under a transhistorical optic that
assumes the diachronic stability of individual words and metaphors. Despite
these differences, a common expectation among literary critics is that eroticism is itself produced in and by the exchange of sexual language—whether
that exchange is thought to occur between two characters bantering or wooing on stage, between characters and the audience exchanging a knowing
wink, or when the reader reacts to erotic language in a sonnet, dialogue, or
piece of prose. For many critics, then, erotic potential inheres in language,

and when that potential is mobilized, circulated, and exchanged, the result is more eroticism.

Whereas both period-specific terms and wordplay are of concern in what follows, I bracket off the eroticism that might be said to be intrinsic to, or generated out of, linguistic interchange. Admittedly, this bracketing vacates from consideration an important way in which sexual meanings develop and accumulate, for there is no doubt but that terms are invested with sexual meaning through processes of linguistic exchange. Nonetheless, in negotiating the irresolvable tension within "sex talk" between the denotative function of indexical "pointing" and the connotative energy of erotic circulation and exchange, I have chosen to subordinate the question of "the erotic" as an intrinsic or generic feature of language, and instead emphasize the *work* of language as it attempts to denominate particular sexual acts. Rather than circle around sex by means of the social and rhetorical phenomena to which it is tethered,[24] I shift the focus to the *functionality* of talking sex—that is, how sex talk *denotes* sex itself. This approach reveals the linguistic substrate—actual words and the strategies of their use—by which sex is substantialized and operationalized through language.

One of the ways to access the processes by which sex acts are verbally materialized,[25] as well as the methods that historians and critics typically employ to interpret sexual idioms, is by examining the culture's most playful, colloquial, and, at times, most vulgar forms of expression: "bawdy language," sexual innuendo, double entendre, and puns. These forms often rely on the physicality of the body for their power, and, in so doing, enjoin a corporeal hermeneutics whose aim is less the production of erotic affects—that is, desire, pleasure, disgust, and shame—than calling attention to the body and its behaviors. By comparing the workings of so-called bawdy language and wordplay to other linguistic resources such as euphemism and stock phrases, I analyze the strategies that are activated when words are called upon to render body parts or sexual acts explicit or, as we sometimes say, graphic. Although I shall begin by describing some of the contents of the early modern sexual lexicon, I am most interested in *how* such terms and related rhetorics accomplish their conceptual and epistemological work. Analyzing early modern sexual lexicons in terms of the wordplay they engender as well as the critical practices of reading and glossing they invite, this chapter explores various ways to put sex talk, both then and now, under pressure.

Rising to the surface by means of this pressure are not only the linguistic resources of but the epistemological competencies and the pedagogies involved in talking sex. That readers' and listeners' comprehension is at stake in the reception of Renaissance wordplay is obvious. It is standard pedagogical protocol for teachers to unpack early modern jokes, puns, and innuendo for students, and thus to fill in their gaps of understanding by slowing down the pace of passages, and to articulate the cultural, visual, and linguistic work of figurative condensation and *translatio*, whereby one word-thing becomes or stands in for another. As Mary Bly remarks of punning in early modern stage plays, "Many such puns are understandable only with a dictionary in hand."[26] Indeed, in our confrontation with condensed, strange, and archaic language, teachers and students alike depend on various forms of editorial labor to render obscurities more comprehensible. The question that motivates this chapter, however, is: On what basis is this transparency achieved? What is made "transparent" and what is elided from such scenes of instruction, as well as from the linguistic and sexual landscape of early modernity, when we view our pedagogical and hermeneutic task exclusively in terms of the imperative to clarify?

Pursuing such questions has entailed traversing a wide swath of texts across the discursive registers of documentary "evidence" and literary "reading": legal documents, medical treatises, pornography, satire, poetry, ballads, jests, pamphlets, and stage plays. While other scholars might focus on whether such texts are best interpreted as indices of actual experience or products of the imagination, and thus analyze the ways genre and discursive domain affect the management of tropes and rhetoric, I deliberately downplay such matters of evidentiary assessment. It is not that I am indifferent to the specificity of genre, tone, and intention across discourses, but whatever the differences in rhetoric, purported purpose, means of circulation and reception, these diverse genres and discourses are joined together in their common effort to denominate, substantialize, and materialize sex. From this perspective, no firm ontological divide separates one form of sex talk from another.

This shared denotative function, I aim to show, often proves elusive. Across the linguistic landscape, strategies of "sex talk," both those of early moderns and those of contemporary critics, tend to lead not to greater certainty, whereby words nail down sexual signification, but to the constitutive role of vagueness, imprecision, and illegibility. The early modern sexual lexicon is often unstable and obscure, hazy on referential detail, and indifferent to gender. Accordingly, while other critics have helpfully adduced the erotic or queer meanings of particular words, extending our awareness of the sex *in* words, I shall pause over those moments *when words fail*. Not fail to be erotic—eroticism can thrive on uncertainty, ambiguity, and contradiction—but fail in their *indexical function* to denote the gender of particular bodies, the specificity of particular body parts, and the actual uses to which those parts are put.

We typically expect words to be referential, and many times they are. Punning, of course, pleasurably messes with this expectation by multiplying possible referents. Yet, the indeterminacy of sexual language extends beyond the labile openness of the pun. All language, we have come to recognize, is tropological and all signification in some sense failed—the "letter," as both Lacan and Derrida attest, never arrives at its destination. However, the specific failures with which I am concerned open onto not only this more general situation but the epistemological tension of knowing and unknowing that the previous chapter argued informs the historical hermeneutics of sex. What differentiates the sexual lexicon from the unreliability that troubles all linguistic phenomena is the semiotic interplay of language, bodies, and acts, which not only informs what can be said, by whom, and what can't, but the relations of knowledge their interplay enjoins. Rather than argue on behalf of sexual signification as a privileged point of access for apprehending the indeterminacy of all signifying practices, my aim is to indicate the extent to which the instability of sex talk mirrors the instability of sex. Despite what I will argue is their down-to-earth materiality, early modern linguistic practices render sex indistinct, amorphous, and sometimes even unintelligible.[27] When it comes to early modern sex, it is not so much literary critics who "set their texts a-wobbling" but the signifying dynamics of sex talk itself.[28]

Thinking Through Whoredom

The concept of "whore" is a prime example of how such uncertainty plays out. Generally interpreted as an identity rather than an act, "whore" is a word that in the contemporary critical environment tends to conjure up knowingness and fixity. Given its pervasive use and widely noted effects, scholars might be justified in thinking that the referential content of this term would be stable and transparent: that it refers to a woman who has exchanged sexual acts for money, goods, or favors. Certainly, across discursive domains, the charge of "whoredom" functioned powerfully, from the medieval period on, to regulate women's conduct—from the clothes women wore, to the words they spoke, to the company and hours they kept.[29] The designation of a woman as a whore could be powerfully decisive, leading to social ostracization, family rejection, and confinement in Bridewell Hospital.[30]

Nonetheless, conceptually "whore" is a less exact term than many might suppose. First, the term was applied not only to women but to men who exchanged sex with other men or women for money, goods, and favors. The image of a young man sexually serving other men has been increasingly acknowledged in both literary and historical scholarship.[31] Less well known is the male prostitute procured by female clients. Such a figure was both a topical reference and an embodied character in plays by Middleton, Fletcher and Massinger, Brome, and Davenant. Extrapolating from the casual inclusion of references to male whores and male stews, as well as from court records of women charged with having paid men for sex, Jennifer Panek argues that there probably were professional "he-whores" in early modern London.[32] While the terms most often used to refer to the man who sexually catered to men were "ingle," "catamite," and "ganymede," the term of choice for the man who served women seems to have been "stallion."

Second, when used to describe women, the category of "whore" functioned in such a catchall way, encompassing under its purview such a broad menu of female transgressions, that its relation to sex was often oblique. So prevalent was "whore" as an insult that, according to Laura Gowing and Bernard Capp, it cannot be assumed an equivalent to "prostitute"; in the seventeenth-century materials they individually examine, "the words of [this] insult were understood to be related *only opaquely to actual sex*."[33] Melissa Mowry relatedly argues that "women characterized as 'whores' had always been vulnerable to prosecution in both secular and ecclesiastical courts. But the charge of 'whoredom' foregrounded questions of honor and reputation *rather than behavior*."[34] The capaciousness of "whore" as a category is evinced in the records of Bridewell Hospital, which, along with the ecclesiastical courts (also known as the "bawdy courts"), was a primary site for the prosecution of sexual offenses. Based on a survey of Bridewell records, Cristine Varholy argues that whoredom was regularly conflated with an array of sexual vices: "early modern English communities and institutions more often did not distinguish between prostitution, as it is presently conceived, and other prosecutable sexual activities, such as fornication, adultery, and bigamy."[35] In the Bridewell accounts, "all of these behaviors were labeled using the blanket term 'whoredom,' and that term also could be used to prosecute any of a variety of unruly female behaviors, from incest to scolding."[36] The language of "whoredom," like other terms such as "sodomy" and "adultery," derives from a biblical idiom.[37] And like the concept of adultery, the language of whoredom, to adopt the argument of David Turner, tended to make "no conceptual or linguistic distinction between different types of offence, or between casual sexual encounters and longer-term affairs."[38] This plasticity of sexual reference meant that "bawd" could be applied to someone who tolerated illicit sex; "whore" could be applied to someone who provided a pregnant woman lodging; and "adultery" could be used to describe the immoderate sex a man had with his own wife.[39] The confusions to which this indeterminacy gave rise are evident in a London consistory court case of 1627, in which Theodosia Merill was slandered by the accusation that she gave money to a man named Norton "to be his whore." Gowing observes of this case: "even when it is the man who receives the money, it is still the woman who is the whore."[40] In addition to the gendered double standard, this piece of slander conveys the extent that, *pace* Foucault, it is not only sodomy that was an "utterly confused category."[41]

Consider, for instance, the numerous early modern English cognates for "whore" identified by literary critic Stephen Spiess; they include "Ambulant-rice," "Apron Mountant," "Autem-Mort," "Backslider," "Bawdy Basket," "Blowzabella," "Carriage," "Cockhorse," "Concony," "Croshabell," "Daughter of the Game," "Doxy," "Driggle-draggle," "Flax-Wench," "Flirt-gill," "Galled Goose of Winchester," "Giglet," "Hackney," "Horn-maker," "Jade," "Laced-mutton," "Limax," "Mutton," "Naught-pack," "Presbyte-rian Dog," "Punchable Nun," "Rotten Medlar," "Sixpenny Damnation," "Smock-rampant," "Surfeiter," "Trugmoldie," "Waistecoater," and "Wres-tler."[42] This dizzying array of terms, selected from a list compiled by Spiess of more than 340, not only indicates the creative fecundity of early modern sex talk in an era of rapid linguistic coinage and proliferation,[43] it also speaks, as Spiess argues, to an underlying anxiety about what it might mean—what knowledge processes might be required—to *know* "the whore." The question "How does one know or identify another as a whore?" leads Spiess to argue that "perceived evidentiary problems . . . serve as forms of evidence in their own right, pointing to cultural impasses that constitute meanings and incur potent cultural effects."[44] Spiess provides compelling examples of the ways in which the "terms of whoredom" both incited and troubled categorical distinctions. Tensions between ambiguity and exactitude, connotation and denotation, the assumed and unknown, all fueled contemporary interest in, and the use of, these terms. To this I would add that scrutinizing "whore" as

a conceptual category leads not only to questions of signification and interpretation, or to evidentiary problems in the history of sexuality, but to the
instability and obscurity of the linguistic substrate upon which such hermeneutic and historiographic procedures depend. Whoredom is not just an evidentiary problem, or a problem of historiography, or of epistemology, or of
language—it is all of these at once.

Sex, Copia, Materiality

Prompted by the nexus of problems that beset the term "whore," I turn now
to the impasses created by the early modern language of sex more generally.
I begin historiographically, noting some of the characteristics of the culture's
sexual lexicon. Since lexicons as we understand them today were just beginning to emerge in the form of hard word lists, bilingual translation dictionaries, and glossaries of Old English, I am using the term broadly to describe
the culture's available sexual vocabulary. Chapter 6 presented the more common terms for "sex," its acts, and participants: lust, lewdness, licentiousness,
lasciviousness, lechery; incontinence, concupiscence, wantonness, bawdry,
venery; coition, fornication, copulation, consummation; deflower, devirginate, lie with, swive, fuck; sodomy, buggery, bestiality, pederasty, tribadry,
masturbation; adultery, incest, bigamy; whore, cuckold, cuckquean, wittol,
libertine; unnatural villainy, carnal knowledge, carnal congression, vice, and
rite of love. My aim was to suggest that this language is curiously devoid of
specific corporeal information, gesturing vaguely toward nebulous behaviors
(which scholars fill in presumptively) or referring the meaning of sex to the
social relations it underpins, expresses, and creates. The force of hazy implication, I suggested, is one means by which the critical habit of presumptive
knowledge is aided and abetted by language itself.

Let us now delve further into the sexual lexicon. A host of early modern
terms with nonsexual meanings were used to denote sexual activities. Among
the verbs are "abuse," "converse," "corrupt," "cover," "defile," "do,"
"embrace," "enjoy," "free," "frequent," "handle," "hug," "jest," "keep company," "labour," "nygle," "occupy," "persuade," "pervert," "play," "pleasure," "pump," "sleep with," "stir," "use," and "yield." Add to this list those
verbs used to denote more specific sexual activities (some of them discrete in
their connotations, some of them quite broad): "bill," "clap," "clip," "coll,"
"expend," "finger," "firk," "fondle," "frig," "itch," "knock," "niggle,"

"sard," "shave," "spend," "sport," "taste," "tickle," "tongue," "top," "toy," "tup," "raise up," "rub," "wap."[45] Nouns specifying sexual activity include "appetite," "affection," "amorousness," "beastliness," "carriage," "conversation," "dalliance," "debauchery," "exercise," "fault," "flesh," "foulness," "game," "immodesty," "infidelity," "intercourse," "luxuriousness," "naught," "obscene," "passion," "pollution," "unchasteness," "uncleanness," "traffic," "trade," "tryst," "tumble," and the Latin legal formulas *rem in re* and *res in re* (thing in thing).[46]

The lexicon of sex also includes terms referring to the body. The female genitals in general and the vagina in particular (the *OED* dates "vagina" itself to 1682) are called "bit," "box," "breach," "cunt," "cut," "case," "clef," "commodity," "cony," "cunnie," "crack," "eye," "fig," "flower," "fruit dish," "naught," "hell," "hole," "lap," "low countries," "medlar," "mons veneris," "Netherlands," "pantofle," "parke," "placket," "privity," "purse," "quaint," "ring," "scut," "secret parts," "slit," "sweetmeats," "tail," "thing," "treasure," "waist," "whibb bob," "wound," and "woman's modesty." The hymen is a "maidenhead," "virgin's zone," and "virgin's knot." The uterus is referred to as a "bag," "bottle," "field of nature," "fountain," "matrix," "purse," "vessel," and "womb." Breasts are referred to as "bosom," "bubbies," "dugs," "mammets," "niplets," and "paps." The clitoris is an "aestrum veneris," "contemptus viorum," "dulcedo amoris," "female yard," "fury and rage of love," "paenis faeminaeus," "tentigo," and "the seate of woman's delight."

As for male genitals, the penis is a "bauble," "bit," "catso," "cock," "dick," "epididymis," "gear," "hanger," "horn," "instrument," "lance," "meat," "member," "organ," "pole," "pintle," "pizzle," "prick," "rod," "root," "stake," "sword," "syringe," "tail," "thing," "tool," "weapon," and "yard." Testicles are "balls," "ball-bags," "bollocks," "cods," "cullions," "jewels," "nuts," "stewed prunes," and "stones." The ass is an "arse," "bottom," "breech," "bum," "posterior," "rump," and "tail." The anus is a "bumhole," "fundament," "hole," "naught," "slit," "nockandroe," and "tail." Semen is "pith," "marrow," "nature," "seed," "sperme," and "spirit."

To this we can add a lexicon of sex based on the gender of partners. Sex between males was not confined to the well-known terms "sodomite" (traceable at least to 1300) and "buggerer" (traceable at least to the 1550s). In the sixteenth century, a variety of other terms began to circulate: "bardash" (ca. 1548), "ganymede" (ca. 1591), "ingle" and "ningle " (ca. 1592), "catamite" (ca. 1593), "pathic" (ca. 1603), and "paederast" (ca. 1613).[47] Broader terms for male-male eroticism include "boy-love," "male-mingled love," "male ven-ery," "masculine love," and "virile love."[48] Terms for sex between women include "confricatrice," "female sodomite," "fricatrice," "hermaphrodite," "rubster," "sodomita," "sodomitesse," and "tribade."[49]

What are we to make of this lexicon? First we might note its sheer *copia*—and I have not attempted to make these lists comprehensive. This is not a culture made verbally skittish by protocols of modesty or decorum; with the exception of terms for sex between women, its sexual vocabulary is prolix.[50] Ian Moulton credits Pietro Aretino for creating a pornographic idiom in which an "endless variety of objects and actions . . . can be eroticized,"[51] but this generative expansiveness, I would argue, is a fundamental feature of the culture's sexual language. On the one hand, this expansiveness is a function of English's location at the intersection, and as a "promiscuous" absorber, of other languages. Although some sexual terms are drawn from or build upon English words of Anglo-Saxon origin, there's also a fair amount of assimilat-ing of French, Latin, and Italian as well. On the other hand, this expansive-ness draws its energies from a range of physical actions, as evinced by the most common locutions: picking a lock, pounding an anvil, piercing a bod-kin, jousting with a lance, stealing a treasure, and laying siege. The experience of daily activities provided a seemingly endless source for new sexual meta-phors. As Patricia Simons notes, "Everyday deeds like coagulating or grating cheese, ploughing a field, watering a garden, tapping a beer key or wine barrel, blowing on a fire or into a balloon, turning a tap, stirring or ladling a pot, or urinating while standing up, could bring to mind an old joke or spur the formation of a new quip, a novel image, all the while reinforcing standard biological knowledge."[52]

Such earthy materiality is one of the distinctive qualities of early modern sex talk. As any reader of eighteenth-century pornography might observe, later sexual discourse, while every bit as verbose, sounds remarkably different. Fanny's erotic vocabulary in John Cleland's *Memoirs of a Woman of Pleasure* (1748–49), for instance, layers description upon florid description, drawing primarily upon elevated idioms of animal spirits, bodily sensations, and emo-tional sensibilities. Fanny's tropes depend on the heating and itching caused by intense suffusions of blood and a mind-blowing transcendence sparked by fiery passions. In part because of the Galenic humoralism that governed many ideas about the early modern body, the earlier idiom of sex instead privileges material bodies and body parts over emotions, sensations, and abstractions. Scholars have argued that words functioned as things in the early modern world;[53] to that we might add that both the body and the sexual acts in which it engaged are substantialized in early modern sex talk as tangibly "thingy" entities engaged in robustly physicalized forms of connection.

Nonetheless, a paradox underlies this materiality: these thingy body parts, and the earthy uses to which they are put, are rarely precisely specified in a one-to-one relation of signifier to signified. To what *specific* sexual activity does "tapping a beer keg" or "ladling a pot" actually refer? In the ballad "The Seven Merry Wives of London," part of a genre that differentiates sexual prowess by trades, the one wife who does not complain about her husband's sexual performance admits that "she had no kind of cause to complain of these wrongs, / For he follow'd his labor with hammer and tongs."[54] To what body part does "tongs" refer, and what "labor" are the hammer and tongs actually doing? The question extends beyond the failure of signifiers to express their referents, or that kegs and ladles, hammers and tongs, are figurative. What differentiates the indeterminacy of sex talk from that of talk in general, then, is that fingers and penises and tongues all can fill a hole, while hands, mouths, and eyes each can caress; however, what is filled and caressed is not determined or limited by physiological function. Moreover, when one attempts to follow the analogical logic implied by a ladle in a pot, one's erotic imagination might well falter. Considered alongside firking flounders and kissing scallops, such referential ambiguity and obscurity begin to take on the status of constitutive features of early modern sex talk.

Bodily Latitudes

If obscurity limns the early modern sexual lexicon, why have scholars not addressed it? Why do most professional readers of sexual language act as though they know exactly what early modern sexual terminology means? Given that queer studies scholars have only recently challenged this sense of certainty,[55] my suspicion is that it is a result of the field formation in which early modern sex has been studied. Our collective inattention, I submit, is due to a convergence of two related but differently motivated trajectories present in both literary and historical work. Just as early modernists began thinking in critically sophisticated ways about sex, many were also thinking hard about gender inequality. The upshot is that inquiry into sexual idioms has tended to focus on metaphors of phallic penetration that seem to express and reinforce gendered power differentials.[56] Although the queering of early

modern scholarship has certainly shifted the emphasis, it remains the case
that the majority of early modern historians and literary critics who have
written about sex in the last thirty years have emphasized that sex was a
matter of one person (usually male) doing something to someone else (usually, but not exclusively female), with sex generally linked to domination and
submission. The symbolics of relative bodily positions—that is, tops and
bottoms—have been readily incorporated into this critical force field. The
"unnatural," sodomitical inversions connoted by such concepts as "arsiver-
sie" and the preposterous,[57] while critically reversing or challenging certain
assumptions, nonetheless are often congruent with the view that sex is a
unidirectional matter of penetration and/as domination.[58] The tropology of
sex, in other words, came to be considered as both a result of and a prime
mover in the ongoing success of patriarchy.

The seamless congruence of power and language evident in this critical
trajectory depends upon and reinforces the gendered essentialism that inheres
in the critical concept of "heterosexuality." In 1996, Gowing voiced a growing consensus when she argued that "gender was figured, and gender difference played out, in the light of the definition of the category of women
through the practice of heterosexuality. The primal scene of gender relations
and gender difference was heterosexual relations."[59] But what did that "playing out" of the meanings of gender as power *mean*? When it came to sex, did
the advantage always fall to men? Did sex always eventuate in and reinforce
male dominance? If so, how does this supposition square with the widespread
assumption, present throughout early modern discourse and explicitly promoted in medicine and theology, that women were by nature more lustful
than men? Are such views only indices of a compensatory misogyny, a masculinist projection onto women of the curse of Eve?

Feminist scholarship on the early modern period remains divided on the
question of whether the representation of women's erotic power is a sign of
male misogyny or an expression of female agency. Rather than attempt to
resolve this debate, it is useful to trace what words themselves have to say
about this question. Consider, for instance, the term that Gowing asserts was
"the most common word early modern women and men used for heterosexual sex" during church court litigation: "occupy."[60] The lexicographer of
slang Eric Partridge maintained that "occupy" meant "to copulate with (a
woman), with an allusion to the two senses, 'take and retain possession of'
(as in warfare) and 'to keep (a person) busy.' "[61] Gowing accordingly argues
that "men occupied women; the image carries the implication that only one

man can occupy, and possess a woman at once."[62] The hierarchical and transitive qualities of "occupy" are obvious in the sense of "possession," and they occur in grim fashion in John Florio's bilingual dictionary *A Worlde of Wordes* (1598), in his translation of the Italian "Trentuno": "a punishment inflicted by ruffianly fellowes uppon raskalie whores in Italy, who (as we pump them in England) so they cause them to be occupide one and thirtie times by one and thirtie severall base raskalie companions. Also an occupying of one and thirtie times to such a common hedge whore or overridden jade, as we say in England a pumping of a common whore."[63] But "occupy" may be less securely or exclusively related to male acts of penetration and possession than this horrific gang rape imagines. Women are recorded as "occupying" men; and couldn't one keep a person, a body, busy in different ways?[64]

The relevant definitions of "occupy" in the *OED* in this period move across transitive and intransitive meanings: "8 a. *trans.* To have sexual intercourse or relations with. b. *intr.* To have sexual intercourse or relations; to cohabit." For this last definition, the *OED* quotes Florio's dictionary: "A good wench, one that occupies freely." Does Florio mean that the woman is happy to be occupied or is happy to do the occupying? Like the inversion of the terms of whoredom in the case of Theodosia Merill, the transitive and intransitive nature of "occupy" suggests that there may exist considerable latitude *within* the signifying function of certain sexual words, latitude that confutes the question of who is doing what to whom.

The Good, the Bad, and the Euphemistic

Capitalizing on such latitude was a primary strategy of early modern writers of poetry, stage plays, and pornography. From idealizations of romantic love to satiric burlesque, from extended metaphorical conceits to fast-paced banter, from winking double entendre to obscene puns, writers not only exploited the semiotic aptitude of words to mean more than one thing but they consistently called attention to their wit in doing so. They also created their own sexual lexicons. Writing about pornographic texts, Sarah Toulalan, for instance, argues that

> the clever use of language, of metaphor, euphemism, double entendre, pun, and allusion, is an integral part of early modern pornographic representation. Authors, perhaps in imitation of Aretino, repeat and pile up image upon

image, metaphor upon metaphor, in a way that becomes paradoxically as
explicit as using more direct language. In this way authors also create an alternative language of the obscene in which repeatedly used words, phrases, and
metaphors become instantly recognizable in their double meaning, and in
some cases are so close to the original obscene word that authors really must
be teasing their readers in substituting one for the other: there is no need to
use "cunt" when "cut" serves just as well, if not better, in that it brings with
it a wealth of meaning.[65]

Toulalan's appreciation of pornography's use of "metaphor and allusion" to
"create an alternative language of the obscene" provides a welcome critical
entrée into the functionality of sexual figuration, to the ways that such figuration actually *works*. But why does Toulalan take recourse in the concept of
"origin" here? Two possibilities come to mind. First, metaphors are conventionally understood to rely on an "original," "literal" meaning that is then
modified through the tropological transfer of meaning from one thing to
another. Second, the notion of an "original obscene word" would seem to
locate particular words as closer to the body and to sex acts, while other
words, supposedly less literal, more replete with figuration, are more distant.
This accords with the view that certain words for body parts are "primary
obscenities," which "are perceived as having an unusually close connection
with the thing they designate."[66] To the extent that certain words possess
what Joan DeJean calls a "peculiar physicality,"[67] this attribution of primacy
seems fair enough. But how, exactly, is "cut" less obscene or offensive than
"cunt"? How is "cut" less literal, more metaphoric? How are "pole" or
"stake" or "rod" or "tool" any less explicit or more metaphoric than "prick,"
especially insofar as "prick" enjoys a broad range of definitions (to penetrate,
to finger an instrument, to notate music, to sew)? To adopt the idiom of
linguists (if only to suggest that these binary categories fail to secure distinctions): which of these is a denotation, which a connotation?

These questions are closely linked to the concept of "euphemism," which
has served as an unacknowledged keyword in the critical practice of identifying sex in language. What is the difference between an "obscene word" and
a "euphemism"? Between an outright obscenity, a "bawdy" innuendo, and
circumlocution? What, after all, *is* "euphemism"? Defined by linguists as
"sweet talking," and contrasted to both "straight talking" (orthophemism)
and "speaking offensively" (dysphemism),[68] "euphemism" is defined in the
OED as "that figure of speech which consists in the substitution of a word

or expression of comparatively favourable implication or less unpleasant associations, instead of the harsher or more offensive one that would more precisely designate what is intended." Arising in the late sixteenth century as "euphemismus," "euphemism" was defined in Thomas Blount's *Glossographia* in 1656 as "a good or favourable interpretation of a bad word."[69] In this respect, euphemism enacts a form of moralized metonymy. Yet, when it comes to language, good and bad are not self-evident. Indeed, the concept of "euphemism" seems above all an indicator of a word's affective register, indicating correspondence to or deviation from protocols of politeness and decorum in given situations. It thus attempts to universalize presumptive notions of good and bad, appropriate and inappropriate, decorous and indecorous, polite and offensive. Like the concept of "malapropism," which similarly enjoins a moral prescription, the concept of "euphemism," to adopt the words of Lynne Magnusson, "both assists and obfuscates our struggle to historicize and understand" early modern language.[70] "Obfuscates" because, as Magnusson and others have argued, the idea of "correct" and "incorrect" word choice is one that derives from the lexical standardization and prescriptivism that postdates the early modern period. Since the designation of good and bad is as much a social as a linguistic operation ("one person's euphemism is another's dysphemism"),[71] and politeness is an effect of culturally and historically specific "civilizing processes" that are "above all a monument to the significance of taboos—concerning bodily functions in particular—that were previously neither clearly established nor universally accepted,"[72] we might seek some epistemological strategies to handle the affective and philological problems that the concept of "euphemism" raises.

For starters, we might dispense with a presumptive division between literal and figurative meanings,[73] and thereby create more space in the early modern sexual landscape for alternative procedures for addressing sexual speech. Despite the widespread notion that there is such a thing as "dirty words," there is little that objectively secures an ontological difference between the explicit and figurative, straight talk and circumlocution, conventional language and obscenity. As linguists Keith Allan and Kate Burridge remark in response to Aretino's pornographic writings, "it depends on the context of use whether terms such as *arse/ass*, *prick*, *cunt*, and *fuck* are orthophemistic or dysphemistic."[74] Such qualities depend on how words are used and received. "Cunt," they argue, is "the most tabooed word in English" but is not as taboo in other languages; nor was it taboo, despite having the same denotation as today, in the medieval period, when it was employed in people's

surnames and a street in London was called "Gropecuntelane."[75] Although
Williams says that the word was becoming obscene by the sixteenth century,
Florio included "cunt" in his definition of the Italian *potta* ("a womans privie
parts, a cunt, a quaint"),[76] and it is difficult to derive from its typical usage
whether it was considered more or less obscene than "privie parts," more or
less vulgar than "quaint." Indeed, the apprehension that reception of such
words would vary provoked early modern medical writers, from James I's anat-
omist Helkiah Crooke to the prolific popularizer Nicholas Culpeper to the
midwife Jane Sharp, to worry that writing about sexual generation in the
vernacular—a revolutionary decision that attracted a far larger readership—was
dangerous. Despite their tendency to resort to Latin at moments when their
anxiety about charges of obscenity surfaced, they could not fail to notice that
"clitoris," "paenis faeminaeus," and "tentigo" are no more or less obscene or
potentially titillating than "female yard" or "seat of women's delight." Aware
of the potential erotic frisson of *all* such terms, they merely reiterated their
hope that readers would "use as much modesty in the perusal of" their work,
as the authors "have endeavoured to do in the writing of it."[77]

Needless to say, such instabilities, slippages, and overlaps within the language of sex are made even more complex by the synchronic variability and
diachronic transformations of language. Synchronically, many words are
polysemic: they possess several potential meanings simultaneously. This
capacity provides one foundation for punning (another foundation is the
homonymic aptitude of words that mean different things to sound alike, such
as Hamlet's inference that "country matters . . . lie between maids' legs").[78]
Such meanings, of course, are also subject to historical changes in use, which
philologists attempt to recover as etymology. The two processes of synchronic
and diachronic transformation are interrelated: in both instances "two
similar-sounding but distinct signifiers are brought together, and the surface
relationship between them is invested with meaning through the inventiveness and rhetorical skill of the writer. If that meaning is in the form of a
postulated connection between present and past, what we have is etymology;
if it is in the form of a postulated connection within the present, the result is
word-play."[79]

But wordplay is also a diachronic process, as Zachary Lesser details in his
analysis of the editorial reception of Hamlet's reference to "country matters"
in the second quarto and the folio editions.[80] Lesser argues that the "supposed
obscene pun" on "cunt" "was never simply self-evident" and was "just beginning to be heard when Q1" (the first quarto, with its alternative reference to

"contrary matters") reappeared in 1823.[81] Many earlier readers failed to register any connection between the two words and, says Lesser, it was only the belated appearance of Q1 that determined the obscene and now standard reading of this passage. Indeed, to consider language as a synchronic structure enacts what Derek Attridge calls "a methodological hypostatization," because "a synchronic state" of language "is never consistent with itself."[82] Furthermore, whatever multiple meanings did at one time obtain are subject to transformation over time. Allan and Burridge, for instance, note that a euphemism "often degenerates into a dysphemism through contamination by the taboo topic," citing the "Latin *penis* 'tail' [which previously] had been a euphemism for *mentula*."[83] They note that "occupy" actually lost its nontaboo meanings for a time, only to regain them "after it had ceased to be used" as a word for sex.[84] (Today "to occupy each other" sounds more like you are headed to a protest on Wall Street than to bed.)

One of the more wayward diachronic trajectories of a sexual keyword is that of "fuck." Along with other four-letter words like "cunt," "twat," and "crap," its etymology is uncertain.[85] Some linguists believe it to be related to the Middle Dutch verb *fokken* or the German *ficken* (to strike).[86] "Fuck" seems to have first appeared in Scotland around 1503 in a piece of flyting, that versatile art of insult that, in this case, probably circulated in manuscript and was possibly performed as entertainment at the Scottish court. "Fuck" comes to us, as much sexual satire from the period does, in an attack against the prelacy: "Bischops . . . may fuck thair fill and be vnmaryit."[87] "Fuck" appeared in 1598 in Florio's *A Worlde of Wordes*, defining the Italian *fottarie*, "japings, sardings, swivings, fuckings"; *fottitrice*, "a woman fucker, swiver, sarder, or japer"; *fottitore*, "a japer, a sarder, a swiver, a fucker, an occupier"; and *fottitura*, "a japing, a swiving, a fucking, a sarding, an occupying."[88] It first appeared on the public stage by means of playwrights' witty translinguistic malapropisms and comic double entendres. Shakespeare introduced it through two sly homophonic puns: one on "focative/vocative," voiced by the Welsh schoolmaster Evans during a schoolboy's Latin lesson in *The Merry Wives of Windsor* (1597–98),[89] and one on "foot/foutre," voiced by Princess Katherine during her language lesson in *Henry V* (1599).[90] In Thomas Dekker and John Webster's *Northward-Hoe* (1607), the Dutchman Hans Van Belch describes his father as "de grotest fooker in all Ausbrough,"[91] in a scene that not only renders comic the phonetic similarities between Dutch and English (*fokker* is Dutch for "cattle-breeder") but, in its printed form, employs typography to both imprint and confute distinctions between the two languages.[92]

In *The Alchemist*, Drugger refers to a cosmetic as a "fucus," which Face understands (or pretends to understand) as "fuck" (2.4.33). The word appears in a defamation case from Somerset in 1600 as an insult directed toward an alekeeper's wife: "she fucketh in every corner with every knave that cometh to thy house."[93] Through repeated use since then, "fuck" has become something *other* than a double entendre, something that functions simultaneously as the Ur-word for what many would refer to as *the* sexual act, as well as a capacious catchall whose use extends from the insulting "motherfucker" to the abject "fuck me."[94]

Stock Phrases and Carnal Unknowing

Recognizing the function of "euphemism" in sex talk encourages an approach to words attentive to their synchronic and diachronic dimensions, as well as to the ways that, as a concept, "euphemism" supports a bid to stabilize sexual language. Another critical concept to which similar analytical pressure might be applied is that of "stock phrases." This is a concept to which early modern historians and critics who write about official proceedings such as legal depositions, as well as those penning editorial commentary, frequently resort in order to insist that a first-person, autobiographical, self-expressive voice is rarely manifest in documents of trials for sexual immorality. All traces of "what really happened" in a bastardy or rape case come to us via formulaic conventions, employed by scribes whose job it was to translate the messiness of oral testimony into a clearly articulated deposition. According to gender historians, in particular, the result of stock phrases has been the elision of women's voices and agency in both sex and the courtroom.

In stock phrases such as "had carnal copulation," "dealt carnally," "committed whoredom," "had the use of her body," "abused my body," "worked his pleasure," "defyled my body," "were naughtie together," "unnatural use," and "committed unnatural villanies," bodies meet in ways that vacate from sexual encounters the quality of affective dimensionality. Particularly when parties are asymmetrically positioned—*his* pleasure, *my* body—stock phrasing evacuates from the "occupied body" any sense of subjective agency and along with it any possibility of mutuality, as indicated by unidirectional verbs such as "had," "dealt," "abused," "worked," "defyled," and "committed." In addition to conveying an assumed gender hierarchy, "stock phrases" indicate a complex mode of *carnal unknowing*. Sharing with "euphemism" an attempt to transit impolite sexual speech up the ladder of decorum, relying on and enforcing a kind of studied imprecision, they simultaneously gesture toward and occlude whatever forms of sex actually occurred.[95] The locution regularly applied to sodomy—"Unfit to be mentioned among Christians"—is the most obvious instance of how a desire not to say is related to a desire not to know. Stock phrases meet—indeed, become—euphemisms at precisely this juncture of desire and knowledge. Like the deliberate inexactness of euphemisms, the indefinition of stock phrases means that they neglect to actually designate or describe particulars. The repetition of such formulas over time only further concretizes the phenomena of presumptive unknowing.

There may be historically specific reasons for this unknowing and affective voiding. Historians agree that Bridewell governors, intent on identifying brothels, their personnel, and their clientele, were not particularly interested in the reasons for a woman's "fall" into prostitution or her subjective experience of participating in the "trade."[96] Nor, I would add, did they seem to be particularly concerned with the actual sex in which alleged perpetrators engaged. We can see this indifference in a presentment against William Comer by two husbands whose wives paid Comer with expensive gifts for a night of pleasure that culminated in "the naughty and filthy acte in defylyng of Kelleys wife and Rasalls wife in one Bed."[97] As Panek notes of this threesome:

> Whatever was going on, the language of the court books seems curiously inaccurate in describing it: Comer is accused of being a "common Bawde Broker for the defylyng and entisyng of mennes wifes, and a picker and receaver of soch things as they can purloyne from their husbands," but there is no suggestion that he attempted to turn the wives to prostitution, which is the usual meaning of "enticing," not to mention "bawd," nor is there any indication that he stole ("picked") the goods in question, or fenced for the wives that they "purloyned," as a "receiver" would do. Calling this particular scoundrel a "Bawde Broker," a "picker," or a "receaver" suggests a not wholly successful attempt to assimilate Comer's behavior to conventional terms.[98]

Notable as the governors' "inaccuracy" is for a case that involves not only male prostitution but a ménage à trois, I would suggest that its elusiveness on the matter of sex is in fact business as usual.

Such inexplicitness also characterizes the discourse of those who presided over church courts, who seem to have been more concerned with determining the basic facts of broken spousals and sexual slander than with the details of what kinds of sex might have established a marriage promise or compromised a person's reputation. Martin Ingram maintains that "it was really only the full sexual act that was of interest to the law: kissing, cuddling, 'tumbling', and the like were very rarely, in themselves, the subject of prosecution."[99] But in modestly referring to "the full sexual act," Ingram unwittingly implies that the "interest" of the law was not all that specific. Was their presumptive knowledge the same as ours? It would seem that the social ramifications of illicit sex (the flouting of sacred marriage vows, the financial provision for bastards, the destruction of sexual reputation) were more significant to officials than the accused's sexual acts. With the exception of the capital crime of sodomy (generally subject to a higher court where proof of penetration supposedly was required to secure a verdict),[100] and interrogations of alleged witches concerning carnal copulation with the devil (largely a Continental phenomenon),[101] specificity of sex at the level of the act seems to have generated little official English concern.[102]

Recognizing that such details may not have been pertinent to the quest to suppress immorality, we might nonetheless reexamine the way stock phrases encourage scholars to bypass the granular particulars of erotic encounters. Consider, for example, one 1598 deposition about adultery, reportedly based on an eyewitness account, from Bridewell. This deposition, as Frances Dolan puts it, is "crammed with arresting details: the detrimental effects of dairy consumption on gear [phallic] performance, sea-water-green-hose, yard hygiene, lunch preparation, and a postcoital toast."[103] Dolan's astute analysis of this document culls out of its narrative the motives of the female deponent, the audience for and emplotment of her deposition, the broader discursive conditions of the court, and the conventions that compose the "genre of the adultery story."[104] In contrast to this narrative plenitude, sex, she observes, "is the most tersely and formulaically described exchange" in the deposition.[105]

This document does indeed use the formula "had carnal copulation with her" in lieu of a more vivid description. But this stock phrase does not delineate the whole sexual action, the details of which challenge the active/passive gendering implied by the formula itself.[106] The deponent, Clement Underhill, initiates sex with Michael Fludd (not her husband) when she reportedly says to him, "eat no more cheese for that it will make your gear short and I mean to have a good turn of you soon." Further evidence of the urgency of

Clement's sexual intent is found in the early stage of their encounter when she accosts him with a rapier; this induces him to take "her in his arms" and bring her to bed, whereupon "she put her hand into his hose" and as "he plucked up her clothes to her thighs, she plucked them up higher." The details of their physical interaction vacillate between lively specificity and banal generality: "then he went up to her upon the bed and putting down his hose had carnal copulation with her and having so done he wiped his yard on her smock." Stock phrases like "had carnal copulation with her" do justice neither to these details nor to Clement's agency. Nor do they answer other questions inquiring minds might want to know: how long did their interaction last, what positions did they assume, did Clement achieve orgasm, did Michael come inside or outside her body? To recognize that these questions are simultaneously raised and left unanswered by the deposition is to recognize that a process of carnal unknowing underlies even the most successful efforts to produce knowledge out of sex talk. Insofar as speech about sex tends to depend on, solicit, and deflect the desire to know,[107] early modern sex talk manifests a particular form of indeterminacy—one that depends not only on the vagaries of language but upon the relations of knowledge to sex.

Bawdy Lexicons

In placing some pressure on feminist approaches to sex and language, I do not mean to imply that women's sexual speech and behavior were not carefully regulated. As previously described, "this was a culture in which it was positively virtuous not to be able to describe sex,"[108] giving rise to a situation in which, as Garthine Walker notes, it is "grimly ironic that in juridical discourse women's accusations of rape epitomised the lightness and wantonness of female speech."[109] The gendered double bind of female sexual reputation was redoubled in the legal arena because in that context "penetrative sex was constructed as an engagement of male will and female submission. Talking about rape as sex (a legal imperative) therefore implied the very submission, or consent, that was necessarily absent in rape."[110]

But as the case of Clement Underhill and Michael Fludd attests, while the legal arena may have had the final say about defining and punishing sexual immorality, it did not have the only say about the gendering of sexual will and submission. Such topics were of widespread interest and considerable debate. Over the course of the late sixteenth and seventeenth centuries, the growing availability of cheap print—ballads, chapbooks, jestbooks, and pamphlets—fostered an increasingly public "plebeian sexual culture."[111] Despite gendered notions of propriety that aimed to enforce divisions of sexual speech, women actively participated in that sexual culture, not only through neighborhood gossip but through entertainments such as singing, listening, or reading bawdy ballads,[112] watching and listening to jigs in the public playhouse,[113] and making or listening to sexually knowing jests.[114] These oral forms often positioned women as narrators as well as active, desiring agents in the plot. Ballads, jigs, and jests, in particular, enabled singers and speakers to perform a sexually replete repertoire that seems to have been especially concerned with infidelity, cuckoldry, and male sexual inadequacy. Their perspectives on these issues are more complex than most studies allow; they run the gamut from female complaints about seduction, rape, unwanted pregnancy, and abandonment to male complaints about domineering wives and deceitful whores, from canny female itemizations of male sexual traits and failures to celebrations of women's erotic victories over their hapless husbands or would-be seducers. Within the scope of oral performance, the gendering of agency was mobile: the dependence on a first-person persona, the use of dramatic dialogue, and switches in point of view between the first and third person enabled opportunities for both tellers and listeners to identify and imagine sexual emplacement across categories of gender and status.[115] Furthermore, the lyrics of many ballads and jigs and the enigmatic punch lines of many riddles and jests depended heavily on sexual innuendo, double entendres, and puns, while the performance of any particular tune could emphasize or deemphasize the sexual content through the use of gesture and facial expression. By the late seventeenth century, these forms of sexual speech were "emphatically part of a public discourse shared by all classes."[116]

It remains an open question whether women participated as agents of sexual speech in writing prior to the Restoration, and in particular whether explicit expressions of sex were possible by genteel women. Scholarship on women writers has tended toward reticence on sexual matters, except insofar as "sex" is represented by the self-lacerating desire of Petrarchan poets such as Lady Mary Wroth or through prose meditations on reproduction, maternity, and female virtue. Yet, the more direct sexual expression of Restoration writers such as Aphra Behn did not come out of nowhere—even if it was given significant support by the changing conditions of political speech, a publicly eroticized court culture, and the movement of women onto the professional stage. It may be that scholars have not yet learned to see sex in Renaissance women's writing because they have assumed a too-tight correlation between the protocols of female authorship and patriarchal injunctions of female modesty.[117]

Be that as it may, both direct and indirect sexual speech was a staple of plays written after the 1580s. Such speech was put in the mouths of characters across gender, age, and status lines. Indeed, Renaissance dramatic wordplay had, by the 1940s, come to be perceived as so pervasive, inventive, and baffling that contemporary critics began to develop a lexicography wholly dedicated to it. Adopting the term "bawdy" from early modern usage,[118] Eric Partridge, in his influential compiling of sexual words in *Shakespeare's Bawdy* (first published in 1947), spearheaded a critical tradition that picked up steam in the 1970s and has continued apace. Scholars have identified, defined, and collated sexual metaphor, innuendo, double entendre, puns, and jokes into dictionaries of "bawdy language," as well as into more localized glossaries, concordances, and commentaries for slang in Shakespeare, Stuart literature, and "street literature."[119] For many critics, the concept of "bawdy language" has been an essential, if undertheorized, tool in the critic's toolbox. Indeed, even if the phrase itself now seems impossibly quaint, "bawdy language" remains a go-to concept for a range of early modern critics, providing foundational support for various critical practices, including those of a less taxonomic and more "readerly" persuasion. For instance, Stephen Booth's anatomization of the dense levels of erotic signification in Shakespeare's sonnets, which paid particular attention to multilayered puns and extended conceits, offered what he has come to call "close reading without readings."[120] Patricia Parker's rhetorical analyses of how class, gender, and eroticism inform wordplay, conversely, emphasized the conceptual coherence among select groups of words and showed how the consideration of linguistic forms opens onto a broad cultural and political arena.[121] Mary Bly directed the effects of wordplay out into the theater audience, demonstrating the extent to which obscene and obscure puns and innuendo provided the prime commodity of the short-lived Whitefriars theater company, as its repertoire created a "space for identification" through "bonds of shared laughter" catering to homoerotically inclined male theatergoers.[122] And Jeremy Lopez's analysis of "obvious, surface-level" puns, especially sexual puns, reveals that this form of linguistic "indulgence . . . is so prevalent, so all-pervasive in the best and worst drama of the period that it must be seen as one of the cornerstones of the fundamental kind of pleasure Elizabethan and Jacobean drama sought to provide."[123] Indeed, according to Lopez, "more than anything else, puns and verbal jokes in Renaissance drama tend toward the sexual. Sexual wordplay is therefore perhaps the best index we have for understanding the phenomena of punning and wordplay in general."[124]

The extent of what Lopez calls this "virtuosic vulgarity"[125] may partially help to explain the growth of what Spiess describes as an "endlessly proliferating Shakespearean 'sexicography,'" which he defines as "a quest to identify the 'bawdy' or 'filthy' inferences of every enigmatic idiom."[126] Linking this impulse to the processes of signification by which women get "whored," Spiess argues that the effort to read sex into ambiguous terms is both a result of the fecundity of figurative language and a disciplinary effort to fix or constrain "the terms of whoredom," which, he argues, actually "remained productively opaque during the period."[127]

I would modify Spiess's critique, however, by way of several caveats. First, it seems important to acknowledge changing critical temporalities: while most of the early work on "bawdy language" was historical only in the sense that it was philologically attentive, and while much of it was sexist and heteronormative and motivated by the desire to fix sexual meaning, those lexicons nonetheless served as a primary resource for critics intent on explicating the sexual meanings of individual words, as well as the intricate instances of wordplay to which they gave rise. However problematic was Partridge's *Shakespeare's Bawdy*,[128] for a long time it offered, at least for some of us, both a point of access to erotic meanings and professional legitimation of the effort to read sex in early modern literature.[129] Partridge's text was and remains a tool for queer resistance as well as a tool for normative discipline.

This disjunction between taxonomic purpose and practical use reminds us that lexicons, for all their organizing and classifying impulses, are not necessarily, *intrinsically*, disciplinary. Dictionaries of slang and in-group argot, such as those that began to appear in the context of gay liberation in the 1970s, for instance, were more invested in community building and providing access to new social worlds than in disciplining the use of language.[130] Furthermore, we might nuance the analysis of "sexicography" in terms of modern lexicographical forms and formats: disciplinary desires might be emphasized differently in a scholarly concordance than in a post-Johnsonian dictionary or glossary: whereas the latter aspires to a certain level of definitional exactitude, the former hinges its definitional aspirations on the specific *contexts* in which words appear and, by pointing the reader in various directions, opens the possibility of multiple interpretations.

It is within the context of the history of linguistic practices of "queer worlding,"[131] as well as the possibility of making such formal distinctions within "sexicography," that we might consider the most far-reaching analysis of the imbrication of early modern sex and words to date. Arguing that a host of everyday, commonplace, "unlikely" words—like "conversation," "foundation," "sweet," "boy," and "friend"—function as "'key words' within early modern lexicons and discourses of sex and gender," Jeffrey Masten, in his close, historicist scrutiny, proffers an essayistic glossary or, as he puts it, a "variorum" for analyzing both the alterity and the contiguities between past and present sexual lexicons and meanings.[132] Masten's own "glossary" of such terms neither attempts comprehensiveness nor proceeds alphabetically from *A* to *Z*; rather, it begins, queerly, with *Q*.[133] Even as Masten appropriates for queer theory the glossary and the gloss, queer philology shows words to be both the matter of, and able to exceed, the organizing rubrics of the letter, the alphabet, and the dictionary. Composing, literally, materially, "*text*urally," bodies in letters and letters in bodies,[134] activating etymology as both "the history of words" and "the history *in* words,"[135] queer philology resists the taxonomizing and normalizing impulses that Spiess rightly attributes to modern mainstream lexicographies of early modern English, while offering an enlarged vocabulary of sex, affect, and desire, as well as a theory of textual annotation.

Bawdy Reading

What, then, is the method of interpretation to which "bawdy language" refers? What kind of conceptual category, after all, *is* "bawdy language"?[136] "Bawdy" means "ribald," and "ribald" means "rough, indelicate, and unrefined"—which suggests that the concept of "bawdy" depends upon and promotes a particular notion of what sex is and what it means to press it into language.[137] "Bawdy," after all, is itself a homonymic pun on "body," and this mutually referential circuit of meaning clues us into the fact that the notion of "bawdy" depends on the body's materialization: it insists on body parts and functions as sexual in and of themselves. But what kinds of critical maneuvers does this category enable, and what does it foreclose? What would it mean to make "bawdy language" an object of inquiry, rather than a term that is used to describe or analyze other phenomena? What would it mean to not assert it as an always already constituted object? What might we then see about how "bawdy" words and concepts function, not only hermeneutically but epistemologically?

To date, the critical activity involved in reading for sex might best be described as hermeneutically circular and (theoretically at least) endlessly expansive. All too often critics encounter a definition of a term provided by a modern lexicon, concordance, or gloss, and then apply this definition to other, wholly different texts and contexts. They are encouraged to do so by lexicographical texts that participate in defining sex, which, through their seemingly decisive definitions and collations, establish the meaning of terms by reference to a specific (literary or discursive) context and then present these meanings as if they were independent of such contexts.[138] As one of the more responsible, and certainly the most capacious, of modern sexual lexicographers of the early modern period, Gordon Williams, maintains, his "concern has been primarily to establish certain image forms and verbal uses as a basis for evaluating such other examples as the user may encounter."[139] Yet many glossaries apply a closed circuit of cross-referencing in their examples, whereby textual quotations supplied for one word (say, the word "O") lead to other entries (like "ring" and "circle," defined as "anus" or "vagina") that problematically send one back to the quotations for the original word ("O").[140] With evidence conflated and context fading to the background, definitions become ossified, especially because the editorial tendency is to repeat prior glosses.[141] Scholars take recourse in dictionaries, glossaries, and concordances of "bawdy" as if they were manuals of transhistorical meaning and stable usage. And through pedagogical recourse to the gloss, teachers train students to do so as well.[142]

To take an obvious case: one of the most famous of Shakespeare's double entendres is Hamlet's command to Ophelia, "Get thee to a nunnery" (3.1.122), an injunction that is regularly glossed: "in Elizabethan slang, 'nunnery' could also mean 'brothel.'"[143] In his *Dictionary of Sexual Language and Imagery in Shakespearean and Stuart Literature*, Williams provides ample evidence that "nunnery" appeared in a range of texts with just that meaning.[144] The problem with relying on this evidence, however, is threefold. As Jennifer Drouin remarks, just because "we can read 'nunnery' as 'brothel' in some instances does not mean that we should in every case"[145]—a point made by E. A. M. Colman in 1974 and reiterated by editors who reject the illogic of such a pun, given that Hamlet is supposedly trying to dissuade Ophelia from "breeding."[146] Currently, editors tend to hedge their bets, with such statements as: "The word was *sometimes* used mockingly to refer to a brothel."[147]

My objection to this glossing of "nunnery" is less its dramatic irrelevance (I don't think Hamlet's motives in this scene are all that clear, nor do I think prostitutes were necessarily ignorant of pregnancy prevention) than the way dependence on it can close down the question of the historical relation between convents and brothels—that is, the social circumstances that gave rise to the conjunction of these concepts in the first place. To *equate* "nunnery" and "brothel" by reference to Elizabethan slang collapses the sociohistorical into a rarified sphere of literariness and fails to attend to the discourses through which this equation was forged: that nuns (and Catholics more generally) in Reformation England were regularly depicted through an antipapist rhetoric of sexual licentiousness, with female vows of chastity deemed the height of hypocrisy and deception.[148] Furthermore, as Drouin observes, we need not "read 'nunnery' as having two diametrically opposed meanings of chastity and whoredom. Rather, given that the term is ambiguous and polysemic, we may read it as both meanings at once, a place where chastity is preserved, but bawdy acts, that is, transgressive, non-reproductive sexuality, may occur under the protective guise of sanctified innocence."[149] The repetition of "brothel" for "nunnery" can render *Hamlet* less the recipient or purveyor of these cultural meanings and discourses than the authorizing frame of reference for explication of other texts. Without condoning the sexual squeamishness of some editors, one can still maintain that the hermeneutic circle thereby construed ends up *mis*construing the signifying latitude that exists within sexual language.

In the contemporary classroom, there is much to be said for pointing to a gloss in an edited text to authorize one's attempt to convince students that a given word or line or speech *is sexual*—that an erotic reading is not just a figment of the teacher's overheated imagination. It is not, therefore, that such pedagogical practices are wrong; they may be tactically advantageous for the larger projects of close reading and historicizing early modern sex. However, recourse to the gloss or the dictionary must also be seen as an authorizing fiction; it all too often depends upon and performs a historical sleight of hand, clouding the synchronic complexity of words as well as their diachronic transformations.[150] In light of this, what is needed is a more deliberately *theorized* account of glossing, one that is as attuned to the history of sex as it is to the history of language.

Queer philology, I suggest, provides an alternative to this hermeneutic circle and the linguistic essentialism it unwittingly supports. Although Masten is not explicit on this issue, his book gestures toward a baseline criterion for *how* to elucidate the queerness in early modern words. First, it is significant that most of the words in his lexicon do not operate mainly as puns or double entendres: boy, friend, lover, sweet. Although he does trace the presence and effects of sexual innuendo, Masten's analysis mostly attends to words whose erotic valences have been lost. And they have been lost because their meanings are all too familiar: "words that seem identical and familiar to modern eyes and tongues we might better see as false cognates ('false friends,' as we used to say in French class)—words that only *pass* as 'the same' as ours, words that, when pressed, release whole new contexts, while also holding within themselves the genealogical seeds of their eventual direction."[151] In addition to widening the scrutiny of sexual language to such "false cognates," Masten places analytical pressure on the material and cultural *ligatures* by which sex and words rub up against, sodomize, and befriend one another, as he adduces connections among words within an associational nexus. The "logically co-incidental" closeness of words composes a "cluster" that, in replacing genealogical reproduction with lateral affiliation, enacts a kind of linguistic voluntary kinship.[152] Hence, etymology in queer philology is less about a word's putative "origin" than about the ways in which meanings can "persist in a word and its surrounding discourse, as a diachronic record of practice in the midst of language as a synchronic system."[153] This hermeneutic process proceeds by reading simultaneously from context *inward* (from a word's "surrounding discourse") and from the history of the word (its "etymology") *outward*. Disrupting typical critical practices that contextualize words from the outside and then leave that generative context behind, Masten shows that it is words themselves that "*when pressed*, release whole new *contexts*."[154]

This double critical maneuver—inward and outward, pressing words and releasing contexts—offers the possibility of more exactitude in our hermeneutic protocols, particularly those that involve glossing early modern words. As Masten reminds us, the gloss "is an intersection within the history of sexuality that is (always) a moving target. 'Glossed' always has 'lost' within it: the world we have glossed; glossed in translation; loves' labours glossed."[155] What we have lost, as well, is access to the movement and sensation of language in the early modern period. Margreta de Grazia, for instance, argues that homonyms, the oral basis of puns, were an integral feature of the English language in the sixteenth and seventeenth centuries. Because of the lack of lexical, grammatical, and orthographic standardization, one word could be spelled several different ways or pronounced differently, several words could be spelled or pronounced identically, and all "words possessed more freedom to associate and interrelate, even when running counter to syntactic or logical structures."[156] Rather than being marked off as anomalous, promiscuous, and transgressive (as they are typically described by literary critics, especially those of a psychoanalytic, deconstructive, or queer perspective),[157] those linguistic maneuvers that we refer to as puns represent "a resource present in language itself before it became primarily a referential medium."[158] What we now call puns "literally *made sense*"—that is, they were constitutive of meaning (including nonmeaning).[159] In this sense, "wordplay" is a misnomer, because what we now consider play was a basic feature of the language, and the individuality, particularity, and separateness of a given word a much later phenomenon.[160]

Because of the flexible multivalence of early modern language across spelling, pronunciation, and parts of speech prior to greater standardization in the later seventeenth century, any modern reference to early modern punning carries with it a set of historical and theoretical problems: although Renaissance studies of rhetoric recognized certain operations that today are understood under the rubric of "puns," the concept did not exist as such until the eighteenth century, when it was demoted as unseemly or appropriate only to comedy.[161] In addition, "pun" seems to imply writerly intention in the installing of the multiple meanings. In the language practices examined in this chapter, there may or may not be such intentionality at stake; sometimes it is the linguistic system itself that has installed multiplicity of meaning, which individuals, to be sure, can further mobilize in particular contexts—but not always. That potential, however, doesn't imply the disappearance of the multiplicity of meaning for readers or hearers.

What de Grazia says of the homonymic pun is true of the sexual lexicon, where, as we have seen, there is considerable "freedom to associate and interrelate." Indeed, some early modern words that were widely used for the purposes of double entendre—for instance, "instrument" (for genitals), "horns" (for cuckoldry), "erect" (for erection), or terms drawn from agriculture like "to bear" or "plow" (for penetration)—probably promiscuously associated most of the time, with their erotic meanings available irrespective of context. All it would take is a receptive ear willing to make connections for such words to "talk sex." And certain homologies—like "waist/waste" and "cunt/cunnie/coney/quaint/count"—may have functioned in a similarly associative manner, evoking erotic significations pretty much as a matter of course.

But terms used to signify sex did not inevitably convey a sexual sense. Not every reference to a back door necessarily connotes anal penetration; not every pun on whole/hole activates the meanings of a bodily orifice; not every reference to spirit refers to semen; not every death is orgasmic; and not every reference to postures is a nod and a wink to Aretino.[162] This brake on the free play of sexual signification demands that we differentiate, in more nuanced ways, our understanding of how words and wordplay operationalized sex. In the next section, I attend to the multiplicity of users and listeners, and their differential access within communities to sexual knowledge, as part of this dynamic of operationalization. For now, my emphasis remains on the linguistic realm itself. Words such as "will," "wit," "meat," and "fault," while used frequently as slang for body parts, may have carried sexual connotations *only* when embedded in particular contexts or only when surrounded by other words that brought out or endorsed their erotic potential; in addition to functioning polysemously as metaphors, they must veer toward, affiliate, and link with other words to activate sexual meaning. They must expand into something akin to a literary *conceit*. Rather than linguistic *free* play, their mode of operation mobilizes, if not the associational clusters present in queer philology, then the mechanisms of extension, ligature, and kinship that underlie it.

To recognize limits to the play of language—whether conceived as erotic, bawdy, or queer—and to recognize the importance of affiliation and context in determining sexual meaning may appear to endorse those who aspire to fix and stabilize such meanings. It may appear to be allied with attempts to prophylactically rule *out* sexual meaning, rather than rule it in. Indeed, it may seem to put me in the company of Stanley Wells, who has inveighed against those "lewd interpreters" of Shakespeare who imagine sex where, he is certain, it manifestly is not.[163] But Wells is invested in drawing a firm line between what is sexual and what is not. What I am advocating is more challenging precisely because it aims to demonstrate the difficulty, at times even the impossibility, of drawing any such line. Rather than pin down sexual meaning and thereby reduce the volatility of linguistic play, rather than call upon an authorizing lexicon to secure a word's sexual meanings irrespective of context, I concur with other queer studies scholars that who gets to decide on such connections is always a matter of sexual politics. At the same time, I maintain that the commitment to bring greater exactitude to the interpretation of sexual language is not, in itself, an act of disciplining erotic language or inimical to queerness.

Getting the Joke

Maybe because I do not "get" most puns straight away and invariably mangle a joke's punch line, maybe because I had to read Masten's pun on "gloss" and "loss" several times before it began to make sense, I understand keenly that the assumption of the universal uptake of sexual puns enacts a knowledge relation, one that will vary for different participants. Not only will readerly or audience responses differ, but some people will remain clueless, unless the play of language is slowed down sufficiently (by actor, teacher, critic) to enable the necessary cognitive and hermeneutic work. Most critics who analyze wordplay are aware that their research objects present challenges. Bly notes that "the very elaboration of rhetoric involved in puns removes them from clear revelation,"[164] while Lopez acknowledges that "the strangeness of wordplay creates an interpretive gap."[165] I would add that it takes *effort* to fill that gap, even if, after repeated training in linguistic play (by attending the theater or learning the protocols of close reading), such labor can seem natural or easy.

By invoking interpretative labor and training, I aim to supplement queer philology with the two interrelated concerns of this book: epistemology and pedagogy. Just as Martha Joyless did not immediately perceive how to conceive a child, so too a member of an audience (then or now) may not know that an extended conceit about rabbit holes is poking fun at a woman's vagina. Early moderns may not have encountered the same difficulties we do—it is, after all, *their* language, their drama, their poetry—but both new coinages and multilayered wordplay undoubtedly risked incomprehension. Gowing, as noted in a previous chapter, alludes to the "partial barrier to the participation of the young and the single" in the use of sexual allusion and metaphor.[166] Bly notes that she limited her "discussion of sexual puns to those . . . audiences would readily grasp."[167] Lopez argues that the drama's "obvious, surface-level puns"—which he contrasts to those eminently satisfying superfluities of meaning in Shakespeare's sonnets—"are presented casually, in an offhand manner, and with a self-conscious confidence that they are *all* clever and necessary. Their casualness is studied, such as to imply that everyone will get the jokes."[168]

But should we take that implication for reality? After all, this "studied" "casualness" positions some auditors and readers as in the know and others as outside the charmed circle of knowledge. Lopez admits that some Renaissance plays are so full of puns that "one has little time to guffaw at each one. Rather, one must adopt an attitude of some sophistication, of seeing punning and wordplay as inevitable and necessary, and of confidence in one's ability to absorb it all; one can feel privately clever while also feeling one's cleverness affirmed and sanctioned by the openly private cleverness of everyone else in the audience."[169] But one can just as easily feel one's *lack* of cleverness; in the face of others' laughter, one can be alienated from the presumption of shared knowledge. This estrangement could lead to a disaffected response to the repertoire of the King's Men or the verse of John Donne; or it could prompt a determination to be ever more attentive to cues and codes in order to be in the know. Some critics go so far as to argue that one purpose of puns and jokes is to differentiate among members of the audience, creating a separation between those in the know and those outside.[170] Nonetheless, implicit educational imperatives underwrite Lopez's observation that one must adopt an attitude of "some sophistication." Theater, in particular, is an embodied community composed of shared conventions—linguistic, dramatic, narrative, performative (including when to laugh, when to be quiet, and when to applaud); these conventions cannot be presupposed, but must be taught. In the space and time in which such learning has not yet occurred, you can adopt an attitude, appear smarter than you are, assume a confidence you may not quite feel—and then you can feel privately clever and enjoy communal approbation of your cleverness, even when you aren't getting the joke.

In fact, Renaissance drama metatheatrically exploits the comic effects of such knowledge relations through its performance of linguistic difficulty and misunderstanding in the form of malapropisms and puns. An exemplary instance, useful for ferreting out the kinds of knowledge relations involved, is Malvolio's puzzling out of Maria's forged letter in Shakespeare's *Twelfth Night*: "By my life, this is my lady's hand. These be her very c's, her u's, and her t's, and thus makes she her great P's" (2.5.78–79).[171] Shakespeare doubles-down on the import of Malvolio's misprision of the letter's veracity by giving the intellectually challenged Sir Andrew the very next line: "Her c's, her u's, and her t's? Why that?" (2.5.81).

Andrew's question is not, it turns out, wholly inane because, as editors and critics have pointed out, no "c" or "p" appears in the superscription of the letter.[172] As Dympna Callaghan remarks, "At that literal, textual level we never really do know why there is a 'CU[N]T' in *Twelfth Night*."[173] Callaghan argues that the symbolic effect of placing "female genitals at the heart of Malvolio's gulling" is to position the status-aspiring steward as a feminized "cut"—a reading bolstered by the homophonic pun of "cunt" and "count," which linguistically underpins his narcissistic fantasy "To be Count Malvolio!" (2.5.30).[174] More than Malvolio's inadvertent puns, however, it is Andrew's question that points to the knowledge relations of this scene, for it stages not only the complexity of erotic interpretation, but the dynamics of erotic instruction. Both Malvolio and Andrew attempt to parse out the meaning of "c," "u," "t," and neither suspects an innuendo. Both fasten on different meanings: Malvolio adduces his "lady's hand," while Andrew's query implies that he hears in these sounds absolute nonsense, whether a string of unrelated letters or the words "seas," "ewes," and "teas."[175] That Andrew's inquiry goes unanswered is also worth noting, for this refusal to respond to his request for knowledge redounds not only on him but on the possibility of audience and readerly identification with these characters.

Insofar as this moment of obtuseness is comic and not simply gratuitously cruel, it depends both on the audience members' ability to get the joke and their desire to distance themselves from the obliviousness of this unfortunate pair. Yet, such distance depends on each reader or auditor's relation to the scene's projection of the skills of literacy: that is, the ability to spell out "c-u-t" and understand these letters to be interchangeable with "cunt."[176] (Editors seem to think that we need the *n* to make sense of this equivalence and, indeed, given the differences between early modern usage and our own, we do.) Indulging in an orthographic joke that requires knowledge not only of sex but of spelling, Shakespeare invites members of his audience—which surely included many who were illiterate—to dissociate themselves from their own lack of knowledge or to risk alienation from the rest of the theatrical knowledge community. Shakespeare's sleight of orthographic hand renders the *in* of this in-joke and the spectatorial relations around which it revolves utterly dependent on the epistemological situation of being in the know.

Tongues and Tails

Once sexual wordplay is recognized as a knowledge relation—and thus implicated in both epistemology and pedagogy—the stakes of the difficulty and obscurity of puns, as well as the interpretative efforts involved in understanding them, come to the fore. Given that puns, as de Grazia argues, are a fundamental feature of early modern English, what is true for puns, I maintain, is true of the period's sexual lexicon. I thus now zero in on how early modern words associated with sex actually treat the sex they attempt to denote. For it is a curious fact that many such words are characterized by instability and opacity, are vague on referential details, and are singularly uninterested in parsing body parts or identifying particular actions in which bodies might engage.

The ambiguities that obtain vis-à-vis bodies and genders are a prime instance of this referential indifference. At the most general level, a lack of semiotic distinction characterizes words for sexual desire and words for sexual acts: "lust," "lechery," "venery," "vice," and "wantonness" all were used interchangeably in this regard. Nouns such as "gear," "genitals," "members," "privities," and "womb" exemplify and further this quality of indistinction, for they all served as generalized reference points, equivocal in their indexical functions. Punsters capitalized on this generality. As Lopez notes of the period's drama, "the sexual puns that recur most frequently derive much of their energy and usefulness from a *broadly applicable vagueness*. Play on the word 'meat' and similar words—'dish,' 'mutton'—is one of the most common sexual puns, and is particularly convenient because it can be used in reference to either men or women."[177] So too with more extended locutions: while "plowing a field" might, given the allusion to organic generation, be assumed to refer to penis-vagina intercourse, "piercing a bodkin" does not imply a particular orifice or agent of penetration. Such inexactness is far from rare. Linguists often refer to "the curious imprecision of many anatomical terms," pointing to the "ambiguity of orifice" and "genital confusion" of words like "fanny" (buttocks, female pudendum), "prat" (buttocks, female pudendum), and "roger" (penis, copulate, rape).[178]

Take, for instance, the common locution "my tongue in your tail." This catchphrase is often described as an early modern analogue for the aggressive and scatological "kiss my ass." A potent linguistic weapon, its comic potential extends back at least to Chaucer's tales of *The Miller* and *The Pardoner*, and forward into Restoration satire.[179] A staple of the early modern stage, it is voiced by Petruchio in his attempt to shut Katherine up with his quip, "What, with my tongue in your tail?" in Shakespeare's *The Taming of the Shrew* (2.1.214). "Tail" provides the opportunity for multiple puns, including the one on "entail" spoken by Face in Jonson's *The Alchemist*:

A wife, a wife for one on's, my dear Subtle:
We'll e'en draw lots, and he, that fails, shall have
The more in goods, the other has in tail

(2.6.85–87)

Bernard Capp's history of sexual insults notes that "'tail' served as a common derogatory euphemism for the genitalia and buttocks of either sex, and its animal associations were frequently exploited to dehumanize an adversary."[180] But does "tail" in any given instance mean vagina, anus, buttocks, or all of it? Editors variously gloss Subtle's reference to "tail" as "pudendum," "genital satisfaction," "sexual pleasure," or the singularly unhelpful "*tail* in its still current sexual sense."[181] In the aggregate, this glossing enforces its own mode of ambiguity by reproducing presumptive knowledge about what sexual satisfaction and pleasure *are*. But what are we to make of the fact that critics and editors of other literary texts interpret "tail" as anus?[182] Or penis?[183] Or buttocks?[184] What manner of pun is Middleton exploiting when, in his 1606 stage play *Your Five Gallants*, he names the male "whore-gallant" serving female clients "Tailby"?[185] Does the homophonic pun on "buy" imply that women can buy access to his penis or his anus for their own pleasure, or does it imply that what is for sale is his ability to pleasure them "in the tail"? Not only is the sexual referent up for grabs but the relations of subject to object, and both to knowledge of sex, are multiplied as well.

The Sexual Crux

Just as vagueness, ambiguity, and obscurity are features of early modern sex talk, the difficulties of correlation need to be considered in interpretative practices. Taking the hermeneutic fortunes of "tail" as a possible baseline, we might ask: how should "ring," "hole," "bit," "purse," "crack," "case," "sweetmeat," or "thing" be distinguished, one from the other? "Crack" is used in contexts that refer to women's vaginas and male anuses, female prostitutes and male catamites. "Bit," according to Bly, refers to both vagina and penis, and "case" and "sweetmeats" often begin by denoting a female body part, but regularly transit over to the male.[186] All of this accords with Will Fisher's observation that "early modern texts often seem to assume a kind of fungibility between different orifices (anus, vagina, mouth, etc.) as well as between different 'instruments' (penis, tongue, dildo, finger, etc.)."[187] Consider, for instance, a riddle published in Puttenham's *Arte of English Poesie*:

> I have a thing and rough it is
> and in the middle a hole Iwis:
> There cam a young man with his ginne,
> And he put a handful in.

Puttenham remarks that the speaker of this riddle, a "good old Gentle-woman" in his mother's nursery, "would tell us that were children how it was meant by a furrd glove."[188] One cannot tell—and Puttenham does not enlighten us—whether the hole is the vagina or anus. "Handful" could refer to a penis or a hand or both; and "furrd glove" could be yet another allusion to either a hand or vagina.

This is not to suggest that the distinction between anuses and vaginas, or between male anuses and female ones, was a matter of inconsequence to any given writer, reader, or listener. Although there are numerous references in the literature of the time to the exchangeability of boys and women—perhaps the most wittily epigrammatic is the rakish indifference of John Wilmot, Earl of Rochester, in "The Disabled Debauchee" as to "Whether the Boy Fuck'd you, or I the Boy"[189]—there are many other instances where the gender of such orifices is explicitly coded as desirable or aversive.[190] My point is that when we actually scrutinize the words, we often don't know—indeed, can't know—which gender or body part is meant and that, faced with this uncertainty, it generally is only presumption about what each partner might physically do that directs interpretations. Typical glosses such as "with sexual connotations," "with erotic innuendo," "an obscene quibble," or "a pun on genitals" fudge the issue by neglecting to provide whatever specificity *may* be available in a given context. This allows both editors and readers to fall back on normative assumptions of what sex is. Such glosses also skirt indeterminacy by assuming that each reader will interpret the innuendo, quibble, or pun in exactly the same way.

Once we begin to put sex talk under pressure such presumptions break apart. This is not to suggest that sex disappears into a vortex of undecidability, nor that the highest interpretative aim is to achieve anatomical and positional exactitude. It is to argue that the irresolvable *tension* between the possibility of multiple sexual referents and the limits on our knowledge might productively be recognized not only as a source of pleasure but as a resource to guide and inform editing and interpretation.

How to turn this resource to editorial and critical advantage will be discussed shortly. But first I illustrate what is at stake in the absence of interpretative and editorial protocols sensitive to this tension by offering two exemplary readings of "bawdy language" in early modern criticism—chosen among many possibilities because they (1) represent the current state of reading for sex; (2) are pieces of criticism I admire; and (3) both address an extended pun on "coney." To the extent that my engagement with each is a critique, it is to suggest that even the most sophisticated treatments of "bawdy" can fall into a presumptive knowingness about sex. (I include myself in this susceptibility: in Chapter 8, I acknowledge my own interpretative presumptions regarding the language of Shakespeare's sonnets.)

In an attempt to elucidate how some puns exceed logic, Jeremy Lopez explicates the following passage spoken by the Corteze in George Chapman's *The Gentleman Usher*:

O, these young girls engross up all the love
From us poor beldames, but I hold my hand;
I'll ferret all the cunni-holes of their kindness
Ere I have done with them.[191]

Lopez remarks,

Chapman's spelling makes the potential dirtiness of "coney holes" even more obvious than it already is. Understanding the wordplay here is a *weird and complex process*. "Ferret all the cunni-holes" . . . obviously suggests sexual intercourse. That is the joke of the pun. But it is also not what Corteze means; she means that she will root out all her young girls' secrets. Corteze is, however, a lusty character who is constantly making lascivious advances to Medice, and so it is not unlikely that she would speak these lines in such a way as to convey the sexual joke. Of course, *the sexual joke does not quite make sense, since Corteze is a woman; but the actor playing her would have been male, and so the joke would have had on some level a faint pertinence (as well as a less faint impertinence, since the actor would have been a boy rather than a man)*. Each of the various layers of experience involves a simple but important collision of literal and figurative ways of understanding. *One hears "ferret" and "cunni-holes" and understands "penis" and "vagina"; one hears a woman telling a sexual joke as though she were a man* but (mostly) understands that joke to be the voice of the author, (mostly) independent of the demands of context; one sees a boy in women's clothes and understands him to be a woman.[192]

That Lopez acknowledges the weird and complex process of interpreting this speech and that he further reads it as a kind of hermeneutic "collision" provides a welcome admission of uncertainty. But what are the hermeneutic protocols that Lopez brings to this interpretive crisis? Do "we" in fact "hear" and "understand" in precisely the way that he describes? In the absence of a

clearly specified method, one might well demur from the ascription of sexual
"pertinence" only to an adult male body, or the lack of pertinence to a
woman, or the impertinence to a boy. Indeed, we might hear women eroticizing their own discourse and each other by means of their talk, pointing to
scholarship produced over the past two decades that militates against the
view, presumed by Lopez, that "since Corteze is a woman" she could not be
the penetrative agent in "sexual intercourse," nor tell the kind of dirty jokes
that men regularly do.

In *The Places of Wit in Early Modern English Comedy*, Adam Zucker explicates a dialogue between the Justice of the Peace Cockbrain and Belt, a servant recently transplanted to London from the countryside in Richard
Brome's *The Weeding of Covent-Garden*. According to the stage directions, a
woman has appeared "above upon a Bellconie."

> *Cock.* O heresie! It is some Lady, or Gentlewoman standing upon her
>   Bellconey.
> *Belt.* Her Bellconey? Where is it? I can spy her from foot to her face, yet I can
>   see no Bellconey she has.
> *Cock.* What a Knave's this: That's the Bellconey she stands on, that which jets
>   out so on the forepart of the house; every house here has one of 'hem.
> *Belt.* 'Tis very good; I like the jetting out of the forepart very well; it is a gallant
>   fashion indeed.[193]

Zucker remarks:

> Belt, it seems has never heard the word "balcony" before. Rather than
> inquiring what the word means, he searches for a homophonic "belle coney,"
> which literally means "beautiful rabbit," but in this context more likely refers
> to a part of the body that, despite the general visibility of the woman above
> them . . . remains hidden. Once Cockbrain has dispelled Belt's confusion with
> a lesson in architectural terminology, the servant proves his own wit with a
> visual pun that links the balcony to the codpiece of a gallant "jetting out of
> the forepart." In a very unlikely jest, the balcony, both coney and codpiece,
> becomes knowable through the sign of hermaphroditism, placing it within a
> discursive field famously dominated by notions of excess and impropriety.[194]

Zucker's examination of wit, centrally concerned with space, means that his
focus is the provocative strangeness of balconies in early modern London; in

an effort to make "Belt's bawdy jokes . . . a bit more comprehensible," he turns to architectural history.[195] But what are the knowledge relations Zucker derives from this pun? Zucker seems to assume the knowingness of Belt, his ability to "prove his own wit." Yet, given Brome's treatment of country naïfs in *The Antipodes* (discussed in Chapter 5), we might wonder whether the scene isn't just as likely to dramatize Belt's cluelessness. The making of inadvertent puns, after all, is the dramatists' stock-in-trade for defining the witlessness of certain characters, especially when it comes to sex. My point is not that Belt necessarily is lacking in knowledge, but that no critical criterion is offered to explain how to distinguish between inadvertent malapropisms that enmesh the speaker unknowingly in eroticized speech and the intentional, knowing manipulation of erotic wit. Is Belt making a joke or is the joke on him?[196]

This is not to suggest that "coney" doesn't signify the female genitals for both the playwright and audience; later in the play a male character drunkenly attempts to grope a woman's "coney." But the pun itself raises the issue of the fit between language and knowledge, and the interpretative means by which we impute knowingness (or lack of it). The pun also raises the specter of the body parts that Zucker doesn't actually name. Moving from an unstated pun on "cunt" to codpiece, Zucker's interpretation ends not with the genitals of either sex, but with the oddly decorporealized "sign of hermaphrodism." Could it be that this disinclination to name body parts is part of what generates this recourse to an abstract sign? Does Zucker too readily settle on the gendered meaning of "the jetting out of the forepart"? According to travel narratives and medical texts, the tribade's clitoris is alleged to jet out in similarly "gallant fashion."[197] Again, my aim is not to replace the male with the female body, but to insist that this text's pun on "bell-coney" *refuses to adjudicate* between these possibilities.

These examples enable us to identify some characteristic procedures to which critics resort when interpreting what we today refer to as sexual puns. In response to the open-endedness of sexual language and the latitude upon which wordplay depends, critics (1) recognize certain forms of multiplicity and fail to recognize others; (2) identify and limit the word's meaning and significance in ways that are not adequately explained by the context in which they appear; and (3) respond to indeterminacy by attempting to *fill in the blanks*. Paradoxically, these responses often (4) mobilize a different order of vagueness—one that depends upon and deploys presumptive knowledge about what sex is, in what positions and with what body parts, what actions it entails, for whom it is possible, and to whom it is legible.[198] In the aggregate, these procedures display collective discomfort in being bewildered or confounded and suggest that interpreting sexual language activates a *desire to know*, a desire that, being unacknowledged or disavowed, impels scholars to pass or paper over—or attempt to pin down—what is enigmatic or inconclusive. What is obscured in these procedures is the extent to which the manner, kind, and type of sex being referenced may in fact be unknowable, whether because it was unnameable or not deemed necessary to name in its own time. Furthermore, in these two cases, what is additionally obscured is the very thought—indeed, the thinkability—of female erotic agency.

All of which is to say that awareness of sex acts enjoins upon critics a corporeal hermeneutics of difficulty, uncertainty, and obscurity. For this reason, queer philology, which seeks to expand our apprehension of the culture's sexual lexicon, might usefully be supplemented with an epistemology of the crux,[199] with "crux" understood as a basic, fundamental condition of early modern "sex talk."[200] If the goal of identifying something as a crux poses it as a problem to be solved, whether by identifying its meaning or pointing to the difficulties in doing so, my point is that, when it comes to talking sex, final solutions are often impossible and possible answers always contingent. On the one hand, the epistemology of the crux is that there are too many possible meanings; on the other hand, there are too many uncertainties. What practical guidelines, then, does an epistemological orientation urge upon a critic or editor?

In the following sections, I will offer my own practice of reading sexual language as one indication of where an epistemologically attuned queer feminist criticism might lead. Editing, however, must be approached more circumspectly, for I have never edited a text. Others are better equipped to demonstrate what might be involved in what Lesser calls an "explicitly genealogical annotational practice," one that seeks "to incorporate into its glosses some of the historical process that has helped to shape our conception" of words' meanings.[201] But since my aim, after all, is not prescriptive but suggestive, I offer here a few principles and strategies that editors might consider when they engage in the act of glossing sexual language.[202] I am guided by Leah Marcus's observation that "part of the purpose of a good edition has traditionally been to bridge historical distance—to make a text and its cultural milieu accessible to people with different practices and assumptions. But that process always involves the risk of over-normalization, of making the past over to accommodate one's own, and one's readers', sense of what constitutes acceptable meaning."[203] Attempting to resist such overnormalization, I offer in the first and last items broad principles, while the items in between suggest some concrete strategies:

- Be as metacritically self-conscious about the history of sexuality as about the history of the language, textual variants, and editorial practice.
- Be mindful of the relations between linguistic elasticity and multiplicity, on the one hand, and the fixity imposed by definition, on the other—remembering that exactitude and ossification are not the same.[204]
- Make available to readers as many meanings as possible, resisting the urge to foreclose any given meaning's legitimacy and allowing readers to adjudicate between them.[205]
- Attend to the historicity of language in both its synchronic and diachronic dimensions. Use early modern lexicons, the *OED*, critical analyses, and performance histories to chart these histories, acknowledging at the same time their aggregate participation in the formation of sexual meaning.
- Be explicit about the logic of individual glosses, especially principles of selection and exclusion, both in introductory notes and in individual cases. This may mean switching from one logic of the gloss to another within the same text, rather than developing a single method for glossing sexual language throughout a text.
- Stage the sequence of glosses in a text to build upon prior articulations of meaning, offering the reading of glosses as an ongoing pedagogical endeavor.
- Employ an "If . . . then" mode in order to make evident epistemological, linguistic, characterological, gendered, and sexual contingencies (e.g., If we read Rosalind as a boy actor, then . . .).
- Think like a queer concordance, locating words in a thick associational web of linguistic, textual, and social contexts.
- Extend the purview of the meanings of sex beyond the terms of imputed character motivation, subjectivity, and desire to consider *structures and ideologies* of desire/bodies/sex.
- Be mindful of the diversity and hierarchies of sexual knowledge communities, both early modern and contemporary, without homogenizing the interests internal to them.

- Be candid about what you don't know. Allow the ongoing production of sexual knowledge to be on display, including its opacities,
  trusting that *not* knowing may be an occasion for pleasure as well as
  anxiety.[206]

There is one more issue that I hope scholars will keep in mind. Within
the current critical dispensation, because of the gendered double bind that
obtains in academic discussions of sexual speech, the question of what it
means to read in a feminist or queer fashion is far from clear. Indeed, talking
sex in today's academic context poses yet another impasse, one that involves
tensions among and within feminist and queer commitments. On the one
hand, scholars face the prospect of giving offense—particularly, it would
seem, to women—by using words that have been deemed vulgar, offensive,
or demeaning. (This concern sometimes extends to young readers as well.)
Although I wish it were not so, this prospect is not, in my experience, wholly
a projection; words, as Shakespeare's Beatrice might say, have the power to
wound, and I have witnessed these risks become magnified in oral speech.
When I have said words such as "cunt," "fuck," or even "clitoris" in academic venues, the room tends to go strangely quiet; and when I hear such
words voiced by others, particularly men, I afterward have been asked to lend
support to certain women who are dismayed and disgusted.

Articulating such words, I believe, is a risk that scholars need to take
in their glossing, criticism, and speech. To fail to do so is to risk patroniz-
ing women (again, it would seem, in particular) when, by demurring to
synonyms that seem less charged, they seek to "protect" women from
offense—as if women today would never dream of using such words themselves and as if, historically speaking, it is unimaginable that women themselves might have *invented* some of this "sex talk." The commitment to such
decorum leads to the use of clumsy, sometimes absurd, locutions other than
the term in question, thereby reinforcing the notion that some words are
"bad." At its worst, this tendency amounts to the performance of a gestural
feminism that doesn't permeate the scholar's analytical frame, buttressing the
idea that feminism requires merely "sensitivity" to women who, in turn, are
imagined as collectively "sensitive" about sex. Insofar as it universalizes the
terms of modesty and offense, a commitment to such protocols in the name
of feminism enacts yet another form of presumptive knowledge. This is not
to endorse a sniggering pleasure in which the shock value of using sexual

slang such as "cunt" and "fuck" is used to publicize one's transgressive credentials.[207] Rather, as Laurie Maguire advocates in her discussion of feminist glossing, we need a relationship to sexual speech that is free from both prurience and shame.[208]

Dildo, Dildo, Dee

It should be clear by now that I am committed, precisely in the name of queer feminism, to de-dramatizing sexual speech by forthrightly naming body parts, describing sexual acts, and using even the most potentially offensive of words. Anything short of this would be to abrogate the commitment to thinking sex as a knowledge relation. At the same time, I advocate loosening one's certainty about how sexual language signifies. To further demonstrate how this epistemological orientation translates into critical practice, I close this chapter by adding to the queer lexicon three terms that exemplify, at the level of the individual word as well as that of interpretative challenges, the dynamics I have traced thus far. I begin with one of the culture's most literally materialized of sexual words: that tool, that instrument, that thing called a "dildo." Made of wood, leather, wax, horn, or Murano glass, dildos were manifestly "thingy" objects, available throughout western Europe and the British Isles from the sixteenth century on.[209] In shape they mimicked not only a penile shaft, but sometimes testicles and pubic hair. They often were molded so as to convey fluids such as hot water, milk, or urine, thereby providing the semblance of moist, warm seed. Some were fitted with mouthpieces to double as drinking vessels, likely used in drinking games.[210] As devices of gender impersonation, in their more modest wooden and leather guises they figured prominently in trials of tribades and cross-dressers who were alleged to "abuse" their female partners with such "unnatural devices."[211] This notion of fraud corresponds to Webster's proposed etymology, wherein "dildo" derives from the Old English "*dyderian*, 'to deceive, to cheat.' "[212] Yet we might also consider Williams' alternative etymology, which begins to gesture toward the contradictions residing at its very origins: "a contraction of *diletto*, Ital. *q.d.* a woman's delight; or of the English *Dally*, *q.d.* a thing to play withal."[213]

As early as Aretino's *Ragionamento* (1534), references to dildos were a staple of pornographic and literary wit.[214] By the late sixteenth century, dildos could function, as they do in Thomas Nashe's "Choise of Valentines" (ca. 1593), as "a marker of a certain urban and mercantile sophistication," while also being associated with "foreign parts" and "foreign pleasures."[215] Other writers quickly followed Nashe in identifying dildos as a feminine luxury good. John Donne's "Elegie II (The Anagram)" (ca. 1595) includes a woman's "Dildoes" along with her "Bedstaves, and her Velvet Glasse,"[216] while Ben Jonson twice alludes to dildos: first in *The Alchemist* when Lovewit finds the ceiling of his house "filled with poesies of the candle: / and MADAM, with a dildo, writ o' the walls" (5.5.41–42), and later in his conversations with William Drummond when Jonson refers to a man "who, being consumed, occupied his wife with a dildo, and she never knew of it till one day he all sleepery had there left his."[217] According to Will Fisher, by the end of the seventeenth century, "all the major pornographic texts circulating in England . . . include scenes that feature dildos."[218] While sometimes depicted as objects of masculinist satire, dildos were also celebrated as a means for women taking sexual matters literally into their own hands. The condemnation voiced by Nashe's hapless Tomalin—"Curse Eunuke dilldo, senceless, counterfet, / Who sooth maie fill, but neuer can begett" (lines 263–64)—indicates the masculine anxiety to which women's use of dildos could give rise,[219] but the ubiquity of their presence in later pornography implies a wider range of affective response, even among men.[220]

Yet, what is most curious about the history of "dildo" is that it was also apparently a nonsense word, a literal manifestation of "no-thing," particularly evident, according to scholars, in ballad refrains, which often included "non-signifying" syllables:

> With a hie, dildo, dill,
> Hie do, dil dur lie;
> It is a delightful thing
> To live at liberty.[221]

Several stage plays reproduce this use of dildo as a ballad refrain, as when Jack Allwit in Thomas Middleton's *A Chaste Maid in Cheapside* sings "La dildo, dildo la dildo, la dildo dildo de dildo."[222] Critics almost always gloss "dildo" in such texts as a meaningless catchword, although in the past decade, they have begun to add a secondary annotation: "artificial penis."[223] These two meanings—nonsense and sexual prosthetic—appear in glosses coextensively, without any necessary connection implied between them.

I suggest that in most ballads in which it appears, "dildo" has a more overdetermined relationship to sex than refrains such as "Tra la la la la," "fa la la," or "down derry down," which are commonly referred to as otiose "filler."[224] Indeed, precisely because of its association with nonsense, "dildo" provides a point of access for considering the non-sense implicated in the act of representing sex. Take the ballad "The Batchelors Feast," or, as the title continues, "The difference betwixt, a single life and a double: being the Batchelors pleasure, and the married Mans trouble, To a pleasant new tune called, With a hie dildo, dill."[225] Such a heading suggests, first, that the tune was actually known by the name "With a hie dildo, dill," which extends the meaning of "dildo" beyond the function of nonsensical "filler." More significantly, the subsequent stanza forges a specific connection between the "nonsensical" refrain and the content of the ballad:

A man that doth intend,
to lead a quiet life,
Must practice day and night,
to please his longing wife.

Please her how? "With a hie dildo" is the implicit answer of the refrain.

Several ballads refer unambiguously to the dildo as a sexual device.[226] "News from Crutchet-Fryers" narrates the story of two "Sluts" who throw homemade "*Merkins* and *Dildoes*" over a neighbor's wall to "torment, and vex" her; the dildos are explicitly described as "Stiff-standing" and, since a "merkin" is artificial pubic hair, the sexual content, if not the meaning of the action, appears clear.[227] Intriguing as those women's actions are, even more intriguing is when the dildo morphs into a penis—that is, when it becomes an actual body part or simulacrum for "a man." In "The Lancashire Cuckold" the adulterous wife, attempting to help her "poor Lover" whose penis has gotten attached to a charmed "Piss-pot," reaches out and "On his delicate Dildoul her right hand she got, / With the left hand she seiz'd on the side of the Pot," until she, too, is "stuck fast" to the pot, setting off a comic chain reaction of painful attachments.[228] In its corporeal "delicacy," "Dildoul" can only refer here to the lover's actual anatomy. Such a conflation also seems to underlie "The Maids Complaint / For want of a Dil doul."[229] Sung by a sighing, sobbing, moaning sixteen-year-old, these lyrics conflate "any good fellow" with whom she would happily "lye" and the material object of her song's refrain: "*For a dill doul, dil doul, dil doul doul, / (quoth*

she) I'm undone if I hant a dil doul." The penultimate stanza renders explicit
the conflation:

> For why tother night I heard my dame *Nancy*
> declare how her Master did tickle her fancy
> *With his dill doul dill doul dill doul doul,*
> *then what e're it cost me I'le have a dil doul.*

The ballad concludes:

> then come along, rub on the place that doth itch
> *For a dill doul, dil doul, dil doul doul*
> *take all my money, give me a dill doul.*

Of course, perhaps the Master is tickling Nancy's fancy with a foreign object
rather than his penis, but how are auditors or readers to know?

Such confusion of the senses and of sense itself is likewise evident in the
first appearance of "dildo" in a dictionary produced in England: Florio's 1598
bilingual *A Worlde of Wordes*, which provides the following synonyms for the
Italian *pinco*: "a prick, a pillicock, a pintle, a dildoe."[230] In Edward Howard's
poem, "Fricatrices: or a She upon a She" (1673), a sexual encounter between
two women hinges precisely on the idea that a man may be the biggest dildo
of all. The poem begins by portraying female-female eroticism as a failed
imitation of that between women and men:

> The Fairest . . . lay down; [and] the other strove
> Manhood to act with Female power and love.
> Their nimble heat dissolv'd the active dew,
> Which from their Pearls within its moisture drew.
> But soon their pleasures were deceiv'd, to finde
> The one Thing wanted to which both had minde.
> One said she was the Woman; t'other swore
> She ought to be the man, and she the Whore.

The poem drives home the failure of this "deception" by unifying the women
in their common desire for a man:

> At last, at their mistake they yield and smile,
> And grant that Loves pleasures nothing can beguile.

A man they wanted, and a Man would have,
Since he the Dildo has which Nature gave.

Despite this return to the authentic "Loves pleasures" from which they had been "beguile[d]," the final couplet is not quite as conclusive as it seems. The phrase "he the Dildo has" turns on the image of the man's penis-as-dildo—an idea that inverts the relationship between nature and artifice and undermines the "naturalness" of his "Thing." As Fisher puts it, "Instead of the dildo being imagined as an artificial imitation of the natural penis, here the penis is imagined as 'the dildo . . . which Nature gave'—that is to say, as a natural imitation of the artificial dildo."[231] The distinctions between nature and artifice, penis and dildo, are retained only by the way these terms swap positions.

The distinction between nature and artifice, however, does not hold, at least not in "A Song" from *Choyce Drollery: Songs & Sonnets; Being a Collection of Divers Excellent Pieces of Poetry, of Severall Eminent Authors*:

A Story strange I will you tell,
    But not so strange as true,
Of a woman that danc'd upon the ropes,
    And so did her husband too.
        With a dildo, dildo, dildo,
          With a dildo, dildo, dee.
       Some say 'twas a man, but it was a woman
        As plain report may see.

She first climb'd up the Ladder
    For to deceive mens hopes,
And with a long thing in her hand
    She tickled it on the ropes.
        With a dildo, dildo, dildo,
          With a dildo, dildo, dee,
       And to her came Knights and Gentlemen
        Of low and high degree.

She jerk'd them backward and foreward
    With a long thing in her hand,

And all the people that were in the yard,
    She made for them to stand.
        With a dildo, &c.

They cast up fleering eyes
    All under-neath her cloaths,
But they could see no thing,
    For she wore linnen hose.
        With a dildo, &c.

The Cuckold her husband caper'd
    When his head in the sack was in,
But grant that we may never fall
    When we dance in the sack of sin.
        With a dildo, &c.

And as they ever danc't
    In faire or rainy weather,
I wish they may be hang'd i' th' rope of Love,
    And so be cut down together.
        With a dildo, &c.[232]

Some of the punning here is pretty standard fare: the double entendre on "yard" and "stand," and men seeing "no thing" under a woman's "cloaths." And clearly the refrain's "*with* a dildo" implies some relationship between the dildo and the dancing, jerking, and capering described. Yet the actual action remains irretrievable—and not primarily because of the possibility of gender fraud ("*Some say 'twas a man, but it was a woman*"). Having climbed up a ladder wearing "linnen hose," this early modern rope dancer tickles "it on the ropes"—but what "it" is she tickling? Is she tickling herself, the "it" being her own body? Is the "it" her clitoris, her vagina, or her anus? (One wonders about the impediment of her hose.) Or is she caressing the rope with the dildo, in an erotically titillating manner, a forerunner to pole dancing? We are told that she is jerking the "Knights and Gentlemen" "backward and foreward / With a long thing in her hand," but how, exactly? By penetrating them with the "long thing," or arousing them with her autoerotic gymnastics, or by stroking their penises, as the conflation of dildo and penis above would suggest? And what of the "Cuckold her husband"? What is his "head" doing in that "sack"? It may be that some reader with more expertise with the early modern sexual lexicon will one day make all of this clear—but I suspect not.[233] As the nature/artifice binary deconstructs, the meaning of dildo and the sex acts it performs become inscrutable. Indeed, I suspect that the tease of leaving readers/listeners scratching their heads is part of the "drollery."[234]

Such uncertainty, it must be said, is not a position that historians and literary critics necessarily enjoy, as is borne out by the most famous dildo crux in the English Renaissance literary tradition: the description of the ped-dler's wares in Shakespeare's *The Winter's Tale* (1609–11). During a scene in Bohemia, the Shepherd's servant says of Autolycus that he "has the prettiest love songs for maids, so without bawdry, which is strange, with such delicate burdens of dildos and fadings, 'Jump her, and thump her.'"[235] The phrase "dildos and fadings" has exercised the ingenuity of many editors, occasioning lengthy glosses from several.[236] A summary of the prevailing wisdom is pro-vided by Susan Snyder and Deborah T. Curren-Aquino: "Although he sets out to prove the pedlar's songs are without indecency ('bawdry'), the servant takes up ballad catchwords ('dildos' and 'fadings') and expressions ('jump' and 'thump') whose sexual connotations make the refrains ('burdens') any-thing but 'delicate.' 'Dildo,' first recorded in the *OED* in 1610, refers to an artificial penis. 'With a fading' was the refrain of a popular song of an inde-cent character (*OED* fading *n*); 'fading' was also the name of a dance or jig. 'Jump' and 'thump' here carry the bawdy sense of copulating with vigour (Partridge)."[237] However nonsensical or disruptive the Shepherd's syntax, then, the dildo's association with the probable sexual innuendo of "delicate burdens" and the vigorous action of "jump her and thump her" imply some kind of sexual meaning. On this most editors agree. But again, *what* kind? One of the more interesting glosses is that of John A. Pitcher, who concludes—based on the same evidence provided by Snyder and Aquino—that "thus *dildos and fadings* would be false penises and ineffectual ones."[238] Dildos, however, might have been seen, at least by some, as attractive and effective; and "fading," according to Partridge, could refer to orgasm as well as its aftermath.[239] Here, then, for the sake of argument, is an alternative gloss for Autolycus's wares: "satisfactory alternative to the penis, implying orgasm."

Claiming the dildo on behalf of women, however, is not really my point. Nor is it to historicize the gender implications of dildo use—although such efforts remain crucial to our emerging histories of sexuality.[240] Rather, the linguistic and narrative "action" of the dildo in these texts, which co-implicates non-sense and no-thing in the some-thing that is sex, exemplifies the import of indecipherability that runs throughout the period's sexual language.[241] As such, the dildo implicates all of us in the cluelessness that seems to be part and parcel of the desire to sexually know.

Naught, &c.

Nowhere is the no-thing inhering in "dildo" more evident than in one of the most common terms associated with sex in the period, that of "naught": a naughty man, a naughtypack, being naughty, being naught together, running a naughty house. Defined by the *OED* as "immoral, licentious, promiscuous, sexually provocative," the terms "naught" and "naughty" etymologically return us to the homonym "nought" and thus to "no thing." Partridge notes that "*naughty* originally meant worthless,"[242] and it is often assumed that the term developed sexual connotations from the misogynist notion of female genitalia as absence or lack. We might take Hamlet's cruel punning with Ophelia as definitive in this regard:

> *Hamlet.* Do you think I meant country matters?
> *Ophelia.* I think nothing, my lord.
> *Hamlet.* That's a fair thought to lie between maids' legs.
> *Ophelia.* What is, my lord?
> *Hamlet.* No thing.[243]

> (3.2.105–9)

But "naught" is not used in the early modern period to refer exclusively to women's desires or bodies; across the domains of religion, law, entertainment, and poetry, it ramifies into puns about holes and *O*'s, orgasm and death, and makes linguistic hay with its homonyms "not" and "knot"—as in the tying and untying of the "virgin knot," "marriage knot," and "true-loves knot."[244] Forging analogical but also incommensurate notions of nothingness, negativity, lack, worthlessness, and immorality, on the one hand, and pleasure, interpersonal contact, bodily integrity, and affective connection, on the other, "naught" accretes, compounds, and expands into a resounding obliquity.

The final obscurity with which I will conclude is that of "et cetera," commonly written, as in "A Song" above, as "&c." In printed broadside ballads, refrains are often denominated by way of "et cetera," which would leave up to the singers' discretion which version of the refrain to sing. In the case of more than one singer, this conceivably could lead to a situation in which different variants are sung at once. Choice and variability, in other words, lurk behind the notion of "et cetera." But that is not all.

The *OED* defines "et cetera" as "And the rest, and so forth, and so on . . . indicating that the statement refers not only to the things enumerated, but to others which may be inferred from analogy"; and "as substitute for a suppressed substantive, generally a coarse or indelicate one." Both meanings are activated in the stage directions of Jonson's *The Devil Is an Asse* (1631), which instruct "*He grows more familiar in his Court-ship*" and "*playes with her paps, kisseth her hands, &c.*" (2.6.71–76).[245] If "&c." implies "and so forth," what, we might ask, is the "so" that is going forth? What is the "suppressed substantive" that follows upon the action of playing with paps and kissing hands? What does this word invite the actor to do? Does "&c." suggest more of the same or moving on to something else? Does it imply repetition, dilation, or sequence? Likewise, in George Chapman's epyllion *Ovid's Banquet of Sense*, in "Which for his fourth course made our Poet court her, &c.,"[246] what kind of Ovidian repast is being served? Is the fourth course the end or merely the middle of the meal?

This uncertainty of reference, duration, and sequence is only the beginning of the inexplicability to which "et cetera" as a sexual denominator is prone. Demonstrating that "in the early modern period *etcetera* embodied a variety of things: acoustic, physiological, temporal, rhetorical, grammatical," Laurie Maguire taxonomizes this variety while arguing that these disparate categories are connected by the way each "directs the eye to a vacancy."[247] One of the more prevalent vacancies to which "et cetera" as a noun directs the eye is the sexual body. In the first quarto of *Romeo and Juliet*, Mercutio describes Romeo's love melancholy for Rosaline: "Ah *Romeo* that she were, ah that she were / An open *Et caetera*, thou a poprin Peare" (1597, Dr). As Maguire remarks of these lines, "by Shakespeare's day *&c / etcetera* is not just a substitute for a bawdy verb or noun but is a bawdy term in itself. It now means the thing it previously only stood in for." In this way, it "both conceals and draws attention to the thing it conceals."[248]

Just what body part or action is being concealed, however, is as unknowable as the referent of the word "tail." While Maguire, along with Partridge and Williams, interprets Rosaline's "*Et caetera*" as denoting her vagina, Joseph Porter and Jonathan Goldberg both turn to editorial emendations of

"*Et caetera*" as "open-arse," itself a pun on Mercutio's previous reference to Rosaline as a "medlar." The reasoning of textual editors for this shift focuses on the differences between the two quartos, neither of which provides a reading much countenanced by editors today.[249] Regardless of textual issues, even those critics who agree that "*Et caetera*" means "open-arse" gender the "arse" differently. While Porter argues that it remains female and thus "heterosexual," Goldberg insists that the gender is indeterminate.[250] Indeed, we might pause to consider that "medlar" itself, while regularly glossed as "a fruit thought to resemble female sex organs,"[251] is, according to Partridge and Goldberg, understood as "ass" by "maids . . . when they laugh alone" (2.1.36). Ass or vagina, male ass or female, misogynist male pun or humorous female speech, medlar and "*Et caetera*" together spin a circuit of orificial allusion that is finally undecidable—presenting not only an editorial crux, or a linguistic or potentially performative one, but a sexual and epistemological crux as well. Indeed, we might extrapolate Maguire's argument that *et cetera* "can have it both ways" on behalf of such signifying impasses, as the term "plays a conceptually sophisticated tease of hide and seek with boundaries and cusps, with abruption and continuation, with suspension and extension of meaning."[252]

Insofar as "et cetera" irrupts into an epistemological vacancy, its tease of hide-and-seek provides a fitting conclusion to my foray into the aporia at the core of the early modern sexual lexicon. Like "naught" and "dildo," "et cetera" exemplifies and heightens the epistemological tension between knowing and not knowing that inheres more generally in the culture's sexual words and wordplay. Producing the semblance of some *thing*, such terms imply that this something is nothing, or nonsense, or inexpressible, or unintelligible. In the give-and-take of sexual signification, words and wordplay take away as much as they give, circulating sexual knowledge and withholding it. From the terse, formulaic phrasing of court depositions to the hyperactive punning of popular plays, early modern sex talk tantalizingly promises and fails to deliver. Whereas what is promised and what is withheld may differ according to discursive genre and social idioms of decorum, the impasses created by such talk remain a fundamental attribute, indeed, an axiomatic strategy, of the culture's means of signifying sex.

Other scholars have alluded to the productive nature of such impasses. Steven Mullaney, for instance, argues that "absence, disjunction, inconsistency, contradiction, incongruity . . . are among the most important dramaturgical and epistemological devices available to the stage. They are among the tools that theater uses to think with, when it wants or needs to think about something else—and when it wants its audiences to do the same."[253] Describing Shakespeare's "radical excision" of plot elements in *Hamlet*, Stephen Greenblatt notes that "Shakespeare found that he could immeasurably deepen the effect of his plays, that he could provoke in the audience and in himself a peculiarly passionate intensity of response, if he took out a key explanatory element, thereby occluding the rationale, motivation, or ethical principle that accounted for the action that was to unfold. The principle was not the making of a riddle to be solved, but the creation of a strategic opacity. This opacity, Shakespeare found, released an enormous energy that had been at least partially blocked or contained by familiar, reassuring explanations."[254]

Although Shakespeare may have been especially attracted to and gifted in exploiting opacity, incongruity, and contradiction,[255] this cognitive and epistemological strategy was not specific to his work or to that of other dramatists. As Stephen Orgel noted over twenty years ago, "incomprehensibility" was a constitutive feature of early modern texts; indeed, "the Renaissance tolerated, and indeed courted, a much higher degree of ambiguity and opacity than we do; we tend to forget that the age often found in incomprehensibility a positive virtue."[256]

Given how incomprehensibility functions in early modern sexual speech and given the critical disposition that, I have argued, this linguistic strategy demands, I conclude by asking whether the opacities, ambiguities, and artful dodges of early modern sex talk "released" something within early moderns. Although it is difficult to say if in any particular instance they experienced the impasses of sex talk as irritating, disappointing, or enticing, the creative energy expended on such opacities by playwrights, poets, and ballad makers suggests that they, at least, counted on opacity as providing its own form of pleasure. What is impossible to know, of course, is how the experience of incomprehension might have elicited *further* speech among women, among men, and across genders—and to what sex acts that speech might have led.

Contemporary critics, for their part, may find in the sex-word aporia an invitation for desire, pleasure, lack, or longing, as well as the frustrations, aggravations, and gratifications of not being in the know. But whatever the affective response, I hope readers will have new incentive, as well as increased ability, to reassess the means by which *we* talk sex—including whether the period's texts might deserve more nuanced competencies for attending to bodily and gender indeterminacy, for tracking the transfer of metaphors from one body part to another, and for honoring the obliquities that persist, despite our most determined efforts to know. I have argued that the physical materiality of sex acts is mirrored by the language that is used to figure it, but I have also argued that neither sex nor its language are rendered more transparent because of this. The lexicon of sex in early modern England is naughty, not because it is bawdy, but because it powerfully indexes some of the social, hermeneutic, and epistemological obstacles that make sex such an obdurate object of knowledge. Thinking sex through Renaissance words and wordplay, it turns out, leads to an appreciation of early modern *sex* that is as strange and inconclusive as the most convoluted pun in Shakespeare or Middleton.

PART III

The Stakes of Gender

CHAPTER 8

Shakespeare's Sex

Shakespeare's sex.[1] The metrical solidity of the phrase might seem to promise something certain, something definite, something profound. Perhaps I might put to rest the question that countless critics have suggested could illuminate the mystery of Shakespeare and his sonnets. As Michael Schoenfeldt notes in his 2007 Blackwell Companion, "if one set out intentionally to create a copy-text of tantalizing irresolution, it would be hard to achieve the level attained" in the 1609 quarto of the sonnets "by the accidental contingencies of history and biography."[2] Biography often has been at stake in readings of the erotic relations alluded to in Shakespeare's sonnets—in evident accord with Michel Foucault's assertion that in modernity the truth of the subject is presumed to reside in the secret of his sex.[3] Indeed, since Edmond Malone's edition of 1790, which split the sonnets into two narratives—one addressed to a fair young man and another addressed to a woman repeatedly described as black—the Ur-text for Shakespeare's sex (by which I mean his sexuality, not his anatomy) has been neither his plays, his narrative verse, nor the documents we have of his life, but that supposed repository of lyric subjectivity, his sonnets.[4]

I am not going to try to pluck out the heart of that mystery. Instead, this chapter explores the conditions of interpretation that currently inform critics' engagements with the sonnets as they navigate the terms through which Shakespeare's sex is understood. The centuries-long history of editorial intervention in Shakespeare's sonnets and the history of literary criticism concerning them render these poems a flash point for thinking sex with the early moderns. Indeed, the question of Shakespeare's sonnets is, for countless editors, critics, and readers, a question that comes down, in various ways, to sex—and it is a question that stubbornly refuses to be answered.

In reaction to the seemingly endless rounds of biographical speculation to which the sonnets have been subject—and perhaps in deference to Stephen Booth's oft-cited assertion of 1977, "William Shakespeare was almost certainly homosexual, bisexual, or heterosexual. The sonnets provide no evidence on the matter"[5]—critics and editors have, with a few exceptions, increasingly highlighted all that we *don't* know about Shakespeare's life,[6] including the possible identities lurking behind the "characters" of the sonnets and the circumstances of the 1609 quarto publication.[7] This acknowledgment of obscurity is one I applaud. But rather than emphasize the contingencies of biography and book history, I shall flip the analytical focus toward the contingencies by which we come to "know" Shakespeare's sexuality. In a previous essay, I argued that the controversy about the sonnets' status as a narrative sequence bears a structural relation to the biographical question of Shakespeare's sex, and that by disentangling the concepts of Shakespeare's biography, sexuality, and narrative sequence, we might better apprehend what is at stake in their pervasive, yet undertheorized, association.[8] The present chapter focuses less on the link between Shakespeare's biography and the sonnets' narrative and more on how contemporary concepts of sexuality affect interpretations of both the life and the work.

This diagnostic exercise is a deliberately historicist one, although, as has been true throughout this book, the history with which I am concerned is as much the here and now as the there and then. If the link between Shakespeare's biography and the sexuality of the sonnets has proven wildly seductive, at least since Oscar Wilde's "The Portrait of Mr. W.H.," it is forged today by means of a different set of assumptions and a different horizon of expectations about what sexuality means than was evident in Wilde's strategic negotiation of the Victorian closet.[9] Just as we might approach Wilde's fictional portrait of Willie Hughes as Shakespeare's beloved (with its illicit intimations and cagey equivocations, couched in deniability) in the context of speech acts widely considered unmentionable yet nonetheless prosecutable,[10] we can gain analytical purchase on our current production of sexual knowledge by scrutinizing the cultural logics by which scholars today are articulating the sexuality of, and in, the sonnets. Whereas my entrée into the historicity of sexual knowledge is through the analytic methods used to adduce the sexual meanings of the sonnets, the question of Shakespeare's sex opens onto other questions that have threaded through this book's pages: not only perennial questions of erotic desire, sexual (non)identity, and gender asymmetries, but questions regarding difference and similitude, aesthetic form, temporality, historicity, knowledge—in short, of what it means to know sexuality, not only in the past but in the present.

Shakespeare's Sex as Knowledge Relation

When did Shakespeare become gay? Or homosexual? Or bisexual? I do not mean, at what point in his physical and psychic development—in his mother's womb, during grammar school, at the sight of a beautiful nobleman—did he first find himself exploring through versification the erotic attractions of young men or, conversely, exploring the potential of poetic verse through the muse of masculine beauty. Rather, my question is, when did *we* decide that Shakespeare—or, if you prefer, his poetic persona—was any of those things, and how did we decide it?

That many of us *have* decided something along these lines is clear. Indeed, distinctions of nomenclature aside, the battle waged by Joseph Pequigney in *Such Is My Love: A Study of Shakespeare's Sonnets*, published in 1985, has been, in many respects, won:[11] even if Pequigney's tentative speculation that the biographical details of Shakespeare's alleged love affairs are encoded in the sonnets continues to be met with skepticism, the general thrust of his argument—that the poet-speaker's articulation of love and desire for his male friend *is erotic*—has largely been accepted. Testament to the impact of the first generation of out gay early modernists who explored how male homoeroticism in the past both spoke to and differed from gay identity in the present,[12] this acceptance testifies as well to some influential readings of individual sonnets.[13] Preeminent among them: in 1991 Bruce Smith's *Homosexual Desire in Shakespeare's England* capitalized on Booth's edition and commentary—which authoritatively established the sexual innuendo of the sonnets' "wordplay"—to make a historical bid for Shakespeare's "invention of a new mode of discourse about homosexual desire . . . that seems distinctively modern."[14] The same year, Gregory Bredbeck laid the basis for subsequent queer readings by arguing that, through their polymorphous perversity, the sonnets disrupt the "proper" order of gender and language.[15] Building on the scholarship of historian Alan Bray,[16] Jeffrey Masten nuanced that insight, arguing that intimate friendship is precisely the means by which, to invoke the phrasing of Mario DiGangi, orderly male homoeroticism gained expression in this period; together, these two critics shed implicit light on the sonnets' supposed "Platonic love" and its alleged "sublimation" of male erotic desire.[17] If critics following in their steps have not always approached the sonnets with the historical sensitivity of these scholars—Shakespeare's sex is sometimes described as homosexuality, sometimes described as bisexuality,[18] sometimes distinguished from modern identity categories, and sometimes conflated with them[19]—it remains the case that the homoeroticism of Shakespeare's sonnets is now routinely acknowledged, not only in literary criticism,[20] but in most editorial introductions and introductory companions, including those marketed to undergraduates and the general public.[21]

If much of this now seems old hat—indeed, encountering this tradition of scholarship, today's students are apt to respond, "What's the big deal?"—I recall it to bear witness to the amount of ground clearing that was required to achieve the current critical consensus or, as some might call it, critical orthodoxy.[22] Liberated from the requirement of proving the relevance of male homoerotic desire to these poems, free to treat the "reality" of sexual desire between men in the sonnets as, in the words of Daniel Juan Gil, "axiom[atic]" and "incontrovertible," literary critics have moved on to analyze the intricate range of affects expressed through the sonnets' rhetorical and aesthetic strategies.[23]

Without intending to diminish the value of this hard-won critical consensus or minimize the intellectual contribution of scholars who transformed the meaning of queer from an insult into a powerful mode of reading, I nonetheless want to suggest that there is something disconcerting about the terms by which Shakespeare's sex has become so normative. My mingled feelings of pleasure, astonishment, and unease are akin to those I felt when cities and states across the United States began to legalize gay marriage—something, when I unlawfully married my partner in 1986, the year after Pequigney's controversial study, I never thought I would see. Just as we need to think carefully about the terms by which gay marriage gains social acceptability—as marriage equality or civil union? Affording which rights, privileges, and responsibilities? In deference to which definitions of normality? At the expense of which other forms of erotic affiliations and in the name of whose history?[24]—we need to think carefully about the cultural and intellectual implications of the critical consensus regarding Shakespeare's sex.

And so I ask: if Shakespeare's sexuality is a settled matter, what are the precise terms of that settlement? Four observations regarding current critical practice motivate this query. First, since the 1990s it has become common to note the homophobia that inflected prior readings of the sonnets.[25] Bringing this reception history to the attention of students, now a common pedagogical practice, usefully historicizes sexuality by showing it to be subject to changing social mores as well as culturally contingent understandings of sex as identity.[26] At the same time, this pedagogy presents a very partial history of sex, thereby reinforcing the common misperception that the history of sexuality takes the form of a developmental trajectory modeled on liberatory narratives of coming out of the closet.[27] Absent a more sustained engagement with the history of sexuality and queer historiography (which, in particular, has sought to resist such teleological schemas), Shakespeareans risk promoting an idea that is belied by the complexity of sexuality in the past. Could the progressive, identitarian, self-congratulatory appeal of that notion of history—which makes us feel good about our own, supposedly more enlightened present moment— be an unintended consequence of, or, equally problematically, a contributing factor to, the critical consensus regarding Shakespeare's sex?

Second, even as scholars have arrived at this consensus, most of them have stopped fretting over Shakespeare's sex life. As Stephen Orgel has noted, "recent editors have accepted the sonnets' gayness without worrying much about Shakespeare's."[28] For a host of reasons it makes sense to disengage biographical speculation about Shakespeare from consideration of the erotic relations of and in the sonnets. At the same time, it is worth noting that setting aside Shakespeare's sex life may have supplied one of the conditions of possibility for our current consensus. A notable harbinger of this trend was Bruce Smith, writing in 1991: "For our purposes here, what is important is not whether particular poems and particular passages 'prove' that Shakespeare the man did or did not have sexual relations with a certain other man but how the sonnets as poems insinuate sexual feeling in the bonds men in general made with one another in early modern England."[29] Along with bracketing the issue of evidentiary proof, most recent criticism on the sonnets has bracketed as well the question of sex acts performed by male bodies with one another.[30]

To the extent that resistance to a literalizing hermeneutic corresponds to the construal of homoeroticism as a matter of social *identity* rather than particular erotic *behaviors*, insofar as it posits "love" as the sine qua non for social acceptance, it bears more than a passing resemblance to the limited political basis, at least within the United States, upon which it is now possible to advocate gay marriage.[31] Is the equanimity with which critics acknowledge the sonnets' expression of homoerotic love, when examined in light of our culture's taking for granted of the desirability of the couple form (with its idealizations of erotic exclusivity, longevity, and stability), purchased at the price of a tacit elision, a disavowal, of same-sex sex?[32]

Third, existing alongside this liberal equanimity is a growing trend to estab-lish the "real scandal" of Shakespeare's sonnets as something *other* than homo-sexuality. As if the sonnets *must* enact a politics of nonnormativity and as if the critic's task were to reveal the repression that would conceal it, now that homosexuality no longer possesses as much power to disturb, some scholars have taken to arguing that what would have been *really* scandalous in Shake-speare's time was not sex among men, but sex across race or class. Based on a historicist appreciation of the Renaissance normativity of male erotic bonds, Margreta de Grazia, for instance, argues that "the scandal in the Sonnets has been misidentified. It is not Shakespeare's desire for a boy; for in upholding social distinctions, that desire proves quite conservative and safe. It is Shake-speare's gynerastic longings for a black mistress that are perverse and menacing, precisely because they threaten to raze the very distinctions his poems to the fair boy strain to preserve."[33] Adopting de Grazia's rhetoric of scandal but shifting the focus of its charge, Colin Burrow argues that it is the speaker's love for an aristocrat that would have most troubled Shakespeare's contemporaries.[34] Important as it is to articulate the racial and class politics of the sonnets and to place these politics within available early modern understandings, critics' rhe-torical insistence that such matters displace homosexuality from its position as the "real scandal" bespeaks a competitive logic that may have more to do with the agon of contemporary identity politics than the knotty relations among sex, race, and class in these poems.

The problems that attend a developmental model of homosexual history, the elision of bodily sex acts, and the creation of a hierarchy of scandals are fairly obvious: my aim in raising them is simply to encourage collective reflection on their enabling conditions as well as a collective appraisal of how to mitigate their costs. Each of them could be addressed by placing the critical conversation about Shakespeare's sex within a more expansive, insistently material, and intersectional history of sexuality. Robert Matz has demon-strated the payoff of such an approach by placing the "untidiness" of the history of the sonnets' reception within a broad historical narrative of the changing configurations of male friendship, homosexuality, adultery, and heterosexuality.[35] Rather than a single scandal, Matz argues, Shakespeare's sonnets flirt with a number of potential scandals, whose moral cogency shifts according to the not always commensurate fortunes of homophobia and het-erosexism.[36] In addition, more remains to be done to explore how sexuality in the sonnets—including the poet's appreciation of erotic attractiveness, his definition of beauty, and his attraction-repulsion toward deception and self-laceration—is constituted through ideas and rhetorics of race and social status.[37]

It is a fourth issue, the analytical status accorded to gender in readings of sex in the sonnets, that is my central concern here. Confronting Shakespeare's intricately elaborated representation of gender similitude and difference (most often registered through the affective dichotomy between the fair "lovely boy" and mistress "colored ill") as well as the critical tradition to which gender analysis has given rise, critics have taken to arguing one of two positions (and sometimes both): on the one hand, some critics seem intent on trying to "save" the "dark lady" from the misogyny that most scholars agree is part of the sonnets' ideological surround.[38] This trend gained momentum in 1996 when Heather Dubrow, developing de Grazia's observation that only about 20 percent of the sonnets specify a gendered addressee—that is, a he or a she—proposed that the indeterminacy of pronominal address and narrative order might be used to provocatively regender some of the poems.[39] Among other things, this indeterminacy permitted Dubrow to transfer onto the dark lady some of the praise lavished on the young man. Similar feminist motives are present in Ilona Bell's attempt to dispute the "evidence of the lady's promiscuity"; unlike Dubrow's celebration of narrative inconclusiveness, however, Bell composes an alternative story in which the lady resists the advances of the poet-speaker out of fidelity to the young man.[40]

On the other hand, Dubrow's influential linkage of narrative indeterminacy to gender and sexual mobility also gave support to scholars who maintain that gender difference in the sonnets has been overplayed. Colin Burrow and Michael Schoenfeldt, for instance, caution that an undue emphasis on gender difference has obscured the extent to which the male friend is subject to the same frustration, bitterness, and reproach directed toward the mistress—suggesting that it is not only Shakespeare but we who have over-idealized the young man.[41] And, by way of proposing that "the most appealing love object forwarded in the sequence is the sequence itself," Douglas Trevor suggests that the gender of the fair youth and dark lady "matters less than does the way both of them make the speaker renounce as dangerous any emotional attachment to other human beings."[42] These critics usefully remind us that neither of Shakespeare's primary "love objects" has an exclusive lock on the poet's praise or dispraise, and that irrespective of the beloved's gender, erotic desire in the sonnets generally is characterized as sickness and pain, attachment is precarious, and love and desire are permeated by intimations of loss and mortality.[43]

Different motives and different critical methodologies characterize the arguments of these scholars. They all share, however, a (generally unstated) assumption that focusing on gender and sexuality necessarily involves considering Shakespeare's biography or indulging in biographical speculation—that is, the attempt to detect Shakespeare's love life or find "real-life" identities behind the sonnets' dramatis personae—even if their aim is to contest such critical moves. In addition, they tend to correlate matters of gender and sexuality with the issue of establishing within the collection a coherent and continuous narrative story. Whether they construe such attempts as worthy or dubious, whether they enact, resist, or ridicule them, they all presuppose that gender and sexuality are necessarily implicated in, and themselves imply, consequences for Shakespeare's biography and the sonnets' status as a narrative or sequence. Indeed, the presumption that the story of the sonnets is somehow linked (for good or ill) to Shakespeare's biography and that the status of the gender and sexual relations in the poems are linked (again, for good or ill) to that story's rendition as a sequence are two critical commonplaces that have informed much of the sonnets' criticism over the past twenty years.

Such presumptions are what I propose to scrutinize in what follows. It is not that these suppositions are necessarily wrong, but that their unacknowledged influence paves the way for a set of ideas about gender, sexuality, and poetic form to make its way into arguments without explicit awareness or acknowledgment. Seeking a different path through this penumbra of presumptive knowledge, I ask: Are there *necessary* relations among gender and sexuality, biography, narrative, and sequence, or are such linkages the effect of unexamined slippages among an overdetermined set of concepts?[44] Might there be something productively symptomatic in the paradox underlying critics' acceptance of the sonnets' homoeroticism—which, after all, is a sexuality defined exclusively, indeed coarsely, on the basis of gender similarity—and their intimation that, as it is deployed in the sonnets, gender (itself a concept based on similitude and difference) might need to be rewritten, subordinated, or displaced? And might this have some bearing on the general critical tendency to advance either a feminist or queer interpretation of the sonnets, but rarely both at the same time?

Queer-Psychoanalytic Shakespeare

The construction of Shakespeare's homo- and bisexuality has an alternative lineage to the one I just described. Around the same time as Pequigney,

Shakespeareans from a more traditional psychoanalytic perspective argued that many of Shakespeare's plays reference an Oedipal trajectory, whereby the male child's identification with and love of the father is split into the victorious acquisition of "normal" gender and heterosexual identity—that is, gender identification with men and erotic desire for women. Some of these critics analyzed the psychic price to male characters as they made their way from "primary narcissism" and "male bonding" toward the sexual difference associated with heterosexual courtship and marriage.[45] (Joel Fineman's influential gender-bifurcated reading of the sonnets enlarges this insight through a Lacanian filter that sutures gender and sexuality to signification).[46] In the 1980s I and some of my peers critiqued the ahistorical, heterosexual bias that underwrote such developmental schemas, contributing to a critical milieu in which historicism replaced psychoanalysis as the dominant method used to read sex in the early modern period.

With the influential exception of the comparativist Carla Freccero, until recently most early modernists working on sex have steered clear of a psychoanalytic idiom—and for some very good reasons. From the perspective of historicism, psychoanalysis is often discredited for its transhistorical pretensions, its normativizing function when practiced as a mode of generating truth,[47] and its hierarchical prioritization of the one who knows (the analyst, the critic, the historian) above the one who is subjected to knowledge (the analysand, the author, the text, the event). It must be admitted that psychoanalytic scholars—whether reading as queers, as early modernists, or both—have not done a particularly persuasive job explaining why psychoanalysis is or should be an appropriate method for approaching sexuality. For all the brilliance of individual interpretations—of literature, of film, of cultural formations—psychoanalytic critics often simply assert their methodological orientation, rather than explicate its utility for the questions they are pursuing; their "readings" thus implicitly bear the burden of that task. Yet, on the other side of hostilities, it is indeed "strange," as L. O. Aranye Fradenburg maintains, that "historicists who believe that there is significant interchange between people and their [own] time, but that this interchange is not transparent, break out in hives at the possibility that they might have had significant interchange with their [own, individual] particular histories that are not fully transparent or known to them."[48]

In direct retort to Stephen Greenblatt's assertion that "psychoanalysis can redeem its belatedness only when it historicizes its own procedures,"[49] however, a number of early modernists who remained psychoanalytically inclined during the heyday of historicism have engaged in just such a historicizing project, whether by situating their work against the dominant historicism of the field or attempting to bridge psychoanalytic concerns with those of historicism by recognizing "the shared reverberations of some of their key terms."[50] Among early modernists whose bridgework most concerns embodiment and sexuality, the trend has been to historicize psychoanalysis in several interconnected ways: by repudiating the idea of a timeless and universal unconscious and exploring the relation of psychoanalytic subjectivity to early modern concepts of interiority, including Galenic psychophysiology and the humoral passions;[51] arguing for the enduring influence of early modern discourses, including those of medicine, theology, and literature, on the thought of Freud, Lacan, Kristeva, Irigaray, and Zizek;[52] and employing psychoanalytic insights to excavate certain psycho-erotic dynamics (perversion, abjection, anal eroticism, narcissism, oral aggression, sadism, masochism, heterosexuality), while eschewing, often in the name of historical alterity, a normalizing or moralizing judgment.[53] Each of these strategies, as well as their confluence, enables the critic to avoid subordinating literature (or the author) under a psychoanalytic template, instead allowing psychoanalysis, aesthetics, and early modern discourses to permeate, illuminate, and assess each other.[54]

Increasingly, queer understandings of desire, nonidentity, and antinormativity have influenced and redirected early modern critics' retooling of psychoanalysis.[55] Actually, it might be more accurate to say that queer theory's own indebtedness to psychoanalysis is finally gaining traction in early modern studies. Queer psychoanalytic critics tend to agree that the psychological mechanisms of desire and identification (along with condensation, substitution, displacement, projection, and introjection) are relevant to every subject, regardless of historical location (even though historical location is seen to influence the contents to which they might be addressed). More particularly, they insist that erotic desire and gender identification are produced simultaneously through intra- and interpsychic processes occurring in specific social and political surrounds;[56] that erotic desire and gender identification are profoundly unstable; that erotic desire and gender identification interact dynamically—sometimes coherently, sometimes with considerable friction; and that singular sexual identities are taken on only as an enabling fiction and at considerable psychic and social cost.[57]

These are all ideas to which I subscribe. Nonetheless, despite this significant area of agreement, my work tends to differ from that of queer psychoanalytic critics in two important respects. First, I am intent on emphasizing the continual *work* that the psychic contingency of desire and identification entails, work whose procedures require articulation and analysis, and whose dynamics impact our understanding of the ongoing effects of gender and sex. For this reason, in my reading of the sonnets to come, I slow down the pace of interpretation, seeking to expose the moment-by-moment textual, psychic, and political maneuvers that inform gendered and sexual relations.

Second, rather than assume the nonnormativity of erotic desires and practices that look queer to us today, I ask whether and how queer they were in their own time. In other words, what does it mean to say that Shakespeare (or again, the poetic persona of his sonnets) was *queer*?[58] By this I do not mean: was the poet interested in using the sonnet form to elaborate complex emotional affects in relation to a beautiful young man—or possibly several of them? Rather, my question is: did he resist his culture's normative categories of gender and sexuality? It has become usual to note Shakespeare's heterodox innovations to both Petrarchan and English conventions of sonneteering, particularly in addressing love poems to a male beauty.[59] But does literary innovation in this case necessarily imply, as many critics, including queer ones, often assume, opposition to dominant regimes of gender and sexuality?

Although scholars have argued that orderly male homoeroticism was central to early modern culture, few have directly confronted how this insight might pressure our go-to notions of orthodoxy and transgression, norms and their subversion—and with them, the very meaning of "queer."[60] In confronting this question, I'm furthering the argument, introduced in previous chapters, that if the concept of queer is to continue to do important conceptual work, it cannot simply function as a trendy or edgy transhistorical synonym for the identity categories "homosexual" or "gay," or, under the more rigorous auspices of theory, as a diffuse instantiation of a degendered, nonidentitarian, polyvalent other to normativity. If queer is a position taken in relation to dominant sexual and gender norms, which are themselves subject to historical change, and if the potential of queer lies in its recognition of an expanded range of erotic and gendered desires, identifications, and acts, then part of its analytical value is that it can help us assess whether early modern male homoeroticism was transgressive of dominant social hierarchies—including those of gender—and if so, under what conditions.

As I have maintained in previous chapters, the very capaciousness, mobility, and mutability of queer—often trumpeted as its unique promise as an analytical category—may obscure as much as enable historical understanding. Whereas there is much to recommend analytic appreciation for gender transitivity and resistance to sexual normativity, these investments, with their accent on the universalizing rather than minoritizing axis of signification, also run the risk of *de*specifying desires, identifications, and practices.[61] By "elud[ing] identitarian capture,"[62] the concept of queer licenses both novel resignifications and productive identifications across time, but the horizon of queer possibility is not entirely open-ended. It is tethered, both now and in the past, to the specificities of social and discursive configurations of sexuality as well as to the tentacles of gender. My general argument is that emphasis on queer's infinite plasticity and inexhaustible adaptability has contributed to an overestimation of its explanatory sufficiency as a method. My more particular argument is that its willingness to forgo deictic reference has resulted in the construction of unwarranted analogies among gender and erotic positions that obscure and belie material asymmetries and hierarchies. For these reasons, it is the specific mechanisms by which gender asymmetries are constructed *by means of sex* that my reading of the sonnets is dedicated to disclosing.

The Diacritics of Sequence

As I build my case that sequence need not be harnessed to Shakespeare's biography, to expectations of characterological coherence, or to narrative continuity, I have expressed several critical desires: to join with others in revitalizing the utility of a queer psychoanalytic appreciation for the instability of desire and identification as an antidote to those forms of historicism that too readily assume a stable desiring subject; to advance the collective project of a nonidentitarian concept of early modern sexuality; to caution against the too-easy application of queer as a transhistorical, universalizing signifier of sexual dissidence;[63] and to historicize the history of sexuality in the present, including the conditions of possibility for our own erotic identities (and nonidentities) and our own critical consensus. At the level of intimation, I have implied that gender and sexuality need to be thought *diacritically*: by which I mean in terms of their difference from one another as well as in terms of their dynamic, ongoing relation. A diacritical understanding is not exactly a dialectical one, which carries with it the expectation of resolution or synthesis—although it shares with dialectics an awareness of mutually constitutive effects. Nor is it merely a comparative one, whereby, for instance, the poet's representation of his black mistress might be compared systematically to that of the fair youth.[64] Although adducing such comparisons is one aspect of a diacritical approach, such an approach—like the diacritical linguistic marks from which it receives its name—foregrounds the *effort* taken to distinguish between one term and another in order to show the precise, even exacting, ways they are related.

In what follows, my diacritical analytic of sequence directly confronts the divergent claims of gender and sexuality, providing a both/and approach to feminist queer studies. Differentiatng the eroticism associated with male (same-sex) erotic friendship from that associated with male lust (for women) while also suggesting that the diffuse capaciousness of the concept of queer problematically elides such differences, my argument underscores the significance of gender specificity in the meanings of sexual desires and acts. It also aims to demonstrate the potential of an analytic of cross-gender identification, insofar as such an analytic tracks the mobilization of transitive genders to precisely situated social positions. Such an analytic confronts the impasse that attends the critical desire to apprehend the desiring position of a poet-speaker whose ambivalent profession of his "two loves" settles uneasily on the bimodal affects of "comfort and despair" (Sonnet 144). My motive in witnessing how this "settling" occurs, however, is not quite captured by a resolve to "take the woman's part" or defend the dark lady's reputation, as previous feminist critics have done. Nor do I mean to turn the tables on the sexual double standard and endorse, from the perspective of a sex-positive feminist, the dark lady's promiscuity—although I am not averse to such a move.[65] My interest, rather, is in how gendered erotic objects and affects, male as well as female, are actively *manufactured*.

In two previous essays, I analyzed the sonnets' interwoven logics of gender and sexuality by means of attending to historically specific forms of production. "Sex Without Issue: Sodomy, Reproduction, and Signification in Shakespeare's Sonnets" contextualized the sonnets via early modern legal and medical discourses of sodomy and reproduction. "The Sonnets: Sequence, Sexuality, and Shakespeare's Two Loves" examined postmodern appropriations of the sonnets in light of contemporary feminist and gay cultural politics. Both essays framed my interpretation of the diacritical relations between gender and sexuality, homoeroticism and heterosexuality, poems to the young boy and poems to the poet's mistress, by means of manifold tensions between feminist, gay male, and queer modes of reading, and both sought a way to address these tensions without acceding to the sonnets' own promotion of a zero-sum game.

Focused historically on the early modern discourse of sodomy, "Sex Without Issue" investigated the convergence in the sonnets of male homoerotic desire and misogyny while resisting critics' tendency to play feminist and gay male investments off of each other. Noting that the sodomitical relationship in the sonnets occurs not between men but between the poet-speaker and the dark lady, I argued that Shakespeare safeguarded his erotic investment in the young man by enacting a motivated inversion of legal and medical discourses of legitimate and illegitimate sex. Appropriating biological and poetic genera-tion as an all-male endeavor, he displaced the culture's horror of sodomy onto his on-again, off-again mistress, thereby making way for a future of homoerotic poetry.[66] Although other critics had noted the sodomitical force of the dark lady sonnets, my argument highlighted the crucial role of psychic and textual *displacement* in the sonnet's overall design. Shakespeare's strategic expunging of sodomy from his relationship to the beautiful boy appeared to require, as if chiasmically, its correlative application to his mistress's dark body. This chiastic structure, working in concert with the operations of dis-placement, yields three critical insights: First, there is nothing *natural* in the association of male-male eroticism with either sodomy or misogyny; any such association is a matter of cultural, aesthetic, and psychic labor. Second, far from being a natural outgrowth of male desires for men, the displacement of sodomy onto the dark lady is strategic and structural: a matter of creating conditions of priority and precedence through processes of substitution and supersession. Such displacement enacts, in a register at once formal and psy-chological, what I called an operation of sexual sequence. Third, the historical interarticulation of male-male desire and misogyny demands an analytic capable of thinking them simultaneously: in short, a diacritical one that is motivated by the crossing of gender identifications.

My subsequent essay developed this diacritical analytic of displacement and sequence by examining the interweaving of literary and cinematic form with ideologies of gender and sexuality. Using the afterlife of Shakespeare's sonnets in the 1998 film *Shakespeare in Love* to unpack the critical conflation of the poet's biography, narrative sequence, and homosexuality, and untying the theoretical knots that hold sequence and sexuality together, I argued that the film's version of liberal feminist progress is purchased at the expense of articulating male-male desire. Indeed, feminist self-expression served as the justification for the erasure of male-male sex from Shakespeare's imagined biography, as the dependencies of an all-male homoerotic literary collabora-tion initially depicted in the film were displaced by a heterosexual collabora-tion anointed with the idealizing gloss of genius and romantic love.[67] In this way, the cinematic manipulation of erotic paradigms enacts a mirror image of the sonnets' own logics—indebted to even as it inverts them. So, too, critical conflict about the sonnets' narrativity is implicated in a zero-sum game that pits homosexuality and feminism off of one another.

Defining the logic of sequence as the temporal and structural relations of precedence, chronology, substitution, and supersession, these essays gestured toward the way displacements are enabled and enforced through particular syntactical arrangements.[68] Sequence, in this view, names an analytic born of the effort to negotiate the impasses of construing the relation of male to female as interlocked and antagonistic. Dedicated to exposing the sequential procedures that enforce or resist the logic of mutually exclusive, antithetical genders and sexualities, these two essays crafted a critical perspective derived from the recognition that gender and sexuality are profitably understood to function in dynamic, diacritical relation, and that a diacritical analysis can also be calibrated to a cross-gendered one.

This chapter, "Shakespeare's Sex," builds on and departs from these earlier essays. The critical tension and attempted balance between feminist, gay male, and queer investments in the complex forms of erotic desire, longing, aversion, and loss that animate these poems remain central. However, as my discussion of tensions among these perspectives throughout this book attest, there is more to be said about the problematic ways in which differential investments in gender and in sexuality continue to square off within our critical dispensations (no less than on the Hollywood screen). Although the rhetorics and media through which these tensions are manifested and addressed have change over time in content and style, the structural link that informs their conflict seems remarkably static—as animating of today's critical conversations as it was in the 1990s.

Second, the theoretical and methodological affordance of the concept of sexual sequence is, in the present chapter, developed more explicitly as a matter of textual *form*. To date, the relationship of gender and sexuality to Shakespearean poetic form has mainly generated analyses of Shakespeare's tight, bimodal structuring of metaphor (e.g., light and dark, fair and foul, truth and lies). But other formal procedures are relevant to the ongoing manufacture of gender and desire: one such procedure, I aim to show, is the formal operation of sequence. The present chapter thus extends my analytic of sequence by bringing to the fore a consideration of its workings by means of a focus on *syntax*. It is helpful in this regard to think of sequence as a single temporal and spatial line, however distended or discontinuous in length, whereas syntax is a larger framing device that orders sequence along that temporal or spatial path. Furthermore, the sequential and the diacritical are related insofar as they enact a coordinated set of relations; these relations can shift, but always within the terms of a static, nondevelopmental frame.

Third, my previous essays tended to conflate my evolving concept of sequence with the critical analytic of *displacement*. Because it operates by way of substitutive logics, sequence depends on and derives from the concept of displacement. However, thinking of sequence in terms of syntax allows us to see how it diverges from displacement both methodologically and theoretically. As I use it here, the concept of sequence invites us to pause over the work of displacement, as well as to resist the pull of essentialism that displacement can carry with it. Dispensing with the notion of a prior "state" that functions as a stabilizing origin (e.g., an original desire from which something turns or that is superseded), sequence allows the status of what is displaced to be rendered contingent and unstable. And by exposing the hidden links and smooth stages by which displacement occurs, the analytic of sequence allows us to analyze how the prioritizations achieved by displacement are enabled by a particular operation of form.

Finally, both of my prior essays took for granted some of the ground that Chapters 6 and 7 argued should not be presumed: on the one hand, the appeal to historical and discursive context as the overarching critical ground for interpreting and fixing the meanings of sex; and, on the other hand, the appeal to "bawdy" words as something made knowable, stable, and secure through the editorial apparatus of the dictionary and gloss. If, as Chapter 7 argued, the language of sex, most especially in terms of puns, poses difficulties of comprehension that cannot be resolved by recourse to a dictionary or gloss, how might this insight affect how we approach the extraordinary polysemy of Shakespeare's sonnets?[69] If we do not take definitions of sexual words and body parts for granted, how is gender manifested through individual words? And if, as Chapter 6 argued, the use of historical context often serves not only as a stabilizing ground for textual interpretation but as a cover for the failure to adequately attend to sex acts, by which historical or formal methods might we adduce the meanings of such basic elements as the gender of bodies in poems dedicated, as Sonnet 20 makes palpably evident, to polysemous punning and erotic ambiguity? "Shakespeare's Sex" tackles these challenges in an effort to devise a different interpretative protocol, one that takes seriously the indeterminacy of the sexual lexicon and seeks alternative ways of determining context that do not subsume or fix the meanings of eroticism, but manifest and materialize sex as an ongoing process of knowledge relations.

Shakespeare's Sequence

At its most basic, "sequence" refers to a process of structuration, both spatial and temporal: on the one hand, it involves a serial assemblage of individual quanta (the eye looks here, then there, then here, or the ear hears this, then that, then this); on the other hand, it enacts a temporal means of forging connections, managing disconnections, and driving a movement, however fitfully, along. Under the conceptual rubric of sequence abide many of the issues that have motivated controversy about the sonnets, from questions about Shakespeare's authorial warrant of the 1609 quarto, to the narrative (in)coherence of the collection, to the indeterminacy of their pronominal address. In terms of criticism on Shakespeare's sonnets, "sequence" refers first to the contested status of the sonnets as a continuous collection of verse. One's view about whether the 1609 quarto should be considered authoritative generally has been construed as either mandating a sequential order of reading or, conversely, freeing readers from this requirement. As if under the guiding metaphor of Shakespeare's hand, authorization is presumed to enforce a serial reading (in abstract conception, if not in actual practice), whereas the lack of Shakespeare's signature, whether bemoaned as a problem or celebrated as an opportunity, is presumed to open the text to other reading strategies, including immersion in the pleasures of individual lyrics. Sequence refers, second, to the layered temporal processes that happen within each poem, which link poems into intratextual mini-sequences, and that cumulate into an overall impression of plot, story, or narrative—or fail to. Because sequence tends to imply linearity, seriality, succession—one thing comes after another—it often elicits a proleptic expectation of development, progress, or teleology.

The fact is that, despite strenuous scholarly efforts, there is much that we do not know about Shakespeare's involvement in the quarto's publication, and our ignorance means that the controversy over the sequencing of these poems most likely will never be settled.[70] Given the vagaries of early modern publication practices, the quarto provides a remarkably stable text—one that is inclusive, well printed, and, for the majority of poems, without a textual rival. Nonetheless, the form in which the collection was first printed—its material inscription on continuous pages, with many poems carrying over from one page to the next—renders it impossible to adjudicate conclusively between the options of reading the volume from beginning to end, picking out various thematic or tonal "clusters," or reading poems as individual, autonomous lyrics. Each option for reading is available, they are not mutually exclusive, and each affords its own pleasures. Even if, as recent scholarship suggests, early modern reading practices may have tended toward reading discontinuously or indexically rather than linearly,[71] Shakespeare's sonnets, printed with many poems fragmented over two pages, might have encouraged a more serial reading practice (Figures 3 and 4).[72]

Given our limited knowledge, we might own up to the fact that preferences on this point, even when proceeding from incisive interpretations of material texts or comparative literary history of sonnet collections (e.g., page-broken sonnets versus one bounded sonnet per page), cannot help but be strategically motivated: rather than based in some ontology of the text, the genre, or the author, they evolve out of particular questions and critical investments. So let me be clear about mine: when the sonnets *are* read in the serial order in which they were first printed *as a collection* for public consumption (or returned to retrospectively with that order in mind),[73] they raise specific problems regarding the relationship of gender to sexuality whose irresolvability could be approached, in their very status as impasse, as a productive critical resource.

The Problem of Pronouns

Many recent interpretations have emphasized the number of poems that, lacking "hes" and "shes," posit generalizable situations and themes.[74] This insight can gratify readers in two ways, which are often assumed to reflect divergent investments and ideologies. On the one hand, generalization can seem to reaffirm the purported universality of such emotions as love, hate, jealousy, and despair; on the other hand, generalization can be harnessed to recognition of the potential fluidity of gender and erotic roles. Given this bicameral hermeneutic division, it is hardly surprising that the issue of indeterminate pronouns has functioned as a hinge in debates about the status of the volume's gendered division and the status of the collection as a narrative story.[75] As Jenny C. Mann notes, "one could describe much of the massive volume of criticism on the sonnets as a meditation on the problem of pronouns."[76] One particularly interesting foray into this field of contention, William Nelles's "Sexing Shakespeare's Sonnets: Reading Beyond Sonnet 20" explicitly construes the sexing of the sonnets and the related issue of narrative sequence precisely as a problem of pronouns.[77] Critiquing the default logic

S H A K E‑S P E A R E S,
SONNETS.

FRom faireſt creatures we deſire increaſe,
    That thereby beauties *Roſe* might neuer die,
But as the riper ſhould by time deceaſe,
His tender heire might beare his memory:
But thou contraſted to thine owne bright eyes,
Feed'ſt thy lights flame with ſelfe ſubſtantiall fewell,
Making a famine where aboundance lies,
Thy ſelfe thy foe,to thy ſweet ſelfe too cruell:
Thou that art now the worlds freſh ornament,
And only herauld to the gaudy ſpring,
Within thine owne bud burieſt thy content,
And tender chorle makſt waſt in niggarding:
    Pitty the world,or elſe this glutton be,
    To eate the worlds due,by the graue and thee.

2

VVHen fortie Winters ſhall beſeige thy brow,
    And digge deep trenches in thy beauties field,
Thy youthes proud liuery ſo gaz'd on now,
Wil be a totter'd weed of ſmal worth held:
Then being askt,where all thy beautie lies,
Where all the treaſure of thy luſty daies;
To ſay within thine owne deepe ſunken eyes,
Were an all-eating ſhame,and thriftleſſe praiſe.
How much more praiſe deſeru'd thy beauties vſe,
If thou couldſt anſwere this faire child of mine
Shall ſum my count,and make my old excuſe
Proouing his beautie by ſucceſſion thine.

B   This

FIGURE 3. William Shakespeare, *Sonnets* (London, 1609), Br. Reproduced by permission of
the Huntington Library, San Marino, California.

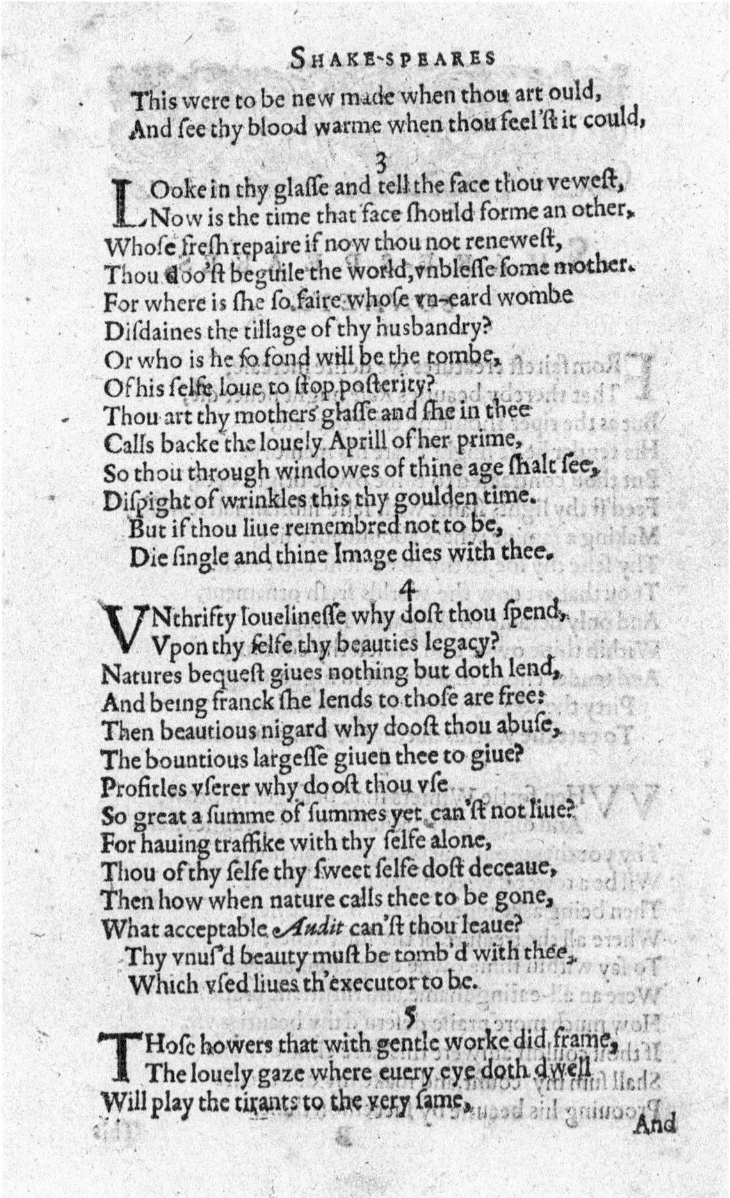

This were to be new made when thou art ould,
And fee thy blood warme when thou feel'ft it could,

3

Ooke in thy glaffe and tell the face thou veweft,
Now is the time that face fhould forme an other,
Whofe frefh repaire if now thou not reneweft,
Thou doo'ft beguile the world, vnbleffe fome mother.
For where is fhe fo faire whofe vn-eard wombe
Difdaines the tillage of thy husbandry?
Or who is he fo fond will be the tombe,
Of his felfe loue to ftop pofterity?
Thou art thy mothers glaffe and fhe in thee
Calls backe the louely Aprill of her prime,
So thou through windowes of thine age fhalt fee,
Difpight of wrinkles this thy goulden time.
  But if thou liue remembred not to be,
  Die fingle and thine Image dies with thee.

4

Nthrifty louelineffe why doft thou fpend,
Vpon thy felfe thy beauties legacy?
Natures bequeft giues nothing but doth lend,
And being franck fhe lends to thofe are free:
Then beautious nigard why dooft thou abufe,
The bountious largeffe giuen thee to giue?
Profitles vferer why dooft thou vfe
So great a fumme of fummes yet can'ft not liue?
For hauing traffike with thy felfe alone,
Thou of thy felfe thy fweet felfe doft deceaue,
Then how when nature calls thee to be gone,
What acceptable *Audit* can'ft thou leaue?
  Thy vnuf'd beauty muft be tomb'd with thee,
  Which vfed liues th'executor to be.

5

Hofe howers that with gentle worke did frame,
The louely gaze where euery eye doth dwell
Will play the tirants to the very fame,
                                          And

FIGURE 4. William Shakespeare, *Sonnets* (London, 1609), Bv. Reproduced by permission of the Huntington Library, San Marino, California.

underlying the pervasive acceptance of Malone's gendered division, Nelles argues that any five of Shakespeare's sonnets can be drawn into a narrative, concluding that "critics who describe their pet sequences for us are not deciphering the Rosetta Stone; they're reciting the playlists for their iPods. Enjoy your playlist," he says, "but stop insisting that you took it from Shakespeare."[78] To the extent that Nelles's target is the presupposition of Shakespeare's authorization and a resulting coherent story, I concur. But to the extent that his target is those "trendy moderns" who use sequence to undergird their readings of gender and sexuality,[79] I feel compelled to press the pause button and ask: is the effect of disregarding or undoing sequence—insofar as it relates to questions of gender and sexuality—really analogous to putting your iPod on shuffle play?[80]

There is more at stake in the relations among sequence, sexuality, and gender than can be discerned by the adoption of an attitude that "anything goes." Part of what is at stake is the structural congruence between scholars' celebration of the sonnets' gender indeterminacy and fluidity and the celebratory understanding of queerness as similarly indeterminate—or, as one critic describes it, "the floating other of the normative."[81] Part of what is at stake is that the issue of gendered pronouns has stood in for sex talk about the sonnets. And part of what is at stake is that these factors together contribute to a critical climate in which approaches to gender and sexuality in the sonnets have reached a point of impasse. Must queer and feminist investments necessarily be posed in opposition? And might there be something important to resist in both feminist and queer celebrations of indeterminacg?

Sequencing Sonnet 31

Reading for sequence allows us to see how these issues impact one another. I thus turn to three sonnets that have in common an utter disregard for the orthodoxy that would restrict sexual congress to a bodily encounter between two and *only* two bodies. In multiplying the number of imagined participants beyond the ménage à trois of poet, youth, and lady, the erotic sharing implied in Sonnets 31, 135, and 136 enact what would seem to be a queer fantasy.[82] These poems, each of which lacks an unequivocally gendered addressee, describe scenarios in which the beloved's body serves as a vessel or depository for other lovers, whether those of the poet-speaker or the beloved.

In Sonnet 31, "Thy bosome is indeared with all hearts," the beloved's "bosome" supplies a venerable container for the poet-speaker's memory of previous "lovers" (line 10), which he "by lacking have supposed dead" (line 2). This image of precious internment seems a clear response to Sonnet 30, "When to the Sessions of sweet silent thought," where the "lack of many a thing I sought" (line 3), including "precious friends hid in death's dateless night" (line 6), causes the speaker to "grieve at grievances foregone" (line 9). But Sonnet 31 also ups the ante on the previous sonnet's factitious, self-consoling resolution: "But if the while I thinke on thee (deare friend) / All losses are restord, and sorrowes end." In Sonnet 31 those "precious friends" actually populate the beloved's body through their synecdochic instantiation as "hearts" (line 1), "Love" (line 3), "Loves loving parts" (line 3), "things" (line 8), "trophies" (line 10), and "images" (line 13). With memory thus materialized and cognitively extended,[83] those past loves, now only "*supposed* dead" (emphasis mine), are miraculously revivified, through a paradox of resurrection that occasions both solemn mourning and joyful gratitude: "Thou art the grave where buried love doth live" (line 9). Having been absorbed into the body of the friend—"Their images I lov'd, I view in thee" (line 13)—the "lovers gone" (line 10) of a previous time, metonymized through their body parts, mingle promiscuously and with extraordinary equanimity in the beloved's body, as well as in the poet's mind.[84] Whether considered in terms of polyamorousness or cognitive extension, this fantasized erotics, defying the bounded singularity of both self and other (as well as the normative bounds of temporality), is what many would call queer.

Yet, is this queerness gendered? I propose that it is *because* the friend's body is axiomatically similar to that of the poet's other "friends" (line 4) that the beloved can mimetically incarnate those of his predecessors, while also substituting for them along a temporal vector that, for the space of this sonnet at least, remains tethered to the past. The capacity of the beloved's bosom to hold the memories of, and for, the poet depends additionally on the similitude of all of those prior friends, including the corporeal "Loves loving parts" that they share: those physical parts that, in requiring mention, specifically are distinguished from hearts. Gender similitude provides the enabling condition for this queer transit across past and present, desire and memory, selves and objects; it is by means of an implied logic of similitude that one thing so effortlessly can translate into, become, another.[85] Indeed, the pleasure the poem takes in the capacities of gender similitude to achieve these substitutions counteracts the "elegiac gravity" and "somber coloring" that other critics have apprehended in this sonnet.[86] The circuit of reciprocity and complete incorporation indicated in the final line—"And thou (all they) hast all the all of me"—suggests the successful amelioration of loss: the beloved, now commensurate with "all they," possesses all of the poet's "all."

But what, one might ask, actually renders the addressee of Sonnet 31 male? It may seem tautological to argue that this gendering proceeds from the simple term "friend" (although banking on the power of tautology, if one takes Sonnet 105's circular self-referentializing repetition of "faire, kinde, and true" (line 9) at its word, is clearly within Shakespeare's imaginative repertoire). Nor is it insignificant that friendship is one attribute of relation that is never ascribed to the poet's mistress in poems that clearly gender *her*. But each of these remarks assumes precisely what needs to be explained: that is, whether and how friendship in the sonnets is figured as exclusively masculine. For evidence of this, one must move outside the boundaries of the individual lyric to the constellation of meanings ascribed to friends, as they evolve and paratactically attach through what I would maintain are operations of sequence.

Sonnet 31 is the culmination of a thematic cluster of poems bemoaning experiences of distance, desire, absence, loss, and the eventual compensatory work of remembrance, which extends back to Sonnet 26. With a self-conscious reference to itself as "this written ambassage" (line 3), Sonnet 26, the first epistolary sonnet of the sequence, functions as a segue from the earlier poems' celebration of writing as a means of praising the young man to those celebrating the young man's body as a repository of the poet's prior loves and losses. Its meditation on distance and desire leads through the insomniac "pilgrimage" of Sonnets 27 (line 6) and 28, a mental journey that attempts to bridge the distance produced by the beloved's absence. If this absence is, in the initial instance, a matter of geographical separation, the poet's studied contemplation of it throughout his sleepless nights and days moves step by step to the intimations of mortality and death in Sonnets 30 and 31. Sonnet 29's "beweep[ing]" of the poet's "out-cast state" (line 2), like Sonnet 30's melancholic summoning "up remembrance of things past" (line 2), turns to joy on the affective fulcrum "Haplye I thinke on thee" (line 10)—a self-comforting resolution echoed in Sonnet 30's "while I thinke on thee (deare friend)" (line 13). Such remembrance of the friend, reiterated in Sonnet 29's invocation of "thy sweet love remembred" (line 13) and the following poem's "Sessions of sweet silent thought" (line 1), leads directly to the friend's body in Sonnet 31 where "buried love doth live." (So efficacious is the beloved's power of reanimation that Sonnet 32 even contemplates the poet's own death.) It is only by tracing this thematic arc back to Sonnet 26 where the mini-sequence begins that we find an explicit masculinizing (and superordination) of the beloved in its opening line's direct address: "Lord of my love" (line 1).

Gendering Sonnets 135 and 136

In contrast to the solace manifest in the erotic imaginings and internments that conclude this cluster, the erotic substitutions, indiscriminate mingling, and corporeal incorporations of Sonnets 135 and 136, widely noted for their manic punning on the poet's name, depend on a radically different gendered logic and rhetoric. Sonnet 135, "Who ever hath her wish, thou hast thy *Will*, / And *Will* too boote, and *Will* in over-plus" (lines 1–2), and Sonnet 136, "If thy soule check thee that I come so neere, / Sweare to thy blind soule that I was thy *Will*" (lines 1–2), stand as prime illustrations of the nonreproductive, sodomitical economy of the black mistress poems; as such, their queer eroticism is double-edged. On the one hand, as Eve Sedgwick was the first to observe, the homonymous exploitation of the poet's proper name as verb and common noun enacts a homoerotic fantasy of multiple male bodies (the "will in others" [Sonnet 135, line 7]) commingling in a common erotic experience.[87] Yet, to call this fantasy homoerotic does not quite do justice to its complexity: as Helen Vendler acknowledges, the poet-speaker's plea that his mistress grant him admittance to her "large and spatious" will (Sonnet 135, line 5) suggests "that the speaker is aroused by participating vicariously in the promiscuity of the mistress."[88] Although Vendler's interpretation attempts to reheterosexualize the poet-speaker, the fact is that his fantasy of erotic encounters with "others" occurs *within* the communal body of another— only this time it is a female body that the poet hopes to claim. Or, to put a queer spin on what one critic calls the sonnet's "semantic metastases of *wills*,"[89] Kathryn Schwarz argues that "all layers of the pun [on "will"], from volition to genitalia to name, merge masculine and feminine qualities, disable the separation of persons, and disperse specificity into the vortex of union."[90]

There is considerable interpretive potency to this view. And a queer perspective virtually demands it. Indeed, I argued in my previous essays that in Sonnets 135 and 136 the *copia* of male bodies and the capaciousness of female desire are collapsed into one and the same thing. But what might be lost in translating this suspension of subjects into a "vortex of union"? Does this union, however based as it may be on a dissolution of boundaries, also dissolve hierarchy? It is here that a feminist insistence on gender specificity presses against a queer appreciation of specificity's dispersion—and vice versa. For it remains crucial to remember that their "union" or "oneness" is literalized and condensed in the form of the speaker himself: "Thinke all but one, and me in that one *Will*" (Sonnet 135, line 14).[91] By virtue of the power of the proper name (a name, we might recall, that remains gendered), the poet-speaker's selfhood is reasserted aggressively, again and again, while the mistress remains nameless. The attempted conflation of the mistress's will into the poet's "number one" (Sonnet 136, line 8), his "one *Will*" (Sonnet 135, line 14), and his "will one" (Sonnet 136, line 6) subordinates her desire to that of the poet-speaker. Indeed, these poems are rigorously performative in their efforts to persuade; as Melissa Sanchez puts it, this is less an attempted seduction than an attempt "to badger her into compliance."[92] That the multiple wills of Sonnets 135 and 136 are *not* in full accord, that the addressee requires convincing, is captured by the forceful puns on "one" and "won" (with a possible homophonic correspondence to the explicitly possessive "own"). One might recall that Sonnet 134 had depicted the poet-speaker as "mortgaged to thy will" (line 2) as well as having "lost" his friend to his mistress—"Him have I lost, thou hast both him and me" (line 13)—a situation that might be construed as stimulating the aggression of the poet's first-person "will" in the subsequent two poems. The poet's plea, which is also a demand, to "Thinke all" (Sonnet 135, line 14) contrasts tellingly to the "all the all of me," which the male friend, and his friends, already hold in possession in Sonnet 31 (line 14). Rather than expressing a mutuality attained, a satisfying recompense for loss, or a queer dispersal of personhood, Sonnets 135 and 136 register the effort required to overcome—through wit, through will, through "masculine persuasive force"[93]—separation, autonomy, and difference.

Given their lack of explicitly gendered addressees, Sonnets 135 and 136 theoretically could be subject to a nongendered or male homoerotic reading, one based on recognition of the "willing" penetrability of male bodies. We might find some linguistic justification for such readings in the repetition of the word "sweet" (used once in 135, twice in 136), the rhetoric of which Jeffrey Masten has shown is associated with homoerotic and cross-sex love "across the Shakespearean canon."[94] Although Masten is careful to point out that the language of affection concentrated in a discourse of "sweet" is relevant to both same-sex and cross-sex bonds, his queer philology concentrates on male-male instances in order to underscore their presence and resist their elision in editions and commentary. Building on his work, I want to consider the ramifications of attending to an affectional rhetoric of sweetness in the diacritical terms of gender and sexuality, for doing so allows us to specify more precisely *how* these poems are gendered.

They do so in several ways. First, the similarity and difference in the wills depicted in these poems echoes distinctions between male and female bodies, attributes, and desires in poems that *do* possess unambiguous gendered referents—for instance, the poems in which the term "friend" clearly bespeaks the male love object. This, I have begun to suggest, is one effect of sequence. Second, we might interpret the effort to render the mistress and her will "sweet" (Sonnet 135, line 4)—through accepting the poet-speaker's "love-sute sweet" (136, line 4) and as "a some-thing sweet to thee" (136, line 12)—as indicating a desire to impart onto her something of the emotional affect that previously characterized the poet's erotic regard for his friend. This transitivity does not so much *de*-gender objects as resituate and regender the quality of sweetness through formal means. Within the context of these poems, such a regendering of "sweet" is another sign of sequence at work. Third, the sole gendered pronoun in Sonnets 135 and 136, while not unambiguous, nonetheless directs attention toward a female addressee: "Whoever hath *her* wish, *thou* hast thy *Will*" (135, line 1, emphasis mine). If the "her" of the first clause is broadly generalizable, serving to differentiate other women from the addressee, the vocative "thou" indirectly assumes gendered meaning by virtue of its comparative and proximate relation to "her." The implicit comparison attains intelligibility only if the "thou" being addressed is sufficiently similar to render the comparison apt. Sonnet 136 does not gesture toward the gender of the beloved, but rather, invoking the proper name, asserts the gender of the speaker: "then thou lovest me for my name is *Will*" (line 14). The intelligibility of this poem's gendered address thus relies on its companionate relation to Sonnet 135—again in an intertextual relation of sequence.

By subtly but nonetheless decisively generating a female addressee, these two sonnets achieve their queerness only through the forceful assertion of "will"—a will that, even in pursuit of transitive desires and beloveds, attempts to overpower female difference. These poems, then, *actively construct* gendered forms of address and differential fictions of gendered sexuality. Their labors literally bring their love objects, their sex objects, into being. They do so not primarily through figuring bodily tropes conventionally or essentially marked as already gendered, although they do capitalize on previously gendered, constellated tropes from elsewhere in the sequence. Nor do they achieve their differential effects by ascribing promiscuity to the female object and monogamy to the male: both love/sex objects are imagined as engaging with multiple other objects, both lead actively volitional erotic lives, and both are only precariously fastened to the poet-speaker. Rather, even in the absence of overtly gendered markers, the sonnets diacritically produce differentially gendered meanings by mobilizing distributed erotic affects in an operation of sequence.[95] Exploiting the conceptual resources and affective resonances of similitude and difference, keyed as they respectively are to the affects of equanimity and anxiety, the sonnets manufacture and reinforce hierarchical gender difference precisely by means of their queer erotics.

The Effects of Sequence

This production of gender and erotic differentiation, I have suggested, is in part a technical effect of sequence. But, as should be clear by now, my understanding of sequence has little in common with those readings that use this term to convey ideas about Shakespeare's biography or the collection's narrative coherence. Part of what distinguishes our use of this concept is that mine is derived from an understanding of the psychic and structural mechanisms of substitution and displacement. Whether pursued via an explicitly psychoanalytic idiom or a more historicist one, substitution and displacement have tended to be construed primarily in terms of psychic and social content.[96] Freudian in origin and depending on notions of psychic or social repression, displacement typically is viewed as a means by which anxieties are mediated, deflected, assuaged, or repressed. Invocations of displacement figure commonly in critical treatments cuckoldry, for instance, where it names how the cuckold's horns and the humor directed at them transmute individual trauma into public performance: in the words of Claire McEachern, "horn jokes mediate cultural anxiety."[97] In my own critical practice, displacement has loomed large. In *Desire and Anxiety: Circulations of Sexuality in Shakespearean Drama*, I argued that analytically focusing on the (homoerotic) middle of Shakespeare's cross-dressing comedies, rather than their (heterosexualizing) endings, allows us to witness how Shakespeare's penchant for substitution and displacement—present as well in his treatment of plot and subplot, as well as in mirrored and doubled characters—tended to overwrite homoeroticism under the generic exigencies of comic closure. The critical task, then, was not to accede to this overwriting as the final "message" of the plot, but rather to exhume the labor involved in such active forgetting. In *The Renaissance of Lesbianism in Early Modern England*, I used the concept of displacement to analyze contemporary scholars' desire to identify lesbians in the past in terms of their similitude to the present; such wishful mirror imaging, I argued, was a displaced response to the trauma of lesbian invisibility.

Considered as a matter of syntactical *form*, however, sequence enables access to the construction of meaning, not only through the displacement and substitution of content and tropes, but through temporal and spatial relations. Bruce Smith has argued that "sex and syntax go together because language articulates where body . . . becomes word."[98] Examining a comic Latin language lesson in *The Taming of the Shrew*, Smith briefly notes that Latin provided "a *syntax* of sexuality, a set of rules for articulating the body"[99] concerned with "what goes *with* what, *by* what, *on* what, *in* what."[100] Syntax, that is, positions bodies by both prepositional and tropological means. Furthermore, such positions, he maintains, can be disrupted or disarticulated, particularly through the punning wordplay that infuses Shakespearean drama's language lessons.

My interest in syntax focuses less on the intersection of word and body than on how thinking syntactically enables us to conceptualize the relations of bodies to *time*. Neither historical time, the subject of Chapters 3 and 4, nor textual time, my focus here, proceeds solely on the basis of one temporal mode; and the concept of sequence helps us ascertain why. Because it unfolds over time, sequence is subject to diachronic logic: it moves forward along a trajectory. This directional movement solicits the collation of sequence to the matters of historical chronology, development, and progression discussed in Chapter 3. But because sequence also occurs in space, as a serial assemblage of discrete quanta, it simultaneously is a matter of synchronic relations, producing what we might think of as snapshots or freeze-frames of time. In Shakespeare's sonnets we access synchrony whenever repeated resonances and subtle modulations of rhymes, rhythms, words, images, and moods invite comparison and contrast to what has come before and what is still to come.[101] It is through the synchronicity implicit in repetition, substitution, and vacillating rhetorical schemes (such as antithesis and paradox) that the sonnets achieve their variegated affective tones. Synchrony is especially pertinent to the apprehension of mini-sequences, those discursive, thematic, or tonal clusters that quickly come to a (sometimes frustrating) halt if pursued with an overarching or comprehensive diachrony in mind. (For instance: whatever happened to that rival poet?) It is a synchronic optic that allows us to isolate Sonnets 26 through 31 as an intratextual sequence focused on overcoming distance and death; synchrony likewise allows us to connect the multiple wills of Sonnets 135 and 136, and compare and differentiate them from the desires articulated in Sonnet 31. But even as we can "cluster" different sonnets, their temporal succession enacts its own movement, which also exists within a larger temporal arc.[102] Such temporal arcs, I now suggest, are particularly amenable not only to the accretive force of repetition (and, given Shakespeare's skill, the pleasures of repetition with subtle differences) but to processes of diacritical displacement.

Whether construed as psychic, social, or formal, the displacements that establish sequence function not only as indices of affective engagements and erotic identifications, as my previous essays on the sonnets describe, but as structural mechanisms that, as Annamarie Jagose reminds us, confer hierarchies of priority and subordination. Because the chronological is "also always the hierarchical" and the temporal is "also always the precedential,"[103] the sequential logic of first and second order constitutes a process whereby effect is seen to follow from cause, epiphenomenon from phenomenon, and conclusion from origin. Sequence thus assumes a "self-licensing" power to function "as its own imprimatur."[104] Furthermore, these various operations can seem to stabilize one term by means of another in a chain reaction of hierarchical enforcement.

But just as the syntax of the language lesson can be disarticulated, so too can the syntax of sequence be disrupted.[105] Such disruption of syntax is central to the psychoanalytic understanding of fantasy where, in Joan Scott's words, "desire is fulfilled, punished, and prohibited all at once."[106] In Shakespeare's sonnets, the asynchronicity of chronological overlap sometimes undercuts the success of succession, undermining the usual privileging of what comes after to what came before. This happens, for instance, when some of the actions described in sonnets to the dark mistress refer to scenarios and actions that seem to have transpired sometime earlier. Because the sonnets continually "return to earlier topics and images, undo the precarious stabilities of ostensibly conclusive couplets, regress to emotions which cannot be assuaged and constantly need to be rewritten,"[107] they enact a kind of Möbius strip "chicken and egg simultaneity."[108] Shakespeare's sonnets are characterized not only by internal oxymoron, chiasmus, and inversion, but by parallelisms, repetitions, and the surging, dissolving, and remounting of questions and tensions across groups of poems. Thus, although sequence may impose artificial fixity onto synchronous phenomena, it also can be derailed, precisely because a straightforward directional arc cannot adequately represent the temporal backtracking, back-to-the-future loops, and continual revisions of its erotics or its form.[109] Indeed, the placement of the dark lady sonnets, which in the 1609 quarto follow upon the lovely boy sonnets (even though they may have been composed earlier), demonstrates that displacement isn't necessarily indicative of narrative or ideological *progress*; it need not even inscribe a forward motion.

Within the current academic climate, the obvious critical gesture is to call this disdain for forward motion, this disinterest in charting a legible story, this precariousness of hermeneutic ground, queer. Queerness, according to this view, is what is signaled by a nonprogressive temporality, a temporal order that is disordered, that stops making sense, and in so doing moves against the future-driven productivity of temporality itself. This is an enormously powerful reading strategy, especially insofar as it invites us to meet the challenge of reading sequence without teleology. At the same time, such a perspective, as Chapter 3 argued, carries with it potential risks. If that chapter's focus was the impasses created in the historiography of sexuality by a too-universalizing model of queerness, at stake here is our understanding not only of the import of gender but the sexuality of time.

The Syntax of Temporality

Acting together to induce what might be called a technology of sequence, synchrony and diachrony provide the temporal syntax by which gendered and erotic meanings are created and transported. Having described the synchronic micro movements of individual poems in their intertextual relations, let us now hone in on the macro results of their diachronic movements, of sequence *qua* sequence. In *Ends of the Lyric*, Timothy Bahti argues that the question of poetic endings is in fact a question "of everything that tries to get one there: beginning, middle, and means."[110] Furthermore, "an inquiry into ends" will "be unprotected from turning into an account of beginnings and middles and means: of everything that does or does not get one to an end."[111] While Bahti's formalist method concerns the "directions for reading" that individual poems provide, the ways that "lyric poems do not end but return to and retrope their means," as well as the "correspondence" or noncorrespondence of "goal and end,"[112] I wish to pause over his sense of the *vulnerability* of any inquiry into poetic ends in order to ask a different set of questions. What are the combined effects of this manufacture of gender difference through queer erotics when read from the perspective of sequence? How do the mini-sequences on which I have focused relate to the tropological and thematic sequence of the sonnets as a whole? And what do these different forms of sequence have to do with the sequence of temporality?

From beginning to end, Shakespeare's sonnets to the young man celebrate, in a profoundly overdetermined way, a homoerotics of reproductive futurity: the reproductive future of the young man, the reproduction of the poet-speaker's love, and the reproduction of the young man's beauty through poetry. As if in an inverted mirror, the dark lady sonnets—with their ascription of indiscriminate, sodomitical desires—split off the sex with which the poet-speaker is self-avowedly obsessed from the reproductive promise that accorded to sex with women whatever minimal cultural legitimacy it possessed. These mirror images produce their greatest illumination when read diacritically in light of each other. If reproduction implies the generation of a future, sodomy, understood in the culture's phobic terms, forms a figure of the future's foreclosure. After the first seventeen "procreation" sonnets, the future envisioned by the poet-speaker depends not on biological generation but on men: men in love, men in love with love, men in love with poetry, men defying time, men putting to the test poetry's celebrated defense against time.[113] However compromised or ambivalent or uncertain this vision of reproductive futurity,[114] women are edited out of it. From the early procreation sonnets, where generic women are imaged as Aristotelian, passive vessels of impregnation—the "viall" to be made "sweet" by the young man's semen (Sonnet 6)—to the moment the mistress emerges as an addictive yet sterile object of desire, women's role in futurity is displaced by a privileging of poetic and mimetic reproduction between men.

The Shakespeare that comes into view in the sonnets, the "Shakespeare effect" of his poetic persona, confirms the extent to which orderly male homoeroticism, when strategically dissociated from sodomy, was one of the glues that held early modern patriarchy together. If the sonnets to the young man "attempt to work out the propriety of Shakespeare's relationship to him" and such "propriety" is a moving target within the terms of Renaissance male homosociality,[115] it remains the case that the sonnets reserve the emotional affects associated with reciprocal and idealized friendship for the beloved youth while projecting onto the mistress the cause of the speaker's obsessive and sterile lust.[116] However one might wish to read individual sonnets as queer, then, there is little in the 1609 quarto that upsets cultural norms of gender. If, as recent critics have posited, there was something radical in the poet's cross-class expression of desire for an aristocrat, the depiction of that relationship nonetheless remains socially conventional insofar as it juxtaposes the normative virtue of male intimacy (however agonized, despairing, and lacking in mutuality) against an equally normative compulsion toward sex with women—sex, moreover, whose denigration is correlative with its compulsiveness. To the extent that the assessment of women's ethical capacities in these poems accords with a pervasive Renaissance disbelief in any female aptitude for friendship,[117] or, indeed, for any kind of intimacy that might correspond to an ethical valuing of women, the erotic economy he portrays aligns with, rather than queers, conventional early modern practices of gender.[118] This does not make Shakespeare's sonnets any less dazzling as poetic anatomies of male desire for men *or* for women. But it does enjoin upon us awareness that these desires are profoundly differentiated—that sex itself is internally segregated through the sequential and diacritical construction of gender.

It is with such awareness that I approach Masten's suggestion, made in the context of delineating the terms of male homoeroticism and sodomy in the sonnets, that the linguistic and syntactical coupling of "sweetness" with the "vile/vial" in Sonnet 6's injunction "Make sweet some viall" (line 3) renders this phrase's possible corporeal meanings "compound" and "logically coincidental"—and thereby opens up onto the pleasures of anal, specifically male, sodomy.[119] The foregoing discussion urges recognition that any such reading might also wish to consider the exigencies of sequence as they construct gendered meanings. If I argued in my earlier work precisely for such a disarticulation of sexuality from sequence in the name of multiple forms of erotic possibility and affiliation,[120] here I insist on what might be lost in such a sundering: namely, the understanding of gender and eroticism as diacritically interrelated.

Insofar as the displacements enabled by sequence refigure reproduction as male, sequence ultimately confers specific meanings to the subject's relation to temporality.[121] Arguing that Shakespeare's concern with the passage of time is paramount in the sonnets, Dympna Callaghan demonstrates how

Shakespeare's speeding up of the rhythms of lifetimes and the seasons creates an "agitated urgency," which she takes to be the "hallmark" of these poems.[122] This sense of an accelerated temporality is, as Callaghan implies elsewhere, deeply gendered, for the concern that synthesizes a *carpe diem* "let's get it on" with a *memento mori* obsession with death has as its primary focus not the promiscuous sterility of the dark lady, but the inevitable decay of the young man.[123] Further adducing the "absence of temporal progression" in the black mistress poems,[124] Joyce Sutphen notes that "the word 'time,' which occurs over seventy times in the first 126 sonnets, never appears again after sonnet 126."[125] And, as Margreta de Grazia likewise observes of the dark lady sonnets, "In the second group, no future is designated."[126] The import of this elision of the future tense in a sequence preoccupied with mortality— and with expending its considerable linguistic resources on producing inge- nious ways of managing and defying it—is incisively specific. By expressing conventional attitudes toward friendship, upending conventional attitudes toward reproduction, and conscripting friendship and reproduction to a tem- poral horizon that is itself gendered, Shakespeare's sonnets appropriate the future exclusively for men, for all time. And no careful parsing of pronouns will will that away.

The sonnets' substitution of women's role in reproduction by the promo- tion of an endlessly fertile male creativity, achieved through the displacement of anxiety regarding sodomy onto the body of an enticing but threatening woman, creates, in other words, a syntax of temporality. It is a syntax born of gender and sex, love and desire, ambivalence and anxiety. It matters little that the hoped-for fulfillment of the speaker's love and desire for either object is perpetually deferred—indeed, the perpetuation of desire is precisely what is at stake in these poems. Beyond what this syntax of temporality reveals about desire in the sonnets, it enables us to observe the formal mechanisms by which genders and sexualities are constituted—which is to say, relationally and diacritically, synchronically as well as diachronically, sequentially as well as tropologically. To suggest that such procedures are technical or formal is not to negate their psychological impetus or content, much less their social genesis or historical contingency; indeed, my aspiration throughout has been to synthesize psychic, social, and historical concerns with an appreciation of the affordances of a particular form. To insist, in addition, that such proce- dures are diacritical, that they come into being and pursue their aims in relation to one another, is not to insert retrospectively a homo/hetero identity paradigm that is ill-suited to the early modern period.[127] My aim, rather, is to suggest that we can apprehend the meanings of sexual desire and acts through the ongoing *work* of gender—work that is no less pertinent to the Renaissance than it is today.[128] And we can witness this work when we attune ourselves to the successive progression of terms along a syntactical line that, despite its retrospective appearance of enacting a foregone teleology or con- clusion imbued with necessity, is in fact a temporal and contingent operation that can be exposed, interrupted, contested, and redirected.

In Chapters 3 and 4 I argue that historical temporality is more complex and multifarious than is suggested by viewing all sequence or chronology as teleological. It may thus seem paradoxical that aspects of my reading of the sonnets could be construed as anti-teleological. My aim, however, has been to show that both the success and failures of teleology demand to be read as specific and contingent. The sonnets' asynchronic revisionism demonstrates the ways in which multiple temporalities can jam up the seamlessness of succession. At the same time, when viewed diacritically, the sonnets show that a diachronic movement that is relentlessly teleological can overwrite asynchrony.

Only by recognizing such maneuvers can we confront the impasses that the workings of sequence throw up in its wake. For the sonnets' preemptive logic of sequence enacts a stiff price for its polymorphous desires, throwing up multiple impediments to the possibility of concomitantly thinking through, much less honoring, feminist and male homoerotic investments. Although there exists no algorithm, no distinct set of criteria, by which to establish a point of purchase on the sonnets' negotiation of these investments, one can train one's eye on how the tensions among them come to be. And it is through such witnessing that we might avoid reenacting in our critical practice the sonnets' own zero-sum game.

It is to insist on the need to confront such ongoing conflict that I have sought to trouble the current consensus and its allied essentialisms (however strategically useful they have been and may continue to be within particular social and pedagogical contexts). If earlier interpretative regimes tended to adduce the sonnets' movement toward the dark lady as evidence of the poet- speaker's victorious acquisition of heterosexuality (or of Shakespeare's psy- chosexual development), it is no less tendentious that today's scholars are apt to speak of "the homoeroticism of the sonnets" as if that phrase could ade- quately sum up the gendered erotics in these poems. Correlatively, it is with awareness of other forms of tendentiousness that we might resist the feminist move to "take the woman's part." However understandably motivated, readings dedicated to rescuing the dark lady from Shakespeare's "abuse" are as misguided as the effort to combat the sonnets' deployment of misogynous clichés by appropriating some of the lovely boy poems on the lady's behalf. The black mistress is not particularly intelligible in characterological terms (neither, for that matter, is the young man); she most definitely is not a woman, and therefore someone with whom it is appropriate to identify or disidentify. She is a trope—of femininity, lust, sterility, darkness, beauty, compulsion, as well as intersubjectivity and "(perverse) mutuality"[129]—in a complex system of gendered, racial, and aesthetic signification. The meanings of her darkness remain obscure—it is, after all, both vilified and praised—and even the poet's appellation to her of "mistress" seems more an indication of a wish than achieved or secure fact. The problems she poses for feminist and queer analysis therefore require a discursive and rhetorical, rather than characterological or biographical, approach. Disengaging her figuration, along with that of the young man, from concerns of biography and character—though not from the "real" world or "real" life as structured in part by such tropes—and reading gender through the mechanism of sequence, we can ascertain how Shakespeare produced and managed, always in tense interaction, many of the abiding concerns of his poetic oeuvre: desire for men, for women, for love, for sex; desire for mutuality and separation, similarity and difference; desire for reproduction, poetry, immortality, and time.

Despite what I would argue is a lack of biographical or narrative necessity, then, relations of gender to eroticism in Shakespeare's sonnets are quite literally *consequential*. Through operations of sequence, as well as through the criticism they have elicited, the sonnets offer a remarkable entrée into some of the ways that gender, sexuality, and knowledge about both are subject to negotiation, both in Shakespeare's time, and in ours.[130] They offer not only a history of sexuality, but an epistemology of sex—a way of considering how sex is thought, and how and why such thinking matters. In so doing, they demonstrate the extent to which sex itself can be viewed as an agent in history, with history understood as an ongoing process in which the relations of sex to gender have been, and will continue to be, contested. The sonnets not only beckon us toward sexuality *in* the past; they help us ascertain what it means for sexuality to *have* a past. *None* of the terms of sexuality's history are self-evident or given: not homosexuality, not heterosexuality, not friendship, not reproduction, not misogyny, not normality. Nor, for that matter, are they self-evident or given today. Their meanings, in the past and in the present, are the effects of cultural and critical *work*—work in which we all engage, whenever we allude, however dispassionately, naively, or rigorously, to Shakespeare's sex.[131]

So play your playlist, by all means; but know that in doing so you are playing with a gendered structure of sex and time that precedes and exceeds your own desires.

CHAPTER 9

The Sign of the Lesbian

Eubulus. There are more who copy Sappho's behavior than share her
talent.

Catharine. I don't quite understand what you mean.

Eubulus. And I say these things in order that the time may not come
when you *do* understand.

—Erasmus, *Virgo misogamos*

Why might those of us who research, teach, and think about sexuality want
or need a history of lesbianism? What would such a history *do* for us? These
are questions pointedly asked and answered by Robyn Wiegman in "The
Lesbian Premodern Meets the Lesbian Postmodern," her afterword to the
2011 anthology *The Lesbian Premodern*. Why, she asks, does the lesbian "need
a history to begin with?"[1] Arguing on the basis of the volume at hand that
"there is finally no clear sense of what having a lesbian history would mean,"
she observes that "as yet there is no clear argument for why everyone else
would benefit from having it."[2]

Given that this observation issues from a scholar who has devoted her
career to thinking about the historical relations among gender, sexuality, and
race[3] as well as the institutional histories of "identity knowledges" such as
Women's Studies and queer studies,[4] we might hesitate to interpret her skepticism as a universal rejection of lesbian history. Rather, the main target of
her critique is what she perceives to be the field's constellation around a
limited set of affective orientations, most especially a fantasy of reparation
and love (in ways that overlap with my critique, in Chapter 6, of the archival
ars erotica).[5] Moreover, since she organizes her questions via the temporality

of the future conditional—the *not yet*—and ends by gesturing toward the slavery archive that, she suggests, would generate different objects of study and less comfortable affective fantasies, it seems clear she has investments in lesbian history of her own.

Even as it issues from within a lesbian-affirmative analytic, however, the terms by which Wiegman frames her queries—why does the lesbian need a history and what would it do for others?—make clear that neither assuming the relevance of lesbian history on behalf of an already consolidated minority nor advocating for it on behalf of the "historical record" would suffice. Her distance from conventional articulations of history's importance, I suggest, can help direct inquiry toward the epistemological ambit within which the concept of lesbianism currently circulates. We can glean indications of what I will argue is the field habitus of queer studies in her expansion of the projected "benefit" of lesbian history from that of lesbians' needs to that of "everyone else." On the one hand, the language of "benefit" would seem to introduce the criterion of making something happen in the world that goes by the name of "practice." On the other hand, the locution "everyone else" would seem to manifest the criterion of commanding the interest of nonlesbians and thus a more generalized dividend, of the sort typically reserved for "theory." Lesbian history, this framework implies, should constitute a knowledge that is generalizable, portable, and useful. Tacitly positioned within the critical frames of theory and practice, lesbian history is vulnerable to failure on all counts.

Given the unlikely but unmistakable congruence of Wiegman's skepticism with the general disinterest in lesbianism pervasive in queer studies as well as with the queer doubts about history examined in Chapter 3, her questions are crucial to confront if lesbian historiography is to have any future traction in the age of queerness. I leave to others the question of how lesbian history might speak to the demands of queer and feminist activism, as well as how the intractable theory/practice divide, which has long troubled academic feminism and has likewise been an issue in queer studies, might be reconceived.[6] My aim is more modest: to persuade that the time has come for a history conceived precisely under what Wiegman calls "the sign of the lesbian."[7] To substantiate such a claim depends on radically reorienting the epistemological field within which her queries are posed. It relies as well on destabilizing the meanings of the operative terms "lesbian" and "history"—away from identity knowledges and toward the knowledge relations that subtend the links among "lesbian," "queer," "history," and "theory." Such a reorientation involves asking what it would mean to take "the sign of the lesbian" not as a de facto sign of identity but as a sign of a historiographic problem.

In what follows, the signature of "Wiegman" indicates less an authorial subject than a motivating lever with which to pry apart the knowledge relations that currently obtain among sex, gender, embodiment, history, and theory. What if one were to think "the lesbian" not in terms of identity or subjectivity, but in terms of historiographic method and the practice of theorizing it? What if one were to loosen the negative hold that identitarian same-sex desire and practice has had on the queer imaginary and think more in terms of the critical work that "the *sign* of the lesbian" could perform? Building on Chapter 4, "The Present Future of Lesbian Historiography," which used the female case to generalize about the historical recurrence of certain idioms and tropes, and Chapter 5, "The Joys of Martha Joyless," which investigated the gendered conditions of erotic knowledge, this chapter translates the epistemological conundrums that have vexed the pursuit of female same-sex eroticism in the past into an opportunity for theorizing not only the unique conceptual affordances of "the lesbian" but of our knowledge of the history of sex.

This anatomizing proposition has as much to do with what we mean by "history" and "theory" as what we mean by "lesbian." Indeed, it offers "the sign of the lesbian" as an exemplary, extradisciplinary pivot for thinking through the way history and theory circulate within queer studies. If the previous chapters considered how, when, and why sex becomes history—and in the process shed light on the variable meanings of history—the present chapter asks, conversely, how, when, and why does sex become *theory*? How, after all, do history and theory overlap and differ, and why are they so consistently presented as antagonists? How does their routine separation within the domain of queer studies impact configurations and trajectories of sexual knowledge? And what ethical obligations does the move toward theorization entail? In earlier chapters I proposed that cross-gender identification could serve as a principle that may help refine the work that the concept "queer" is employed to do. Transiting across identifications from male to female, I drew certain perspectives out of gay male histories and areas of interest in order to elucidate dispositions toward knowledge and sex that might benefit women. Here, I make a different yet complementary move, as I shift the focus from the universalizing category of queer (which includes women but rarely attends to their specificity) to explore how the category of same-sex desire and practice most explicitly marked by gender might yield theoretical resources for queerly rethinking the history of sex.

Lesbianism, several scholars have noted, has all but disappeared in the stories that queer theory tells about itself. Countering such partial remembrances of queer theory's social and intellectual emergence, they have attempted to resurrect and renarrate that not-too-distant history and, in so doing, provide a more capacious genealogy of queer theoretical investments. Attending to the paradigmatic moves that lead to the institutional consolidation of fields, they argue that there has always been *another* queer theory, one that derives not only from the intellectual work of lesbians but from crucial frameworks provided by antifoundational feminisms.[8] Furthermore, a vibrant strand of feminist queer theorizing has been produced from the standpoint of lesbian subjectivities,[9] perhaps especially by those of lesbians of color.[10] In reactivating "the lesbian" as a category of analysis that might animate and guide queer theoretical engagements with historiography, my aim is not to essentialize lesbianism, deny its imbrications in troubling histories of race and class, or uphold the lesbian as the master trope of women's history.[11] Nor is my aim solely to answer Wiegman's query about the relevance of lesbian history for "everyone else" in terms that speak directly to queer aspirations. My purpose is to supplement these revisionist accounts of queer theory by suggesting that it is precisely the history of lesbianism, *when reconceived as a problem of representation and epistemology*, that offers a valuable heuristic for crafting an analytic that is simultaneously feminist and queer. Reasoning that one impediment to recognizing these interventions as queer *theory* is that many of these innovations have been produced by means of analysis that is explicitly *historical*,[12] I argue that "the lesbian" presents not only a limit case for queer theory, but a methodological release point for anyone interested in sexual knowledge—past, present, and future.

The Epistemic Privilege of Queer Theory

For over a decade, queer studies has been distancing itself from the historicizing impulses that had been a major field-forming motivation.[13] Earlier forms of gay/lesbian/queer scholarship, even that well informed by nonhistorical forms of post-structuralism (e.g., Lacan, Derrida), tended to theorize from specific instances, cultures, and time periods. In the foundational work of Halperin, Miller, Sedgwick, Rubin, and Edelman, for instance, queer theory developed its insights from deep knowledge of specific historical periods in order to generate broader research questions and agendas, whose theoretical abstraction could then be tested by their relevance to other historical moments. Accompanying this shift in focus has been a growing emphasis on the cultural production of the last century and the current moment: these temporal frames become the occasion for theory, while everything prior to the twentieth century increasingly is positioned as simply history. In a prescient observation of this phenomenon, Christopher Nealon noted in his 2001 book *Foundlings: Lesbian and Gay Historical Emotion Before Stonewall* that he hoped "to resolve a tension in the United States between lesbian and gay studies, on the one hand, and queer theory, on the other."[14] Reminding his readers that other queer studies scholars have characterized this tension in terms of method—a difference between historical and psychoanalytic approaches, for instance—as well as in terms of the disciplinary locations of historians and literary critics, Nealon addressed the "unfinished business between desire and history" by reading twentieth-century texts' participation in "feel[ing] historical."[15]

Despite the positive reception of Nealon's book, the standoff he described, in both its methodological and disciplinary guises, continues to inflect contemporary studies of sexuality, whether conceived as history, literary criticism, or theory, and whether manifested through explicit debate or implicit institutional structures. To put it bluntly, in queer studies right now, theory partakes of the prime time, while history is yesterday's news. For evidence, we might turn to the 2013 *Routledge Queer Studies Reader*, which offers an admirably comprehensive and imaginative snapshot of the field. And yet, its section on "genealogies" refers solely to genealogies of the field itself, while its section on "temporalities" includes only one essay concerned with pre-twentieth-century phenomena.[16] I make this observation not to fault the editors' selection process, but because I believe that they have accurately represented the current focus of collective energy and excitement. Temporality, not historicity, is where the action is. For further evidence, we might examine what it means to "experiment in the forms of theoretical production," as Lauren Berlant and Lee Edelman enact it in their 2014 coauthored book *Sex, or the Unbearable*.[17] Here, the acceptance of theory's decontextualizing impetus is especially evident in the contributions of Berlant precisely because her past work has tended to theorize out of the specificities of space, time, and national location, including a historical "trilogy" covering the past two hundred years.[18] The authors' self-descriptions are salient in this regard: while each of them is oriented toward a different psychoanalytic register, Berlant generally "traces *the conditions* impelling subjects to normalizing narratives of

emotional adequation even while she attends . . . to the strategies by which
alternative possibilities for world-building might also begin to emerge" (a materialist position implicitly aligned with historicism), while Edelman "question[s]
the ground of those possibilities" (an epistemological position aligned with
theory).[19] However, very little of their dialogue on the unbearable in and of sex
is concerned with might be called social, rather than theoretical, conditions,
despite Berlant's description of her growing certainty "of the need to invent
new genres for the kinds of speculative work we call 'theory.' "[20]

This is not a critique of Berlant—or Edelman, for that matter. Rather,
their experiment in the forms of theoretical production begs the question of
the relation of the material to the epistemological, of the conditions of
thought to their conceptual grounds. Their enactment of what it means to
theorize likewise offers a reminder that the elision of history and historicizing
is a seldom-considered outcome in the recurrent confusion and slippage
between queer theory and queer studies. In making this observation, I am
not promoting the problematic mandate to "always historicize"; prodigious
work has emerged precisely from resistance to that mandate. Nor am I hostile
to the different forms of psychoanalysis Berlant and Edelman each promotes.
What interests me, rather, is the epistemic privilege within queer studies that
licenses theory's ability to dispense with history, whereas any history writing
untouched by theoretical understanding is considered naive and dispensable.
The discomfort of having such naïveté projected onto one's scholarship rose
to the surface during a *GLQ* roundtable devoted to the queer "turn toward
temporality," published in 2007. Here, Edelman outlined the conceptual
distance he would draw between projects of queer temporality, on the one
hand, and queer historicism on the other. Bringing to the conversation his
expertise on rhetoric and figuration, Edelman remarked that he is "less interested . . . in the 'turn toward time' than in the turning or troping by which
we're obliged to keep turning time *into* history."[21] Edelman further suggested
that "history" cannot help but traffic in ontologies: "Whether polyphonous
or univocal, history, thus ontologized, displaces the epistemological impasse,
the aporia of relationality, the nonidentity of things, by offering the promise
of sequence as the royal road to *con*sequence."[22] In an essay published the
same year, Edelman likewise links history to the reproductive imperative that
underwrites heteronormativity:

This compulsion to produce the "after" of sex through the naturalization of
history expresses itself in two very different, though not unrelated, ways: first,

in the privileging of reproduction as the after-event of sex—an after-event whose potential, implicit in the ideal, if not always in the reality, of hetero-genital coupling, imbues straight sex with its meaning as the agent of historical continuity; second, in the conflation of meaning itself with those forms of historical knowing whose authority depends on the fetishistic prestige of origin, genealogy, telos. In each case the entry into history coincides with the entry into social narratives that work to domesticate the incoherence, at once affective and conceptual, that's designated by "sex."[23]

Edelman's is an eloquent, hard-hitting synopsis of a certain queer perspective on both sex and history. And while Chapter 3 indicates that I do not agree that "the entry into history" necessarily depends on "the fetishistic prestige of origin, genealogy, telos," I concur with his diagnosis of the stakes involved in the incoherence and unintelligibility of sex, to which he gives the term "negativity."[24] My project shares with Edelman's a recognition of "the epistemological impasse, the aporia of relationality," as well as an insistence that thinking sex involves "moments that signal the failure or even the inadequacy of knowledge as such, moments when the frameworks of knowing are not simply *incoherently at odds* with each other but *incapable of accommodating* the encounter with something unnamable in the terms they offer."[25] The overlap in our interests is evident as well in the importance he accords to "resistance, misconstruction, frustration, anxiety, becoming defensive, feeling misunderstood" in the process of thinking sex.[26] In particular, his attempt to pose sex "over and against" a concept of "education as a 'leading out' of ignorance, inability, and bewilderment and into the conditions of mastery, understanding, and realized sovereignty" voices, albeit in a different idiom, many of my concerns about how sexual knowledge is and has been made.

Nonetheless, as a description of historicism, Edelman's is a characterization about which some queer literary historicists have demurred—and for good reason. Carolyn Dinshaw, for instance, objects that Edelman "sets up 'history' as a straw man, in a form in which none of us actually practice it."[27] To which Edelman countered: "If anything passes for an article of faith among those working in historical analysis, it's that what they're doing mustn't be confused with 'old-style historicism'. . . . I might be more inclined to believe this if it weren't repeated quite so often. But the very need for such repetition bespeaks the *logic* of repetition at the heart of historicism itself . . . indicative of an encounter with what can't be assimilated to any systematic understanding, what doesn't conduce to the logic of periodization or identity."[28] Parodying this "article of faith" among queer historicists, Edelman refuses—deconstructively, psychoanalytically, and *in principle*—to engage with pre- and early modern histories of sexuality, even those produced by Dinshaw (and Freccero, one of the other roundtable interlocutors) that explicitly aim *not* to "conduce to the logic of periodization or identity."

Dinshaw's attempt to counter Edelman's principled indifference to and suspicion of history by appealing to post-identitarian queer historicism clearly had no effect on his certainty that historicism inevitably partakes of a compensatory teleology. Nor, I suspect, would appealing to the importance of history *as such*—that is, as a self-evidently valuable disciplinary field of knowledge—effectively challenge Edelman's disinterest. Indeed, such a move would hold in place the least productive terms of this debate: by pitting deconstructive and Lacanian theories *against* historicism, it returns to precisely the standoff that Nealon earlier described. Against the academic prestige of theory within queer studies[29]—whose worth derives from its ability to travel across conceptual domains and disciplines—what persuasive claims could history (distinguished as it is by commitments to definite locations in time and place) make on its own behalf, much less on behalf of its utility to theory?

In an effort to reorient this impasse, I intend to approach the tension between history and theory obliquely, by drawing something productive out of Edelman's recognition of "an encounter with what can't be assimilated to any systematic understanding." Although Edelman's encounter is with the negativity that, he argues, inheres in any sexual encounter, this focus does not exhaust the modes of resistance to intelligibility and coherence that might be discovered in the academic itineraries of sexual knowledge. In asking what other encounters might be available, and what they might reveal about the relations between queer history and theory, I take my bearings from two queer historicists who are also skilled theorists: Susan Lanser's proposal to shift "the emphasis from studying lesbian history to studying "lesbian" and "history" as mutually constitutive,"[30] and Peter Coviello's desire to identify "the very obliquities between past and present from which we might stand to learn something important—and something more, perhaps, than that the past, like the present, is always already queer."[31] With my eye on the "something more" that "studying history *through* lesbians" in the past might reveal, I approach these questions on theory's own ground: returning first to Wiegman's ambivalence about the relevance and utility of lesbian history, and then using some large and, I hope, portable claims about lesbian history to—how shall I put it?—*lesbianize* queer theory.

Lesbian Object Lessons

In the course of an incisive reading of the strategic utility of queer theory's divergence from feminism in *Object Lessons*, Wiegman confesses, "I want the queer theoretic to do some work on behalf of the analytic mobilities of that seemingly defunct figure, 'the lesbian,' who has been reduced, unsexed, domesticated, uglied, and abjected by forces too numerous to list, including those of feminism and queer theory."[32] Consciously and performatively forging "an attachment to her," Wiegman attempts "to extract some space for the lesbian to claim her own affections for a sex-affirmative, shame-affirmative, irrational, anti-identitarian, anti-male-female and antiessentialist queer theoretic."[33]

Well, yes. Decidedly, enthusiastically, yes.

But why is the project of historicizing the conditions of possibility of lesbianism precluded from contributing to that project? For this dismissal is what appears to issue from Wiegman's critique of lesbian history as an academic field formation: "when all our critical obligations are amassed under the sign of the lesbian (or to her various likenesses), we risk losing the past by compromising it for the critical investments that secure our authority here and now."[34] I already have noted that the "critical investments" with which Wiegman is most concerned are those that make lesbian history a "practice of love."[35] Furthermore, the fear of "losing the past" announces Wiegman's respect for the alterity and pastness of the past in terms that resonate with my argument in Chapter 6.[36] Yet, the undesirable compromising of the past also, it would seem, is entailed by what Wiegman elsewhere calls the "critical enmeshments of identity."[37]

Wiegman's doubt about the adequacy of "the lesbian" as "a figure of our critical and political destination"[38] was earlier voiced in her Introduction to the 1994 anthology, *The Lesbian Postmodern* where, taking seriously postmodern anti-identitarianism (which would find ample expression in queer theory), she sought to undermine "the sanctity and security of the lesbian as a category of being"[39]—or, as she later put it, to interrupt "our performative participation in 'her' commodification to get some other kind of work done."[40] That Wiegman was expressly concerned with "the commodification of the lesbian" in both cultural and academic domains suggests how much has changed since 1994 when she could say, without irony or self doubt, that "the lesbian has become a category of speculation and intrigue, operating . . . under the sexy appellation 'queer theory.' "[41]

The extent to which "the lesbian" does and does not operate under "the sexy appellation 'queer theory'" will be considered in due course. For now, suffice it to say that since 1994, a number of scholars with similar postmodern/poststructuralist commitments have sought to reorient the history of sexuality in general, and of lesbianism in particular, as something other than an identity project.[42] Yet, insofar as Wiegman's recent critique extends to the work of those who qualify "lesbian" as an adjective (in order to suggest its status as a strategic project) rather than a noun (which generally announces a recuperative identity project); italicize it to denaturalize and historicize it (as I have done in previous work); attach it to qualifiers (such as Judith Bennett's influential use of "lesbian-like"); or use it to reference genderqueer virginal marriage resisters and cross-dressing female husbands, these interventions either have been unconvincing or have gone unnoticed.

This lack of success in reorienting perceptions of the field is hardly surprising, in part because the readership for lesbian history rarely extends beyond those involved in crafting it. And within that field, conversations tend to remain discipline, period, racially, and geographically specific; work in one subfield, time period, or geographical area rarely makes much of a dent in the debates of others. Moreover, Alan Bray's perspicacity regarding the stranglehold of identity on the history of sexuality has had limited impact among historians and some historicists: as I argued in previous chapters, even in the course of debates about identity's relevance, identity has continued to exert a strong gravitational pull. In short, scholarship challenging identity history (including the tenacious premodern/modern divide and the contested "threshold narratives" of "before" and "after")[43] has not gained much traction, and identity as a hegemonic nodal point for history thus appears to be all but axiomatic. From the perspective of queer theory, this is an obvious demerit. With the modern solidifications of identity exerting such gravitational force, appeals to "history" seem to run counter to queer theory's post-identitarian thrust, and the premodern history of lesbianism, in this view, can *only* be construed as a history of identity—certainly not a basis from which to theorize the variable (which is to say, historical) meanings and functions of female same-sex bonds. All of which is to suggest that the problem of lesbian history for queer theory—the feminist investments of which I take Wiegman to be a staunch advocate—is a problem of both *lesbians* and *history*. The effect of this "problem," I submit, is redoubled by their conjunction.

History and Theory

Wiegman's ambivalence regarding the salience of pre- and early modern lesbian history exists in tangled relation to broad trends within queer studies. Precisely because of Wiegman's lesbian, feminist, queer, and historicist commitments, this awkward proximity—which is not, in the limited space of an afterword, addressed—leads me to wonder whether the field habitus within which her queries are proffered is that of theory's epistemic privilege. On what definitional or functional basis, we might ask, is this privilege secured? To answer this question, some space-clearing generalizations may prove useful—especially since my aim is not to distance theory from history or to demarcate their terrain, but to resist the hierarchy that currently obtains within queer studies by bringing them into closer alignment.

To theorize or to historicize is to engage in an intricate series of intellectual acts involving a number of different strategies, the complexities of which are minimized or obscured when the substantive nouns "theory" and "history" shift the focus away from the process of intellection and toward a putatively stable set of characteristics. It is not my intention, then, to comprehensively define the modes of knowing, research, and argumentation that traffic under the names "theory" and "history," especially insofar as any definition of essential qualities or meanings would exclude aspirations, commitments, and understandings that are important to *someone*. Both of these activities occur on profoundly unstable terrain—which is partly why their definitions tend toward the overly vague or the hotly contested. To some, for instance, "theory" is associated with a canon of influential thinkers dedicated to a variety of forms of anti-foundationalism and hostility to empiricism. To others, "theory" is a style of discourse or reasoning characterized by abstract, or abstruse, or even deliberately mystifying language. To some, "theory's" processes of abstraction and generalization are defined in diacritical opposition to praxis, whether that praxis is that of empirical collection of documents and selection of evidence or of political activism. I believe that "theory" is usefully approached as a strong interpretation of why something exists and/or how it functions; by identifying patterns, "theory" aims at generalizable principles that not only explain more than one instance of the phenomenon and have explanatory force for new cases to which it is applied, but are transferrable across different discursive and historical domains. For historians, generalizing might take the form of recognizing how historical phenomena might be interconnected, whether synchronically or diachronically; for literary critics, generalizing might take the form of pursuing a question that is applicable to all texts (e.g., how do texts end?). The abstractions of "theory," from this perspective, are less a matter of recondite words and concepts than indices of the attempt to secure a global diagnosis and to impart a broadly applicable analytic. Anyone who succeeds in this effort, I submit, is a theorist.

One of the constitutive aspects of "theory," however, is that it cannot but fail to achieve the goal of total applicability: there will always be individual cases that do not fit or fall in line. Whether this is a frustration or a fact of life may depend on a number of factors. Historians, for instance, are often testing hypotheses but they are less apt to test a particular theory and more apt to jettison it if it doesn't help make sense of their evidence; literary critics, conversely, not only apply theory but sometimes see their task as confirming a given theory or contributing new ones. Either way, a theory's success can only be measured by the ways in which it is adopted and appropriated, used to ask fresh questions and open new avenues of thought. Theory's efficacy, then, inheres in the degree to which it is transportable. But this transfer comes at a cost; in the words of Elizabeth Freeman, "when a thought becomes a theory, it becomes portable and tends to shed origins that look retrospectively like dross."[44]

The definitional ground of history is no more stable. To some, "history" means, in a homogeneous, massifying way, "the past"—that is, whatever happened before "the now." To some, it means the passage, the flows, the structures of time—whether conceived as discrete dates or temporal arcs, linear or lateral, progressive or proleptic, recursive or repetitive. To others, "history" means the contexts we reanimate and the narratives we create in our encounter with objects—texts, images, material artifacts—that have survived the ephemerality of the past and continue to exert some pull on the present. And to others, "history" means all of these things at once. For me, "history" tends to be about, in the first instance, particular people, phenomena, ideas, and events—what we might call the object of inquiry in its temporal and spatial dimensions. Given the importance of context to "history" as a discipline (or, more precisely, to those who practice it), however much they might strive for comprehensiveness and representativeness, historians do not tend to value abstraction as a disciplinary sine qua non. In the second instance, "history" tends to be about an object (an idea, event, person) in some larger field of meaning, often presented as a narrative of change, rupture, continuity, or stasis. It is here that "history" begins to take on some of the abstracting aims (if not the universality and mobility) generally attributed to "theory."

That said, historians might well insist that vis-à-vis their use of theory, abstraction is not really the point. From a historian's point of view, theory tends to be conceptualized as a framework for inquiry; it typically is a means to an end, not an end in itself.[45] The stakes for historians tend to lie in the viability of the theory to make sense either of their practice as historians or of the nature of their evidence. (This, of course, could also be said of many literary critics—the disciplines are not oppositional in this regard.) One way to approach the salient difference between the impulses of historicization and theorization is as a matter of scale. In a lot of historical writing, the desire to produce an argument out of sufficient evidence, comprehensive detail, interpretative nuance, and depth of context means that much of the intellectual effort is involved in situating and *scaling down*.[46] Historical explanation tends to be grounded in the material details of experience. Theory, in contrast, tends to value the results of *scaling up*, of extrapolating away from context and extending the object's import into the largest possible explanatory domain. These tendencies, I would suggest, are as complementary as they are inverse.[47]

Inverse as well are the ways theory and history seek to make analytical connections by means of *speculation*, whether that speculation takes the form of a historical hypothesis or a conceptual one. Whereas theory's speculations tend to be forward looking, sometimes even predictive, most historical subfields ground their conjectures, even their most future-oriented ones, in the constructed "data bank" of as-comprehensive-as-possible "recollection." How these modes foresee and remember, how they forget and reconstruct, is obviously more complex than these schematic remarks suggest; but my point is that history and theory, as complementary modes of inquiry, are dialectically interleaved.[48]

Beyond advocating recognition that historicizing and theorizing are inextricably connected, I suggest that how we frame the one also implies how we understand the other. Within queer studies, it is generally assumed that history needs theory to help it to frame its questions and, in particular, to prod it to ask different and larger questions—and then, of course, to answer those questions in light of the evidence. In this sense, theory encourages history to scale up. Queer theory, however, needs history every bit as much, first, because the material that theory bases its speculations on can only ever be historical, in the sense of what we already think we know, as well as what has happened in the past to make us think the way we think; and, second, because the results of historical research, including queer uses of the archive,[49] can supply the efficacious friction of something other than what we think we already know. Such friction helps theory get a better handle on its conceptual parameters and perimeters, helping it to see that its foundational axioms may not be as widely exigent as previously thought.[50] This is not to suggest that theory must always engage with history; nor is it to criticize the decisions of any scholar to privilege the universal and abstract over the specific and contingent. It is to suggest, as Lynn Huffer has, that "any theory—including queer theory—has an obligation to examine the conditions of possibility of its own speaking position as theory, where theory is defined as a set of truth claims that, by virtue of their utterance as theory, move away from particularity to generality. In fact, this examination of one's own speaking position is *an ethical obligation of theory.*"[51] This ethical obligation extends, I suggest, not only to queer theory's recognition of its own conditions of possibility, but to the field habitus that it inaugurated and sustains. Insofar as queer studies, under the mandate of queer theory, continues to expand its commitment to universalizing modes of thought while contracting its interest in minoritizing ones—as I have argued throughout this book that it has—it would seem that some of the expendable "dross" from which queer theory has emerged, indeed, which it has left behind in the transit from "thought" to "theory," is no less than "history" itself.[52]

Thinking "the Lesbian" as Identity

"The lesbian," of course, is typically considered a "minoritized identity form." Insofar as queer theory's universalizing thrust can render gender extraneous, the lesbian's minoritarian status has justified the disposal of a lesbian analytic under the supervening rubric of queer. Wiegman complicates such narratives of supersession in her summary gloss on queer theory's resistance to "the lesbian":

> Like all minoritized identity forms, *the lesbian first coalesced into categorical coherence through epistemic and corporeal violence;* she came to life as a species

of person through those processes that reduced the human to populations, *acts to identities*, self-recognition to saturated discipline; she is part of a dense and shifting *modern* map of human relations, *an "identity" produced by discourses of social abjection* and politically reclaimed for the purposes of amelioration, which means that she has been used—wielded even—for wildly different political ambitions and critical aims, often in ways that make her unrecognizable across domains. In the different arenas in which we follow her, she is a figure whose power is powerfully divergent: *being both the frame for identitarian commitments and for their refusals*; for the fantasy of utter self-attachment and for profound, unassimilable disidentifications; and for relations that are not always discernible on the grounds of (dis)identification at all. *She can be historically discontinuous, even with those versions most thought to be herself and even in those situations when the postulation of her transhistorical coherence is required for something new to enunciate itself*—as when queer takes on the very identity destinations it otherwise disavows and both includes and reduces her, or why dykebois and genderqueers seek defiantly to be anything except her. These enunciations rely on *making the lesbian solid enough to perform their own self-fashioning reclamations*—indeed it is their proximity to and intimacy with her that makes their divergence from her possible.[53]

By focusing on the contradictions that attend the lesbian-as-identity-form, Wiegman's anatomy usefully parses how this figure has come to bear the kind of weight that has led to her uneasy inclusion in, and ready exclusion from, theoretical and political endeavors.[54] But given the rapidity with which Wiegman moves through the densely imbricated processes leading to the lesbian's coalescence "into categorical coherence," we might wish to slow the pace, pausing to ask how the constituent parts of this process are sutured together. For, it seems no accident that the gesture that opens this exhortation passes quickly over the *historical* coalescence of lesbian-as-identity, taking as historical "fact" the reputed shift from sexual acts to identities. This move, which would seem to elide traces of any prior histories, concurs, I submit, too readily with a homogeneous narrative of lesbianism "produced by [modern] discourses of social abjection," a narrative that has been contested and complicated by multiple histories of female sodomy, erotic friendship, tribadism, and sapphism, from the medieval period through the nineteenth century, and across cultures.[55] It likewise skates too quickly across the social production of abjection, as work on the first decades of the twentieth century shows, and thus ends up overstating the coherence of lesbian identity in modernity as well.[56]

One implication of this elision of historical processes within the project of theorizing queer theory's resistance to the lesbian is that "the lesbian" can only be thought as a modern phenomenon. This principled commitment to lesbian-as-modern-identity-form renders any prior formation illegible or irrelevant and implicitly construes any such concept as "the premodern lesbian" or even the adjectival "lesbian premodern" to be a contradiction in terms. Strict nominalism, of course, did and still may have important work to do, especially when pursued with the goal of attending to a prior period's own lexicon (such as tribade, friend, sapphist). Nonetheless, the effect within current queer discourses is to quarantine into irrelevance the elucidation of forms of female desire and sex in pre- and early modernity. Coming *before* identity and the formation of modern norms, these forms paradoxically seem *not queer enough* to do queer work, because, in order to constitute them as research objects, one necessarily projects backward, ex post facto, the supposedly modern-only identity of "the lesbian."[57]

Such a projection *backward*, it has been alleged, amounts to a form of presumptive knowledge: the problematic assumption that we always already know who and what "the lesbian" is. This allegation, broadly construed, underlies calls for an unhistoricism that decisively rejects all tethering of past formations of desire to present identities by means of temporal chronologies or sequence.[58] It motivates Laura Doan to critique those scholars who practice what she calls "ancestral and queer genealogical" approaches: "Whether coherent or incoherent, knowable or unknowable, speakable or unspeakable, secure or suggestible, these scholars understand the objective of historical explanation as measuring the past against current understandings."[59] And it prompts Carla Freccero to elucidate the many reasons "to elude the identitarian terms of lesbian in premodernity, or rather to invoke her only as a queer specter haunting the European past from a present vantage point" or as "a fantasmatic creature conjured for the sake of present and future survival."[60]

Yet, if Wiegman is right that it is the effort to distance oneself from "the lesbian" through acts of disavowal that *produces* this figure as transhistorically coherent and that this disavowal confers upon her a recalcitrant solidity that other identities supposedly lack, *why must we repeat this critical gesture?* Why elide the lesbian's status as "historically discontinuous" and project onto her an undeserved stability or, conversely, resurrect her only as a ghostly specter, whose materiality vanishes in the sands of time? The tendency to do so, I submit, is based in part on the occlusion of the terms of "her" prehistory, as well as on the occlusion of some of the enduring relations of knowledge by which "she" continues to be "known" today.[61]

The Embarrassment of Lesbian Studies

As a "sign," "the lesbian" opens onto the academic itineraries of knowledge production, and in particular the field "lesbian studies," which, in the age of queerness has come to be seen as impossibly quaint, anachronistic, a phase consigned by many to the dustbin of history.[62] Indeed, despite the increase in the exploration of lesbian texts, histories, and representations since the 1990s, it remains the case that scholarship produced under "the sign of the lesbian" is sidelined not only in history and literature, but in queer, gender, and women's studies. Multiple factors collude, wittingly and unwittingly, in this marginalization. Most obvious is the still-secondary status of sexuality studies in the literary and historical "mainstream."[63] Among some scholars the possible anachronism of the word "lesbian" continues to fuel doubt over the historical existence of female same-sex relations. And outdated formulations about the unfeasibility of tracing female homoeroticism historically, despite having been discredited, continue to be reiterated by scholars outside the field.[64]

But other knotty factors, internal to sexuality and queer studies, are also involved. Across disciplines and methodological approaches, the question of what counts as "lesbian" in contemporary usage has remained a stumbling block, even as the term has become embroiled in tensions between "feminist" and "queer." Queer theory's success in positioning lesbianism as retrograde and dull means that to claim a lesbian identity or a lesbian analytic is to accept one's status as superannuated. Many women of color, youth, and genderqueers view lesbianism as a white, middle-class identification, and have no interest in being "hailed" by it, whatever their sexual inclinations. Many scholars of lesbianism address topics other than or broader than lesbianism, and most do not profess a strong identification with "lesbian studies" or highlight "lesbian" in their book titles or academic profiles (a tendency encouraged by publishers' enthusiasm for the greater marketability of "queer"). These problems are exacerbated by institutional formations, such as the paucity of dialogue across historical periods, geographies, national languages, and disciplines;[65] indeed, since so much academic conversation takes place within disciplinary venues, scholars who work on lesbian *anything* are often the lone representative of this interest in a department, panel, conference, or anthology.

Each of these internal factors carries its own complex history, and some of them are the result of viable intellectual and/or political concerns. The binding and unbinding of energies that attach and preclude attachments to "the sign of the lesbian" can be highly personal, deeply felt, and vary across the life span. Nonetheless, in the aggregate and regardless of anyone's intentions, these factors have had tangible effects on knowledge production. They have reinforced a misleading heteronormativity in the study of women, impoverished and distorted histories of sexuality and gender, enabled a tendentious nonspecificity to considerations of queerness, and retarded the resolution of key questions about lesbianism itself. In contrast to the 1970s and 1980s, "lesbian studies" now names not a rich field of inquiry but an embarrassing relic of times gone by.

Histories Lost and Found

If "the lesbian" is a sign crosscut by specific modes of knowledge production, then it behooves us to step back from its current configuration and examine its historical formation *as a concept*. The signifier "lesbian" consists of both the term and a corresponding set of figurations. The term itself has an exceptionally long history.[66] Awareness of this etymological longevity, however, does not preclude a tendency to view "lesbian-as-identity" as the term's only possible meaning. Reviewing the recurrence of an "etymological moment" in early modern literary criticism and queer studies, Paula Blank reminds us of Erasmus's early sixteenth-century popular compendium the *Adages*, which defines "*Lesbiari*, 'To behave like a Lesbian,'" as "the infamous vice, which is performed with the mouth, called fellatio, I think, or irrumatio, [it] is said to have originated with the people of Lesbos, and among them it was first of all something which women had to perform."[67] In the sixteenth century, it apparently was proverbial knowledge that "lesbian-like" meant a woman who engaged in fellatio. Now, the historical meanings of "lesbian" have long been contested, with debates focused on when it stopped referring only to the island of Lesbos,[68] whether in certain periods it signified primarily female poetic prowess,[69] whether the term was lost during the Middle Ages,[70] how early the erotic longings inscribed in Sappho's poetic fragments were used to describe other women's desires,[71] and how early the term came to name a "sexual identity" in its modern sense of female homosexual.[72] But what we have not debated, even though some of us have been cognizant of this etymology,[73] is whether lesbians are women who fellate men.

My point is not that fellatio is still a meaning present in current usages of "lesbian"—it is not as if etymological meanings only accumulate and don't also sometimes fall away. Nor is it to suggest that we broaden our understanding of "lesbian" to be so inclusive (although others wishing to queer sexual practice might wish to do so). Rather I want to use this history to reinvigorate awareness of the temporal contingency and variability that limns all identity categories, even those that appear most reified. The term "lesbian" has not only, as Blank argues, been subject to "obvious, spasmodic changes in its vernacular meanings since the Renaissance";[74] it also has been subject to recursive temporalities that interrupt the stability of its meaning in modernity. We need only note that in the 1908 treatise *Outlines of Medical Jurisprudence for India*, when the authors introduce the "forms of unnatural immorality, such as Tribadism," they define "tribadism" as the "unnatural and immoral practices between woman and woman: *formerly called 'lesbian love'*)."[75] Temporally positioning "lesbian" as the term that precedes and has been superseded by "tribade" (a word with its own classical etymology and its own uneven history of use), the authors evince the simple truth that, *at the level of the word*, "lesbian" is not as self-evidently modern as many have assumed.[76] The temporal divisions involved in thinking "the lesbian" as premodern/modern/postmodern, it turns out, are historically inadequate, for within each category the multiplicities of experience, definition, and discourse are collapsed into an overarching homogeneity.

(Im)possibility, (In)significance, (In)consequence

Ever since Terry Castle's *The Apparitional Lesbian* demonstrated the spectral quality of lesbian representation in British and American contexts, a number of scholars have argued that invisibility, insignificance, unaccountability, and impossibility have provided some of the prevailing terms by which lesbianism has figured in the cultural imaginary of Europe and North America. While the archive for this perception is geopolitically specific, in its general coordinates it has salience for non-Western contexts as well.[77] Its historiographic

reach traverses time, from my own genealogy of the rhetoric of (in)signifi-
cance and (im)possibility that structures the discourse of female same-sex
desire in sixteenth- and seventeenth-century England,[78] to Elizabeth Wahl's
comparative study of English and French "invisible relations" in the long
eighteenth century,[79] to Valerie Rohy's elucidation of "impossible women"
in late nineteenth- and early twentieth-century American literature.[80]

To date, the most theoretically elaborated contribution to this cultural
history is that of Annamarie Jagose, who argues on the basis of nineteenth-
and twentieth-century British and American texts that lesbians are generally
conceived as always already a second-order, derivative phenomenon (at once
to men and to homosexuality). But rather than bemoan lesbian "inconsequence" and subscribe to strategies of historical recovery to remediate it,
Jagose instead articulates "the coordinates of a widespread conceptual
impasse in contemporary lesbian theory in which the problem of lesbian
representability is nearly indistinguishable from its alleged solution."[81] The
"alleged solution" that Jagose identifies goes by the name of "history," which,
she observes, "has seemed to function, for lesbian studies, as invisibility's
indemnification."[82] By this she refers to the fantasy wherein a prior, transhistorical lesbian history might provide lesbians with visibility and thus render
them viable as historical subjects in their own right. Jagose rejects the "apparent promise of recuperation" proffered by this "reliance on the historicizing
gesture."[83] Moreover, she is intent less on historicizing the structure of inconsequence than in theorizing it as an epistemological contradiction: "while
identity formations based on homosexual desire between women are frequently represented in some belated or secondary relation to other forms of
allegedly precedent sexual organization, this is less an empirical fact concerning the date of their historical emergence than a constituent characterization
of the masculinist and heteronormative representational strategies that secure
the cultural definition of female homosexuality. The epistemological contradiction of lesbianism is that its specificity is founded less on distinction than
on derivation."[84]

While theorizing the terms of derivation, Jagose, however, remains "interested in the ways in which the modern category of lesbianism is historicized,"
an interest giving rise to a dual focus that, as she admits, divides her project
"against itself."[85] The results of this self-division are twofold. First, it inaugu-
rates a historicist self-reflexivity, whereby she tries, initially with respect to
Anne Lister, "to put aside the semantic driftnet of 'lesbian' long enough to

see what floats up in Lister's account of herself . . . to catch at her early-nineteenth-century sexual knowledge rather than attempt to detect our own already and presciently in operation."[86] This act of pausing to watch what "floats up" has considerable affinities with the historicist method of Chapter 5, where the character of Martha Joyless stands as a figure for the status of women's sexual knowledge in an analysis that yields some of the same *inexplicableness* that Jagose finds with respect to sexual subjectivity produced in Lister's diary.[87] This putting aside of "the semantic driftnet of 'lesbian'" is also in keeping with Doan's determination that the history of same-sex relations not presume that the lineaments of its object are always already constituted and known in advance.[88] And it accords with Anjali Arondekar's proposal that lesbian history across geopolitical formations might partake of and produce something other than "search and rescue" or salvific forms.[89] In short, thinking "the lesbian" in epistemological terms shifts inquiry away from the recuperation of identities and toward the structures of representation and knowledge operative both then (whatever the specific "then" is) and now.

Second, Jagose's dual historicist/theoretical orientation confers the epistemological recognition that "'history,' with its apparent promise of recuperation, stands in an overdetermined relationship to the 'lesbian,' who is persistently figured as unable to secure the grounds of her own representation."[90] The overdetermination of the relations between "lesbian" and "history," I now propose, are salient in ways extending beyond those addressed by Jagose. What, for instance, might "float up" were we to hypothesize that, in the current critical context, the expendability of *history* from queer *theory* bears a structural resemblance to the expendability of "the lesbian" from the domain of "queer"? Or, by postulating, even more strenuously, that, in terms of the divergent statuses of queer and lesbian studies, *lesbian* is to *history* as *queer* is to *theory*? Any such generalized structure of equivalences, of course, risks flattening the complexity of engagements of particular lesbians and queers, historicists, and theorists; yet, despite exceptions, the act of reading these relations as overdetermined tenders a structural point of purchase that may prove diagnostically useful. For what comes into focus by means of this postulation is the extent not only to which "lesbian" figures the "dross" from which "queer" has emerged, but that "history" tends to be approached, even in queer theorizations attentive to and affirmative of lesbians, as a static, even homeostatic, signifier: as that which might retrospectively secure lesbian identity, establish the grounds of her representation, or provide the hoped-for avenue for political redress. In both instances, a "superior" term requires and is served by a "subordinate," more pedestrian term that it putatively masters and renders irrelevant.

But what if "history," albeit in "overdetermined relationship to the 'lesbian,'" were *not* defined, a priori and in toto, as a mode of stabilization or recuperation? What if "the lesbian" did not allude or lead to epistemological surety, but rather to the obstacles, difficulties, and recalcitrance of knowledge relations? What if the task of "history" were to ask questions *of theory* from a perspective on lesbianism conceived in terms *other* than identity? What if one activated these questions, not on behalf of "a productive model for thinking about the derivativeness, culturally displaced onto lesbianism, *that structures identity itself*,"[91] as Jagose encourages us to do, or even to further adduce the "unbearable" in sex, as Berlant and Edelman recommend, but rather on behalf of a "historicizing gesture" conceived altogether otherwise?

"The Lesbian" as Knowledge Problem

The "historicizing gesture" I propose to develop depends on exploiting the history of "the lesbian," both as word and figure, in terms of the problems and possibilities it poses for knowledge relations. Both the recursive temporalities of the word "lesbian" and the topos of impossibility, insignificance, inconsequence, and immateriality through which "the lesbian" has been historically represented prompt recognition of the ways "knowledge" of "the lesbian" has been constructed by means of instability and contradiction.[92] And here, it is crucial to insist that my argument is *not* that "the lesbian" actually *has been* invisible, impossible, inconsequential, or apparitional, but that this figure's representational status has hinged on a dialectic between visibility and invisibility, possibility and impossibility, signification and insignificance. The parenthesis surrounding the negativizing prefix in (im)possibility, for instance, aims to maximize awareness of the diacritical relationality of "the lesbian"—the way that this figure is apprehensible only through oscillations of assertion and denial that are embedded in processes of knowing and unknowing. Within the activity of identifying or "coming to terms" with "the lesbian" at any particular moment, the prepositional content of these terms may shift, as Chapter 4 argued, but the positive-negative structure of contradiction persists. In this respect, what matters most in scholars' insistence on the "the lesbian" as "coherent or incoherent, knowable or unknowable, speakable or unspeakable, secure or suggestible" is that, historically speaking, the "or" in this set of relations is in fact more properly an "and." In the history of lesbian representation, "the lesbian" is simultaneously known and not known, simultaneously signified and rendered insignificant. Inhering within the figure of "the lesbian," in other words, is a dynamic conjunction, whereby fathomability, intelligibility, and comprehensibility are always fastened, whether loosely or tightly, to their negation. And this means that for the sign of "the lesbian," both the status of ontology and the status of signification are implicated in a crucible of knowledge relations.

At issue is the way the past can only be understood by means of a method capable of harnessing and working such contradictions. Other scholars have begun to gesture toward the utility of these problems for historiography. Katherine Binhammer, for instance, describes the topos of lesbian unaccountability and invisibility as generating its own historiographic possibilities: "in trying to account for the unaccountable, the history of sexuality is most successful when it is forced to confront this evidentiary silence. By investigating a history without a proper object, scholars are led to ask complex questions about evidence, history, and power. . . . In the end, we learn as much from the unanswerable questions we ask than the explanations we can give."[93]

Linking the unanswerable questions caused by problems of evidence to the representational problem of lesbian invisibility, Binhammer notes:

> Within lesbian history, the dearth of empirical documents has freed historians
> to shift from a history of sexual identities to a history of the discursive effects
> of female same-sex desire. . . . Lesbian historiography foregrounds the necessity
> of interpretation in the production of historical knowledge and as such, it
> shifts the ground to epistemological questions about the discourse of
> sexuality—how we know what we know, how knowledge about sex is ideologi-
> cally inflected, how who speaks and from where determines what is said.[94]

The questions about knowledge to which Binhammer alludes are the means by which Valerie Rohy, reading texts from a later period and a different continent, explores the "problem of lesbian definition": "I take impossibility, then, as a kind of vanishing point in both discourse and desire. . . . As a name for an internal resistance, impossibility also describes the unacknowledged contradictions within hegemonic systems of sexuality, which patriarchal culture, in its will to meaning, displaces onto lesbian figures."[95] Echoing

Jagose, Rohy's historically and nationally specific project seeks to "make lesbian sexuality a repository for the failures of meaning inherent in figurality
itself."[96] And like Binhammer, Rohy chooses "uncertainty over certainty as a
critical strategy" in order "to gain critical purchase on the mechanisms of
sexual knowledge that both posit lesbianism as the limit of epistemology and
continue to insist, paradoxically enough, that they know a lesbian when they
see one."[97] Parallel to these apprehensions of "lesbian" as a site of linguistic
and epistemological failure and the attempt to "build a theory . . . on 'impossibility' "[98] is Susan Lanser's proposition that since 1600, "the logic of woman
+ woman reappears as unexpected, unprecedented, or unaccountable," a
recurrence that functions "as a sign of the degree to which sapphic subjects
continued to confound epistemic assumptions and yet kept demanding attention because modernity could not set their logic aside."[99] Such contradictions
and irresolution, I now suggest, function simultaneously as an empirical
description of lesbian history and a "release point" for historiographic
method. They not only direct our attention to the "epistemic assumptions,"
the ideological contradictions and representational limits, that subtend and
secure "the sign of the lesbian," but to the *resistance to knowing* that this
figure has embodied over time.

Intractable Materiality

Thinking "the lesbian" as a historical and epistemological category, then,
leads not to stability and solidity but to impasse and contradictions in the
production of knowledge. Considered historiographically, "the sign of the
lesbian" figures precisely the "epistemological impasse, the aporia of relationality," that Edelman discerns in sex itself and that I have argued throughout this book composes sex as a knowledge relation. This aporia, however, is
not the only form of impasse regularly attributed to "the lesbian." Filling out
this discursive profile are the lineaments of a material embodiment that have
seemed to be particularly stolid and stubborn. Indeed, the evocation of a
recalcitrant lesbian *materiality* is so pervasive that it comes close to possessing
the status of a "field-forming complaint"[100]—that is, a "complaint" against
that which the field of lesbian studies organizes and legitimizes itself.

In 1994, Biddy Martin critiqued queer theory for its tendency to privilege
masculinity as a transitive and transgressive mode, conceptually defined
against a static and fixed femininity. "Anti-foundationalist celebrations of
queerness," she argued, sometimes "rely on their own projections of fixity,

constraint, or subjection onto a fixed ground, often onto feminism or the female body, in relation to which queer sexualities become figural, performative, playful, and fun."[101] This fixity, she argued, was constitutively related to the analytical and social invisibility of femininity, particularly the invisibility of the femme, in contrast to the hypervisibility of the butch.[102] Since then, other scholars have noted that lesbians seem more *embodied* than other identities named by sex (or gender); indeed, in contrast to queers, lesbians seem overburdened by the weight of both identity and corporeality. Says Karma Lochrie: "Let's face it, the term 'lesbian' has often carried a more identitarian and resolutely literal meaning than most of the other terms for homosexuals, making it the least portable of them."[103] So, too, Elizabeth Freeman notes "the gravitational pull that 'lesbian' sometimes seems to exert upon 'queer,'" wherein the lesbian "is cast as the big drag, drawing politics inexorably back to essentialized bodies, normative visions of women's sexuality, and single-issue identity politics."[104] Unlike trans identities, for whom an attachment to corporeality has been vigorously theorized—and in such a way as to issue a potent challenge to queer idealizations of transitivity[105]—the problem of "lesbian as intractable materiality" is one of those commonplaces that, to my knowledge, has yet to be theorized at all. In fact, in the words of Lochrie, the lesbian's "resolutely literal meaning" is one reason that she "resists abstraction and generalization"[106]—which makes it difficult to theorize from her situation or on her behalf.

Why is the concept "lesbian" "widely regarded as essentialist, historically redundant, and limiting" when "gay" is not,[107] or, in relation to "a queer enlightenment," considered "conceptually rearguard,"[108] a dead weight on queer theorizations? What is it about lesbian identities, sexual practices, and their position in the social imaginary that limit their use value for other problems and groups? Why does the concept of "the lesbian" seem less transferable, less scalable, to other critical contexts? What prevents certain questions, approaches, and objects from even being recognized as "lesbian"? Why is "the lesbian" only improbably theoretical? Is this circumscription merely a masculinist projection, as implied by Martin? Is it the academic version of the earnest literalism stereotypically ascribed to lesbians, positioned as they are in contrast to the equally stereotypically campy, ironic, histrionic, *more queer* gay man—and this, despite our queer ironic stand-up comics, screwball performance artists, and wry graphic novelists?[109]

The analysis I've proffered thus far leads to my hypothesis that the "complaint" of lesbian materiality (which exists in diacritical relation to the attribution of immateriality) may be structurally related to the history of lesbian (im)possibility. That is, whether construed as continuous, discontinuous, or, as Chapter 4 argued, through cycles of salience, the cultural logics through which "the lesbian" has been composed have hinged on the dual axes of (im)materiality and (im)possibility, which specify and configure "the lesbian" in distinct, yet intersecting, ways. The overemphasis on material embodiment is the means by which "woman + woman" achieves legibility—or else she remains a specter. But this overemphasis is not fully explained as a projection of fixity onto femininity—in fact, it is belied by certain renditions of femininity. For such materiality also explains in part the cultural prominence of gender transitive (that is, masculine) morphologies and behaviors to lesbian history. Emblematized by, among others, the historically specific figures of the militant virago, the tribade (with her hypertrophic clitoris), the female husband, the masculine sapphist, the invert, the dyke, the bulldagger, and the butch, such masculine identifications, and the corresponding idiom of "imitation" to which, until very recently, they have been subject,[110] may be conceived not only as personal modes of subjectivity but as epistemological effects. In other words, the recalcitrant materiality of lesbianism is a function of the way that gender—both femininity and masculinity—impinges on the meanings of sex.

Indeed, the various imputations of (im)possibility and (in)significance attending the conjunction of "woman + woman" do not depend on gender dissonance; they pertain equally to women whose gender identifications and styles are consonant with cultural norms, whatever those norms are in a given time and place. (Indeed, my previous work on early modern representations shows that the shift from insignificance to significance hinges on a tilt toward masculinity, whose coordinates I would now locate on the axis of materiality.) The pervasive perception of a general incapacity attributed to lesbians *tout court*—and the corresponding incredulity about their desires, sexual practices, and modes of sociability—depends on a particularly tricky logic, one that relies not on hypermateriality (and the hypervisibility of gender transgression), but on a quite literal insignificance—that is, a failure to signify. Through such crosscutting imperatives, the axes of (im)materiality and (im)possibility can be seen not only to run on parallel tracks but to converge.

Moreover, I would suggest that the contradictory axes of (im)materiality and (im)possibility contribute to the apparent theoretical insufficiency of "the lesbian." This hypothesis becomes more tenable if we continue to track the conceptual variables attributed to "the lesbian" as relative to "queer" and "theory." In relation to "queer," "the lesbian" is posited as too particular, too local, too gendered; in relation to "theory," she is too mundane, too literal, too stolid. Like "history," "the lesbian," we might say, is too minor in scale. Because of this doubled "scaling down," "the lesbian" is apt to be perceived as a social category, rather than a theoretical one. In short, the forms of derivation and inconsequence theorized by Jagose inflect not only "the sign of the lesbian" as a concept, but also its potential as a category of analysis.[111]

It is precisely because "the lesbian" catalyzes such unmanageable contradictions that this sign provides an epistemological point of entrée into the processes of sexual knowledge production. It hardly seems accidental that the axes of (im)materiality and (im)possibility that structure the epistemology of "the lesbian" dovetail with but do not entirely map onto the dual axes of materiality and metaphor that previous chapters argued constitute the epistemology of sex. It is not only that gender impinges upon and organizes the signifying logics of lesbianism (although it does), but also that "the lesbian" has historically served as a compacted site for the obdurate materiality of embodiment *and* for the representational (im)possibility of sex. From this epistemological vantage, "the sign of the lesbian" manifests, in its very form, the impasses of sexual knowledge. "She" is not and never has been what we already know. Instead, "she" is what *we have never known* and what has *resisted knowledge* across a remarkably enduring set of cultural coordinates. "The lesbian" isn't the solution or the salvific mode of redress for those who seek knowledge of same-sex desires and practices in the past. Rather, "the lesbian" is the elusive figure *whose history embodies the problem.*

As a sign, "the lesbian" is not *only* an identity, although clearly that; not merely an object of historical or contemporary knowledge, although often that, too. "The lesbian" is not just a constellation of tropes, a node in relations of power, or a discursive relay for other concerns, although this sign regularly is made to perform and conform to these functions. Nor is it just that "the lesbian" has had an attenuated claim on the attention of many queer theorists or that, in order to redress this attenuation and subordination, queer theory must speak to lesbian concerns. Nor does it suffice to argue that lesbians have served as contested "object lessons" in dialogues between queer theory and feminism—although that recognition remains crucial for imagining the grounds for future articulations of "queer" and "lesbian" on equal footing.

Magnetizing the tension between universalizing and minoritizing understandings of sex, the contemporary "lesbian" is a switch point connecting, through a tensile set of tripwires, the concrete materialities and destinies of embodied identity, the dynamic and unstable processes of identification and disidentification, and the utopian longings of a feminist queer otherwise. At the same time, the historical "lesbian" is an apposite figure for the ways it is possible *not to know* within the protocols of both historical and theoretical inquiry.

Given the tension between these contemporary and historical forms, it should be clear that to invoke this history of (im)materiality and (im)possibility is not to essentialize or condone it. My purpose is not to install "the lesbian" as a privileged signifier around which other, more mobile figures might circulate.[112] We are under no obligation to *believe* in the ultimate intelligibility or *un*intelligibility of lesbianism, just as we are under no obligation to believe in *any* sexual taxonomies or descriptions. I am not even positing the transhistoricity of the dialectic of lesbian (im)possibility: recent historical research has rendered pre- and early modern lesbianism ever more legible, and scattered references across the lesbian "greatest hits" canon suggest that female-female sex may have been cognitively processed in a broad variety of ways.[113] Nor am I arguing that lesbians actually *do* carry more material weight than other forms of sexualized embodiment; the lesbian's stolidity and density, after all, are nothing if not tropes. Most important, the history I have highlighted is not over, as Wiegman's passionate avowal of desire *for* and *on behalf of* "the lesbian" makes clear. "The lesbian" could be—*is being*—written differently, not least by those subjects who write under that name as well as by those who eschew it.

Times to Come

Does offering "the lesbian" as a sign for the impasses involved in making sexual knowledge suffice in addressing the need to "benefit" from her history?[114] Although that is for others to decide, I have tried to suggest the epistemological importance of this sign for knowledge production more generally. Rather than proffer a method that would ratify or secure the future of lesbian history as a field, my strategy has been to shift the terms of a possible response to Wiegman's questions: away from sententious appeals and minoritarian rectitude and toward some larger structures of knowing, within which concerns about relevance and utility might be recalibrated. The analytical traction provided by recognition of this dual epistemological status is what I wish to emphasize in conclusion. If, as I've argued, *queer* is to *theory* as *lesbian* is to *history*, then rather than appealing to history over and against theory or theory over and against history, of queer over lesbian or lesbian over queer, we might employ "the sign of the lesbian" to resist these oppositions. Furthermore, this sign enables us to interrupt those misrecognitions of "history" whereby the terms of subordination that characterize "the lesbian" bear an uncanny resemblance to the grounds on which "history" is dismissed. For if the problem of lesbian history for queer theory is a problem of both *lesbians* and *history*, "the sign of the lesbian" reminds queer theory of its own disavowals as it seeks to institutionalize itself as, paradoxically, a continuously insurgent field. Recognizing these structural relations as overdetermined, we might better apprehend that they can be denaturalized: "history" need not yield a "stability" of meaning or an "identity" of the subject, but provide the tools for entering into, taking hold of, and redeploying contradictions— contradictions that are as relevant to those who would *never* identify as lesbian as they are to those who do. The tensions between knowing and unknowing, intelligibility and unintelligibility, that have structured "the sign of the lesbian" provide a point of access and leverage for reactivating historicity in queer theory. Thus repurposed, "the lesbian" becomes a useful category of theoretical analysis: a sign whose history might contribute to theorizing how and what "queer" will signify in times to come.[115]

The "sign of the lesbian" thus opens onto a reconfigured vista where, when it comes to thinking sex, history and theory will no longer be thought as mutually exclusive or antagonistic. Rather, the conditions for thought are also the conditions of life; how we frame the epistemological and the theoretical is inseparable from how we frame the material and the historical. The conditions of our historicity—our embodiment, our emplacement, and our relations to temporality—are the prerequisites to our theorizations, just as our theorizations are the means by which we understand our historicity. The "sign of the lesbian" invites us to approach history and theory as complementary, diacritical tools that together can be used to confront the impasses of thought, as well as the agencies of the unthought and the yet-to-be thought, in the making of sexual knowledge.

CHAPTER 10

Sex Ed; or, Teach Me Tonight

When I was young and stupid, as Bette Midler might put it,[1] I loved listening to the music of Phoebe Snow. Snow seemed passionate and wise. If she also seemed just a bit insecure, she overwrote her fear with vocal assertion. Her lyrics, performed in a deep, throaty, oftentimes soaring voice, suggested that whatever she didn't know about desire, about sex, she was going to find out:

> Did you say, I've got a lot to learn
> Well don't think I'm trying not to learn
> Since this is the perfect spot to learn
> Teach me tonight. . . .
> Starting with the ABC of it
> Getting right down to the XYZ of it
> Help me solve the mystery of it
> Teach me tonight. . . .
> One thing isn't very clear, my love
> Should the teacher stand so near, my love
> Graduation's almost here, my love
> Teach me tonight.[2]

I always imagined that Snow got what she was asking for: that her teacher-lover, standing provocatively close, helped her to "graduate" and, in so doing, solved the "mystery." It was a reassuring fantasy. Budding English major that I was, I appreciated the idea that sex could be organized like an alphabet; I too was curious about what might occur between *A* and *Z*. Even if I never adopted the forcefulness of Snow's demands, the possibilities of self-assertion glimmering in her refrain "teach me tonight" helped me imagine an interpersonal horizon beyond the awkwardness of a bisexual adolescence.

The dynamics of sexual instruction examined in this book, in contrast, have had more in common with my actual memories of sexual tutelage. They have tended to lead to less, rather than more, surety; to more, rather than less, doubt. The certainty that one will receive the kind of instruction one asks for from the person one wants, or that, having received it, one will know exactly what it means, has remained elusive. This state of uncertainty, I've argued, is a constitutive dynamic of early modern sex, affecting the culture's representations of sex, including its means of talking about it. I have focused not on the representation of those whose cognitive aptitudes and social competencies gain them power, but those who lack such aptitudes and who stand in need of tutelage. Martha Joyless may be exceptional in early modern texts in asking another woman for erotic instruction, but she is not exceptional in her ignorance of the sexual ABC's. Nor is she exceptional in the tacit disavowal her request elicited. Renaissance texts are populated with women and men who simply do not know what other people seem to know; and more often than not, this lack of knowledge consistently evokes a pedagogical imperative that is elided or refused or fails.

This is not wholly a gendered phenomenon—or, at least, not a simple one. When Jack Dapper in Thomas Middleton and Thomas Dekker's *The Roaring Girle* asks to be taught the meaning of "niggling"—"teach me what niggling is; I'd fain be niggling" (10.214–15)—his request is likewise fobbed off.[3] As a sartorially extravagant "fop" who represents a species of failed masculinity, Jack is consistently the object of other characters' displays of wit and, as was true with Martha, the dismissal of his desire is in accord with his butt-of-the-joke role.[4] If some of the interest of Martha's request is that it derives from her prior experience with a wanton woman, some of the interest of Jack's request is that it occurs within the context of the play's thematization of the intelligibility of sexual communication. Critics have acknowledged *The Roaring Girle*'s interest in slang and wordplay, as well as the ways Moll Cutpurse, the cross-dressed "roaring girl" of the title, functions as an interpreter of the slang "cant" of city rogues. Angered by the rogue Trapdoor's invitation, offered at the end of a bout of canting, to "wap with me, and I'll niggle with you" (10.194), Moll at first will not deign to translate. When Sir Beauteous Ganymede (yes, that really is his name) urges, "Nay, nay, Moll, what's that wap?" (10.213), Jack interjects his request for an explanation of "niggling." Moll responds less than explicitly: "Wapping and niggling is all one: the rogue my man can tell you," effectively passing the task of translation to Trapdoor. The rogue is happy to comply, but only in his own terms: "'Tis fadoodling, if it please you" (218). By the play's logic, "niggling" means "wapping," and "wapping" means "fadoodling." Now, "fadoodling," according to the play's editor, is a nonce word, one that, she assures us, is a "euphemism for having sex."[5] Readers of Chapter 7 will be interested that "fadoodle" doesn't appear in the *OED* until 1670, where it is defined solely as "something foolish or ridiculous; nonsense."[6] Which doesn't mean that "fadoodle" didn't mean something related to sex in 1611 when this scene was first performed; but it does suggest—as we have seen throughout this book—that when it comes to knowledge relations, the meanings of sex line up along an asymptotic curve, to which some subjects (then, and now) are unable to catch hold.

Two genres that responded more favorably to the appeal for sexual instruction, providing more obliging answers than Martha or Jack enjoyed, were ballads and pornography. The ballad "The Mourning Conquest; Or, The Womans sad Complaint, and doleful Cry, To see her Love in Fainting fits to lye,"[7] narrates the attempt of a maid to gain sexual satisfaction from a "bashful" "Young-man" she meets walking abroad, but whose efforts over the course of twelve stanzas come to naught. Despite the youth's "good intent," he "knew not what she meant," and though she flings herself "on the ground," "kist him" and "did closely to him cling," she repeatedly finds "him begin to fail." Neither "rubb[ing] his joynts" nor calling him "Hony, and her Dear" does the trick, and despite his resolve "to try his strength," "all was spent in vain." Whether that last refers to the spending of his seed outside her body or the spending of her erotic energy underscores the ambiguous effect of the refrain "alas poor thing!" which points to a different referent in each stanza and leaves unclear who is to be pitied more, the knowing maid or the ignorant youth.[8]

Other male novices, like Tomalin in Nashe's obscene poem "Choise of Valentines," also receive explicit instruction yet likewise are judged a failure in the arts of love. Yet some others are merely resistant, as in Shakespeare's *Venus and Adonis*, where the poem's center of gravity is less the youth's ignorance than the possibilities it provides for rhetorical invention. Venus's ingenious persuasions to her resistant boy toy take the form of several lessons in how to find pleasure in her body—but the pleasures are all for the reader. Sometimes pornography and ballads satirize the desire for sexual knowledge; sometimes their frank expression of the desire to know amps up the sense of characters being game for the encounter; sometimes the tutelage falls on deaf ears or is beside the point. Whichever way, by circulating erotic knowledge and thematizing its instruction, pornography and ballads performed a brand of sexual pedagogy more responsive than the drama to the desire for tutelage. And this is not purely a condition of print rather than live performance. Marital advice books were surprisingly thin in their instructional apparatus, and medical texts, while more verbose in their taxonomies, were not particularly rich in descriptive detail. All of which suggests that, barring access to pornography—which until after the civil wars was mostly an elite phenomenon—most sex was probably learned in person, if not in the act of doing, than in the act of watching, talking, singing, and hearing about it.

Yet just what is it that was learned in such encounters? Writing about his youth after the civil wars, John Cannon, for instance, recalls that at the age of twelve he "took a ramble to the river" with his friends. While there, a seventeen-year-old youth named Scraces "took an occasion to show the rest what he could do if he had a female in place, and withal took his privy member in his hand rubbing it up and down till it was erected and in short followed emission, the same as he said in copulation." Scraces then "advised more of the boys to do the same, telling them that although the first act would be attended with pain yet by frequent use they could find a deal of pleasure, on which several attempted and found as he said indeed." Cannon confesses to being one of the older boy's "pupils."[9] Cannon, readers might recall, was one of the figures alluded to in Chapter 6 for narrating his many nonpenetrative sexual encounters with women, some of them consensual, some of them clearly not. His early training in an all-male masturbation circle, it seems, did not necessarily lead him in a straight line toward "copulation"; but neither did it instigate a lifelong involvement in sex with men. Even when instruction is forthcoming, the trajectories of sexual tutelage can remain radically uncertain.

Pedagogies of Unknowing

Interest in the dynamics of such pedagogical encounters—who knows, who doesn't, who learns, who doesn't—have been a primary motivation of *Thinking Sex with the Early Moderns*. Having attempted to think sex mostly with the early moderns, I want to conclude, not by reference to texts of that distant period, but to the pedagogical imperatives operative in queer studies today. In 2009 a conference called "Rethinking Sex" was held in honor of the twenty-fifth anniversary of Gayle Rubin's groundbreaking essay. In a perceptive and generous review of the conference, Regina Kunzel observes that

"'Rethinking Sex' participants reflected on agnotology's slipperier meanings for the state of the field: What forms of knowledge does our current understanding of the field foreclose? What unwitting exclusions does it perform? What modes of living, forms of intimacy, and ways of distributing resources—in the past and in the contemporary world—does it keep us from seeing? And what forms of unknowing might be worth cultivating?"[10] Given the connection between this broader interest in "forms of unknowing" and the arguments of this book, I want to explore one moment in the conference that staged the stakes of knowledge and ignorance in a specifically pedagogical way. Having just completed a provocative presentation titled "Sex Without Optimism," one panelist, widely admired for his brilliant contributions to queer scholarship over the past thirty years, was confronted in the Q&A by an earnest and, as she called herself, "humble undergraduate." What, she wanted to know, would sex without optimism look like? After making a joke about whether the student was asking him about his sex life, the panelist reiterated some of his theoretical points and then concluded, "What would sex without optimism, as sex, look like? I think you already know." The audience laughed, the student surrendered the microphone, and on that confident assertion of knowledge the session was brought to a close.

My scrutiny of this interaction is not offered as a criticism of Lee Edelman's on-the-spot rejoinder.[11] Rather, I mean to use this Q&A interaction to further explore the conditions of sexual knowledge and related scenes of pedagogy that it has been the business of this book to study. I am conscious of the potential breech of academic protocol in analyzing a scholar's extempore speech rather than his written work, and I would hope my intent not be misconstrued. There was nothing ungenerous, belittling, or inappropriate in Edelman's response, which was characteristically attentive and respectful. Furthermore, his endeavor to refer the question back to the questioner is congruent with the Lacanian perspective that informs his scholarship. In positing the presence of knowledge in his interlocutor that she herself failed to recognize, Edelman might be construed as rehearsing the classic psychoanalytic transference in which, in reaction to the analysand's assumption that the analyst is the one who knows, the analyst assures her that he does not know, that it is *she* who knows. More prosaically, he could be encouraging her to look further, to dig deeper, to discover what was hidden but nonetheless already there. I'm not so sure, however, because Edelman's recent publications, which analyze the pedagogical imperatives of reproductive futurity and the queer affordances of "bad education," pose the question: "Could any pedagogy renounce the sublimation inherent in acts of reading, taking seriously the status of teaching as an impossible profession and seeing ourselves in relation to our students as agents of a radical queerness whose assault on meaning, understanding, and value would take from them more than it ever could give?"[12] This is not intended, I believe, as a rhetorical question. Since "good education," in his view, requires "the Child's" innocence or non-knowledge in order to harness it to the promise of a heteroreproductive future, Edelman's response in the conference Q&A may have reaffirmed, in a pedagogical key, the "assault on meaning" posed by "a radical queerness."

Based on the expression on her face, Edelman's response was not what his interlocutor was hoping for. Not that I know what she was thinking at that moment. Nor do I think pedagogy is best served when students feel most pleased. Furthermore, plenty of students end up finding most valuable those instructional moments when they were most confused. Students regularly tell my colleagues and me that they didn't understand what we were talking about, or the value of what we were doing, when they took our classes, but that they have come to realize belatedly how important it was. Indeed, I have felt that way about formal instruction myself. Edelman's response might well resonate unexpectedly with her over the long term.

My question, however, is not about what she learned or didn't learn, the specific content of her affective, subjective response, or whether that content would ever morph into something else. Rather than focus on possible "learning outcomes"—which are, despite the calculating designs of university administrators, largely unknowable—I pause, instead, at the moment of her request and the response that it engendered. For regardless of the intellectual integrity and consistency of Edelman's scholarship—and despite the possibility that he was attempting to avoid enacting a prescriptive authority by instead valorizing her experience and her freedom—her question elicited what seems to me to be something of an artful dodge. Indeed, I would describe the tenor of his response as *ironic*.

Irony is nothing if not dodgy, allowing one to say dicey things and get away with it. The fact that I cannot tell for sure whether Edelman meant what he said is part of irony's peculiar power. There is much to recommend irony as a mode of rhetoric in general and of queer rhetoric in particular. Because irony "privileges the unsaid," it has structured a lot of queer theorizing.[13] Its double edge can skewer the pretensions of stable sexual orientations, of dichotomous gender identities, of romantic love as well as romantic despair.[14] In *No Future: Queer Theory and the Death Drive*—a tour de force that exposes the work "the Child" performs in suturing subjectivity to "futurism," diagnoses our collective captivation by that ideal, and reclaims the abjection of the homosexual from that ideal—Edelman calls irony "that queerest of rhetorical devices."[15] Indeed, he argues that because irony "severs the continuity essential to the very logic of making sense," it "always characterizes queer theory."[16] If Edelman's concluding comment was ironic, then, it was also, in his terms, paradigmatically queer.

My historicist skepticism regarding Edelman's "always" on behalf of "queer theory," however, leads me to ask: whose irony, whose theory, in the service of what logical disruptions, and directed toward whose desires? Whereas irony that targets heteronorms, or even the self, may be an efficacious queer strategy (not least because of its capacity for self-deflation), it may be less serviceable when its "assault on meaning" targets those who are the possible future "agents of a radical queerness." Insofar as irony operates by means of a tension between the said and the unsaid, and signals that the ironist knows more than he or she cares to make explicit, irony's obscurities constitute a particularly delicate knowledge relation. Understood pedagogically, with attention to what Linda Hutcheon calls the discursive "scene of irony,"[17] irony in this case enacts not a queer deconstruction, but a deflection of a pedagogical claim on queers.

For this student *didn't* know and *wanted* to. If she was not yet an "agent of a radical queerness," she was thinking hard about what that might mean. The tacit dismissal of her ignorance (which, I hasten to add, is not the same as a dismissal of her question) has something in common with the way the pursuit of sexual knowledge has been represented in the past. Her situation was not unlike that of Martha Joyless, when she requested Barbara to teach her how to have sex. Presumably less clueless about sex than Martha was, this undergraduate nonetheless asked for her desire for sexual knowledge to be acknowledged and answered. Of course, since the power of an ironic remark is to produce an undecidable effect, there is no way to know how it might ultimately sit with her. Such opacity has been, throughout this book, precisely my point.

But I have another point to make. For this convergence of past representations with present academic exchanges leads me to wonder whether sexual pedagogy might create, even within a queer dispensation, its own regime of truth: eliciting, cajoling, and deflecting the desire to know. That is, the projection of knowledge in a subject who failed to recognize it dramatizes in a contemporary key what appears to be a general logic structuring scenes of

erotic instruction. For this student, it turns out, was not alone. Based on the
applause that greeted her question, her curiosity, ambivalence, and untutored
naïveté seemed to resonate wryly with many in the audience, perhaps because
they long ago had learned the perils of admitting ignorance in an academic
setting.[18] Indeed, she was rearticulating precisely the question that graduate
students had posed to me earlier in the day during an open session dedicated
to exploring their reactions to the conference proceedings. Accurately identifying as one of the conference's main themes the exploration of the antisocial
"negativity thesis" in queer theory—a focus on the political potential of back-
wardness, hopelessness, masochism, shame, passivity, infantilism, of feeling
and being bad—they wanted to understand the implications of such negative
affects and antisocial theses on scholarship, activism, and eroticism. What
were the consequences for actual bodies, they wanted to know, of a queer
political economy of negative affect, and what were those bodies actually
doing with negativity? Was this just theoretical acrobatics and is this, they
asked, how academics talk about sex?[19]

As should be clear by now, I do not think that these questions should or
could necessarily be answered by providing a more candid and forthcoming
description of sex—with or without optimism. I am not suggesting we paper
over the complexity of sexual knowledge by means of an appeal to compas-
sion, empathy, or sincerity, especially a sincerity that is unappreciative of, or
impervious to, irony's rhetorical force. To the contrary: irony is a productive
tool for thinking with and through obscurity as well as sexuality.[20] Moreover,
irony can be profoundly sincere (as I suspect it was with Edelman)—in recognition of which I wish to avoid being slotted into the role of the pious lesbian
demanding of the witty gay man that he just *get serious.*

It has been a central argument of this book that sex might be profitably
thought in terms of the contradictions that fracture its epistemology: this
involves, on the one hand, a materially minded acknowledgment of embodied desires, specific sex acts, and the gendered agents who perform them; and,
on the other hand, a psychoanalytic, queer, and, I have argued, *historical*
appreciation of the impossibility of ever fully knowing or understanding what
such desires and acts might mean. The interest of the Q&A I've described is
that it is poised precisely over this gulf of intelligibility: between what could
be requested and delivered in a given cultural situation, granted meaning and
sense; and what cannot be articulated, for a host of reasons, but among them
because it *resists being thought.* The artful dodge in Edelman's response, then,
is not particular to him. As a response to a query for knowledge, its knowing

ambiguity exemplifies one strategy for tightroping across the fault line of epistemology and signification created by sex. It represents, in other words, a situated manifestation and predicament of sexual opacity when such opacity is viewed not only as a queer and theoretical problem but as a pedagogical relation.

The Very Thought of Education

Thinking Sex with the Early Moderns has offered some alternative choreographies for minding this particular epistemological gap. Taking my cue from this undergraduate and her early modern forebears, I have argued that there might be something to be gained in rethinking a queer theory that, despite its promotion of "stop making sense" as a political strategy, nevertheless always seems to be "in the know" about sex. This book has attempted to respond to such "humble" and "ignorant" desires for sexual knowledge by focusing on various moments of cluelessness—considering not only the methodological, historiographic, and ethical questions they raise, but the impossible, *truly impossible*, pedagogical debts they entail.

To consider pedagogy as a disposition of indebtedness is not necessarily to advocate pastoral care. Nor is it to suggest that on the basis of such a disposition one might be authorized to make utopian claims for social transformation or even for local political improvements. I have tried to confront the impediments that hinder an easy response, not in order to pave and polish the way, but to pause over the fact of stumbling. Across several fields of endeavor, this book has exploited the epistemological opacity of sex as a basis from which to historicize and theorize the difficulty involved in sexual knowledge relations. To back up and ask questions about knowledge that dissatisfies in terms of desire, identification, and history is to ask what the production of knowledge can tell us—and, just as important, *not* tell us— about the past and ourselves. To ask such questions, without the confidence that we know, or *can* know, the answers, and to recognize them as involving a form of indebtedness, is to be propelled beyond a discussion of methodology or theory into the domain of ethics—both ethical understanding and ethical practices vis-à-vis others. Moreover, because the inquiry I have described involves knowledge that is not only desired but transmitted (however fitfully or inadequately), the disposition toward knowledge I have adopted in this book implicates scholars and teachers as well as learners in what Deborah Britzman has called "the very thought of education."[21]

Taking "the very thought of education" seriously means examining education as a knowledge relation. Clearly this is a formulation that risks tautology: what could education be if not a knowledge relation? My point is that sexual pedagogy involves some of the same dynamics of dissatisfaction and impossibility entailed by sex in its dual status as both material practice and representation. Furthermore, if, as I've implied, the strategic use of psychoanalytic concepts on behalf of historiography also enacts a knowledge relation—between past and present, between one present and another—then exploring sex-as-knowledge necessarily involves continually transiting between the (alterity and similarity of the) past and the contemporary sexual world. Such a transit between then and now is often proclaimed in politically progressive scholarship, from feminist and queer studies to early modernists' briefs on behalf of "presentism."[22] I submit, however, that there is an express tenor imposed on this endeavor when pursued on behalf of sexual knowledge. For if teaching is, as Freud alleged, "an impossible profession,"[23] then this impossibility is especially true of queer and sexuality studies. For one thing, unlike teaching writing or close reading skills, we are debarred from modeling or practicing most aspects of sex with our students. For another, unlike our response to a student's desire to learn to write better or gain a more comprehensive understanding of the past, we face the challenge of taking seriously the *desire* for sexual knowledge—something made strangely tricky, given the widespread belief that one of the initiating theorists of queer studies, Michel Foucault, indicts such desire as politically suspect.

It is a matter of some irony that only in the wake of Foucault's genealogy of institutions did the history of sexuality gain an institutional foothold in the academy.[24] Foucault did not work in a vacuum, and plenty of historians, sociologists, anthropologists, psychologists, and literary critics put sex on the academic agenda. But Foucault made a decisive imprint on the direction and temper of sexuality studies—and not only by emphasizing that sexual knowledge is never disinterested and is always embedded in a microphysics of power. Insofar as the will to knowledge is allied with the will to power, *The History of Sexuality*, volume 1, implies that our desires for knowledge about sex, and our role in communicating that knowledge, may be inseparable from the modern disciplining, the apparatus or *dispositif*, of sexuality. Because the requirements of teaching and scholarship necessarily involve putting sex into discourse, they would seem to inscribe us in yet another chapter of the *scientia sexualis* (rather than, for instance, authorizing pedagogical initiation into sex through an *ars erotica*).[25] Fear of captivation appears to be a common anxiety among queer studies scholars, given clear expression in this criticism by Lynne Huffer: "as a discursive formation whose primary purpose is to talk about sex, queer theory participates in a truth game that forces the secret of sexuality . . . simply adding to the discursive store of sex talk that *is* the repressive hypothesis."[26] So too, feminist philosopher Nancy Tuana asks: "Can my investigations of the power dimensions of ignorance concerning women's orgasms not fall prey to a constructed desire for the 'truth of sex'?"[27] Historians have also posed the problem with their own disciplinary "sex talk" in this way.[28] Whether we believe such comments take sex to refer to desire, the body, or its pleasures, or the modern regime of sexuality, it seems clear that the tension between Foucault's influence and the expectations governing our work in the academy haunts the pedagogical aspirations of many of us, across disciplines, who teach about sex.[29]

There is no question but that sexual pedagogy *can* contribute to contemporary biopower, and that its sense-making apparatus can help produce properly disciplined, docile subjects. But this is not the final word on the pedagogy of sex. Very few of us imagine, for instance, that "if sex saturates the worldview of our contemporary moment, then simply refusing to talk about it" might "constitute an appropriate or efficacious intervention."[30] Lisa Downing calls our present moment one of "compulsory sexuality" from which we "cannot *opt out*," arguing that "the ethical and strategic imperative lies on the side of asking *how one might engage with the system to which one is compulsorily subjected* in order to show up the interests and iniquities within that system."[31] Such investments in demystifying the meanings and stakes of sexual knowledge motivate, I wager, many queer and feminist teachers, not least because it was in the classroom, or in conversation with a teacher, or by reading or looking at a book, *that things changed*—and sometimes, even marginally, for the better.

Of course, there are good reasons to resist designating such learning as "liberation" or "freedom." My point is not to endorse allegories of student empowerment, for they often depend on untenable myths of the pedagogic situation wherein the teacher always loves her pupils and they love the teacher right back.[32] (In this regard, a one-liner of Lacan's seems particularly apposite: defining love as giving what one does not have to someone who does not want it.)[33] And I could not agree more with Jeff Dolven who writes, in the context of an argument about the failures of Renaissance humanist pedagogy, that "in the course of our lives we learn a great deal, perhaps most of what we know, in situations that do not have a particularly didactic structure. Learning does not [necessarily] entail teaching any more than teaching does learning."[34]

Nonetheless, learning *can* entail some forms of teaching, and teaching *sometimes* generates productive forms of learning. Given this, it seems important to recognize the disjunct between the Foucaultian critique of sexual discourse, writ large, and the specificity of pedagogical practices in the current context. For it is not as though the status of sexual discourse has remained inert since Foucault's critique—which, after all, was proffered in the context of a wide-scale yet short-lived social phenomenon that came to be called "the sexual revolution." For evidence of what has changed since the discursive amplification of sex was subject to critique, we need not look beyond the present. Formal sexual pedagogy for adolescents and young adults typically occurs in highly class- and race-stratified educational institutions, where inequalities of gender inform the acquisition of sexual knowledge and the performance of sexual speech—not only what is known, but what can be said and by whom. It is currently directed, at least in the United States, at students for whom the childhood pedagogy of sex was a scandal-ridden site in proliferating forms of media, even as, conversely, adolescent "sex education" was radically truncated and diminished under a government policy of "abstinence-only" education—which is to say, no sex and very little education. The story of how sex education in the United States was hijacked by the forces of fear is a blot on both feminists and sex educators, who were outflanked by politicized rhetorics of sexual danger that effectively turned sex into disease.[35]

Within this contradictory context of a phobic "just say no" to a sex whose airbrushed images saturate contemporary culture, the chief danger is not potential complicity with the discursive amplification of sexuality. Although other scholars worry that sexual speech reimplants the truth of the subject in sexuality, my own classroom experiences suggest that today's youth are not much influenced by a depth model of sexual subjectivity (despite their default reliance on ready-to-hand notions of natural sexual orientations and expectations of romantic fulfillment).[36] Crisscrossed by currents of information transmitted via media technologies, their erotic lives are more likely to be cognitively processed through relations of surface, mobility, speed, and proliferation—from Internet cruising to sexting—even as they vow virginity and offhandedly designate their sexually active peers as "players" and "whores." Other scholars are theorizing the effects of digital interfaces on sexual subjectivity and modes of erotic engagement. What is at stake for my project is less the question of "the subject" of sexuality than the basic attainment of sexual literacy. Literacy in my terms refers to several aspects of sexuality: the cognitive, affective, and bodily competencies to experience and enjoy sex; the possession of a toolbox of concepts available to handle sexual questions, frustrations, and crises; and the cognitive capacity to think about and reflect critically upon those experiences. In my advancing of a pedagogical disposition toward sexual knowledge, I have been guided, in the first instance, by an affirmative impulse that credits the utility of certain forms of knowledge (a vocabulary of anatomy and physiology, for instance, and a syntax of access, rights, and subcultures) in combination with each individual's psychic creativity for improving sexual literacies and improvising "good enough" erotic lives.

As the history of pornography's own pedagogical investments shows, people may not know what they like—what it is *even possible* to like—before they encounter it in speech, in representation, or through the tutelage of another. Can, in fact, people know what they want if they are missing the language by which to know it, think it, speak it? We know that people in the past deployed prior discourses and rhetorics to understand and further their own desires, intimacies, and sexual acts. In the middle of the seventeenth century, Katherine Philips boldly appropriated classical tropes of male friendship she had encountered, including their expressions of mutuality, equality, and similitude, to express, authorize, and, to an extent, publicize her own passionate liaisons with a series of women.[37] Writing during the early nineteenth century, Anne Lister recorded her efforts to track erotic allusions in Juvenal, Martial, Horace, Ovid, as well as contemporaneous British and French authors such as Byron and Thomas Moore, which she used not only as aids to masturbation but to gauge the extent of her potential sexual partners' erotic interest.[38] And today's readers of lesbian historical fiction avidly consume erotic plots set in Victorian England and the U.S. frontier to authorize and take pleasure in their contemporary queer present.[39]

Such aptitudes and faculties are necessarily tethered to subjectivity and its capacity for outward expression. But interpersonal agency is not the only possible outcome of enhanced sexual literacy. For, in the second instance, among those aptitudes I most wish to encourage are the potential benefits of the experience of *not* knowing.[40] In Chapter 1 I referred to "opaque knowledge," defining it as knowledge that results from structures of occultation and unintelligibility that are also the source of our ability to apprehend and analyze it. Knowing that one *does not know* is just such an opaque knowledge. It can foster intellectual and sexual generosity toward others as well as toward oneself. It can engender tremendous erotic frisson in the form of wonder. Moreover, the experience of not knowing can cultivate cognitive aptitudes and affective faculties that complicate what the fact of possessing a vocabulary or syntax of sex might do or mean.[41] Although I've asked whether people can know what they want if they don't have the means to think or speak it, the obscurity of sex I've delineated in this book has led me, conversely, to ask as well: Can they ever really know it then?

Sex Ed

That the accent in my response in *Thinking Sex with the Early Moderns* has been on the negative to *both* of these questions offers up the contradiction with which the historicized pursuit of sexual knowledge—or, to adopt the lingo of the United States, "sex ed"—must contend. It is a contradiction as relevant today, when preteens access most of their information about sex from watching Internet porn, as it was in the past. It should be clear that by "sex ed" I do not refer to a seamless transmission of knowledge based on a steady collation of empirical facts about sex in the past—although, as should also be clear by now, I do not discount the importance of either facts or empiricism. Nor do I precisely mean the promotion of a sex-positive, queer sexual hygiene that would stand in opposition to the culture's dominant sex-phobic norms—although I am certainly not opposed to such an endeavor. While I want educational institutions to provide sex education based on responsible research that discloses what scientists, social scientists, and humanists do and do not know about sex as a physiological, psychological, and cultural phenomenon, I do not believe that the pedagogical disposition with which this book is concerned should pin its hopes on fostering better sex. By referring to the history and historiography of sexuality as a matter of pedagogy, and to this pedagogy as involving ethical indebtedness, I am arguing, rather, that sexual thought and sexual speech deserve to be credited with and analyzed not only as modes of bodily knowledge but as modes of intellection.

Sex may not be the key to hidden meaning, but it is a motor of curiosity—as Freud, who notoriously called children "little sex researchers,"[42] well knew. That students currently require and deserve opportunities to engage in sexual "research" of various kinds has been a major factor in my thinking about how historical scholarship on sex might be implicated in pedagogical ethics. As for "sex ed" more narrowly construed: fortunately, the fight for a more candid and humane sex education, in schools and without, is not over. A new generation of researchers, educators, and policy activists is tackling the tangled nexus of desire, fear, pleasure, power, health, and disease on some new terms, with a special focus on girls and queer youth.[43] And young people themselves are using their expertise with digital platforms to contest enforced ignorance and the politics of fear that underlie it.[44] Earlier versions of sex education, which focused prophylactically on anatomy, biology, and health,[45] are being reconfigured into what its proponents call "sexuality education,"[46] which honors sexual and gender diversity and emphasizes the role of emotions and social context (including power hierarchies of race, class, gender, and age) in sexual risk and sexual decision making.[47] Attending not only to the contexts in which sex is articulated and performed but the effects of sexual stigma and sexual shame, these educators' approach toward sex is gaining in self-consciousness about its own status as a knowledge relation.

To say this is not to idealize sex educators. Indeed, current "sex ed" policy in the United States—crafted in the context of a prevailing political and moral conservatism, even in the era of Obama—is developed with deference to the reputed dangers of knowledge (loss of innocence, contamination by knowing) and the importance of the family, not the state, as the provider of information. This protectionist policy discourse may at times function separately from health care, behavioral, and political efforts, yet it pervades the atmosphere within which sex educators operate.[48] Indeed, were they interested in my views, these educators would find that the version of "sex ed" enacted in this book would challenge several of their field's basic principles. For while we join in common cause in the desire to legitimize sexual speech and provide access to sexual information, as well as in the desire to de-dramatize the psychic effects of sex across an array of contexts (including the shaming of those whose sexual literacy is "underdeveloped"), I would urge that they consider as well how to:

• resist the displacement of the desiring, corporeal body by the affective, relational one;

- reconsider the pervasive privileging of identity categories by deploying an analytic of identification and the quest for various forms of
  pleasure;
- resist the tendency to overemphasize risk, danger, and oppression;
- create policy that acknowledges that some sexual matters remain outside the domain, not only of sexual hygiene and social welfare, but
  of conscious thought.

As these "policy" statements imply, I am not satisfied with the notion of
sex primarily as an effect of power-knowledge. This formulation, axiomatic
in queer studies and the history of sexuality, is good enough as far as it goes;
indeed, as the medical governance of transgender access to technologies of
embodiment such as hormones and surgery shows, the pertinence of biopower is undeniable. But because it is based on a limited set of discourses
(primarily medical and juridical) and certain forms of historical understanding, the power-knowledge nexus does not exhaust the circuitries of knowledge that subtend sexuality. By always routing the question of sexual
knowledge through the question of "the subject," and by positioning knowledge of the subject within either a *scientia sexualis* or an *ars erotica*, this
paradigm has circumscribed understanding of the messy, implicit, and contradictory ways in which sexual knowledge and ignorance are articulated,
affirmed, neglected, contested, and disappeared.

Even as we insist that knowledge of sexuality, in the past and in the present, not be held hostage to tendentious regimes of truth or normativity or
personal enlightenment, we avoid confronting the contradictions that structure the teaching of these issues at some cost. On the one hand, those of us
working in the United States, in particular, cede too much ground to social
conservatives, whose campaign of misinformation places its trust in the rhetorical appeal of appearing to silence speech about sex while in fact always
talking about it. On the other hand, we fail to respond affirmatively to students' curiosity about forms of knowledge that might materially improve
their erotic literacy.[49] Recognition of such double binds has taken the form
in this book of historical analyses that traffic between the present and the
past. I now suggest that historicist inquiry needs to be more self-consciously
infused with the question of *why* we do what we do in the sexuality studies
classroom and what *kind* of teaching that teaching about sex is.

Pausing to consider the impossibility of our pedagogical entailments
requires critical reflection on the conditions of knowledge production and

transmission—not only our own implication within a *scientia sexualis* and prohibitions against an *ars erotica*, but those knowledge relations, particularly involving women, which, as Chapter 5 argued, remain eccentric to those formations. Such a pedagogical disposition entails owning up to the desire for sexual knowledge (our own and our students'), and how such desire, especially when channeled through engagement with the past, speaks to current conditions of erotic diversity, erotic pleasure, and, most important, erotic dissatisfaction—the mundane trial and error that for many is the very condition of sex. It recognizes that such conditions are not adequately addressed by appeals to sexual identities assumed to be stable and self-evident or by sexual (non)identities that are designated as queer, by means of forthright descriptions of sexual anatomy and erotic acts, or by invocations of a queer *jouissance*. Most crucially, this pedagogical disposition encourages recognition of the analytical purchase of sexual ignorance.

Pedagogies of Ignorance

Ever since Eve Kosofsky Sedgwick published *Epistemology of the Closet*, we have become attuned to the idea that ignorance possesses a political geography:

> Rather than sacrifice the notion of "ignorance," then, I would be more interested at this point in trying, as we are getting used to trying with "knowledge," to pluralize and specify it. That is, I would like to be able to make use in sexual-political thinking of the deconstructive understanding that particular insights generate, are lined with, and at the same time are themselves structured by particular opacities. If ignorance is not—as it evidently is not—a single Manichaean, aboriginal maw of darkness from which the heroics of human cognition can occasionally wrestle facts, insights, freedoms, progress, perhaps there exists instead a plethora of *ignorances*, and we may begin to ask questions about the labor, erotics, and economics of their human production and distribution. Insofar as ignorance is ignorance *of* a knowledge—a knowledge that may itself, it goes without saying, be seen as either true or false under some other regime of truth—these ignorances, far from being pieces of the originary dark, are produced by and correspond to particular knowledges and circulate as part of particular regimes of truth.[50]

In staking a claim for the value of ignorance as a crucial aspect of sexual pedagogy, I am echoing but also inverting Sedgwick's deconstruction of the relations between ignorance and knowledge. The relations that I seek to understand are not exhausted by the will not to know that Sedgwick described, in regard to homophobia, as the "privilege of unknowing," or that Gayatri Chakravorty Spivak calls, in relation to imperialism, "sanctioned ignorance."[51] Nor are they limited to the political manufacture and manipulation of ignorance and uncertainty, for which the medical historian Robert Proctor coined the term "agnotology,"[52] invoked by Kunzel in reference to the "Rethinking Sex" conference. Nor, despite my opening allusion to Bette Midler's song, am I approaching ignorance as a cognate to "stupidity"—a concept whose ethical claims have been thoughtfully theorized by Avital Ronell.[53] Nor am I precisely invoking the promulgation of misinformation emphasized by sex educators, who regularly refer to various forms of not knowing, each with its own origin and purpose—although their recognition of uneven ignorance helps us to see that sometimes the production of ignorance about sexuality is purposeful and intentional, sometimes it is the result of unwitting practices or business as usual, sometimes it dampens sexual knowledge, and sometimes it incites it.

Whereas these approaches attend to the productivity of "ignorance effects" primarily through the politically noxious work they are conscripted to do,[54] I have directed attention toward the potentially *positive* effects of sexual ignorance. This reorientation seeks to unchain ignorance from its circumscription as a "bad," undeveloped, static state and time, something that is of interest only because it signifies the stable "before" of a presumably more dynamic, transformative knowledge.[55] Such depreciation of ignorance has been with us at least since the early modern period, when William Cunningham's *Cosmographical Glasse* (1559) stated succinctly, "Knowledge hath no enemie but ignorance."[56] If we bracket the assumption that knowledge is the logical end (implicit purpose, developmental telos, final terminus) to ignorance, we are emboldened to ask not only *why* we do not know what we do not know, but what we might make with and of such a "lack."

Even as I argue, as I did in Chapter 5, that such a lacuna, even when it amounts to cluelessness, may evince its own improbable kind of subaltern knowledge, my inquiry does not primarily result in exposing the political economy of ignorance to the light of knowledge. Rather, I have redeployed Sedgwick's deconstruction of ignorance by considering its function in tandem with a specific mode of knowledge production, asking how the history of sexuality, writ large to include not only the work of historians but that of queer theorists and literary critics, is constituted as an object. This tactic, I suggest, enables a reconceptualization of the relations of sexual historiography, literary criticism, feminism, and queer studies as productively functioning together, precisely by means of their contradictions, as a capacious and aspirational form of sex education. Furthermore, such contradictions not only exist in tandem with, but may be a historical effect of, a structural dynamic between knowledge and ignorance that has composed the epistemology of sex.

In sum, there is no "epistemological yield" to the inquiry I have pursued.[57] I have not attempted to map a political geography of ignorance, attribute false consciousness to any particular ignorance, or prescribe the contents of ignorance (such as lack of knowledge about HIV transmission or how to achieve orgasm), which relations of knowledge, however affectively nuanced or tonally styled, might address. Nor have I attempted to trace the origin of any particular ignorance. Instead, I have paused over those moments when desire for knowledge hits up against a wall. The wall may wear a friendly, respectful face; it may even be "on our side." Confronting that wall and contemplating the strategies that have been devised to bypass, surmount, or ignore it does not just increase tolerance of ignorance. It also impresses upon us the fact that, for all its ordinary, taken-for-granted relevance, sexual knowledge is not only partial and tenuous but difficult, its modes of communication intractable, its forms of interconnection precarious. For this reason, the sex education I advocate mobilizes the positive *work* of ignorance by affirming the obscurity of sex as a rich epistemological resource—a heuristic with which to think as well as act, in the present and on behalf of the past.

Despite the early modern focus of this book, commitment to a sexual pedagogy derived from difficulty, obscurity, and ignorance has ethical implications for teaching, scholarly protocols, one's commitment to modes of disciplinarity, and our fitful attempts at interdisciplinarity. "Ethics" as I use it here is not about enforcing morals—rule-like, law-like, conferring absolute responsibilities and possessing pretensions to objectivity, authority, and judgment. The ethics of knowledge relations on offer here are situated and pragmatic, affective as much as intellectual. Like many others, I have found in Sedgwick's disarmingly commonsense axioms proffered in *Epistemology of the Closet* considerable analytical traction. Her jaw-droppingly-obvious "Axiom 1: People are different from each other" is key to the ethical imperative of this book.[58] So, too, Sedgwick's recognition of the potential allure of cross-gender identification—"the paths of allo-identification are likely to be strange and recalcitrant"[59]—succinctly expresses an intuition whose use value for this femme has proven remarkably salient and durable. If I have attempted to prod cross-gender identification to do conceptual work that is somewhat eccentric to Sedgwick's intentions, it is in part to advance Sedgwick's own analysis of the "double-binding but immensely productive incoherence about gender" present in contemporary culture and in our critical paradigms.[60] As I have shown, this "productive incoherence about gender" continues, often silently and unwittingly, to inflect queer approaches to sexuality.

The pedagogical ethos of this book not surprisingly has something in common with Sedgwick's notion of "reparative" reading practices (although, in its "unmasking" of presumptive knowledge, it also has much in common with what she describes as "paranoid" practices as well). This does not mean that it traffics in redemption, the false promises of which motivate Edelman's antisocial ethics of negativity. Or if it edges ever so closely to such hopes, it does it in the simultaneously earnest and ironic tenor of Ellis Hanson's description of Sedgwick's appropriation of Melanie Klein's concept of the reparative position: "which is still redemption but less naive. . . . Faced with the depressing realization that people are fragile and the world hostile, a reparative reading focuses not on the exposure of political outrages that we already know about but rather on the process of reconstructing a sustainable life in their wake."[61] Like Hanson, I see in Sedgwick's proposal for a reparative analytic, especially its willingness to be surprised, "an artistic and intellectual practice that helps us pick up the pieces."[62]

Nor does the ethos of this book bank on an affective, erotic touch across time, seeking to repair time's divisions through the force of desire. Rather than an ethics grounded in eroticizing history, the self, or the self's relation to its own body or that of others,[63] the pedagogical ethos I have sought to mobilize is generated from the intersubjective, decidedly social, and at times institutional commerce of knowledge relations. This interchange is contradictory in the terms articulated in Chapter 6: "You must go on, I can't go on, I'll go on." If, in this concluding chapter, the figure of "the student" has implicitly served to figure the position of "the learner," other chapters conceive the purveyors of ignorance more broadly and extend the meanings of pedagogy and tutelage to encompass wider practices of communication. And, because it has been concerned simultaneously with the present and the past, this pedagogical ethics is both historiographic and responsive to the historicity of knowledge relations, including those in which we engage through intellectual labor within present-day, corporatized, highly sex-regulated bureaucracies. This labor begins with appreciation for the mundane and the clueless. It proceeds by asking and patiently following up on "the stupid question." And it seeks to demonstrate that, despite the understandable love of aptitude, aptness, and acuity, there is something to be said on behalf of slow going and slow learners.

Critique from Within

This labor also involves critique—not only of those critical rationalities that remain impervious to the diversity of sex, but of certain methods within queer studies. From a position within the ambit of that broad antihomophobic project, I have tallied the benefits and costs of different methods that have circulated under the name of queer—whether they take the form of queer temporality, of homohistory, an archival *ars erotica*, a queer Shakespeare, or a queer theory that finds lesbian history dispensable—examining how each of these projects presents its claims and assessing what they enable as well as what they foreclose. This critique has been motivated by the sense that queer studies has yet to reckon with the methods that have developed in the wake of its institutionalization.

Queer studies has a number of strong theories from which its practitioners draw its post-humanism and anti-foundationalism, its anti-identitarianism and anti-normativities, its anti-teleology and anti-sociality, as well as its embattled historicisms. To the extent that queer studies is a field formation, it is around these theories that the field has consolidated itself. But the field has spent considerably less energy thinking about what it might mean to espouse or enact a queer method, much less to forthrightly contend with the range of methods circulating within its purview. Theory, as I said in the last chapter, names a broad and strong interpretation of why something exists and/or how it functions; it aims at generalizable principles that not only explain multiple instances and have explanatory power when applied to new cases, but are transferrable across different discursive domains and historical situations. Conducted at a level of abstraction, theory (at least when specialized idioms do not get in the way) enables scholars to speak across disciplines while challenging narrow academic specializations. Method concerns *how* we implement the theories that most compel us. It generally involves applying broad frameworks to particular questions and texts, and it tends to bear the imprint of its disciplinary genesis. Self-consciousness about method helps to bring some coherence and parameters to what we do, as well as prod us toward metacritical reflections on *why* we do *what* we do the *way* we do it. Although the content with which method and theory concern themselves may be similar, method tends to apply while theory abstracts. Indeed, method occupies a somewhat awkward space between the savory detail of particular cases (whether literary, historical, or sociological) and the universalizing ambitions and traveling truth claims of theory.

There are many reasons for queer studies' general lack of interest in method, including a widespread conflation of theory with method and the propensity to view "queering" as a method in itself. And yet, it is clear that queer studies' scholars in different disciplines pursue different methods, generally recognized under the labels of "historicism," "empiricism," "qualitative analysis," "psychoanalysis," and so on. The fact of methodological diversity among key scholars serves as a reminder that no one method is useful for or adequate to every research question—every method has limitations. The need for diverse methods to approach different questions is, after all, one reason why disciplines exist as well as one reason why they are subject to critique. The tendentious operations of disciplinarity in producing historical knowledge about sex are crucial to identify and analyze. But it is hard to see how partisanship on behalf of one's own method, particularly when voiced without much understanding of what other disciplines or methods actually do, serves anyone's interests. And yet, for many scholars it is understandably too time-consuming or overwhelming to test one's frameworks and arguments against the friction provided by learning the protocols, debates, and methods of others.

To date, the question within queer studies has been how the concept of "queer" might challenge, inflect, or transform method; this has given rise to a number of antidevelopmental, anti-teleological, antiprogressive, and antihistorical positions. This book, conversely, has suggested how thinking about *method* might productively pressure the terms of "queer." Currently there are (at least) two pervasive impulses that motivate and subtend the methods of queering. One impulse is to mobilize queer's adjectival status and universalizing capacity: to maintain that just about everything can be queered, if looked at in the right way—not only ostensibly heterosexual texts and images, or human bodies and subjectivities, but nonhuman qualities, abstract concepts, and large-scale materialities. The indefinition and capaciousness of "queer," which aims to suspend knowing in advance what "queer" might be, has been one of the field's signal strengths, and it has enabled questions and analyses otherwise unthinkable.

The other less profitable impulse is to maintain that only certain procedures or arguments about sex are *queer enough*; that if one employs certain analytical procedures—for instance, compiling empirical evidence, resorting to historical periodizations, or leveraging disciplinary expertise—one's argument could not possibly be queer. My discomfort with this lies not in the act of rigorous appraisal, but in the enforcement of a singular definition of queerness, whereby "queer" is rendered less a tool of analysis than an expression of moral certainty about the genesis and results of its performance of transgression.[64]

There is nothing intrinsic to these two approaches that would link them; indeed, they not only enact different trajectories but from a certain perspective are logically contradictory: the act of policing "queer" as a state of mind that can be achieved only by an enlightened few logically precludes promoting "queer" as an ever-expanding horizon of possibility. Yet when presented coterminously, their double-binding incoherence reminds me of those vital terms that I have deployed throughout this book, likewise derived from Sedgwick: the universalizing and minoritizing axes of modern homo/heterosexual definition. But here, rather than emerging as a result of the incoherence of the epistemology of the closet, the double bind they enforce stems from within the contradictory formations of queer studies itself.

To take just one example: an implicitly universalizing notion of queerness recently has been touted as enjoying a special relationship to failure, whereby stupidity, forgetting, and illegibility are celebrated as a "queer art."[65] Within this exposition, qualities such as "serious" and "rigorous" are aligned with a disciplinary correctness that can only confirm what is already, tediously, known. Academic knowledge, particularly knowledge that depends on disciplinary expertise and logical analysis, is positioned in opposition to inspiration and unpredictability. And because terms and concepts travel, hook up, and start to congregate with one another, they are employed as talismanic indices for a disparate collocation of ideas.

As several chapters have made clear, I find untenable the universalizing impulse of "queer" when it promotes the idea that *any* effort to ground analysis in distinctions of time and place or the bodily entailments of gender unduly circumscribes the meanings of queerness. The horizon of queer possibility is delimited by historically wrought configurations of bodies, and when we elide embodiment, the capaciousness of "queer" can obscure as much as it enables. It is for the same reason that I maintain that, despite my stipulating the value of ignorance, queer studies' dynamism, openness, and audaciousness would benefit from recommitting to various forms of *exactitude*: not only of embodiment, but also of time and of place. Indeed, that the queer art of failure is pointedly antihistorical draws to full circle some of the false cognates that might be submitted to examination in the effort to construct methods attentive to the multiple—and contradictory—forms of queerness lived today.

Intellectual rigor, precision, deliberation, and seriousness are not inimical to queerness. To suggest as much indicates queer studies' disavowal of its success in institutionalizing itself in the academy. Such undeniable success—tenuous though it may be and internally dissonant though it may feel—seems to have elicited a need to resurrect oppositionality and transgressiveness as points of principle. To acknowledge this is not to say that we should not analyze the academy's adaptive strategies of solicitation toward diversity and "minority difference" and analyze the modes of complicity within which we are ensnared.[66] But the antidevelopmental, antiprogressive, and anti-teleological forces within queer studies, while undoubtedly useful for certain critical moves, has, through its preference for polemics over careful analysis, diminished our ability to confront the changes we have wrought within academia and how these changes, given the coterminous neoliberal corporatization of the university, might require complex modifications in the terms of queer insurgency.

Countering the diffuse application of "queer," I have explored, rather than assumed, queer's oppositional stance toward normativity, reexamining the epistemological relevance of the concepts of both "queer" and "normative" for the early modern period. I have offered analysis of *specific* instabilities, heterogeneities, inconsistencies, and slippages, rather than universalizing these attributes under one theoretical unity.[67] Yet exactitude requires something more than a commitment to *historical* specificity. It also involves prioritizing analytical precision in our terms and concepts, not just in regard to how they are mobilized in argument but in terms of the conceptual categories by which we come to know. If those categories are diffuse, inexact, overly universalizing, or unduly circumscribing, or if they gain rhetorical power only by functioning associatively as indices for qualitatively dissimilar phenomena, then their usability and portability for the production of knowledge about sex is radically diminished.

The disposition of cluelessness I have advocated encourages queer studies to be more discerning, more meticulous, more exacting, and more scrupulous in managing its conceptual debts, its internal disagreements, its affective relations, and its memory of critical contestations—without sacrificing its playfulness, its irony, its tongue-in-cheekiness, its pleasures *and* its pains. One thing this balancing act may require is more patience with words and with texts and more forbearance for each other. Particularly apropos in this regard are two lessons offered by Robyn Wiegman regarding her own past "adventure in participatory dissuasion." While I recognize the truth in her perception that "our critical practices will always invite interpretations that we hoped precisely not to provoke," I am banking more on the fact that "we are always bound to that which we try to refuse, which is why resistance is a mark of critical belonging, not evidence that anyone is heading for the door."[68] *Thinking Sex with the Early Moderns* has paused at doors that seem to be shut, knocking on them with the belief that our inquiries gain energy when we are not all intent on the same project and do not all pursue a given project in the same way. I do not believe that my interventions are the only ones available or should supersede those that came before, or that others should abandon their own projects to take up mine. Indeed, the precise ramifications of the different "scenes of instruction" in which we are each enmeshed are for us alone to discern. My own entailments have foregrounded particular scenarios and particular kinds of texts, but these choices are just that: mine. Indeed, the more strategies we devise to articulate, confront, and negotiate the impasses of sexual knowledge, the better.

Working the Contradictions

An intellectual disposition founded on sexual knowledge relations recognizes in what we *don't* know, as well as what we *can't* know, not only the partiality of our methods and a spur to future inquiry but an intractability that has been constitutive of the history of sex and which continues to inform our relations to that history and to each other. The fact of this intractability (and the fact of its ongoing historicity) has prompted me to keep sex and sexual speech moving through incommensurate registers—the past, the present, the epistemological, the pedagogical, the historicist, the psychoanalytic, the feminist, the lesbian, the queer—linking, delinking, and relinking them in new constellations of knowledge-ignorance. Momentarily holding unstable phenomena in tense and not always equal equipoise, this strategy proceeds by grasping rough edges, rotating angles, and scrutinizing the tensile properties whereby new links might be forged. These specific commitments have not resulted in a full theoretical synthesis or a comprehensive demonstration; rather, they have led me to develop and hone specific methodological strategies. Each of the methods I enact derives from the epistemological question of the different ways in which we have come to know; each concerns the concepts, categories, and processes by which knowledge is created; and each is concerned with the possible transactions between the past and the present, including the work of identifications, disidentifications, cross-identifications, and transference.

To recap: I have tried to synthesize and create new knowledge of past sexualities, while also keeping the past and sexuality productively unknown. I have offered strategies for connecting different temporal periods through specific configurations of affects, desires, bodies, and figures without privileging either their historical alterity or their similarities to the present, resisting teleology while accounting for change. I have activated the contradictions between formulations of historiography as a matter of affect and historiography as an empirical finding of bodies, integrating questions of representation with questions about lived experience, and by means of those questions endeavored to uncover the relative incoherence and relative power of past and present conceptual categories. I have returned to that outmoded critical category "bawdy language" to ask what in the way of knowledge early modern sexual language can reasonably offer, and I have proposed principles for editing and reading such language that would render those practices more open to incomprehension and obscurity. I have closely read a stage play and a series of sonnets in order to track how gender impinges on the quest for and making of sexual knowledge. By attending to gender, I have theorized the role of sequence in the epistemology of sex. And I have offered that most recalcitrant of figures, the lesbian, as a sign of a historiographic problem, using her history of inconsequence, unintelligibility, and impossibility as an analytical wedge to pry apart the knowledge relations that currently obtain among sex, history, and theory. By means of all of these strategies I have intimated some of the ways that sex possesses its own form of historical agency. Other scholars have begun to suggest how sex performs particular modes of cultural work: the capacity to stimulate new forms of thought, organize modes of discourse, affect the outcome of events, and bring alternative modes of living into existence.[69] My focus has been to suggest how sex activates processes of knowledge production.

Out of these broad strategies have emerged certain "lower-level" tactics, particularly regarding issues of sexual identity, disciplinarity, and temporality. These tactics conduce to a series of implicit, and implicitly interrelated, propositions. Because their exposition has extended discontinuously over many pages, I offer them here in compressed form:

- Positive ascriptions of identity and resistance to identity's coercions are constitutively and socially interrelated, and thus equally necessary to the project of queering.
- Universalized and minoritized understandings of erotic desire are two sides of the same (historical, theoretical, and methodological) coin; both are necessary to apprehending the historical status of sex and its varying relations to identity and knowledge.
- The analytical potential of cross-gender identification enjoins attentiveness to the specificity of social emplacements of identity, even as it exploits the ways that the dynamics of identification disturb such boundaries.
- Genealogy need not be developmental or sequential, nor need it conduce to a position on historical periodization, chronology, or teleology. Genealogy can take the form of emphasizing historical alterity or similarity, ruptures or continuity.[70]
- The opacity of sexuality means that the relations between the material and the metaphoric, reality and representation, will remain inextricable and shifting, subject to temporary stasis only through the discursive and disciplinary framing imposed upon it. Thus, the explanatory power of any discipline-based analysis will remain limited and both discipline-specific and cross-disciplinary competencies necessary.
- Challenging presumptive knowledge about sex, including the conceptual categories that govern methods and interpretations, may require risking empiricism precisely in order to render sex more susceptible to theorization.
- Maintaining a state of uncertainty regarding meaning and a state of contradiction regarding method may paradoxically achieve more

exactitude than privileging a single method or designating certain authors, texts, or analytics as queer.

- Both synchrony and diachrony are indispensable forms of temporality and historiography; historicism is not antithetical to queer temporality, and chronology and sequence, while sometimes pressured into the service of teleology, are not inherently heterotemporal or straight.
- Invocations of similarity and difference, especially when conflated with *homo* and *hetero*, demand discursive specification and contextualization.
- The psychoanalytic concept of displacement gains renewed analytic vigor when conjoined to a temporal analytic of sexual sequence.[71]

Sex, History, and the Future

These collective propositions are moored to one further principle that has appeared intermittently throughout, as manifested in my description of the "present future" of lesbian historiography, my gesture toward a dissident futurity in my framing of *The Antipodes*, my reading of Shakespeare's appropriation of the future on behalf of men, and my use of "the sign of the lesbian" to think about the prospect of placing lesbian and queer on equal footing. Thinking sex with the early moderns, it turns out, is an endeavor of queer futurity.

I did not expect to end up at this place; indeed, given the recriminations that have characterized debates about queer futurity, I would have preferred to avoid this issue. There is so much to admire in Edelman's reckoning of reproductive futurism, so much to grapple with the vision of antisociality that he advocates for queer thinking, that it seems churlish to demur. And yet, one implication of the analyses offered in these pages is that his diagnosis of reproductive futurity, while exquisitely capturing much that is crucial about our own historical moment, derives from an attenuated evidentiary basis of the forms of sex in history, an attenuation born out of not only its principled theoretical framework but its selective archive of twentieth-century figurations.[72] And masterful though his exposition is within the terms it sets for itself, this attenuation necessarily affects the antisocial response he proposes. Rather than concede Edelman's "insistence on the negativity that pierces the fantasy screen of futurity, shattering narrative temporality with irony's always explosive force," and rather than join him in his effort "to

escape the will-to-be-taught" by honing our capacity for "bad education,"[73]
I suggest the value of an alternative educational dispensation, one neither
good nor bad, neither consoling nor redemptive, which also honors the
impossibility of knowledge—not by undoing it, but by confronting the contradictions of doing it. Or, to put it another way: by committing to both
historiography and futurity by advancing an analytics of sex education.

Within this self-contradictory project, a hypostatized emblem of "the
Child" need not subtend all desires for a future different from the present.[74]
Nor need the past be conscripted to a future we would wish to avoid or
prevent. Rather, we might find in early modern texts a means to historicize
and query the compulsory requirements of reproductive futurity. Whereas
"the Child" stands for reproductive futurism *now*, in other times and places,
the future has been figured otherwise. Despite the congruence of reproductive
futurism with *Hamlet*—a text, as Edelman's reading of its "paternal com-
mandment[s]" cannot help but intimate, structured by masculine bonds and
patriarchal inheritance[75]—Shakespeare's drama of masculine selfhood is not
the final word on what early moderns, or even Shakespeare, bequeath to us.[76]
A more spacious purview of early modernity would decline to neatly map
eroticism *tout court* onto the self-confirming ego, stabilized identity categories, or the "heterotemporal repetition" of a backward-looking futurism.[77] In
many early modern texts, after all, the future isn't kid stuff.

With its extraordinarily high childhood mortality rates, children in the
sixteenth and seventeenth centuries, in fact, are lucky to figure at all.
Bemoaned by historians as an evidentiary problem, the lack of references to
children has shrouded the history of childhood in obscurity.[78] The popular
genre of "mothers' advice books" was directed toward imparting the precepts
of good Christian living to children; diaries, conduct books, and medical
manuals address such topics as swaddling, feeding, weaning, and the pleasures
that children can confer, but very little else.[79] When children figure in literary
texts, they tend to be the recipient of maternal or paternal sentiment (think
Macduff and Lady Macduff in *Macbeth*), reflecting parental investments,
both material and emotional.[80] Parents certainly expressed the wish that their
children not only respect and obey them but be comforts to them as well.
Yet while children were valued—"as the blessing of God to those influenced
by religious teachings, as guarantees of the perpetuation of the family line to
those concerned with their lineage, as a source of personal pleasure and emotional satisfaction to all"[81]—parents made this investment with very little
expectation of a return.[82]

Thus, while historians have established that there *was* a concept of "childhood" in the early modern period, and while children were often represented as vulnerable and in peril, there was no equivalent to "the Child" in the terms theorized by Edelman. As much as children might represent for the landed the prospect of an ongoing familial lineage, and as much as their presence might more generally evoke hope, children did not represent "reproductive futurity"—that is, the reproduction of futurity through a regime of sexuality. In many texts, particularly those of Puritan origin, the reverse is the case.[83] As noted in the commonplace book entry of Sir Simon D'Ewes: "Parents are especially bound to instruct the children, pray for them and train them up in fear of God because they drew original corruption from their loins."[84] Rather than looking forward to the fulfillment of societal ideals, such instructions suggest that children allegorize for early modern culture a backward look to the sin-filled origin of humankind.

Just as "the Child" was not merely the emblem of heteroreproductive futurity, so too the exclusion of women from the promise of subjective coherence and historical significance—precisely what is supposedly guaranteed by futurism's injunction—moderates the applicability of this paradigm to the early modern past. Throughout *Thinking Sex with the Early Moderns* I have argued that however principled one's resistance to identity categories, gender remains diacritically entangled with sexuality, pressuring the concepts through which we analyze the epistemology of sex. This pressure can be brought to bear on the "*sinthomo*sexuality" with which Edelman propounds the conjunction of the death drive with queerness. *Sinthomo*sexuality names the projection onto queerness of an intolerable negativity, the claiming of which, Edelman maintains, is the only means by which to resist futurism's distorted claims. Yet, the death drive does not accurately describe the way that women's negotiation and management of their desires was psychically or conceptually processed. Although it may be true that "any number of female characters might be considered in terms of *sinthomo*sexuality,"[85] it is equally true that many female "characters," both in the past and in the present, whose desires are not precisely straight, would fail to meet those conditions. Because of the economic, social, and political restrictions on female autonomy, women have not fit particularly well within the paradigms developed for male homosexuality[86]—although male histories do offer, as I have suggested, a useful counterpoint from which to theorize women's. Female desires—sometimes granted social accommodation or significance precisely because they are recognized only under the "insignificant" names of chastity, friendship, or kinship—have existed in oblique relation to both patriarchal and reproductive mandates. Interstitial, under the radar, nonsymptomatic, these forms of female eroticism neither visibly transgress nor are subsumed by the paternal law, heteronormativity, or reproductive futurity. Nonproductive in all manner of ways, their traces of sociality tend to be muted or disappeared, leaving only the faintest of tracks: such as a one-line query in a stage play.

Those traces reveal that the past doesn't only mortgage the living to the dead through the repetition of paternal voices; the legacy of the past includes modes of existence, instructive tactics and strategies, of people gendered female and male who manage to carve out improbable, counterfactual, inquiring if sometimes clueless lives. This legacy includes writers, as well, who intimate the possibility of their doing so. If I don't believe that all forms of meaning making about the past are captive to a self-confirming telos in the present; if I postulate sex to be not only an *effect* of historical processes, but an agent in history; if I imagine a queer feminist pedagogy, a sex education, that is yet to be—it is because *that* is what thinking sex with the early moderns has taught me.

NOTES

1. By describing these as panics, I do not mean to dismiss the problem of abuse. Yet, it is clear that, as Gayle Rubin remarks, "legitimate concerns for the sexual welfare of the young have been vehicles for political mobilizations and policies with consequences well beyond their explicit aims, some quite damaging to the young people they are supposed to help. . . . There are genuine issues and real problems, but much of the response consists of uncontrolled institutional expansion, escalating expenditure of resources, poorly defined targets, and few effective ways to measure success" ("Blood Under the Bridge," 37–38).

2. This phenomenon is often noted by academics who teach contemporary porn; see Linda Williams, *Porn Studies* and *Screening Sex*; Bronski, "Foreword."

CHAPTER 1. THINKING SEX

Note to epigraph: Bishop, "At the Fishhouses," in *The Complete Poems*, 64–66.

1. Scott, "Gender."

2. I adopt "methodological release points" from McClelland and Fine, "Writing on Cellophane."

3. One approach to this question would direct attention to the contemporary political realm and conservative efforts to actively bar individuals from knowledge of sex. While this recognition provides one motivation for the pedagogical disposition of this book, the obstacles analyzed in the ensuing pages are not primarily a matter of conservative fundamentalism. Another obstacle derives from the linguistic and conceptual confusion caused by the fact that the meaning of "sex" transits unevenly across time, referring at different and overlapping moments to anatomy, gender, and erotic practices. This confusion is readily seen in discourses of transsexuality and transgender, where "sexuality" and "gender" often are used interchangeably, even when the clarity of bodies and the specific relations of sexuality to embodiment are matters of considerable import.

4. In an influential essay, "Sexuality, Schooling, and Adolescent Females," Fine attributes the inscrutability of sex to a lack of language caused by political marginalization.

5. See Dolan, *True Relations*, 151: "Recognizing what we cannot know is an important part of creating historical knowledge."

6. Rubin, "Thinking Sex," was first presented as a workshop at "The Scholar and the Feminist IX Conference: Towards a Politics of Sexuality," at Barnard College on April 24, 1982.

Rubin was one of the first to elucidate the structural hierarchies of sexual status, to theorize the ways in which such statuses change historically (often in relation to societal sex panics), and to call for the development of theories adequate to such structural stabilities and change. She offered two important analytical moves that decisively influenced the development of queer studies: the analytical separation of sexuality from gender and the corresponding call for a framework, as a supplement to feminism, for analyzing sexuality on its own terms. See also Rubin, "Blood Under the Bridge"; Rubin and Butler, "Sexual Traffic."

7. Rubin, "Thinking Sex," 275.

8. Love, "Rethinking Sex."

9. Rubin's analytic is derived not just from a theoretical consideration of sexuality but from analyzing the specific plight of stigmatized peoples, their sexual practices and communities: sadomasochism, prostitution, pedophilia. See also the rich ethnography of BDSM, with its attention to institutions, geography, protocols, ambience, and temporality, in Rubin, "The Catacombs: A Temple of the Butthole."

10. The idea that we might want to *use* the sexual past has come under critique as being theoretically naive or passé; see the opening paragraph of the introduction to Nardizzi, Guy-Bray, and Stockton, *Queer Renaissance Historiography*. A more incisive critique of the concept of "use" is advanced in Guy-Bray's *Against Reproduction*, where he aligns use with productivity, reproductivity, labor, narrative continuity, and teleology. While provocatively reading the constraining limits imposed on sexuality and textuality, and proffering an important strategy for defending the "uselessness" of the arts, his critique associatively slides across different registers of meaning.

11. Because the sites and technologies of sex have multiplied and transformed under the conditions of mass culture—from Internet porn and cybersex to vibrators and Viagra—the available techniques and supports of eroticism not only have altered the occasions and meanings of sex but have changed how it is corporeally enacted.

12. The problems early modernists confront in thinking about early modern sexuality depart most radically from those whose historical focus necessitates contending with the knowledge derived from the "modern" fields of medicine and psychiatry (with their taxonomies and case histories), and where public and private media (trial records, newspapers, correspondence, diaries, life writing) are abundant. Doan, *Disturbing Practices*, ix, describes one of the main difficulties of her research as "the voluminous evidentiary base" of a single case study. For analysis of the difference that the new genre of popular periodicals, with their question-and-answer format, made to the circulation of sexual knowledge, see Berry, "Lawful Kisses?"

13. In using "early modern" as a descriptor for a general time period also known as the Renaissance, I do not mean to enthrone the modern as the telos of an earlier time. Nonetheless, modernity is implicated in the questions about sexuality I pose here, and in ways that make "early modern" more salient than the idea of a rebirth of the classical past.

14. Throughout this book, I use "historian" for those scholars who are trained in and/or work in the discipline of history, and "historicist" or "historical scholar" to include literary critics whose work is concerned with historical questions, methods, and paradigms.

15. *Scenes of Instruction* is the title of at least three other books. Most relevant is Dolven's *Scenes of Instruction in Renaissance Romance*, which examines the "growing crisis of confidence in the humanist program" of early modern teaching and "how romance could offer a literary landscape within which to critique that program and experiment with alternatives" (8). Our projects intersect in our interest in the failures of pedagogy, humanist and otherwise; in his

words, "the most reliable fact about teaching and learning in romance is that they will go wrong" (13).

16. According to Huffer, *Mad for Foucault*, 47, "le sexe" is even more layered in French, including "sex-as-organs, sex-as-biological-reproduction, sex-as-individual-gender-roles, sex-as-gendered-group-affiliation, sex-as-erotic-acts, and sex-as-lust."

17. Sharon Marcus, "Queer Theory for Everyone," 205.

18. This regime, first described by Foucault, *The History of Sexuality*, is defined as when sex becomes sutured to subjectivity, is classified by means of strict taxonomies, and is promoted as the key to personal identity; see Davidson, *The Emergence of Sexuality*; Halperin, *How to Do the History of Homosexuality*.

19. Jordanova, *History in Practice*, 95. Jordanova primarily is concerned with relationships between historians (as knowers) and the data, facts, processes, people, and events of the past (the known).

20. Epistemology has been a central concern of feminist philosophers and theorists, including Simone de Beauvoir, Elizabeth Anderson, Sandra Harding, Donna Haraway, and Patricia Hill Collins, but their primary aim is to critique matrices of intelligibility and structures of epistemic authority such as "rationality," "objectivity," and "scientific method." Feminist epistemologists have also developed alternative epistemologies based on the social situation arising from gendered embodiment, women's cognitive styles, and the "situated knowledges" or perspectival "standpoints" of women and other marginalized groups. The broader subfield of epistemology within philosophy has its own complex tradition of engaging with the status and grounding of truth claims, which has only a tangential relation to the present study.

21. Fradenburg, *Sacrifice Your Love*, 46.

22. On the "concept," see Bal, *Travelling Concepts in the Humanities*.

23. Love, *Feeling Backward*, 31. The distinction between epistemology and affect is present as well in Wiegman, "Wishful Thinking."

24. Vicinus, "Lesbian History."

25. Judith Butler, *Bodies That Matter*. For how this question has affected historical work, see Coviello, *Tomorrow's Parties*, 8: "What are the codes of legibility that allow us even to recognize something—a body, an act, an impression, a thought, a sentence—as sex, or sexually invested? What have those codes of legibility to do with what gets to count, not only as sex or sexuality or sexual identity, but as History as well?"

26. Edelman, *Homographesis*, xiv.

27. On insignificance and invisibility, see Traub, *The Renaissance of Lesbianism*; on unaccountability, see Binhammer, "Accounting for the Unaccountable"; on inconsequence, see Jagose, *Inconsequence*. For more on this issue, see Chapter 9.

28. Edelman, *Homographesis*, xiv. Edelman's influential theorization of modern discourses reveals "the historical relationship that has produced gay sexuality in a discourse that associates it with figures of nomination or inscription" (*Homographesis*, 4). See also D. A. Miller, "Anal Rope."

29. For early articulations of this problem within early modern studies, see Bredbeck, *Sodomy and Interpretation*; Goldberg, *Sodometries* and *Queering the Renaissance*. More recently, see Menon, *Wanton Words*; Masten, *Queer Philologies*.

30. On "sodomy," see Goldberg, *Sodometries*; on "lesbian," see Andreadis, *Sappho in Early Modern England*; on "whore," see Spiess, "Shakespeare's Whore."

31. Bray, *Homosexuality in Renaissance England*; Shannon, "Queerly Philological Reading" and *Sovereign Amity*.

32. Traub, *The Renaissance of Lesbianism*, 163, emphasis added.

33. As Saunders, *Desiring Donne*, 114, remarks when discussing the problem of differentiating between critical appreciations of sexiness versus charges of sexism leveled at John Donne: "the social and political signification of a potentially erotic image, text, or practice is not necessarily an inherent feature of that particular image, text, or practice. Instead, for any given individual, the social signification of an erotic image, text, or practice is inseparable from that same individual's prior conceptions of, among other things, sexual difference and relative power relations."

34. Coviello, "World Enough," 392.

35. Sex, like trauma, is often posed as an extreme, excessive, decontextualizing experience, governed by a libido whose excitations transgress bodily and psychic boundaries and take subjects outside of themselves. Nonetheless, certain sex acts (e.g., anal intercourse) also confer onto those selves specific social meanings. Access to sexual knowledge, to sexual spaces, to the redress of sexual wrongs are all constituted by material relations of power that ground the experience of sex and impart differential meanings to it. Sex thus poses a problem not only of representation and signification but of understanding and accounting for the tension between subjective decontextualization and social location. For this reason, the process of contextualizing sex will never—at least, on its own—provide a sufficient basis for historical understanding.

36. In addition to Doan, see Dinshaw, *Getting Medieval*, whose method of "touching" across disparate temporalities seeks to connect those "left out of sexual categories back then and . . . those left out of current sexual categories now" (1); Freccero, *Queer/Early/Modern*, whose work is rigorously anti-identitarian; and Anna Clark, "Twilight Moments" and *Desire*, who traces expressions of erotic desire rather than the acquisition of identity. Whereas the instability of sexual signification informs Clark's concept of "twilight moments" (sexual encounters that occasion no remark, and thereby exist within a field of discretion), the relations with which she is most concerned exist at the level of social utterance rather than that of legibility and intelligibility.

37. Like Doan, I am concerned "that history making framed by 'identity knowledge' constrains even as it illuminates, because it is mobilized by the epistemological and social structures of modern sexuality" (*Disturbing Practices*, ix). We differ, however, regarding the extent to which the remnants of such structures, including the "logic of lineage" and the epistemological stance of "knowingness," remain tethered to queer genealogy (59).

38. See Spector, Puff, and Herzog, *After "The History of Sexuality."*

39. Halperin, *How to Do the History of Homosexuality*, 43.

40. Anna Clark, "Before and After Sexuality" panel comment.

41. On the ambiguity involved in "social kissing," see David M. Turner, "Adulterous Kisses."

42. Fisher, "'The Use of Flogging in Venereal Affairs'"; Enterline, "Rhetoric, Discipline"; Largier, *In Praise of the Whip*.

43. Fisher, "The Erotics of Chin Chucking."

44. Exceptions to my generalization include Wallace, "Outside History," who addresses how same-sex sexual arrangements, especially within the context of colonial societies, "tend to elude material documentation or statistical scrutiny," and who argues that "the intractable difficulty of producing histories of same-sex sexuality is symptomatic of sexuality studies' evolving relation to the limitations and possibilities of archival study" (62); and Doan, *Disturbing Practices*, who writes that her book "changed as a result of the peculiarities and conceptual roadblocks" that she "encountered in the archive" (5); more particularly, her "experiences

in the archive forced" her "to confront a paradox: How was it that the same epistemological structure of sexuality that impelled me to historicize sexuality in the first place also hin-
dered and obscured other ways the 'sexual' might have been configured, talked about, and
known?" (22).

45. In *Is the Rectum a Grave?* Bersani charges that "queer critiques of homosexual identity
have generally been desexualizing discourses," a phenomenon he links to the overuse of the
concept of homoeroticism, whereby "we end up with the implicit but . . . extraordinary proposition that gays aren't homosexual but all straights are homoerotic. Given the terminological
and epistemological confusion all this creates, it might not be a bad idea to drop the very
category of homoeroticism, since it seems to me to be little more than a provokingly tendentious way of asserting a certain sexual indeterminacy in all human beings, a state of affairs
hardly discovered by queer studies" (42).

46. Indeed, as Kahan implies in *Celibacies*, queer studies seems uncomfortable with the
notion of sexual lack, as it tends to fill in "the 'absence' of sex as itself a sign of homosexuality"
(2), in a critical habit that Kahan judges as "the least queer aspect of queer theory" (4).

47. Saunders, *Desiring Donne*, 145.

48. For historicist efforts to resist reading heterosexuality back into the pre- and early
modern periods, see Lochrie, *Heterosyncracies*; Schultz, "Heterosexuality as a Threat"; Bach,
Shakespeare and Renaissance Literature; and Bromley, *Intimacy and Sexuality*.

49. My focus on the production of knowledge is not primarily dedicated to exposing the
contingent manufacture of sexual knowledge by means of a "hermeneutics of suspicion" or to
solving the problems posed by early modern sex by reference to new archival findings. This is
not to suggest that it might not be useful, for any given project, to bracket the epistemological
difficulties with which I am concerned in order to ask *other* questions of sex: how designations
of active and passive, as well as their implication in gender asymmetries, historically structure
the meanings of individual erotic acts; how erotic acts or identities might be construed as
minoritizing or universalizing for certain individuals; and how, in a given time and place, the
line between the erotic and the nonerotic has been drawn and by whom. Whether pursued
as theoretical or historical problems, such questions and the procedures they require remain
crucial.

50. I concur with those critiques of interdisciplinarity that recognize its institutional uptake
as predicated on the application of natural and social science paradigms to humanities research,
as well as the way its rhetoric can circulate as a brand without content and in order to stave off
genuine critique; at the same time, I continue to value the ways interdisciplinary women's/
gender studies, queer studies, and ethnic studies can challenge disciplinary business as usual.

51. My thinking about proximate relations has been influenced by Dollimore, *Sexual Dissidence*, esp. 228–30; Rubright, *Doppelgänger Dilemmas*.

52. Edelman, "Against Survival," 149.

53. Amin, "Queer's Affective Histories." See also Wiegman, *Object Lessons* and "Wishful
Thinking"; Jagose, *Orgasmology*; Huffer, *Are the Lips a Grave?*

54. Doan, *Disturbing Practices*, 21.

55. Rubin and Butler, "Sexual Traffic"; Traub, *Desire and Anxiety*.

56. On this debate, see Halley, *Split Decisions*; Wiegman, *Object Lessons*.

57. Schultz, "Heterosexuality as a Threat," 24.

58. Huffer, *Are the Lips a Grave?*

59. In the early modern period, gender is a mode of bodily materialization that is repeatedly
stabilized as social hierarchy. For all its brilliance, Laqueur's influential study of the "one-sex

body" in *Making Sex* unfortunately has led some scholars to minimize the import of gender in regulating early modern social life.

60. See Loughlin, *Hymeneutics*; Schwarz, "The Wrong Question."

61. Ferguson, "Hymeneal Instruction," 105.

62. Culpeper, *A Directory for Midwives*, 23–24. See also Sharp, *The Midwives Book*, 48.

63. For a summary of medical thinking regarding the hymen, see Traub, *The Renaissance of Lesbianism*, 382 n. 70.

64. As Crooke concluded in the "Questions" section at the end of his discussion in *Microcosmographia*, 256, "Wee must therefore finde out some other locke of Virginitie."

65. The enigma of the female body engendered countless cuckold jokes in ballads, stage-plays, and jests. For analysis of this fear in relation to the politics of reproduction, with particular attention to ballads, see Fissell, *Vernacular Bodies*; with regard to jests, see Brown, *Better a Shrew*.

66. Garber, "The Insincerity of Women." For analysis of how orgasm has been conscripted as a figure for heterosexuality, see Jagose, " 'Critical Extasy' " and *Orgasmology*. For early modern ambivalence about the "asocial space of orgasm," and the extent to which it "conventionally signaled surfeit, decay, or death," see Leinwand, "Coniugium Interruptum," 246, 245.

67. The "secrets of women"—the knowledge of sex and generation that women were alleged to possess from the medieval period through early modernity—"came to symbolize," in the words of Katharine Park, "the most difficult intellectual challenges posed by human bodies." Park, *Secrets of Women*, 37–38.

68. This nineteenth-century sculpture was designed by Eugène Emmanuel Viollet-le-Duc and executed by Adolphe-Victor Geoffroy-Dechaume. It is not the original on this column, which was destroyed in the Revolution; originally, the snake had feet (signifying his punishment to crawl), dragon wings, and a male human face.

69. Pagels, "The Politics of Paradise," 82.

70. Pagels, "The Politics of Paradise," 84. At the same time, original sin is not equated with sexuality; rather, sexual arousal is a means of transmitting it. When the will is properly directed, as in marriage, it may be redeemed. On such paradoxes, as well as their fortunes in the sixteenth and seventeenth century, see James Grantham Turner, *One Flesh*.

71. Calvin importantly contested the localization of sin in the genitals. For women's responses to the Fall, see Dowd and Festa, *Early Modern Women on the Fall*.

72. One of the best articulations of the relationship between male lust and effeminacy is that of Rackin, "Foreign Country." Panek, " 'This Base Stallion Trade,' " productively complicates Rackin's formulation to demonstrate the sexual and status-based contradictions that attend patriarchal masculinity and inject specificity and dynamism into the concept of antipatriarchal manhood.

73. Although the female-headed serpent is not the dominant representation of Eve's seducer, it is more prevalent than one might suppose in both visual and textual representation; see Flores, "Effigies Amicitiae."

74. Salisbury, *The Beast Within*, 64.

75. For analysis of the hybridity of the female-headed serpent, see Burns, "A Snake-Tailed Woman."

76. Language in the period says as much: in 1589, George Puttenham refers to women as "the sex." *OED*, s.v. "sex," 3.a: "With *the*. The female sex."

77. Lochrie, *Covert Operations*; Park, *Secrets of Women*.

78. Fifteenth-century anatomical illustrations, for instance, often show an animated female corpse exuberantly throwing off nature's veil to reveal her reproductive organs, while the female cadaver remains emblematic of anatomical knowledge well after Vesalius's title page of the 1543 *Fabrica*.

79. Toulalan and Fisher, *The Routledge History*, 8.

80. Gowing, *Common Bodies*, 83.

81. Queer theory's universalizing investments exist in complex tension with the universalizing/minoritizing analytic offered by Sedgwick in *Epistemology of the Closet*. Much of what follows explores the tensions she identified between the minoritizing and universalizing axes of homo/hetero definition, whereby sexual preferences are viewed as pertaining only to a small, distinct minority of people or, conversely, haunting the sexual characters of all people, regardless of their sexual orientation and regardless of their awareness of it. Recognition of this incoherence has provided my project an analytical framework that extends methodologically beyond the modern systems of sexuality from which she derived it.

82. By "diacritical," I refer to concepts that are constituted by difference or distinction. The term evolved out of theorists' engagements with Saussure's analysis of the relationship between the signifier and the signified. Saussure described language as diacritically structured insofar as the relationship between signified and signifier relies on differences in order to produce meaning. Linguistically, a "diacritical mark" signals a difference in pronunciation or meaning from that of the "unmarked" term. Diacritical concepts, then, are simultaneously mutual and differential, and represent tension and mobility.

83. Early modern precedents of cross-gender identification include the impersonation of women by boys on the public stage; humanist pedagogy, whereby grammar school boys were trained in rhetoric to cross-gender their speech through Ovidian *imitatio* (Enterline, "Rhetoric, Discipline"); and ballad singers' impersonations of the other gender in voicing narratives of love and woe (Smith, "Female Impersonation" and *The Acoustic World*, 168–205).

84. One study that employs identification as an analytic while indicating its inadequacies is Halperin, *How to Be Gay*, 258–59.

85. This does not mean that we abandon the effort to queer, but it challenges us to develop more nuanced protocols for adducing the relations among sex and gender in terms of the tensions among universalizing and minoritizing understandings.

86. When approached psychoanalytically, identification is aligned with fantasy, itself understood less as an object than as a structure or scenario, in which individuals can occupy more than one position and play more than one part; the fantasized scene as a whole, rather than a particular subject position, can be the focus of identification.

87. Fuss, *Identification Papers*, 2. "Identification is a process that keeps identity at a distance, that prevents identity from ever approximating the status of an ontological given, even as it makes possible the formation of an *illusion* of identity as immediate, secure, and totalizable," 2.

88. Rubright, *Doppelgänger Dilemmas*, 28.

89. See Judith Butler, *Bodies That Matter*, 105.

90. As Halperin says in *How to Do the History of Homosexuality*, these identifications enable us to "pick out resemblances, connections, echo effects" (15). For problems with such echo effects, see the final chapter of Traub, *The Renaissance of Lesbianism*.

91. Smith, "Resexing Lady Macbeth's Gender," 29.

92. Halperin, *How to Do the History of Homosexuality*, 13.

93. I am repurposing Sedgwick's phrase regarding the hermeneutics of suspicion in *Touching Feeling*, 130. Sedgwick argues that paranoid readings expose the workings of regimes of truth in part to protect against surprise and the failure to anticipate; while not dismissing the worth of such practices, she attempts to make way for a more "reparative" practice that is open to surprise and can accommodate hope.

94. This method need not depend on a psyche or unconscious understood as timeless or universal; it need not be used to diagnose symptoms, promote tendentious narratives of psychic development, or propose treatments or cures. It need not be defined by efforts to articulate or enforce definite prepositional contents (the Oedipal complex, stages of sexual maturation, the incest taboo, the classification of neuroses and psychoses, the mirror stage, the phallus, or the Law of the Father) or to produce allegorical readings that "prove," yet again, the perspicacity of Freud or Lacan.

95. I agree with Bersani and Phillips, *Intimacies*, that "the language of psychoanalysis has both served and demystified strategies designed to control human subjects" (65).

96. In claiming psychoanalysis as a disposition, my method has similarities to the psychoanalytically inflected, queer trajectory of affect studies, but affect is not my main topic.

97. In the words of Britzman, *Lost Subjects*, "psychoanalysis reminds one of the failure of knowledge, the work of forgetting, the elusiveness of significance, the incidental, the coincident, the bungled action, and the psychic creativity of selves" (10).

98. Britzman, *Lost Subjects*, 7.

99. Huffer, *Mad for Foucault*, 124.

100. "Transference" is the name that Freud gave to the evolving play of trust and accusation between analyst and analysand that must be "worked through" for any treatment to occur. If Freud installs the psychoanalyst as the one who knows, Lacan insists that the analyst does not actually possess knowledge of the subject and that the analyst's role is to move the patient beyond such misrecognition.

101. LaCapra, *History and Its Limits*, 33.

102. Bersani and Phillips, *Intimacies*, 92.

103. Here I have slightly modified Fradenburg's observation that "psychoanalysis contends that the un/conscious desire of the observer changes the object of observation, and that *analysis of this desire can produce knowledge about the object*" (*Sacrifice Your Love*, 47).

104. This marks a slight shift from my previous use of psychoanalysis, which suggested ways in which logical structures in Freud and Lacan were uncannily anticipated by Shakespeare (*Desire and Anxiety*), or which diagnosed certain historiographic desires as melancholic (*The Renaissance of Lesbianism*).

105. I am influenced here by Sedgwick's shift from the hermeneutics of suspicion to the affective perspective of *Touching Feeling*, which spatializes its understanding of object relations as *beside*: "the irreducibly spatial positionality of *beside* also seems to offer some useful resistance to the ease with which *beneath* and *beyond* turn from spatial descriptors into implicit narratives of, respectively, origin and telos" (8).

106. My project also shares some of the impulses of "antihermeneutic psychoanalysis" (derived from Jean Laplanche) that allows Will Stockton to queer the temporality of psychoanalysis itself in *Playing Dirty* and "How to Do the History of Heterosexuality."

107. Saunders, *Desiring Donne*, 6.

108. Saunders, *Desiring Donne*, 4. Although Saunders's aim is to name alternative interpretative desires that might exceed "chilly institutional and professional categories" (5) such as those I've been using (historicist, psychoanalytic, deconstructive, feminist, queer), we are allied

in considering "when and how [interpretative] desires and pleasures come into conflict, and when and how they may be conjoined" (32–33).

109. Hammill, "Psychoanalysis and Sexuality," 74.

110. Hammill, "Psychoanalysis and Sexuality," 74. Hammill is interested in using psychoanalysis to think beyond sexuality (especially norms and deviance) to address "the problem of collective life, the fantasies, myths, and violent acts that sustain it" (78), in order to "desubjectivize" psychoanalysis (77). The impossibility of knowledge as well as the impossibility of desire's forthright articulation motivates Hillman's analysis in *Shakespeare's Entrails* of early modern skepticism, born of the self's opacity to itself.

111. In this respect, *Thinking Sex with the Early Moderns* has methodological affinities with Jagose, *Inconsequence* and *Orgasmology*; and Wiegman, *Object Lessons*.

112. For Foucault's reasons for distinguishing pleasure from desire, see Halperin, *Saint Foucault*, 91–97.

113. Fradenburg, *Sacrifice Your Love*, 7. See also Bersani and Phillips, *Intimacies*, 60, which emphasizes the destructive, intractable aggression of *jouissance*, as well as the paradox that it is "a sexual pleasure that sex can't give."

114. One exception is Guy-Bray, whose *Against Reproduction* resists the reduction of sexuality to orgasm.

115. Bersani, *Homos*, 101.

116. Bersani, "Is the Rectum a Grave?" 197.

117. This remains the case even if "*jouissance* as a mode of ascesis" is about playing with surface rather than depth, involves considerable pain, and is indebted to the destructive aggression of the death drive; see Bersani, "Is the Rectum a Grave?" 222. In subsequent work, Bersani linked the masochistic "divestiture" of self-shattering to a form of "impersonal narcissism"; see Bersani and Phillips, *Intimacies*; and Bersani, *Is the Rectum a Grave?* Bersani tends in the latter work to overstate queer theory's hostility to psychoanalysis (as the influence of Butler, Edelman, and Sedgwick attests).

118. It is important to not conflate queer theory's celebration of pleasure with an interest in orgasm; indeed, the glorification of pleasure may in part be secured by queer theory's inattention to actual sex acts. In *Orgasmology*, Jagose argues that queer theory "has had next to nothing to say of orgasm" (1); when it does find something to say, she maintains, orgasm tends to be dismissed as normalizing and "inadequately queer" (2). Using the concept of orgasm to retheorize queer agency, she notes the contradictory ways pleasure and desire have been figured in post-structuralist and queer theories.

119. One exception is Jagose, *Orgasmology*, especially in her treatment of female anorgasmia and fake orgasm as challenges to "near-axiomatic understandings of what constitutes, politically speaking, good sex and bad" (177). Another is Berlant, *Cruel Optimism*: "Sex events might be expressive of one's true feelings or not, and they might be exciting, overwhelming, painful, or boring. One can never be sure, though, whether one will be confirmed or threatened either by the negativity or positivity that one attaches to the event" (147). On the pervasiveness of erotic dissatisfaction from the perspective of social science, see Michael et al., *Sex in America*, the mass-market companion to Laumann et al., *The Social Organization of Sexuality*. Surveying heterosexuals in the United States between the ages of eighteen and fifty-nine, this survey found that one of three women report disinterest in sex, and one out of five women report that sex provides little pleasure. To both questions, this is twice the number of men. In the survey, 25 percent of women reported inability to reach orgasm, in comparison to 8 percent of men. For a more recent survey, see Reece et al., "Findings from the National Survey." For self-reflexive

analyses of the assumptions behind these surveys, see Adam, "Accounting for Sex"; Epstein, "The New Attack on Sexuality Research." On developing more accurate measures (and more sensitive algorithms) of women's sexual satisfaction, see McClelland, "Intimate Justice," "'What Do You Mean,'" and "Who Is the 'Self.'"

120. Sedgwick, *Epistemology of the Closet*, 25.

121. Having suggested that this relegation may be unwarranted, I nonetheless want to distance myself from queer theory's deprecation of therapy. Although the therapeutic cultures of contemporary capitalism are open to critique, I would emphasize some of the positive impacts of feminism and gay/lesbian/trans discourses on the health professions and empirical sex research.

122. Throughout this book, I have bracketed off instances of sexual aggression, coercion, or violence, referring to these topics only when the rhetoric suggests something about other acts, like sodomy. Although this risks reinscribing pleasure as the sine qua non of sexual historiography, I would argue that the power issues involved in sexual assault tend to overdetermine the meanings of whatever bodily contact has occurred. A vigorous feminist historiography about sexual coercion, compulsion, assault, and consent focuses less on particular sex acts than on how to infer whether they were desired or repulsed, how accountability is rhetorically ascribed, how these experiences and their aftermath contribute to our understanding of women's subjectivity, agency, and reputation, and how the alleged actions came to fit legal criteria for evidence and prosecution in the context of changing definitions of rape (from a crime of property to a crime against personhood). See Walker, "Rereading Rape and Sexual Violence"; Dolan, "Re-reading Rape in *The Changeling*"; Varholy, "'But She Woulde Not Consent.'"

123. There are two exceptions to this within queer studies: the recent trend, taking form under the broad rubric of affect studies, to think about illegibility, impasse, and failure in sexual relations as productive sites of queer theorizing; and the discourse of BDSM, which recognizes the need to acknowledge the role of revulsion and pain in erotic desires and identifications. In what follows, I engage more directly with affect studies.

124. On affective adjustment, see Berlant, *Cruel Optimism*.

125. Jagose, *Inconsequence*, xi.

126. Jagose, *Inconsequence*, 145.

127. Jagose, *Inconsequence*, x.

128. Edelman, *Homographesis*, xv.

129. Eisner and Schachter, "*Libido Sciendi*," 823.

130. Bersani and Dutoit, *Caravaggio's Secrets*, 6.

131. Goldberg and Menon, "Queering History," 1609. Goldberg and Menon characterize desire "as a formation that rarely has a single objective correlative by which to be measured" (1611).

132. Exploring the role of eros in Foucault's ethics, Huffer, *Mad for Foucault*, admits not only that "I cannot know what Foucault's sexuality really is," but "I cannot really even know my own" (38) and "the more I think about 'sex itself,' the less I know what it means" (180). In her bid to separate feminism from queer politics, Halley, *Split Decisions*, confesses her "strong attraction to 'queer' revelations of the strangeness and unknowability of social and sexual life" (15).

133. On critique as a problematic field habitus, see Wiegman, *Object Lessons* and "Wishful Thinking."

134. My debt to each of the scholars I contend with is profound, and I hope that readers will perceive in what follows a serious engagement with the provocations of their work. I may

not have succeeded in conveying my respect for their labor, but I hope my critiques will be approached as an effort to hone our collective thinking. The goal of the following chapters is to expand our methodological toolkit; but I do not believe that my tools are the only ones available, that they should supersede those that came before, or that others should abandon their own projects to take up mine.

CHAPTER 2. FRIENDSHIP'S LOSS

1. LaCapra, *History and Its Limits*, 2–3.
2. LaCapra, *History and Its Limits*, 3–4.
3. LaCapra, *History and Its Limits*, 3, 4.
4. LaCapra, *History and Its Limits*, 51.
5. Bray and Rey, "The Body of the Friend," 65.
6. Bray, *The Friend*. I cannot claim for myself the status of Alan's friend; although we had corresponded about each other's work, we did not meet until the year before his death. After we met, he revealed to me that he would be reading the manuscript of *The Renaissance of Lesbianism* for the publisher and suggested that we might dispense with the protocol of confidentiality in order to further our conversation. Portions of this chapter were communicated to him in my response to the manuscript that he shared with me the summer before his death. For other attempts to honor his legacy, see Jody Greene, "The Work of Friendship"; and Gowing, Hunter, and Rubin, *Love, Friendship and Faith in Europe*.
7. Bray, *Homosexuality in Renaissance England* (1982); unless otherwise noted, citations taken from this edition.
8. Bray, "Homosexuality and the Signs of Male Friendship," 42; Bray, *The Friend*, 186.
9. Bray, "Homosexuality and the Signs of Male Friendship," 47; Bray, *The Friend*, 186.
10. Bray, "Afterword," 116.
11. Goldberg, *Queering the Renaissance*, 4–5.
12. Bray, *The Friend*, 25.
13. Bray, *The Friend*, 104–5.
14. Bray, *The Friend*, 125.
15. Bray, *Homosexuality in Renaissance England*, 11. Scholars have variously adopted, nuanced, or attempted to refute Bray's constructionist account. As Goldberg notes, almost all the essays in *Queering the Renaissance* are indebted to Bray (4). See, subsequently, Goldberg, *Sodometries*; Bredbeck, *Sodomy and Interpretation*; Smith, *Homosexual Desire*; Rambuss, *Closet Devotions*; DiGangi, *The Homoerotics of Early Modern Drama*; Masten, *Textual Intercourse*; Stewart, *Close Readers*; Orgel, *Impersonations*; Haggerty, *Men in Love*; Trumbach, *Heterosexuality and the Third Gender*; and Hitchcock, *English Sexualities*.
16. For analysis of the effects of "the historical search for a Great Paradigm Shift," see axiom 5 of Sedgwick's *Epistemology of the Closet*, 44–48. Bray's initial account continues to be nuanced by reflections on the meanings of identity, even as the contours of his chronology have gained general acceptance.
17. Bray remarks that his study of sodomy "places it outside a discrete history of sexuality," in "Homosexuality and the Signs of Male Friendship," 56.
18. Bray, *The Friend*, 6.
19. Bray, *Homosexuality in Renaissance England*, 55–56. See also his "Historians and Sexuality."

20. Bray, *The Friend*, 150.

21. Bray, *The Friend*, 217. For an update of this shift that explicates its gendered dimensions, see Anderson, *Friendship's Shadows*.

22. Bray, "The Body of the Friend," 80; Bray, *The Friend*, 218.

23. Bray, *The Friend*, 212.

24. Bray, *The Friend*, 209.

25. Bray, *The Friend*, 6, 272. See also Bray's headnote to my essay "The Perversion of 'Lesbian' Desire."

26. Bray, "Homosexuality and the Signs of Male Friendship," 46; slightly altered in *The Friend*, 156.

27. Bray, "Homosexuality and the Signs of Male Friendship," 50; Bray, *The Friend*, 190.

28. Bray, *The Friend*, 174.

29. Bray's other break with traditional protocols of historical evidence was his frequent use of literary representation as one means of access to the social. Both of these, of course, would come to characterize the new cultural history.

30. Shannon, *Sovereign Amity*, 93–94.

31. As Berlant and Duggan point out in *Our Monica, Ourselves*, the "Clinton Affair" was "a moment of stunning confusion in norms of sexuality; of fantasies of national intimacy—what constitutes 'ordinary sex' and 'ordinary marriage,' let alone the relation between law and morality, law and justice" (4). Several essays in *Our Monica, Ourselves* remark upon, but none actually analyze, this constitutive confusion. In "It's Not About Sex," James Kincaid remarks of Clinton's infamous denial, "I did not have sexual relations with that woman, Miss Lewinsky": "What the 'it' is that isn't sex shifts, of course, according to the context: anatomical, moral, legal, or causal. My point is that it always shifts so *as to keep the bodies themselves out of the picture.* The idea that oral sex isn't sex is just one of those refocusings" (75, emphasis mine). In "The First Penis Impeached," Toby Miller likewise has other fish to fry: "But Bill's dalliance with desire, his carefully calibrated, Monigated, sense of how far he could go—what constituted sex—was in fact part of the dance of management (not denial) that characterizes high office and its organization of low desires" (118). Eric Clarke, in "Sex and Civility," notes the "telling incoherence" that "defined the events surrounding the president's actions, the media coverage of them, and the political response: his alleged crimes and misdemeanors both were and were not about sex"; but for Clarke, this incoherence is less about sex than "the fraught place of sex in the public sphere" (286). Not incidentally, a survey of midwestern college students in 1991 revealed that 60 percent of them did not think that they had "had sex" if it involved oral contact rather than intercourse; see Sanders and Reinisch, "Would You Say," and Sanders, et. al., "Misclassification Bias."

32. Bray, *Homosexuality in Renaissance England*, 69.

33. Bray, "The Body of the Friend," 83; slightly reformulated in *The Friend*, 218. *The Friend* foregrounds the importance of the advent of civil society, arguing that it divorced sworn kinship from marriage and, in doing so, removed "the family from the traditional setting that this diverse and complex world had created. 'Friends' could still negotiate marriage and did, but friendship was no longer to be created in relations that overlapped with it and were akin to it" (217).

34. The dependence of the hetero on the homo has been a tenet of queer theory since Sedgwick's *Epistemology of the Closet* and Judith Butler's *Gender Trouble*.

35. Bray, "Homosexuality and the Signs of Male Friendship," 54; see also *The Friend*, 193. Also suspicious of the reliability of literary texts as indicators of their author's sexual orientation,

Bray assumes an exclusive hetero orientation in some of the subjects he analyzes, a problem addressed by Bredbeck, Goldberg, and Smith.

36. Bray, *Homosexuality in Renaissance England*, 17.

37. Incisive critiques of *Homosexuality in Renaissance England* along similar lines include that of Sedgwick, who points out Bray's "inadvertent reification of 'the homosexual' as an already-constituted entity," which has a "disturbing functionalist effect" on his argument (*Between Men*, 86); Goldberg, who questions the anachronistic role of individualism as well as the foreclosure of meaning in Bray's narrative (*Sodometries*, 68–71); DiGangi, who charges that Bray does not consider the homoerotics of Elizabethan male friendship (*The Homoerotics of Early Modern Drama*, 10); and Bredbeck, for whom the stigma of sodomy is less perfectly inscriptive or monolithic than Bray would seem to suggest (*Sodomy and Interpretation*, 4–5, 144).

38. "The image of the masculine friend," Bray writes, "was an image of intimacy between men in stark contrast to the forbidden intimacy of homosexuality" ("Homosexuality and the Signs of Male Friendship," 42).

39. DiGangi, *The Homoerotics of Early Modern Drama*, 10. See also Orgel, *Impersonations*, 42.

40. Goldberg, *Sodometries*, 162.

41. More than once, Bray expressed anxiety about the controversy he believed our books would encounter; my *Renaissance of Lesbianism*, he cautioned, required "armour-plating" from the attacks that he believed would be inevitable from British historians (pers. comm.).

42. The kisses of greeting that we bestow on our sexual partners, for instance, may not always be qualitatively different from those we bestow on our friends, just as the waning of sexual desire between long-term lovers may not turn them, automatically, into "just friends."

43. Bray, *The Friend*, 7.

44. Bray, *The Friend*, 225.

45. Bray cites as evidence a letter Newman wrote following St. John's death, in which he articulates St. John's "hope that during his whole priestly life he had not committed one mortal sin," which Bray takes as "definitive" (*The Friend*, 293).

46. Bray quickly follows with a second question: "How much does that answer tell one? I have written this book for those interlocutors who are willing to ask that question" (*The Friend*, 269). Bray's point is that the good of these formalized bonds "lay for them self-evidently beyond the individuals for whom a friendship was being made" (277), and that focusing on sexuality does not get us to that point.

47. One can infer from Bray's reading of Newman's life that the line between the erotic and the spiritual depends in part on a division between the private and the communitarian: spiritual love creates bonds of community, whereas carnal love is more limited in its reach. Because such a division is belied by Bray's argument regarding the wide nexus of elective kinship that friendships created up through the seventeenth century, it may be that this separation is itself a further effect of the social change he charts. Or, this could simply be the place where his own Roman Catholicism, to which Bray converted as an adult, most comes to the fore.

48. Bray, *The Friend*, 316.

49. Halperin incisively articulates the issue: "if the funerary monuments Bray describes had conveyed even the faintest suggestion that the *connubium* of friends celebrated in them had consisted in a sodomitical union, we would not find those monuments enshrined in Christian churches. I do not infer from this alone that Piper and Wise never had sex . . . in most cases, I

assume, the evidence does not allow us to draw any firm inferences one way or the other. But I do deduce that the *rhetoric* of friendship or love employed in those monuments succeeded in sealing off the relationships represented in them from any suggestion of being sodomitical" ("Introduction," in O'Donnell and O'Rourke, *Love, Sex, Intimacy, and Friendship*, 10 n. 9).

50. Bray, *The Friend*, 6.

51. Goldberg, *Queering the Renaissance*, 6.

52. This point was made by David Wootton in his remarks during the Birkbeck College Symposium on Alan Bray in September 2003.

53. A similar incarnation of this problem occurs in a blurb on the cover of a 2002 anthology, Phillips and Reay, *Sexualities in History*: "Sexual behaviours and mentalities are embedded in systems of power," David Levine observes, but this recognition is preceded with the claim: "Sex is, perhaps, the *least* interesting aspect of the history of sexuality" (emphasis mine).

54. Only two moments in *The Friend* remotely smack of "debunking," and in each instance the issue is not eroticism but rather an anachronistic understanding of the role and meaning of homoeroticism in early modern culture. In his discussion of other scholars' assertions of *covert* homosexuality, for instance, the issue is not the projection of homoeroticism but the assumption of the need for secrecy (Bray, *The Friend*, 166).

55. Bray, *The Friend*, 6. At the same time, he warns "that to read this book within the narrow terms of a debate as to whether homosexual friendship constitutes a family would be to misunderstand it, perhaps gravely. The ethics it deals with overflow that question. To widen the terms of this debate . . . is to see it within a broader contemporary crisis in the ethics of friendship, the signs of which have been the diverse loyalties of identity, region, culture, or language that have come to mark the pluralism of the late modern world, of which sexuality has been one, but only one, strand" (8).

56. In the introduction to *The Friend*, Bray characterizes the motivation of his own historical enterprise as "seeking among the tombs of the dead those lost friends" who died of HIV/ AIDS—"against all expectations I found such friendship there in these monuments" (5). So, too, his coda concludes: "As in our own time the permafrost of modernity has at last begun to melt . . . the world we are seeing is not a strange new world, revealed as the glaciers draw back, but a strange *old* world: kinship, locality, embodiment, domesticity, affect" (306).

57. Bray, *The Friend*, 197.

58. Bray, *The Friend*, 224.

59. Bray, *The Friend*, 134.

60. Bray, *The Friend*, 158.

61. Bray, *The Friend*, 125.

62. Bray, *The Friend*, 268.

63. Bray, *The Friend*, 139.

64. Goldberg, *Sodometries*, 19–20.

65. Bray, "Historians and Sexuality," 194.

66. Margaret Hunt, "Afterword," 372.

67. Efforts to stake claims on one side of a rigid divide separating sexuality from asexuality have been constitutive of lesbian history, from Faderman's implication in *Surpassing the Love of Men* that romantic friends were not sexual to Castle's rejoinder in *The Apparitional Lesbian* that sex is the basis of lesbianism. Interventions by Traub, *The Renaissance of Lesbianism*, Vicinus, *Intimate Friends*, and Sharon Marcus, *Between Women*, attempted to displace that binary.

68. Bray seemed content that others might push the ramifications of his work in a more explicitly erotic direction. His "Afterword" in the reprint of *Homosexuality in Renaissance*

England acknowledges those scholars who not only welcomed his work, but critiqued or used it for their own analysis of the historical relation between the homosocial and the homoerotic. Based on the citations of other scholars and personal testimony offered since his death, many have experienced Bray's work and feedback as not only generative, but enabling of their own more explicitly erotic interpretations of the archive.

69. Bray, "Afterword," 118, emphasis mine.

70. Bray, "The Curious Case of Michael Wigglesworth," 206. Given that, from a certain point of view, Wigglesworth's dreams are a perfect illustration of what desire is, Bray's own conception of desire and how it functions in the modern world is worth further investigation.

71. Bray, *The Friend*, 172.

72. Halperin, "Introduction," 5.

73. O'Donnell and O'Rourke, *Love, Sex, Intimacy, and Friendship*, 85.

74. Bray, *Homosexuality in Renaissance England*, 17.

75. Bray, *Homosexuality in Renaissance England*, 74, emphasis mine.

76. The question of influence is complex. Bray's first book obviously influenced Shannon, whose *Sovereign Amity* (primarily on masculine friendship, but attentive to female friendship) seeks at several points to extend Bray's analysis of the dangers of inequality, as well as Schwarz, *Tough Love*, whose analysis draws heavily on Bray's treatment of cultural intelligibility. Yet, it is notable that neither of these books is primarily about female homoeroticism. Wahl sees in Bray's focus on those who threaten social stability "a particularly useful approach for analyzing England's apparent cultural indifference to the desire of one woman for another," but she does not develop that observation in *Invisible Relations*, 52. Andreadis approvingly cites Bray's historical argument about a homosexual subculture in order to speculate about "an analogous female homosexual subculture" emerging around the same time in London in *Sappho in Early Modern England*, 52, 95–96. Based on the presence of citations as well as on critical approach, Bray appears to have held little utility for Jankowski, *Pure Resistance*; Donoghue, *Passions Between Women*; or the essays on female intimacy in Frye and Robertson, *Maids and Mistresses, Cousins and Queens*. With the exception of my contribution, Bray is not cited in any of the essays in Beynon and Gonda's *Lesbian Dames*.

77. Bray, "The Body of the Friend," 75; Bray, *The Friend*, 158.

78. I owe this question to Laura Gowing.

79. Bray, *The Friend*, 10, 174–76, 199.

80. Bray, *The Friend*, 268, 269, 244.

81. Bray, *The Friend*, 223.

82. Williamson, *Lady Anne Clifford*, 76. This question is raised by Gowing in *Common Bodies*, 65–68, as well as in "Lesbians and Their Like in Early Modern Europe." Bennett, "Remembering Elizabeth Etchingham and Agnes Oxenbridge," pushes Bray's timeline for public commemoration of female intimacy back to the late fifteenth century.

83. In "The Modern Divide," de Grazia usefully summarizes: "After poststructuralism's attack on historicism, continuums of any stripe (teleological, evolutionary, developmental) are decidedly out of favor. (Jameson is the salient exception, holding fast to the Marxist 'uninterrupted narrative' of class struggle.) In the wake of the counterhistories of Nietzsche and Foucault or the *petits récits* of Lyotard, the progression of continuous history has been judged too partial to the dominant powers, leaving much of the (nonbourgeois and non-Western) world behind (panting to catch up). Hence the appeal of Althusser's call for a 'history without a subject or *telos*' and of Foucault's articulation of a genetic history that avoids both by artificially isolating elements in the past as the a posteriori preconditions for the present. There is no

unified working out through time (incrementally, serially, dialectically), but rather 'systematic dissociation' in the form of epistemic rupture, dispersal, reversal, and accident" (461–62).

84. Classical, medieval, and early modern medicine, astrology, and physiognomy, for instance, describe some homoerotic behaviors, especially those associated with gender deviance, as linked to, and sometimes caused by, anatomical aberrations, diseases of the mind, or habituation due to sexual practices. Although this view does not constitute "homosexual identity" in its post-sexological construction, neither is it the undifferentiated concept of sin to which all were subject.

85. See Chapter 4.

CHAPTER 3. THE NEW UNHISTORICISM IN QUEER STUDIES

1. Jordanova, *History in Practice*, defines "teleology" as "explanation in terms of goals or purposes; the assumption that ends or outcomes are present in and/or explain earlier stages of a process" (215). Teleology is often referred to by its detractors as the Whiggish view of history: "history that is written either from the point of view of the winners or from an unthinking commitment to progress" (216).

2. Nardizzi, Guy-Bray, and Stockton, *Queer Renaissance Historiography*, 1. See also Eisner and Schachter, "*Libido Sciendi*," 817–37; Will Stockton, "How to Do the History of Heterosexuality"; and Nagle, "'Unusual Fires.'" For interest in temporality in early modern studies, see Harris, *Untimely Matter in the Time of Shakespeare* and "Untimely Mediations." Judging from publications and references at conferences, endorsement of the critique has been nearly universal.

3. One muted exception is Dinshaw and Lochrie's letter in "Forum: Queering History," which accepts the general critique of teleology but resists the substitution of "early modern" for "Renaissance" and inquires what it might mean to reconstitute scholarly periodization for scholars trained in periods. Dissenting murmurs about the exclusionary politics of unhistoricism have begun to be articulated in reviews; see DiGangi, "Queer Theory, Historicism, and Early Modern Sexualities"; and Radel, review of *Queer Renaissance Historiography*. Appearing close to the publication of the article version of this argument is a similar critique by Coviello, *Tomorrow's Parties*, 13–14: "It does not follow . . . that to embrace anachronism as a scholarly or historical mode is, of necessity, to be queer, nor that to attend to the specificity of a given moment's codes of sexual being . . . is to side, methodologically, with the normalizing impulses of modernity."

4. See respectively Love, *Feeling Backward*; Kathryn Bond Stockton, *The Queer Child*; and Edelman, *No Future*. See also Freeman, *Time Binds*; Halberstam, *In a Queer Time and Place*; Rohy, *Anachronism and Its Others*; Muñoz, *Cruising Utopia*. Journals such as *South Atlantic Quarterly* and *GLQ* have dedicated special issues to queer temporality: see Goldberg, "After Thoughts"; and Freeman, "Theorizing Queer Temporalities." "Queer Temporality" served as the central topic at Manchester University's 2011 Sexuality Summer School.

5. Jagose, "Feminism's Queer Theory," 158.

6. One of the most sustained, and largely appreciative, analytical engagements with this larger body of work to date is Stein, "American Literary History and Queer Temporalities," which offers a compelling example of how attentiveness to queer temporality might productively impact literary history. Stein also provides a conceptual map of varieties of work on queer temporality, distinguishing between those that (1) consider "how history is transmitted across

time" (e.g., Dinshaw, Nealon, Love), (2) intervene "against a perceived chrononormativity" (e.g., Edelman, Berlant, Freeman), (3) or "draw attention to the properties of time itself that can organize (or disorganize) event perceptions in queer ways" (e.g., Freccero, Rohy, Goldberg, Menon, Jagose, Coviello, Bond Stockton). Noting that "the picture they collectively paint is messy, contradictory, and certainly complex," and that they "use the past in nonidentical ways," Stein applauds practitioners of queer temporalities as "both admirably searching and nearly unique among scholarly models for their commitment to thinking reflexively about the relationship between history and time" (864–65).

7. Goldberg's prior book *Sodometries* did not eschew *any* relationship to modern categories: "I have wanted to see how relations between men (or between women or between men and women) in the period provide the sites upon which later sexual orders and later sexual identities could batten" (22). In addition, in *Queering the Renaissance* he warned that sexuality "can always be explained in other terms, and in ways in which anything like sex disappears" (6).

8. Sedgwick, *Tendencies*, 8.

9. Goldberg and Menon, "Queering History," 1616.

10. Freccero, "Queer Times," 485.

11. Menon, *Unhistorical Shakespeare*, 7.

12. Goldberg and Menon, "Queering History," 1616.

13. Menon, "Spurning Teleology in *Venus and Adonis*," 496.

14. Freccero, "Queer Times," 485–86.

15. Goldberg, "After Thoughts," 502.

16. Freccero, *Queer/Early/Modern*, 31.

17. Goldberg and Menon, "Queering History," 1609.

18. For discussion of historians' problems with teleology, see Lynn Hunt, *Measuring Time, Making History*.

19. Sedgwick, *Epistemology of the Closet*, 44.

20. Sedgwick, *Epistemology of the Closet*, 47.

21. Sedgwick, *Epistemology of the Closet*, 45.

22. Goldberg, "After Thoughts," 503.

23. Sedgwick, *Epistemology of the Closet*, 48.

24. Halperin, *How to Do the History of Homosexuality*, 107.

25. Fradenburg and Freccero, *Premodern Sexualities*, xix.

26. Fradenburg and Freccero, *Premodern Sexualities*, xix.

27. Dinshaw, *Getting Medieval*, 39.

28. Dinshaw, *Getting Medieval*, 54.

29. Arondekar, "Time's Corpus," 125 n. 2.

30. Babayan and Najmabadi, *Islamicate Sexualities*; Sang, *The Emerging Lesbian*; and Cuncun, *Homoerotic Sensibilities in Late Imperial China*.

31. Arondekar, "Time's Corpus," 125 n. 2.

32. Burger and Kruger, *Queering the Middle Ages*, xii.

33. That genealogy might not be the best or only method with which to pursue a queer history of sexuality is worth considering, as Doan, *Disturbing Practices*, shows regarding the relations among ancestral genealogy, queer genealogy, and critical history.

34. The ongoing, dynamic, and often contested relations among historicism, psychoanalysis, and deconstruction, as well as queer theory's indebtedness to each of them, deserve their own genealogy. It is beyond the scope of my argument to anatomize these critics' use of psychoanalysis and deconstruction, which differs in emphasis, theoretical source, as well as in

synthesis attained; nor is it my intention to pigeonhole them according to theoretical frame-works. They do, however, consistently align deconstruction and psychoanalysis and do not explore possible conceptual tensions between them. Freccero's *Queer/Early/Modern* is the most programmatic, announcing its fidelity to "psychoanalytic and poststructuralist dimensions of queer theory" (2) and regularly citing Derrida and Benjamin. Menon's persistent focus on desire as the excess that disrupts identity cleaves closely to Lacanian understandings, but her readings generally pursue a deconstructive aim. Goldberg's theoretical repertoire, like his oeu-vre, is eclectic; his touchstones in *The Seeds of Things* include Serres, Deleuze, Bersani, and Foucault.

35. Freccero, *Queer/Early/Modern*, 4.

36. Psychoanalysis has also proven fruitful for historians, as in LaCapra, *History and Its Limits*; Roper, *Oedipus and the Devil*; and Scott, *The Fantasy of Feminist History*.

37. de Grazia, "The Modern Divide," 462.

38. Foucault, "Nietzsche, Genealogy, History," 144.

39. Foucault, "Nietzsche, Genealogy, History," 148.

40. Foucault's interest in discontinuity on behalf of "effective history" did not fetishize alterity but sought to expose the insufficiency of "suprahistorical" perspectives as an underlying "basis for self-recognition" ("Nietzsche, Genealogy, History," 152–53). His goal was to assess the role of emergence, displacement, and rupture on modern concepts and realities: "the stake, the challenge for any history of thought, is precisely that of grasping when a cultural phenome-non of a determinate scale actually constitutes within the history of thought a decisive moment that is still significant for our modern mode of being subjects" (Foucault, *The Hermeneutics of the Subject*, 9). See also Halperin, *One Hundred Years of Homosexuality*, *Saint Foucault*, and *How to Do the History of Homosexuality*.

41. Foucault, "Nietzsche, Genealogy, History," 145.

42. Foucault, "Nietzsche, Genealogy, History," 146.

43. Foucault, *Discipline and Punish*, 31.

44. I would emphasize that Foucault's "Nietzsche, Genealogy, History" begins thus: "Genealogy is gray, meticulous, and patiently documentary" (139).

45. Freccero, "Queer Times," 487.

46. Freccero, "Queer Times," 488.

47. Freccero, "Queer Times," 489.

48. Freccero, "Figural Historiography," 61.

49. Freccero, "Queer Times," 488.

50. Freccero, *Queer/Early/Modern*, 104.

51. Goldberg, "The History That Will Be," 400.

52. Goldberg, "After Thoughts," 503, 502.

53. Goldberg, "After Thoughts," 502–3.

54. Goldberg, "Margaret Cavendish, Scribe," 435.

55. Goldberg, "After Thoughts," 504.

56. Menon, *Unhistorical Shakespeare*, 22, 25.

57. Menon, *Unhistorical Shakespeare*, 1.

58. Menon, "Afterword," 233.

59. Menon, *Unhistorical Shakespeare*, 28.

60. Menon, *Unhistorical Shakespeare*, 54.

61. This phrase appropriates Leo Bersani's call in *Homos* for an "anticommunal mode of connectedness" that would not assimilate queers "into already constituted communities" (10). Bersani's meaning of "homos," however, is invested in social specificity.

62. One question raised by the confluence of these paradigms is how far the postcolonial critique of Western teleological history echoes and differs from the queer historiographic critique.

63. Menon, reply, in "Forum: Queering History," 839. Retheorizing anachronism is of broad interest (see Harris, "Untimely Mediations"; and Rohy, *Anachronism*), and is partially fueled within early modern studies by the long-standing critique by new historicists of psychoanalysis. Here I can only point out that these critics' treatment of anachronism is paradoxical. On the one hand, they resist the anachronistic imposition of modern identities onto the past, with Goldberg, in *Queering the Renaissance*, repeatedly remarking that the early modern period is "not organized under the aegis of the homo/hetero divide" (2). On the other hand, they celebrate the way in which anachronism breaks with the niceties of temporal order. In this respect, their treatment of analogy differs from Rohy's, insofar as she argues that anachronism and chronology do not have essential political meanings; rather, time is a trope and anachronism is a figure. Furthermore, the historical analogy between blackness and homosexuality she analyses retroactively creates the similarities it purports to observe.

64. These critics might reject the preposition "across" altogether, as it might be thought to presume the existence of discrete temporal blocks across which people and events move.

65. Foucault, *The Order of Things*.

66. Lantham, *A Handlist of Rhetorical Terms*, 99.

67. Cummings, "Metalepsis."

68. Freccero, *Queer/Early/Modern*, 2.

69. Menon, *Wanton Words*, 85.

70. Freccero, *Queer/Early/Modern*, 2.

71. Because it "seems less like a cause than a metaphor substituted for a cause . . . [metalepsis] 'can facilitate the transposition of values into facts'" (Lantham, *Handlist*, 99–100).

72. Analyzing a different "series of metonymic displacements," Abbas, "Other People's History," similarly has disarticulated the logic of analogy from teleology in her contrapuntal analysis of the rhetoric of an "Islamic Reformation."

73. Stein, "American Literary History and Queer Temporalities," 856.

74. See Blackbourn, "'The Horologe of Time,'" for a historian's account of how periodization functions in the discipline of history.

75. Davis, *Periodization and Sovereignty*, 3.

76. Edelman, *No Future*.

77. Menon, "Afterword," 233.

78. See Grosz, *The Nick of Time*.

79. In "The Modern Divide," de Grazia identifies a similar phenomenon within noncontinuous historical narratives that posit a special affinity between the modern and the early modern: "the Renaissance from the start was periodized as the push-off point of the modern. Every time Shakespeare or the early modern is cast as the nascent form of some facet of the modern, its identity as such is reconfirmed. . . . Early modern studies routinely preserves the two endpoints of the nineteenth-century narratives [e.g., Hegel, Burckhardt, Marx] but dissolves the intervening connection that linked them, leaving a yawning historical chasm in between (1500–2000). . . . Yet we continue to link the two endpoints, thus retaining the prestige of the period's inaugural title while tossing (into history's ashbin) the diachronic narrative that conferred it in the first place" (463).

80. Positing analogies between literary (or cinematic) form and sexual (and political) positions has a long history in queer theory (see Edelman, *Homographesis*). Within early modern

sexuality studies, this strategy informs studies by Bredbeck, *Sodomy and Interpretation*; Hammill, *Sexuality and Form*; and Haber, *Desire and Dramatic Form*.

81. Sedgwick, *Tendencies*, 6.

82. See Alderson, "Queer Cosmopolitanism."

83. In an oft-cited remark, Halperin, *Saint Foucault*, 62, maintains that "queer is by definition *whatever* is at odds with the normal, the legitimate, the dominant." He also states that "queer" "demarcates not a positivity but a *positionality* vis-à-vis the normative" (62, emphasis added). Halperin argues for a recognition of "the strategic functioning" of "queer" vis-à-vis "gay" (63) and analyzes both the advantages and liabilities of queer (64–67).

84. Lochrie, *Heterosyncrasies*.

85. As Sharon Marcus, "Queer Theory for Everyone," 196, points out, "While *queer* foregrounds the belief that sexual identity is flexible and unstable, *gay* and *lesbian* do not assert the contrary." She further argues that "*queer* has been the victim of its own popularity, proliferating to the point of uselessness as a neologism for the transgression of any norm (queering history, or queering the sonnet)."

86. This move will be further discussed in Chapters 8 and 9.

87. Menon, *Unhistorical Shakespeare*, 25.

88. Edelman, *No Future*, 17.

89. See Halperin's meditation on the benefits and costs of sexual identity in *How to Be Gay*, 73–76.

90. See Manalansan, "In the Shadows of Stonewall"; Puar, "Circuits of Queer Mobility"; Gopinath, *Impossible Desires*; Wah-shan, *Tongzhi*; Rofel, *Desiring China*; Jeffreys, *Sex and Sexuality in China*; and Alexander, *Pedagogies of Crossing*.

91. A related point is made, in the context of a very different argument, by Wiegman, *Object Lessons*, 120: "let's not assume . . . that as a form of internal critique, queer theory bears a truth that identity's inaugural form does not."

92. Sedgwick, *Tendencies*, 8.

93. Menon, *Unhistorical Shakespeare*, 3.

94. One might well inquire where in us that "homo" is located: In the unconscious, à la Freud's *Three Essays on a Theory of Sexuality*? In the Real, per Lacan? In modes of antisocial relation, as in Bersani? By means of our political affiliations, as in certain forms of lesbian feminism?

95. In this, the new unhistoricists repeat some of the errors of the new historicists who, in constructing the specter of an old historicism against which to argue, failed to attend to ongoing developments within the discipline of history; see Maza, "Stephen Greenblatt, New Historicism, and Cultural History."

96. Goldberg and Menon, "Queering History," 1615–16.

97. Freccero, "The Queer Time of the Lesbian Premodern," 72 n. 13.

98. Rubin, along with Sedgwick, Halperin, and Butler, is often cited as founding queer theory. The importance of ethnographic study to "Thinking Sex" has been highlighted by Epstein in "Thinking Sex Ethnographically."

99. Freccero, *Queer/Early/Modern*, 3.

100. Menon, "Afterword," 234, emphasis added. The idea of "compulsory heterotemporality" could be taken to imply that those scholars who find anachronistic similarity in the past are the ones most harmed by homophobia.

101. For more on the meanings of history, see Chapter 9. Within queer studies, there is a pervasive slippage and confusion among the terms "history" (meaning the past), "history" (meaning the academic discipline), "historicism" (a particular method, both old and new), "historiography" (methods in general), the "past" or "pastness," and "temporality." "Historicism" as used in queer studies mainly refers to literary critics who focus on historically distant periods, while historians almost never use the term (which for them refers to Leopold von Ranke's "scientific" conception of history as an objective account of the past). It may be useful to distinguish between queer historicists and queer historians: both write about the sexual past; both use queer theory to inform their writing; both situate texts and discourses within a specific context; but their objectives, forms of archival research, styles of exposition, and methods of textual interpretation tend to differ. While few literary historicists would call themselves historians, they are often referred to as such by others.

102. Doan, *Disturbing Practices*, explores the tensions among gender history, the history of sexuality, and queer historiography, as well as how these subfields are construed by the historical discipline writ large, while composing a nonidentitarian history of women's eroticism during World War I. For a historian's attempt to resist both identity categories and teleology in the history of sexuality, see Anna Clark, *Desire*.

103. See Puff, "After the History of (Male) Homosexuality"; and Herzog, "Syncopated Sex."

104. This lack of engagement with the discipline of history does not bode particularly well for the prospect of interdisciplinarity advocated by Freccero and Goldberg. Freccero's desire for a critical practice that would be "a queering of the so-called human sciences in their institutionalized and disciplinary forms" ("Queer Times," 492) and Goldberg's suggestion that "the new work for queer theory involves the multiplication and dissolution of disciplinary boundaries" ("After Thoughts," 508) would, it seems, need to occur on their own terms.

105. For astute articulations of some of those challenges, see Doan, *Disturbing Practices*. Lanser, *The Sexuality of History*, approaches sapphism not as an identity but as a set of historically contingent, spatiotemporal representations, balancing a synchronic comparativist strategy with a broadly genealogical intent. Correlating the eruption of printed discourses about sapphism in England, France, and Holland from 1600 to 1800 to changes in the public sphere, political economy, and colonial conquest, Lanser shows not "how seventeenth- [and eighteenth-] century sapphism fits into a diachronic account of lesbian existence," but rather "how lesbian representation fits into a synchronic account of the seventeenth [and eighteenth] century" ("The Political Economy of Same-Sex Desire," 163). The overall effect of this genealogy is a careful balancing act: chronological and sequential, but comparative, polyvocal, and nonidentitarian.

106. This is not to say that we might not find it valuable to rethink the stakes in queer theory's self-constellation around antinormalization. See Wiegman, *Object Lessons*, and Amin, "*Queer*'s Affective Histories."

107. Menon, "Afterword," 233.

108. Nuanced analytics of sameness and difference, grounded in specific epistemological domains, have been offered for early modern studies by Shannon, "Nature's Bias" and "Poetic Companies"; and Guy-Bray, "Andrew Marvell and Sexual Difference"; and for modernity by Edelman, *Homographesis*. These analyses do not deposit all forms of difference and alterity into an abjected "hetero" or all forms of sameness and similitude into a reified "homo," but rather

demonstrate how sameness and difference function via distinct registers or are internally fractured or different from themselves.

CHAPTER 4. THE PRESENT FUTURE OF LESBIAN HISTORIOGRAPHY

1. The terms of the debate about continuism versus alterity have emerged from within the subfield of the history of homosexuality largely as constructed by literary scholars; historians more likely would frame the issue as one of continuity versus change over time. For most historians, the issue is not whether the past is other or different, but how, when, and if change does occur, which continuities remain or persist. Within history as a discipline, alterity often is reduced to antiquarianism and a fetishizing of the past for its pastness; it thus is fundamentally conservative. Within literary studies, conversely, the assertion of alterity was long thought to have a radical cast.

2. Faderman, *Surpassing the Love of Men*; Castle, *The Apparitional Lesbian*.

3. Brooten, *Love Between Women*.

4. Foucault, *The History of Sexuality*, 43.

5. Bennett, "Confronting Continuity," 73.

6. Bennett, "'Lesbian-Like' and the Social History of Lesbianisms."

7. Bennett, "Confronting Continuity," 88.

8. Fradenburg and Freccero, *Premodern Sexualities*, xix.

9. Dinshaw, *Getting Medieval*.

10. Vicinus, *Intimate Friends*, xxii.

11. Vicinus, *Intimate Friends*, xxiv and xxix.

12. Despite these advances, too often the concept of identity remains undertheorized and hazily defined, associated with such different concepts as sexual inclination, tendency, preference, predisposition, orientation, consciousness, subjectivity, self-perception, and subculture—listed here according to a spectrum from "soft" to "hard" identity claims. Several problems and questions arise from this definitional confusion and associational logic. Are identity, orientation, and subjectivity synonymous? If they are, do they mean the same thing as inclination, predisposition, and tendency? Does an inclination, even if defined as innate, necessarily signify something causal, or is it merely probabilistic? Does the subcultural grouping of like-minded persons necessarily constitute an identity or subjectivity? Does the *content* of a homoerotic subjectivity alter historically? See also Traub, "'The Past Is a Foreign Country?'" 19–20.

13. In regard to the dominating force of patriarchy, in addition to Brooten, see Halperin, who concedes that, because of the constancy of patriarchal relations, "there may be fewer turning points in the history of lesbianism than in the history of male homosexuality" (*How to Do the History of Homosexuality*, 78). For my disagreement with him, see *The Renaissance of Lesbianism*, 331–32.

14. By referring to a "canonical form," I do not mean to imply that there are not discontinuities and contradictions that destabilize modern lesbianism, nor that it should not be subject to the same epistemological skepticism with which this book treats all sex.

15. Although she quickly collapses the issue of cyclical patterns into "continuity," for a historian's brief consideration of how such cycles might operate in the history of masculinity, see Karen Harvey, "The History of Masculinity," 311.

16. In the garden, perennials are herbaceous plants that die back with the frost, live dormant underground during the winter, and emerge from the ground in the spring. However,

their new growth is not necessarily identical to their former selves—foliage and blooms can be larger and more robust or smaller and weaker. Whereas seasonal regularity is not congruent with the process I am describing, this analogy has the virtue of suggesting the here-now, then-gone, then-here-again-with-a-difference quality that I mean to suggest.

17. Much lesbian history has been written by scholars trained as literary critics (e.g., Andreadis, Castle, Dinshaw, Donoghue, Faderman, Halberstam, Lanser, Moore, Rohy, Traub, Vicinus, and Wahl). This disciplinary training has affected not only the ways such histories are written (including their narrative shape and their explicit and implicit aims) but criteria around such things as what counts as evidence and differences among types of texts. Why this dominance of critics is truer of lesbian than gay male history raises the question of whether lesbian history poses particular or distinctive problems in the history of sexuality. In addition, the turn toward cultural history within the discipline of history has effected a transformation of social history that has allowed it to speak to and at times intersect with intellectual history; this has allowed cultural history to address questions of power, politics, and representation in ways that social and intellectual history did not.

18. "Tribade" was originally used by Greek and Roman writers to designate women who sexually penetrated both women and men, either with their clitoris or a dildo; see Halperin, "Homosexuality." On the reintroduction of the tribade to English culture, see Traub, *The Renaissance of Lesbianism*, chapters 1 and 5.

19. Leading up to *The Sexuality of History*, Lanser has published a series of articles on eighteenth-century sapphism. See "The Political Economy of Same-Sex Desire," "Befriending the Body," "Singular Politics," "Sapphic Picaresque," and "'Queer to Queer.'"

20. Vicinus, "'They Wonder to Which Sex I Belong'" and *Intimate Friends*.

21. Halberstam, *Female Masculinity*.

22. Chauncey, "From Sexual Inversion to Homosexuality." See also the way typology functions in Trumbach, "London's Sapphists."

23. See Rowson, "Categorization of Gender and Sexual Irregularity"; Sweet and Zwilling, "The First Medicalization"; Furth, "Androgynous Males and Deficient Females"; Bray, *Homosexuality in Renaissance England*; Trumbach, *Heterosexuality and the Third Gender*; Chauncey, *Gay New York*; Jackson, "The Persistence of Gender"; Sinfield, "Lesbian and Gay Taxonomies."

24. Halperin, *How to Do the History of Homosexuality*, 106.

25. Halperin, *How to Do the History of Homosexuality*, 109. One of the virtues of Halperin's account is that it brings some systematicity to the scholarship on male-male desire that has proliferated over the past thirty years.

26. Halperin, *How to Do the History of Homosexuality*, 106.

27. It may be useful to think of typologies as second order epiphenomena, whereas the conceptual logics that give rise to them are of the first order.

28. Jagose, *Inconsequence*.

29. This is not to suggest that hypervirility was an invention of the late nineteenth century; the hypervirile woman goes back as far as the Latin tribade and the medieval virago.

30. Lanser, "The Political Economy of Same-Sex Desire," 157.

31. In addition to Lanser, see Moore, *Dangerous Intimacies*.

32. Vicinus, *Intimate Friends*, xvii.

33. Moore, *Dangerous Intimacies*, 152.

34. Lanser, "Befriending the Body."

35. On the intimacy between Clarissa and Anna Howe, see Braunschneider, "Maidenly Amusements."

36. Moore, *Dangerous Intimacies.*

37. Smith-Rosenberg, "The Female World of Love and Ritual," 34.

38. Vicinus, *Intimate Friends*, xviii.

39. Vicinus, *Intimate Friends*, xviii–xix.

40. Vicinus, *Intimate Friends*, xxix. See also Diggs, "Romantic Friends or a 'Different Race of Creatures'?"

41. Doan, "Topsy-Turveydom."

42. Doan, *Fashioning Sapphism.*

43. An earlier problem with typological methods was diagnosed by Sedgwick in her critique of linear models of historical succession in *Epistemology of the Closet*; her critique was expanded by McFarlane, *The Sodomite in Fiction and Satire.*

44. See the implicit contest over typologies for Radclyffe Hall and her fictional alter ego, Stephen Gordon, in Doan and Prosser, *Palatable Poison*, among three essays: Newton, "The Mythic Mannish Lesbian"; Prosser, "'Some Primitive Thing Conceived'"; and Halberstam, "'A Writer of Misfits.'"

45. For astute analysis of eighteenth-century narrative conventions, see Braunschneider, "Maidenly Amusements." For differences between popular representations of passing women in ballads and newspapers in the eighteenth and twentieth centuries, see Oram, *Her Husband Was a Woman!*

46. O'Driscoll, "Word on the Street."

47. Somerville, "Scientific Racism and the Invention of the Homosexual Body," 73, 62.

48. Traub, *The Renaissance of Lesbianism.*

49. Lanser, "The Political Economy of Same-Sex Desire"; Moore, *Dangerous Intimacies*; Vicinus, *Intimate Friends.*

50. Rubin, "Thinking Sex"; and Weeks, *Sex, Politics and Society.*

51. Binhammer, "The Sex Panic of the 1790s"; Lynn Hunt, "The Many Bodies of Marie Antoinette."

52. The latter book is geographically and temporally expansive but its introductory remit prompts Rupp to glide over important distinctions.

53. In addition to analytical studies, there has been a welcome proliferation of sourcebooks. For the early modern period see, for instance, Loughlin, *Same-Sex Desire in Early Modern England*; Borris, *Same-Sex Desire in the English Renaissance;* Borris and Rousseau, *The Sciences of Homosexuality in Early Modern Europe;* Merrick and Ragan, *Homosexuality in Early Modern France.*

54. Burger and Kruger, *Queering the Middle Ages*; Goldberg, *Queering the Renaissance*; Herrmann, *Queering the Moderns.* These studies are slightly more temporally broad than their period-bound titles might suggest.

55. This critique focuses on such metanarrative's retrospective investment in progress, causality, and supersession; its sequential requirements of the pre- and the post-; its tendency toward false synthesis; and its press-ganging of all prior formations of same-sex desire into modern identities. See Jagose, *Inconsequence*; Fradenburg and Freccero, *Premodern Sexualities*; Burger and Kruger, *Queering the Middle Ages*, as well as Chapter 3.

56. Dinshaw, *Getting Medieval*; Freccero, *Queer/Early/Modern*; Lochrie, "Don't Ask, Don't Tell" and "Presidential Improprieties and Medieval Categories"; and Kruger, "Medieval/Postmodern."

57. The major historical monographs on lesbianism, including my own, are generally respectful of period boundaries. In addition to those listed above, see Donoghue, *Passions*

Between Women; Julie Abraham, *Are Girls Necessary?*; Rohy, *Impossible Women*; Andreadis, *Sappho in Early Modern England*; Sautman and Sheingorn, *Same-Sex Love and Desire Among Women*; and Velasco, *Lesbians in Early Modern Spain*.

58. Anthologies such as Giffney, Sauer, and Watt, *The Lesbian Premodern*, and Beynon and Gonda, *Lesbian Dames*, have been more capacious and creative in assembling work across periods, but individual essays therein tend to focus on more discrete time periods.

59. For examples of such border skirmishes, see Dinshaw and Lochrie, letter, and Menon, reply, in "Forum: Queering History," as well as Lochrie's critique of my work and that of Katharine Park in *Heterosyncrasies*. Dinshaw and Lochrie's insistence that "the issues are more complex than simple turf battles" elicits Menon's reply, "What they deny is a turf war is exactly that by any other name" (838).

60. I use the rather old-fashioned literary critical term "theme" because it refers to something that is recognized as it recurs.

61. Doan, *Disturbing Practices*, 4, and private correspondence.

62. Dinshaw and Lochrie, letter, in "Forum," 837.

63. This project is made more urgent by the proliferation of anthologies of gay and lesbian literature, which tend to recuperate traditional teleological schemas without explicitly arguing for them; see Coote, *The Penguin Book of Homosexual Verse*; Donoghue, *Poems Between Women*; Castle, *The Literature of Lesbianism*. On the other hand, other sourcebooks' disregard for periods in preference for conceptual categories can impart an implied transhistoricity; see Hennegan, *The Lesbian Pillow Book*.

64. For comparative work, see Wahl, *Invisible Relations*; Lanser, *The Sexuality of History*; Marcus, "Comparative Sapphism"; and Hayes, Higonnet, and Spurlin, *Comparatively Queer*.

65. Cvetkovich, *An Archive of Feelings*; Love, "Emotional Rescue."

66. Although not often concerned explicitly with history prior to that of the twentieth century—and generally more concerned with the present and future than the past—queer of color critique has developed methods of analysis, the utility of which has yet to be sufficiently explored by historicists. See, for starters, Rod Ferguson, *Aberrations in Black*; Johnson and Henderson, *Black Queer Studies*; Muñoz, *Disidentifications*; and Eng, *Racial Castration*.

67. On the history of Islamic lesbianism, see Babayan, "The *'Aqā' id al-Nisā'*; Babayan and Najmabadi, *Islamicate Sexualities*. On the history of South Asian lesbianism, see Vanita, *Queering India* and "Playing the Field." On historical crossings between Islamic and Christian cultures, see Amer, *Crossing Borders*.

68. On methodological debates in transnational queer scholarship, see Dinshaw, "The History of *GLQ*"; Povinelli and Chauncey, "Thinking Sex Transnationally"; Gopinath, *Impossible Desires*; Harper et al., "Queer Transexions of Race, Nation, and Gender"; Cruz-Malavé and Manalansan, *Queer Globalizations*. For helpful overviews of transnational histories of sexuality, see Canaday, "Thinking Sex in the Transnational Turn."

69. For further thoughts on the methodological challenges posed by traveling sexual categories and epistemologies, particularly the politically loaded significations of tradition and modernity, see Traub, "'The Past Is a Foreign Country?'"; and Boone, *The Homoerotics of Orientalism*.

CHAPTER 5. THE JOYS OF MARTHA JOYLESS

Note to epigraphs: Warner, *The Trouble with Normal*, 192–93; Gallop, *Feminist Accused of Sexual Harassment*, 100.

1. Burton, *The Anatomy of Melancholy*.

2. Brome, *The Antipodes*, act 1, scene 3, lines 304–5. To my knowledge, there are four modern editions: *The Antipodes*, ed. Kastan and Proudfoot; *The Antipodes*, ed. Haaker; *The Antipodes*, in Parr, *Three Renaissance Travel Plays*; and R. Cave's online edition, *The Antipodes: A Comedie*. All citations are taken from the first edition accessed at the University of Michigan Special Collections, with line numbers from the original edition that accompanies Cave's modern online edition.

3. Jowitt, *Voyage Drama and Gender Politics*, emphasizes the patriarchal framing of this encounter: "The woman-to-woman sexual relationship described here is obviously not a celebration of same-sex desire, rather it is predicated on the need of a(n absent) man to father children and thus fulfil women's biological and social roles. Desire flickers here between Martha and the 'wanton maid' because of the absence of any available man" (218). This rather skewed causality—we have no indication that the encounter with the wanton maid occurred because of *anything*, much less the absence of a man—is replicated in Jowitt's assertion that Peregrine's disease is "a consequence rather than a cause of the moral malaise described in the text. The contagion, represented in Martha's case as same-sex desire, was already fully present prior to Peregrine's reading of travel accounts" (219). Linking this "contagion" to the supposed sexual eccentricities of Letoy and, ultimately, Caroline London, Jowitt seeks to demonstrate the "pointlessness" of "the whole text" (222). Goldie, *The Idea of the Antipodes*, 92, focuses more queerly on Martha's "unsatisfiable and undirected desire" in the course of an argument regarding the play's lack of closure; while Miles Taylor, "The Permeable World," sees Martha's "permeable," desiring body as providing an analogue to the play's deployment of the antipodean carnivalesque.

4. For analysis of how the characteristic wit of early modern comedy "always depends on the distances separating those in the know from those who stand in definitive contrast to them," see Zucker, *The Places of Wit*, 1. Interested in how "linguistic acrobatics, the satirical visions of human desire and intrigue, and the humiliations and expulsions that mark off 'wit' on the early modern stage . . . can reinforce and disguise other kinds of uneven relationships," Zucker also argues that wit "permits status to accrue with groups or individuals—women, servants, the untitled or unmoneyed—normally distant from centers of economic or political control" (7, 10–11). The multiperspectivalism of early modern drama renders stage plays a hothouse for the staging of social conflict; indeed, plays seem much better at exploring conflict than resolving it.

5. Gordon Williams, *A Dictionary of Sexual Language and Imagery*, 251, defines "clip" as "sexual embrace," citing several examples from 1510 to 1676. In *A Glossary of Shakespeare's Sexual Language*, Williams defines "clip" as "embrace closely," citing *Coriolanus* and *Venus and Adonis* (71). In both works, he defines "clap" only in its noun form as a "sexual mishap," referring to gonorrhea or pregnancy (*Dictionary*, 246; *Glossary*, 70). The *OED Online* defines "clap" as "a sounding blow or stroke . . . a slap," as well as "to pat fondly."

6. Martha's predicament is not unheard of in the annals of early modern social history. In a deposition, William Bayker describes the predicament of Agnes Carr, whose husband, Thomas, "haith not used nor entretyd the said Agnes, his wyf, as an honestman ought to have doon," a situation that caused Agnes to weep and lament, and which caused Bayker to intervene on Agnes's behalf; see "Ex parte Agnetis Carr adversus Thomam Carr, maritum suum" in *Depositions*, ed. Raine, 97–98. And the 1690s ballad "The Seven Merry Wives of London," which details the sexual failings of husbands according to their trades, includes two wives voicing the lines "he'll seldom cast into the mould that he should," and "he never had enter'd

nor found the right Vein, / Therefore surely, said she, I have cause to complain"; see Hailwood, *Alehouses and Good Fellowship*, 160.

7. Chaytor, "Husband(ry)," exposes a peculiar double bind. In the context of rape accusations, women's "innocence was not a matter of behaviour but a condition of being; and a condition of being defined by absence—of sexual knowledge, intentions, desires. As such it was a difficult virtue for women themselves to invoke, for how could they lay claim to their innocence without laying claim to the knowledge which wasn't supposed to be there?" (399).

8. D. A. Miller, *The Novel and the Police*; Sedgwick, *Epistemology of the Closet*.

9. Nor does Martha's story accord with accounts of the history of scientific knowledge and the role of secrets, particularly the "secrets of women," in medieval and early modern science and medicine. See Eamon, *Science and the Secrets of Nature*; Lochrie, *Covert Operations*; Monica Greene, "From 'Diseases of Women' to 'Secrets of Women'"; Park, *Secrets of Women*.

10. Among many other meanings, the *OED* defines "wanton" as "undisciplined, ungoverned"; "lascivious, unchaste, lewd. Also, in a milder sense, given to amorous dalliance"; "sportive, unrestrained in merriment"; "capricious, frivolous, giddy"; "unrestrained, extravagant." The many relevant meanings of "strange" include "foreign, alien"; "unknown, unfamiliar; not known, met with, or experienced before"; "Of a kind that is unfamiliar or rare; unusual, uncommon, exceptional, singular, out of the way"; "extreme"; "unfamiliar, abnormal, or exceptional to a degree that excites wonder or astonishment; difficult to take in or account for; queer, surprising, unaccountable"; "unpracticed or unskilled at." That strangeness is a function of both knowledge and skill seems particularly relevant.

11. One might compare this to Bray's reading in "The Curious Case of Michael Wigglesworth" of the sexual dreams and fantasies expressed in Wigglesworth's diary, which he uses to argue against the contemporary scholar's imposition of a modern concept of desire; such an internal, generative mechanism or drive is, according to Bray, alien to the psychic, emotional, and ideological landscape of early modern culture. See Chapter 2.

12. According to Neely, "Lovesickness, Gender, and Subjectivity," the therapeutic discourse of love melancholy was surprisingly ecumenical about the diversity of sexual practices: "In the discourse of lovesickness, gender is less polarized and sexuality less normalized than in many other early modern texts. Because the discourse is concerned primarily with the satisfaction of desires, only secondarily with marriage, and not at all with reproduction, it includes without sharp distinction a wide and weird range of gender behaviors, erotic objects, and amorous styles" (279).

13. Virgins' melancholy, greensickness, womb hysteria, suffocation of the womb, and chlorosis were closely related diagnoses, all stemming from an imbalance of humors caused by a lack of the proper expulsion of seed. Womb fury, writes Ferrand, is "a raging or madness that comes from an excessive burning desire in the womb, or from a hot intemperature communicated to the brain and to the rest of the body through the channels in the spine, or from the biting vapors arising from the corrupted seed lying stagnant around the uterus" (*A Treatise on Lovesickness*, 263).

14. Traub, *The Renaissance of Lesbianism*, 84.

15. Martha's request would enjoy what limited indemnity it possessed only so long as the Galenic medical model governed the intelligibility of bodies. By the mid-eighteenth century, any such request would face a more pronounced knowingness and, presumably, a more forcible resistance to the breach of bourgeois decorum and propriety. For the growing concern about propriety in sexual matters by the late seventeenth century, see Andreadis, *Sappho in Early Modern England*; and Wahl, *Invisible Relations*.

16. *The Travels of Sir John Mandeville* was reprinted five times between 1612 and 1639; although viewed as fraudulent by many, it continued to be appreciated as an entertaining mixture of fantasy and fact. See Sanders, "The Politics of Escapism."

17. There is much that could be said about the relations among travel, sex, and sexual dysfunction in Brome's play, including that both travel and sex function homeopathically as both problem and cure.

18. On the politics of inversion in this play, see Leslie, "Antipodal Anxieties."

19. The play seems devoid of anxiety about cross-cultural sex and takes as a given that Peregrine would desire to wed the Antipodean queen.

20. This may be one of the most important ways in which sexual representation on stage differs from the conventions of early modern pornography, wherein the pleasures of erotic looking are paramount. Toulalan is right that "looking at the sexual body and watching the sexual body in action are constructed as central to sexual pleasure, both as a sexual pleasure in itself, and as one that is an incitement to sexual action for the voyeur" (*Imagining Sex*, 34). Conversely, Maus argues perceptively that Renaissance playwrights "inevitably encounter a gap between their limited theatrical resources and the extravagant situations they dramatize. English Renaissance theatrical method is thus radically synecdochic, endlessly referring the spectators to events, objects, situations, landscapes that cannot be shown them. We are provided . . . not with an actual sexual act but with the preliminaries or consequences of a sexual relationship. . . . The English Renaissance stage seems deliberately to foster theatergoers' capacity to use partial and limited presentations as a basis for conjecture about what is undisplayed or undisplayable" (*Inwardness and Theater*, 32).

21. In one sense, Martha's narration of her homoerotic encounter makes it more visible than the offstage heterosexual encounter; in another sense, the lack of dramatization of the Joyless's sex leaves room for the reader's/spectator's possible fantasy of unconventional sex.

22. This feigned seduction is, not incidentally, another instance of pedagogy.

23. Kaufmann, *Richard Brome*.

24. See, in addition to the introductions to the editions, Martin Butler, *Theater and Crisis*; Ira Clark, *Professional Playwrights*; Cope, "Richard Brome"; Donaldson, *The World Upside Down*.

25. In particular, the notion of the public sphere as a realm of rational sociability separate from both the private realm and the sphere of public authority was just beginning to emerge in the 1640s and gained ground after the English civil wars. Nuancing, from a historical perspective, Jürgen Habermas's *The Structural Transformation of the Public Sphere* are Achinstein, *Milton and the Revolutionary Reader*; Norbrook, *Writing the English Republic*; Pincus, "'Coffee Politicians Does Create.'"

26. Hitchcock, *English Sexualities*; Margaret Hunt, "The Sapphic Strain." For more on sex acts during the period, see Chapters 6 and 7.

27. Cressy, *Birth, Marriage, and Death*, 350–76.

28. Cressy, *Birth, Marriage, and Death*, 374. Lack of consummation was one of the few grounds for marital annulment.

29. Two exceptions are Mendelson and Crawford, *Women in Early Modern England*; and Crawford and Gowing, *Women's Worlds in Seventeenth-Century England*. These not only provide source materials for a richly diversified history of women but also reconceptualize, in both the categories of the *Sourcebook* and in the analysis proffered in the monograph, some of the primary terms by which women's lives are defined. The categories in the latter's chapter on "Sexual Experiences"—"sex and single women; sex and marriage; sex between women; secrecy

and adultery; rape, assaults, and attempts"—usefully belie the life-cycle truism as well as the licit/illicit binary. In addition to the monograph's chapter on marriage, there is a chapter on relationships, which includes the wonderfully ecumenical list "neighbors, families, friends and lovers, animals and spirits."

30. Cressy, *Birth, Marriage, and Death*; Gillis, *For Better, For Worse*; Anthony Fletcher, *Gender, Sex, and Subordination*. Among these, Cressy is most able to resist the subordination of sexual pleasure to the reproductive life cycle; nonetheless, insofar as his study is structured by public ritual, it cannot resist very far.

31. "Premarital" sex is an interesting case of the difficulty of construing "transgression," insofar as it was often a customary phase of wooing and wedding.

32. In this, my argument extends my treatment of chaste female-female desire in *The Renaissance of Lesbianism* and has something in common with Anna Clark, "Twilight Moments."

33. Foucault, *The History of Sexuality*, 57. Increasingly scholarship suggests the extent to which the Western/non-Western divide in Foucault is overdrawn, particularly for cultures such as India and the Middle East, which had their own highly elaborated sexual taxonomies. For further consideration of the adequacy of Foucault's conceptualization of the *ars erotica*, see Traub, "'The Past Is a Foreign Country?'"

34. Toulalan, *Imagining Sex*, 1. Toulalan provides a helpful overview to this notoriously difficult genre, including how others have attempted to separate it from erotica, define its readership, and assess its relative transgressive libertinage or didactic moralism (35–36). While arguing a debt to earlier Italian publications, most scholarship on English pornography begins its narrative during or after the civil wars, when, in the context of an enlarging public sphere, increased access to printing, and libertinism, publications increased in explicitness; see James Grantham Turner, *Libertines and Radicals*; Mowry, *The Bawdy Politic*; Weil, "Sometimes a Scepter Is Only a Scepter." Persuasively countering this trend, Toulalan argues for a broader definition of the pornographic that attempts to bypass tendentious binaries such as high and low genres, obscenity and literature, pornography and medical writing, by recognizing its generic hybridity (including advice literature, drinking songs, rogue narratives, and political pamphlets). Moulton, *Before Pornography* and "Erotic Representation," also emphasizes the presence of earlier English erotic writing.

35. As Cryle has argued, the early modern Italian and French "classical" erotic texts that so influenced later contributions to the form "are characterized by the *mise en abyme* of instruction. While fulfilling for readers the broad didactic function of listing and transmitting the standard figures of eroticism, they regularly dramatize the teaching of these figures to young pupils" (*Geometry in the Boudoir*, 71). On pornography's thematization of erotic instruction, see also James Grantham Turner, *Schooling Sex*, who analyzes the "educational fantasy in sexual writing" (10); and Kraakman, "Reading Pornography Anew."

36. On Aretino, see Talvacchia, *Taking Positions*. On Aretino's influence on Nashe, see Moulton, *Before Pornography*; and Traub, *The Renaissance of Lesbianism*, 96–103.

37. Norbrook and Wouduysen, ed., *The Penguin Book of Renaissance Verse*, 258–59.

38. DeJean, *The Reinvention of Obscenity*, details the French context. Contesting the view that John Cleland's novel teaches its readers how to read eroticism and how to masturbate, Jagose argues that "the instructional aim of *Memoirs of a Woman of Pleasure* is to give voice to an emergent sexual ideology, the force of which depends precisely on literalizing the body and its pleasures" ("Critical Extasy," 463). But this recognition of the uneven force of sexual ideology does not obviate the fact that much pornography from the sixteenth through the eighteenth centuries purports to serve pedagogy.

39. Unlike most scholars of pornography, I am not interested in assessing the didactic, moral, or political intent of these texts, which, it seems to me, are far more variable than scholars argue.

40. This gendered position is inverted as time goes on: "a tradition of erotic literature shows women having first had the power to know and teach the art of pleasure, then having gradually lost that power. Classical erotic literature . . . represents a kind of hazardous transfer: the laborious and perhaps incomplete shift of erotic authority from women to men" (Cryle, *Geometry in the Boudoir*, 31). Cryle notes that the classical form of the *ars erotica* is binary: "from innocence to knowledge, from childhood to adulthood, there appears to be only one giant step, to be taken always as a kind of initiation" (*Geometry*, 71).

41. Gowing, *Common Bodies*, 84. Gowing emphasizes that women's bodies were a source of self-knowledge, the means for a common understanding, *and* a source of uncertainty. Patricia Crawford, "Sexual Knowledge in England," argues that there existed separate male and female domains of sexual knowledge, constituted partially by different levels of literacy, as well as by the unofficial knowledge circulating within female culture.

42. Gowing, *Common Bodies*, 70.

43. Gowing, *Common Bodies*, 84.

44. Roy Porter, "The Literature of Sexual Advice."

45. See Bray, *Homosexuality in Renaissance England* and *The Friend*; Masten, *Textual Intercourse*; DiGangi, *The Homoerotics of Early Modern Drama*; Julie Crawford, "The Homoerotics of Shakespeare's Elizabethan Comedies."

46. To my knowledge, only one study has raised, as an explicit question, whether sexuality might have played a constitutive role, performing as an effective agent, in larger social relations: Lanser, *The Sexuality of History*.

47. See Irvine, *Talk About Sex*; Levine, *Harmful to Minors*. For more on "sex ed," see Chapter 10.

48. Jowitt remarks, for example, that the "sex-starved and still virgin" Martha "meanders through scenes making embarrassing, misdirected sexual remarks as she tries to discover the secrets of married love" (*Voyage Drama and Gender Politics*, 218).

49. Poovey, "[International Prohibition Against] Sex in America," 381.

50. Warner, *The Trouble with Normal*, 182.

51. Warner, *The Trouble with Normal*, 171.

52. Warner, *The Trouble with Normal*, 184.

53. Warner, *The Trouble with Normal*, 192; Delany, *Times Square Red*.

54. Warner, *The Trouble with Normal*, 139. See also Edelman, *Homographesis*, 148–70; Castiglia, "Sex Panics, Sex Publics"; Colter, *Policing Public Sex*.

55. Warner, *The Trouble with Normal*, 178. It could be argued that Warner collapses the mode of erotic production (sex acts) with their mode of circulation (teaching, ethics); however, that slippage is precisely what is provocative in his account. See also Harper, *Private Affairs*, who attempts to disrupt the clear conceptual boundaries between public and private that legislate sexual life by focusing on the conditions of visibility and modes of negotiation apparent in spaces of sexual encounter.

56. Sedgwick, *Epistemology of the Closet*, 22.

57. Warner, *The Trouble with Normal*, 180.

58. In the words of Warner, *The Trouble with Normal*, 178: "A public sexual culture changes the nature of sex, much as a public intellectual culture changes the nature of thought." See also Warner's reflections on the meanings of public sex in "Queer World Making."

59. The term is from Dollimore, *Sexual Dissidence.*

60. See Irvine, *Talk About Sex*; Levine, *Harmful to Minors.*

61. See Vogler, "Sex and Talk," who counters the pop-psych and philosophical equation of sex and conversation by linking sex and sex talk "non-expressively."

62. I disagree with Kincaid, "It's Not About Sex," when he says, "Sex exists where we can find ways to talk about having sex. Where we can't do that, there is no sex" (73). If this were true, there would have been no *ars erotica*, its independence from discourse precisely Foucault's point.

63. Gallop, *Anecdotal Theory*, 44–47.

64. Gallop, *Anecdotal Theory*, 55.

65. Gallop, *Anecdotal Theory*, 55.

66. Gallop, *Anecdotal Theory*, 54. "Consensual amorous relations are included in my university's sexual harassment policy. Thus, although I had sexually harassed no one, I was nominally in violation of sexual harassment policy. The 'consensual amorous relation' in question was neither a sexual relation nor even a romantic, dating one; it was a teaching relation where both parties were interested in writing and talking about the erotic dynamics underpinning the student-teacher relation" (53). It is out of concern that "an entire stretch of experience [feminist academics' sexual relations with their teachers] was being denied, consigned to silence" that Gallop crosses a "discursive line in order to bring into theoretical discourse what is whispered in the social spaces of institutional life" (163). For a similar critique of policies that bar consensual sexual relations between students and faculty, see Jafar, "Consent or Coercion?"

67. When it conflates speech with trauma, the discourse of "trigger warnings" in college classrooms is a recent instance of this problem; see 7 Humanities Professors, "Trigger Warnings Are Flawed"; Saketopoulou, "Trauma Lives Us."

68. On the complex erotics of queer pedagogy, see Halperin, "Deviant Teaching"; Hanson, "Teaching Shame"; and Lord, "Minor Eruptions."

69. As Edelman, *Homographesis*, and Jagose, *Inconsequence*, have argued, so embedded is the figure of "the homosexual" in symbolic systems of illegibility that simply taking recourse in visibility will not solve the problem of homosexual representation.

70. For how this does and does not link up with empirical inquiry, see Chapters 6 and 7.

71. The dependence of the hetero on the homo has been given influential theoretical expression by Judith Butler, *Bodies That Matter*. Historical studies that make an effort to demonstrate the historical imbrication of the hetero and the homo include Mendelson and Crawford, *Women in Early Modern England*; Crawford and Gowing, *Women's Worlds in Seventeenth-Century England*; Hitchcock, *English Sexualities*; Trumbach, *Heterosexuality and the Third Gender*; Traub, *The Renaissance of Lesbianism.*

72. Sedgwick, *Epistemology of the Closet*, 59.

73. Many queer scholars have relied on Sedgwick's work to authorize a separation of sexuality from gender studies and, increasingly, to enact skepticism regarding the applicability of feminist to gay male studies and vice versa. See Halley, *Split Decisions*; and Rambuss, review of *A House in Gross Disorder*. As the following chapters will suggest, recognizing the potential utility of cross-gender identification as an analytical method might help us move beyond accusations of inattention and exclusion and toward more productive modes of engagement across gender. For a more detailed articulation of the ways in which cross-identification affects gay/lesbian/queer scholarship, see the introduction to Halperin and Traub, *Gay Shame.*

74. See Lochrie's advocacy of "a hermeneutic of epistemological uncertainty regarding contemporary heterosexuality," in *Heterosyncrasies*, xvii; Jagose's argument that orgasm is neither

an act nor an identity in "'Critical Extasy'"; Crimp's reminder that the gay community invented safe sex practices (memorably encapsulated in his assertion that "it is our promiscuity that will save us") in *Melancholia and Moralism*, 64; Kipnis's theorization of adultery as resistance to the labor of monogamy in *Against Love*; and Delany's advocacy of institutions for public heterosexual sex controlled by women, in *Times Square Red*, 197.

75. Coviello, *Tomorrow's Parties*, 203.

CHAPTER 6. SEX IN THE INTERDISCIPLINES

1. Beckett, *The Unnamable*, 179.
2. Wiegman, *Object Lessons*.
3. The absence of feminism in this heuristic will not go unnoticed. While feminist literary critics, queer theorists, and historians play a central role in what follows, their defining terms of analysis—gender, agency, male dominance—are not the main terms in question in this chapter.
4. Maza, "Stephen Greenblatt," 265.
5. Doan, *Disturbing Practices*, 33.
6. How we theorize the relations between the past and the present and develop methods salient to those relations is relevant to those who are theorizing the spatial relations between different geographical locales. Says Boone, writing about sexual exchanges across East and West: "How can scholars excavating the history of sexuality responsibly put into words those 'desires' that they feel they 'hear' in past eras or in cultures different from their own, when such expressions only reach them as echoes, as ghosts, as translations, traversing time and space?" (*The Homoerotics of Orientalism*, xx).
7. Herrup, "Finding the Bodies."
8. Huffer, *Mad for Foucault*, 197.
9. See the critical debates described in Neill's Oxford edition of *Othello*, 136–37, debates that sparked the interest not only of critics interested in the temporality of the plot and stage time, but Cavell, *Disowning Knowledge*. With sex's status as a realized "act" continuously debated, the broken syntax of the play's treatment of sex fades to the background. The play stages the tragic "end" of this couple's "love," its apotheosis as murder and suicide, but only by way of murky beginnings and an absent middle. Shakespeare offers up "sex" only in the form of retrospective and competing stories. Othello, Desdemona, Roderigo, Iago, and Brabantio each have their own stories about how the erotic attraction began. The consummation, so devoutly wished for by countless critics, is never affirmed. Instead, there is only the nightgown and the sheets of the wedding bed, tragically loaded, bloodied not with the supposed evidence of virginity, but with the blood of Othello atop Desdemona's corpse and, depending on the staging, Iago and Emilia as well. If, as Neill notes, "the question of consummation remains fundamentally undecidable; and that surely is the point" (137), the discussion during the 2011 Shakespeare Association of America seminar convened by Lena Cowen Orlin suggests the degree to which that point is one with which many critics remain uncomfortable.
10. In *Desire*, Anna Clark uses "desire" as a way to organize a history of sexuality that is not confined to the binary of acts versus identities. The concept of desire, as Puff notes, "has spawned many a conversation across temporal and geographic specializations" ("After the History," 23). Nonetheless, Puff sees the ubiquity and "infinite plasticity" of desire as something that should be "up for critical examination" (23, 22).

11. As LaCapra, *History and Its Limits*, 54, put it: "The point here is not to deny the role of aporia or paradox but to seek ways of negotiating double binds without simply postulating and endlessly reiterating their terminal or interminable nature."

12. Traub, *The Renaissance of Lesbianism*, 354.

13. Dinshaw, *Getting Medieval*.

14. Freccero, *Queer/Early/Modern*.

15. Freeman, *Time Binds*. Freeman calls "erotohistoriography" "a historiographic method that would admit the flesh, that would avow that history is written on and felt with the body" ("Introduction," 164).

16. Dinshaw, *How Soon Is Now?*

17. Huffer, *Mad for Foucault*, 197, *Are the Lips a Grave?* 46. Dinshaw, *Getting Medieval*, 136–42, and Nealon, *Foundlings*, 22–23, invoke the same moment in Foucault's work. See also Love, *Feeling Backward*, 46–52.

18. Farina, "Lesbian History and Erotic Reading," 55.

19. Dinshaw, *How Soon Is Now?* 4.

20. For "structures of feeling," see Raymond Williams, *Marxism and Literature*.

21. See Giffney and O'Rourke, "Series Editors' Preface," which applauds the volume editors' invitation to the reader to partake in an "erotics of reading" (ix). Giffney, Sauer, and Watt, *The Lesbian Premodern*, also invoke "the 'touch' of the lesbian across time and space" (10). See also Vicinus's observation in "Lesbian Ghosts" that many of the contributors "seek an affective relationship with the past" (195).

22. Coviello, *Tomorrow's Parties*, 203.

23. Scott, *The Fantasy of Feminist History*, 147.

24. Wiegman, "Afterword," 208.

25. Dinshaw, *How Soon Is Now?* 6.

26. Love, *Feeling Backward*, 24.

27. Freccero, *Queer/Early/Modern*, 101.

28. In *Feeling Backward*, Love names a more expansive group of what she calls "affect historians," which includes Dinshaw, Freccero, Freeman, Halperin, and Traub. My chapter, "The Quest for Origins, Erotic Similitude, and the Melancholy of Lesbian Identification," in *The Renaissance of Lesbianism*, 326–61, explored lesbian critics' experiences of identification and disidentification in an attempt to adduce the past's alterity. Love views my reading of this dynamic in terms of melancholia and mourning as necessarily jettisoning negative affects; I would maintain that negative affects are a necessary part of the "working through" of mourning.

29. My phrasing here is ironic. Several of the critics cited above allude to Derrida, *Archive Fever*, and/or *Specters of Marx*. As these critics recognize, Derrida critiques the fever for the archive, seeing in it an investment in originary meaning.

30. For a similarly skeptical view, see Radel's review of *Queer Renaissance Historiography*.

31. Dinshaw, *How Soon Is Now?* 39, 104.

32. Dinshaw, *How Soon Is Now?* 32.

33. Dinshaw qualifies her claims on behalf of asynchrony as not "inherently positive" (*How Soon Is Now?* 34).

34. Those critics focused on negative affects are particularly cognizant of affective resistance, and Love, in *Feeling Backward*, seems explicitly motivated by this question.

35. Jameson, *The Political Unconscious*, 82. Jameson refers to Samuel Johnson's refutation of Bishop Berkeley, as narrated by Boswell's *Life of Johnson*: "After we came out of the church,

we stood talking for some time together of Bishop Berkeley's ingenious sophistry to prove the nonexistence of matter, and that every thing in the universe is merely ideal. I observed, that though we are satisfied his doctrine is not true, it is impossible to refute it. I never shall forget the alacrity with which Johnson answered, striking his foot with mighty force against a large stone, till he rebounded from it, 'I refute it *thus* ' " (333).

36. I thus disagree with Doan, *Disturbing Practices*, when she asserts that "*the past does not exist* until conjured into existence in the making of history" (xii) and that "*there is no past* we do not already construct in the present" (85), emphases mine. Quoting Joan Scott, Doan writes that "it is a central paradox of all history that it is always engaged in 'creating the objects it claims only to discover' " (*Disturbing Practices*, 65). Although she qualifies this view by saying that "this does not mean history is a matter of pure invention" (65), the emphasis throughout her exposition is on the scholar's creation of history.

37. Traub, *The Renaissance of Lesbianism*, 354, emphasis added.

38. A similar point is made by Love, *Feeling Backward*, and seems to be part of what is at stake in Freccero's conferral of subjectivity onto ghosts in *Queer/Early/Modern*, 101.

39. An alteritist position continues to enable new questions; see Masten's discussion in *Queer Philologies* on "the *textures* of alterity" and Simons's insistence in *The Sex of Men* on how understanding humoralism affects paradigms of male sexuality.

40. I agree with Kathryn Bond Stockton in *The Queer Child* when she notes that history "surprises, luminesces" (10). In a discussion of the fact that no one can " 'go back' to texts, historical or fictional, so as to think their meanings in their own time" (9), she articulates a strategy, in certain respects aligned with those of the archival *ars erotica*, to "make my history the history of my reading a series of fictions, which I arrange" (10). However, she qualifies this endeavor: "I find it too easy and imprecise to say that I saw what I wanted to see in the fictions I read for this book. The thing I would now call 'what I wanted'—that I would now say shaped my reading—has been shaped in part by what I started seeing, part of which I didn't see coming at all" (10).

41. The weight given at any moment to difference and sameness is heavily freighted with assumed interpretative stances regarding history. Although I have often been described as an "alteritist," upon the publication of Chapter 4's argument about "cycles of salience," I have been read as privileging similarity.

42. Freccero, "Figural Historiography"; Love, *Feeling Backward*.

43. Margaret Ferguson, "Hymeneal Instruction," 108.

44. Hammill, review of *Shakesqueer*.

45. Early modern historians have been particularly concerned to identify rates of prostitution, rape, masturbation, sodomy, bastardy, and bestiality, and to debate the various reasons for their rise and fall. See Trumbach, *Heterosexuality and the Third Gender*; Adair, *Courtship, Illegitimacy and Marriage*; Laqueur, *Solitary Sex*; and the discussion of bestiality below.

46. Anthony Fletcher, *Gender, Sex, and Subordination*.

47. Foyster, *Manhood in Early Modern England*; Gowing, *Domestic Dangers*.

48. Cressy, *Birth, Marriage, and Death*; O'Hara, *Courtship and Constraint*.

49. Cressy, *Birth, Marriage, and Death*, 277–78; Griffiths, *Youth and Authority*; Ingram, *Church Courts, Sex and Marriage*. See, however, Mendelson and Crawford, who qualify that "there was in fact a wide spectrum of opinion on the question of sexual relations between espoused couples; we can chart substantial variations not only by age and social rank, but also by geographical region. Parents, the elite, women, and inhabitants of lowland regions generally

insisted that sexual relations were taboo before marriage" (*Women in Early Modern England*, 120).

50. Froide, *Never Married*, 2. Other scholars put the average slightly earlier—twenty-three to twenty-five for women and twenty-five to twenty-seven for men—but agree that most did not marry until they had completed their apprenticeships.

51. According to Cressy, *Birth, Marriage, and Death*, some 20 percent of marriages were bridal pregnancies; Ingram, *Church Courts, Sex and Marriage*, puts the rate as high as 30 percent. See also Ingram, "Courtship and Marriage." On bastardy, adultery, and marital dissolution, see Cressy, *Birth, Marriage, and Death*; Adair, *Courtship, Illegitimacy and Marriage*; and O'Hara, *Courtship and Constraint*.

52. For analysis of female erotic pleasure, see Traub, *The Renaissance of Lesbianism*, chapters 2 and 3. For an overview of medical discourse, popular ideas about sexual health, and how women's pleasure was conceived as uterine and fluid rather than clitoral or orgasmic, see Simons, *The Sex of Men*, chapters 4 and 6.

53. For overviews of relevant medical writings, see Traub, *The Renaissance of Lesbianism* and Cadden, *Meanings of Sex Difference*. In *The Sex of Men*, Simons demonstrates the extent to which semen, testicles, and masculine heat were constitutive of understandings of men's sex.

54. On the impact of Protestantism, see Wiesner-Hanks, *Christianity and Sexuality*. For scholarship on companionate marriage and domestic heterosexuality, see Traub, *The Renaissance of Lesbianism*, chapter 6.

55. Fisher, *Materializing Gender*, 69–74; Simons, *The Sex of Men*.

56. O'Hara, *Courtship and Constraint*.

57. Froide, *Never Married*, 2. Froide's demographic study of Southampton in 1696 found that "wives actually comprised a minority of adult women," while women who never married "made up one-third of the townswomen" (2–3). In another study of one hundred English communities (1574–1821), "singlewomen comprised on average 30.2 per cent of the adult female population" (3). She concludes that "at least one-third of urban women were single in the early modern era" (3). See also Bennett and Froide, *Singlewomen in the European Past*.

58. Bray, *The Friend*; Froide, *Never Married*; Masten, *Queer Philologies*; Lanser, *The Sexuality of History*.

59. David M. Turner, *Fashioning Adultery*; Ingram, "Courtship and Marriage." Such changes include a decrease in community-based shaming rituals, a shift from regulating adultery to prosecuting prostitution, and a general decline in the business of the church courts.

60. Gowing, *Domestic Dangers* and *Common Bodies*; Capp, "The Double Standard Revisited."

61. Bray, *Homosexuality in Renaissance England*; Goldberg, *Sodometries*; DiGangi, *The Homoerotics of Early Modern Drama*.

62. Gowing, *Common Bodies*; Bennett, "'Lesbian-Like'"; Traub, *The Renaissance of Lesbianism*; Crawford and Mendelson, "Sexual Identities in Early Modern England"; see also Chapter 4.

63. Lanser, *The Sexuality of History*.

64. Julie Crawford, "The Homoerotics of Shakespeare's Elizabethan Comedies" and "Shakespeare. Same Sex. Marriage."

65. Gowing, "'The Freedom of the Streets.'"

66. Archer, *The Pursuit of Stability*; Griffiths, "The Structure of Prostitution"; Dabhoiwala, "The Pattern of Sexual Immorality"; Ungerer, "Prostitution in Late Elizabethan London"; Panek, "'This Base Stallion Trade.'" The London molly house seems to have arisen only in

the very late seventeenth century and disappeared in the 1730s; see O'Driscoll, "The Molly and the Fop."

67. See Chapter 5.

68. Roy Porter, "The Literature of Sexual Advice."

69. Laqueur, *Making Sex*; Park, "The Rediscovery of the Clitoris"; Borris and Rousseau, *The Sciences of Homosexuality*; Traub, *The Renaissance of Lesbianism*, chapters 2 and 5.

70. Traub, *The Renaissance of Lesbianism*, chapter 1.

71. Most scholars who have investigated early modern cases of bestiality stress that while rhetoric condemning buggery was impassioned and frequently published, the numbers of actual prosecutions are small, and the number of convictions even smaller. With the exception of two indictments brought against women in the late seventeenth century, all the cases involve men penetrating animals. For an overview that assumes the truth-value of her sources, see Courtney Thomas, "'Not Having God Before His Eyes.'" For the reigns of Elizabeth and James, see Boehrer, "Bestial Buggery," who argues that "the rhetoric of bestiality was in some basic ways more important than the crime itself" (132). Smith, *Phenomenal Shakespeare*, 121, however, stresses that during Elizabeth's reign, bestiality yielded indictments that far outnumbered those for male-male sodomy (four for sodomy; thirty for buggery with animals) and yielded a higher conviction rate.

72. Gowing, *Common Bodies*; Walker, *Crime, Gender, and Social Order*.

73. Not all of this violence tended in one direction. See Dolan, *Marriage and Violence*, "Household Chastisements," and *Dangerous Familiars*. For coercion within female same-sex relations, see Bruster, "Female-Female Eroticism"; Walen, *Constructions of Female Homoeroticism*.

74. The bibliography is now vast, but for starters, see Hall, "'Those Bastard Signs of Fair'"; Loomba, *Shakespeare, Race, and Colonialism*; Dolan, *Whores of Babylon*; Masten, *Queer Philologies*, chapter 8.

75. This problem is addressed by Hitchcock, "The Reformulation of Sexual Knowledge," who begins his essay: "Any attempt to create a coherent history of sexuality in eighteenth-century England is faced with an apparently irresolvable conundrum. Many of the historiographical elements needed to create such a history directly contradict one another or, at best, define their subject in ways that apparently prevent the conclusions drawn from one sort of history from being compared with those drawn from another" (823).

76. We might take E. P. Thompson's credo in "Anthropology and the Discipline of Historical Context" as a baseline: "The discipline of history is, above all, the discipline of context; each fact can be given meaning only within an ensemble of other meanings" (45). Yet, as LaCapra argues, "contextualization, archival research, and translating archives into narratives are mainstays—indeed, the three pillars—of conventional history at the present time. . . . But they call for continual rethinking that itself requires an inquiry into assumptions and modes of conceptualization implying a nexus between history . . . and critical theory" (*History and Its Limits*, 36).

77. Binhammer, "Accounting for the Unaccountable," 1.

78. Garrett, "Witchcraft and Sexual Knowledge," 33.

79. With the exception of language, witchcraft, the theater, and politics, each of these topics is addressed in previous notes. For language, see Chapter 7. For the imbrication of sex in witchcraft accusations in western Europe, many of them brought by women against women, see Roper, *Oedipus and the Devil* and *Witch Craze*. For the importance of sex with demons in witchcraft treatises, see Stephens, *Demon Lovers*, 26, which argues that sexual intercourse with

devils was construed as "a form of knowledge gathering"; theologians' interest in sexual acts with demons was propelled by their desire to render material the belief in demons that they otherwise found unbelievable. See also Wiesner-Hanks, *Christianity and Sexuality*. English witchcraft discourse was less interested in female sexual transgression than was its continental counterpart; see Willis, *Malevolent Nurture*. Nonetheless, Garrett, "Witchcraft and Sexual Knowledge," argues that English "witchcraft discourse occupies a vital place within the history of sexuality" (32), noting that "witchcraft discourse creates a permissive context for the investigation of bodies and sexual behaviors" (56); furthermore, "witch trials are a point of convergence for all those domains of knowledge—the law, Christian doctrine, reproductive practice, and medical literature—that collectively describe what one could know about sexual anatomy and conduct in the early modern period" (35). For the imbrication of sex and the theater, see Lenz, "Base Trade"; Singh, "The Interventions of History"; Howard, *The Stage and Social Struggle* and *Theater of a City*; Maus, "Horns of Dilemma"; DiGangi, *Sexual Types*, 159–91. For sex and politics, see Mowry, *The Bawdy Politic*; Bellany, *The Politics of Court Scandal*; Harris, *Foreign Bodies and the Body Politic*.

80. Introductions to sourcebooks as well as surveys of the history of sexuality bear this out. For sourcebooks, see Anna Clark, *The History of Sexuality in Europe*; Borris, *Same-Sex Desire in the English Renaissance*; Mudge, *When Flesh Becomes Word*; Merrick and Ragan, *Homosexuality in Early Modern France*. For surveys, see Anna Clark, *Desire*; Phillips and Reay, *Sex Before Sexuality*; Katherine Crawford, *The Sexual Culture of the French Renaissance*; Hitchcock, *English Sexualities*.

81. DiGangi, *Sexual Types*, 7.

82. Dabhoiwala, *The Origins of Sex*, 3. Despite this declaration, Dabhoiwala seems most interested in sexual attitudes rather than how sex actually affected early modern social relations.

83. This view occurs across the history of sexuality, as evinced by the following statements: Sharon Marcus, *Between Women*: "We can best understand what kinds of relationships women had with each other not by hunting for evidence of sex, which even if we find it will not explain much, but rather by anchoring women's own statements about their relationships in a larger context" (44); Katherine Crawford, *The Sexual Culture of the French Renaissance*, who describes her project as "not just a story about what people long ago and far away thought about sex. It is about cultural processes through which subjects . . . constituted themselves in relation to power, configured and understood as potency, sexual desire, and control over bodies" (22); Karen Harvey, *The Kiss in History*, who maintains of her anthology that "the act [of kissing] is not quite the central point of focus. The interest here is not in how people kissed . . . but in what representations of the kiss were 'about' and what they enabled contemporaries to articulate" (5).

84. For a related argument, see Friedlander, "Promiscuous Generation."

85. Dipiero and Gill, *Illicit Sex*; Hammond, *Figuring Sex Between Men*; Rickman, *Love, Lust, and License*; Toulalan, *Imagining Sex*; Katherine Crawford, *The Sexual Culture of the French Renaissance*; Levy, *Sex Acts in Early Modern Italy*.

86. Maus, *Inwardness and Theater*, 131 n. 1.

87. Maus, *Inwardness and Theater*, 169.

88. Varnado, "'Invisible Sex!'" 31.

89. Varnado, "'Invisible Sex!'" 32.

90. Ferguson, "Hymeneal Instruction," 97, 109. Focused on masculinity and civility, Ferguson argues that "through the discourses of hymeneal instruction . . . early modern English writers explore the idea that deferring carnal knowledge is a wise course of action for the new

husband, whose propensity toward violence as a means toward fulfilling his desires is frequently presumed to exist and to require an educational regime construed as one of checking or limiting masculine 'nature'—but doing so without rendering him effeminate or impotent" (110).

91. Ferguson, "Hymeneal Instruction," 112. Sinfield, *Shakespeare, Authority, Sexuality*, and Orgel, *Impersonations*, have also resisted the ideology of comic heterosexual closure.

92. See Masten's consideration of "conversation" and "intercourse" in *Queer Philologies*.

93. Poovey, "[International Prohibition Against] Sex in America," 386. Poovey describes this "sociological" view as reducing "sexuality to sex acts," thereby denuding sex of its social and psychic meanings (390).

94. The concept of a "sex act" is itself a modern formation; see Cryle, *The Telling of the Act*.

95. Whether this would mandate putting the ontology of "the act" under erasure is a question to be asked. Helpful in this regard are the insights regarding the complexity of embodiment in disability theory; see Siebers, "A Sexual Culture for Disabled People" and "Sex, Shame, and Disability Identity."

96. My language here echoes that of Rudolph Bell's *How to Do It: Guides to Good Living for Renaissance Italians*, which, despite the sexy title, is largely unconcerned with sexual practices.

97. Bromley, "'Let it Suffise,'" 67. See also Saunders, *Desiring Donne*, 119.

98. Herrup, "Finding the Bodies," 257.

99. Herrup, *A House in Gross Disorder*. Scandalized by Castlehaven's actions as they may have been, the peers condemned him to the scaffold not because of sodomy, but because he failed to uphold the patriarchal duties of a landed aristocrat who is responsible for the sexual order of his household.

100. Herrup, *A House in Gross Disorder*, 6, xvi.

101. On masturbation, see Traub, *The Renaissance of Lesbianism*, chapter 2; and Simons, *The Sex of Men*, 164, 236.

102. Building on Keith Thomas's identification of the Renaissance as the moment when kissing "lost much of its ritual importance and bec[a]me instead a bearer of emotional and sexual meaning" ("Afterword," 191), Fisher, "'Loves Wealthy Croppe of Kisses,'" analyzes how this shift occurred, focusing on the role of passionate kissing in providing "ideological traction" to the emerging model of companionate marriage and romantic love. Central to this erotic reciprocity is tongue kissing, detailed directions for which are given in pornographic texts.

103. Lanser, *The Sexuality of History*; Traub, *The Renaissance of Lesbianism*; Toulalan, *Imagining Sex*, chapter 4.

104. Toulalan, *Imagining Sex*, 83–88; 154–58; Daileader, "Back Door Sex"; Will Stockton, *Playing Dirty*. For one woman's murderous response to forced anal sex, see Dolan, *Marriage and Violence*, 89–96.

105. Oral sex has seemed to historians to be especially obscure. Following the lead of Lawrence Stone, who attributed the relative absence of such representations to lax practices of hygiene (*The Family, Sex, and Marriage in England*, 266), other scholars routinely allude to the lack of references to oral-genital contact. Regarding pornography, see Toulalan, *Imagining Sex*, 225; Moulton, *La Cazzaria*, 49; James Grantham Turner, *Schooling Sex*, 300. Toulalan, however, reproduces three engravings from a Latin edition of *The Dialogues of Luisa Siega* (ca. 1690) that depict oral sex, including fellatio (*Imagining Sex*, 226, 238, 239). Hitchcock, *English Sexualities*, 123 n. 27, notes: "Except in the context of trial reports relating to sodomy I have been unable to locate any creditable accounts of oral sex in the eighteenth century." But, Fisher, "'Stray[ing] Lower,'" reveals references to cunnilingus in a wide array of sources, demonstrating not only

the intelligibility of male-female cunnilingus from the sixteenth century on, but the mistake in thinking that the practice was universally condemned. Although there is ample evidence in court records of women fondling male genitals, the evidence of cross-sex fellatio is mainly literary. A quick dialogue between a citizen and his wife in John Fletcher's *The Island Princess* (1621) as a fire rages across the town includes the husband's cry, "O me neighbors there's a fire in my codpiece." His wife responds, "Blesse my husband," to which he replies "Blow it out wife" (2.2). This joke gains comedic intensity if the audience is cognizant of "blowing" on genitals as a possible erotic taste. In John Lyly's *Midas* (1589), an eroticized comic riff between two pages about their mistress's "disposition" includes a pun on "tennis balls" suggestive of fellatio: "Licio: First, she hath a head as round as a tennis ball. Petulus: I would my bed were a hazard. Licio: Why? Petulus: Nothing, but that I would have her head there among the other balls"; see Lancashire, *Gallathea and Midas* (1.2.29–31). See also the innuendo involved in *A Midsummer Night's Dream* in Flute/Thisbe's declaration to "Wall" that "My cherry lips have often kissed thy stones" (5.1.188), and Hamlet's offer to Ophelia "to lay my head in your lappe" in the first quarto, sig. F3r. O'Driscoll, "The Molly and the Fop," 152, quotes the pamphlet "Mundus Foppensis" (1691), which elevates cross-sex ass kissing over male-male fellatio: "For who that loves as Nature teaches, / That had not rather kiss the Breeches / Of Twenty Women, than to lick / The Bristles of one Male dear Dick" (152).

106. Toulalan, *Imagining Sex*, 81. Intriguing references to what may refer to manual caressing or penetration occur in Dekker and Middleton's *The Patient Man and the Honest Whore* (ed. Mulholland, in Taylor and Lavagnino, *Thomas Middleton*, 285–327), in Fustigo's comment to the Porter, "if ever I stand in need of a wench that will come with a wet finger" (1.2.4–5); and in *Arden of Faversham*, ed. White, when Black Will asks, "Didst thou ever see better weather to run away with another man's wife or play with a wench at potfinger?" (scene 12, lines 7–8); White glosses this line as "obvious sexual allusion" (77). See the entry for "lick," in Gordon Williams, *A Dictionary of Sexual Language and Imagery*, 2:807.

107. Toulalan, *Imagining Sex*, 82–83.

108. Fisher, "Wantoning with the Thighs."

109. Fisher, "The Erotics of Chin Chucking."

110. Fisher, "'The Use of Flogging'"; Enterline, "Rhetoric, Discipline"; Largier, *In Praise of the Whip*; Toulalan, *Imagining Sex*, chapter 3.

111. Simons, *The Sex of Men*, 214–18; Traub, *The Renaissance of Lesbianism*, chapters 2 and 5; Fisher, "'Doctor Dildos Dauncing Schoole.'"

112. Bromley, "Rimming the Renaissance."

113. Paster, *The Body Embarrassed*; Saunders, "Iago's Clyster"; Wall, *Staging Domesticity*.

114. "Keyhole sex" is a widespread trope in pornography and legal testimony; see Toulalan, *Imagining Sex*; Dolan, *True Relations*; Ingram, "Sexual Manners."

115. Toulalan, *Imagining Sex*.

116. A. Lynn Martin, *Alcohol, Sex, and Gender*; Capp, "Gender and the Culture of the English Alehouse"; Hailwood, *Alehouses and Good Fellowship*.

117. Hitchcock, *English Sexualities*, chapter 2.

118. Johnston, "'To What Bawdy House Doth Your Maister Belong?'"

119. Attending the public theater was an experience imbued with erotic potential, not only because the theaters were located near brothels and frequented by prostitutes, but because many stage plays depend heavily upon sexualized language and gesture, and some of the repertory catered specifically to men's interest in the bodies of men and boys. See Chapter 7.

120. Gowing, "'The Freedom of the Streets.'"

121. Bly, "Carnal Geographies." For changes in the meanings of London public space as pertains to sexual behavior from the seventeenth to the eighteenth century, see O'Driscoll, "Conjugal Capitalism."

122. In addition to these early modern studies, cultural and intellectual histories of sexual practices such as flagellation, frigidity, orgasm, masturbation, impotence, and celibacy have been subject to analyses that sometimes gesture toward the prehistory of modern erotic systems. See Largier, *In Praise of the Whip*; Cryle and Moore, *Frigidity*; McLaren, *Impotence*; Jagose, "Critical Extasy"; Laqueur, *Solitary Sex*; Kahan, *Celibacies*.

123. Abelove, "Some Speculations." Abelove was critiqued by McKeon, "Historicizing Patriarchy," 319, for extrapolating data regarding frequency of intercourse from length of marriage and for conflating the incidence and popularity of intercourse.

124. Hitchcock, *English Sexualities*, 41. In "Redefining Sex," Hitchcock argues that "sex changed. At the beginning of the [eighteenth] century it was an activity characterized by mutual masturbation, much kissing and fondling, and long hours spent in mutual touching, but very little penal/vaginal penetration—at least before marriage. . . . The important thing is that there was an equality of emphasis on a wide range of different parts of the body" (79). See also Hitchcock, "The Reformulation of Sexual Knowledge."

125. See discussion of the topos of "invention" by Cryle and Moore, *Frigidity*, 12–14. According to Simons, *The Sex of Men*, 198, "the Latin *preludia* [occurs] in Andreas Capellanus' treatise on courtly love from the 1180s."

126. Quaife, *Wanton Wenches*, 5.

127. Gowing, *Common Bodies*, 89.

128. Simons, *The Sex of Men*, 46.

129. Jones, "Heterosexuality," 90, notes of Pepys that "most of his sexual activities took the form of mutual exploration and masturbation, usually in his study, in coaches, and in the back rooms of inns"; David M. Turner, "Adulterous Kisses," 88, notes Pepys's "special delight in recording kisses that he had stolen from Betty while her husband was in close proximity." John Cannon lived from 1684–1743; on his manuscript "Memoirs of the Birth, Education, Life and Death of Mr. John Cannon" (1743), see Hitchcock, *English Sexualities*, 28–38, as well as "Sociability and Misogyny."

130. In *The Renaissance of Lesbianism*, I address the problems involved in any notion of a "golden age" of sex, including the pervasive gender and age inequalities that structure the sexual system. Toulalan, *Imagining Sex*, poses her argument as challenging "previous historiography, which has maintained that sex changed from an early modern 'polymorphous' sexuality in which a wide range of sexual activities were practised (not necessarily including penetrative sex), to a more restrictive sexuality from the eighteenth century onwards in which penetrative sex took primacy of place. . . . The evidence of these seventeenth-century texts does not, however, support this narrative of change, as they emphasise the primacy of penetrative intercourse for the purpose of procreation, linking it with political and economic concerns about inheritance and legitimacy" (32). Toulalan generalizes too quickly from the genre of pornography to broad arguments about early modern sexual practices and tends to backdate the rhetorics of pornography, largely written during or after the civil wars, to the seventeenth century writ large. In addition, while penetration and reproduction are crucial to early modern discourses, they are less determining than she suggests. She argues that seventeenth-century erotic texts "invariably" maintain "that [sexual] pleasure *stems* from a desire to reproduce," and thus they "emphasize the need for penetrative heterosexual sexual intercourse" (64), because "complete

sexual pleasure was understood *to require conception to occur*" (62), emphases mine. Here Toula-lan reverses the causal logic organizing the relation between pleasure and conception in most early modern texts. Her effort to counter scholars' celebration of an early modern "polymor-phous perverse" (66), alongside her overarching thesis that early modern pornography "rein-force[s] contemporary moral strictures" (63), leads her to misread the idealization of mutual orgasm in pornography as a wholesale "privileging of heterosexual penetrative sex over all other varieties of intercourse" (66). She neglects to consider the fondling of the penis as a pleasure in its own right or the possible narcissistic value of male writers extolling the size, strength, and beauty of the penis—instead mapping onto this interest a straightforwardly penetrative and reproductive role. Her tendency to read narratives teleologically rather than in terms of textual contradictions and readerly appropriation leads her to adduce too readily the didactic and morally circumscribing intents and impact of pornographic texts.

131. This survey may seem to imply that the regime of presumptive knowledge regarding early modern sex is over. Yet, given critical predilections, the force of habit, and uneven dissemi-nation of scholarship, the narrative I have proffered is not yet the dominant one in history or literary studies. While some of this research was conducted in the 1980s, it has not had complete uptake; some of this work is still in progress or has been published quite recently.

132. Laqueur, *Making Sex.*

133. Quaife, *Wanton Wenches*, is one example.

134. Bromley, "'Let It Suffise,'" 67.

135. These, of course, are not mutually exclusive: Dolan's historicist strategies are motivated by epistemological canniness, while Jagose's theoretical ambit is deftly historicized.

136. Masten, *Textual Intercourse* and *Queer Philologies*, chapter 2; Haggerty, *Men in Love* and "The History of Homosexuality"; O'Donnell and O'Rourke, *Love, Sex, Intimacy*; Vicinus, *Intimate Friends.*

137. Puff, "After the History," 26. For assessments of the role of the erotic in Bray, see Katherine Crawford, "Privilege, Possibility, and Perversion"; and Gowing, Hunter, and Rubin, *Love, Friendship and Faith.*

138. Sharon Marcus, *Between Women*, 30, argues that "we need distinctions that allow us to chart how different social bonds overlap without becoming identical."

139. There is an uneasy correlation in Bray's work to contemporary discourses that were just on the cusp of emerging at the time he was writing, in which it is only through fidelity to love, intimacy, and companionship that sexual minorities can gain social legitimacy and rights. Some of the political consequences of this congruence between historical scholarship and what queer theorists have called "homonormativity" will be addressed in Chapter 8.

140. Medievalists have perhaps been the most creative in defying these conventions, as they have sought to explore those idioms whose alterity puts into relief the supposedly "modern" preoccupation with genitalia. Lochrie asks: "Could the exchange of love tokens, such as green girdles or gutted boars, be more erotic than kissing? How much does heterosexual sex require prosthetics, such as squeamish clerks at the window and acts of revenge between men, to become erotic? How does the eroticism of mystical sex compare with the eroticism of material sex?" (*Heterosyncracies*, xviii).

141. Helpful in this regard is Jagose, "'Critical Extasy'": Jagose challenges "the persistent critical tendency to read roughshod over literary descriptions of sex acts as if their meanings, values, and significances were always already transparently known—known, that is, to the degree that they are unchangingly always the same" (459). Noting "the overvaluation of story and the undervaluation of sexual description" in treatments of Cleland's *Memoirs of a Woman*

of Pleasure, her reading yields "the conceptual unruliness of eighteenth-century erotic description in which the proper articulation of desire is still available for discursive contestation" (459, 461). Rather than assuming an already formed "heterosexuality," Cleland's narrative "labors to explain and naturalize erotic interest between the sexes," a labor that critics miss because "the syntactic units of its articulation—those sex acts that are widely regarded as incidental to its novelistic form—are retrospectively understood to evidence the existence of the very ideological sexual system they are being marshaled to inaugurate" (461).

142. Scholarly interest in sodomy has not flagged since the 1980s. Since the queer turn, however, literary critics interested in sodomy have begun to place it within a broader spectrum of perverse desires; see DiGangi, *Sexual Types*; Will Stockton, *Playing Dirty*; Bromley, *Intimacy and Sexuality*; Masten, *Queer Philologies*.

143. For relevant scholarship on early modern lesbianism, see Chapter 4.

144. For critiques of my focus on the tribade and the femme, see Toulalan, *Imagining Sex*, chapter 4; and Walen, *Constructions of Female Homoeroticism*.

145. Coke, *Third Part of the Institutes*, 58.

146. In addition to sources noted above, see Maxwell-Stuart, " 'Wild, Filthie, Execrabill' "; Murrin, " 'Things Fearful to Name.' " For primary sources, see McCormick, *Secret Sexualities*. Critics have begun to rethink the issue of animal agency. Focusing on human-animal shared embodiment rather than rationality and resisting the collapse of human-animal erotics into bestiality, Raber, *Animal Bodies*, asks if it is possible for us to consider mutuality in human-animal intersexualities; Dugan, "Aping Rape," reexamines the "pervasive cultural belief in interspecies rape of human females by male apes" in an attempt to reveal "the limits in thinking sex," particularly in terms of its manifestation as violence (213, 214).

147. Whether responding to buggery trials or reading literary tropes, the sexualization of interspecies relations tends to be read as figuring early modern anxiety about humans losing their exceptional status as rational creatures with a privileged interiority. The fact that bestiality was sometimes linked to monstrous births and to witchcraft amplified this fear. For the patristic tradition, the link between bestiality and sodomy, and increasing penalties over time, see Salisbury, *The Beast Within*, 61–80; Fudge, "Monstrous Acts"; Callaghan, "(Un)natural Loving"; Friedlander, "Promiscuous Generation." Some critics have linked this anxiety to emerging forms of racialization; see Little, *Shakespeare Jungle Fever*, chapter 2; and Masten, *Queer Philologies*, chapter 8.

148. Coke, *The Third Part of the Institutes*, 59. Stewart, "Queer Renaissance Bodies?" emphasizes, however, "the intense debate which is to be found in the attempt to define 'buggery' and 'sodomy' in contemporary legal commentaries," including whether the emission of semen, without penetration, was sufficient proof (143). Citing various commentators (including Coke's later argument that both penetration and emission are necessary), Stewart argues that "the nature of buggery was constantly in question during the early modern period, and its implementation as a legal category effectively reliant on the particularities of each individual case" (144).

149. Coke noted in *The Third Part of the Institutes* that "if the party buggered be within the age of discretion [under fourteen], it is no felony in him, but in the agent only" (59).

150. See Howell and Prevenier, *From Reliable Sources*, 149: "Our entire craft is based precisely on the understanding that our knowledge of any event comes to us through sources which we know are *not* perfect reflections of 'reality,' which are constructions of reality, and which have to be decoded in order for us to understand what reality they construct. . . . However, it is true that most historians . . . have thought that a reality lay behind these sources

and that if we read our sources skillfully enough we could arrive at that reality. Today many of us would disagree, arguing that any reality that lay behind the sources is, finally, inaccessible to us, not matter how skilled we are—and that we have to settle for studying the reality that sources construct rather than 'reality' itself."

151. Halperin, *How to Do the History of Homosexuality*, 7.

152. Edelman, *Homographesis*, xiv.

153. Herzog, "Syncopated Sex," 1288.

154. Howell and Prevenier, *From Reliable Sources*, 3.

155. Dolan, *True Relations*, 16.

156. Dolan, *True Relations*, 17, 18. This "shared terrain" is the foundation of the subfield of cultural history, which has been a primary growth area within the discipline of history since the late 1980s. Howell and Prevenier, *From Reliable Sources*, credit the development of its methods "to historians' encounters with cultural theorists in other branches of the humanities and social sciences, especially with literary critics, cultural anthropologists, and cultural sociologists. From them, historians have learned new strategies of reading documents, learned to be more attentive to (and more cautious of) language, learned to interrogate their own position as assemblers of 'facts,' interpreters of 'evidence,' formulators of 'explanations' " (117). For another overview of the practical training of historians that makes clear the extent to which they are concerned with textual mediation and the status of evidence, acceptance of the provisional nature of historical knowledge and the role of interpretation in it, suspicion of periodization even as they rely on it, negotiations of the relationship between truth and objectivity versus reliability and consistency, and the historicity of disciplinarity itself, see Jordanova, *History in Practice*. See also Hutson, "Series Editor's Preface," xi: "No longer are historians naive about textual criticism, about rhetoric, literary theory or about readerships; likewise, literary critics trained in close reading now also turn easily to court archives, to legal texts, and to the historians' debates about the languages of political and religious thought. Social historians look at printed pamphlets with an eye for narrative structure; literary critics look at court records with awareness of the problems of authority, mediation and institutional procedure."

157. Of course, just because they recognize this and also utilize a broad range of kinds of texts does not mean that some historians of sexuality are not still producing teleological narratives, as is clear of McKeon in "Symposium."

158. Montrose, "The Elizabethan Subject."

159. Dolan, *True Relations*, 113.

160. Spiegel, "History, Historicism," 75. To invoke Spiegel in this context is not to endorse her appraisal of deconstruction and post-structuralism as a "dissolution of history" (85); nor is it to confirm her assertion that "the text is an objective given," whereas "the object of historical study must be constituted by the historian" (75). It is worth noting, however, that as early as 1990, Spiegel felt comfortable asserting that "no historian, even of positivist stripe, would argue that history is present to us in any but textual form" (76). Since that time, exceptions and challenges to this generalization have appeared, evident in debates between a post-cultural turn back toward social history and a theory-inflected intellectual history. On the tensions between historians' recourse to "culture" and "the social," see Bonnell and Hunt, "Introduction."

161. Maza, "Stephen Greenblatt," 264.

162. Maza, "Stephen Greenblatt," 265.

163. Other examples include Karen Harvey, who argues, much as a literary critic would: "Ideas, meanings, and representations have a 'reality,' whether in material forms as objects or as agents which cause and effect" (*The Kiss in History*, 4).

164. A case in point is scholarship on prostitution: in reaction to Griffiths, "The Structure of Prostitution," which subordinates literary representations to the documentary record, Newman, *Cultural Capitals* elevates the literary over the archival.

165. Phillips, *On Historical Distance*, 6.

166. Dolan, *True Relations*, 19. She also argues "that there is more common methodological ground than disciplinary divisions might sometimes suggest and that, when we do find conflicts regarding evidentiary reading practices, they do not predictably fall out by discipline" (113).

167. Dolan, *True Relations*, 25, 16.

168. Dolan, *True Relations*, 6. Dolan notes that "terms such as 'texts,' 'documents,' or 'discourses' both evade the distinction between what is literature and what is not and leave the category of literature unchallenged" (20).

169. Dolan, "Tracking the Petty Traitor," 164.

170. Gowing, *Domestic Dangers*, 56; Richardson, *Domestic Life and Domestic Tragedy*, 30.

171. David M. Turner, *Fashioning Adultery*, 18. See also Shepard, "From Anxious Patriarchs," 289, which advocates the need for masculinity studies to attend simultaneously to the cultural construction of manhood and to men's social experiences.

172. Simons, *The Sex of Men*, 18.

173. See *Webster's New Twentieth-Century Dictionary*, s.v. "inter-": "1. A prefix meaning *between, among*, as in *inter*flow, *inter*change. 2. a prefix meaning *with* or *on each other* (or *one another*), *together, mutual, reciprocal, mutually, reciprocally*, as in *inter*act."

174. This strategy of lateral comparison challenges the alleged division of labor inveighed against by Spiegel, "History, Historicism," 73–74, that it is the "menial" labor of historians to provide "a lucid, accessible—above all, knowable and known—context, while critics take their leisure in exploring the productive enigmas of textuality. Literary critics have been accustomed to get their history secondhand and prepackaged and tended, in practice if not in theory, to treat it as unproblematic, something to be invoked rather than investigated." As Dolan, *True Relations*, 209, notes, "literary critics have come to think of themselves as engaged in the creation of historical knowledge, rather than applying someone else's historical hypotheses to literary texts to confirm their interpretations."

175. Cocks's review article "The Growing Pains" laments the field's split into two schools: one engaged "with the theoretical legacy of Foucault, feminism, and other kinds of 'theory,'" and another that "styles itself as a primarily empirical and even descriptive enterprise" (657). According to Brady, "All About Eve?" while "debates have emphatically moved on from the desiccation of the essentialist/constructionist binary," it may nonetheless be the case that the history of sexuality "has now developed into a binary of narrative/theoretical" (194). Katherine Crawford, "Privilege, Possibility, and Perversion," observes that "perhaps the largest debate for historians has been, and remains, that between those who choose to focus on discourse and those who seek a more empirical grounding" (413).

176. For a useful meditation on the relations between discourse and experience from the perspective of a social historian, see Canning, *Gender History*, who proffers a "conception of agency as a site of mediation between discourses and experiences" (77).

177. Jagose, *Orgasmology*, 11.

178. Jagose, *Orgasmology*, 12–13.

179. Jagose, *Orgasmology*, 13. Such "transubstantiation" seemed to be at work in the *GLQ* roundtable moderated by Freeman, "Theorizing Queer Temporalities"; when she asked a group of queer studies scholars, most of whom work on modern or contemporary culture, to address

the question "how sex itself—sex as bodily practice, not sexuality as identity—infuses or inter-sects with queer temporality," their answers largely were routed through a rhetoric of identities and identifications despite her explicit request that they approach "sex as bodily practice" (189). Such "routing," I submit, is not merely a personal preference or due to embarrassment.

180. Jagose, *Orgasmology*, 15, emphases added.

181. Jagose, *Orgasmology*, xiii.

182. Jagose, *Orgasmology*, 28.

183. Jagose, *Orgasmology*, 28. To Jagose's citation of Elizabeth Wilson, I would add Grosz, *The Nick of Time*, which makes feminist alliance with Darwin; and Rosario, "Quantum Sex," which argues "for an analytics of gender and sexuality that takes the social and the biological seriously by acknowledging the complexity and depth of both influences" (268); his description of an "interactionist model of genetic sex modifiers" puts into play "a polymorphic and multi-factorial model" that he calls "quantum sex" (269).

184. Orgasm, Jagose shows, has been similarly subject to presumptive knowledge—first by doctors and sexologists, but more recently by post-structuralist and queer theorists who assume they know what orgasm "is" and "means." Some forms of foreknowledge, it turns out, are the result not of heteronormativity but of knowledge formations operant in queer theory itself.

185. Or, as LaCapra argues, "there is a necessary speculative element in historical under-standing. But it should be checked and to some extent regulated by empirical research that may never prove or fully substantiate certain contentions but can lend them greater credibility. Empirical inquiry, while never a self-sufficient or free-standing activity, is particularly pointed and fruitful when it is combined with critical questioning and invoked as a 'reality check' that may facilitate specificity and interrupt free-flowing, at times self-involved, theoretical specula-tion" (*History and Its Limits*, 8).

186. Jagose, *Orgasmology*, 34.

187. Jagose, *Orgasmology*, 215.

188. Hitchcock, "The Reformation of Sexual Knowledge," 827.

189. Hitchcock, "The Reformation of Sexual Knowledge," 826.

190. Hitchcock, "The Reformation of Sexual Knowledge," 823.

CHAPTER 7. TALKING SEX

Note to epigraph: Jonson, *The Alchemist*, ed. Cook, 3.3.66–71.

1. On the virginal, see Pursglove, "Prick-Song Ditties."

2. The *OED* defines "firk" as "a smart sudden blow or stroke, as with a whip; a flick, flip; a cut or thrust (with a sword)," dating from 1635; "a trick, dodge, subterfuge. Also, a freak, prank, caprice," dating from 1611; and, surrounded by question marks, "a dance; a partner for a dance," from 1637. Yet, in *A Dictionary of the French and English Tongues*, Randle Cotgrave uses the word to define the French "Bichecoterie": "A leacherous tricke, a lasciuious part; firkerie, an odde pranke, or ierke, in whoorisme"; Lexicons of Early Modern English, http://leme.library.utoronto.ca.proxy.lib.umich.edu/lexicons.

3. Jonson, *The Alchemist*, ed. Brown; and ed. Ostovich, in *Jonson, Four Comedies*.

4. *The Alchemist*, ed. Mares; and Woolland.

5. *The Alchemist*, ed. Mares; Woolland; and Cook.

6. It is glossed as an allusion to a Latin poem attributed to the Emperor Gallienus, "non vincant oscula conchae" (itself variously translated by Mares and Cook as "your kisses [are sweeter] than clams" and "Don't let a clam's kisses win").

7. *The Alchemist*, ed. Cook.

8. *The Alchemist*, ed. Mares; Cook; Woolland.

9. *The Alchemist*, ed. Ostovich. See also Henke, *Courtesans and Cuckolds*, 145.

10. *The Alchemist*, ed. Bement; see also Woolland's ed.

11. *The Alchemist*, ed. Ostovich.

12. *The Alchemist*, ed. Cook.

13. This projection of sexual fluency accords more generally with the ways in which bawds and whores in the drama are positioned as experientially intimidating figures, especially for inexperienced men; whores, in other words, tend to be *the ones who know* (or who others think know).

14. Fleming, "Dictionary English"; Menon, *Wanton Words*; Spiess, "Shakespeare's Whore." On ellipses, see Andreadis, *Sappho in Early Modern England*. On indirection, sexual innuendo, and double entendre, see Hammond, *Figuring Sex*.

15. Parker, *Literary Fat Ladies* and *Shakespeare from the Margins*; Bly, *Queer Virgins*.

16. Rubright, *Doppelgänger Dilemmas*; Maguire, "Typographical Embodiment."

17. Masten, *Queer Philologies*; Blank, "The Proverbial 'Lesbian.'"

18. Masten, *Queer Philologies*.

19. Masten, *Queer Philologies*. Conversely, "there is rarely philology without sex."

20. Masten defines "queer philology" as "a detailed study of the terms and related rhetorics early modern English culture used to inscribe bodies, pleasures, affects, sexual acts, and, to the extent we can speak of these, identities" (*Queer Philologies*).

21. As noted by Turner, *Fashioning Adultery*, 24, "language is a central agency through which sex acquires its meaning in different contexts at each historical moment."

22. By focusing on words, I do not mean to scant the importance of visual and material culture in ascertaining the metaphorics of sex. See Simons, *The Sex of Men*; Toulalan, *Imagining Sex*; Wolfthal, *In and Out*; and Talvacchia, "Erotica." Regarding print culture, O'Connell notes that "erotic prints appeared only at the upper end of the market in the seventeenth century, and the most suggestive cheap ballad illustrations are woodcuts of fully clothed couples embracing, whether on a bed or in the countryside" (70).

23. Bray, *The Friend*; Gowing, *Common Bodies*; Rocke, *Forbidden Friendships*; Puff, *Sodomy and Reformation Germany*; Anna Clark, *Desire*.

24. Thus, I will not be concerned, as many critics and historians have been, with the modalities of language—the metaphors and rhetorics from Petrarchanism to the metaphysical conceit—that early modern subjects used to express erotic attraction, love, or desire. Nor will I describe the social-linguistic dynamics of wooing or being seduced or the metaphors that inform portrayals of sexual honesty, adultery, cuckoldry, or betrayal.

25. I am guided, in part, by Judith Butler's assertion that "language and materiality are not opposed, for language both is and refers to that which is material, and what is material never fully escapes from the process by which it is signified" (*Bodies That Matter*, 68).

26. Bly, "Bawdy Puns," 104.

27. Neither can the critical efforts they solicit secure meaning or resolve knotty historical questions about the salience and significance of sex. This is not to say that words and critical strategies can never shorten gaps in understanding or illuminate historical problems. But the failures of sex talk I seek to analyze can only pose an irritant to the history of sexuality if that history is conceived as one of discrete and fully legible sexual acts, of specific, stable body parts, or clear-cut genders.

28. See my discussion of Maza in Chapter 6.

29. Karras, *Common Women.*

30. Froide, *Never Married*, notes that "the line between a singlewoman who worked and lived on her own and a prostitute became a thin one," arguing that this allowed "urban authorities to control any independent woman under the guise of moral policing" (21).

31. Traub, *The Renaissance of Lesbianism*, 167; and Bray, *Homosexuality in Renaissance England.*

32. Panek, "'This Base Stallion Trade.'"

33. Gowing, *Domestic Dangers*, 59, emphasis mine; Capp, *When Gossips Meet*, 189–93.

34. Mowry, "London's Bridewell," 210, emphasis mine.

35. Varholy, "'But She Woulde Not Consent,'" 62 n. 3. Varholy argues that conceptions of sexual transgression wavered between an emphasis on promiscuity characteristic of the medieval discourse of commonness and an emphasis on commercial exchange more prevalent in later discourses.

36. Varholy, "'Rich Like a Lady,'" 8.

37. David M. Turner, *Fashioning Adultery*, 27.

38. Turner, *Fashioning Adultery*, 28.

39. Within the circulation of terms describing illicit sexual activities, the "labelling of vice," Turner notes, is affected by a number of capricious social practices: by "popular linguistic traits which defied straightforward categorization; by the variable signification of certain words in different social, political or cultural contexts; and by the dictates of individual conscience" (*Fashioning Adultery*, 35).

40. Gowing, *Domestic Dangers*, 66.

41. Foucault, *History of Sexuality*, 101.

42. Spiess, "Shakespeare's Whore," 59–61, and private communication. See also Stanton, "'Made to Write "Whore" Upon?'"

43. According to Magnusson, "Language," 243: "More new words were introduced into the English language . . . from about 1500 to 1660, than in any other period of its history."

44. Spiess, "Shakespeare's Whore," 24, 200.

45. In addition, the emission of seed was thought to be a form of sexual pleasure for both men and women (for him, in emitting it; for her, in emitting and receiving); for both it is referred to as an ecstasy, epilepsy, cough, spilling, dousing, purging, and flowing forth. It sometimes did and sometimes did not map onto modern notions of orgasm; on the latter, see Simons, *The Sex of Men*, chapter 6.

46. A few of these words have been subject to extended analysis. On "use" and "abuse," see Braunschneider, "The Macroclitoride, the Tribade, and the Woman"; on "enjoy," "intercourse," and "conversation," see Masten, *Queer Philologies*, chapter 3; on the use of "to frequent" in court depositions, see Giese, *Courtships, Marriage Customs*, 94–97.

47. Hughes, *Swearing*, 229. These inaugural dates should be taken with skepticism, as they depend on a philology that is definitely *not* queer. A case in point is *cinaedus*, which became an English loanword, but is absent from the *OED*; see Borris, *Same-Sex Desire*, 20.

48. Borris, *Same-Sex Desire*, 7.

49. These are the main ones used in England until the eighteenth century, when "lesbian," "sapphist," "mannish," and "the game of flats" come to the fore. For more terms used across western Europe, see Lanser, *The Sexuality of History.*

50. One of the best representatives of this verbosity is Antonia from Pietro Aretino's *Ragionamenti* (1534), who exclaims to her fellow courtesan Nanna: "Speak plainly and say 'fuck,' 'prick,' 'cunt,' and 'ass' if you want anyone except the scholars at the university in Rome to

understand you. You with your 'rope in the ring,' your 'obelisk in the Coliseum,' your 'leek in the garden,' your 'key in the lock,' your 'bolt in the door,' your 'pestle in the mortar,' your 'nightingale in the nest,' your 'tree in the ditch,' your 'syringe in the flap-valve,' your 'sword in the scabbard,' not to mention your 'stake,' your 'crozier,' your 'parsnip,' your 'little monkey,' your 'this,' your 'that,' your 'him' and your 'her,' your 'apples,' 'leaves of missal,' 'fact,' '*verbigratia*,' 'job,' 'affair,' 'big news,' 'handle,' 'arrow,' 'carrot,' 'root,' and all shit there is—why don't you say it straight out and stop going about on tiptoes?" See *Aretino's Dialogues*, 43–44. Antonia's profusion of metaphors is comic, but it also indicates the plenitude of terms, metaphors, and homologies. As Moulton remarks, this speech "is as much a celebration of metaphor as a request for plain speaking" (*Before Pornography*, 128). Toulalan, *Imagining Sex*, and James Grantham Turner, *Schooling Sex*, regularly refer to pornography's prolixity, but pornography is only the most obvious example of a broader cultural habit.

51. Moulton, *Before Pornography*, 128.

52. Simons, *The Sex of Men*, 293. See also Gowing, "Knowledge and Experience," 247.

53. de Grazia, "Words as Things"; Fleming, *Graffiti and the Writing Arts*. In *The Places of Wit*, Zucker reads "wit as a social or material quantity" (4). To invoke Simons: "metaphors about bodies have material presence and everyday effect" (*The Sex of Men*, 293).

54. Hailwood, *Alehouses and Good Fellowship*, 160.

55. Three examples might suffice. Regarding Donne's "Elegie XVIII (Love's Progress)," lines 91–96: "Rich Nature hath in women wisely made / Two purses, and their mouths aversely laid: / They then, which to the lower tribute owe, / That way which that Exchequer looks, must go: / He which doth not, his error is as great, / As who by Clyster gave the Stomack meat." Will Stockton takes issue with Sawday's contention in *The Body Emblazoned* that "aversely" means "backwards," and that the poem instructs the male reader in the proper technique for entering the female anus; Stockton confesses that he is "not as sure as Sawday about how to read these aversely laid purses, but his reading of the poem's orificial confusion illustrates nothing if not how even after the meticulous metaphorization of female body parts proper to a blazon, the speaker fails to clearly distinguish between anatomical ends at the end of the poem" (*Playing Dirty*, 70). Similarly, Bromley, "Rimming the Renaissance," argues that scholars need to be careful about "rewrit[ing] an anal-oral connection as 'really' a genital connection, whether that involves transforming a tongue into a penis or an anus into a vagina. . . . By substituting a penis for a tongue or a vagina for an anus, a critic . . . might claim to draw on a supposedly agreed-upon definition of sex. Such substitutions, however, narrow the erotic, doing the ideological work of tacitly securing the status of genital intercourse as what really counts as sex" (183–85). And regarding Petruccio's reference to "tail" in *Taming of the Shrew*, Orvis, "Queer Renaissance Dramaturgy," pits Eric Partridge's "more capacious exposition of the term in question" against Gordon Williams's suggestion that "in this instance 'tongue in [the] tail' means cunnilingus," to "argue that anilingus is just as likely the referent" (39). His point "is not that Petruccio's bawdy pun refers to one act or another, but rather that the spectrum of acts is available to all characters and players . . . across the dramatic and dramaturgic configurations *Shrew* parades" (39).

56. This idea is widespread, but for representative examples, see Foyster, *Manhood in Early Modern England*; Gowing, "Knowledge and Experience," 248.

57. Goldberg, *Sodometries*; Parker, *Shakespeare from the Margins*.

58. The most sophisticated rendition of sex as a series of discrete acts, which does not conduce to this form of presumptive knowledge, is the book in progress of Fisher, *Sexual Practices in England*.

59. Gowing, *Domestic Dangers*, 7.

60. Gowing, *Domestic Dangers*, 271.

61. Partridge, *Shakespeare's Bawdy*, 160.

62. Gowing, *Domestic Dangers*, 271.

63. Florio, *A Worlde of Wordes*, s.v. *trentuno*.

64. Foyster, *Manhood in Early Modern England*, 73.

65. Toulalan, *Imagining Sex*, 12. Toulalan goes on to note that "this style of writing was entirely consistent with other writing in the period, which is characterized by allegory, symbolism, allusion, and double meaning, intended not to obfuscate or to hide its 'real' meaning but rather to illuminate it" (12).

66. DeJean, *The Reinvention of Obscenity*, 15.

67. DeJean, *The Reinvention of Obscenity*, 15.

68. Allan and Burridge, *Forbidden Words*, 1, 53.

69. Blount, *Glossographia* (1656), s.v. "euphemism."

70. Magnusson, "Language," 254.

71. Allan and Burridge, *Forbidden Words*, 54.

72. DeJean, *The Reinvention of Obscenity*, 19. On the civilizing process, see Elias, *The History of Manners*.

73. According to Spiess, personal communication, this division is evident in early modern lexicography itself.

74. Allan and Burridge, *Forbidden Words*, 34.

75. Allan and Burridge, *Forbidden Words*, 52; *OED*, s.v. "cunt," ca. 1230.

76. Williams, *A Dictionary of Sexual Language*, 1:352; Florio, *A Worlde of Wordes*, s.v. *potta*.

77. Sharp, *The Midwives Book*, 5. For analysis of medical writers' anxiety, see Traub, *The Renaissance of Lesbianism*, 103–24.

78. *Hamlet*, in *The Norton Shakespeare*, ed. Greenblatt et al., 3.2.105–7.

79. Attridge, *Peculiar Language*, 108. Taking the pun as the epitome of wordplay, Culler argues that etymology is "the diachronic version of punning," deconstructively viewing puns as "illustrations of the inherent instability of language and the power of uncodified linguistic relations to produce meaning" (*On Puns*, 2, 3). Crawforth, *Etymology and the Invention of English*, argues that "patterns of etymological thinking" in early modern literature and linguistic treatises demonstrate the extent to which "what and how words mean" was important to early moderns (8), and that etymology is simultaneously dedicated to the act of discovery ("uncovering the history of the word") and invention ("remaking that word for present use by reconnecting it to this past") (3).

80. Lesser, "Contrary Matters." In his welcome uncertainty about how to read sexual meanings, his impatience with editorial circumlocutions, his recognition that puns are "transactional language use" (79), his effort to articulate principles of interpreting puns and editorial glossing, and his recognition of the labor involved in getting puns across to a reader/audience, his analysis has much in common with mine.

81. Lesser, "Contrary Matters," 75.

82. Attridge, *Peculiar Language*, 118.

83. Allan and Burridge, *Forbidden Words*, 43.

84. Allan and Burridge, *Forbidden Words*, 43.

85. Hughes, *Swearing*, 24–25.

86. Hughes, *Swearing*, 27.

87. *The Flyting of Dunbar and Kennedy*, line 1363, in Hughes, *Swearing*, 20, 119–20.

88. Florio, *A Worlde of Wordes*, s.vv. "fottarie," "fottitrice," "fottitore," and "fottitura."

89. Shakespeare, *The Merry Wives of Windsor*, 4.1.42. Crane's edition provides this gloss on "focative case": "Evans' pronunciation of 'vocative' introduces the notion 'fuck' and suggests the slang sense of 'case' as meaning 'vagina' (Mistress Quickly at 53, has taken 'genitive case' to mean 'Jenny's vagina')" (125).

90. Shakespeare, *The Life of Henry the Fifth*, 3.4.46–47.

91. Dekker and Webster, *Northward-Hoe*, 23.

92. See Rubright's reading of this scene as both linguistic and typographic wit in *Doppelgänger Dilemmas*.

93. Hailwood, *Alehouses and Good Fellowship*, 209.

94. As Hughes notes, it "has extended grammatically . . . to virtually every part of speech. . . . In its most emotive uses, the word ranges from the barely plausible *you fucking bitch!* to the incestuous improbability *mother-fucker*, finally reaching the physical impossibilities of *fuck off!* and *go fuck yourself!*" (*Swearing*, 30).

95. Legal documents, such as court depositions that record accusations of rape, sodomy, adultery, bastardy, prostitution, and broken betrothals, are characterized by stock phrases, perhaps inserted by scribes. According to Ungerer, "Prostitution in Late Elizabethan London," the legal term for sexual intercourse was "to know a woman," whereas the ecclesiastical term was "to occupy a woman" (221 n. 180). Describing church court depositions, Gowing notes that when "testimonies concerned illicit sex, scribes, lawyers, or witnesses themselves shifted into a different register from everyday speech; instead of 'occupying' or 'lying with,' witnesses' depositions use the terms 'carnall knowledge,' 'carnall copulation,' and the stock phrase 'fornication adultery or incontinence'" (*Domestic Dangers*, 46). Elsewhere, however, Gowing writes that a "clerk, however basic his training, went on writing 'occupy' to denote sexual intercourse whatever anyone else said" ("Women's Bodies," 820). The status of first-person speech has been a particular point of controversy in historical scholarship on early modern court depositions; see Dolan, *True Relations*, who argues for the communal origins of court depositions and warns against attributing a first-person "I" as the singular author of the action. On stock phrases, see Varholy, "'But She Woulde Not Consent'"; Walker, "Rereading Rape." Although attention to the narrative dimensions of court depositions has broadened the lexicon of violent sex, the evidence provided by depositions is mediated by the complex motives for accusation and denial and the presence of multiple interlocutors; their stable repertoire of images and formulations evinces not only the speaker's attempt to shape a convincing story and to enforce or evade punishment, but the influence of legal criteria and constraints of decorum. Reticence particularly informs women's rape accusations, which, because of gendered constructions of honor, culpability, and consent, tend to avoid graphic descriptions of sexual acts. Noting the "minor rhetorical role" accorded to sex in narratives of sexual violence, Walker, "Rereading Rape," argues that, because available discourses of sexuality implied women's consent, sexually graphic language was "an inappropriate medium through which to report a rape" (7 and 5); there are moments when rape narratives break out of standard convention, as when Anne Fownall describes that her assailant "in most Savage and barbarous mannor spent his lust on my Clothes" (13). Chaytor, "Husband(ry)," reads the absences in rape depositions as evidence of unconscious imperatives and repressions, making the historical argument that, with the seventeenth-century sexualization of women and changes in the legal status of consent, "sexuality had to be expunged from the [rape] narrative because legally, culturally, it had for the first time begun to get in" (395).

96. Griffiths, "The Structure of Prostitution."

97. Panek, "'This Base Stallion Trade,'" 389.

98. Panek, "'This Base Stallion Trade,'" 389–90.

99. Ingram, "Sexual Manners," 105.

100. The Castlehaven case is a notable exception, whose "conviction for 'sodomy' was energetically pursued and narrowly secured even though penetration could not be proven" (Borris, *Same-Sex Desire*, 79). For controversy on the definition of sodomy, see Stewart, "Queer Renaissance Bodies?"

101. Stephens, *Demon Lovers*.

102. Ingram continues that "in practice, evidence of sexual immorality was usually circumstantial and cumulative in nature. Private meetings, too-frequent 'companying,' undue familiarity, untoward pregnancies, suspicious removals, the intuition of fellow servants and neighbours, or the rash speeches of the parties, gradually led to the build-up of 'vehement suspicion' or 'common fame' of incontinence sufficient to justify legal action" ("Sexual Manners," 105).

103. Dolan, *True Relations*, 149.

104. Dolan, *True Relations*, 151.

105. Dolan, *True Relations*, 150. Dolan's observation supports her main point about the collaborative construction of court depositions. By recasting "mediation as collaboration," Dolan seeks to deconstruct "the holy grail of deposition reading": "the trace of a speaking self who can be seen as prior to and the origin of the deposition" (*True Relations*, 118, 123). The full account (Bridewell Hospital Records, Guildhall BCB 4 [microfilm], fol. 23) is reproduced in Dolan, *True Relations*, 149, as well as in Crawford and Gowing, *Women's Worlds*, 151–52.

106. For other instances, see Quaife, *Wanton Wenches*.

107. One might read this dynamic as a psychoanalytic tautology: the lack created by ambiguous signification produces a desire for more knowledge, while the desire for more knowledge inscribes sexual signification as lacking.

108. Gowing, *Common Bodies*, 83.

109. Walker, *Crime, Gender, and Social Order*, 55.

110. Walker, *Crime, Gender, and Social Order*, 56.

111. Gowing, *Common Bodies*, 84.

112. Wiltenburg, *Disorderly Women*, 141–82. The extent to which sex is a central concern of ballads is indicated by Pepys's headings for his collection of nearly eighteen hundred ballads: "Love Pleasant," "Love Unfortunate," "Marriage, Cuckoldry, &c.," and "Love Gallantry." See O'Connell, "Love Pleasant."

113. Clegg and Skeaping, *Singing Simpkin*. The jig—"a short sung-drama that featured as an afterpiece of the main play in the open playhouses"—emerged from the ballads and dances of clowns in the 1570s. With their popularity at a peak in the early seventeenth century, jigs were "frequently bawdy, sometimes libelous, often farcical" (1). Almost all of the extent jigs reproduced in *Singing Simpkin* revolve around erotic plots—sexual competition, intrigue, fidelity, and betrayal—some of which were written as libelous exposés. So tight is the connection between sex and the thematics and performance of the jig (with its rapid, jerky dance movements) that the term lives on in slang as a term for sexual action (4).

114. Brown, *Better a Shrew*.

115. Smith, "Female Impersonation" and *The Acoustic World*, 168–205. This is likewise true of pornography, which leaves "space in the text for a multiplicity of identifications and pleasures for a variety of readers" (Toulalan, "Extraordinary Satisfactions," 65).

116. Murphy and O'Driscoll, "Introduction," 21.

117. One might consider the anonymous "A copie of Verses made by a Lady, and sent to another Lady, with a bracelet made of her own hair," in John Cotgrave's *Wits Interpreter*, 46, which includes the potentially erotically punning lines: "And whilst others speak her fair, / 'Tis I that have her to a hair"; see Traub, *The Renaissance of Lesbianism*, 335–36.

118. According to the *OED*, although the earliest uses of "bawdy" refer to something "soiled, dirty, filthy," from the sixteenth century on the term was particularly associated with words and pictures: "Of, pertaining to, or befitting a bawd; lewd, obscene, unchaste. (Usually applied to language)." DeJean, *The Reinvention of Obscenity*, remarks: "By the early sixteenth century, English speakers had a word to designate something like the territory subsequently covered by the obscene: they could refer to 'bawdy' language or poems"; yet, "bawdy" did not have "*obscene*'s massively negative connotations: the term was not used in censorial fashion. The bawdy was clearly audacious, but it was neither socially threatening nor a problem the state sought to suppress" (8).

119. See Henke, *Courtesans and Cuckolds* and *Gutter Life and Language*; Rubinstein, *A Dictionary of Shakespeare's Sexual Puns*; Gordon Williams, *A Dictionary of Sexual Language* and *A Glossary of Shakespeare's Sexual Language*. Works that function less as dictionary, glossary, or concordance than as a kind of "greatest hits" of "filth" in Shakespeare include Kiernan, *Filthy Shakespeare*; Macrone, *Naughty Shakespeare*; Hill and Ottchen, *Shakespeare's Insults*.

120. Booth, *Shakespeare's Sonnets*. Booth's appraisal of puns is ambivalent. Because he believes that puns are gratuitous to sense making (providing, at their best, aesthetic pleasure), Booth refuses to mediate between the meanings of different layers. In "Shakespeare's Language," Booth seeks to differentiate between the pleasurable moment before the pun is made— "the joy . . . in sensing the availability of a simultaneously likely and unlikely connection, an unexpected opportunity for articulating two contexts that are and remain essentially unconnected" (33)—and the less aesthetically satisfying moment of punning itself, which exposes only "triviality" and "insubstantiality" (34).

121. In *Literary Fat Ladies* and *Shakespeare from the Margins*, Parker makes a compelling case for the omnipresence of linguistic multiplicity in early modern literature; she focuses less on the doubleness of puns than association and proximity whereby certain words, such as "preposterous" or "jointure," are used repeatedly in certain gendered and/or erotic contexts. For the imbrication of sexual meanings with rhetorical tropes, see Menon, *Wanton Words*; and Mann, "The 'Figure of Exchange.'"

122. Bly, *Queer Virgins*, 20. Bly prefers the term "bawdy" over the more pejorative "obscene" as well as the more neutral "sexual" because of its connotation of humor.

123. Lopez, *Theatrical Convention*, 36, 37; Lopez makes the valuable point "that overt punning and unintentional, unnoticeable punning are closely related, and that the unignorable presence of the former in Elizabethan and Jacobean drama is the key evidence that allows us to assume the importance of the effects of the latter" (39).

124. Lopez, *Theatrical Convention*, 39.

125. Lopez, *Theatrical Convention*, 41.

126. Spiess, "Shakespeare's Whore," 19.

127. Spiess, "Shakespeare's Whore," 70–71 n. 17.

128. On problems with Partridge's method more generally, see Coleman, "Historical and Sociological Methods."

129. Such is the temporality of critical turns that such concordances have been articulated as necessary to the discipline of art history: "art historians need to compile a dictionary of these

visual metaphors along the lines of recent dictionaries of erotic euphemisms used in the literature of the period" (Ruggiero, "Introduction," 5).

130. Simes, "Gay Slang Lexicography," who dates the first English language gay glossary to 1910, provides a history of such glossaries, which were written by those within and external/hostile to gay culture. He notes that sexual language disappeared from dictionaries with Samuel Johnson (1755) and only began to make it back into mainstream lexicography in the 1960s. See also Coleman, "Glossaries of Sexuality."

131. Warner, *The Trouble with Normal.*

132. Masten, *Queer Philologies*, examines not only lexical meanings and etymologies, but inscriptions through orthography, typography, and rhetoric.

133. Masten, *Queer Philologies.*

134. On the perversity of letters as material forms, see Goldberg, *Writing Matter*; Conley, *The Self-Made Map.*

135. Masten, *Queer Philologies.*

136. DiGangi, "Shakespeare's 'Bawdy' " demonstrates how this term can pertain to nonhuman erotic agency.

137. Colman, *The Dramatic Use of Bawdy*, defines "bawdy" as "indecency" and "salacious," with "the intention to startle or shock" (x, 3). In his view bawdy language "always partakes of the comic, whether through absurdity, grossness or a startling ingenuity" (3). Assuming the unity and coherence of Shakespearean character, Colman determines whether a phrase is bawdy through tone; since he insists that bawdy is always comic, this seals off a range of potential innuendo from "indecency," and supports his "conviction that the golden rule is to be slow in *assuming* ribald significance anywhere in Shakespeare" (21). Wells, *Looking for Sex*, acknowledges that "sexual wordplay need not be comic . . . and, even when it is comic, it may be delicately, slyly and touchingly so" (15).

138. Henke, *Courtesans and Cuckolds*, admits to ambivalence about the extent to which one can use "non-dramatic analogs as supporting evidence for the ribald interpretation of some gloss entries" (xii).

139. Gordon Williams, *A Dictionary of Sexual Language*, vol. 1, xiii.

140. Such circular cross-referencing is also a mode of some early modern dictionaries.

141. Lesser, "Contrary Matters," notes the problem of repetitive glossing, arguing that it reifies meaning according to an undertheorized historicist theory of reception.

142. For analysis of how such glossing functions to the detriment of a historicized sexual pedagogy, see Masten, *Queer Philologies*, chapter 8.

143. *Hamlet*, in *The Norton Shakespeare*, ed. Greenblatt et al., 1734.

144. Gordon Williams, *A Dictionary of Sexual Language*, 2:963–64.

145. Drouin, "Diana's Band," 91.

146. See the demurral by Thompson and Taylor in the Arden *Hamlet*, 290. Also contesting the logic of the imputed double entendre, Colman, *The Dramatic Use of Bawdy*, notes that the brothel-nunnery equation first appeared in Dover Wilson's New Cambridge Edition of *Hamlet* in 1934.

147. See Mowat and Werstine's edition of *Hamlet*, 130.

148. Dolan, "Why Are Nuns Funny?"

149. Drouin, "Diana's Band," 91.

150. I am less sanguine than Lesser, who argues that reification of meaning in glossing can operate most strongly in the case of "obscene" puns because "editors want to make sure readers understand these jokes" ("Contrary Matters," 82).

151. Masten, *Queer Philologies*. Elsewhere Masten refers to the difficulty "of translating out of (or back into) early modern English some of the range of meanings we no longer associate with these terms."

152. Masten, *Queer Philologies*. See also Parker, *Shakespeare from the Margins*.

153. Masten, *Queer Philologies*.

154. Masten, *Queer Philologies*, emphasis mine; or, as he later puts it, "when lifted out of editorial attempts to pin them down and instead opened out philologically."

155. Masten, *Queer Philologies*.

156. de Grazia, "Homonyms Before and After," 152.

157. Burckhardt describes the Shakespearean pun as "an act of verbal violence, designed to tear the close bond between a word and its meaning. . . . It denies the meaningfulness of words and so calls into question the genuineness of the linguistic currency on which the social order depends" (*Shakespearean Meanings*, 25).

158. de Grazia, "Homonyms Before and After," 149.

159. de Grazia, "Homonyms Before and After," 155.

160. de Grazia notes that the term "wordplay" is a "nineteenth-century coinage." This "shift in terminology . . . suggests something of a fall in stature. If words *play* instead of *work*, how can they be anything but trivial, decorative, and tricky?" (review of *Shakespeare from the Margins*, 407). Hope, "Shakespeare and Language," emphasizes the orality of early modern English—a "tongue" rather than a "language" (3)—as well as linguistic variation: "We have reified 'words' and 'meaning' and we associate meanings with particular spellings, and therefore the written language, in a way conceptually impossible in the Early Modern period. . . . Many 'words' only exist as distinct things in their written form: to/too/two; air/heir; Barbar/barber" (6, 11).

161. On the history of the pun, including corresponding rhetorical concepts, its congruence with oral forms of expression (drama, sermons), and the history of the term itself, see Read, "Puns."

162. As Bly's work on a single theatrical milieu suggests, linguistic resources are best correlated to specific social performances, audiences, and interlocutors. From the theatrical to the legal to the medical to the domestic, representations of sexual experience are produced within site-specific domains, each drawing on its own rhetorical resources. Such discourses are not only the medium through which erotic representations are articulated; they also contribute to the construction and dissemination of particular erotic knowledges.

163. Wells, *Looking for Sex* and *Shakespeare, Sex and Love*.

164. Bly, "Bawdy Puns," 98. A fair amount of work on puns assumes that they are used to "circumvent . . . taboos" (Redfern, *Puns*, 91). See Rogers, "Riddling Erotic Identity." Bly usefully contests the idea that "the audience's attention may be redirected from the titillating *double entendre* to admiration of rhetorical cleverness," arguing that "bawdy puns do not mask desire but flaunt it" ("Bawdy Puns," 98).

165. Lopez, *Theatrical Convention*, 45.

166. Gowing, *Common Bodies*, 84.

167. Bly, "Bawdy Puns," 100 n. 14.

168. Lopez, *Theatrical Convention*, 36.

169. Lopez, *Theatrical Convention*, 36–37. Bly likewise argues that certain characters "are able to dance further into obscenity because their puns tumble onto each other, delighting the ear before comprehension strikes" ("Bawdy Puns," 104).

170. Lesser, "Contrary Matters," 81.

171. Greenblatt's gloss on these lines is representative: "Malvolio unwittingly spells out 'cut,' slang for 'female genitals'; the meaning is compounded by 'great P's'" (*Twelfth Night*, 1791).

172. Lothian and Craik, in their edition of *Twelfth Night*, 67, credit this insight to Dover Wilson's edition of 1949. The note in Elam's Arden Third Series edition of *Twelfth Night* refers to Steevens's disapproving notice that "there is neither a C, nor a P, to be found" (242).

173. Callaghan, "Body Politics," 36–37.

174. Callaghan, "Body Politics," 36.

175. See *Twelfth Night*, ed. Raffel.

176. The homophonic pun "P/pee" doesn't necessarily rely on a basic knowledge of orthography, but it does rely on an equation between "pee" and "piss." However, the *OED* cites the first use of the verb "pee" as "to urinate" in 1788; the noun "act of urination" is dated at 1880. Although editors such as Lothian and Craik, and lexicographic critics such as Colman, *The Dramatic Use of Bawdy*, assume a homophonic pun, it is possible that the only cognate in Shakespeare's time was "piss."

177. Lopez, *Theatrical Convention*, 41, emphasis mine.

178. Hughes, *Swearing*, 253–54. Such bodily and gender imprecision is characteristic not only of the diachronic fate of anatomical terms but of the lexicon's synchronic latitude.

179. On Chaucer's interest in anal erotics and the confusions of orifices, see Will Stockton, *Playing Dirty*; and Lochrie, *Covert Operations*. On anality in Restoration satire, see Hammond, *Figuring Sex*.

180. Capp, *When Gossips Meet*, 190.

181. See, respectively, *The Alchemist* editions by Bement; Cook; Ostovich; and Mares.

182. Enterline, in "Rhetoric, Discipline," 181, remarks of "The Birch," a schoolboy's poem about erotic flogging: "The poem's anal conceits (knowledge being something that 'Goes in behind and out before' or spreads 'From tail to Head') give plenty of time to homoerotic fantasy." Brown, noting that in early modern jests, "women frequently deploy tongue-in-tail barbs" as the butt of the joke, equates "kiss my tail" with "tongue in tail," and interprets such jests as invoking an "anal/genital kiss" (*Better a Shrew*, 107).

183. Hughes, *Swearing*, 254. See also Partridge (*Shakespeare's Bawdy*, 200), who ascribes to "tail" the meanings of "pudend," "penis," and "podex" (Latin for anus).

184. While demonstrating the way in which the "tail" of the letter *Q* persistently enacts an accord between the "faithful friends" of bottoms and tails, Masten observes that in certain instances, "the agreement of the tail and the bottom may also alert us here to the confused sodometrics (or positionings) of this configuration, the strangeness (even as it appears to be already sodomitic) of a coupling of tails. Embodying in the letter a trope that is . . . the rhetorical figure of sodomy in the period, Q's tail is literally preposterous, a confusion of before and behind, for it leads while it also follows; simultaneously, this tail, as in English of the period, begins to function not (or not only) as tail but as yard, as penis" (*Queer Philologies*).

185. "Whore-gallant" distinguishes Tailby from the other four "gallants" of the title; see Middleton, *Your Five Gallants*, ed. Cohen and Jowett.

186. Bly, *Queer Virgins*, 14, 65.

187. Fisher, "'Stray[ing] Lower,'" argues that "scholars need to be careful about assuming that this analogical thinking . . . only worked in one direction. . . . We shouldn't assume that the tongue was only imagined to be like a phallus, or an anus was only imagined to be like a vagina, since these comparisons/substitutions undoubtedly worked in the other direction as well." Gowing attributes this "flexibility" of gender reference to "the idea of commensurate

sexual organs" ("Knowledge and Experience," 248), but the issue seems to go beyond the homologies of gender underpinned by Galenic humoralism and the so-called "one-sex" model of embodiment.

188. Puttenham, *The Arte of English Poesie*, 188.

189. *The Works of John Wilmot*, ed. Love, 45.

190. Comic confusion about which orifice is penetrated—and whether that orifice is gendered—provides the organizing conceit of a late seventeenth-century satirical ditty, "The Ladys Complaint," about King William III's betrayal of English Protestant liberties: "letts pray for the good of our State, & his soule / *that He'd putt his finger into the right hole,* / for the case Sir is such / the people think much / that your love is Italian, & Government Dutch." BL MS Add 29497, fol. 101r–v, quoted in Hammond, *Figuring Sex*, 181.

191. Chapman, *The Gentleman Usher*, ed. Smith, 4.4.29–32.

192. Lopez, *Theatrical Convention*, 49, emphases mine. Similarities between Lopez's and my work include our shared interest in limitation and failure, as when he insists that "the potential for failure of many of the theatrical devices indigenous to or inherent in early modern drama is an essential part of understanding their potential success" (2).

193. Brome, *The Weeding of the Covent-Garden*, 9.

194. Zucker, *The Places of Wit*, 119.

195. Zucker, *The Places of Wit*, 119.

196. In Shakespeare, certain characters' sexual "malapropisms" are particularly notable: Mistress Quickly in *Henry IV*, Parts 1 and 2, and *The Merry Wives of Windsor*, who intervenes in a schoolboy's Latin lesson, and Princess Katherine in *Henry V*, who engages in translinguistic bawdy puns during an English language lesson focused on words for body parts. Many feminist readers of Quickly take the view that her "malapropisms" are unintentional, a sign of her lack of learning and "errant female speech," and thus ultimately evidence of misogyny turned against her; see Parker, *Literary Fat Ladies*, 27. Magnusson, however, defends Quickly's speech as "resourceful acts of comprehension" that demonstrate her close relationship to oral culture during a period of "transition between orality and literacy"; see "Language," 248. Most critics read Princess Katherine's "bawdy" language as unintentional, with my *Desire and Anxiety*, which argues that her speech is a sign of erotic agency (62), a minority view.

197. Traub, *The Renaissance of Lesbianism*.

198. It may be helpful to contrast a hermeneutic strategy that is attentive to sex acts from a strategy directed by desire, for desire is precisely what is mobilized to fill in the blanks to which sex acts direct us.

199. My phrasing echoes that of Masten who organized two panels, one for the Modern Language Association (MLA) in 2007 and one for the Shakespeare Association of America (SAA) in 2009 entitled "The Epistemology of the Crux," the purpose of which was to explore the category of the "crux," the history of its use in editorial and critical practice, and the effect of textual scholarship, textual theory, and criticism on critical and editorial practices pertaining to the "crux."

200. In "Squashing the 'Shard-borne Bettle' Crux," Billings defines a "crux" as "a question whose options are more or less equally weighted, to be decided by each reader" (435). Acknowledging the pleasures of the crux, he nonetheless sees the task as being to "heap . . . together enough evidence in one place to settle the matter once and for all" (435). See also Gary Taylor, "Textual and Sexual Criticism," which displays the thought processes of an editor as he seeks to "solve" the problems of an obscure passage. In "The Passion of the Crux," presented at the SAA in 2009, Masten unpacks the logic animating this desire.

201. Lesser, "Contrary Matters," 112.

202. I recognize the constraints of practicality and intended use of any given edition or series. Publishers and series editors understandably have their own requirements and specifications for glossing, directing brevity or the use of the *OED* as an authoritative source for dates, definitions, spellings, and the quarantining of meanings from parts of speech.

203. Leah S. Marcus, *Unediting the Renaissance*, 11.

204. In his edition of Rowley, Middleton, and Heywood's *An/The Old Law*, Masten attempts "to recrux the modernized, edited text required by the volume's protocols, by crossing glosses and textual notes together" in his commentary" ("The Passion of the Crux").

205. Some editions self-consciously "show their work" by including textual notes in the on-page commentary, including examples of unmodernized texts, or noting, as Taylor and Lavagnino do in *Thomas Middleton*, that "every act of punctuation, whether made by an early copyist or a modern editor, necessarily involves arbitrary choices, which will encourage one pronunciation or interpretation over another; every system of punctuation to some degree disambiguates a text which may be deliberately ambiguous" (20).

206. Rather than citing a previous editor's gloss and then silently amending it, such a practice could promote open debate about the logic of previous glosses, exposing the historically evolving logic of the gloss to reveal something about the opacity—or negotiation—of sexual knowledge across the whole of the editorial history of a text. Because a nineteenth-century gloss might presume sexual knowledge differently than a gloss in 2015, glossing might become an occasion for marking that distance (or proximity) in ways of making sense of sexual knowledge *throughout* a text's publication history.

207. Huffer, *Are the Lips a Grave?*, notes that queer theory invented itself in part through "the discursive shock effect of words like *fist fucking*," thus creating "avenues of expression that hadn't existed before, especially in an academic context" (74). Whereas her critique of "the unspoken assumption that those who will be shocked by all this anal imagery are the hetero-genito-normative" rests on the way "queer discourse unwittingly perpetuates the linguistic production of perversions through an incitement to talk dirty in theory" (74–75), my interest is in the way talking dirty can elicit responses that fracture along queer and feminist lines.

208. Maguire, "Feminist Editing." Thompson also advocates greater forthrightness in "Feminist Theory," 95; see also Wayne, "The Gendered Text."

209. For the custom house's seizure of twelve leather dildos imported from France in 1670, see Fisher, "'Doctor Dildos Dauncing Schoole.'"

210. Simons, *The Sex of Men*, chapter 6.

211. Traub, *The Renaissance of Lesbianism*, 42–44; Gowing, "Lesbians and Their Like."

212. Partridge, *Shakespeare's Bawdy*, 101.

213. Gordon Williams, *A Dictionary of Sexual Language*, 1:387.

214. For an abundance of references from the sixteenth to eighteenth centuries, see Gordon Williams, *A Dictionary of Sexual Language*, 1:387–90.

215. Newman, *Cultural Capitals*, 143.

216. Donne, *The Complete English Poems*, ed. Patrides, 139.

217. Donaldson, *Ben Jonson*, 608, lines 497–99.

218. Fisher, "'Doctor Dildos Dauncing Schoole.'"

219. See Moulton, *Before Pornography*, 158–93; and Traub, *The Renaissance of Lesbianism*, 96–99.

220. Contesting an overemphasis on male anxiety, Fisher, "'Doctor Dildos Dauncing Schoole,'" argues that gentlemen readers may have found the poem's main character, Frances's,

erotic agency attractive and may have identified positively with Tomalin, or even with the dildo itself.

221. Cited without attribution by Orgel, "On Dildos and Fadings," 107, and in his glossing of *The Winter's Tale*, 179. He appears to be citing "The Batchelors Feast," discussed below.

222. Middleton, *A Chaste Maid in Cheapside*, 1.2.57.

223. See Woodbridge's gloss to this line in Taylor and Lavagnino, *Thomas Middleton*, 918.

224. According to ballad researcher, singer, and director Lucie Skeaping (personal communication), fillers provide breathing space, not only for the singer, but to allow auditors to absorb all of the information. Of course, a line such as "with his fa la la, with her fa la la" could carry erotic innuendo.

225. "The Batchelors Feast," British Library Roxburghe 1.12, English Broadside Ballad Archive.

226. "The Beautiful SHEPHERDESS OF ARCADIA . . . To the Tune of, The Shepherds Daughter, etc.," which narrates the rape of said shepherdess and her eventual marriage to her rapist, includes the refrain "*Sing trang dildo lee*" (British Library Roxburghe 2.30–31, English Broadside Ballad Archive). See also "A New made MEDLY Compos'd out of sundry SONGS, For Sport and Pastime for the most ingenious Lovers of Wit and Mirth. To the Tune of State and Ambition," Magdalene College Pepys 5.411, English Broadside Ballad Archive.

227. "News from CRUTCHET-FRYERS. Being an Account of some notorious passages which not long since happened there, and will appear a shame to the Actors, not to be forgotten, nor conceal'd Being a great part of impudence, as you shall hear by the following Ditty. Tune is, Hey Boys up go we," Magdalene College Pepys 4.287, English Broadside Ballad Archive.

228. "The Lancashire Cuckold; or, The Country Parish-Clark betray'd by a Conjurer's Inchanted Chamber-pot. To the Tune of, Fond boy, &c.," Magdalene College Pepys 4.145, English Broadside Ballad Archive.

229. "The Maids Complaint / For want of a Dil doul. / This Girl long time had in a sickness been, / Which many maids do call the sickness green: / I wish she may some comfort find poor Soul / And have her belly fill'd with a Dil doul. / To a New Tune, called the Dil doul; or Women and Wine," Magdalene College Pepys 4.50, English Broadside Ballad Archive.

230. Florio, *A Worlde of Wordes*, s.v. *pinco*.

231. Fisher, "'Doctor Dildos Dauncing Schoole.'"

232. *Choyce Drollery*, 31–32.

233. Although Orgel, "On Dildos and Fadings," purports to understand the sexual action of the first three stanzas, calling it "a characteristic piece of male pornography," in which "the dildo is indistinguishable from the real thing, and an object that . . . gives pleasure to the exclusively male audience rather than to the female performer," he admits "I have no idea what is going on in the two final stanzas" (109).

234. A similar question at the heart of the sexual action informs the ballad "Comical News from Bloomsbury: The Female Captain; or, the Counterfit Bridegroom" (ca. 1690), which narrates the sexual relations between the indigent prostitute Mary Plunket who cross-dresses in order to marry a wealthy heiress: "The Bridegroom had prudently got a Sheep's gut / blow'd up very stiff, as a Bladder; / But what he did with it, or whether 'twas put / I'll leave you good Folks to consider." The narrator assures us that the "innocent Bride . . . seem'd to be greatly delighted," even as s/he warns the listening "Lasses" against being "so cleverly cheated," Magdalene College Pepys 5.424, English Broadside Ballad Archive. Despite the ballad's coy refusal to state what happened, Toulalan, *Imagining Sex*, professes to know: "The mixing-up of bodily functions appears here in the implied analogy of breaking wind and urination with ejaculation

in the description of the 'Sheep's gut / blow'd up very stiff, as a Bladder.' The joke is that the young woman has been either farted or urinated into to simulate male ejaculation, and has been deceived into believing that the evacuation either of wind or of urine, or indeed of both, is the satisfactory climax to intercourse" (226).

235. *The Winter's Tale*, ed. Howard, 4.4.194–96.

236. *The Winter's Tale*, ed. Brooks and Jenkins, 100–101; ed. Orgel, 179; ed. Turner and Haas, 384–85.

237. *The Winter's Tale*, ed. Snyder and Curren-Aquino, 185.

238. *The Winter's Tale*, ed. Pitcher, 272.

239. Partridge, *Shakespeare's Bawdy*, 110.

240. Writing about ballads and broadsides, O'Driscoll, "A Crisis of Femininity," notes: "While the dildo in the 1690s is represented as something that any woman might use to satisfy her lust, half a century later it becomes the unmistakable symbol of a woman who is a sexual outlaw" (50), for, in the later period, "the dildo is invested with an enormous burden of masculine significance" (56).

241. Other common ballad refrains are also often sexual; see "The Maid of Tottenham" in *Choyce Drollery*, 45–47: "To fall down, down, derry down, / down, down, derry down, / derry, derry dina." Likewise, it would seem that the word "nonny," also often used in ballad refrains (as in Shakespeare's *Much Ado About Nothing*), was accorded erotic significance; see Rubinstein, *A Dictionary of Shakespeare's Sexual Puns*, 170. In "The Shepheards lamentation for the losse of his Love" (*Choyce Drollery*, 65–67), the shepherd laments the loss of his love's "hy nonny nonny no," and ends "she was her own foe, / And gave her selfe the overthrowe, / By being too franke of her hy nonny nonny no."

242. Partridge, *Shakespeare's Bawdy*, 157.

243. "Thing" is also a reference to the penis, so the sexual innuendo of the passage is far from stable.

244. Carroll, "The Virgin Not."

245. Jonson, *The Devil Is an Ass*, 48.

246. Chapman, *Ovid's Banquet of Sense* (1595), sig. D4r.

247. Maguire, "Typographical Embodiment." Indeed, one might view "et cetera" in the way Joan DeJean approaches the sixteenth-century use of the term "obscene": as a "semantic free radical, capable of playing dramatically different roles" (*The Reinvention of Obscenity*, 9).

248. Maguire, "Typographical Embodiment."

249. According to Wells, *Shakespeare, Sex, and Love*, Richard Hosley's edition of 1957 resolved the difference between the quartos, "O Romeo, that she were, O that she were / An open Et caetera and thou a poperin pear!" (Q1, 1597), and "O Romeo, that she were, O that she were /An open, or, and thou a poperin pear!" (Q2, 1599; and Folio 1623) with the emendation of what Wells calls the "true reading restored" (157): "O Romeo, that she were, O that she were / An open-arse and thou a poperin pear!" "Open, or" is, editors argue, a compositor's misreading of "open-ars," while "Et cetera" is a euphemism occasioned by print. The emendation is now standard, used in *The Norton Shakespeare* and *The RSC Shakespeare*, as well as the individual editions of Levenson, Evans, and Weis.

250. Joseph Porter, *Shakespeare's Mercutio*; Goldberg, "Romeo and Juliet's Open R's," 235. Goldberg's transitive reading of eroticism across gender lines emphasizes that "the open-arse . . . hits and deflects the mark (much as both Q1 and Q2 fail to deliver what Gibbons and most modern editions now allow Mercutio to say)" (230).

251. *Romeo and Juliet*, ed. Greenblatt, 890.

252. Maguire, "Typographical Embodiment."

253. Mullaney, *The Reformation of Emotions*, 119.

254. Greenblatt, *Will in the World*, 323–24.

255. In speaking of the "energy" that may have been "released" by means of "strategic opacity," Greenblatt refers to the energy released within the playwright's own creative process, an energy others have gleaned in Shakespeare's exploitation of paradox as a mode of thinking for both characters and audience; see Platt, *Shakespeare and the Culture of Paradox*, who argues that "the Shakespearean stage *was constituted by* paradox and that it *helped to constitute* . . . a culture of paradox in and for its witnesses" (11; italics in original).

256. Orgel, "The Poetics of Incomprehensibility," 431–37.

CHAPTER 8. SHAKESPEARE'S SEX

1. In *Shakespeare in Psychoanalysis*, Armstrong uses "Shakespeare's Sex" for the title of a chapter on the relationships between Shakespeare, psychoanalysis, gender, and sexuality.

2. Schoenfeldt, *A Companion to Shakespeare's Sonnets*, 2.

3. Foucault, *The History of Sexuality*.

4. Gary Taylor, *Reinventing Shakespeare*; de Grazia, *Shakespeare Verbatim*.

5. Booth, *Shakespeare's Sonnets*, 548. In "More Life," Yates describes Booth's "jocular hit of hyper-formalism" (339) as "out to deep-six" what Booth supposedly regards as "biographical excesses"; yet Yates also notes that "even as Booth closes off the question of a finite sexual identity . . . the studied nonchalance of the self-canceling 'almost certainly' renders any closure of the 'matter' premature" (338).

6. A historicizing approach to trends in Shakespearean biography is pursued by Dutton, "*Shake-speares Sonnets*."

7. This is the approach taken by Burrow, "Editing the Sonnets"; Callaghan, *Shakespeare's Sonnets*; Magnusson, "Shakespeare's Sonnets"; Matz, *The World of Shakespeare's Sonnets*; Schoenfeldt, *The Cambridge Introduction*. This trend stands in contrast to Duncan-Jones's efforts to establish Shakespeare's involvement in the quarto publication in her edition, *Shakespeare's Sonnets*, as well as in her speculative biography *Ungentle Shakespeare*. It also stands in contrast to the speculative biography by Greenblatt, *Will in the World*.

8. Traub, "The Sonnets."

9. Wilde, "The Portrait of Mr. W.H."

10. According to Danson, "Oscar Wilde," 997, Wilde's strategy of ambiguously affirming while denying the meanings of his representation of desire in his novella as well as during his trial is "neither a tease nor an evasion but an effort . . . not to be trapped in another man's system." For a reading of Wilde's novella that places his refusal to nominate desire within the context of both Shakespeare's sonnets and an aesthetics of the sublime, see Halpern, *Shakespeare's Perfume*.

11. Pequigney, *Such Is My Love*; see also "Sonnets 71–74."

12. Smith, *Homosexual Desire*; Bredbeck, *Sodomy and Interpretation*; Dollimore, *Sexual Dissidence*; Goldberg, *Sodometries*; Orgel, *Impersonations*; Sinfield, *Shakespeare, Authority, Sexuality*.

13. In "Reading New Life," Schiffer provides a useful overview of this trajectory up to 1999. See also the bibliography of Traub, "Recent Studies in Homoeroticism."

14. Smith, *Homosexual Desire*, 267.

15. Bredbeck, *Sodomy and Interpretation*.

16. Bray, *Homosexuality in Renaissance England*.

17. Masten, *Textual Intercourse*; "The Two Gentlemen of Verona"; "Towards a Queer Address"; DiGangi, *The Homoerotics of Early Modern Drama*. See also Shannon, *Sovereign Amity*. Despite this work, references to a desexualized Platonic love continue to circulate in sonnets' criticism without awareness that these scholars have transformed understandings of Renaissance Platonism from a defense against homosexuality to one of its most cherished means of expression.

18. On the sonnets' textualization of bisexual desire, see Chedgzoy, "'Two Loves I Have'"; Garber, *Vice Versa*.

19. By using the term "gay," I have been mildly flippant. Nonetheless, because a firm historicist stance can be used to license the dismissal of homoerotic affects, I am uninterested in defending absolute precision regarding terminology. Furthermore, many Shakespeareans remain unconcerned with debates about the relevance of sexual identity categories that have preoccupied critics working on the history of sexuality.

20. Criticism that assumes the homoeroticism of the sonnets includes Matz, "The Scandals of Shakespeare's Sonnets" and *The World of Shakespeare's Sonnets*; Gil, *Before Intimacy*; Herman, "What's the Use?"; Hawkes, "Sodomy, Usury"; Schoenfeldt, "The Matter of Inwardness"; Magnusson, "Shakespeare's Sonnets"; Halpern, *Shakespeare's Perfume*.

21. Among editions that take part in this consensus, see Kerrigan, *William Shakespeare*; Duncan-Jones, *Shakespeare's Sonnets*; Cohen, "The Sonnets"; and Burrow, *William Shakespeare*. Vendler's *The Art of Shakespeare's Sonnets* is sometimes described as an edition, but it is more a commentary. All of these works accept the traditional bipartite division. Among companions and collections to Shakespeare's poetry, see Schiffer, *Shakespeare's Sonnets*, 45, which notes the "general acceptance . . . of gay and bisexual readings of the Sonnets"; Callaghan, *Shakespeare's Sonnets*; Schoenfeldt, *A Companion to Shakespeare's Sonnets* and "The Sonnets"; Matz, *The World of Shakespeare's Sonnets*.

22. "Orthodoxy" is used by Mann in "The 'Figure of Exchange,'" 184.

23. Gil, *Before Intimacy*, 174.

24. Warner, *The Trouble with Normal*; Halperin, *How to Be Gay*.

25. de Grazia, "The Scandal of Shakespeare's Sonnets"; Stallybrass, "Editing as Cultural Formation"; see also Pequigney, *Such Is My Love*. Smith anticipated these reception histories in *Homosexual Desire*, and followed them up with "Shakespeare's Sonnets"; see also Matz, "The Scandals of Shakespeare's Sonnets."

26. DiGangi, "'Love Is Not (Heterosexual) Love.'"

27. de Grazia, "The Scandal of Shakespeare's Sonnets," is aware of this problem; it is notable that few critics who reference her essay note that she proposes "that modern treatments of the sonnets have displaced onto Benson" their own unacknowledged skittishness about "Shakespeare's deviant sexuality" (91).

28. Orgel, "Mr. Who He?" 142. He continues: "and contemporary commentary on these poems is sexually much more open than in comparable editions of the plays," also noting that "the best treatment . . . of both homosexuality and autobiography in the sequence" is that of Kerrigan (143). The grounds for this endorsement are puzzling, insofar as Kerrigan seems to imply that the only grounds for carnal love are visual: "In the last analysis, what one finds registered in the Sonnets is profound homosexual attachment of a scarcely sensual, almost unrealized kind. It is after all remarkable that the poems should tell us so little about the friend's appearance" (*William Shakespeare*, 51). Vendler, *The Art of Shakespeare's Sonnets*, invests this logic with a sublimating rationale, writing that "the infatuation of the speaker with the

young man is so entirely an infatuation of the eye—which makes a fetish of the beloved's countenance rather than of his entire body—that gazing is this infatuation's chief (and perhaps best and only) form of intercourse" (15). For a similar de-corporalization of sex, see Edmondson and Wells, *Shakespeare's Sonnets*, 27, which acknowledges that though the sonnets may not be autobiographical, they show that Shakespeare "could enter the imaginations of men who felt deep love and desire for individual men and women."

29. Smith, *Homosexual Desire*, 231. In "I, You, He, She, and We," Smith critiques others for the attempt "to de-eroticize the first 126 sonnets" (412) most especially Jonathan Bate's contention that "we do not need to know what happened in the bed, because what the sonnets are interested in is how love happens in the head" (Bate, *The Genius of Shakespeare*, quoted by Smith at 413).

30. For a rare exception to this general reticence regarding sex acts in the sonnets, see Sinfield, "What Happens in Shakespeare's Sonnets," in *Shakespeare, Authority, Sexuality*, 162–80.

31. Says Appiah, *Cosmopolitanism*, 77: "Over the last thirty or so years, instead of thinking about the private activity of gay *sex*, many Americans started thinking about the public category of gay *people*. Even those who continue to think of the sex with disgust now find it harder to deny these people their respect and concern (and some of them have learned, as we all did with our own parents, that it's better not to think too much about other people's sex lives anyway)." Progressive politics here are advanced through their likeness to existing social structures of affect and alliance, rather than by means of a challenge to them.

32. It is in part to render that elision less likely that Chapters 6 and 7 describe the varied sex acts potentially attributable to early moderns.

33. de Grazia, "The Scandal of Shakespeare's Sonnets," 106. Analyzing the history of readers' reactions to the sonnets, Roberts, *Reading Shakespeare's Poems*, argues that "it was not so much Shakespeare's portrayal of passionate love between men that was so daring or shocking to readers of the 1609 *Sonnets* as the figure of the sordid, soiled sonnet mistress and the stormy vitriol she provoked" (153). The general concept of competitive Shakespearean scandals appears as early as Greenblatt, *Shakespearean Negotiations*, where he rhetorically asks: "And what if the scandal of a marriage contracted so far beneath a countess's station were topped by a still greater scandal: the revelation that the young groom was in fact a disguised girl?" (66–67).

34. Burrow, *William Shakespeare*. Gil, Magnusson, and Sinfield also emphasize the cross-class nature of the poet's relation to the young man, but do not promote this as the "real scandal."

35. Matz, "The Scandals of Shakespeare's Sonnets," 478.

36. Matz, "The Scandals of Shakespeare's Sonnets," balances awareness of synchronic variations within a narrative of diachronic change, revealing a useful tension between understandings of same-sex and cross-sex desire that propels analysis beyond binary oppositions of male and female, hetero and homo: "before the mid-twentieth century, responses to the sonnets are sometimes what we would call homophobic (fearful of same-sex desire)—but they are not heterosexist (favoring of cross-sex desire)"; earlier "readers might condemn the sonnets' same-sex love or celebrate it as male friendship, but they typically did not react to Shakespeare's 'homosexuality' by finding solace in his 'heterosexuality'" (478).

37. On the racial and aesthetic meanings of white, black, and fair, see de Grazia, "The Scandal of Shakespeare's Sonnets"; see also Hall, "'Those Bastard Signs of Fair'"; Marvin Hunt, "Be Dark but Not Too Dark"; Iyengar, "Whiteness as Sexual Difference," esp. 166–69.

38. The forms and effects of misogyny in Shakespeare's sonnets are more complicated than the handy use of the term suggests. Some of the poems ventriloquize misogyny as an intellectualized rhetorical stance, others traffic in it as an emotional weapon, while others seem invested in it as expressions of truth about the lady. What makes these poems misogynist is not their application of the topos of female licentiousness (which could be erotically empowering for women), but the disgust directed toward the female body as well as the "madness" she elicits from the poet-speaker.

39. Dubrow, "'Incertainties Now Crown Themselves.'" Dubrow's championing of the dark lady was anticipated by Schalkwyk, "'She Never Told Her Love.'" See also Duncan-Jones, *Shakespeare's Sonnets*. For my critique of Dubrow's logic, see Traub, "The Sonnets."

40. Ilona Bell, "Rethinking Shakespeare's Dark Lady," 298. Bell reads the sonnets performatively, "as a private lyric dialogue, rooted in the practice of courtship and seduction and the laws of betrothal and marriage" (293). Although she says that she resists reading the sonnets as a "narrative or explanatory" story (296), she constructs an alternative story. In reading the sonnets intertextually with *A Lover's Complaint*, Roberts, *Reading Shakespeare's Poems*, attempts to moderate the judgment that the misogyny of the sonnets is Shakespeare's own.

41. Burrow, *William Shakespeare*; Schoenfeldt, "The Sonnets." This is epitomized for them by Fineman's brilliant if problematic *Shakespeare's Perjured Eye*. Likewise taking Fineman to task, Kalas, "Fickle Glass," reads the relation of the poet to his two love objects relationally, proposing that the missing concluding couplet of Sonnet 126, with its baffling pairs of brackets, marks the dynamic intersection of, rather than a strict division between, scenarios regarding the speaker's male and female lovers.

42. Trevor, "Shakespeare's Love Objects," 230; Trevor seeks to detach literary figures from "real-life sources" (228), to show that the speaker's love refers to both the beloved and love itself and that one aim of the sonnets, given the inability to attain the love object with any form of constancy, is to instantiate poetry itself as the highest and most constant form of love—a kind of metapoetic consolation (or even revenge). See also Naomi J. Miller, "Playing 'the Mother's Part'": "Whether the addressee is woman or man makes no difference to the speaker's calculated plea that the beloved 'play the mother's part, kiss me, be kind'" (362).

43. Callaghan, *Shakespeare's Sonnets*; Burrow, *William Shakespeare*; Trevor, "Shakespeare's Love Objects"; Schoenfeldt, "The Sonnets."

44. Schiffer, in *Shakespeare's Sonnets*, 6, cites Ramsey, who in *The Fickle Glass*, 3, notes that the problems of the sonnets "loop and twist into each other, and to tug at one is to tighten others."

45. Adelman, "Male Bonding in Shakespeare's Comedies"; Wheeler, *Shakespeare's Development*; Kahn, *Man's Estate*; MacCary, *Friends and Lovers*. For a critique of this tradition, see Armstrong, *Shakespeare in Psychoanalysis*.

46. In addition to *Shakespeare's Perjured Eye*, see Fineman, "Fratricide and Cuckoldry."

47. Parts of this debate hinge on Foucault's purported relationship to psychoanalysis, a debate still going strong. For instance, arguing for the neglected importance of Foucault's critique of psychoanalysis in *History of Madness* for the project of queer theory, Huffer's *Mad for Foucault* critiques queer theorists' efforts to integrate Foucault with psychoanalysis. While making a strong case for Foucault's description of the psyche as "a function of our sexual subjectivation" (138), her argument proffers *History of Madness* as the master text with which to read all of Foucault, the result of which is to impose a unity and coherence on his oeuvre that hypostatizes his engagements with psychoanalysis. So too, her characterization of "queer theory's pervasive investment in a timeless psyche" (129) seems a mirror image to Bersani's

overstatement of queer theory's rejection of psychoanalysis (see my Chapter 1); both arguments rely on a very selective definition of what counts as "queer theory."

48. Fradenburg, *Sacrifice Your Love*, 48.

49. Greenblatt, "Psychoanalysis and Renaissance Culture," 142.

50. Trevor, *The Poetics of Melancholy*, 30. Defenses of psychoanalysis against a perceived hegemonic historicism include Bellamy, "Psychoanalyzing Epic History," and "Psychoanalysis and Early Modern Culture"; and the introduction to Nardizzi, Guy-Bray, and Stockton, *Queer Renaissance Historiography*. An attempt at reconciliation was broached by Mazzio and Trevor, "Dreams of History."

51. In addition to Trevor, "Shakespeare's Love Objects," see Cynthia Marshall, *The Shattering of the Self*; and Hillman, *Shakespeare's Entrails*. Much of this scholarship is indebted to the historicist work on humoralism by Paster, *The Body Embarrassed* and *Humoring the Body*; and Paster, Rowe, and Floyd-Wilson, *Reading the Early Modern Passions*. See also Schoenfeldt, *Bodies and Selves*, which opposes humoralism to psychoanalysis.

52. Enterline, *The Rhetoric of the Body*; Schwarz, *Tough Love*; Schiesari, *The Gendering of Melancholia*; Traub, *Desire and Anxiety*, 50–70.

53. Gil, *Before Intimacy*; Sanchez, *Erotic Subjects*.

54. Occasionally linked to a diachronic narrative of change and other times resistant of any such chronology, such historically minded psychoanalytic criticism has been most persuasive when it forgoes a "before and after" model of modern subjectivity (or of the modern body or of intimacy) and works within a synchronic framework to excavate the metaphors, lexicons, and imagery by which we come to know desiring subjects, conceptual categories, and modes of thought.

55. Gil, *Before Intimacy*; Sanchez, *Erotic Subjects*; Hammill, *Sexuality and Form*; Will Stockton, *Playing Dirty*.

56. Even a properly historicized psychoanalysis is a theory that, like any theory, aims toward broad applicability. The challenge, then, is not only to resist surreptitious reintroductions of heterosexist paradigms, but to query the presumption that we always know what erotic desire means and what bodily acts typified early modern sex.

57. Three touchstones in queer theory for whom psychoanalysis have been central are Judith Butler, *Bodies That Matter*; Edelman, *No Future*; Bersani, *Is the Rectum a Grave?*

58. Although this understanding of queerness pervades contemporary queer readings of early modern writers, this line of thinking is advocated most strenuously by Menon, *Shakesqueer* and *Unhistorical Shakespeare*.

59. Callaghan, *Shakespeare's Sonnets*; Schoenfeldt, "The Sonnets" and *A Companion to Shakespeare's Sonnets*; Roberts, "Shakespeare's Sonnets." Richard Barnfield's and Michelangelo's sonnets did precisely the same thing. For a more complex view of Shakespeare's Petrarchism, see Braden, "Shakespeare's Petrarchism."

60. Exceptions include Masten, *Textual Intercourse* and *Queer Philologies*; DiGangi, *The Homoerotics of Early Modern Drama* and *Sexual Types*; Shannon, *Sovereign Amity*; Saunders, *Desiring Donne*.

61. These issues are part of what is stake not only within queer theory but between the ongoing negotiation between queer theory, gay male masculinity, and feminism; see Halley, *Split Decisions*; Rambuss, "After Male Sex"; Weigman, *Object Lessons*.

62. Dean, "Queer Theory Without Names," 431.

63. See Chapter 3.

64. Callaghan, *Shakespeare's Sonnets*, compares the poet's relation to the youth and mistress but doesn't view these tensions as mutually constitutive.

65. Sanchez analyzes the productivity of female promiscuity in "The Poetics of Feminine Subjectivity." Indeed, some women might find sexy precisely the terms of abuse that the poet-speaker directs toward the mistress.

66. Appropriation of female reproduction for male authorship is a common Renaissance topos; see Elizabeth Harvey, "Flesh Colors and Shakespeare's Sonnets"; Brooks, *Printing and Parenting*. For a queer critique of the heterosexualizing imperatives of critics who have analyzed reproductive metaphors, see Guy-Bray, *Against Reproduction*.

67. A related argument, to which I am indebted, is made by Masten, "Authorship in Love."

68. Displacement need not always happen sequentially; displacements in dreams are polysynchronous.

69. Mann's reading of Sonnet 20 in "The 'Figure of Exchange'" notes that the "correlation between this lyric and the 'Figure of exchange' does not resolve" the gender/sexual ambiguity of the sonnet, which instead "resists a teleology of desire that could be adduced as either hetero- or homosexual" (184).

70. Another common conflation is between authorization and the dating of Shakespeare's composition, a question to which computer stylometrics increasingly is applied.

71. For "the centrality of indexical reading to nearly all Christians in early modern England," see Stallybrass, "Books and Scrolls," 51.

72. See Hutchison, "Breaking the Book," for analysis of the page breaks that "interrupt" the quarto's sonnets, but also produce a kind of "material enjambment" (55), that forces readers to "read across the fold" (34). In "The Sonnets and Book History," North points out the quarto's material anomalies in relation to most other sonnet sequences: "Since its compositor made no effort to keep poems to a single page, awkwardly isolated leading and trailing lines force the reader to flip pages back and forth to get the full sense of some sonnets." This "asymmetrical" layout creates "a kind of forward rhythm that cuts across the thematic divisions and connections in the sequence" (208). This would seem to imply a preference for a sequential reading of the quarto; however, North uses it to argue that it is evidence that "Thorpe acquired a partially organized collection of small côterie sequences and individual sonnets" (211). With the exception of Booth, editors who reproduce the quarto's original spelling and punctuation neglect to reproduce its continuous and asymmetrical pagination, its running header, or its catchwords (see Duncan-Jones, *Shakespeare's Sonnets*; Schoenfeldt, *A Companion to Shakespeare's Sonnets*; Vendler, *The Art of Shakespeare's Sonnets*). Booth's *Shakespeare's Sonnets*, however, is not a true facsimile, as it inserts facing pages of modernized text and deletes *A Lover's Complaint* from the 1609 quarto.

73. A few sonnets were first published in *The Passionate Pilgrim* in 1599.

74. Booth notes that "although the sex of the beloved is unspecified in most of the sonnets, all those that are specifically and exclusively addressed to a man precede [Sonnet 126] in the Q order, and all those specifically and exclusively addressed to a woman follow it" (*Shakespeare's Sonnets*, 430). Arguing that the sonnets are best understood as a collection rather than a sequence, Edmondson and Wells provide a table entitled "Sexing the Sonnets: Male and Female Addressees" in *Shakespeare's Sonnets*, 30. One exception to this trend is Magnusson, "Shakespeare's Sonnets," which examines pronouns for the clues they provide of a dialogue that is socially situated by age, class, gender, and vocation.

75. Dubrow argues that the "axiom" of the traditional gender division has generated unwarranted "assumptions about the presence of a linear plot" ("'Incertainties Now Crown Themselves,'" 291). Emphasizing the sonnets' resistance to narrativity, she defines "the issue of sequence" precisely as the question of "whether the poems now exist in the order their author intended [which is] is closely related to, but separable from, the likelihood of determining their addressees" (293). In "The Incomplete Narrative of Shakespeare's Sonnets," Schiffer provides several possible reasons for the sonnets' "anti-narrativity."

76. Mann, "The 'Figure of Exchange,'" 184.

77. Nelles admits that the matter is more complex than mere counting. He summarizes the different numbers of sonnets that are gendered by different critics, noting that "one obvious complication in such tabulations is in agreeing upon which cues count as marking the gender of the addressee" ("Sexing Shakespeare's Sonnets," 131 n. 10); however, he then offers his own computational assessment of forty-three sonnets marked for gender. Schiffer, "Reading New Life," likewise notes the lack of consensus about which poems lack a gendered address.

78. Nelles, "Sexing Shakespeare's Sonnets," 140.

79. Nelles, "Sexing Shakespeare's Sonnets," 139.

80. This critical move has an antecedent in the history of Shakespearean scholarship on gender and sexuality. If those of us who worked on the gendered and erotic dimensions of cross-dressing first focused on gender and erotic indeterminacy, polymorphous play, and performativity, many quickly became cognizant that cross-dressing takes place within a system of constraints.

81. McCabe, "To Be and to Have," 123.

82. These sonnets might be viewed as providing an alternative to the anguished jealousy, born of triangular desire, dramatized in Sonnets 40–42 and 133–34.

83. Bozio, "The Extended Self in Shakespeare's Sonnets."

84. This puts a twist on Sullivan's contention that after the failure of the procreation sonnets, "the poet is the sole repository for the memory and identity—the 'life'—of the young man" ("Voicing the Young Man," 339).

85. There is nothing intrinsic to this poem that genders its lyric "I"; this also depends on an effect of sequence, most especially invoked by those "holy and obsequious teare[s]" that the poet's "eye" has previously shed.

86. Vendler, The Art of Shakespeare's Sonnets, 170.

87. Sedgwick, Between Men, 28–48.

88. Vendler, The Art of Shakespeare's Sonnets, 575.

89. The phrase is Grossman, "Whose Life Is It Anyway?" 235. I am in some accord with Grossman, whose essay perceptively addresses the relations among sexuality, syntax, and epistemology in the sonnets. We differ, however, to the extent that the central question remains for him that of sexual subjectivity, finding in Shakespeare's sex, once again, the Lacanian phallus.

90. Schwarz, What You Will, 141. Analyzing the "transactional subjectivity" (135), of "heterosocial" intention and desire, Schwarz's book is the most far-reaching feminist queer analysis of gender and eroticism in the dark lady subsequence. Exploring representations of early modern women's complicity with expectations of femininity and demonstrating the oscillating dynamics in "the space of engagement in which masculine and feminine subjects meet" (135), Schwarz argues that the sonnets deploy familiar misogynist rhetoric in the poet-speaker's and lady's exchanges of "will," only to expose and destabilize misogyny through "transgressive reinscription" (152). Her deconstructive analysis shares with mine an interest in the mutual

constitution of erotic subjects and objects and in the transitive relays across categories of sameness and difference. We agree that "the poems are less a story than an anatomy, not of a passively objectified female body but of the active and consequential encounters that produce gendered agents" (132) and a "good-enough" erotics. If I am not persuaded that the subsequence ultimately is as deconstructive of gender and misogyny as she is, it is because she tends to see "mutuality," "contract" (137), and "symbiosis" (136) precisely at the moments I see hierarchy and coercion. She also accords greater effectivity to gender transitivity than I do, in part because she views the exposure of gender's "factitiousness" (132) as dismantling the gender system: "The circulation of will across lines of gender nullifies that system" (131). Most pertinent to our differences, however, is that our readings of the sonnets attend to opposite moments in the process of gender construction. Whereas I track the formal means by which genders are constituted in order to query the status of poet-speaker and mistress as already predicated gendered subjects, she shows the effects of "volitional exchange" (131) and focuses on their deconstruction.

91. Schwarz reads this line, among others, as connoting that "subjectivity in these poems does not mean having a will of one's own. Shared possession of a woman, understood as rivalry or as traffic, becomes shared possession with a woman, a shift that defines autonomous masculinity as an untenable state" (*What You Will*, 142).

92. Sanchez, "The Poetics of Feminine Subjectivity," 516.

93. The phrase is adopted from Fish, "Masculine Persuasive Force," 250. My emphasis on Shakespeare's ability to create rather than simply deploy gender figurations is similar to Fish's reading of Donne. If, in the end, Fish's point is that "the lesson of masculine persuasive force is that it can only be deployed at the cost of everything it purports to incarnate—domination, independence, assertion, masculinity itself" (250), we differ in the extent to which we view this as a problem.

94. Masten, "The Two Gentlemen of Verona," 283, and "Towards a Queer Address."

95. In "I, You, He, She, and We," Smith demonstrates through attention to a wider range of pronominal markers that male and female are not so much indeterminate as "implicated in one another" (417); his claim that "the whole effect of the poems is to constitute the sexually desiring 'I' in terms of both 'him' and 'her,'" and that these three positions "have no independent existence, but exist in terms of each other" (424), coheres in broad strokes with the diacritical argument I am pursuing here. See, too, Matz's recognition that "the scandal of the sonnets to the woman is generated out of, and serves to displace, the scandal in the sonnets to the man" in "a diacritical relationship" ("The Scandals of Shakespeare's Sonnets," 484).

96. For a classic cultural materialist analysis of displacement, see Stallybrass and White, *The Politics and Poetics of Transgression*. For representative treatments of displacement in Shakespeare studies, see Snyder, "'The King's Not Here'"; Cook, "'The Sign and Semblance of Her Honor'"; Mohler, "'What Is Thy Body.'"

97. McEachern, "Why Do Cuckolds Have Horns?" 608. McEachern's argument extends displacement into the religious realm, reading horn humor as a response to "the affective and epistemological conundrums posed by soteriology" (610), particularly as "a response to anxiety whose expression is faith" (615).

98. Smith, "Latin Lovers," 344.

99. Smith, "Latin Lovers," 349.

100. Smith, "Latin Lovers," 344.

101. For how synchrony contributes to diachrony, see Kerrigan, *William Shakespeare*, 8: it is "that subtle modulation of material from poem to poem into the form of the whole which

makes reading Shakespeare's Sonnets such a concentrated yet essentially cumulative experience"; a "rhythm, rhyme, a quirk of syntax, or an echoing image: such minutiae, hardly discernible in conscious reading, knit the poems together." See also Burrow, *William Shakespeare*, 108: "a random sequence could not have produced the waves of consonant moods, of sounds and rhythms of thought, which link almost every sonnet with a neighbour or near-neighbour, and which parallel the tireless interconnections within individual sonnets of sound with sound and quatrain with couplet."

102. So too, the notion of a sonnet "playlist" conscripts a synchronic mode of analysis to a diachronic one.

103. Jagose, *Inconsequence*, xi, 36.

104. Jagose, *Inconsequence*, ix, xi.

105. Parker, *Literary Fat Ladies*, 178–233.

106. Scott, *The Fantasy of Feminist History*, 51.

107. Hammond, *Figuring Sex*, 72.

108. Grossman, "Whose Life Is It Anyway?" 232.

109. Grossman, "Whose Life Is It Anyway?"

110. Bahti, *Ends of the Lyric*, 18.

111. Bahti, *Ends of the Lyric*, 21.

112. Bahti, *Ends of the Lyric*, 19, 41, 23.

113. Kerrigan's introduction focuses on the role of time, especially "clock time," in the sequence and sees in reproduction a "moral means to similitude" (*William Shakespeare*, 35, 27). Other critics have traced Shakespeare's assertion of poetry's power to defy time to memorializing strategies and the arts of memory; see Sutphen, "'A Dateless Lively Heat'"; Sullivan, "Voicing the Young Man"; Watson, "'Full Character'd.'"

114. Burrow argues that the first seventeen poems "are a crucial part of the design of the whole sequence. . . . Much of the rest of the sequence urgently asks whether poetry can provide a form of permanent beauty which would function as a substitute for biological reproduction. . . . The question as to whether words in themselves can create an archetype and permanent source of beauty is in one respect the subject of the whole sequence up to 126." And in Sonnet 126, the sequence "breaks off, still asking whether poetic power can provide an alternative to the biological decay of the principal source of its vitality" (*William Shakespeare*, 115).

115. Matz, "The Scandals of Shakespeare's Sonnets," 480.

116. As Smith notes, the term "friend" is applied to the young man seven times, whereas it is applied to the mistress only once (*Homosexual Desire*, 249).

117. On women's relationship to the Renaissance discourse of friendship and its changes over the course of the seventeenth century, see Traub, *The Renaissance of Lesbianism*, 276–325.

118. That it was conventional does not mean that it was aligned with official orthodoxy, a point that needs to be made in reference to the most extensive treatment of the sonnets' homoeroticism in editorial practice. Exemplary in his exactitude regarding most aspects of Shakespeare's text, Burrow argues that Shakespeare explores the full spectrum of possible social attitudes toward same-sex love, from idealized celebration to self-shaming condemnation. Yet, having adopted this view, he then employs the term "sodomy" as a placeholder for all of these affects and attitudes, neglecting to consider that nowhere in Shakespeare's complex vacillation of positions regarding his friend does he invoke the specter of sodomy. Thus collapsing the range of emotions expressed toward the friend into the orthodox, prejudicial definitional framework, Burrow commits a kind of category error. In so doing, he misses the extent to which

Shakespeare's representation of homoerotic love, desire, and pain is conventional precisely insofar as it dissociates male-male love from the terms that could land a man such as Shakespeare
in prison. A far more nuanced historical understanding of relations among friendship and
sodomy is advanced by Matz, "The Scandals of Shakespeare's Sonnets," but he overestimates
the extent to which "Shakespeare's imposition of his 'eternal lines' over the young man's family
lines . . . confounds the social order" (483). Appropriation of the idioms of generation doesn't
so much confound lineage as rearticulate it in a different register.

119. Masten, "Gee, Your Heir Smells Terrific."

120. Traub, "The Sonnets."

121. In a short section entitled "Women's Time," Callaghan remarks, in regard to Sonnet
129, that woman is associated with "the absence of temporal progression" (*Shakespeare's Sonnets*,
98); her point, however, is to elaborate Duncan-Jones's suggestion of the dark lady sequence as
corresponding to the menstrual cycle.

122. Callaghan, "Confounded by Winter," 104. Callaghan links this haste to Ovid, and
contrasts it to the protracted temporality of Petrarch.

123. Callaghan, *Shakespeare's Sonnets*, 89. Asking what "makes the poet so concerned" about
time in relation to the youth and "so unconcerned about it in relation to the woman," Callaghan answers that the woman, "possessed of neither youth nor beauty, has nothing to lose"
(89).

124. Callaghan, *Shakespeare's Sonnets*, 98.

125. Sutphen, "'A Dateless Lively Heat,'" 210.

126. de Grazia, "Revolution in Shake-speares Sonnets," 67.

127. This would seem to be the accusation lodged by Goldberg against Fineman when he
invokes Sedgwick's argument from *Epistemology of the Closet* that the diacritical difference
between opposed forms of sexual identity is characteristic of modern forms of knowledge about
sexuality; see Goldberg, "Literary Criticism, Literary History." I would suggest that a diacritical
perspective, implicit in Judith Butler's *Gender Trouble* and *Bodies That Matter*, has, with the
growing prestige of queer as an alternative, largely dropped out of queer early modern studies.

128. It may seem to readers well schooled in feminist critical traditions that the sonnets'
displacement of anxiety onto the body of a woman is all too familiar, and perhaps implicitly
a- or transhistorical. Familiar, yes; transhistorical, no. The accent throughout has been on how
gendered and sexual understandings are mediated through syntactical procedures that, though
formally available at each historical moment, are expressed in socially contingent ways.

129. On intersubjectivity, see Schwarz, *What You Will*; on perverse mutuality, see Gil,
Before Intimacy, 109. A diacritical understanding implicitly underlies Gil's argument that
"Shakespeare uses the Dark Lady to absorb functional homosocial intimacy *and* the dysfunc-
tional intimacy of sodomy" (111).

130. The extent to which we, as readers and commentators on the sonnets, are captive to
their reproductive logic is observed by Schiffer, *Shakespeare's Sonnets*, 49.

131. It is not that Shakespeare is somehow exemplary of "the Renaissance" or that his
iconic status—which has given rise to a "Shakespeare function," a "Shakespeare effect," and a
"Shakespeare regime"—doesn't carry with it histories of privilege and exclusion. Rather, I have
put into practice Denise Albanese's proposal that "Shakespeare needs to be read dialectically,"
and that "there remains the possibility of a utopian surplus, of Shakespeare as a repository for
'social dreaming'—a recognition, that is, that Shakespearean formations, even when imbricated
in questions of political economy and acts of hegemony, can still be *useful*, can still signify
beyond those confines" (*Extramural Shakespeare*, 5, 8–9).

CHAPTER 9. THE SIGN OF THE LESBIAN

Note to epigraph: Erasmus, *Virgo misogamos*, trans. Thompson, as "The Girl with No Interest in Marriage," 108, emphasis in translation. An early modern translation by H.M. (1671) titles *Virgo misogamos* as "A Maid Hating Marriage," with the relevant passage translated thus: "*Eu.* Because there are found more which imitate the manners of *Sappho*, than which are like her in wit. *Ca.* I do not well understand what that means. *Eu.* And therefore I speak these words, my *Catarine*, lest at any time thou mayst understand them" (144).

1. Wiegman, "Afterword," 205.

2. Wiegman, "Afterword," 208–9.

3. Wiegman, *American Anatomies*.

4. Wiegman, "Feminism, Institutionalism," and *Object Lessons*. Further, Wiegman has examined the tensions between these field formations, including the differential status accorded to lesbianism.

5. Wiegman argues that "lesbian history as a disciplinary endeavor takes itself as a practice of love" (211), an overinvestment that, to her mind, explains the lack of dissension among the book's contributors. While there is truth to her characterization of love and reparative reading as one motivation, neither love as a historical object nor lack of dissension within the field are as hegemonic as she supposes.

6. For Wiegman's meditations on the theory/practice conundrum, see "The Intimacy of Critique."

7. Wiegman, "Afterword," 211.

8. Jagose, *Queer Theory* and "Feminism's Queer Theory"; Sharon Marcus, "Queer Theory"; Wiegman, *Object Lessons*; Huffer, *Are the Lips a Grave?*

9. De Lauretis, *The Practice of Love*.

10. Foundational texts are Combahee River Collective, "The Combahee River Collective Statement"; Moraga and Anzaldúa, *This Bridge Called My Back*; Lorde, *Sister Outsider*; Anzaldúa, *Borderlands/La Frontera*. For queer work that attends to their contributions, see Muñoz, *Disidentifications*; Rod Ferguson, *Aberrations in Black*; Johnson and Henderson, *Black Queer Studies;* Gopinath, *Impossible Desires*.

11. Sharon Marcus argues that if lesbianism is used as the "master discourse for understanding all relationships between women," crucial questions about women's intimacies go unasked (*Between Women*, 12).

12. In making this claim, I am not suggesting that histories of medieval and early modern lesbianism are, as Giffney, Sauer, and Watt contend, "theory in and of itself" (*The Lesbian Premodern*, 12). We need to think carefully about the theoretical work that the history of lesbianism can and cannot do. For a demurral similar to mine, see Lochrie, "Preface," xvii.

13. See Chapter 3. Historicism remains a strong force within early modern studies, although its "hegemony" has been cracked by a number of innovations, not least among them psychoanalytically inflected queer work.

14. Nealon, *Foundlings*, 17.

15. Nealon, *Foundlings*, 9, 18.

16. Hall and Jagose, *Routledge Queer Studies Reader*, xvii. Whereas the editors refer approvingly to work in the history of sexuality and note more broadly their discomfort with the processes of selection involved in anthologization, they move quickly from history to temporality.

17. Berlant and Edelman, *Sex*, ix. A response to characterizations of their work as anti-reparative and antisocial, each of the book's key terms—negativity, optimism, sovereignty, aesthetic, repair, butthole—is placed within a broad discursive tradition (e.g., psychoanalysis or political theory) and subjected to rigorous theoretical investigation, but is only loosely tethered to specific social contexts.

18. See Berlant's "national sentimentality trilogy": *The Anatomy of National Fantasy; The Queen of America; The Female Complaint.*

19. Berlant and Edelman, *Sex*, 9. In *Cruel Optimism*, Berlant refers to her work on the political and affective impasses of the present as "a kind of proprioceptive history, a way of thinking about represented norms of bodily adjustment as key to grasping the circulation of the present as a historical and affective sense" (20).

20. Berlant, *Cruel Optimism*, 21.

21. Edelman in Freeman, "Theorizing," 181.

22. Edelman in Freeman, "Theorizing," 181.

23. Edelman, "Ever After," 470.

24. In *Sex*, Berlant and Edelman define "negativity" as "the nonfutural insistence in sex of something nonproductive, nonteleological, and divorced from meaning making" (11).

25. Berlant and Edelman, *Sex*, 10, emphases mine.

26. Berlant and Edelman, *Sex*, ix.

27. Dinshaw in Freeman, "Theorizing," 186.

28. Edelman in Freeman, "Theorizing," 188.

29. The prestige of theory is higher in queer studies than in early modern studies or other fields that have taken a more demographic turn such as film studies.

30. Lanser, *The Sexuality of History*, 9.

31. Coviello, "World Enough," 395; see also his meditations on the role of obliquity, inarticulacy, and errancy as a constitutive feature of the queer past in *Tomorrow's Parties*.

32. Wiegman, *Object Lessons*, 102.

33. Wiegman, *Object Lessons*, 103.

34. Wiegman, "Afterword," 211.

35. Wiegman, "Afterword," 211.

36. This is a position potentially aligned with what Coviello, *Tomorrow's Parties*, calls the "agnostic" approach to sexual history—the idea that, given the "intractable illegibility of the past," one should resist "the impulse to erode the distinctiveness of the past by rendering it in the terms and taxonomies of the present" (13).

37. Wiegman, *Object Lessons*, 312.

38. Wiegman, "Afterword," 203.

39. Wiegman, "Introduction," 5.

40. Wiegman, "Afterword," 203.

41. Wiegman, "Introduction," 2.

42. See Chapter 4.

43. For challenges to the premodern/modern divide, see Toulalan and Fisher, *The Routledge History*, 4; and the section "When Was Sexuality? Rethinking Periodization," in Spector, Puff, and Herzog, *After "The History of Sexuality."* For "threshold narratives," see Puff, "After the History," 19.

44. Freeman, "Sacramentality," 179.

45. For more on how historians view theory, see Doan, *Disturbing Practices*.

46. "History" has its own modes of scaling up: e.g., periodization and, during the heyday of the Annales school, the *longue durée*. Microhistory might be seen as the epitome of scaling down.

47. These are not the only correspondences between history and theory. The theories that literary scholars tend to privilege and the scholarly productions of historians are centrally concerned with and depend upon the work of signification, whether it is construed as tropology, discourse, or narrative. While some historians resist announcing the theoretical underpinnings of their work (as is more common among literary scholars), their practice of narration has been extensively theorized; see Chapter 6. For analysis of how notions of history do and do not transit across the disciplines of English and History, including their implications for each discipline's notions of "time" and "narrative," see Stein, "American Literary History."

48. Different perceptions and valuations of scale, of the relative emphasis on looking backward or forward, and of the formal narratives by which arguments are made have contributed to conflicts between queer historicism and queer temporality. The latter's interest is in scaling up by moving beyond the specificities of bodies and psyches to explore the erotics and nonnormativities of much larger conceptual fields, such as language, affect, matter, space, and time. See Chapter 3.

49. Given queer and postcolonial critiques of "the archive" that summarily conflate its mode of organization (e.g., the classifying catalog) with specific ideologies (e.g., teleological history, racism, imperialism), it seems important to say that while there is, indeed, a politics of the archive, that politics is not inert, either in its genesis or in its use. Any archive is produced over time by a mix of intention, selection, chance, opportunism, accretion, and exclusion. Archivists use specific methods to identify, catalog, and house archival objects, and scholars with a range of purposes and methods can put these modes of classification to a variety of uses, including nonrecuperative, nonteleological, and anti-imperial ones. For a thoughtful meditation on the "critical attachments to archival recovery" in postcolonial sexuality studies, see Arondekar, *For the Record*, 1–5: Arondekar acknowledges that "the archive has emerged as *the* register of epistemic arrangements, recording in its proliferating avatars the shifting tenor of debates about the production and ethics of knowledge." She recognizes that "one must work with the empirical status of the materials, even as that very status is rendered fictive," yet nonetheless questions "how sexuality is made visible in the colonial archive and . . . how this process paradoxically discloses the very limits of that visibility." Her interest is in how the archive's "fiction effects" and its "truth effects" are "agonistically co-constitutive of each other" and how to intervene in the promise of recovery and the "transformative hopes" that come with it.

50. See Chapter 6.

51. Huffer, *Are the Lips a Grave?* 68–69.

52. Foundational theoretical tenets of queer theory that were developed out of historical analysis of the late nineteenth century include the epistemology of the closet (Sedgwick), the open secret (D. A. Miller), and the transformation of sex into sexuality (Foucault).

53. Wiegman, *Object Lessons*, 130–31, emphases mine.

54. See also Huffer, *Are the Lips a Grave?* who challenges the way that "the ethical tension between queers and feminists" has been figured as "a tension between an antinormative, self-shattering queer flirtation with the irrational and feminism's seemingly more rationalist, normative, moralizing claims about sexuality in a gendered order" (13). Relaying her "questions about ethics through the epistemological and ontological questions at the heart of the debate," Huffer

attempts "to break through the rigid lines across which the queer feminist opposition is constructed" (59). She also notes that "one of the crucial effects of the feminist/queer split" is "the erasure of the 'lesbian' subject'" (195 n. 27). Revisiting the history of queer theory's construction of feminism as moralist narrative thus involves challenging "an identitarian conception of lesbian with an alternative account that redefines lesbian as an event of marginalization that is erotically charged"; for her, it also involves making a claim on behalf of "a forgotten lesbian jouissance" (118).

55. See Chapter 4.

56. See Doan, *Disturbing Practices*; Colin R. Johnson, *Just Queer Folks*.

57. Lesbianism, so construed, has a very short historical arc: it is neither premodern nor postmodern, but only and ever modern.

58. See Chapter 3.

59. Doan, *Disturbing Practices*, 3; Doan aligns "the genealogical urge" with the desire "to know with certainty" (2).

60. Freccero, "The Queer Time," 69, 70.

61. I have tried, when possible, to eschew the personal pronoun in order to avoid personifying "the lesbian" as a sign.

62. Susan Lanser and I convened a Radcliffe Institute Workshop, "Writing Lesbianism into History and Representation," in January 2014, to query the salience and outcome of this view of lesbian studies. By fostering a conversation among scholars of diverse theoretical investments, intellectual approaches, historical fields, and disciplines, we hoped to identify reasons for the persistent minimization of "lesbianism" and to imagine intellectual projects and institutional strategies that could redirect the course of scholarship and increase recognition of its import. The following two paragraphs are revisions of an invitation to participants to that workshop, cowritten with Lanser.

63. Doan, *Disturbing Practices*.

64. See the treatment of lesbianism in Dabhoiwala, *The Origins of Sex*; McKeon, "Symposium."

65. See as well the material factors addressed by Gomez, "But Some of Us."

66. Brooten, *Love Between Women*, 5, notes that Arethas, in his tenth-century Byzantine commentary on Clement of Alexandria's discussion of women who married other women, equated *lesbiai*, *tribades*, and *hetairistriai*. But note Halperin's disagreement that *lesbiai* meant "lesbian" in its modern sense in *How to Do*, 48–80, esp. 52.

67. Blank, "The Proverbial 'Lesbian,'" 108.

68. "Sappho the lesbian" was often taken to refer to her birthplace on the island of Lesbos.

69. DeJean, *Fictions of Sappho*; Prins, *Victorian Sappho*.

70. Amer, *Crossing Borders*, 7; Amer argues that the term reemerges in French after a six-century hiatus in Brantôme's sixteenth-century *Vies des dames galantes*, and emerges in English only in the eighteenth century (171 n. 31).

71. Andreadis, *Sappho in Early Modern England*.

72. See Halperin's critique of Brooten's investment in conceptual and historical continuity, and his effort "to distinguish language from experience, categories of thought from forms of subjectivity, continuities from discontinuities in the historiography of sex and gender" (*How to Do*, 48–49). See also Borris, *Same-Sex Desire*, 18; Bennett, "'Lesbian-Like'"; Lanser, *The Sexuality of History*; and Traub, *The Renaissance of Lesbianism*.

73. Puff, "Toward a Philology"; Halperin, *How to Do*, 50.

74. Blank, "The Proverbial 'Lesbian,'" 109.

75. Hehir and Gribble, *Outlines*; cited by Arondekar, *For the Record*, 89, emphasis mine.

76. Blank, "The Proverbial 'Lesbian,'" 133.

77. See Chapter 4.

78. In *The Renaissance of Lesbianism*, I used "lesbian" to refer "to a representational image, a rhetorical figure, a discursive effect, rather than a stable epistemological or historical category" (15). In contrast, this chapter attempts to treat this figure as epistemological and historical while retaining a sense of instability.

79. Wahl, *Invisible Relations*; see also King, "The Unaccountable Wife."

80. Rohy, *Impossible Women*; see also Love, *Feeling Backward*, 21.

81. Jagose, *Inconsequence*, 24.

82. Jagose, *Inconsequence*, 9.

83. Jagose, *Inconsequence*, 8.

84. Jagose, *Inconsequence*, 8.

85. Jagose, *Inconsequence*, 8.

86. Jagose, *Inconsequence*, 16.

87. Jagose, *Inconsequence*, 21.

88. Doan, *Disturbing Practices*, 137. It accords as well with Coviello's guiding question in *Tomorrow's Parties*: "what if the sexual possibilities dreamed into being in the era before sexology proved *not* to be amenable to the forms of sexual subjectivity and sexual specificity that would, in fact, arrive?" (15, emphasis in the original).

89. Arondekar, "In the Absence."

90. Jagose, *Inconsequence*, 9.

91. Jagose, *Inconsequence*, 23, emphasis mine.

92. See also Roof, *A Lure of Knowledge*.

93. Binhammer, "Accounting for the Unaccountable," 2.

94. Binhammer, "Accounting for the Unaccountable," 2–3.

95. Rohy, *Impossible Women*, 9, 4.

96. Rohy, *Impossible Women*, 5.

97. Rohy, *Impossible Women*, 146.

98. Rohy, *Impossible Women*, 150; see also Roof, *A Lure of Knowledge*.

99. Lanser, *The Sexuality of History*, 245.

100. Wiegman, "Afterword," 208.

101. Biddy Martin, *Femininity Played Straight*, 71–72.

102. Biddy Martin, *Femininity Played Straight*, 77. Martin was partly reacting to what Sedgwick called, in a different context, "the coarser stigmata of gender difference" (*Epistemology of the Closet*, 32).

103. Lochrie, "Preface," xiv.

104. Freeman, "Packing History," 728. See also the less temperate Schlichter, "Contesting 'Straights'"; and Walters, "From Here to Queer."

105. Wiegman notes that "Martin's topography of gender has undergone extensive revision" in the queer theoretic, particularly because under the auspices of transgender and related discourses, gender has become a "profoundly transitive signifier" (*Object Lessons*, 103). See also Prosser, *Second Skins*; Stryker, "Lesbian Generations"; Love, "'Oh, the Fun We'll Have.'"

106. Lochrie, "Preface," xiv. Describing the methods used to adduce "the lesbian" in the premodern period in "Sacramentality," Freeman notes that they tend to involve "a certain adhering to the object, a refusal of the abstracting process, a set of textual practices that are as

devotional and corporeal as they are cognitive and linguistic" (182). Whereas Freeman celebrates these practices of adherence as befitting what she calls a "sacramental" object, I have sought to "adhere" to "the lesbian," not to refuse abstraction, but to enable it.

107. Giffney, Sauer, and Watt, *The Lesbian Premodern*, xxi.

108. Freeman, "Sacramentality," 179.

109. I'm thinking of Margaret Cho, Holly Hughes, and Alison Bechdel.

110. Halberstam, *Female Masculinity*.

111. In this regard, one might apply Wiegman's recognition in "Feminism, Institutionalism," of how identity-based studies are consigned "to their most reduced and realist referential function as affect and not intellect, as particularity and not complexity" to "the lesbian," whose "referential function" is relegated to the realm of the social rather than to the realm of the intellect, and whose remit becomes particularity rather than complexity (60).

112. I echo Jagose's explanation of her motives in *Orgasmology* in offering "orgasm" as a critical term: "I'm not offering it as yet another critical figure around which we can rally differently than the last figure we rallied differently around. Rather . . . I am speaking to the value of sticking with an unlikely scholarly object, attending to the thick textures of its discursive formulations, for the new perspectives it affords on familiar questions and even received knowledges, without requiring it to harden off into a specifiable program or course of action" (xvi).

113. Educated men with access to the classics thought they understood a good deal about female-female sex; see Puff, "Toward a Philology." Surveying seventy stage plays written between 1570 and 1660, Walen, *Constructions of Female Homoeroticism*, suggests the extent to which representations of female-female desire may have been more culturally intelligible than supposed, providing a taxonomy of scenarios in which homo-desiring female characters are represented or the possibility of same-sex erotic love alluded to: "(1) [in] playful scenarios of mistaken identity, (2) in anxious moments of erotic intrigue, (3) in predatory situations, and (4) in enthusiastic utopian representations of romantic love." The "broad representation of and response to female homoeroticism" in the drama includes: "accepted as a chaste passion; dismissed as an improbable fiction; condemned as a lewd practice; and supported as preferable to heterosexual intercourse; encountered as innocent practice, as substitution, as rebellion against male authority, or as its own pleasure in female relations; found among both transvestite or masculine women and traditionally feminine women, from aristocrats to vagrants to city and country wives" (*Constructions*, 2, 19). For the nineteenth century, Sharon Marcus argues that "authors openly represented relationships between women that involved friendship, desire, and marriage. It is only twentieth-century critics who made those bonds unspeakable, either by ignoring what Victorian texts transparently represented, or by projecting contemporary sexual structures onto the past" (*Between Women*, 75).

114. In addition to Freccero's specter, other figures have been posited as particularly suitable for queering the past. Love notes Foucault's reference to Orpheus, who, she says, "offers an apt emblem of the practice of queer history" (*Feeling Backward*, 50). In "Lesbian History," Farina proposes that readers of "a lesbian erotic should draw inspiration from Echo" because of her "transformative mirroring," mobility, and ability to create resonances between past and present (57); see also Scott's deployment of Echo as a figure for feminist historiography in *The Fantasy*. In "No Present," Guy-Bray offers Narcissus as a model for queer historiography in a self-consciously "lyrical engagement with the literature of the past" (43).

115. My argument has something in common with Wiegman's attempt in "Feminism, Institutionalism" to refute a realist approach to the name of the field "Women's Studies" by

separating it from its historical referent in order to think capaciously about what the field could be. In a sense, I have redeployed Wiegman's own question about Wendy Brown's critique of the institutionalization of Women's Studies: "Why refuse the possibility that attention to the issues [Wiegman] defines will productively contribute to the redefinition, resignification, and redeployment of the intellectual force, frame, and function of the field?" (60).

CHAPTER 10. SEX ED

1. Midler, "One Monkey Don't Stop No Show"; music by Rose Marie McCoy; lyrics by Charlie Singleton: "I used to be chicken hearted, cry when he'd walk out the door / 'Cause I was just young and stupid, ha, ain't like that no more."

2. Snow, "Teach Me Tonight"; music by Gene De Paul, lyrics by Sammy Cahn. Lyrics © Warner/Chappell Music, Inc.

3. All citations from Middleton and Dekker, *The Roaring Girle*.

4. Bromley, "'Quilted with Mighty Words.'" Early modern "city comedy" (set in London) and "town comedy" (set in the newly developed West End) have productively been read as genres concerned with embodied social types often identified by sexuality; see Howard, *Theater of a City*; Rubright, "Going Dutch in London City Comedy"; DiGangi, *Sexual Types*.

5. *The Roaring Girle*, 770.

6. "Nyggle," in contrast, makes its initial appearance in the *OED* with Thomas Harman's canting dictionary, *Caveat for Commen Cursetors* in 1567, with the next two entries attributed to Dekker. What criterion authorizes the definition of "niggle" as "to have sex" whereas "fadoodle," failing to meet this criteria, becomes a "nonce word" and "euphemism"?

7. "The Mourning Conquest," Magdalene College Pepys 3.139, English Broadside Ballad Archive, sung to the tune of "A loving Husband will not be unto his Wife unkind."

8. Murphy and O'Donnell, "Introduction," call this ballad's theme "fairly typical: lusty women having their way with men," 13. My point is that women in such texts more often than not do *not* have their way. At least in ballads, sexual naïveté is gendered. O'Connell, "Love Pleasant," asserts that "the notion of naïveté in young women does not appear in English popular visual culture until late in the eighteenth century" (70).

9. "Memoirs of the Birth, Education, Life and Death of Mr. John Cannon" (1743), quoted in Griffiths, *Youth and Authority*, 243–44.

10. Kunzel, "Queer Studies in Queer Times," 163. "Rethinking Sex" was held at the University of Pennsylvania March 4–6, 2009; Kunzel's essay appears in a special issue of *GLQ* devoted to the conference. I was in attendance and have consulted a taped version of the proceedings. My effort to identify the speaker through a query to the organizer was unsuccessful.

11. Although the presentation was a dialogue between Lee Edelman and Lauren Berlant, Edelman was the one to respond to this student; a revision of their presentation appears in Berlant and Edelman, *Sex*, 1–34.

12. Edelman, "Against Survival," 169. See also his "Learning Nothing." According to "Queer Theory and *Hamlet*," Edelman is completing a book on sexuality, aesthetic philosophy, and humanistic values to be titled "Bad Education."

13. Huffer, *Mad for Foucault*, 203.

14. On the relations among irony, love, and passion, see Halperin, "Love's Irony."

15. Edelman, *No Future*, 23.

16. Edelman, *No Future*, 24, 28. Berlant and Edelman designate irony as "the rhetorical figure of nonsovereignty" (*Sex*, 15).

17. On the transideological utility of irony across the political spectrum, with particular attention to its misunderstanding and misfirings, see Hutcheon, *Irony's Edge*, 2.

18. A number of queer studies scholars have noted the importance of taking such risks. In "Still After," Freeman admits to wondering "whether daring to ask a question that seemed banal, even rearguard, might produce a leap forward of some sort" (497). For a rare admission of ignorance, see Kate Thomas, "Post Sex." Jagose notes that her project in *Orgasmology* "is to take up a 'simple question' without repudiating it as the dumb question for which such simple questions are often mistaken. It is to risk seeming naive, even backward, about queer scholarly knowledges or codes of critical inquiry" (10). This self-perception of naïveté and belatedness is evident as well in Dinshaw's self-description of "always playing a no-win game of catch up" in *How Soon Is Now?* 103.

19. Many of these questions are addressed in Berlant and Edelman, *Sex*. See also Love, *Feeling Backward*, on the "intransigent difficulties of making feeling the basis for politics" (14), as well as the distinction she draws between her emphasis on failure and Edelman's emphasis on negativity (23).

20. And yet, irony also needs to be historicized. See Albanese, *Extramural Shakespeare*, 115: "There was a time when, it seems, irony was considered to be the basis of an oppositional political practice, when, as Roland Barthes expresses it in *Mythologies*, 'sarcasm [was] the condition of truth'. . . . I wonder whether such a modeling of distance ever did have the effectivity he claimed for it: Barthes himself scripted a sad fate for the leftist mythographer, cut off, alienated from the center of culture and from those whose consciousness she or he would attempt to re-form. Nevertheless, it needs no ghost to tell us that cynical distance has gone mainstream. Like the English majors many of us have trained as resistant, canny spectators, debunkers of cultural myths who are now working in the advertising industry, irony has become a part of the sales repertory of capitalism."

21. Whereas Britzman, *The Very Thought*, puts "the very thought of education . . . on the couch" in order to access "the idea that something within education resists thinking" (3), and whereas she locates this "thought" in emotional scenarios animated by fantasies of love, rage, authority, and dependency, her "pedagogy of uncertainty" frames learning and teaching as not only *about* knowledge but as a particularly fraught knowledge relation (xi). Following Freud in viewing education as an "impossible profession," she approaches "the thought of education dynamically: as uneven development, as conflict, as promise, and as reparation" (2). "While normative views of education promise a progression of knowledge and an accumulation of best practice, seen from the idea of resistance to education or what education resists, the promise of education begins with the transference and its difference" (140).

22. In appropriating the term "presentism," critics attempt to turn others' allegation of anachronism against historicism; but insofar as presentists tend to neglect the extent to which feminist and queer scholars for decades have been practicing a "history of the present," these critics also seem to be promoting a manufactured novelty.

23. Quoted in Britzman, *The Very Thought*, 6.

24. Foucault, *The History of Sexuality*, vol. 1; this foothold, of course, is uneven across different disciplines.

25. See Halperin, "Deviant Teaching," as well as *How to Be Gay*, for how the specter of initiation haunts gay male pedagogical practices.

26. Huffer, *Mad for Foucault*, 138, 95. Recognition of this "theoretical bind" in which we are "mesmerized by our own subjectivation" leads Huffer not only to question talk about sex, but to discount queer theory informed by psychoanalysis: "psychoanalytic queer theory's 'sex talk' ironically reproduces a nineteenth-century positivist discourse that objectifies alterity across the split between reason and madness" (95, 94, 138). She continues this argument in *Are the Lips a Grave?*: "queer utterances, far from disrupting the regime of sexuality, in fact reinforce it; indeed, the queer speaking of previously unspoken acts perpetuates the repressive myth of sex as a secret to be confessed" (76). Calling this "queer theory's constitutive contradiction" (76), she argues that "the only way out of this familiar conundrum is to go on inventing new pleasures with strange parts of the body, never speaking of them at all" (77).

27. Tuana, "Coming to Understand."

28. Spector, Puff, and Herzog, *After "The History of Sexuality."*

29. Due to Sedgwick's theory of reparative reading, the pedagogical encounter, of which Sedgwick often stands as the teacherly exemplum, has come to the fore in queer studies; see Love, "Truth and Consequences," who reads Sedgwick as calling for a de-idealization of the relation between student and teacher.

30. Downing, "Afterword," 528.

31. Downing, "Afterword," 529, emphases mine.

32. Britzman, *The Very Thought*, xi–xii: "Students are involved in their own transference. . . . They may wish the teacher to leave them alone, to come closer, or tell them what she wants. They may not want to know anything about it, or demand to be given the proper instrument that will come with some sort of guarantee. They may be anxious about measuring up or feel too big and too smart. There is so much going on that we do not know about or do not want to know anything about." On the other side of the transference: "involved in any teaching and learning is a certain ruthlessness, an aggression with both the material taught and with our respective uses of it. The teacher, after all, is a witness to how students ruin her lessons, misinterpret her intentions, refuse to read, hand in late papers, and generally go their own way without thinking about the teacher's plans, schedules, or even her feelings" (97).

33. According to some, Lacan made this remark in a session of the seminar on "crucial problems" on March 17, 1965, in the course of a commentary on Alcibiades's speech in Plato's *Symposium*: "L'amour, c'est donner ce qu'on n'a pas à quelqu'un qui n'en veut pas" (Love, that's giving what one doesn't have to someone who doesn't want any of it); others credit it to an earlier seminar; see Lacan, *Le séminaire*, 23.

34. Dolven, *Scenes of Instruction*, 11; "necessarily" is my addition.

35. Irvine, *Talk About Sex*; Levine, *Harmful to Minors*; Luker, *When Sex Goes to School*; Fields, *Risky Lessons*.

36. This is one reason that it is difficult for students to understand the import of Foucault's critique of the "repressive hypothesis." The Reich/Marcuse discourse against which Foucault was writing—which heralded the promise of freedom through sex—is not a major part of their world.

37. Traub, *The Renaissance of Lesbianism*, 295–308. For eighteenth-century examples, see Gonda, "Ledore," "Lesbian Narrative," and "What Lesbians Do."

38. Castle, *The Apparitional Lesbian*, 102–6; Anna Clark, "Anne Lister's Construction"; Colclough, "'Do You Not Know.'"

39. See Waters, *Tipping the Velvet*, *Affinity*, and *Fingersmith*; and Brenda K. Marshall, *Dakota*.

40. This is related to a historical awareness of the similarities and differences in different sexual systems across time, including the enduring role of gender asymmetries of sexual knowledge.

41. Britzman, *The Very Thought*, 131, notes that in construing education as "the transference of desire for knowledge and love, [it] may be transformed into a capacity to tolerate uncertainty."

42. Freud, *Three Essays*, 194.

43. Rasmussen, Rofes, and Talburt, *Youth and Sexualities*; Carrillo and Fontdevila, "Rethinking Sexual Initiation"; Angelides, "Feminism, Child Sexual Abuse" and "Subjectivity Under Erasure."

44. See the response to the "It Gets Better" media campaign: "This is reteaching gender and sexuality."

45. Horowitz, *Rereading Sex*; Moran, *Teaching Sex*.

46. Fine and McClelland, "Sexuality Education."

47. Garcia, "'Now Why Do You Want to Know'"; Abraham, "Teaching Good Sex."

48. McClelland and Fine, "Writing on Cellophane."

49. Important changes have occurred within LGBTQ psychology and public health research on HIV/AIDS prevention and women's health; see Diamond, *Sexual Fluidity*. However, it is unlikely that these fields will offer a historical perspective on contemporary sexual formations.

50. Sedgwick, *Epistemology of the Closet*, 8; *Tendencies*, 25.

51. Sedgwick, *Tendencies*, 23–51; Spivak, *A Critique*. Spivak's target is the ignorance, produced and supported by mainstream educational practices, of the "elite theorist and self-styled activist" (86), regarding the material and ideological conditions of globalization.

52. Proctor argues that "ignorance has a history and a complex political and sexual geography, and does a lot of other odd and arresting work that bears exploring" (*Cancer Wars*, 2). See Proctor and Schiebinger, *Agnotology*, 3: "We need to think about the conscious, unconscious, and structural production of ignorance, its diverse causes and conformations, whether brought about by neglect, forgetfulness, myopia, extinction, secrecy, or suppression."

53. Ronell, *Stupidity*, 5: "stupidity does not allow itself to be opposed to knowledge in any simple way, nor is it the other of thought. It does not stand in the way of wisdom, for the disguise of the wise is to avow unknowing. . . . the question of stupidity is not satisfied with the discovery of the negative limit of knowledge; it consists, rather, in the absence of a relation to knowing." This absence of a relation to knowing differentiates stupidity from ignorance, and it is this differential relation with which Ronell closes her introductory chapter, entitled "Slow Learner": "While it draws a blank and is *about* blanking out, ignorance, at once perniciously coherent and seriously lacking in coherence—not in itself contemptible—downshifts from stupidity in the sense that you may still find the owner's manual somewhere or . . . some rules of operation. Ignorance holds out some hope, you can get to know it, maybe move on. I am not so sure about stupidity" (29).

54. Proctor acknowledges that ignorance isn't "always a bad thing" (Proctor and Schiebinger, *Agnotology*, 2), but he links this value to the right to privacy and the dangers of information overload.

55. The movement from ignorance to knowledge generally has been construed as a developmental sequence: from lack to gain, from darkness to light, from vacancy to plenitude. In addition, knowledge generally is construed as incremental, advancing progressively toward betterment, improvement, and the fulfillment of goals.

56. Cunningham, *The Cosmographical Glasse*, 46.

57. I adopt the phrase from Jagose, *Orgasmology*, 10.

58. Sedgwick's positive estimation of difference rearticulates one of Rubin's central insights in "Thinking Sex" that one need not like a particular sex act in order to recognize that someone else does.

59. Sedgwick, *Epistemology of the Closet*, 59.

60. Sedgwick, *Tendencies*, xii.

61. Hanson, "The Future's Eve," 105; for a taste of Hanson's irony: "Having only just recovered from Judith Butler's gender melancholia, we are launched into the tenuous positionality of Sedgwick's queer depressive" (106).

62. Hanson, "The Future's Eve," 113. See also Love, "Truth and Consequences," who emphasizes the extent to which paranoid and reparative modes are intertwined, even in Sedgwick's own essay.

63. I am not proposing sexuality itself as an ethics, whether conceived as a poetic "ethic of eros" that, through honoring past lives, provides a "map for living" (Huffer, *Mad for Foucault*, 43, 48), or, conversely, a desubjectifying ethos, a modern ascesis or self-shattering, sought through certain corporeal pleasures (e.g., the degenitalization of BDSM or fistfucking) or modes of communal yet impersonal affiliation (e.g., cruising). See Halperin, *Saint Foucault*, 76–106, on Foucault's vision of a "homosexual ascesis" that "may be able 'to define and develop a way of life' that in turn 'can yield a culture and an ethics,' new forms of relationship, new modes of knowledge, new means of creativity, and new possibilities of love" (78). On self-shattering, see Bersani, *Homos*; and Bersani and Phillips, *Intimacies*. For cruising, see Bersani, *Is the Rectum a Grave?* which offers a proposal for an ethics of the self based on antisocial relationality that would remediate the aggressive violence of the monadic ego.

64. As Amin, "*Queer*'s Affective Histories," notes: "Queer Studies has become a discipline whose field norms include statements (or protests) of anti-disciplinarity and whose field habitus is one in which practitioners demonstrate belonging by performing, in their work and through their embodiment, transgression, eccentricity, a disregard or even contempt of conventions, and a stance against the institution of academia in general and the institutionalization of Queer Studies more specifically. This is not to say that such gestures are empty, but only that it is by learning to perform them with conviction that one becomes paradoxically professionalized as a Queer Studies practitioner."

65. In *The Queer Art of Failure*, Halberstam advocates failure, stupidity, forgetting, and illegibility as a queer strategy of "oppositional pedagogies" (12). She dismisses such qualities "like *serious* and *rigorous*" as "code words" for the "disciplinary correctness" that can only confirm "what is already known according to approved methods of knowing" (6)—constructing a false binary that opposes "rigor and order" to "inspiration and unpredictability" (10), and situating the latter outside of and against academic knowledges. Her "third thesis: *Suspect memorialization*" (15), is pointedly antihistorical, drawing its energies from Foucault's critique of memory as a disciplinary mechanism, but failing to recall (or conveniently forgetting) that Foucault proposed not less history but the strategies of counter-memory.

66. Ferguson, *The Reorder of Things*. For other views of academic institutionalization, complicity, and co-optation, see Wiegman, *Object Lessons*, "Feminism, Institutionalism," and "Wishful Thinking"; Ahmed, *On Being Included*.

67. Nor do I think that elucidating unknowing or attending to inarticulateness means dispensing with a historical "archeology of sexual knowledge," as proposed by Herring, *Queering the Underworld*, 209. In order to "query the possibility of a knowable gay and lesbian past,"

Herring provocatively employs a "suspicion of sexual hermeneutics" to counter "a hermeneutics of sexual suspicion," but in his effort to "render more incognito sexual moments of anyone's sexual period," he tends to treat all forms of sexual knowledge as part of a disciplinary epistemology of the closet (20, 23, 14).

68. Wiegman, "Afterword," 203–4.

69. This idea was broached by Bray; see Chapter 2. It has been developed by Lanser, *The Sexuality of History*. Vicinus, "Lesbian Ghosts," 196, briefly notes that "one of the most promising new directions in scholarship might be called the mainstreaming of sexuality studies, demonstrating not the impact of society on sexual mores, but the opposite—how female homoeroticism is an agent for social change," referencing, along with Lanser, Sharon Marcus's demonstration of the impact of female marriages on divorce debates.

70. Although Foucault was suspicious of "the consoling play of recognitions," he emphasized discursive profusion, entanglement, and contradiction as well as temporal recursivity and dispersion: doublings, false starts, deviations, displacements, backtracking, reversals, and feedback loops ("Nietzsche, Genealogy, History," 153).

71. Certain arguments have accrued broadened significance across the course of this book. For instance, the workings of sexual sequence, first broached in Chapter 3 to approach structural relations between chronology and temporality, was deployed in Chapter 8 to analyze relations among gender and sexuality, feminism and queer theory. Rearticulating a historiographic problem as a theoretical and hermeneutic one, Chapter 8 doubles back upon the historical argument of Chapter 4, wherein perennial cycles of salience demonstrate how sequence itself can be nonsequential.

72. I do not mean that Edelman fails to think historically or neglects texts of an earlier time; see his reading of *Hamlet* in relation to negativity and queerness in "Against Survival," which argues that Hamlet "belongs to the universe in which the Child has become the guarantor of futurity: a fantasy figure produced as the promise of secular temporal closure intended to restore an imaginary past in a future endlessly deferred" (148).

73. Edelman, *No Future*, 31; "Against Survival," 169.

74. In this I echo Freeman, "Introduction," 166: "do all futurities entail heteronormative forms of continuity or extension?"; as well as Coviello, *Tomorrow's Parties*, 21: "investments in futurity might not always and everywhere amount to capitulation to the logic of reproductive heteronormativity."

75. Edelman, "Against Survival," 153.

76. In "Edward's Futures," Masten describes how in Marlowe's *Edward II*, the position of "the Child" in reproductive futurity is better described as "the crown"; at the same time, Edward's son and heir queerly ventriloquizes his father at the end of the tragedy by looking perversely backward: "In me, my loving father speaks."

77. Edelman, "Against Survival," 167.

78. Wrightson, *English Society*, 107; Pollock, *Forgotten Children*, 97.

79. Printed advice on parental conduct did not become very specific or prevalent until the 1670s.

80. Historians have countered the controversial thesis of Lawrence Stone that children in early modern England were met with parental coldness and indifference, pointing to evidence of parental grief at childhood mortality. Literary critics have begun to redress the invisibility of children, both in the early modern period and in scholarship, by looking for a broader range of "evidence for early modern children's cultural presence and agency" (Chedgzoy, "Introduction," 28).

81. Wrightson, *English Society*, 104.

82. Wrightson, *English Society*, 112, 117.

83. Clerical writers warned against pampering children, children's corporal punishment generally was seen as a necessary response to disobedience, and childhood health or sickness tended to be interpreted as a sign of God's favor or disfavor.

84. Cited in Anthony Fletcher, *Growing Up*, 4.

85. Edelman explains his decision to not "engage" the ways in which "any number of female characters might be considered in terms of *sinthomo*sexuality": "to engage them here would necessitate a parsing of the category to identify their differences from *sinthomo*sexuality as I discuss it here. . . . Valuable as the exploration of such gendered differences would be, I have chosen not to engage it here lest the introduction of taxonomic distinctions at the outset dissipate the force of my larger argument against reproductive futurism" (*No Future*, 165–66 n. 10).

86. See Halperin, *How to Do*, 48–80; my critique of Trumbach's "London's Sapphists" in *The Renaissance of Lesbianism*, 29–31; Freccero's review of Bray's use of Lister in "Passionate Friendship."

BIBLIOGRAPHY

Abbas, Sadia. "Other People's History: Contemporary Islam and Figures of Early Modern European Dissent." *Early Modern Culture* 6 (2007). http://emc.eserver.org/1-6/abbas.html.

Abelove, Henry. "Some Speculations on the History of Sexual Intercourse During the Long Eighteenth Century in England." *Genders* 6 (1989): 125–30.

Abraham, Julie. *Are Girls Necessary? Lesbian Writing and Modern Histories.* London: Routledge, 1996.

Abraham, Laurie. "Teaching Good Sex." *New York Times Magazine,* November 16, 2011. http://www.nytimes.com/2011/11/20/magazine/teaching-good-sex.html?smid = pl-share.

Achinstein, Sharon. *Milton and the Revolutionary Reader.* Princeton, NJ: Princeton University Press, 1994.

Adair, Richard. *Courtship, Illegitimacy and Marriage in Early Modern England.* Manchester: Manchester University Press, 1996.

Adam, Barry D. "Accounting for Sex." *GLQ: A Journal of Lesbian and Gay Studies* 3 (1996): 311–16.

Adelman, Janet. "Male Bonding in Shakespeare's Comedies." In *Shakespeare's "Rough Magic": Renaissance Essays in Honor of C. L. Barber,* ed. Peter Erickson and Coppélia Kahn, 73–103. Newark: University of Delaware Press, 1985.

Ahmed, Sara. *On Being Included: Racism and Diversity in Institutional Life.* Durham, NC: Duke University Press, 2012.

Albanese, Denise. *Extramural Shakespeare.* New York: Palgrave Macmillan, 2010.

Alderson, David. "Queer Cosmopolitanism: Place, Politics, Citizenship and *Queer as Folk.*" *New Formations* 55 (2005): 73–88.

Alexander, M. Jacqui. *Pedagogies of Crossing: Meditations on Feminism, Sexual Politics, Memory, and the Sacred.* Durham, NC: Duke University Press, 2005.

Allan, Keith, and Kate Burridge. *Forbidden Words: Taboo and the Censoring of Language.* Cambridge: Cambridge University Press, 2006.

Amer, Sahar. *Crossing Borders: Love Between Women in Medieval French and Arabic Literatures.* Philadelphia: University of Pennsylvania Press, 2008.

Amin, Kadji. "*Queer's* Affective Histories." Presentation, National Women's Studies Association Convention, San Juan, Puerto Rico, November 2014.

Anderson, Penelope. *Friendship's Shadows: Women's Friendship and the Politics of Betrayal in England, 1640–1705.* Edinburgh: Edinburgh University Press, 2012.

Andreadis, Harriette. *Sappho in Early Modern England: Female Same-Sex Literary Erotics, 1550–1714.* Chicago: University of Chicago Press, 2001.

Angelides, Steven. "Feminism, Child Sexual Abuse, and the Erasure of Child Sexuality." *GLQ: A Journal of Lesbian and Gay Studies* 10, no. 2 (2004): 141–77.

———. "Subjectivity Under Erasure: Adolescent Sexuality, Gender, and Teacher-Student Sex." *Journal of Men's Studies* 15, no. 3 (Fall 2007): 347–60.

Anzaldúa, Gloria. *Borderlands/La Frontera: The New Mestiza*. San Francisco: Aunt Lute, 1987.

Appiah, Kwame Anthony. *Cosmopolitanism*. New York: W. W. Norton, 2006.

Archer, Ian W. *The Pursuit of Stability: Social Relations in Elizabethan London*. Cambridge: Cambridge University Press, 1991.

Aretino, Pietro. *Aretino's Dialogues*. Trans. Raymond Rosenthal. New York: Stein and Day, 1971.

Armstrong, Philip. *Shakespeare in Psychoanalysis*. London: Routledge, 2001.

Arondekar, Anjali. *For the Record: On Sexuality and the Colonial Archive in India*. Durham, NC: Duke University Press, 2009.

———. "In the Absence of Reliable Ghosts: Sexuality, Historiography and South Asia." *Positions* 23, no. 1 (forthcoming 2015).

———. "Time's Corpus: On Sexuality, Historiography, and the Indian Penal Code." In *Comparatively Queer: Crossing Time, Crossing Cultures*, ed. Jarrod Hayes, Margaret Higonnet, and William J. Spurlin, 113–28. New York: Palgrave Macmillan, 2010.

Attridge, Derek. *Peculiar Language: Literature as Difference from the Renaissance to James Joyce*. Ithaca, NY: Cornell University Press, 1988.

Babayan, Kathryn. "The 'Aqā' id al-Nisā': A Glimpse at Safavid Women in Local Isfahani Culture." In *Women in the Medieval Islamic World: Power, Patronage, Piety*, ed. Gavin R. G. Hambly, 349–81. New York: St. Martin's Press, 1998.

Babayan, Kathryn, and Asfaneh Najmabadi, eds. *Islamicate Sexualities: Translations Across Temporal Geographies of Desire*. Cambridge, MA: Harvard University Press, 2008.

Bach, Rebecca Ann. *Shakespeare and Renaissance Literature Before Heterosexuality*. New York: Palgrave Macmillan, 2007.

Bahti, Timothy. *Ends of the Lyric: Direction and Consequence in Western Poetry*. Baltimore: Johns Hopkins University Press, 1996.

Bal, Mieke. *Travelling Concepts in the Humanities: A Rough Guide*. Toronto: University of Toronto Press, 2002.

Beckett, Samuel. *The Unnamable*. New York: Grove Press, 1958.

Bell, Ilona. "Rethinking Shakespeare's Dark Lady." In *A Companion to Shakespeare's Sonnets*, ed. Michael Schoenfeldt, 293–313. Malden, MA: Blackwell, 2007.

Bell, Rudolph M. *How to Do It: Guides to Good Living for Renaissance Italians*. Chicago: University of Chicago Press, 1999.

Bellamy, Elizabeth. "Psychoanalysis and Early Modern Culture: Is It Time to Move Beyond Charges of Anachronism?" *Literature Compass* 7, no. 5 (2010): 318–31.

———. "Psychoanalyzing Epic History." In *Translations of Power: Narcissism and the Unconscious in Epic History*, 1–37. Ithaca, NY: Cornell University Press, 1992.

Bellany, Alastair. *The Politics of Court Scandal in Early Modern England: News Culture and the Overbury Affair, 1603–1660*. Cambridge: Cambridge University Press, 2002.

Bennett, Judith M. "Confronting Continuity." *Journal of Women's History* 9, no. 3 (1997): 73–94.

———. "'Lesbian-Like' and the Social History of Lesbianisms." *Journal of the History of Sexuality* 9 (2000): 1–24.

———. "Remembering Elizabeth Etchingham and Agnes Oxenbridge." In *The Lesbian Premodern*, ed. Noreen Giffney, Michelle M. Sauer, and Diane Watt, 131–43. New York: Palgrave Macmillan, 2011.

Bennett, Judith M., and Amy M. Froide, eds. *Singlewomen in the European Past*. Philadelphia: University of Pennsylvania Press, 1999.

Berlant, Lauren. *The Anatomy of National Fantasy: Hawthorne, Utopia, and Everyday Life*. Chicago: University of Chicago Press, 1991.

———. *Cruel Optimism*. Durham, NC: Duke University Press, 2011.

———. *The Female Complaint: The Unfinished Business of Sentimentality in American Culture*. Durham, NC: Duke University Press, 2008.

———. *The Queen of America Goes to Washington City: Essays on Sex and Citizenship*. Durham, NC: Duke University Press, 1997.

Berlant, Lauren, and Lisa Duggan, eds. *Our Monica, Ourselves: The Clinton Affair and the National Interest*. New York: New York University Press, 2001.

Berlant, Lauren, and Lee Edelman. *Sex, or the Unbearable*. Durham, NC: Duke University Press, 2014.

Berry, Helen. "Lawful Kisses? Sexual Ambiguity and Platonic Friendship in England, c. 1660–1720." In *The Kiss in History*, ed. Karen Harvey, 62–79. Manchester: Manchester University Press, 2005.

Bersani, Leo. *Homos*. Cambridge, MA: Harvard University Press, 1995.

———. "Is the Rectum a Grave?" *October* 43 (Winter 1987): 197–222.

———. *Is the Rectum a Grave? and Other Essays*. Chicago: University of Chicago Press, 2010.

Bersani, Leo, and Adam Phillips. *Intimacies*. Chicago: University of Chicago Press, 2008.

Bersani, Leo, and Ulysse Dutoit. *Caravaggio's Secrets*. Cambridge, MA: MIT Press, 1998.

Beynon, John C., and Caroline Gonda, eds. *Lesbian Dames: Sapphism in the Long Eighteenth Century*. Farnham, England: Ashgate, 2010.

Billings, Timothy James. "Squashing the 'Shard-borne Bettle' Crux: A Hard Case with a Few Pat Readings." *Shakespeare Quarterly* 56, no. 4 (2005): 434–47.

Binhammer, Katherine. "Accounting for the Unaccountable: Lesbianism and the History of Sexuality in Eighteenth-Century Britain." *Literature Compass* 7, no. 1 (2010): 1–15.

———. "The Sex Panic of the 1790s." *Journal of the History of Sexuality* 6, no. 3 (1996): 409–34.

Bishop, Elizabeth. *The Complete Poems, 1927–1979*. New York: Farrar, 1983.

Blackbourn, David. "'The Horologe of Time': Periodization in History." *PMLA* 127, no. 2 (2012): 301–7.

Blank, Paula. "The Proverbial 'Lesbian': Queering Etymology in Contemporary Critical Practice." *Modern Philology* 109, no. 1 (2011): 108–34.

Blount, Thomas. *Glossographia; or, A Dictionary Interpreting All Such Hard Words of Whatsoever Language Now Used in Our Refined English Tongue*. London, 1656.

Bly, Mary. "Bawdy Puns and Lustful Virgins: The Legacy of Juliet's Desire in Comedies of the Early 1600s." *Shakespeare Survey* 49 (1996): 97–109.

———. "Carnal Geographies: Mocking and Mapping the Religious Body." In *Masculinity and the Metropolis of Vice, 1550–1650*, ed. Amanda Bailey and Roze Hentschell, 89–113. New York: Palgrave Macmillan, 2010.

———. *Queer Virgins and Virgin Queans on the Early Modern Stage*. Oxford: Oxford University Press, 2000.

Boehrer, Bruce Thomas. "Bestial Buggery in *A Midsummer Night's Dream*." In *The Production of English Renaissance Culture*, ed. David Lee Miller, Sharon O'Dair, and Harold Weber, 123–50. Ithaca, NY: Cornell University Press, 1994.

Bonnell, Victoria E., and Lynn Hunt. "Introduction." In *Beyond the Cultural Turn*, ed. Victoria E. Bonnell and Lynn Hunt, 1–32. Berkeley: University of California Press, 1999.

Boone, Joseph Allen. *The Homoerotics of Orientalism*. New York: Columbia University Press, 2014.

Booth, Stephen. "Shakespeare's Language and the Language of His Time." In *Shakespeare and Language*, ed. Catherine M. S. Alexander, 18–43. Cambridge: Cambridge University Press, 2004.

———. *Shakespeare's Sonnets, Edited with Analytic Commentary*. New Haven, CT: Yale University Press, 1977.

Borris, Kenneth, ed. *Same-Sex Desire in the English Renaissance: A Sourcebook of Texts, 1470–1650*. New York: Routledge, 2004.

Borris, Kenneth, and George Rousseau, eds. *The Sciences of Homosexuality in Early Modern Europe*. New York: Routledge, 2008.

Boswell, James. *Life of Johnson*. Ed. R. W. Chapman. Oxford: Oxford University Press, 1998.

Bozio, Andrew. "The Extended Self in Shakespeare's Sonnets." Unpublished manuscript.

Braden, Gordon. "Shakespeare's Petrarchism." In *Shakespeare's Sonnets: Critical Essays*, ed. James Schiffer, 163–83. New York: Garland, 2000.

Brady, Sean. "All About Eve? Queer Theory and History." *Journal of Contemporary History* 41, no. 1 (2006): 185–95.

Braunschneider, Theresa. "The Macroclitoride, the Tribade, and the Woman: Configuring Gender and Sexuality in English Anatomical Discourse." *Textual Practice* 13, no. 3 (1999): 509–32.

———. "Maidenly Amusements: Narrating Female Sexuality in Eighteenth-Century England." Ph.D. dissertation, University of Michigan, Ann Arbor, 2002. ProQuest.

Bray, Alan. "Afterword." In *Homosexuality in Renaissance England*. New edition. New York: Columbia University Press, 1995.

———. "The Curious Case of Michael Wigglesworth." In *A Queer World: The Center for Lesbian and Gay Studies Reader*, ed. Martin Duberman, 205–15. New York: New York University Press, 1997.

———. *The Friend*. Chicago: University of Chicago Press, 2003.

———. "Historians and Sexuality." *Journal of British Studies* 32, no. 2 (1993): 189–94.

———. "Homosexuality and the Signs of Male Friendship." *History Workshop Journal* 29 (1990): 1–19. Reprinted in *Queering the Renaissance*, ed. Jonathan Goldberg, 40–61. Durham, NC: Duke University Press, 1994.

———. *Homosexuality in Renaissance England*. London: Gay Men's Press, 1982.

Bray, Alan, and Michel Rey. "The Body of the Friend: Continuity and Change in Masculine Friendship in the Seventeenth Century." In *English Masculinities, 1660–1800*, ed. Tim Hitchcock and Michèle Cohen, 65–84. London: Longman, 1999.

Bredbeck, Gregory W. *Sodomy and Interpretation: Marlowe to Milton*. Ithaca, NY: Cornell University Press, 1991.

Britzman, Deborah P. *Lost Subjects, Contested Objects: Toward a Psychoanalytic Inquiry of Learning*. Albany: State University of New York Press, 1998.

———. *The Very Thought of Education: Psychoanalysis and the Impossible Professions*. Albany: State University of New York Press, 2009.

Brome, Richard. *The Antipodes: A Comedie. Acted In the Yeare 1638. by the Queenes Majesties Servants, At Salisbury Court In Fleet-street.* London: Printed by J. Okes, for Francis Constable, and are to be sold at his shops in Kings-street at the signe of the Goat, and in Westminster-hall, 1640.

———. *The Antipodes: A Comedie.* Ed. R. Cave for "Richard Brome Online." http://www.hrionline.ac.uk/brome/viewTranscripts.jsp?play=AN&act=1&type=BOTH.

———. *The Antipodes.* Ed. Ann Haaker. Lincoln: University of Nebraska Press, 1966.

———. *The Antipodes.* Ed. David Scott Kastan and Richard Proudfoot. London: Globe Education, Nick Hern Books, 2000.

———. *The Antipodes.* In *Three Renaissance Travel Plays,* ed. Anthony Parr, 217–326. Manchester: Manchester University Press, 1995.

———. *The Weeding of the Covent-Garden.* In *Five New Playes.* London, 1659.

Bromley, James. *Intimacy and Sexuality in the Age of Shakespeare.* Cambridge: Cambridge University Press, 2012.

———. "'Let It Suffise': Sexual Acts and Narrative Structure in *Hero and Leander.*" In *Queer Renaissance Historiography: Backward Gaze,* ed. Vin Nardizzi, Stephen Guy-Bray, and Will Stockton, 67–84. Farnham, England: Ashgate, 2009.

———. "'Quilted with Mighty Words to Lean Purpose': Clothing and Queer Selfhood in *The Roaring Girl.*" In "Style, Subjectivity, and Male Sexuality in Early Modern English Literature." Unpublished manuscript.

———. "Rimming the Renaissance." In *Sex Before Sex: Figuring the Act in Early Modern England,* ed. James M. Bromley and Will Stockton, 171–94. Minneapolis: University of Minnesota Press, 2013.

Bronski, Michael "Foreword. " In *Beyond Shame: Reclaiming the Abandoned History of Radical Gay Sexuality,* by Patrick Moore, xv–xvi. Boston: Beacon Press, 2004.

Brooks, Douglas. *Printing and Parenting in Early Modern England.* Burlington, VT: Ashgate, 2005.

Brooten, Bernadette J. *Love Between Women: Early Christian Responses to Female Homoeroticism.* Chicago: University of Chicago Press, 1996.

Brown, Pam Allen. *Better a Shrew Than a Sheep: Women, Drama, and the Culture of Jest in Early Modern England.* Ithaca, NY: Cornell University Press, 2003.

Bruster, Douglas. "Female-Female Eroticism and the Early Modern Stage." *Renaissance Drama* 24 (1993): 1–32.

Burckhardt, Sigurd. *Shakespearean Meanings.* Princeton, NJ: Princeton University Press, 1968.

Burger, Glenn, and Steven F. Kruger, eds. *Queering the Middle Ages.* Minneapolis: University of Minnesota Press, 2001.

Burns, E. Jane. "A Snake-Tailed Woman: Hybridity and Dynasty in the *Roman de Mélusine.*" In *From Beasts to Souls: Gender and Embodiment in Medieval Europe,* ed. Jane E. Burns and Peggy McCracken, 185–220. Notre Dame, IN: Notre Dame University Press, 2013.

Burrow, Colin. "Editing the Sonnets." In *A Companion to Shakespeare's Sonnets,* ed. Michael Schoenfeldt, 145–62. Malden, MA: Blackwell, 2007.

———, ed. *William Shakespeare: The Complete Sonnets and Poems.* Oxford: Oxford University Press, 2002.

Burton, Robert. *The Anatomy of Melancholy.* Ed. Floyd Dell and Paul Jordan-Smith. 2 vols. Reprint, Kila, MT: Kessinger, 1991.

Butler, Judith. *Bodies That Matter: On the Discursive Limits of "Sex."* New York: Routledge, 1993.

————. *Gender Trouble: Feminism and the Subversion of Identity.* London: Routledge, 1990.

Butler, Martin. *Theater and Crisis, 1632–64.* Cambridge: Cambridge University Press, 1984.

Cadden, Joan. *Meanings of Sex Difference in the Middle Ages: Medicine, Science, and Culture.* Cambridge: Cambridge University Press, 1993.

Callaghan, Dympna. "'And All Is Semblative a Woman's Part': Body Politics and *Twelfth Night.*" In *Shakespeare Without Women: Representing Gender and Race on the Renaissance Stage*, 26–49. London: Routledge, 2000.

————. "Confounded by Winter: Speeding Time in Shakespeare's Sonnets." In *A Companion to Shakespeare's Sonnets*, ed. Michael Schoenfeldt, 104–18. Malden, MA: Blackwell, 2007.

————. *Shakespeare's Sonnets.* Malden, MA: Blackwell, 2007.

————. "(Un)natural Loving: Swine, Pets, and Flower in *Venus and Adonis.*" In *Textures of Renaissance Knowledge*, ed. Philippa Berry and Margaret Trudeau-Clayton, 58–78. Manchester: Manchester University Press, 2003.

Canaday, Margot. "Thinking Sex in the Transnational Turn: An Introduction." In "AHR Forum: Transnational Sexualities," *American Historical Review* 114, no. 5 (2009): 1250–57.

Canning, Kathleen. *Gender History in Practice: Historical Perspectives on Bodies, Class, and Citizenship.* Ithaca, NY: Cornell University Press, 2006.

Cannon, John. "Memoirs of the Birth, Education, Life and Death of: Mr. John Cannon." 1743. Somerset Record Office DD/SAS C/1193.

Capp, Bernard. "The Double Standard Revisited: Plebian Women and Male Sexual Reputation in Early Modern England." *Past & Present* 162 (1999): 70–100.

————. "Gender and the Culture of the English Alehouse in Late Stuart England." In *The Trouble with Ribs: Women, Men and Gender in Early Modern Europe*, ed. Anu Korhonen and Kate Lowe, 103–27. Helsinki: Collegium, 2007.

————. *When Gossips Meet: Women, Family, and Neighbourhood in Early Modern England.* Oxford: Oxford University Press, 2003.

Carrillo, Héctor, and Jorge Fontdevila. "Rethinking Sexual Initiation: Pathways to Identity Formation Among Gay and Bisexual Mexican Male Youth." *Archives of Sexual Behavior* 40, no. 6. (2011): 1241–54.

Carroll, William C. "The Virgin Not: Language and Sexuality in Shakespeare." *Shakespeare Survey* 46 (1994): 107–19.

Castiglia, Christopher. "Sex Panics, Sex Publics, Sex Memories." *boundary 2* 27, no. 2 (2000): 149–75.

Castle, Terry. *The Apparitional Lesbian: Female Homosexuality and Modern Culture.* New York: Columbia University Press, 1993.

————. *The Literature of Lesbianism: A Historical Anthology from Ariosto to Stonewall.* New York: Columbia University Press, 2003.

Cavell, Stanley. *Disowning Knowledge in Six Plays of Shakespeare.* Cambridge: Cambridge University Press, 1987.

Chapman, George. *The Gentleman Usher.* Ed. John Hazel Smith. Lincoln: University of Nebraska Press, 1970.

————. *Ovid's Banquet of Sense.* London: Printed by J[ames] R[oberts] for Richard Smith, 1595.

Chauncey, George, Jr. "From Sexual Inversion to Homosexuality: The Changing Medical Conceptualization of Female Deviance." *Salmagundi* 58/59 (Fall 1982–Winter 1983): 114–46.

————. *Gay New York: Gender, Urban Culture, and the Making of the Gay Male World, 1890–1940.* New York: HarperCollins, 1994.

Chaytor, Miranda. "Husband(ry): Narratives of Rape in the Seventeenth Century." *Gender & History* 7, no. 3 (1995): 378–407.

Chedgzoy, Kate. "Introduction: What, Are They Children?" In *Shakespeare and Childhood*, ed. Kate Chedgzoy, Susanne Greenhalgh, and Robert Shaughnessy, 15–31. Cambridge: Cambridge University Press, 2007.

———. "'Two Loves I Have': Shakespeare and Bisexuality." In *The Bisexual Imaginary: Representation, Identity, and Desire*, ed. Phoebe Davidson, Jo Eadie, Clare Hemmings, Ann Kaloski, and Merl Stor, 106–119. London: Cassell, 1997.

Choyce Drollery: Songs & Sonnets; Being a Collection of Divers Excellent Pieces of Poetry, of Severall Eminent Authors. London: Printed by J. G. for Robert Pollard and John Sweeting, 1656.

Clark, Anna. "Anne Lister's Construction of Lesbian Identity." *Journal of the History of Sexuality* 7, no. 1 (1996): 23–50.

———. "Before and After Sexuality: Rethinking Continuity and Change in Lesbian History." Panel comment, Berkshire Conference on the History of Women, Minneapolis, June 2008.

———. *Desire: A History of European Sexuality*. London: Routledge, 2008.

———, ed. *The History of Sexuality in Europe: A Sourcebook and Reader*. New York: Routledge, 2011.

———. "Twilight Moments." *Journal of the History of Sexuality* 14, nos. 1–2 (2005): 139–60.

Clark, Ira. *Professional Playwrights: Massinger, Ford, Shirley, and Brome*. Lexington: University of Kentucky Press, 1992.

Clarke, Eric O. "Sex and Civility." In *Our Monica, Ourselves: The Clinton Affair and the National Interest*, ed. Lauren Berlant and Lisa Duggan, 285–90. New York: New York University Press, 2001.

Clegg, Roger and Lucie Skeaping. *Singing Simpkin and other Bawdy Jigs: Musical Comedy on the Shakespearean Stage: Scripts, Music and Context*. Exeter: University of Exeter Press, 2014.

Cocks, H. G. "The Growing Pains of the History of Sexuality." *Journal of Contemporary History* 39, no. 4 (2004): 657–66.

Cohen, Walter. "The Sonnets and 'A Lover's Complaint.'" In *The Norton Shakespeare*, ed. Stephen Greenblatt, Jean Howard, Katharine Eisaman Maus, Walter Cohen, 1915–21. New York: W. W. Norton, 1997.

Coke, Edward. *Third Part of the Institutes of the Lawes of England*. London, 1644.

Colclough, Stephen. "'Do You Not Know the Quotation?' Reading Anne Lister, Anne Lister Reading." In *Lesbian Dames: Sapphism in the Long Eighteenth Century*, ed. John C. Beynon and Caroline Gonda, 159–72. Farnham, England: Ashgate, 2010.

Coleman, Julie. "Glossaries of Sexuality." In *A History of Cant and Slang Dictionaries*, vol. 4, *1937–1984*, 265–90. Oxford: Oxford University Press, 2010.

———. "Historical and Sociological Methods in Slang Lexicography: Partridge, Maurer, and Cant." In *"Cunning Passages, Contrived Corridors": Unexpected Essays in the History of Lexicography*, ed. Michael Adams, 129–46. Monza, Italy: Polimetrica, 2010.

Colman, E. A. M. *The Dramatic Use of Bawdy in Shakespeare*. London: Longman, 1974.

Colter, Ephen Glenn, ed. *Policing Public Sex: Queer Politics and the Future of AIDS Activism*. Boston: South End Press, 1996.

Combahee River Collective. "The Combahee River Collective Statement." In *Home Girls: A Black Feminist Anthology*, ed. Barbara Smith, 264–74. New York: Kitchen Table/ Women of Color Press, 1983.

Conley, Tom. *The Self-Made Map: Cartographic Writing in Early Modern France*. Minneapolis: University of Minnesota Press, 1996.

Cook, Carol. "'The Sign and Semblance of Her Honor': Reading Gender Difference in *Much Ado About Nothing*." *PMLA* 101, no. 2 (1986): 186–202.

Coote, Stephen. *The Penguin Book of Homosexual Verse*. London: Penguin, 1983.

Cope, Jackson I. "Richard Brome: The World as Antipodes." In *The Theater and the Dream: From Metaphor to Form in Renaissance Drama*. Baltimore: Johns Hopkins University Press, 1973.

Cotgrave, John. *Wits Interpreter, the English Parnassus*. London, 1655.

Cotgrave, Randle. *A Dictionary of the French and English Tongues*. London, 1611.

Coviello, Peter. *Tomorrow's Parties: Sex and the Untimely in Nineteenth-Century America*. New York: New York University Press, 2013.

——. "World Enough: Sex and Time in Recent Queer Studies." *GLQ: A Journal of Lesbian and Gay Studies* 13, nos. 2–3 (2007): 387–401.

Crawford, Julie. "The Homoerotics of Shakespeare's Elizabethan Comedies." In *A Companion to Shakespeare's Works*, vol. 3, *The Comedies*, ed. Richard Dutton and Jean E. Howard, 137–58. Malden, MA: Blackwell, 2003.

——. "Shakespeare. Same Sex. Marriage." In *Oxford Handbook of Shakespeare and Embodiment*, ed. Valerie Traub. Oxford: Oxford University Press, forthcoming 2016.

Crawford, Katherine. "Privilege, Possibility, and Perversion: Rethinking the Study of Early Modern Sexuality." *Journal of Modern History* 78 (2006): 412–33.

——. *The Sexual Culture of the French Renaissance*. Cambridge: Cambridge University Press, 2010.

Crawford, Patricia. "Sexual Knowledge in England, 1500–1750." In *Sexual Knowledge, Sexual Science: The History of Attitudes to Sexuality*, ed. Roy Porter and Mikuláš Teich, 82–106. Cambridge: Cambridge University Press, 1994.

Crawford, Patricia, and Laura Gowing. *Women's Worlds in Seventeenth-Century England: A Sourcebook*. New York: Routledge, 2000.

Crawford, Patricia, and Sara Mendelson, "Sexual Identities in Early Modern England: The Marriage of Two Women in 1680." *Gender & History* 7, no. 3 (1995): 362–77.

Crawforth, Hannah. *Etymology and the Invention of English in Early Modern Literature*. Cambridge: Cambridge University Press, 2013.

Cressy, David. *Birth, Marriage, and Death: Ritual, Religion, and the Life-Cycle in Tudor and Stuart England*. Oxford: Oxford University Press, 1997.

Crimp, Douglas. *Melancholia and Moralism: Essays on AIDS and Queer Politics*. Cambridge, MA: MIT Press, 2002.

Crooke, Helkiah. *Microcosmographia: A Description of the Body of Man*. London, 1615.

Cruz-Malavé, Arnaldo, and Martin F. Manalansan IV, eds. *Queer Globalizations: Citizenship and the Afterlife of Colonialism*. New York: New York University Press, 2002.

Cryle, Peter. *Geometry in the Boudoir: Configurations of French Erotic Narrative*. Ithaca, NY: Cornell University Press, 1994.

——. *The Telling of the Act: Sexuality as Narrative in Eighteenth- and Nineteenth-Century France*. Newark: University of Delaware Press, 2001.

Cryle, Peter, and Alison Moore. *Frigidity: An Intellectual History*. New York: Palgrave Macmillan, 2011.

Culler, Jonathan, ed. *On Puns: The Foundation of Letters*. Oxford: Blackwell, 1988.

Culpeper, Nicholas. *A Directory for Midwives*. London, 1656.

Cummings, Brian. "Metalepsis: The Boundaries of Metaphor." In *Renaissance Figures of Speech*, ed. Sylvia Adamson, Gavin Alexander, and Katrin Ettenhuber, 217–33. Cambridge: Cambridge University Press, 2007.

Cuncun, Wu. *Homoerotic Sensibilities in Late Imperial China*. London: Routledge, 2004.

Cunningham, William. *The Cosmographical Glasse*. London, 1559.

Cvetkovich, Ann. *An Archive of Feelings: Trauma, Sexuality, and Lesbian Public Cultures*. Durham, NC: Duke University Press, 2003.

Dabhoiwala, Faramerz. *The Origins of Sex: A History of the First Sexual Revolution*. Oxford: Oxford University Press, 2012.

———. "The Pattern of Sexual Immorality in Seventeenth and Eighteenth-Century London." In *Londinopolis: Essays in the Cultural and Social History of Early Modern London*, ed. Paul Griffiths and Mark S. R. Jenner, 86–106. Manchester: Manchester University Press, 2001.

Daileader, Celia R. "Back Door Sex: Renaissance Gynosodomy, Aretino, and the Exotic." *ELH* 69 (2002): 303–34.

Danson, Lawrence. "Oscar Wilde, W. H., and the Unspoken Name of Love." *ELH* 58, no. 4 (1991): 979–1000.

Davidson, Arnold I. *The Emergence of Sexuality: Historical Epistemology and the Formation of Concepts*. Cambridge, MA: Harvard University Press, 2001.

Davis, Kathleen. *Periodization and Sovereignty: How Ideas of Feudalism and Secularization Govern the Politics of Time*. Philadelphia: University of Pennsylvania Press, 2008.

Dean, Tim. "Queer Theory Without Names." *Paragraph* 35, no. 3 (2012): 421–34.

D'Emilio, John, and Estelle B. Freedman. *Intimate Matters: A History of Sexuality in America*. New York: Harper and Row, 1989.

de Grazia, Margreta. "Homonyms Before and After Lexical Standardization." *Deutsche Shakespeare-Gesellschaft West Jahrbuch* (1990): 143–56.

———. "The Modern Divide: From Either Side." *Journal of Medieval and Early Modern Studies* 37, no. 3 (2007): 453–67.

———. Review of *Shakespeare from the Margins: Language, Culture, Context*, by Patricia Parker. *Shakespeare Studies* 26 (1998): 406–12.

———. "Revolution in *Shake-speares Sonnets*." In *A Companion to Shakespeare's Sonnets*, ed. Michael Schoenfeldt, 57–69. Malden, MA: Blackwell, 2007.

———. "The Scandal of Shakespeare's Sonnets." In *Shakespeare's Sonnets: Critical Essays*, ed. James Schiffer, 89–112. New York: Garland, 2000.

———. *Shakespeare Verbatim: The Reproduction of Authenticity and the 1790 Apparatus*. Oxford: Clarendon Press, 1991.

———. "Words as Things." *Shakespeare Studies* 28 (2000): 231–35.

DeJean, Joan. *Fictions of Sappho, 1547–1937*. Chicago: University of Chicago Press, 1989.

———. *The Reinvention of Obscenity: Sex, Lies, and Tabloids in Early Modern France*. Chicago: University of Chicago Press, 2002.

Dekker, Thomas, and Thomas Middleton. *The Patient Man and the Honest Whore*. Ed. Paul Mulholland. In *Thomas Middleton: The Collected Works*, ed. Gary Taylor and John Lavagnino , 285–327. Oxford: Clarendon Press, 2007.

Dekker, Thomas, and John Webster. *Northward-Hoe: Sundry Times Acted by the Children of Paules*. London, 1607. Reprinted in *The Dramatic Works of Thomas Dekker*, ed. R. H. Shepherd, vol. 3. London: J. Pearson, 1873.

Delany, Samuel R. *Times Square Red, Times Square Blue*. New York: New York University Press, 1999.

De Lauretis, Teresa. *The Practice of Love: Lesbian Sexuality and Perverse Desire*. Bloomington: University of Indiana Press, 1994.

Derrida, Jacques. *Archive Fever: A Freudian Impression.* Chicago: University of Chicago Press, 1996.

———. *Specters of Marx: The State of the Debt, the Work of Mourning, and the New International.* Trans. Peggy Kamuf. New York: Routledge, 1994.

Diamond, Lisa. *Sexual Fluidity: Understanding Women's Love and Desire.* Cambridge, MA: Harvard University Press, 2008.

DiGangi, Mario. *The Homoerotics of Early Modern Drama.* Cambridge: Cambridge University Press, 1997.

———. "'Love Is Not (Heterosexual) Love': Historicizing Sexuality in Elizabethan Poetry." In *Approaches to Teaching Shorter Elizabethan Poetry,* ed. Patrick Cheney and Anne Lake Prescott, 173–78. New York: Modern Language Association of America, 2000.

———. "Queer Theory, Historicism, and Early Modern Sexualities." *Criticism* 48, no. 1 (2006): 129–42.

———. *Sexual Types: Embodiment, Agency, and Dramatic Character from Shakespeare to Shirley.* Philadelphia: University of Pennsylvania Press, 2011.

———. "Shakespeare's 'Bawdy.'" Presentation, Shakespeare Association of America, St. Louis, April 11, 2014.

Diggs, Marylynne. "Romantic Friends or a 'Different Race of Creatures'? The Representation of Lesbian Pathology in Nineteenth-Century America." *Feminist Studies* 21, no. 2 (1995): 1–24.

Dinshaw, Carolyn. *Getting Medieval: Sexualities and Communities, Pre- and Postmodern.* Durham, NC: Duke University Press, 1999.

———. "The History of *GLQ,* Volume 1: LGBTQ Studies, Censorship, and Other Transnational Problems." *GLQ: A Journal of Lesbian and Gay Studies* 12, no. 1 (2006): 5–26.

———. *How Soon Is Now? Medieval Texts, Amateur Readers, and the Queerness of Time.* Durham, NC: Duke University Press, 2012.

Dinshaw, Carolyn, and Karma Lochrie. Letter to the editor. In "Forum: Queering History," *PMLA* 121, no. 3 (2006): 837–38.

Dipiero, Thomas, and Pat Gill, eds. *Illicit Sex: Identity Politics in Early Modern Culture.* Athens: University of Georgia Press, 1996.

Doan, Laura. *Disturbing Practices: History, Sexuality, and Women's Experience of Modern War.* Chicago: University of Chicago Press, 2013.

———. *Fashioning Sapphism: The Origins of a Modern English Lesbian Culture.* New York: Columbia University Press, 2001.

———. "Topsy-Turvydom: Gender Inversion, Sapphism, and the Great War." *GLQ: A Journal of Lesbian and Gay History* 12, no. 4 (2006): 517–42.

Doan, Laura, and Jay Prosser, eds. *Palatable Poison: Critical Perspectives on "The Well of Loneliness."* New York: Columbia University Press, 2001.

Dolan, Frances E. *Dangerous Familiars: Representations of Domestic Crime in England, 1550–1700.* Ithaca, NY: Cornell University Press, 1994.

———. "Household Chastisements: Gender, Authority, and 'Domestic Violence.'" In *Renaissance Culture and the Everyday,* ed. Patricia Fumerton and Simon Hunt, 204–25. Philadelphia: University of Pennsylvania Press, 1999.

———. *Marriage and Violence: The Early Modern Legacy.* Philadelphia: University of Pennsylvania Press, 2008.

———. "Re-reading Rape in *The Changeling.*" *Journal for Early Modern Cultural Studies* 11, no. 1 (2011): 4–29.

———. "Tracking the Petty Traitor Across Genres." In *Ballads and Broadsides in Britain, 1500–1800*, ed. Patricia Fumerton, Anita Guerrini, and Kris McAbee, 149–71. Farnham, England: Ashgate, 2010.

———. *True Relations: Reading, Literature, and Evidence in Seventeenth-Century England.* Philadelphia: University of Pennsylvania Press, 2013.

———. *Whores of Babylon: Catholicism, Gender, and Seventeenth-Century Print Culture.* Ithaca, NY: Cornell University Press, 1999.

———. "Why Are Nuns Funny?" *Huntington Library Quarterly* 70, no. 4 (2007): 509–35.

Dollimore, Jonathan. *Sexual Dissidence: Augustine to Wilde, Freud to Foucault.* Oxford: Clarendon Press, 1991.

Dolven, Jeff. *Scenes of Instruction in Renaissance Romance.* Chicago: University of Chicago Press, 2007.

Donaldson, Ian, ed. *Ben Jonson.* Oxford: Oxford University Press, 1985.

———. *The World Upside Down: Comedy from Jonson to Fielding.* Oxford: Clarendon Press, 1970.

Donne, John. *The Complete English Poems of John Donne.* Ed. C. A. Patrides. London: J. M. Dent & Sons, 1985.

Donoghue, Emma. *Passions Between Women: British Lesbian Culture, 1668–1801.* New York: HarperCollins, 1993.

———. *Poems Between Women: Four Centuries of Love, Romantic Friendship, and Desire.* New York: Columbia University Press, 1997.

Dowd, Michelle M., and Thomas Festa, eds. *Early Modern Women on the Fall: An Anthology.* Tempe: Arizona Center for Medieval and Renaissance Studies, 2012.

Downing, Lisa. "Afterword: On 'Compulsory Sexuality', Sexualization, and History." In *The Routledge History of Sex and the Body, 1500 to the Present*, ed. Sarah Toulalan and Kate Fisher, 527–32. New York: Routledge, 2013.

Drouin, Jennifer. "Diana's Band: Safe Spaces, Publics, and Early Modern Lesbianism." In *Queer Renaissance Historiography: Backward Gaze*, ed. Vin Nardizzi, Stephen Guy-Bray, and Will Stockton, 85–110. Farnham, England: Ashgate, 2009.

Dubrow, Heather. "'Incertainties Now Crown Themselves Assur'd': The Politics of Plotting Shakespeare's Sonnets." *Shakespeare Quarterly* 47 (1996): 291–305. Reprinted in *Shakespeare's Sonnets: Critical Essays*, ed. James Schiffer, 113–34. New York: Garland, 2000.

Dugan, Holly. "Aping Rape: Animal Ravishment and Sexual Knowledge in Early Modern England." In *Sex Before Sex: Figuring the Act in Early Modern England*, ed. James M. Bromley and Will Stockton, 213–32. Minneapolis: University of Minnesota Press, 2013.

Duncan-Jones, Katherine, ed. *Shakespeare's Sonnets.* London: Arden Shakespeare, 1997.

———. *Ungentle Shakespeare: Scenes from His Life.* London: Arden Shakespeare, 2001.

Dutton, Richard. "*Shake-speares Sonnets*, Shakespeare's Sonnets, and Shakespearean Biography." In *A Companion to Shakespeare's Sonnets*, ed. Michael Schoenfeldt, 121–36. Malden, MA: Blackwell, 2007.

Eamon, William. *Science and the Secrets of Nature.* Princeton, NJ: Princeton University Press, 1994.

Edelman, Lee. "Against Survival: Queerness in a Time That's Out of Joint." *Shakespeare Quarterly* 62, no. 2 (2011): 148–69.

———. "Ever After: History, Negativity, and the Social." *South Atlantic Quarterly* 106, no. 3 (2007): 469–76.

———. *Homographesis: Essays in Gay Literary and Cultural Theory.* New York: Routledge, 1994.

———. "Learning Nothing: Bad Education." Presentation, University of Michigan. September 22, 2007.

———. *No Future: Queer Theory and the Death Drive.* Durham, NC: Duke University Press, 2004.

———. "Queer Theory and *Hamlet.*" Interview with Madhavi Menon. http://shakespeare quarterly.wordpress.com. August 2, 2011.

Edmondson, Paul, and Stanley Wells. *Shakespeare's Sonnets: Oxford Shakespeare Topics.* Oxford: Oxford University Press, 2004.

Eisner, Martin G., and Marc D. Schachter. "*Libido Sciendi*: Apuleius, Boccaccio, and the Study of the History of Sexuality." *PMLA* 124, no. 3 (2009): 817–37.

Elias, Norbert. *The History of Manners.* Vol. 1 of *The Civilizing Process.* New York: Pantheon, 1982.

Eng, David L. *Racial Castration: Managing Masculinity in Asian America.* Durham, NC: Duke University Press, 2001.

English Broadside Ballad Archive. University of California at Santa Barbara, 2003–. http://ebba.english.ucsb.edu.

Enterline, Lynn. "Rhetoric, Discipline, and the Theatricality of Everyday Life in Elizabethan Grammar Schools." In *From Performance to Print in Shakespeare's England,* ed. Peter Holland and Stephen Orgel, 173–90. Basingstoke: Palgrave Macmillan, 2006.

———. *The Rhetoric of the Body from Ovid to Shakespeare.* Cambridge: Cambridge University Press, 2000.

Epstein, Steven. "The New Attack on Sexuality Research: Morality and the Politics of Knowledge Production." *Sexuality Research and Social Policy* 3, no. 1 (2006): 1–12.

———. "Thinking Sex Ethnographically." *GLQ: A Journal of Lesbian and Gay Studies* 17, no. 1 (2011): 85–88.

Erasmus, Desiderius. *Virgo misogamos* (1523). Translated as "The Girl with No Interest in Marriage," in *The Colloquies of Erasmus,* trans. Craig R. Thompson, 103–11. Chicago: University of Chicago Press, 1965.

———. *Virgo misogamos.* Translated as "A Maid Hating Marriage," in *The Colloquies, or Familiar Discourses of Desiderius Erasmus of Roterdam, Rendered into English,* trans. H. M., Gent., 140–48. London, 1671.

"Ex parte Agnetis Carr adversus Thomam Carr, maritum suum." In *Depositions and Other Ecclesiastical Proceedings, Extending from 1311 to the Reign of Elizabeth from the Courts of Durham,* ed. James Raine, 97–98. London: J. B. Nichols & Son, 1845.

Faderman, Lillian. *Surpassing the Love of Men: Romantic Friendship and Love Between Women from the Renaissance to the Present.* New York: Morrow, 1981.

Farina, Lara. "Lesbian History and Erotic Reading." In *The Lesbian Premodern,* ed. Noreen Giffney, Michelle M. Sauer, and Diane Watt, 49–60. New York: Palgrave Macmillan, 2011.

Ferguson, Margaret. "Hymeneal Instruction." In *Masculinities, Childhood, Violence: Attending to Early Modern Women—and Men, Proceedings of the 2006 Symposium,* ed. Amy E. Leonard and Karen L. Nelson, 97–129. Newark: University of Delaware Press, 2011.

Ferguson, Rod. *Aberrations in Black: Toward a Queer of Color Critique.* Minneapolis: University of Minnesota Press, 2003.

———. *The Reorder of Things: The University and its Pedagogies of Minority Difference.* Minneapolis: University of Minnesota Press, 2012.

Ferrand, Jacques. *A Treatise on Lovesickness.* Trans. and ed. Donald A. Beecher and Massimo Ciavolella. Syracuse, NY: Syracuse University Press, 1990. Originally published as *De la maladie d'amour, ou mélancolie érotique* (1610/1623).

Fields, Jessica. *Risky Lessons: Sex Education and Social Inequality.* Newark, NJ: Rutgers University Press, 2008.

Fine, Michelle. "Sexuality, Schooling, and Adolescent Females: The Missing Discourse of Desire." *Harvard Educational Review* 58, no. 1 (1988): 29–54.

Fine, Michelle, and Sara McClelland. "Sexuality Education and Desire: Still Missing After All These Years." *Harvard Educational Review* 76, no. 3 (Fall 2006): 297–338.

Fineman, Joel. "Fratricide and Cuckoldry: Shakespeare's Doubles." In *Representing Shakespeare: New Psychoanalytic Essays*, ed. Murray M. Schwartz and Coppélia Kahn, 70–109. Baltimore: Johns Hopkins University Press, 1980.

———. *Shakespeare's Perjured Eye: The Invention of Poetic Subjectivity in the Sonnets.* Berkeley: University of California Press, 1986.

Fish, Stanley. "Masculine Persuasive Force: Donne and Verbal Power." In *Soliciting Interpretation: Literary Theory and Seventeenth-Century English Poetry*, ed. Elizabeth D. Harvey and Katharine Eisaman Maus, 223–52. Chicago: University of Chicago Press, 1990.

Fisher, Will. "'Doctor Dildos Dauncing Schoole': Sexual Instruments, Women's Erotic Agency, and Thomas Nashe's *The Choise of Valentines*." Unpublished manuscript.

———. "The Erotics of Chin Chucking in Seventeenth-Century England." In *Sex Before Sex: Figuring the Act in Early Modern England*, ed. James M. Bromley and Will Stockton, 141–69. Minneapolis: University of Minnesota Press, 2013.

———. "'Loves Wealthy Croppe of Kisses': Kissing in England c. 1600–1730." Unpublished manuscript.

———. *Materializing Gender in Early Modern English Literature and Culture.* Cambridge: Cambridge University Press, 2006.

———. "Sexual Practices in England During the Long Seventeenth Century." Unpublished manuscript.

———. "'Stray[ing] Lower Where the Pleasant Fountains Lie': Cunnilingus in Shakespeare's *Venus and Adonis* and in Early Modern English Culture, c. 1600–1700." In *Oxford Handbook of Shakespeare and Embodiment*, ed. Valerie Traub. Oxford: Oxford University Press, forthcoming 2016.

———. "'The Use of Flogging in Venereal Affairs': Sexual Flagellation in England, c. 1600–1730." Unpublished manuscript.

———. "'Wantoning with the Thighs': The Socialization of Thigh Sex in England c.1600–1730," *Journal of the History of Sexuality* 24, no. 1 (2015): 1–24.

Fissell, Mary. *Vernacular Bodies: The Politics of Reproduction in Early Modern England.* Oxford: Oxford University Press, 2004.

Fleming, Juliet. "Dictionary English and the Female Tongue." In *Enclosure Acts: Sexuality, Property, and Culture in Early Modern England*, ed. Richard Burt and John Michael Archer, 290–326. Ithaca, NY: Cornell University Press, 1994.

———. *Graffiti and the Writing Arts of Early Modern England.* London: Reaktion, 2001.

Fletcher, Anthony. *Gender, Sex, and Subordination in England, 1500–1800.* New Haven, CT: Yale University Press, 1995.

———. *Growing Up in England: The Experience of Childhood, 1600–1914.* New Haven, CT: Yale University Press, 2008.

Fletcher, John. *The Island Princess.* London, 1621.

Flores, Nona C. "Effigies Amicitiae . . . Veritas Inimicitiae: Antifeminism in the Iconography of the Woman-Headed Serpent in Medieval and Renaissance Art and Literature." In *Animals in the Middle Ages: A Book of Essays*, ed. Nona C. Flores, 167–95. New York: Garland, 1996.

Florio, John. *A Worlde of Wordes; or, Most Copious, and Exact Dictionarie in Italian and English.* London, 1598.

Foucault, Michel. *Discipline and Punish: The Birth of the Prison.* Trans. Alan Sheridan. New York: Pantheon, 1978.

———. *The Hermeneutics of the Subject: Lectures at the Collège de France, 1981–82.* Ed. Frédéric Gros, Francois Ewald, Alessandro Fontana, and Arnold I. Davidson, trans. Graham Burchell. New York: Picador, 2005.

———. *The History of Sexuality.* Vol. 1, *An Introduction.* Trans. Robert Hurley. New York: Random House, 1976.

———. "Nietzsche, Genealogy, History." In *Language, Counter-Memory, Practice: Selected Essays and Interviews,* ed. Donald F. Bouchard, trans. Donald F. Bouchard and Sherry Simon, 139–64. Ithaca, NY: Cornell University Press, 1977.

———. *The Order of Things: An Archaeology of the Human Sciences.* New York: Random House, 1971.

Foyster, Elizabeth. *Manhood in Early Modern England: Honour, Sex, and Marriage.* London: Routledge, 1999.

Fradenburg, L. O. Aranye. *Sacrifice Your Love: Psychoanalysis, Historicism, Chaucer.* Minneapolis: University of Minnesota Press, 2002.

Fradenburg, Louise, and Carla Freccero, eds. *Premodern Sexualities.* London: Routledge, 1996.

Freccero, Carla. "Figural Historiography: Dogs, Humans, and Cyanthropic Becomings." In *Comparatively Queer: Crossing Time, Crossing Cultures,* ed. Jarrod Hayes, Margaret Higonnet, and William J. Spurlin, 45–67. New York: Palgrave Macmillan, 2010.

———. "Passionate Friendship." *GLQ: A Journal of Lesbian and Gay Studies* 10, no. 3 (2004): 503–7.

———. *Queer/Early/Modern.* Durham, NC: Duke University Press, 2006.

———. "Queer Times." *South Atlantic Quarterly* 106, no. 3 (2007): 486–94.

———. "The Queer Time of the Lesbian Premodern." In *The Lesbian Premodern,* ed. Noreen Giffney, Michelle M. Sauer, and Diane Watt, 61–73. New York: Palgrave Macmillan, 2011.

Freeman, Elizabeth. "Introduction." *GLQ: A Journal of Lesbian and Gay Studies* 13, nos. 2–3 (2007): 159–76.

———. "Packing History, Count(er)ing Generations." *New Literary History* 31, no. 4 (2000): 727–44.

———. "Sacramentality and the Lesbian Premodern." In *The Lesbian Premodern,* ed. Noreen Giffney, Michelle M. Sauer, and Diane Watt, 179–86. New York: Palgrave Macmillan, 2011.

———. "Still After." *South Atlantic Quarterly* 106, no. 3 (2007): 495–500.

———. "Theorizing Queer Temporalities: A Roundtable Discussion." *GLQ: A Journal of Lesbian and Gay Studies* 13, nos. 2–3 (2007): 177–95.

———. *Time Binds: Queer Temporalities, Queer Histories.* Durham, NC: Duke University Press, 2010.

Freud, Sigmund. *Three Essays on the Theory of Sexuality.* In *The Standard Edition of the Complete Psychological Works of Sigmund Freud,* ed. and trans. James Strachey, vol. 7. London: Hogarth Press, 1953.

Friedlander, Ari. "Promiscuous Generation: Rogue Sexuality and Social Reproduction in Early Modern England." Ph.D. dissertation, University of Michigan, Ann Arbor, 2011. ProQuest.

Froide, Amy. *Never Married: Singlewomen in Early Modern England.* Oxford: Oxford University Press, 2005.

Frye, Susan, and Karen Robertson, eds. *Maids and Mistresses, Cousins and Queens: Women's Alliances in Early Modern England*. New York: Oxford University Press, 1999.

Fudge, Erica. "Monstrous Acts: Bestiality in Early Modern England." *History Today* 50, no. 8 (2000): 20–25.

Furth, Charlotte. "Androgynous Males and Deficient Females: Biology and Gender Boundaries in Sixteenth- and Seventeenth-Century China." In *The Lesbian and Gay Studies Reader*, ed. Henry Abelove, Michèle Aina Barale, and David M. Halperin, 479–97. New York: Routledge, 1993.

Fuss, Diana. *Identification Papers*. New York: Routledge, 1995.

Gallop, Jane. *Anecdotal Theory*. Durham, NC: Duke University Press, 2003.

———. *Feminist Accused of Sexual Harassment*. Durham, NC: Duke University Press, 1997.

Garber, Marjorie. "The Insincerity of Women." In *Subject and Object in Renaissance Culture*, ed. Margreta de Grazia, Maureen Quilligan, and Peter Stallybrass, 349–68. Cambridge: Cambridge University Press, 1996.

———. *Vice Versa: Bisexuality and the Eroticism of Everyday Life*. New York: Simon and Schuster, 1995.

Garcia, Lorena. "'Now Why Do You Want to Know About That?' Heteronormativity, Sexism and Racism in the Sexual (Mis)Education of Latina Youth." *Gender and Society* 23, no. 4 (August 2009): 520–41.

Garrett, Julia M. "Witchcraft and Sexual Knowledge in Early Modern England." *Journal for Early Modern Cultural Studies* 13, no. 1 (2013): 32–72.

Giese, Loreen L. *Courtships, Marriage Customs, and Shakespeare's Comedies*. New York: Palgrave Macmillan, 2006.

Giffney, Noreen, and Michael O'Rourke. "Series Editors' Preface: Sextualities." In *Queer Renaissance Historiography: Backward Gaze*, ix–xii. Farnham, England: Ashgate, 2009.

Giffney, Noreen, Michelle M. Sauer, and Diane Watt, ed. *The Lesbian Premodern*. New York: Palgrave Macmillan, 2011.

Gil, Daniel Juan. *Before Intimacy: Asocial Sexuality in Early Modern England*. Minneapolis: University of Minnesota Press, 2006.

Gillis, John. *For Better, For Worse: British Marriages, 1600 to the Present*. Oxford: Oxford University Press, 1985.

Godbeer, Richard. *Sexual Revolution in Early America*. Baltimore: Johns Hopkins University Press, 2002.

Goldberg, Jonathan. "After Thoughts." *South Atlantic Quarterly* 106, no. 3 (2007): 501–10.

———. "The History That Will Be," *GLQ: A Journal of Lesbian and Gay Studies* 1, no. 4 (1995): 385–403.

———. "Literary Criticism, Literary History, and the Place of Homoeroticism." In *Early Modern English Poetry: A Critical Companion*, ed. Patrick Cheney, Andrew Hadfield, and Garrett A. Sullivan, Jr., 136–46. Oxford: Oxford University Press, 2007.

———. "Margaret Cavendish, Scribe." *GLQ: A Journal of Lesbian and Gay Studies* 10, no. 3 (2004): 433–52.

———, ed. *Queering the Renaissance*. Durham, NC: Duke University Press, 1994.

———. "Romeo and Juliet's Open R's." In *Queering the Renaissance*, ed. Jonathan Goldberg, 218–35. Durham, NC: Duke University Press, 1994.

———. *The Seeds of Things: Theorizing Sexuality and Materiality in Renaissance Representations*. New York: Fordham University Press, 2009.

————. *Sodometries: Renaissance Texts, Modern Sexualities.* Stanford, CA: Stanford University Press, 1992.

————. *Writing Matter: From the Hands of the English Renaissance.* Stanford, CA: Stanford University Press, 1990.

Goldberg, Jonathan, and Madhavi Menon. "Queering History." *PMLA* 120, no. 5 (2005): 1608–17.

Goldie, Matthew Boyd. *The Idea of the Antipodes: Place, People, and Voices.* New York: Routledge, 2010.

Gomez, Jewelle. "But Some of Us Are Brave Lesbians: The Absence of Black Lesbian Fiction." In *Black Queer Studies: A Critical Anthology*, ed. E. Patrick Johnson and Mae G. Henderson, 289–97. Durham, NC: Duke University Press, 2005.

Gonda, Caroline. "Ledore and Fanny Derham's Story." *Women's Writing* 6, no. 3 (1999): 329–44.

————. "Lesbian Narrative in the Travels and Adventures of Mademoiselle de Richelieu." *British Journal of Eighteenth-Century Studies* 29, no. 2 (2006): 191–200.

————. "What Lesbians Do in Books, 1723–1835: Narrative Possibilities." Unpublished manuscript.

Gopinath, Gayatri. *Impossible Desires: Queer Diasporas and South Asian Public Cultures.* Durham, NC: Duke University Press, 2005.

Gowing, Laura. *Common Bodies: Women, Touch and Power in Seventeenth-Century England.* New Haven, CT: Yale University Press, 2003.

————. *Domestic Dangers: Women, Words, and Sex in Early Modern London.* Oxford: Clarendon Press, 1996.

————. "'The Freedom of the Streets': Women and Social Space, 1560–1640." In *Londinopolis: Essays in the Cultural and Social History of Early Modern London*, ed. Paul Griffiths and Mark S. R. Jenner, 130–51. Manchester: Manchester University Press, 2001.

————. "Knowledge and Experience, c. 1500–1750." In *The Routledge History of Sex and the Body, 1500 to the Present*, ed. Sarah Toulalan and Kate Fisher, 239–55. New York: Routledge, 2013.

————. "Lesbians and Their Like in Early Modern Europe, 1500–1800." In *Gay Life and Culture: A World History*, ed. Robert Aldrich, 125–43. London: Thames and Hudson, 2006.

————. "Women's Bodies and the Making of Sex in Seventeenth-Century England." *Signs* 37, no. 4 (2012): 813–22.

Gowing, Laura, Michael Hunter, and Miri Rubin, eds. *Love, Friendship and Faith in Europe, 1300–1800.* New York: Palgrave Macmillan, 2006.

Greenblatt, Stephen. "Psychoanalysis and Renaissance Culture." In *Learning to Curse: Essays in Early Modern Culture*, 131–45. New York: Routledge, 1990.

————. *Shakespearean Negotiations: The Circulation of Social Energy in Renaissance England.* Oxford: Clarendon Press, 1988.

————. *Will in the World: How Shakespeare Became Shakespeare.* New York: W. W. Norton, 2004.

Greene, Jody, ed. "The Work of Friendship: In Memoriam Alan Bray." Special issue, *GLQ: A Journal of Lesbian and Gay Studies* 10, no. 3 (2004): 319–37.

Greene, Monica. "From 'Diseases of Women' to 'Secrets of Women': The Transformation of Gynecological Literature in the Later Middle Ages." *Journal of Medieval and Early Modern Studies* 30 (2000): 5–39.

Griffiths, Paul. "The Structure of Prostitution in Elizabethan London." *Continuity and Change* 8, no. 1 (1993): 39–63.

———. *Youth and Authority: Formative Experiences in England, 1560–1640*. Oxford: Clarendon Press, 1996.

Grossman, Marshall. "Whose Life Is It Anyway? Shakespeare's Prick." *Textual Practice* 23, no. 2 (2009): 229–46.

Grosz, Elizabeth. *The Nick of Time: Politics, Evolution, and the Untimely*. Durham, NC: Duke University Press, 2004.

———. *Space, Time, and Perversion: Essays on the Politics of Bodies*. New York: Routledge, 1995.

Guy-Bray, Stephen. *Against Reproduction: Where Renaissance Texts Come From*. Toronto: University of Toronto Press, 2009.

———. "Andrew Marvell and Sexual Difference." In *Queer Renaissance Historiography: Backward Gaze*, ed. Vin Nardizzi, Stephen Guy-Bray, and Will Stockton, 171–83. Farnham, England: Ashgate, 2009.

———. "No Present." In *Sex, Gender and Time in Fiction and Culture*, ed. Ben Davies and Jana Funke, 38–52. Basingstoke: Palgrave Macmillan, 2011.

Haber, Judith. *Desire and Dramatic Form in Early Modern England*. Cambridge: Cambridge University Press, 2009.

Habermas, Jürgen. *The Structural Transformation of the Public Sphere: An Inquiry into a Category of Bourgeois Society*. Trans. Thomas Burger and Frederick Lawrence. Cambridge, MA: MIT Press, 1989.

Hacke, Daniela. *Women, Sex, and Marriage in Early Modern Venice*. Aldershot: Ashgate, 2004.

Haggerty, George E. "The History of Homosexuality Reconsidered." In *Developments in the Histories of Sexualities: In Search of the Normal, 1600–1800*, ed. Chris Mounsey, 1–15. Lewisburg, PA: Bucknell University Press, 2013.

———. *Men in Love: Masculinity and Sexuality in the Eighteenth Century*. New York: Columbia University Press, 1999.

Hailwood, Mark. *Alehouses and Good Fellowship in Early Modern England*. Martelsham: Boydell and Brewer, 2014.

Halberstam, Judith. *Female Masculinity*. Durham, NC: Duke University Press, 1998.

———. *In a Queer Time and Place: Transgender Bodies, Subcultural Lives*. New York: New York University Press, 2005.

———. *The Queer Art of Failure*. Durham, NC: Duke University Press, 2011.

———. "'A Writer of Misfits': 'John' Radclyffe Hall and the Discourse of Inversion." In *Palatable Poison: Critical Perspectives on "The Well of Loneliness,"* ed. Laura Doan and Jay Prosser, 145–61. New York: Columbia University Press, 2001.

Hall, Donald E., and Annamarie Jagose, eds., with Andrea Bebell and Susan Potter. *Routledge Queer Studies Reader*. London: Routledge, 2013.

Hall, Kim F. "'Those Bastard Signs of Fair': Literary Whiteness in Shakespeare's Sonnets." In *Post-Colonial Shakespeares*, ed. Ania Loomba and Martin Orkin, 64–83. London: Routledge, 1998.

Halley, Janet. *Split Decisions: How and Why to Take a Break from Feminism*. Princeton, NJ: Princeton University Press, 2006.

Halperin, David M. "Deviant Teaching." In *Companion to LGBTQ Studies*, ed. George Haggerty and Molly McGarry, 146–67. Malden, MA: Blackwell, 2007.

———. "Homosexuality." In the *Oxford Classical Dictionary*, 3rd ed., ed. Simon Hornblower and Antony Spawforth, 722–23. Oxford: Oxford University Press, 1996.

————. *How to Be Gay*. Cambridge, MA: Harvard University Press, 2012.

————. *How to Do the History of Homosexuality*. Chicago: University of Chicago Press, 2002.

————. "Introduction." In *Love, Sex, Intimacy, and Friendship Between Men, 1550–1880*, ed. Katherine O'Donnell and Michael O'Rourke, 1–11. Basingstoke: Palgrave Macmillan, 2003.

————. "Love's Irony: Six Remarks on Platonic Eros." In *Erotikon: Essays on Eros, Ancient and Modern*, ed. Shadi Bartsch and Thomas Bartscherer, 48–58. Chicago: University of Chicago Press, 2005.

————. *One Hundred Years of Homosexuality and Other Essays on Greek Love*. New York: Routledge, 1990.

————. *Saint Foucault: Towards a Gay Hagiography*. Oxford: Oxford University Press, 1995.

Halperin, David M., and Valerie Traub, eds. *Gay Shame*. Chicago: University of Chicago Press, 2009.

Halpern, Richard. *Shakespeare's Perfume: Sodomy and Sublimity in the Sonnets, Wilde, Freud, and Lacan*. Philadelphia: University of Pennsylvania Press, 2002.

Hammill, Graham. "Psychoanalysis and Sexuality." *Shakespeare Studies* 33 (2005): 73–79.

————. Review of *Shakesqueer: A Queer Companion to the Complete Works of Shakespeare*, ed. Madhavi Menon. *Bryn Mawr Review of Comparative Literature* 10, no. 1 (2012). http://www.brynmawr.edu/bmrcl/BMRCLFall2012/Shakesqueer.htm.

————. *Sexuality and Form: Caravaggio, Marlowe, and Bacon*. Chicago: University of Chicago Press, 2000.

Hammond, Paul. *Figuring Sex Between Men from Shakespeare to Rochester*. New York: Oxford University Press, 2002.

Hanson, Ellis. "The Future's Eve: Reparative Reading After Sedgwick." *South Atlantic Quarterly* 110, no. 1 (2011): 101–19.

————. "Teaching Shame." In *Gay Shame*, ed. David M. Halperin and Valerie Traub, 132–64. Chicago: University of Chicago Press, 2009.

Harper, Phillip Brian. *Private Affairs: Critical Ventures in the Culture of Social Relations*. New York: New York University Press, 1999.

Harper, Phillip Brian, Anne McClintock, José Esteban Muñoz, and Trish Rosen, eds. "Queer Transexions of Race, Nation, and Gender." Special issue of *Social Text* 52/53, vol. 15, nos. 3–4 (Fall/Winter 1997).

Harris, Jonathan Gil. *Foreign Bodies and the Body Politic: Discourses of Social Pathology in Early Modern England*. Cambridge: Cambridge University Press, 1998.

————. *Untimely Matter in the Time of Shakespeare*. Philadelphia: University of Pennsylvania Press, 2009.

————. "Untimely Mediations." *Early Modern Culture* 6 (2007). http://emc.eserver.org/1-6/harris.html.

Harvey, Elizabeth. "Flesh Colors and Shakespeare's Sonnets." In *A Companion to Shakespeare's Sonnets*, ed. Michael Schoenfeldt, 314–28. Malden, MA: Blackwell, 2007.

Harvey, Karen. "The History of Masculinity, circa 1650–1800." *Journal of British Studies* 44, no. 2 (2005): 296–311.

————, ed. *The Kiss in History*. Manchester: Manchester University Press, 2005.

Hawkes, David. "Sodomy, Usury, and the Narrative of Shakespeare's Sonnets." *Renaissance Studies* 14 (2000): 344–61.

Hayes, Jarrod, Margaret Higonnet, and William Spurlin, eds. *Comparatively Queer: Crossing Time, Crossing Cultures*. New York: Palgrave Macmillan, 2010.

Hehir, P., and J. D. B. Gribble. *Outlines of Medical Jurisprudence for India*, 5th ed. Madras: Higginbotham, 1908.

Henke, James T. *Courtesans and Cuckolds: A Glossary of Renaissance Dramatic Bawdy (Exclusive of Shakespeare)*. New York: Garland, 1979.

———. *Gutter Life and Language in the Early "Street" Literature of England: A Glossary of Terms and Topics Chiefly of the Sixteenth and Seventeenth Centuries*. West Cornwall, CT: Locust Hill Press, 1988.

Hennegan, Alison. *The Lesbian Pillow Book*. London: Fourth Estate, 2000.

Herman, Peter. "What's the Use? Or, The Problematic of Economy in Shakespeare's Procreation Sonnets." In *Shakespeare's Sonnets: Critical Essays*, ed. James Schiffer, 263–83. New York: Garland, 2000.

Herring, Scott. *Queering the Underworld: Slumming, Literature, and the Undoing of Lesbian and Gay History*. Chicago: University of Chicago Press, 2007.

Herrmann, Anne. *Queering the Moderns: Poses/Portraits/Performances*. New York: Palgrave, 2000.

Herrup, Cynthia. "Finding the Bodies." *GLQ: A Journal of Lesbian and Gay Studies* 5, no. 3 (1999): 255–65.

———. *A House in Gross Disorder: Sex, Law, and the 2nd Earl of Castlehaven*. New York: Oxford University Press, 1999.

Herzog, Dagmar. "Syncopated Sex: Transforming European Sexual Cultures." *American Historical Review* 114, no. 5 (2009): 1287–1308.

Hill, Walter F., and Cynthia J. Ottchen. *Shakespeare's Insults: Educating Your Wit*. New York: Three Rivers Press, 1991.

Hillman, David. *Shakespeare's Entrails: Belief, Skepticism, and the Interior of the Body*. New York: Palgrave Macmillan, 2007.

Hitchcock, Tim. *English Sexualities, 1700–1800*. New York: St. Martin's Press, 1997.

———. "Redefining Sex in Eighteenth-Century England." *History Workshop Journal* 41 (1996): 72–90.

———. "The Reformulation of Sexual Knowledge in Eighteenth-Century England." *Signs: Journal of Women in Culture and Society* 37, no. 4 (2012): 823–32.

———. "Sociability and Misogyny in the Life of John Cannon." In *English Masculinities, 1660–1800*, ed. Tim Hitchcock and Michèle Cohen, 25–43. London: Longman, 1999.

Hope, Jonathan. "Shakespeare and Language: An Introduction." In *Shakespeare and Language*, ed. Catherine M. S. Alexander, 1–17. Cambridge: Cambridge University Press, 2004.

Horowitz, Helen Lefkowitz. *Rereading Sex: Battles over Sexual Knowledge and Suppression in Nineteenth-Century America*. New York: Knopf, 2002.

Howard, Jean. *The Stage and Social Struggle in Early Modern England*. New York: Routledge, 1993.

———. *Theater of a City: The Places of London Comedy, 1598–1642*. Philadelphia: University of Pennsylvania Press, 2007.

Howell, Martha, and Walter Prevenier. *From Reliable Sources: An Introduction to Historical Methods*. Ithaca, NY: Cornell University Press, 2001.

Huffer, Lynne. *Are the Lips a Grave? A Queer Feminist on the Ethics of Sex*. New York: Columbia University Press, 2013.

———. *Mad for Foucault: Rethinking the Foundations of Queer Theory*. New York: Columbia University Press, 2010.

Hughes, Geoffrey. *Swearing: A Social History of Foul Language, Oaths, and Profanity in English.* Oxford: Basil Blackwell, 1991.

Hunt, Lynn. "The Many Bodies of Marie Antoinette: Political Pornography and the Problem of the Feminine in the French Revolution." In *Eroticism and the Body Politic*, ed. Lynn Hunt, 108–30. Baltimore: Johns Hopkins University Press, 1991.

———. *Measuring Time, Making History.* Budapest: Central European University Press, 2008.

Hunt, Margaret. "Afterword." In *Queering the Renaissance*, ed. Jonathan Goldberg, 359–77. Durham, NC: Duke University Press, 1994.

———. "The Sapphic Strain: English Lesbians in the Long Eighteenth Century." In *Single-women in the European Past, 1250–1800*, ed. Judith M. Bennett and Amy M. Froide, 270–96. Philadelphia: University of Pennsylvania Press, 1999.

Hunt, Marvin. "Be Dark but Not Too Dark: Shakespeare's Dark Lady as a Sign of Color." In *Shakespeare's Sonnets: Critical Essays*, ed. James Schiffer, 369–89. New York: Garland, 2000.

Hutcheon, Linda. *Irony's Edge: The Theory and Politics of Irony.* New York: Routledge, 1995.

Hutchison, Coleman. "Breaking the Book Known as Q." *PMLA* 121, no. 1 (2006): 33–66.

Hutson, Lorna. "Series Editor's Preface." In *Friendship's Shadows: Women's Friendship and the Politics of Betrayal in England, 1640–1705*, by Penelope Anderson, x–xii. Edinburgh Critical Studies in Renaissance Culture. Edinburgh: Edinburgh University Press, 2012.

Ingram, Martin. *Church Courts, Sex and Marriage in England, 1570–1640.* Cambridge: Cambridge University Press, 1987.

———. "Courtship and Marriage, c. 1500–1750." In *The Routledge History of Sex and the Body*, ed. Sarah Toulalan and Kate Fisher, 313–27. London, 2013.

———. "Sexual Manners: The Other Face of Civility in Early Modern England." In *Civil Histories: Essays Presented to Sir Keith Thomas*, ed. Peter Burke, Brian Harrison, and Paul Slack, 87–110. Oxford: Oxford University Press, 2000.

Irvine, Janice. *Talk About Sex: The Battles over Sex Education in the United States.* Berkeley: University of California Press, 2002.

Iyengar, Sujata. "Whiteness as Sexual Difference." In *Shades of Difference: Mythologies of Skin Color in Early Modern England*, 140–69. Philadelphia: University of Pennsylvania Press, 2005.

Jackson, Peter A. "The Persistence of Gender: From Ancient Indian *Pandakas* to Modern Thai *Gay-Quings.*" In "Australia Queer." Special issue of *Meanjin* 55, no. 1 (1996): 110–20.

Jafar, Afshan. "Consent or Coercion? Sexual Relationships Between College Faculty and Students." *Gender Issues* 21, no. 1 (Winter 2003): 43–58.

Jagose, Annamarie. "Critical Extasy: Orgasm and Sensibility in Memoirs of a Woman of Pleasure." *Signs* 32, no. 2 (2007): 459–82.

———. "Feminism's Queer Theory." *Feminism and Psychology* 19, no. 2 (2009): 157–74.

———. *Inconsequence: Lesbian Representation and the Logic of Sexual Sequence.* Ithaca, NY: Cornell University Press, 2002.

———. *Orgasmology.* Durham, NC: Duke University Press, 2013.

———. *Queer Theory: An Introduction.* New York: New York University Press, 1996.

Jameson, Fredric. *The Political Unconscious: Narrative as a Socially Symbolic Act.* Ithaca, NY: Cornell University Press, 1981.

Jankowski, Theodora A. *Pure Resistance: Queer Virginity in Early Modern English Drama.* Philadelphia: University of Pennsylvania Press, 2000.

Jeffreys, Elaine. *Sex and Sexuality in China.* London: Routledge, 2006.

Johnson, Barbara. *A World of Difference.* Baltimore: Johns Hopkins University Press, 1987.

Johnson, Colin R. *Just Queer Folks: Gender and Sexuality in Rural America*. Philadelphia: Temple University Press, 2013.

Johnson, E. Patrick, and Mae G. Henderson, eds. *Black Queer Studies: A Critical Anthology*. Durham, NC: Duke University Press, 2005.

Johnston, Mark Albert. "'To What Bawdy House Doth Your Maister Belong?': Barbers, Bawds, and Vice in the Early Modern London Barbershop." In *Masculinity and the Metropolis of Vice, 1550–1650*, ed. Amanda Bailey and Roze Hentschell, 115–35. New York: Palgrave Macmillan, 2010.

Jones, Ann Rosalind. "Heterosexuality: A Beast with Many Backs." In *A Cultural History of Sexuality in the Renaissance*, vol. 3, ed. Bette Talvacchia, 35–50. Oxford: Berg, 2011.

Jonson, Ben. *The Alchemist*. Ed. Peter Bement. London: Methuen, 1987.

———. *The Alchemist*. Ed. Douglas Brown. London: Ernest Benn, 1966.

———. *The Alchemist*. Ed. Elizabeth Cook. New York: W. W. Norton, 1991.

———. *The Alchemist*. Ed. F. H. Mares. London: Methuen, 1967.

———. *The Alchemist*. Ed. Helen Ostovich. In *Jonson, Four Comedies*. London: Longman, 1997.

———. *The Alchemist*. Ed. Brian Woolland. Cambridge: Cambridge University Press, 1996.

———. *The Devil Is an Ass*. Ed. Albert S. Cook. New York: Henry Holt, 1905.

Jordanova, Ludmilla. *History in Practice*. London: Arnold, 2000.

Jowitt, Claire. *Voyage Drama and Gender Politics, 1589–1642: Real and Imagined Worlds*. Manchester: Manchester University Press, 2003.

Kahan, Benjamin. *Celibacies: American Modernism and Sexual Life*. Durham, NC: Duke University Press, 2013.

Kahn, Coppélia. *Man's Estate: Masculine Identity in Shakespeare*. Berkeley: University of California Press, 1981.

Kalas, Rayna. "Fickle Glass." In *A Companion to Shakespeare's Sonnets*, ed. Michael Schoenfeldt, 261–76. Malden, MA: Blackwell, 2007.

Karras, Ruth Mazo. *Common Women: Prostitution and Sexuality in Medieval England*. New York: Oxford University Press, 1996.

Kaufmann, R. J. *Richard Brome, Caroline Playwright*. New York: Columbia University Press, 1961.

Kerrigan, John, ed. *William Shakespeare: The Sonnets and A Lover's Complaint*. London: Penguin, 1986.

Kiernan, Pauline. *Filthy Shakespeare: Shakespeare's Most Outrageous Sexual Puns*. New York: Gotham Books, 2006.

Kincaid, James. "It's Not About Sex." In *Our Monica, Ourselves: The Clinton Affair and the National Interest*, ed. Lauren Berlant and Lisa Duggan, 73–85. New York: New York University Press, 2001.

King, Kathryn R. "The Unaccountable Wife and Other Tales of Female Desire in Jane Barker's *A Patch-work Screen for the Ladies*." *Eighteenth Century: Theory and Interpretation* 35, no. 2 (1994): 155–72.

Kipnis, Laura. *Against Love: A Polemic*. New York: Pantheon, 2004.

Kraakman, Dorelies. "Reading Pornography Anew: A Critical History of Sexual Knowledge for Girls in French Erotic Fiction, 1750–1840." *Journal of the History of Sexuality* 4, no. 4 (1994): 517–48.

Kruger, Steven F. "Medieval/Postmodern: HIV/AIDS and the Temporality of Crisis." In *Queering the Middle Ages*, ed. Glenn Burger and Steven F. Kruger, 252–83. Minneapolis: University of Minnesota Press, 2001.

Kunzel, Regina. "Queer Studies in Queer Times: Conference Review of 'Rethinking Sex,'
University of Pennsylvania, March 4–6, 2009." *GLQ: A Journal of Lesbian and Gay Studies*
17, no. 1 (2011): 155–65.

Lacan, Jacques. *Le séminaire*, vol. 8, *Le transfert, 1960–1961*. Paris: Seuil, 1991.

LaCapra, Dominick. *History and Its Limits: Human, Animal, Violence*. Ithaca, NY: Cornell
University Press, 2009.

Lancashire, Anne Begor, ed. *Gallathea and Midas*. Lincoln: University of Nebraska Press, 1969.

Lanser, Susan S. "Befriending the Body: Female Intimacies as Class Acts." *Eighteenth-Century
Studies* 32, no. 2 (1998–99): 179–98.

———. "The Political Economy of Same-Sex Desire." In *Structures and Subjectivities: Attending to Early Modern Women*, ed. Joan E. Hartman and Adele Seeff, 157–75. Newark: University of Delaware Press, 1996.

———. "'Queer to Queer': Sapphic Bodies as Transgressive Texts." In *Lewd and Notorious:
Female Transgression in the Eighteenth Century*, ed. Katharine Kittredge, 21–46. Ann Arbor:
University of Michigan Press, 2003.

———. "Sapphic Picaresque, Sexual Difference and the Challenges of Homo-Adventuring."
Textual Practice 15, no. 2 (2001): 1–18.

———. *The Sexuality of History: Modernity and the Sapphic, 1565–1830*. Chicago: University of
Chicago Press, 2014.

———. "Singular Politics: The Rise of the British Nation and the Production of the Old
Maid." In *Singlewomen in the European Past, 1250–1800*, ed. Judith Bennett and Amy
Froide, 297–323. Philadelphia: University of Pennsylvania Press, 1999.

Lanser, Susan S., and Valerie Traub. "Writing Lesbianism into History and Representation."
Radcliffe Institute Workshop, January 2014.

Lantham, Richard A. *A Handlist of Rhetorical Terms*. 2nd ed. Berkeley: University of California
Press, 1991.

Laqueur, Thomas. *Making Sex: Body and Gender from the Greeks to Freud*. Cambridge, MA:
Harvard University Press, 1990.

———. *Solitary Sex: A Cultural History of Masturbation*. New York: Zone Books, 2003.

Largier, Niklaus. *In Praise of the Whip: A Cultural History of Arousal*. New York: Zone Books,
2007.

Laumann, Edward, John Gagnon, Robert Michael, and Stuart Michaels. *The Social Organization of Sexuality: Sexual Practices in the United States*. Chicago: University of Chicago Press,
1994.

Leinwand, Theodore B. "Coniugium Interruptum in Shakespeare and Webster." *ELH* 72, no. 1
(2005): 239–57.

Lenz, Joseph. "Base Trade: Theater as Prostitution." *ELH* 60, no. 4 (1993): 833–55.

Leslie, Marina. "Antipodal Anxieties: Joseph Hall, Richard Brome, Margaret Cavendish and
the Cartographies of Gender." *Genre* 30 (1997): 51–78.

Lesser, Zachary. "Contrary Matters: The Power of the Gloss and the History of an Obscenity."
In *Hamlet After Q1: An Uncanny History of the Shakespearean Text*, 72–113. Philadelphia:
University of Pennsylvania, 2015.

Levine, Judith. *Harmful to Minors: The Perils of Protecting Children from Sex*. Minneapolis:
University of Minnesota Press, 2002.

Levy, Allison, ed. *Sex Acts in Early Modern Italy: Practice, Performance, Perversion, Punishment*.
Farnham, England: Ashgate, 2010.

Little, Arthur. *Shakespeare Jungle Fever: National-Imperial Re-Visions of Race, Rape, and Sacrifice.* Stanford, CA: Stanford University Press, 2000.

Lochrie, Karma. *Covert Operations: The Medieval Uses of Secrecy.* Ithaca, NY: Cornell University Press, 1999.

———. "Don't Ask, Don't Tell: Murderous Plots and Medieval Secrets." *GLQ: A Journal of Lesbian and Gay Studies* 1, no. 4 (1995): 405–17.

———. *Heterosyncracies: Female Sexuality When Normal Wasn't.* Minneapolis: University of Minnesota Press, 2005.

———. "Preface." In *The Lesbian Premodern,* ed. Noreen Giffney, Michelle M. Sauer, and Diane Watt, xiii–xviii. New York: Palgrave Macmillan, 2011.

———. "Presidential Improprieties and Medieval Categories: The Absurdity of Heterosexuality." In *Queering the Middle Ages,* ed. Glenn Burger and Steven F. Kruger, 87–96. Minneapolis: University of Minnesota Press, 2001.

Loomba, Ania. *Shakespeare, Race, and Colonialism.* Oxford: Oxford University Press, 2002.

Lopez, Jeremy. *Theatrical Convention and Audience Response in Early Modern Drama.* Cambridge: Cambridge University Press, 2003.

Lord, Catherine. "Minor Eruptions: Lesbian Accused of Promoting Pedophilia." *Radical Teacher* 66 (2003): 22–27.

Lorde, Audre. *Sister Outsider.* New York: Crossing Press, 1984.

Loughlin, Marie H. *Hymeneutics: Interpreting Virginity on the Early Modern Stage.* Lewisburg, PA: Bucknell University Press, 1997.

———. *Same-Sex Desire in Early Modern England, 1550–1735: An Anthology of Literary Texts and Contexts.* Manchester: Manchester University Press, 2014.

Love, Heather. "Emotional Rescue." In *Gay Shame,* ed. David M. Halperin and Valerie Traub, 256–76. Chicago: University of Chicago Press, 2009.

———. *Feeling Backward: Loss and the Politics of Queer History.* Cambridge, MA: Harvard University Press, 2007.

———. " 'Oh, the Fun We'll Have': Remembering the Prospects for Sexuality Studies." *GLQ: A Journal of Lesbian and Gay Studies* 10, no. 2 (2004): 258–61.

———. "Queers _____ This." In *After Sex? On Writing Since Queer Theory,* ed. Janet Halley and Andrew Parker, 180–91. Durham, NC: Duke University Press, 2011.

———. "Rethinking Sex." *GLQ: A Journal of Lesbian and Gay Studies* 17, no. 1 (2010): 15–48.

———. "Truth and Consequences: On Paranoid Reading and Reparative Reading." *Criticism* 52, no. 2 (2010): 235–41.

Luker, Kristin. *When Sex Goes to School: Warring Views on Sex and Sex Education Since the Sixties.* New York: W. W. Norton, 2006.

MacCary, W. Thomas. *Friends and Lovers: The Phenomenology of Desire in Shakespearean Comedy.* New York: Columbia University Press, 1985.

Macrone, Michael. *Naughty Shakespeare: The Lascivious Lines, Offensive Oaths, and Politically Incorrect Notions from the Baddest Bard of All.* New York: Gramercy, 2000.

Magnusson, Lynne. "Language." In *Oxford Handbook of Shakespeare.* ed. Arthur F. Kinney, 239–57. Oxford: Oxford University Press, 2012.

———. "Shakespeare's Sonnets: A Modern Perspective." In *Shakespeare's Sonnets,* ed. Barbara Mowat and Paul Werstine, 355–69. Washington, DC: Folger Shakespeare Library, 2004.

Maguire, Laurie. "Feminist Editing and the Body of the Text." In *A Feminist Companion to Shakespeare,* ed. Dympna Callaghan, 59–79. Malden, MA: Blackwell, 2000.

———. "Typographical Embodiment: The Case of *Etcetera.*" In *Oxford Handbook of Shakespeare and Embodiment,* ed. Valerie Traub. Oxford: Oxford University Press, forthcoming 2016.

Manalansan, Martin F. "In the Shadows of Stonewall: Examining Gay Transnational Politics and the Diasporic Dilemma." *GLQ: A Journal of Lesbian and Gay Studies* 2, no. 4 (1995): 425–38.

Mann, Jenny C. "The 'Figure of Exchange': Shakespeare's 'Master Mistress,' Jonson's *Epicene,* and the English Art of Rhetoric." *Renaissance Drama* 38 (2010): 173–98.

Marcus, Leah S. *Unediting the Renaissance: Shakespeare, Marlowe, Milton.* London: Routledge, 1996.

Marcus, Sharon. *Between Women: Friendship, Desire, and Marriage in Victorian England.* Princeton, NJ: Princeton University Press, 2007.

———. "Comparative Sapphism." In *The Literary Channel: The Inter-National Invention of the Novel,* ed. Margaret Cohen and Carolyn Dever, 251–85. Princeton, NJ: Princeton University Press, 2002.

———. "Queer Theory for Everyone: A Review Essay," *Signs: Journal of Women in Culture and Society* 31, no. 1 (2005): 191–218.

Marshall, Brenda K. *Dakota, Or What's a Heaven For.* Fargo: North Dakota Institute for Regional Studies, 2010.

Marshall, Cynthia. *The Shattering of the Self: Violence, Subjectivity, and Early Modern Texts.* Baltimore: Johns Hopkins University Press, 2002.

Martin, A. Lynn. *Alcohol, Sex, and Gender in Late Medieval and Early Modern Europe.* Basingstoke: Palgrave, 2001.

Martin, Biddy. *Femininity Played Straight: The Significance of Being Lesbian.* New York: Routledge, 1997.

Masten, Jeffrey. "Authorship in Love." Unpublished manuscript.

———. "Edward's Futures." Paper presented at the Modern Language Association Conference, Vancouver, BC, January 2015.

———. "Gee, Your Heir Smells Terrific: Response to 'Shakespeare's Perfume.'" *Early Modern Culture* 2 (2001). http://emc.eserver.org/1-2/masten.html.

———. "The Passion of the Crux: Rhetorics of Early Modern Editing." Paper presented at the Shakespeare Association of America Conference, Washington, DC, April 2009.

———. *Queer Philologies: Sex, Language, & Affect in Shakespeare's Time.* Philadelphia: University of Pennsylvania Press, forthcoming.

———. *Textual Intercourse: Collaboration, Authorship and Sexualities in Renaissance Drama.* Cambridge: Cambridge University Press, 1997.

———. "Towards a Queer Address: The Taste of Letters and Early Modern Male Friendship." *GLQ: A Journal of Lesbian and Gay Studies* 10, no. 3 (2004): 367–84.

———. "The Two Gentlemen of Verona." In *A Companion to Shakespeare's Works,* vol. 3, *The Comedies,* ed. Richard Dutton and Jean E. Howard, 266–88. Malden, MA: Blackwell, 2003.

Matz, Robert. "The Scandals of Shakespeare's Sonnets." *ELH* 77, no. 2 (2010): 477–508.

———. *The World of Shakespeare's Sonnets: An Introduction.* Jefferson, NC: McFarland, 2008.

Maus, Katharine Eisaman. "Horns of Dilemma: Jealousy, Gender, and Spectatorship in English Renaissance Drama." *ELH* 54 (1987): 561–83.

———. *Inwardness and Theater in the English Renaissance.* Chicago: University of Chicago Press, 1995.

Maxwell-Stuart, P. G. "'Wild, Filthie, Execrabill, Detestabill, and Unnatural Sin': Bestiality in Early Modern Scotland." In *Sodomy in Early Modern Europe*, ed. Tom Betteridge, 82–93. Manchester: Manchester University Press, 2002.

Maza, Sarah. "Stephen Greenblatt, New Historicism, and Cultural History, or What We Talk About When We Talk About Interdisciplinarity." *Modern Intellectual History* 1, no. 2 (2004): 249–65.

Mazzio, Carla, and Douglas Trevor. "Dreams of History." In *Historicism, Psychoanalysis, and Early Modern Culture*, ed. Carla Mazzio and Douglas Trevor, 1–19. New York: Routledge, 2000.

McCabe, Susan. "To Be and to Have: The Rise of Queer Historicism." *GLQ: A Journal of Lesbian and Gay Studies* 11, no. 1 (2005): 119–34.

McClelland, Sara. "Intimate Justice: A Critical Analysis of Sexual Satisfaction." *Social and Personality Psychology Compass* 4, no. 9 (2010): 663–80.

———. "'What Do You Mean When You Say that You're Sexually Satisfied?' A Mixed Methods Study." *Feminism & Psychology* 24, no. 1 (2014): 74–96.

———. "Who Is the 'Self' in Self Reports of Self Satisfaction? Research and Policy Implications." *Sexuality Research and Social Policy* 8, no. 4 (2011): 304–20.

McClelland, Sara, and Michelle Fine. "Writing on Cellophane: Studying Teen Women's Sexual Desires, Inventing Methodological Release Points." In *The Methodological Dilemma: Creative, Critical and Collaborative Approaches to Qualitative Research*, ed. Kathleen Gallagher, 232–60. London: Routledge, 2008.

McCormick, Ian, ed. *Secret Sexualities: A Sourcebook of 17th and 18th Century Writing*. New York: Routledge, 1997.

McEachern, Claire. "Why Do Cuckolds Have Horns?" *Huntington Library Quarterly* 71, no. 4 (2009): 607–32.

McFarlane, Cameron. *The Sodomite in Fiction and Satire, 1660–1750*. New York: Columbia University Press, 1997.

McKeon, Michael. "Historicizing Patriarchy: The Emergence of Gender Difference in England, 1660–1760." *Eighteenth-Century Studies* 28, no. 3 (1995): 295–332.

———. "Symposium: Before Sex." *Signs: Journal of Women in Culture and Society* 37, no. 4 (2012): 791–848.

McLaren, Angus. *Impotence: A Cultural History*. Chicago: University of Chicago Press, 2007.

Mendelson, Sara, and Patricia Crawford. *Women in Early Modern England, 1550–1720*. Oxford: Clarendon Press, 1998.

Menon, Madhavi. "Afterword: Period Cramps." In *Queer Renaissance Historiography: Backward Gaze*, ed. Vin Nardizzi, Stephen Guy-Bray, and Will Stockton, 229–35. Farnham, England: Ashgate, 2009.

———. Reply. In "Forum: Queering History," *PMLA* 121, no. 3 (2006): 838–39.

———, ed. *Shakesqueer: A Queer Companion to the Complete Works of Shakespeare*. Durham, NC: Duke University Press, 2011.

———. "Spurning Teleology in *Venus and Adonis*." *GLQ: A Journal of Lesbian and Gay Studies* 11, no. 4 (2005): 491–519.

———. *Unhistorical Shakespeare: Queer Theory in Shakespearean Literature and Film*. New York: Palgrave Macmillan, 2008.

———. *Wanton Words: Rhetoric and Sexuality in English Renaissance Drama*. Toronto: University of Toronto Press, 2004.

Merrick, Jeffrey, and Bryant T. Ragan, Jr., eds. *Homosexuality in Early Modern France: A Documentary Collection*. Oxford: Oxford University Press, 2001.

Michael, Robert, John Gagnon, Edward Laumann, and Gina Kolata. *Sex in America: A Definitive Survey*. New York: Warner Books, 1994.

Middleton, Thomas. *A Chaste Maid in Cheapside*. Ed. Linda Woodbridge. In *Thomas Middleton: The Collected Works*, ed. Gary Taylor and John Lavagnino, 907–58. Oxford: Clarendon Press, 2007.

———. *Your Five Gallants*. Ed. Ralph Alan Cohen and John Jowett. In *Thomas Middleton: The Collected Works*, ed. Gary Taylor and John Lavagnino, 597–636. Oxford: Clarendon Press, 2007.

Middleton, Thomas, and Thomas Dekker. *The Roaring Girle; or, Moll Cutpurse*. Ed. Coppélia Kahn. In *Thomas Middleton: The Collected Works*, ed. Gary Taylor and John Lavagnino, 721–77. Oxford: Clarendon Press, 2007.

Midler, Bette. "One Monkey Don't Stop No Show." On *Bathhouse Betty*. Warner Bros. Records, 1998.

Miller, D. A. "Anal Rope." In *Inside/Out: Lesbian Theories, Gay Theories*, ed. Diana Fuss, 119–42. New York: Routledge, 1991.

———. *The Novel and the Police*. Berkeley: University of California Press, 1988.

Miller, Naomi J. "Playing 'the Mother's Part': Shakespeare's Sonnets and Early Modern Codes of Maternity." In *Shakespeare's Sonnets: Critical Essays*, ed. James Schiffer, 347–67. New York: Garland, 2000.

Miller, Toby. "The First Penis Impeached." In *Our Monica, Ourselves: The Clinton Affair and the National Interest*, ed. Lauren Berlant and Lisa Duggan, 116–33. New York: New York University Press, 2001.

Mohler, Tina. " 'What Is Thy Body but a Swallowing Grave . . . ?': Desire Underground in *Titus Andronicus*." *Shakespeare Quarterly* 57, no. 1 (2006): 23–44.

Montrose, Louis Adrian. "The Elizabethan Subject and the Spenserian Text." In *Literary Theory/Renaissance Texts*, ed. Patricia Parker and David Quint, 303–40. Baltimore: Johns Hopkins University Press, 1986.

Moore, Lisa. *Dangerous Intimacies: Toward a Sapphic History of the British Novel*. Durham, NC: Duke University Press, 1997.

Moraga, Cherríe, and Gloria Anzaldúa, eds. *This Bridge Called My Back: Writings by Radical Women of Color*. New York: Kitchen Table/ Women of Color Press, 1983.

Moran, Jeffrey. *Teaching Sex: The Shaping of Adolescence in the 20th Century*. Cambridge, MA: Harvard University Press, 2000.

Moulton, Ian. *Before Pornography: Erotic Writing in Early Modern England*. Oxford: Oxford University Press, 2000.

———. "Erotic Representation, 1500–1750." In *The Routledge History of Sex and the Body, 1500 to the Present*, ed. Sarah Toulalan and Kate Fisher, 207–22. New York: Routledge, 2013.

———, ed. and trans. *La Cazzaria: The Book of the Prick*, by Antonio Vignali. New York: Routledge, 2003.

Mowry, Melissa. *The Bawdy Politic in Stuart England, 1660–1714: Political Pornography and Prostitution*. Burlington, VT: Ashgate, 2004.

———. "London's Bridewell: Violence, Prostitution, and Questions of Evidence." In *Violence, Politics, and Gender*, ed. Joseph Ward, 207–22. New York: Palgrave Macmillan, 2008.

Mudge, Bradford K., ed. *When Flesh Becomes Word: An Anthology of Early Eighteenth-Century Libertine Literature*. Oxford: Oxford University Press, 2004.

Mullaney, Steven. *The Reformation of Emotions in the Age of Shakespeare*. Chicago: Chicago University Press, 2015.

Muñoz, José Esteban. *Cruising Utopia: The Then and There of Queer Futurity*. New York: New York University Press, 2009.

————. *Disidentifications: Queers of Color and the Performance of Politics*. Minneapolis: University of Minnesota Press, 1999.

Murphy, Kevin D. and Sally O'Driscoll. "Introduction: 'Fugitive Pieces' and 'Gaudy Books': Textual, Historical, and Visual Interpretations of Ephemera in the Long Eighteenth Century." In *Studies in Ephemera: Text and Image in Eighteenth-Century Print*, 1–25. Lewisburg: Bucknell University Press, 2013.

Murrin, John M. "'Things Fearful to Name': Bestiality in Early America." In *The Animal/ Human Boundary: Historical Perspectives*, ed. Angela N. H. Creager and William Chester Jordan, 115–56. Rochester, NY: University of Rochester Press, 2002.

Nagle, Christopher C. "'Unusual Fires': Ann Batten Cristall's Queer Temporality." In *Developments in the Histories of Sexualities: In Search of the Normal, 1600–1800*, ed. Chris Mounsey, 51–69. Lewisburg, PA: Bucknell University Press, 2013.

Nardizzi, Vin, Stephen Guy-Bray, and Will Stockton, eds. *Queer Renaissance Historiography: Backward Gaze*. Farnham, England: Ashgate, 2009.

Nashe, Thomas. "The Choise of Valentines." In *The Penguin Book of Renaissance Verse*. ed. David Norbrook and H. R. Wouduysen. London: Penguin, 1993, 253–63.

Nealon, Christopher. *Foundlings: Lesbian and Gay Historical Emotion Before Stonewall*. Durham, NC: Duke University Press, 2001.

Neely, Carol Thomas. "Lovesickness, Gender, and Subjectivity: *Twelfth Night* and *As You Like It*." In *A Feminist Companion to Shakespeare*, ed. Dympna Callaghan, 276–98. Oxford: Blackwell, 2000.

Nelles, William. "Sexing Shakespeare's Sonnets: Reading Beyond Sonnet 20." *English Literary Renaissance* 39, no. 1 (2009): 128–40.

Newman, Karen. *Cultural Capitals: Early Modern London and Paris*. Princeton, NJ: Princeton University Press, 2007.

Newton, Esther. "The Mythic Mannish Lesbian: Radclyffe Hall and the New Woman." In *Palatable Poison: Critical Perspectives on "The Well of Loneliness,"* ed. Laura Doan and Jay Prosser, 89–108. New York: Columbia University Press, 2001.

Norbrook, David. *Writing the English Republic*. Cambridge: Cambridge University Press, 1999.

North, Marcy L. "The Sonnets and Book History." In *A Companion to Shakespeare's Sonnets*, ed. Michael Schoenfeldt, 204–21. Malden, MA: Blackwell, 2007.

O'Connell, Sheila. "Love Pleasant, Love Unfortunate: Women in Seventeenth-Century Popular Prints." In *Politics, Transgression, and Representation at the Court of Charles II*, ed. Julia Marciari Alexander and Catharine MacLeod, 61–78. New Haven: Yale Center for British Art, 2007.

O'Donnell, Katherine, and Michael O'Rourke, eds. *Love, Sex, Intimacy, and Friendship Between Men, 1550–1800*. Basingstoke: Palgrave Macmillan, 2003.

O'Driscoll, Sally. "Conjugal Capitalism: The Domestication of Public Space." In *Heteronormativity in Eighteenth Century Literature and Culture*, ed. Ana de Freitas Boe and Abby Coykendall, 41–58. Burlington, VT: Ashgate, 2015.

————. "The Molly and the Fop: Untangling Effeminacy in the Eighteenth Century." In *Developments in the Histories of Sexualities: In Search of the Normal, 1600–1800*, ed. Chris Mounsey, 145–71. Lewisburg, PA: Bucknell University Press, 2013.

———. "A Crisis of Femininity: Re-Making Gender in Popular Discourse." In *Lesbian Dames: Sapphism in the Long Eighteenth Century*, ed. John C. Beynon and Caroline Gonda, 45–59. Farnham, England: Ashgate, 2010.

———. "Word on the Street: 18th Century Pamphlets and the Popular Language of Gender." Unpublished manuscript.

O'Hara, Diana. *Courtship and Constraint: Rethinking the Making of Marriage in Tudor England.* Manchester: Manchester University Press, 2000.

Oram, Alison. *Her Husband Was a Woman! Women's Gender-Crossing in Modern British Popular Culture.* London: Routledge, 2007.

Oram, Alison, and Annmarie Turnbull. *The Lesbian History Sourcebook: Love and Sex Between Women in Britain from 1780 to 1970.* London: Routledge, 2001.

Orgel, Stephen. *Impersonations: The Performance of Gender in Shakespeare's England.* Cambridge: Cambridge University Press, 1996.

———. "Mr. Who He?" In *A Companion to Shakespeare's Sonnets*, ed. Michael Schoenfeldt, 137–44. Malden, MA: Blackwell, 2007.

———. "On Dildos and Fadings." *ANQ: A Quarterly Journal of Short Articles, Notes, and Reviews* 5, nos. 2–3 (1992): 106–11.

———. "The Poetics of Incomprehensibility." *Shakespeare Quarterly* 42, no. 4 (1991): 431–37.

Orvis, David L. "Queer Renaissance Dramaturgy, Shakespeare's *Shrew*, and the Deconstruction of Marriage." In *Developments in the Histories of Sexualities: In Search of the Normal, 1600–1800*, ed. Chris Mounsey, 17–50. Lewisburg, PA: Bucknell University Press, 2013.

Pagels, Elaine. "The Politics of Paradise: Augustine's Exegesis of Genesis 1–3 Versus That of John Chrysostom." *Harvard Theological Review* 78, nos. 1–2 (1985): 67–99.

Panek, Jennifer. "'This Base Stallion Trade': He-whores and Male Sexuality on the Early Modern Stage." *English Literary Renaissance* 40, no. 3 (2010): 357–92.

Park, Katharine. "The Rediscovery of the Clitoris: French Medicine and the Tribade, 1570–1620." In *The Body in Parts: Fantasies of Corporeality in Early Modern Europe*, ed. David Hillman and Carla Mazzio, 171–93. New York: Routledge, 1997.

———. *Secrets of Women: Gender, Generation, and the Origins of Human Dissection.* New York: Zone Books, 2006.

Parker, Patricia. *Literary Fat Ladies: Rhetoric, Gender, Property.* London: Methuen, 1987.

———. *Shakespeare from the Margins: Language, Culture, Context.* Chicago: University of Chicago Press, 1996.

Parr, Anthony, ed. *Three Renaissance Travel Plays.* Manchester: Manchester University Press, 1995.

Partridge, Eric. *Shakespeare's Bawdy: A Literary and Psychological Essay and a Comprehensive Glossary.* London: Routledge, 1947.

Paster, Gail Kern. *The Body Embarrassed: Drama and Disciplines of Shame in Early Modern England.* Ithaca, NY: Cornell University Press, 1993.

———. *Humoring the Body: Emotions and the Shakespearean Stage.* Chicago: University of Chicago Press, 2004.

Paster, Gail Kern, Katherine Rowe, and Mary Floyd-Wilson, eds. *Reading the Early Modern Passions: Essays in the Cultural History of Emotion.* Philadelphia: University of Pennsylvania Press, 2004.

Pequigney, Joseph. "Sonnets 71–74: Texts and Contexts." In *Shakespeare's Sonnets: Critical Essays*, ed. James Schiffer, 285–304. New York: Garland, 1999.

————. *Such Is My Love: A Study of Shakespeare's Sonnets*. Chicago: University of Chicago Press, 1985.

Phillips, Kim M., and Barry Reay, eds. *Sex Before Sexuality: A Premodern History*. Cambridge: Polity, 2011.

————, eds. *Sexualities in History: A Reader*. London: Routledge, 2002.

Phillips, Mark Salber. *On Historical Distance*. New Haven, CT: Yale University Press, 2013.

Pincus, Steven. "'Coffee Politicians Does Create': Coffeehouses and Restoration Political Culture." *Journal of Modern History* 67, no. 4 (1995): 807–34.

Platt, Peter G. *Shakespeare and the Culture of Paradox*. Burlington, VT: Ashgate, 2009.

Pollock, Linda A. *Forgotten Children: Parent-Child Relations from 1500–1900*. Cambridge: Cambridge University Press, 1983.

Poovey, Mary. "[International Prohibition Against] Sex in America." *Critical Inquiry* 24 (1998): 366–92. Reprinted in *Intimacy*, ed. Lauren Berlant, 86–112. Chicago: University of Chicago Press, 2000.

Porter, Joseph. *Shakespeare's Mercutio*. Chapel Hill: University of North Carolina Press, 1988.

Porter, Roy. "The Literature of Sexual Advice Before 1800." In *Sexual Knowledge, Sexual Science*, ed. Roy Porter and Mikulas Teich, 134–57. Cambridge: Cambridge University Press, 1994.

Povinelli, Elizabeth A., and George Chauncey, eds. "Thinking Sex Transnationally." Special issue of *GLQ: A Journal of Lesbian and Gay Studies* 5, no. 4 (1999).

Prins, Yopie. *Victorian Sappho*. Princeton, NJ: Princeton University Press, 1999.

Proctor, Robert. *Cancer Wars: How Politics Shapes What We Know and Don't Know About Cancer*. New York: Basic Books, 1996.

Proctor, Robert, and Londa Schiebinger. *Agnotology: The Making and Unmaking of Ignorance*. Stanford, CA: Stanford University Press, 2008.

Prosser, Jay. *Second Skins: The Body Narratives of Transsexuality*. New York: Columbia University Press, 1998.

————. "'Some Primitive Thing Conceived in a Turbulent Age of Transition': The Transsexual Emerging from *The Well*." In *Palatable Poison: Critical Perspectives on "The Well of Loneliness,"* ed. Laura Doan and Jay Prosser, 129–44. New York: Columbia University Press, 2001.

Puar, Jasbir K. "Circuits of Queer Mobility: Tourism, Travel, and Globalization." *GLQ: A Journal of Lesbian and Gay Studies* 8, nos. 1–2 (2002): 101–37.

Puff, Helmut. "After the History of (Male) Homosexuality." In *After "The History of Sexuality": German Genealogies With and Beyond Foucault*, ed. Scott Spector, Helmut Puff, and Dagmar Herzog, 17–30. New York: Berghahn, 2012.

————. *Sodomy and Reformation Germany and Switzerland, 1400–1600*. Chicago: University of Chicago Press, 2003.

————. "Toward a Philology of the Premodern Lesbian." In *The Lesbian Premodern*, ed. Noreen Giffney, Michelle M. Sauer, and Diane Watt, 145–57. New York: Palgrave Macmillan, 2011.

Pursglove, Glyn. "Prick-Song Ditties: Musical Metaphor in the Bawdy Verse of the Early Modern Period." In *"And Never Know the Joy": Sex and the Erotic in English Poetry*, ed. C. C. Barfoot, 65–88. Amsterdam: Rodopi, 2006.

Puttenham, George. *The Arte of English Poesie*. Ed. Gladys Doidge Willcock and Alice Walker. Cambridge: Cambridge University Press, 1936.

Quaife, G. R. *Wanton Wenches and Wayward Wives: Peasants and Illicit Sex in Early Seventeenth Century England.* London: Croom Helm, 1979.

Raber, Karen. *Animal Bodies, Renaissance Culture.* Philadelphia: University of Pennsylvania Press, 2013.

Rackin, Phyllis. "Foreign Country: The Place of Women and Sexuality in Shakespeare's Historical World." In *Enclosure Acts: Sexuality, Property, and Culture in Early Modern England,* ed. Richard Burt and John Michael Archer, 68–95. Ithaca, NY: Cornell University Press, 1994.

Radel, Nicholas F. Review of *Queer Renaissance Historiography: Backward Gaze,* ed. Vin Nardizzi, Stephen Guy-Bray, and Will Stockton. *Renaissance Quarterly* 63, no. 3 (2010): 996–98.

Rambuss, Richard. "After Male Sex." *South Atlantic Quarterly* 106, no. 3 (Summer 2007): 577–88.

———. *Closet Devotions.* Durham, NC: Duke University Press, 1998.

———. Review of *A House in Gross Disorder: Sex, Law, and the 2nd Earl of Castlehaven,* by Cynthia Herrup. *Shakespeare Studies* 30 (2002): 274–81.

Ramsey, Paul. *The Fickle Glass: A Study of Shakespeare's Sonnets.* New York: AMS Press, 1979.

Rasmussen, Mary Louise, Eric Rofes, and Susan Talburt, eds. *Youth and Sexualities: Pleasure, Subversion, and Insubordination In and Out of Schools.* New York: Palgrave Macmillan, 2004.

Read, Sophie. "Puns: Serious Wordplay." In *Renaissance Figures of Speech,* ed. Sylvia Adamson, Gavin Alexander, and Katrin Ettenhuber, 81–94. Cambridge: Cambridge University Press, 2007.

Redfern, Walter D. *Puns.* Oxford: Blackwell, 1984.

Reece, Michael, Debby Herbenick, Vanessa Schick, Stephanie A. Sanders, Brian Dodge, and J. Dennis Fortenberry. "Findings from the National Survey on Sexual Health and Behavior (NSSHB), Center for Sexual Health Promotion, Indiana University." Special issue, *Journal of Sexual Medicine* 7, Supplement 5 (2010): 243–373.

Richardson, Catherine. *Domestic Life and Domestic Tragedy in Early Modern England: The Material Life of the Household.* Manchester: Manchester University Press, 2006.

Rickman, Johanna. *Love, Lust, and License in Early Modern England.* Burlington, VT: Ashgate, 2008.

Roberts, Sasha. *Reading Shakespeare's Poems in Early Modern England.* Basingstoke: Palgrave Macmillan, 2003.

———. "Shakespeare's Sonnets and English Sonnet Sequences." In *Early Modern English Poetry: A Critical Companion,* ed. Patrick Cheney, Andrew Hadfield, and Garrett A. Sullivan, Jr., 172–83. Oxford: Oxford University Press, 2007.

Rocke, Michael. *Forbidden Friendships: Homosexuality and Male Culture in Renaissance Florence.* Oxford: Oxford University Press, 1996.

Rofel, Lisa. *Desiring China: Experiments in Neoliberalism, Sexuality, and Public Culture.* Durham, NC: Duke University Press, 2007.

Rogers, Janine. "Riddling Erotic Identity in Early English Lyrics." In *"And Never Know the Joy": Sex and the Erotic in English Poetry,* ed. C. C. Barfoot, 1–12. Amsterdam: Rodopi, 2006.

Rohy, Valerie. *Anachronism and Its Others: Sexuality, Race, Temporality.* Albany: State University of New York Press, 2009.

———. *Impossible Women: Lesbian Figures and American Literature.* Ithaca, NY: Cornell University Press, 2000.

Ronell, Avital. *Stupidity.* Urbana: University of Illinois Press, 2002.

Roof, Judith. *A Lure of Knowledge: Lesbian Sexuality and Theory.* New York: Columbia University Press, 1991.

Roper, Lyndal. *Oedipus and the Devil: Witchcraft, Sexuality and Religion in Early Modern Europe.* New York: Routledge, 1994.

———. *Witch Craze: Terror and Fantasy in Baroque Germany.* New Haven, CT: Yale University Press, 2004.

Rosario, Vernon. "Quantum Sex: Intersex and the Molecular Deconstruction of Sex," *GLQ: A Journal of Lesbian and Gay Studies* 15, no. 2 (2009): 267–84.

Rowley, William, Thomas Middleton, and Thomas Heywood. *An/The Old Law.* Ed. Jeffrey Masten. In *Thomas Middleton: The Collected Works,* ed. Gary Taylor and John Lavagnino, 1331–96. Oxford: Clarendon Press, 2007.

Rowson, Everett. "Categorization of Gender and Sexual Irregularity in Medieval Arabic Vice Lists." In *Body Guards: The Politics of Gender Ambiguity,* ed. Julia Epstein and Kristina Straub, 50–79. London: Routledge, 1991.

Rubin, Gayle. "Blood Under the Bridge: Reflections on 'Thinking Sex.'" *GLQ: A Journal of Lesbian and Gay Studies* 17, no. 1 (2010): 15–48.

———. "The Catacombs: A Temple of the Butthole." In *Leatherfolk: Radical Sex, People, Politics, and Practice,* ed. Mark Thompson, 119–41. Boston: Alyson, 1991.

———. "Thinking Sex: Notes for a Radical Theory of the Politics of Sexuality." In *Pleasure and Danger: Exploring Female Sexuality,* ed. Carole Vance, 267–319. London: Routledge and Kegan Paul, 1984.

Rubin, Gayle, and Judith Butler, "Sexual Traffic: Interview." In *Feminism Meets Queer Theory,* ed. Elizabeth Weed and Naomi Schor, 68–108. Bloomington: Indiana University Press, 1997.

Rubinstein, Frankie. *A Dictionary of Shakespeare's Sexual Puns and Their Significance.* London: Macmillan, 1984.

Rubright, Marjorie. *Doppelgänger Dilemmas: Anglo-Dutch Relations in Early Modern English Literature and Culture.* Philadelphia: University of Pennsylvania Press, 2014.

———. "Going Dutch in London City Comedy: Economies of Sexual and Sacred Exchange in John Marston's *The Dutch Courtesan* (1605)." *English Literary Renaissance* 40, no. 1 (Winter 2010): 88–112.

Ruggiero, Guido. "Introduction: Hunting for Birds in the Italian Renaissance." In *Erotic Cultures of Renaissance Italy,* ed. Sarah F. Matthews-Grieco, 1–16. Farnham, England: Ashgate, 2010.

Rupp, Leila J. *A Desired Past: A Short History of Same-Sex Love in America.* Chicago: University of Chicago Press, 1999.

———. *Sapphistries: A Global History of Love Between Women.* New York: New York University Press, 2011.

Saketopoulou, Avgi. "Trauma Lives Us: Affective Excess, Safe Space, and the Erasure of Subjectivity." https://bullybloggers.wordpress.com/2014/12/06/trauma-lives-us-affective-excess -safe-spaces-and-the-erasure-of-subjectivity/.

Salisbury, Joyce E. *The Beast Within: Animals in the Middle Ages.* London: Routledge, 1994.

Sanchez, Melissa E. *Erotic Subjects: The Sexuality of Politics in Early Modern English Literature.* Oxford: Oxford University Press, 2011.

———. "The Poetics of Feminine Subjectivity in Shakespeare's Sonnets and 'A Lover's Complaint.'" In *The Oxford Handbook of Shakespeare's Poetry,* ed. Jonathan Post, 505–21. Oxford: Oxford University Press, 2013.

Sanders, Julie. "The Politics of Escapism: Fantasies of Travel and Power in Richard Brome's *The Antipodes* and Ben Jonson's *The Alchemist*." In *Writing and Fantasy*, ed. Ceri Sullivan and Barbara White, 137–50. London: Longman, 1999.

Sang, Tze-lan D. *The Emerging Lesbian: Female Same-Sex Desire in Modern China*. Chicago: University of Chicago Press, 2003.

Sanders, Stephanie A., Brandon J. Hill, William L. Yarber, Cynthia A. Graham, Richard A. Crosby, and Robert R. Milhausen. "Misclassification Bias: Diversity in Conceptualisations about Having 'had sex.'" *Sexual Health* 7 (2010): 31–34.

Sanders, Stephanie A. and June Machover Reinisch. "Would You Say You 'Had Sex' If . . . ?" *Journal of the American Medical Association* 281, no. 3 (January 20, 1999): 275–77.

Saunders, Ben. *Desiring Donne: Poetry, Sexuality, Interpretation*. Cambridge, MA: Harvard University Press, 2006.

———. "Iago's Clyster: Purgation, Anality, and the Civilizing Process in *Othello*." *Shakespeare Quarterly* 55, no. 2 (2004): 148–76.

Sautman, Francesca Canadé, and Pamela Sheingorn, eds. *Same-Sex Love and Desire Among Women in the Middle Ages*. New York: Palgrave Macmillan, 2001.

Sawday, Jonathan. *The Body Emblazoned: Dissection and the Human Body in Renaissance Culture*. New York: Routledge, 1995.

Schalkwyk, David. "'She Never Told Her Love': Embodiment, Textuality, and Silence in Shakespeare's Sonnets and Plays." *Shakespeare Quarterly* 45, no. 4 (1994): 381–407.

Schiesari, Julia. *The Gendering of Melancholia: Feminism, Psychoanalysis and the Symbolics of Loss in Renaissance Literature*. Ithaca, NY: Cornell University Press, 1992.

Schiffer, James. "The Incomplete Narrative of Shakespeare's Sonnets." In *A Companion to Shakespeare's Sonnets*, ed. Michael Schoenfeldt, 45–56. Malden, MA: Blackwell, 2007.

———. "Reading New Life into Shakespeare's Sonnets: A Survey of Criticism." In *Shakespeare's Sonnets: Critical Essays,* ed. James Schiffer, 3–71. New York: Garland, 2000.

———, ed. *Shakespeare's Sonnets: Critical Essays*. New York: Garland, 2000.

Schlichter, Annette. "Contesting 'Straights': 'Lesbians,' 'Queer Heterosexuals' and the Critique of Heteronormativity." *Journal of Lesbian Studies* 11, nos. 3–4 (2007): 189–201.

Schoenfeldt, Michael. *Bodies and Selves in Early Modern England: Physiology and Inwardness in Spenser, Shakespeare, Herbert, and Milton*. Cambridge: Cambridge University Press, 1999.

———. *The Cambridge Introduction to Shakespeare's Poetry*. Cambridge: Cambridge University Press, 2010.

———, ed. *A Companion to Shakespeare's Sonnets*. Malden, MA: Blackwell, 2007.

———. "The Matter of Inwardness: Shakespeare's Sonnets." In *Shakespeare's Sonnets: Critical Essays*, ed. James Schiffer, 305–24. New York: Garland, 1998.

———. "The Sonnets." In *The Cambridge Companion to Shakespeare's Poetry*, ed. Patrick Cheney, 125–43. Cambridge: Cambridge University Press, 2007.

Schultz, James A. "Heterosexuality as a Threat to Medieval Studies." *Journal of the History of Sexuality* 15, no. 1 (2006): 14–29.

Schwarz, Kathryn. *Tough Love: Amazon Encounters in the English Renaissance*. Durham, NC: Duke University Press, 2000.

———. *What You Will: Gender, Contract, and Shakespearean Social Space*. Philadelphia: University of Pennsylvania Press, 2011.

———. "The Wrong Question: Thinking Through Virginity." *differences: A Journal of Feminist Cultural Studies* 13, no. 2 (2002): 1–33.

Scott, Joan Wallach. *The Fantasy of Feminist History*. Durham, NC: Duke University Press, 2011.

———. "Gender: A Useful Category of Historical Analysis." *American Historical Review* 91, no. 5 (1986): 1053–75.

Sedgwick, Eve Kosofsky. *Between Men: English Literature and Male Homosocial Desire*. New York: Columbia University Press, 1985.

———. *Epistemology of the Closet*. Berkeley: University of California Press, 1990.

———. *Tendencies*. Durham, NC: Duke University Press, 1993.

———. *Touching Feeling: Affect, Pedagogy, Performativity*. Durham, NC: Duke University Press, 2003.

7 Humanities Professors, "Trigger Warnings Are Flawed," https://www.insidehighered.com/views/2014/05/29/essay-faculty-members-about-why-they-will-not-use-trigger-warnings.

Shakespeare, William. *Hamlet*. Ed. Barbara A. Mowat and Paul Werstine. New York: Simon and Schuster, 2012.

———. *Hamlet*. In *The Norton Shakespeare*, ed. Stephen Greenblatt, Jean Howard, Katharine Eisaman Maus, Walter Cohen. New York: W. W. Norton, 2008.

———. *Hamlet*. Ed. Ann Thompson and Neil Taylor. London: Arden Shakespeare, 2006.

———. *The Life of Henry the Fifth*. In *The Norton Shakespeare*, ed. Stephen Greenblatt, Jean Howard, Katharine Eisaman Maus, Walter Cohen. New York: W. W. Norton, 2008.

———. *The Merry Wives of Windsor*. Ed. David Crane. Cambridge: Cambridge University Press, 2010.

———. *A Midsummer Night's Dream*. In *The Norton Shakespeare*, ed. Stephen Greenblatt, Jean Howard, Katharine Eisaman Maus, Walter Cohen. New York: W. W. Norton, 2008.

———. *Othello, the Moor of Venice*. Ed. Michael Neill. Oxford: Oxford University Press, 2006.

———. *Romeo and Juliet*. Ed. G. Blakemore Evans. Cambridge: Cambridge University Press, 1984; updated ed., 2003.

———. *Romeo and Juliet*. In *The Norton Shakespeare*, ed. Stephen Greenblatt, Jean Howard, Katharine Eisaman Maus, Walter Cohen. New York: W. W. Norton, 2008.

———. *Romeo and Juliet*. Ed. Jill L. Levenson. Oxford: Oxford University Press, 2000.

———. *Romeo and Juliet*. Ed. René Weis. London: Arden Shakespeare, 2012.

———. *The RSC Shakespeare: The Complete Works*. Ed. Jonathan Bate and Eric Rasmussen. New York: Modern Library, 2007.

———. *Twelfth Night*. Ed. Keir Elam, Arden Shakespeare, 3rd ser. London: Cengage Learning, 2008.

———. *Twelfth Night*. Ed. J. M. Lothian and T. W. Craik. London: Methuen, 1975.

———. *Twelfth Night*. Ed. Burton Raffel. New Haven, CT: Yale University Press, 2007.

———. *Twelfth Night, or What You Will*. In *The Norton Shakespeare*, ed. Stephen Greenblatt, Jean Howard, Katharine Eisaman Maus, Walter Cohen. New York: W. W. Norton, 2008.

———. *The Winter's Tale*. Ed. Harold F. Brooks and Harold Jenkins. London: Methuen; and Cambridge, MA: Harvard University Press, 1963.

———. *The Winter's Tale*. Ed. Jean Howard. In *The Norton Shakespeare*, ed. Stephen Greenblatt, Jean Howard, Katharine Eisaman Maus, Walter Cohen. New York: W. W. Norton, 2008.

———. *The Winter's Tale*. Ed. Stephen Orgel. Oxford: Clarendon Press, 1996.

———. *The Winter's Tale*. Ed. John A. Pitcher. London: Arden Shakespeare, 2010.

———. *The Winter's Tale*. Ed. Susan Snyder and Deborah T. Curren-Aquino. Cambridge: Cambridge University Press, 2007.

————. *The Winter's Tale*. Ed. Robert Kean Turner and Virginia Westling Haas. New York: Modern Language Association of America, 2005.

Shannon, Laurie. "Nature's Bias: Renaissance Homonormativity and Elizabethan Comic Likeness." *Modern Philology* 98, no. 2 (2000): 183–210.

————. "Poetic Companies: Musters of Agency in George Gascoigne's 'Friendly Verse.'" *GLQ: A Journal of Lesbian and Gay Studies* 10, no. 3 (2004): 453–83.

————. "Queerly Philological Reading." Paper presented at the "Lesbianism in the Renaissance" seminar, Shakespeare Association of America, Minneapolis, 2002.

————. *Sovereign Amity: Figures of Friendship in Shakespearean Contexts*. Chicago: University of Chicago Press, 2002.

Sharp, Jane. *The Midwives Book; or, The Whole Art of Midwifry Discovered*. London, 1671.

Shepard, Alexandra. "From Anxious Patriarchs to Refined Gentlemen? Manhood in Britain, Circa 1500–1700." *Journal of British Studies* 44, no. 2 (2005): 281–95.

Siebers, Tobin. "Sex, Shame, and Disability Identity: With Reference to Mark O'Brien." In *Disability Theory*, 157–75. Ann Arbor: University of Michigan Press, 2009.

————. "A Sexual Culture for Disabled People." In *Disability Theory*, 135–56. Ann Arbor: University of Michigan Press, 2009.

Simes, Gary. "Gay Slang Lexicography: A Brief History and a Commentary on the First Two Gay Glossaries." *Dictionaries: Journal of the Dictionary Society of North America* 26 (2005): 1–159.

Simons, Patricia. *The Sex of Men in Premodern Europe: A Cultural History*. Cambridge: Cambridge University Press, 2011.

Sinfield, Alan. "Lesbian and Gay Taxonomies." *Critical Inquiry* 29, no. 1 (2002): 120–38.

————. *Shakespeare, Authority, Sexuality: Unfinished Business in Cultural Materialism*. New York: Routledge, 2006.

Singh, Jyotsna. "The Interventions of History: Narratives of Sexuality." In *The Weyward Sisters: Shakespeare and Feminist Politics*, ed. Dympna Callaghan, Lorraine Helms, and Jyotsna Singh, 7–58. Oxford: Blackwell, 1994.

Smith, Bruce R. *The Acoustic World of Early Modern England: Attending to the O-Factor*. Chicago: University of Chicago Press, 1999.

————. "Female Impersonation in Early Modern Ballads." In *Women Players in England, 1500–1660: Beyond the All-Male Stage*, ed. Pamela Allen Brown and Peter Parolin, 281–304. Burlington, VT: Ashgate, 2005.

————. *Homosexual Desire in Shakespeare's England: A Cultural Poetics*. Chicago: University of Chicago Press, 1991.

————. "I, You, He, She, and We: On the Sexual Politics of Shakespeare's Sonnets." In *Shakespeare's Sonnets: Critical Essays*, ed. James Schiffer, 411–29. New York: Garland, 2000.

————. "Latin Lovers in *The Taming of the Shrew*." In *Shakesqueer: A Queer Companion to the Complete Works of Shakespeare*, ed. Madhavi Menon, 343–50. Durham, NC: Duke University Press, 2011.

————. *Phenomenal Shakespeare*. Malden, MA: Wiley-Blackwell, 2010.

————. "Resexing Lady Macbeth's Gender—and Ours." In *Presentism, Gender, and Sexuality in Shakespeare*, ed. Evelyn Gajowski, 25–48. Basingstoke: Palgrave Macmillan, 2009.

————. "Shakespeare's Sonnets and the History of Sexuality: A Reception History." In *A Companion to Shakespeare's Works*, vol. 4, *The Poems, Problem Comedies, Late Plays*, ed. Richard Dutton and Jean E. Howard, 4–26. Malden, MA: Blackwell, 2003.

Smith-Rosenberg, Carroll. "The Female World of Love and Ritual: Relations Between Women in Nineteenth-Century America." *Signs: A Journal of Women in Culture and Society* 1, no. 1 (1975): 1–29.

Snow, Phoebe. "Teach Me Tonight." On *It Looks Like Snow*. Columbia Records, 1976.

Snyder, Susan. "'The King's Not Here': Displacement and Deferral in *All's Well That Ends Well*." *Shakespeare Quarterly* 43, no. 1 (1992): 20–32.

Somerville, Siobhan B. "Scientific Racism and the Invention of the Homosexual Body." In *Sexology in Culture: Labeling Bodies and Desires*, ed. Lucy Bland and Laura Doan, 60–76. Chicago: University of Chicago Press, 1998.

Spector, Scott, Helmut Puff, and Dagmar Herzog, eds. *After "The History of Sexuality": German Genealogies With and Beyond Foucault*. New York: Berghahn, 2012.

Spiegel, Gabrielle. "History, Historicism, and the Social Logic of the Text in the Middle Ages." *Speculum* 65, no. 1 (1990): 69–86.

Spiess, Stephen. "Shakespeare's Whore: Language, Prostitution, and Knowledge in Early Modern England." Ph.D. dissertation, University of Michigan, Ann Arbor, 2013.

Spivak, Gayatri Chakravorty. *A Critique of Postcolonial Reason: Toward a History of the Vanishing Present*. Cambridge, MA: Harvard University Press, 1999.

Stallybrass, Peter. "Books and Scrolls: Navigating the Bible." In *Books and Readers in Early Modern England*, ed. Jennifer Lotte Andersen and Elizabeth Sauer, 42–79. Philadelphia: University of Pennsylvania Press, 2002.

———. "Editing as Cultural Formation: The Sexing of Shakespeare's Sonnets." *Modern Language Quarterly* 54 (1993): 91–103.

Stallybrass, Peter, and Allon White. *The Politics and Poetics of Transgression*. Ithaca, NY: Cornell University Press, 1986.

Stanton, Kay. "'Made to Write "Whore" Upon?': Male and Female Use of the Word 'Whore' in Shakespeare's Canon." In *A Feminist Companion to Shakespeare*, ed. Dympna Callaghan, 80–102. Malden, MA: Blackwell, 2000.

Stein, Jordan Alexander. "American Literary History and Queer Temporalities." *American Literary History* 25, no. 4 (2013): 855–69.

Stephens, Walter. *Demon Lovers: Witchcraft, Sex, and the Crisis of Belief*. Chicago: University of Chicago Press, 2002.

Stewart, Alan. *Close Readers: Humanism and Sodomy in Early Modern England*. Princeton, NJ: Princeton University Press, 1997.

———. "Queer Renaissance Bodies? Sex, Violence, and the Constraints of Periodisation." In *In a Queer Place: Sexuality and Belonging in British and European Contexts*, ed. Kate Chedgzoy, Emma Francis, and Murray Pratt, 137–53. Aldershot: Ashgate, 2002.

Stockton, Kathryn Bond. *The Queer Child; or, Growing Sideways in the Twentieth Century*. Durham, NC: Duke University Press, 2009.

Stockton, Will. "How to Do the History of Heterosexuality: Shakespeare and Lacan." *Literature Compass* 7, no. 4 (2010): 254–65.

———. *Playing Dirty: Sexuality and Waste in Early Modern Comedy*. Minneapolis: University of Minnesota Press, 2011.

Stone, Lawrence. *The Family, Sex, and Marriage in England, 1500–1800*. New York: Penguin, 1979.

Stryker, Susan. "Lesbian Generations—Transsexual . . . Lesbian . . . Feminist." *Feminist Studies* 39, no. 2 (2013): 375–83.

Sullivan, Garrett A., Jr. "Voicing the Young Man: Memory, Forgetting, and Subjectivity in the Procreation Sonnets." In *A Companion to Shakespeare's Sonnets*, ed. Michael Schoenfeldt, 331–42. Malden, MA: Blackwell, 2007.

Sutphen, Joyce. "'A Dateless Lively Heat': Storing Loss in the Sonnets." In *Shakespeare's Sonnets: Critical Essays*, ed. James Schiffer, 199–217. New York: Garland, 2000.

Sweet, Michael, and Leonard Zwilling. "The First Medicalization: The Taxonomy and Etiology of Queers in Classical Indian Medicine." *Journal of the History of Sexuality* 3, no. 4 (1993): 590–607.

Talvacchia, Bette. "Erotica: The Sexualized Body in Renaissance Art." In *A Cultural History of Sexuality in the Renaissance*, vol. 3, ed. Bette Talvacchia, 175–201. Oxford: Berg, 2011.

———. *Taking Positions: On the Erotic in Renaissance Culture*. Princeton, NJ: Princeton University Press, 1999.

Taylor, Gary. *Reinventing Shakespeare: A Cultural History from the Restoration to the Present*. New York: Weidenfeld and Nicolson, 1989.

———. "Textual and Sexual Criticism: A Crux in *The Comedy of Errors*." *Renaissance Drama*, n.s., 19 (1988): 195–225.

Taylor, Gary, and John Lavagnino, eds. *Thomas Middleton: The Collected Works*. Oxford: Clarendon Press, 2007.

Taylor, Miles. "The Permeable World: Travel and Carnival in *The Antipodes*." *Exemplaria* 19, no. 3 (2007): 438–54.

"This Is Reteaching Gender and Sexuality." Online video clip. Vimeo, 2011. http://vimeo.com/17101589.

Thomas, Courtney. "'Not Having God Before His Eyes': Bestiality in Early Modern England." *Seventeenth Century* 26, no. 1 (2011): 149–73.

Thomas, Kate. "Post Sex: On Being Too Slow, Too Stupid, Too Soon." *South Atlantic Quarterly* 106, no. 3 (2007): 615–24.

Thomas, Keith. "Afterword." In *The Kiss in History*, ed. Karen Harvey, 187–205. Manchester: Manchester University Press, 2005.

Thompson, Ann. "Feminist Theory and the Editing of Shakespeare: *The Taming of the Shrew* Revisited." In *The Margins of the Text*, ed. D. C. Greetham, 83–103. Ann Arbor: University of Michigan Press, 1997.

Thompson, E. P. "Anthropology and the Discipline of Historical Context." *Midland History* 1, no. 3 (1972): 41–55.

Toulalan, Sarah. "Extraordinary Satisfactions: Lesbian Visibility in Seventeenth-Century Pornography in England." *Gender & History* 15, no. 1 (2003): 50–68.

———. *Imagining Sex: Pornography and Bodies in Seventeenth-Century England*. Oxford: Oxford University Press, 2007.

Toulalan, Sarah, and Kate Fisher, eds. *The Routledge History of Sex and the Body, 1500 to the Present*. New York: Routledge, 2013.

Traub, Valerie. *Desire and Anxiety: Circulations of Sexuality in Shakespearean Drama*. London: Routledge, 1992, rpt. 2014.

———. "'The Past Is a Foreign Country?': The Times and Spaces of Islamicate Sexuality Studies." In *Islamicate Sexualities: Translations Across Temporal Geographies of Desire*, ed. Kathryn Babayan and Afsaneh Najmabadi, 1–41. Cambridge, MA: Harvard University Press, 2008.

———. "The Perversion of 'Lesbian' Desire." *History Workshop Journal* 41 (1996): 19–49.

———. "Recent Studies in Homoeroticism, 1970–1999." *English Literary Renaissance* (Spring 2000): 284–329.

———. *The Renaissance of Lesbianism in Early Modern England.* Cambridge: Cambridge University Press, 2002.

———. "Sex Without Issue: Sodomy, Reproduction, and Signification in Shakespeare's Sonnets." In *Shakespeare's Sonnets: Critical Essays*, ed. James Schiffer, 431–52. New York: Garland, 1999.

———. "The Sonnets: Sequence, Sexuality, and Shakespeare's Two Loves." In *A Companion to Shakespeare*, vol. 4, *The Poems, Problem Comedies, and Late Plays*, ed. Richard Dutton and Jean E. Howard, 275–301. Malden, MA: Blackwell, 2003.

Trevor, Douglas. *The Poetics of Melancholy in Early Modern England.* Cambridge: Cambridge University Press, 2004.

———. "Shakespeare's Love Objects." In *A Companion to Shakespeare's Sonnets*, ed. Michael Schoenfeldt, 225–41. Malden, MA: Blackwell, 2007.

Trumbach, Randolph. *Heterosexuality and the Third Gender in Enlightenment London.* Vol. 1. of *Sex and the Gender Revolution.* Chicago: University of Chicago Press, 1998.

———. "London's Sapphists: From Three Sexes to Four Genders in the Making of Modern Culture." In *Third Sex, Third Gender: Beyond Sexual Dimorphism*, ed. Gilbert Herdt, 111–36. New York: Zone Books, 1994.

Tuana, Nancy. "Coming to Understand: Orgasm and the Epistemology of Ignorance." In *Agnotology: The Making and Unmaking of Ignorance*, ed. Robert Proctor and Londa Schiebinger, 108–45. Stanford, CA: Stanford University Press, 2008.

Turner, David M. "Adulterous Kisses and the Meanings of Familiarity in Early Modern Britain." In *The Kiss in History*, ed. Karen Harvey, 80–97. Manchester: Manchester University Press, 2005.

———. *Fashioning Adultery: Gender, Sex and Civility in England, 1660–1740.* Cambridge: Cambridge University Press, 2002.

Turner, James Grantham. *Libertines and Radicals in Early Modern London: Sexuality, Politics and Literary Culture, 1630–1685.* Cambridge: Cambridge University Press, 2002.

———. *One Flesh: Paradisal Marriage and Sexual Relations in the Age of Milton.* Oxford: Clarendon Press, 1987.

———. *Schooling Sex: Libertine Literature and Erotic Education in Italy, France, and England, 1534–1685.* Oxford: Oxford University Press, 2003.

Ungerer, Gustav. "Prostitution in Late Elizabethan London: The Case of Mary Newborough." *Medieval and Renaissance Drama in England* 15 (2002): 138–223.

Vanita, Ruth. "Playing the Field." *Feminist Studies* 39, no. 2 (2013): 365–71.

———. *Queering India: Same-Sex Love and Eroticism in Indian Culture and Society.* New York: Routledge, 2002.

Varholy, Cristine M. "'But She Woulde Not Consent': Women's Narratives of Sexual Assault and Compulsion in Early Modern London." In *Violence, Politics, and Gender in Early Modern England*, ed. Joseph Patrick Ward, 41–65. New York: Palgrave Macmillan, 2008.

———. "'Rich Like a Lady': Cross-Class Dressing in the Brothels and Theaters of Early Modern London." *Journal for Early Modern Cultural Studies* 8, no. 1 (2008): 4–34.

Varnado, Christine. "'Invisible Sex!': What Looks Like the Act in Early Modern Drama?" In *Sex Before Sex*, ed. James Bromley and William Stockton, 25–52. Minneapolis: University of Minnesota Press, 2013.

Velasco, Sherry. *Lesbians in Early Modern Spain.* Nashville: Vanderbilt University Press, 2011.

Vendler, Helen. *The Art of Shakespeare's Sonnets*. Cambridge, MA: Harvard University Press, 1997.

Vicinus, Martha. *Intimate Friends: Women Who Loved Women, 1778–1928*. Chicago: University of Chicago Press, 2004.

———. "Lesbian Ghosts." In *The Lesbian Premodern*, ed. Noreen Giffney, Michelle M. Sauer, and Diane Watt, 193–201. New York: Palgrave Macmillan, 2011.

———. "Lesbian History: All Theory and No Facts or All Facts and No Theory?" *Radical History Review* 60 (1994): 57–75.

———. " 'They Wonder to Which Sex I Belong': The Historical Roots of the Modern Lesbian Identity." In *Lesbian Subjects: A Feminist Studies Reader*, ed. Martha Vicinus, 233–59. Bloomington: Indiana University Press, 1996.

Vogler, Candace. "Sex and Talk." In *Intimacy*, ed. Lauren Berlant, 48–85. Chicago: University of Chicago Press, 2000.

Wahl, Elizabeth Susan. *Invisible Relations: Representations of Female Intimacy in the Age of Enlightenment*. Stanford, CA: Stanford University Press, 1999.

Wah-shan, Chou. *Tongzhi: Politics of Same-Sex Eroticism in Chinese Societies*. London: Routledge, 2000.

Walen, Denise. *Constructions of Female Homoeroticism in Early Modern Drama*. New York: Palgrave Macmillan, 2005.

Walker, Garthrine. *Crime, Gender, and Social Order in Early Modern England*. Cambridge: Cambridge University Press, 2003.

———. "Rereading Rape and Sexual Violence in Early Modern England." *Gender & History* 10, no. 1 (1998): 1–25.

Wall, Wendy. *Staging Domesticity: Household Work and English Identity in Early Modern Drama*. Cambridge: Cambridge University Press, 2002.

Wallace, Lee. "Outside History: Same-Sex Sexuality and the Colonial Archive." In *Embodiments of Cultural Encounters*, ed. Sebastian Jobs and Gesa Mackenthun, 61–74. Münster: Waxmann, 2011.

Walters, Suzanna Danuta. "From Here to Queer: Radical Feminism, Postmodernism, and the Lesbian Menace (or, Why Can't a Woman Be More Like a Fag?)." *Signs: Journal of Women in Culture and Society* 21, no. 4 (1996): 830–69.

Warner, Michael. "Queer World Making: Annamarie Jagose Interviews Michael Warner." *Genders* 31 (2000).

———. *The Trouble with Normal: Sex, Politics, and the Ethics of Queer Life*. Cambridge, MA: Harvard University Press, 1999.

Waters, Sarah. *Affinity*. New York: Riverhead, 1999.

———. *Fingersmith*. New York: Riverhead, 2002.

———. *Tipping the Velvet*. New York: Riverhead, 1998.

Watson, Amanda. " 'Full Character'd': Competing Forms of Memory in Shakespeare's Sonnets." In *A Companion to Shakespeare's Sonnets*, ed. Michael Schoenfeldt, 343–60. Malden, MA: Blackwell, 2007.

Wayne, Valerie. "The Gendered Text and Its Labour." In *Oxford Handbook of Shakespeare and Embodiment*, ed. Valerie Traub. Oxford: Oxford University Press, forthcoming 2016.

Webster's New Twentieth-Century Dictionary. Unabridged 2nd ed. Cleveland: World Publishing Company, 1973.

Weeks, Jeffrey. *Sex, Politics and Society: The Regulation of Sexuality Since 1800*. New York: Longman, 1981.

Weil, Rachel. "Sometimes a Scepter Is Only a Scepter: Pornography and Politics in Restoration England." In *The Invention of Pornography: Obscenity and the Origins of Modernity, 1500–1800*, ed. Lynn Hunt, 125–53. New York: Zone Books, 1993.

Wells, Stanley. *Looking for Sex in Shakespeare*. Cambridge: Cambridge University Press, 2004.

———. *Shakespeare, Sex and Love*. Oxford: Oxford University Press, 2010.

Wheeler, Richard P. *Shakespeare's Development and the Problem Comedies: Turn and Counter-Turn*. Berkeley: University of California Press, 1981.

White, Martin, ed. *Arden of Faversham*. New York: W. W. Norton, 1990.

Wiegman, Robyn. "Afterword: The Lesbian Premodern Meets the Lesbian Postmodern." In *The Lesbian Premodern*, ed. Noreen Giffney, Michelle M. Sauer, and Diane Watt, 203–12. New York: Palgrave Macmillan, 2011.

———. *American Anatomies: Theorizing Race and Gender*. Durham, NC: Duke University Press, 1995.

———. "Feminism, Institutionalism, and the Idiom of Failure." In *Women's Studies on the Edge*, ed. Joan Wallach Scott, 38–66. Durham, NC: Duke University Press, 2008.

———. "Introduction: Mapping the Lesbian Postmodern." In *The Lesbian Postmodern*, ed. Laura Doan, 1–20. New York: Columbia University Press, 1994.

———. "The Intimacy of Critique: Ruminations on Feminism as a Living Thing." *Feminist Theory* 11, no. 79 (2010): 79–84.

———. *Object Lessons*. Durham, NC: Duke University Press 2012.

———. "Wishful Thinking." *Feminist Formations* 25, no. 3 (2013): 202–13.

Wiesner-Hanks, Merry E. *Christianity and Sexuality in the Early Modern World: Regulating Desire, Reforming Practice*. London: Routledge, 2000.

Wilde, Oscar. "The Portrait of Mr. W.H." *Blackwood's Edinburgh Magazine*, July 1889.

Williams, Gordon. *A Dictionary of Sexual Language and Imagery in Shakespearean and Stuart Literature*. 3 vols. London: Athlone Press, 1994.

———. *A Glossary of Shakespeare's Sexual Language*. London: Athlone, 1997.

Williams, Linda, ed. *Porn Studies*. Durham, NC: Duke University Press, 2004.

———. *Screening Sex*. Durham, NC: Duke University Press, 2004.

Williams, Raymond. *Marxism and Literature*. Oxford: Oxford University Press, 1977.

Williamson, George C. *Lady Anne Clifford, Countess of Dorset, Pembroke & Montgomery, 1590–1676: Her Life, Letters, and Work*. Kendal: Titus Wilson and Son, 1922.

Willis, Deborah. *Malevolent Nurture: Witch-Hunting and Maternal Power in Early Modern England*. Ithaca, NY: Cornell University Press, 1995.

Wilmot, John. *The Works of John Wilmot, Earl of Rochester*. Ed. Harold Love. Oxford: Oxford University Press, 1999.

Wiltenburg, Joy. *Disorderly Women and Female Power in the Street Literature of Early Modern England and Germany*. Charlottesville: University of Virginia Press, 1992.

Wolfthal, Diane. *In and Out of the Marital Bed: Seeing Sex in Renaissance Europe*. New Haven, CT: Yale University Press, 2010.

Wootton, David. Presentation at Birbeck College Symposium on Alan Bray. Birkbeck College, London, September 2003.

Wrightson, Keith. *English Society, 1580–1680*. London: Hutchinson, 1982.

Yates, Julian. "More Life: Shakespeare's Sonnet Machines." In *Shakesqueer: A Queer Companion to the Complete Works of Shakespeare*, ed. Madhavi Menon, 333–42. Durham, NC: Duke University Press, 2011.

Zucker, Adam. *The Places of Wit in Early Modern English Comedy*. Cambridge: Cambridge University Press, 2011.

INDEX

Page numbers in italics refer to illustrations.

ACKNOWLEDGMENTS

To thank the many friends and colleagues who have supported this project and sustained my life in the academy is a singular pleasure. Patsy Yaeger—passionate thinker, gardener, and Empress of All—was a precious friend and luminous interlocutor, with ideas that rocked, heart and arms wide open, and hands smelling of sweet dirt and desire. That she is gone will ever be unthinkable. In incalculable ways, Peggy McCracken enlivens my life with honest talk, engaged critique, solicitous advice, and tromps through the snow; if her early reading of the manuscript convinced me that I had a book, her friendship, along with that of Doug Anderson, has extended my family. Jeffrey Masten's influence has been more important than he knows, as has been his engagement with my arguments, large and small; our friendship bestows ballast upon which I depend. Discussions with Laura Doan about queer historiography have been a source of delight, topped only by the incomparable pleasures of touring English gardens and hanging out at her cottage with Mar. Exchanges with Sue Lanser about the conjunction of lesbianism + history have prodded me toward greater exactitude and given an anchor to my free-floating thoughts, while reminding me that we 1970s lesbian feminists had a vision of collaboration and collectivity that extends into the present. Jean Howard has been an invaluable source of wisdom and inspiration and has morphed without missing a beat from informal mentor to beloved friend. Conversations with Fran Dolan have been an all-too-rare gift, with intellectual matters seasoned with down-to-earth wisdom about crazy families, siblings and parents who need us, gardening, and the virtues of refusing to waitress that table. Will Fisher, the most unassuming of men, is a walking archive of sexual history; more important, his faithful friendship enacts a truly Renaissance ideal. The calm assurance and approbation of Valerie Wayne exudes more encouragement than I could ever deserve. Gina Bloom, whose boundless enthusiasm reminds me why we do what we do, has on several occasions saved me from my worser self. Wendy Wall is her own early modern joy. Ari Friedlander, Carla Mazzio, and Marjorie Rubright have proven to be my very best critics, as well as talented wordsmiths. My friendship with Carla is as sweet and tough as her big brain. The depth of my admiration for Marjorie has only increased by being the recipient of her scholarly and personal care, amazing discernment, and heroic application of WD-40 to my arguments. Laurie Shannon's exactitude in word and deed is one of the great pleasures of our friendship. Annamarie Jagose imparts the sense of living in parallel intellectual universes—even if hers seems to move faster than the speed of light. David Halperin's scholarly inspiration will be evident throughout this book, but I thank him as well for his queer collegiality, for many crucial turns of phrase, for introducing me to Paris, and most of all for his loyal friendship. Although Robyn Wiegman arrived late to this project, the keen edge of her scholarship preceded her; the force of her intellectual generosity confirms my sense that there remains something to be cherished about feminism. And Carol Batker remains not only the most stalwart of friends, but since grad school has been a moral compass for navigating the shoals of academic politics.

The responses of several early modernists to chapter drafts honed my thinking: Kathryn Schwarz and Stephen Spiess offered careful scrutiny that led to important nuance. Bruce Smith provided steady encouragement from afar. Doug Trevor gave liberally of his early modern and editorial expertise, helping me cut to the chase while staffing the Lacan hotline. Mike Schoenfeldt and Jeffrey Todd Knight provided judicious input on Shakespeare's sonnets. Mike has been, as well, a mainstay of support and good will since welcoming me many years ago to Michigan. Along with Mike and Doug, fellow Michigan early modernists Linda Gregerson, Steve Mullaney, and Barbara Hodgdon make me feel that we are doing something special and possibly right. Dena Goodman, Helmut Puff, and Scott Spector have tutored me in the discipline of history without knowing it. My thoughts on sex education and feminist methodology have been immeasurably enriched by conversations with Sara McClelland. Talking with Elizabeth Wingrove has made me smarter, but not as smart as she. Abby Stewart's generosity of time and wisdom has made a palpable difference to me and countless others. For her deft infusion of respect for personhood into the life of administration, as well as her friendship, I thank Sid Smith. I have learned much from my capacious colleagues in Women's Studies, most especially from Carol Boyd, Gayle

Rubin, Ruby Tapia, Wang Zheng, and Dean Hubbs. Tobin Siebers, to the end a dignified and generous interlocutor, will always be missed. That I can depend on Anita Norich to supply just the right mixture of irony and common sense, especially when things are bad, still strikes me as a gift after all these years. I will never forget the art of friendship as practiced by Yopie Prins and Marjorie Levinson. And to Linda Wells, the beloved friend of my youth, I can only say thanks for sticking with me through thick and thin.

I will forever be grateful to Steve Hindle, director of research at the Huntington Library, for offering me a fellowship, which I used to complete this book. I am indebted as well to the hard work of wonderful research assistants: Laura Ambrose, Lilianna Hibbeln, Eliza Mathie, and Lauren Eriks. I particularly thank Tiffany Ball for her perspicuity and for always being game. Editors of several journals and handbooks, among them Jody Greene, George Haggerty, and Adele Seeff, made many astute comments on aspects of this manuscript. Laurie Shannon and Anna Clark read an early version of the manuscript for the press; their substantive engagement with its argument and structure led to many changes of substance and style.

Earlier versions of portions of this book were previously published; they have all been revised and expanded. I am grateful to the following people and presses for permission to reprint: to the editors of *Early Modern Women: An Interdisciplinary Journal*, for a précis entitled "Making Sexual Knowledge"; to *PMLA* for a shorter version of "The New Unhistoricism in Queer Studies"; to *GLQ: A Journal of Lesbian and Gay Studies* and Duke University Press for "Friendship's Loss: Alan Bray's Making of History"; to Leonard Barkan, Bradin Cormack, Sean Keilen and Palgrave Macmillan for "The Joys of Martha Joyless: Queer Pedagogy and the (Early Modern) Production of Sexual Knowledge"; and to George Haggerty, Molly McGarry and Blackwell for "The Present Future of Lesbian Historiography."

Even more important than the opportunity to publish has been the opportunity to share my thinking over the course of refining the arguments in this book. I am grateful to the many people who invited me to present talks for their questions, comments, and generous hospitality. In particular, I thank my hosts and interlocutors from the New Chaucer Society; the Queer Peoples Conference at Cambridge University; the Lesbian Lives Conference, University College, Dublin; the Sexuality Summer School and Sexuality After Foucault Conference at Manchester University; the Walter Penn Warren Institute for the Humanities at Vanderbilt University; McGill University; the

Rocky Mountain Medieval and Renaissance Conference at the University of Arizona; Columbia University; the University of Hawaii, Manoa; Northwestern University; Western Michigan State University; Rutgers University; the University of Pennsylvania; SUNY Buffalo; the University of Minnesota; the University of Miami; USC; UC-Irvine; UCLA; University of Sydney; the University of Queensland; Syracuse University; Miami University; the University of Pittsburgh; the University of British Columbia; Clemson University; the University of Alabama; Louisiana State University; California Institute of Technology; University of California, Riverside; the Claremont Graduate School. Particularly memorable questions and responses during presentations of this work were offered by Ellen Armour, Crystal Bartolovich, Mary Bly, Barbara Bono, Sean Brady, Theresa Braunschneider, Joe Bristow, Dympna Callaghan, Anna Clark, Peter Cryle, Joan DeJean, Heidi Brayman Hackel, Melissa Hardie, Jim Holstun, Benjy Kahan, Kate Lilley, David Lloyd, Karma Lochrie, Ania Loomba, Molly McGarry, Chris Nagle, Sally O'Driscoll, Will Stockton, Judith Surkis, Jim Swan, Lee Wallace, Michael Warner, and Amanda Winkler. Anne Curzan, Alan Stewart, Angela Heetderks, and Michelle Dowd responded generously to my queries.

Jerry Singerman has been the best possible editor: enthusiastic about the big picture, attuned to the difficulties of complexity, a cheerleader when it mattered, and unperturbed by my many delays. Hannah Blake and Noreen O'Connor-Abel ushered the book through production with timely information and considerable good will. I thank Kentston Bauman for his superb work on the index.

Terri, Carolyn, and Michael Traub have been steadfast in their encouragement and respect for what I do, even if they wish I would do it less. And although she probably won't read this book, and might not like it if she did, Brenda K. Marshall is daily evidence of Eve Sedgwick's axiom "People are different from each another." The life of an academic is measured not in teaspoons but in pages written, papers presented, dissertations defended, and colleagues mentored and tenured. No one knows this better than the farm girl novelist from North Dakota. What *I* know is that if, in the course of pursuing this life of reading and thinking, traveling and administrating, writing and gardening, I have often taxed her patience, I have never taxed her love. Together we have created an improbable life whose constancies never stale. Like waves pounding the California shore, sunlight piercing through the Michigan clouds, and the first daffodils of a Tennessee spring: she always brings me joy.